To Jerry,
with best wishes,
[illegible]

Ancient Israel in Sinai

Ancient Israel in Sinai

The Evidence for the Authenticity of the Wilderness Tradition

JAMES K. HOFFMEIER

OXFORD
UNIVERSITY PRESS
2005

OXFORD
UNIVERSITY PRESS

Oxford University Press, Inc., publishes works that further
Oxford University's objective of excellence
in research, scholarship, and education.

Oxford New York
Auckland Cape Town Dar es Salaam Hong Kong Karachi
Kuala Lumpur Madrid Melbourne Mexico City Nairobi
New Delhi Shanghai Taipei Toronto

With offices in
Argentina Austria Brazil Chile Czech Republic France Greece
Guatemala Hungary Italy Japan Poland Portugal Singapore
South Korea Switzerland Thailand Turkey Ukraine Vietnam

Published by Oxford University Press, Inc.
198 Madison Avenue, New York, New York 10016

www.oup.com

Library of Congress Cataloging-in-Publication Data
Hoffmeier, James Karl, 1951–
Ancient Israel in Sinai : the evidence for the authenticity of the
wilderness tradition / James K. Hoffmeier.
p. cm.
Includes bibliographical references and index.
ISBN 978-0-19-515546-4
1. Bible. O.T. Exodus XVI–Numbers XX—Criticism, interpretation, etc.
2. Bible. O.T. Exodus XVI–Numbers XX—Evidences, authority, etc. 3. Bible. O.T.
Exodus XVI–Numbers XX—History of biblical events. 4. Bible. O.T. Exodus XVI–
Numbers XX—Geography. 5. Sinai (Egypt)—Antiquities. I. Title.
BS1245.52.H64 2005
222'.12095—dc22 2004021554

9 8 7 6 5 4

Printed in the United States of America
on acid-free paper

Dedicated to Alan Millard
on the occasion of his retirement from
the University of Liverpool
in appreciation of many years of
friendship and encouragement

Foreword

Here, in the early twenty-first century, we are heirs to two centuries of breathtaking discoveries and to frontiers of knowledge pushed out to vastly broadened horizons. In the pioneering nineteenth century, the first broad outlines for our knowledge of the real biblical world—the Ancient Near East—began to emerge with the decipherment of Egyptian hieroglyphs and of the intricate Mesopotamian cuneiform script. In the meantime, pioneer archaeologists probed the secrets of "hundred-gated Thebes," resurrected the vast palaces of Nineveh and Babylon, probed deep into fabled Troy and Mycenae, and opened up the geography and mounds of Syria-Palestine, from Palmyra to Petra.

In the tumultuous twentieth century, the rate of discovery grew apace: first, with spectacular finds such as the golden treasures of Tutankhamun in Egypt and of the royal tombs in "Ur of the Chaldees"; the wonders of Ugarit, Mari, and Ebla in Syria; or the Dead Sea Scrolls in Palestine; and second, with a growing refinement and precision, especially in field archaeology and the introduction of useful techniques from the natural sciences in the last fifty years. And today, both the growth and the refining of knowledge and how we understand it continue to expand.

It is in this wider panoramic context that we may set Professor James K. Hoffmeier's new book on Egypt, Sinai, and earliest Israel. He has already spent most of an active lifetime in the professional study of ancient Egypt and of the Hebrew Bible in its ancient context. Egypt's East Delta and North Sinai districts have always been zones of continual contact and transit between Egypt and her northeast neighbors, from prehistory to the present. But effective, modern-quality archaeological work in these particular districts is of recent date. Professor Hoffmeier's excavations and discoveries at Tell el-Borg have revealed remains of an important Egyptian military staging post from the delta into northeast Sinai on the route to Canaan, and this work has as a context the parallel work done at ancient Avaris and Pi-Ramesse by Professors Manfred Bietak and Edgar Pusch, and at Tell Hebua by Dr. Abd-el-Maksoud. Such is the background to James K. Hoffmeier's new book, which sets the narratives of the biblical exodus and wilderness travels of the early Hebrews in a fresh, up-to-date, factual context of the latest knowledge about the geography, routes, and physical conditions in Delta and Sinai alike. The book also brings together the results of wider study of the giving of law and covenant in Sinai, of the results of modern study of the ancient use of portable structures ("tabernacles") for worship and cult, and of the occurrence of Egyptianizing proper names among the Hebrews departing from Egypt, and it offers a calm, judicious review of the "hot potato" subject of ancient Israel's endlessly discussed possible origins. And more besides! Thus, alongside his *Israel in Egypt*, Professor Hoffmeier's informative new volume on Egypt and Sinai in biblical antiquity deserves likewise to serve a very wide readership.

—KENNETH A. KITCHEN

Preface

The exodus from Egypt and the wilderness narratives that follow in the Torah or Pentateuch contain the Bible's version of how Israel originated as a nation in Egypt, marched to Mt. Sinai where it entered into a covenant relationship with God, and received the law before entering the "Promised Land." In recent years, the Egypt and Sinai pillars of ancient Israel's history have been shaken by questions raised by some critical scholars and by outright rejection from others. In 1997 in my book *Israel in Egypt: The Evidence for the Authenticity of the Exodus Tradition* (Oxford), I argued—largely on the basis of Egyptian background evidence—that there were good reasons to believe that the reports of the Hebrew sojourn and forced labor were plausible. Considerable time was given to discussing the geographical details of the exodus from Egypt and proposing a route taken by the Hebrews to leave Egypt. Because of the importance of the wilderness tradition to Israel's origin and the current debate about this matter over the past two decades, a similar study of the episodes in Sinai is necessary. In a sense, this book is a logical sequel.

An examination of the wilderness tradition, which includes Exodus 16 through Numbers 20, and a study of how later biblical writers reflect on the wilderness episodes is offered in chapter 1, followed by an examination of how historians of religion view these episodes (chapter 2). In this same chapter it is argued that in view of the impasse between the scientific (modern) hermeneutic and the postmodern approach to the wilderness tradition, a different method is required. The phenomenological approach is offered as a way out.

The setting of the wilderness tradition, the Sinai Peninsula, is one of the most intriguing geographical regions in the world. Understanding the terrain and climate enable readers of the wilderness tradition to comprehend better the context of many of the episodes. Hence, an introduction to the geography and ecological zones of Sinai is offered in chapter 3.

In the years since 1997, a number of important developments have occurred that demand that some of the geographical discussions in *Israel in Egypt* be reassessed. First, there continues to be a steady stream of studies that question the historical reliability of most portions of the Torah, including the wilderness tradition and geography of the exodus. Some of these include Thomas Thompson's *The Mythic Past: Biblical Archaeology and the Myth of Israel* (1999), Israel Finkelstein and Neil Silberman's *The Bible Unearthed: Archaeology's New Vision of Ancient Israel and the Origin of its Sacred Texts* (2001), and an essay by John Van Seters, "The Geography of the Exodus" (2001). The conclusions of these works, and others like them, need to be questioned in the light of new data from our investigations in Sinai.

Second, since the mid-1990s, new archaeological data from North Sinai are available. I was inclined to identify Tell Hebua with Egypt's ancient frontier town of Tjaru/Sile in *Israel in Egypt*, but thanks to a new inscription discovered in 1999, this identification has been confirmed. This new information means that one can be much more certain about the sequence of Egyptian forts in North Sinai, if more were to be discovered. And this, in turn, will play a significant role in identifying the location of the Egyptian fort Migdol (the second fort east of Hebua), which is believed to be the same as the Migdol of Exodus 14:2. This same verse indicates that Migdol is near the sea crossed by Moses and the Israelites. Consequently, if we are able to locate the approximate area of Migdol, then the location of the Re(e)d Sea can be proposed with greater certainty.

After several years of archaeological surveying in North Sinai (1994–1998), the East Frontier Archaeological Project, which I direct, began excavations at Tell el-Borg in 2000. After four seasons, we have discovered a New Kingdom fort, clearly one of those named in Egyptian texts. This discovery, along with the paleoenvironmental fieldwork by the project's geologist, Dr. Stephen O. Moshier, has made it possible to trace the route of the military road from Egypt's frontier and on toward Canaan. Chapter 4 will introduce the new data and their implications for the geography of the exodus and travels in Sinai. In my earlier book, I suggested several possible locations for the Re(e)d Sea. Thanks to new evidence, and a more critical reading of texts such as Exodus 14:2, a specific body of water can now be posited in chapter 5.

The location of Mt. Sinai, a problem that has bedeviled explorers, biblical scholars, and archaeologists for centuries, is treated in chapter 6. Although no earthshaking identification is made, careful analysis of the biblical texts does allow us to eliminate a number of the proposed sites for the mountain where

Moses is said to have received the law. Also, the Torah does provide some information that, I will argue, narrows down the general region where Mt. Sinai was located.

How could the Israelites have traveled and lived in Sinai? Were there millions involved? Why is there no direct archaeological evidence for the Israelites in Sinai? Does the wilderness itinerary of Exodus and Numbers make sense? These probing questions are addressed in chapter 7.

Without a doubt, receiving the law at Mt. Sinai through Moses as intermediary is one of the most memorable episodes of the Bible. Before discussing the law itself and how it is structured, it seems prudent to ask if Moses (assuming he actually lived in the second half of the second millennium B.C.) could have written; was there an alphabetic script like the Hebrew known in the twelfth century B.C. available for use a century or two earlier? Chapter 8 discusses this matter, followed by studying the literary form of the Sinai covenant in a comparative way with surviving ancient Near Eastern treaties.

The origins of Israel's cultic worship, according to the Torah, is closely tied to the law given at Sinai, and hence a sanctuary was required. What better option for a people in a wilderness and without a permanent home and worship center than to possess a tentlike sanctuary? This indeed is what is prescribed in Exodus 25ff. Chapter 9 explores the tabernacle or tent of meeting, and gives special attention to Egyptian cultic and linguistic connections to the biblical material. The evidence shows that there is considerable Egyptian influence, which is not surprising if the Israelites had been in Egypt, as the book of Exodus maintains. However, if these traditions date to the fifth century B.C., as many scholars have believed, how then are these Egyptian elements to be explained? Continuing with the theme of Egyptianisms in the wilderness tradition, chapter 10 investigates the significant number of Egyptian personal names among the generation of the exodus. Additionally, several elements of Israelite religion are explored in the light of an Egyptian perspective, such as the prohibition against eating pork.

The book concludes (chapter 11) with several other important elements of Israel's religious heritage that appear to originate in the wilderness, including the problem of the origin of the name of Israel's God, Yahweh. This investigation of the wilderness tradition determines that it is vital to understand both ancient Israel as a people and the foundation of its religious heritage. Furthermore, the evidence considered in this volume not only affirms the authenticity of the wilderness tradition but also further supports the biblical tradition that Israel resided in Egypt for a sufficient period of time to have been influenced by the remarkable culture of the Nile Valley.

This book is dedicated to Alan Millard, emeritus professor of Hebrew and Semitic languages at the University of Liverpool. For over twenty-five years he has been a friend and a mentor. Often he has read through my manuscripts, offering helpful criticism and advice, and he has kept me on his offprint mailing list. Alan and Margaret, his wife, have graciously hosted my family and me in their home over the years. Their hospitality has been enjoyed and appreciated by many scholars and students over the years. Thanks to both of you!

To produce this study, several years of work were required, and it could not have been accomplished without the help of others. The members of the Tell el-Borg staff are the ones truly responsible for the significant discoveries made in North Sinai. I can't think of a better group of professionals with whom to work. They have been wonderful. Ronald Bull has accompanied me to Sinai regularly since 1995, and Dr. Stephen O. Moshier, associate professor of geology at Wheaton College, who has worked with me since 1998, is responsible for the stunning paleoenvironmental evidence that has enabled us to reconstruct the Qantara-Baluza region of North Sinai. Jessica T. Hoffmeier, my daughter and a member of the Tell el-Borg staff, is responsible for preparing the illustrations for this book, and she created three of the maps (figures 1, 4, and 10).

I joined the faculty of the Divinity School of Trinity International University in Deerfield, Illinois, in the fall of 1999, because of the administration's enthusiastic support for this project. The deans, first Bingham Hunter and now Tite Tienou, have allowed me flexibility in my teaching schedule in order to accommodate a spring excavation season during the semester, while the weather is still pleasant. My colleagues have also been supportive of this project, which has been most gratifying. I must extend heartfelt thanks to the Miller Family foundation for steady financial support to Trinity for this project since 1999. Without this provision our discoveries in North Sinai would not have been possible. Finally, I need to express appreciation to the Supreme Council for Antiquities of Egypt. The North Sinai Inspectorate has been cooperative in every way, but Dr. Mohamed Abd el-Maksoud, director for Lower Egypt and Sinai, actually recruited me to work in Sinai back in 1987. In fact, he is the one who asked my team to visit Tell el-Borg as a possible site to excavate in 1999. Heartfelt thanks are offered to him. He has been a great advocate for all archaeological work in North Sinai for many years.

"Writing a book is an adventure," Winston Churchill declared in November 2, 1949, when speaking to the National Book Exhibition regarding his multivolume war memoirs. He elaborated: "To begin with, it is a toy and an amusement; then it becomes a mistress, and then it becomes a master, and then a tyrant. The last phase is that just as you are about to be reconciled to your servitude, you kill the monster, and fling him out to the public." I must admit to have gone through each of these stages, and along the way, Cynthia Read and Theo Calderara of Oxford University Press have been patient with me. So I fling out this minimonster to the public, in hopes that it will stimulate thought and discussion about the wilderness tradition among students, be they academics or interested laypeople, of the Bible, history, and archaeology.

All Bible quotations are from the New Revised Standard Version (NRSV) unless otherwise specified.

Contents

Abbreviations

ÄAT	Ägypten und Altes Testament (Wiesbaden: Otto Harrassowitz)
ABC	*Anchor Bible Commentaries*, ed. W. F. Albright and D. N. Freedman (New York: Doubleday, 1964)
ABD	*Anchor Bible Dictionary*, 6 volumes, ed. D. N. Freedman (New York: Doubleday, 1992).
ABW	*Archaeology in the Biblical World*
AEO	*Ancient Egyptian Onomastica*, 2 volumes (London: Oxford University Press, 1947)
AJA	*American Journal of Archaeology*
AJSL	*American Journal of Semitic Languages*
ÄL	*Ägypten und Levant / Egypt and the Levant* (Vienna)
ANET	James B. Pritchard, *Ancient Near Eastern Texts Relating to the Old Testament*, 3rd ed. (Princeton: Princeton University Press, 1969).
ARCE	American Research Center in Egypt
ASAE	*Annales du service des antiquités de l'Égypte* (Cairo)
ASOR	American Schools of Oriental Research
ASV	American Standard Version
AUSS	*Andrews University Seminar Series*
AV	Authorized Version
BA	*Biblical Archaeologist*
BAR	*Biblical Archaeology Review*
BASOR	*Bulletin of the American Schools of Oriental Research*
BDB	F. Brown, S. R. Driver, and C. A. Briggs, *A Hebrew and English Lexicon of the Old Testament with an Appendix containing the Biblical Aramaic* (Oxford: Clarendon Press, 1907)

BIFAO *Bulletin de l'Institut Français d'Archéologie Orientale* (Cairo)
BN *Biblische Notizen* (Bamberg)
BR *Bible Review*
BZAW *Beiheften zur Zeitschrift für Ägyptische Sprache und Altertumskunde*
CAD *The Assyrian Dictionary of the Oriental Institute of the University of Chicago* (ed. I. J. Gelb et al.; Chicago: University of Chicago Press, 1956 to present)
CAH *Cambridge Ancient History* II (Cambridge: Cambridge University Press, part 1, 1973; part 2, 1975)
CBQ *Catholic Biblical Quarterly*
Cd'É *Chronique d'Égypte*
CDME R. O. Faulkner, *Concise Dictionary of Middle Egyptian* (Oxford: Griffith Institute, 1962)
COS W. W. Hallo and K. Lawson Younger, eds., *Context of Scripture*, 3 volumes (Leiden: Brill, 1997, 2000, 2003)
CRIPEL *Cahiers de recherches de l'institut de Papyrologie et d'Égyptologie de Lille*
D Deuteronomic source
DE *Discussions in Egyptology* (Oxford)
DLE Leonard H. Lesko, *A Dictionary of Late Egyptian*, 5 volumes (Berkeley, Calif.: BC Scribe, 1982–1990)
DtrH Deuteronomistic History or Historian
E Elohist source
EA El-Amarna = Amarna Letters
EA *Egyptian Archaeology*
EEF Egypt Exploration Fund
EES Egypt Exploration Society
EI *Eretz-Israel*
FT *Faith and Thought* (Transactions of the Victoria Institute, England)
GM *Göttinger Miszellen*
HAB *The Harper Atlas of the Bible* (ed. J. B. Pritchard; New York: Harper & Row, 1987)
HTR *Harvard Theological Review*
HUCA *Hebrew Union College Annual*
IEJ *Israel Exploration Journal*
IFAO Institut Français d'Archéologie Orientale
ISBE *International Standard Bible Encyclopedia* (ed. G. W. Bromiley; Grand Rapids, Mich.: Eerdmans, 1979–1988)
J Jahwist source
JANES *Journal of the Ancient Near Eastern Society*
JAOS *Journal of the American Oriental Society*

JARCE *Journal of the American Research Center in Egypt*
JB Jerusalem Bible
JBL *Journal of Biblical Literature*
JEA *Journal of Egyptian Archaeology*
JEOL *Jaarbericht ex Oriente Lux*
JETS *Journal of the Evangelical Theological Society*
JNES *Journal of Near Eastern Studies*
JPS Jewish Publication Society
JQR *Jewish Quarterly Review*
JSOT *Journal for the Study of the Old Testament*
JSS *Journal of Semitic Studies*
JSSEA *Journal of the Society for the Study of Egyptian Antiquities*
KB Ludwig Koehler and Walter Baumgartner, *Lexicon in Veteris Testamenti Libros* (Leiden: Brill, 1985).
KJV King James Version
KRI Kenneth Kitchen, *Ramesside Inscriptions, Historical and Biographical*, 7 volumes (Oxford: Blackwell, 1968 to present)
LEM Alan H. Gardiner, *Late Egyptian Miscellanies*, Bibliotheca Aegyptiaca (Brussels: Édition de la Fondation Égyptologique Reine Élisabeth, 1937).
LXX Septuagint (Greek translation of the Hebrew Bible)
MBA Yohanan Aharoni and Michael Avi-Yonah, *The Macmillan Bible Atlas* (New York: Macmillan, 1968).
MIFAO Memoires de l'Institut Français d'Archéologie Orientale
MT Masoretic Text
NAB New American Bible
NASB New American Standard Bible
NBA *New Bible Atlas* (ed. J. J. Bimson, J. P. Kane, J. H. Patterson, D. J. Wiseman, & D. R. W. Wood; Downers Grove, Ill.: IV Press, 1985)
NBD *New Bible Dictionary*, revised ed. (ed. J. D. Douglas; Downers Grove, Ill.: IV Press, 1982)
NEAEHL *New Encyclopedia of Archaeological Excavations in the Holy Land*, 4 volumes (ed. Ephraim Stern; New York: Simon and Schuster, 1993).
NEASB Near East Archaeology Society Bulletin
NEB New English Bible
NIV New International Version
NIVAB Carl Rasmussen, *NIV Atlas of the Bible* (Grand Rapids, Mich.: Zondervan, 1989).
NJB New Jerusalem Bible
NJPS New Jewish Publication Society translation
NKJV New King James Version
NRSV New Revised Standard Version

OBA Herbert G. May, *Oxford Bible Atlas* (London: Oxford University Press, 1974)
OBO *Orbis Biblicus et Orientalis* (Freiberg)
OMRO *Oudheidkundige Mededelingen uit het Rijksmuseum van Oudheden te Leiden*
P Priestly source
PEQ *Palestine Exploration Quarterly*
PSBA *Proceedings of the Society of Biblical Archaeology*
R Redactor
RB *Review Bibliqué*
RITA K. A. Kitchen, *Ramesside Inscriptions Translated and Annotated: Notes and Comments,* 7 volumes (Oxford: Blackwell, 1993 to present).
RSV Revised Standard Version
RT *Recueil de travaux relatifs à la philolgie et à l'archéologie égyptiennes et assriennes*
SAK *Studien zur Altägyptischen Kultur*
SBL Society of Biblical Literature
SCA Supreme Council of Antiquities
SJOT *Scandinavian Journal of Old Testament*
TB *Tyndale Bulletin* (Cambridge)
UF *Ugarit-Forschungen*
Urk. IV Kurt Sethe, *Urkunden der 18. Dynastie,* 4 volumes (Berlin: Akademie-Verlag, 1961)
VT *Vetus Testamentum*
VTS *Vetus Testamentum Supplements*
Wb Adolf Erman and Hermann Grapow, *Wörterbuch der ägyptischen Sprache,* 5 volumes (Leipzig: J. C. Hinrichs'sche, 1926–1931).
ZÄS *Zeitschrift für Ägyptische Sprache und Altertumskunde*
ZAW *Zeitschrift fur die alttestamentliche Wissenschaft*

Chronological Charts

Syro-Palestinian Chronology

Middle Bronze II	1800–1650 B.C.
Middle Bronze IIc or III	1650–1550 B.C.
Late Bronze I	1550–1400 B.C.
Late Bronze IIA	1400–1300 B.C.
Late Bronze IIB	1300–1200 B.C.
Iron Age IA	1200–1150 B.C.
Iron Age IB	1150–1000 B.C.
Iron Age IIA	1000–925 B.C.
Iron Age IIB	925–720 B.C.
Iron Age IIC	720–586 B.C.

Dates based on Amihai Mazar's Archaeology of the Land of the Bible *(New York: Doubleday, 1990).*

Egyptian Chronology

Old Kingdom (Dynasties 3–6)	2700–2190 B.C.
First Intermediate Period (Dynasties 7–11)	2190–2106 B.C.
Middle Kingdom (Dynasties 11–12)	2106–1786 B.C.

Second Intermediate Period (Dynasties 13–17)	1786–1550 or 1539 B.C.
The Hyksos Period (Dynasties 15–16)	1648–1550 or 1540 B.C.
The New Kingdom (Dynasties 18–20)	1550 or 1539–1069 B.C.
The Eighteenth Dynasty	1550 or 1539–1295 B.C.
The Nineteenth Dynasty	1295–1186 B.C.
The Twentieth Dynasty	1186–1069 B.C.

Dates are based on the chronologies of R. Krauss and K. A. *Kitchen in* High, Middle or Low? Acts of an International Colloquiium on Absolute Chronology Held as the University of Gothenburg 20th–22nd August 1987, *parts 1–3, ed. Paul Åström (Gothenburg: Åströms Förlag, 1987–1989) and laid out in convenient chart form in Kitchen, ABD 2: 328–329.*

Ancient Israel in Sinai

I

The Wilderness Tradition

I remember the devotion of your youth,
your love as a bride,
how you followed me in the wilderness
in a land not sown.

—Jeremiah 2:2

I. The Wilderness Tradition in the Bible

The wilderness tradition dominates the Torah or Pentateuch (the first five books of the Bible) and has left a lasting impression on Israel throughout its history, down to the present day. The expression "wilderness tradition" is used in this book to refer to that body of literature that is set in the wilderness (*miḏbār*). After crossing the Re(e)d Sea in Exodus 14–15, the Hebrews arrived in Sinai; this marks the beginning of the wilderness tradition. The books of Leviticus and Numbers are also set "in the wilderness" (*bᵉmiḏbār*); in fact, these are the opening words of the latter book and served as the Hebrew name of Numbers. Furthermore, the book of Deuteronomy is also set "in the wilderness, in the Arabah" of Transjordan (Deut. 1:1). Thus, approximately two-thirds of the Torah deals with Moses and the wilderness episodes. For the most part, the present study will be limited to the Pentateuchal materials that are set in Sinai.

From the so-called historical books (or Former Prophets = Hebrew *nᵉḇîʾîm*), there are references to the wilderness tradition that may predate the references in the earliest prophetic books (e.g., Amos, Hosea, Micah—see next paragraph). Joshua, Judges, and 1 Samuel all refer to Israel's time in Sinai.[1] Joshua 5 contains a record of the circumcision of the Israelite men who had failed to be circumcised during the forty years in the wilderness:

> So Joshua made flint knives, and circumcised the Israelites at Gibeath-haaraloth. This is the reason why Joshua circumcised them: all the males of the people who came out of Egypt, all the warriors, had died during the journey through the wilderness after they had come out of Egypt. Although all the people who came out had been circumcised, yet all the people born on the journey through the wilderness after they had come out of Egypt had not been circumcised. For the Israelites traveled forty years in the wilderness, until all the nation, the warriors who came out of Egypt, perished, not having listened to the voice of the Lord. (5:3–6)

Caleb, Joshua's colleague, reminds the reader that he was with Moses for the forty years in the wilderness and specifically mentions being at Kadesh-Barnea (Josh. 14:6–10), a place that plays a central role in the book of Numbers. The Song of Deborah, regarded as a very early piece of Israelite poetry,[2] alludes to the theophany of Yahweh at Sinai (Judg. 5:5). The judge Jephthah offers a historical retrospective of early Israel's activities in the Transjordan and refers to them coming to that region from Egypt via the wilderness and Kadesh (Judg. 11:15–18). The text reports the judge as saying: "Thus says Jephthah: Israel did not take away the land of Moab or the land of the Ammonites, but when they came up from Egypt, Israel went through the wilderness to the Red Sea and came to Kadesh" (Judg. 11:15–16). Interestingly, in 1 Samuel 4:8, when the Philistines captured the ark of the covenant they were troubled by a plague that they attributed to the "gods" of Israel: "These are the gods who smote the Egyptians with every sort of plague in the wilderness."[3]

The death of Solomon resulted in the rather abrupt end of the "United Monarchy" (ca. 931 B.C.), and the establishment of two adversarial kingdoms: Israel in the north and Judah in the south (1 Kings 11–12). Although David's successor, Rehoboam, controlled Jerusalem and the temple of the Lord, Jeroboam, the founder of the Northern Kingdom, initially had no counterpart.[4] Thus Jeroboam established rival cult centers at Bethel and Dan, where he set up the infamous golden calves, declaring, "You have gone up to Jerusalem long enough. Behold your gods, O Israel, who brought you up out of the land of Egypt" (1 Kings 12:29). These final words are a quote from Aaron in the Sinai wilderness, who made a golden calf to serve as a cultic symbol to lead them on their journeys (Exod. 32:1–6).

Given the way that the Torah is dominated by the wilderness tradition, it is not surprising that subsequent biblical texts mention or allude to various episodes from that corpus, indicating how widely it influenced later thought.

The wilderness motif inspires the message of some of Israel's earliest prophets. An oracle of Amos reports God as reminding Israel: "Also I brought you up out of the land of Egypt, and led you forty years in the wilderness to possess the land of the Amorite" (Amos 2:10). This reference is significant because it brings together three blocks of tradition, the sojourn-exodus, the wilderness period, and the conquest of Canaan, understanding them as sequential events known to the eighth-century B.C. Judaean prophet.[5] Concerning the reference to the forty years in the wilderness, Gerhard Maier recently noted that "it (was) entirely self-evident that the forty years *bammidbar* is known to every listener."[6] When Amos castigates people of the Northern Kingdom for engaging in pagan sexual rites "upon garments taken in pledge" (Amos 2:8), he is referring to the prohibition in Exodus 22:26–27.[7] Thus, Amos shows an awareness not only of the events of the exodus-wilderness-conquest sequence but also of the minute details of the law itself. Another eighth-century B.C. prophet, Hosea from the Northern Kingdom of Israel, also shows familiarity with the wilderness tradition. He reminds Israel that it was in the wilderness (*miḏbar*) that God had established a covenant with them (Hos. 13:5) and that he would reestablish the broken covenant relationship by taking Israel back to the wilderness where it all began (Hos. 2:14–20). Similarly, the eighth-century prophet Micah demonstrates his familiarity with the exodus-Sinai story in chapter 6. Concerning this, Maier observes that "Mic. 6:3ff. runs very briefly through the Exodus from Egypt, Moses, Aaron, Miriam, Balak, Balaam, Shittim, and Gilgal—in the chronological sequence found in the Pentateuch, incidentally—and speaks of God's actions encountered by Israel at each of these stages in its history, without needing to clarify any elements of this history."[8]

Finally, Jeremiah, the seventh- to sixth-century B.C. prophet, speaks of the wilderness experience in language reminiscent of Hosea (Jer. 2:2, 6). Unmistakably, the eighth- and seventh-century prophets of Israel and Judah could speak about the wilderness tradition without explanatory comments, indicating that these stories were well known to audiences in both kingdoms.

Because of the centrality of the wilderness tradition to Israel's religious identity, the events from the Sinai wilderness are frequently recalled in the Psalms, ancient Israel's liturgical corpus. Reflecting the theophany at Mt. Sinai (Exod. 19), Psalm 68 states: "The earth quaked, the heavens poured down rain, at the presence of God; yon Sinai quaked at the presence of God, the God of Israel" (v. 8, RSV) and "the Lord came from Sinai into the holy place" (v. 17, RSV). Israel's testing of God at Massah and Meribah—recorded in Exodus 17:7 and Numbers 20:13 and 34—is recited in Psalms 81:7 and 95:8. The works of God are the reason for praising the Lord in Psalm 78. The plagues, the exodus, and the crossing of the sea are all recalled, as is God's provision of manna and quail (vv. 21–31, see also Ps. 105:40) and how God led them with a cloud by day and a pillar of fire by night, and provided water in the wilderness (vv. 14–16; see also Ps. 105:41). The giving of the law to Moses is mentioned in Psalms 99:7 and 103:7. And Moses's role as prophet and intercessor is acknowledged in Psalms 99:6 and 106:23. These references show that the psalmists from the first and second temple periods were familiar with the wilderness tradition as preserved in the Torah.

II. The Origins of Israel Debate

The nature of Israel's origins has been the subject of heated debate over the past twenty-five years, resulting in the publication of tens of monographs and scores of scholarly articles. A number of biblical historians and archaeologists have challenged or abandoned the traditional view presented in the Bible, that the Israelites originated as a nation in Egypt (Gen. 37–Exod. 11), were led out of Egypt and through Sinai by Moses (Exod. 12–Deut.) and on into Canaan under the leadership of Joshua, who led Israel's conquest of the land (Josh. 1–11). Two radically distinct paradigms have largely drowned out the voices of more traditional historians. The first approach, based on Enlightenment rationalism, is positivist in its treatment of biblical history. Simply put, this view will accept the claim of a story or narrative if there is independent corroboration. It has been the preeminent position in Western academe since the nineteenth century, but scholars seem to have grown more skeptical toward the historicity of the Bible in recent decades. J. Maxwell Miller and John H. Hayes would be good exemplars of this view. They maintain: "We hold that the main story line of Genesis–Joshua—creation, pre-Flood patriarchs, great Flood, second patriarchal age, entrance into Egypt, twelve tribes descended from the twelve brothers, escape from Egypt, complete collections of laws and religious instructions handed down at Mt. Sinai, forty years of wandering in the wilderness, miraculous conquests of Canaan, . . . —is an artificial and theologically influenced literary construct."[9]

The second paradigm reads the Bible using a postmodern hermeneutic, and its adherents arrive at nearly the same conclusion. Consider the position of Thomas Thompson as a spokesperson for this model: "Biblical Israel, as an element of tradition and story, such as the murmuring stories in the wilderness, . . . is a theological and literary creation."[10] Similarly, Philip Davies seemingly offers an obituary on the age of Moses and the wilderness period when he opines: "Most biblical scholars accept that there was no historical counterpart to this epoch, and most intelligent biblical archaeologists accept this too."[11] Both of these paradigms will be examined in more detail below, but for the moment, it is clear that many of those who champion these approaches are equally skeptical that the Bible can serve as a source for history. The title of a recent article by Siegfried Herrmann, "The Devaluation of the Old Testament as a Historical Source,"[12] well reflects this situation.

One might think that startling new archaeological discoveries must have been made during the last couple of decades for such radical views to be proposed. This, however, is not the case. On the contrary, it has been the absence of any direct evidence to support the Bible's claim of the sojourn in Egypt, the exodus, and Joshua's conquest of Canaan that has led these scholars to reject the historicity of these narratives. This is not the place for a review of the debate of the 1980s and 1990s, but the interested reader is encouraged to review my book, *Israel in Egypt: The Evidence for the Authenticity of the Exodus Tradition.*[13] In addition to surveying and critiquing the theories of the key figures, this study also argues for the plausibility of the sojourn-exodus story on the basis of supporting or background materials from Egypt. Another very helpful work, which contains a devastating critique of the revisionist movement in the area of biblical studies and archaeology, is William G. Dever's *What Did the Biblical Writers Know & When Did They Know it? What Archaeology Can Tell Us about the Reality of Ancient Israel,* which appeared in 2001.[14] Behind the revisionist movement, Dever shows, is a postmodern worldview and hermeneutic. This includes treating the biblical narratives as literature that does not represent reality. Additionally, a strong anti-authoritarian strain runs through this approach. It seeks to deconstruct texts and traditional values to liberate people from the supposedly oppressive, patriarchal, puritanical grip of the Bible. The reality in the text is the meaning that comes from the reader's context. Such an approach, Dever rightly notes, leads only to revisionist, nonhistories of Israel.[15]

Known for his rebuke during the 1970s and 1980s of conservative biblical archaeologists and their naïve use of archaeological data,[16] Dever now takes aim at historical revisionists and their cavalier and selective use of archaeological data. He condemns their approach by saying, "'Anti-biblical' archaeology is no improvement over 'biblical' archaeology."[17] In this statement he attacks the uncritical use of archaeological data for ideological purposes, be it by fundamentalists or revisionists.

Often called historical minimalists,[18] these scholars have continued their unrelenting attack on the Hebrew Bible's affirmations in studies that have appeared since the appearance of *Israel in Egypt* in 1997. Two noteworthy monographs are Thompson's *The Mythic Past: Biblical Archaeology and the Myth of Israel,* from which a quotation was offered above, and Israel Finkelstein and Neil Silberman's *The Bible Unearthed: Archaeology's New Vision of Ancient Israel and the Origins of Its Sacred Texts.*[19] Finkelstein and Silberman's work, because it is semipopular in nature, has attracted a broad reading.[20] Many readers have been troubled to find two Jewish scholars rejecting the foundation of their own religious tradition, by making statements about the Torah such as "The historical saga contained in the Bible—from Abraham's encounter with God and his journey to Canaan, to Moses' deliverance of the children of Israel from bondage . . . [is] a brilliant product of the human imagination."[21] Without offering any evidence, they are confident that this burst of literary brilliance took place within a generation or two during the seventh century. In other words, the stories of Israel's origins are fictitious, the product of a creative imagination and not historical memories of real events.

The recent debate has centered primarily on the exodus-sojourn tradition and on the "conquest" of Canaan as presented in the book of Joshua. Surprisingly little attention has been given to the wilderness tradition, which is central to Israel's religious traditions. The Mosaic or Sinaitic covenant, the law, the origin of Israel's cult, the ark of the covenant, the tabernacle, and the Levitical priesthood all find their origin in this section of the Torah, and yet the corpus containing this material has been largely ignored in the recent historical debate; even more surprisingly, it has been marginalized by scholars of religion, as will be shown in the following chapter.

When one considers the broad range of biblical literature and various genres represented in the passages cited above, not to mention the testimony of the Torah itself, it is hard to understand why the wilderness tradition has been so summarily dismissed in many recent scholarly works. As the texts cited previously demonstrate, the wilderness tradition is too much a part of the fabric of ancient Israel's history and religious heritage to be ripped from the rich tapestry. Furthermore, if the wilderness tradition did not reflect real events but was just the result of human imagination, how did subsequent Hebrew writers so utterly misunderstand the hoax and turn it into a history, a history that stands at the very foundation of ancient Israel's faith and permeates so much of the biblical tradition? Thinking along similar lines, Richard Elliott Friedman points out that to accept the view that the writer of the wilderness tradition invented his material in the Second Temple Period and passed it off as authentic is to make it "a pious fraud document."[22]

III. The Wilderness Tradition and the History of Scholarship

So why has the wilderness tradition been ignored or trivialized by recent investigation, whereas the exodus and conquest narratives have received more attention? Several answers might be suggested. As some scholars have abandoned the Egyptian sojourn-exodus story and the "conquest" model to account for the Israelites' entry into Canaan, a popular alternative paradigm is to view them as a purely indigenous development in the land.[23] This theory obviously has no room for the Sinai experience. Another answer to this question lies not in the results of recent investigation but in the dogma of nineteenth-century biblical scholars such as Karl Heinrich Graf and Julius Wellhausen.[24] They proposed that most of the religious texts in Exodus through Numbers were the products of Priestly writers (P), dated from the postexilic period (fifth century B.C.), and do not reflect accurately on early Israel's history or religious origins.[25] It goes without saying that Moses, the giant figure of the Torah, according to this analysis of the Bible, shrinks and either becomes a midget or disappears entirely from the radar screen of history. John Van Seters, for instance, has recently announced that "the quest for the historical Moses is a futile exercise. He now belongs only to legend."[26]

The traditional view of the Pentateuch was that Moses was largely responsible for recording these books. The name of Moses occurs 693 times in the Hebrew Bible, making him the most dominant person in Jewish scripture. He is portrayed as the writer of both historical reports and the laws revealed at Sinai. As a historian, Moses is instructed to record the events he had witnessed upon the conclusion of the battle against the Amalekites: "Write this as a memorial in a book" (סֵפֶר: *seper* = scroll) (Exod. 17:14).[27] Moses is also reported as recording the itineraries of Israel's travel: "Moses wrote down their starting places, stage by stage" (Num. 33:2). Concerning the laws, Moses is told, "Write these words; in accordance with these words I have made a covenant with you and with Israel" (Exod. 34:27). References to Moses speaking to the people are ubiquitous. So one can understand why the later biblical texts speak of the "law of Moses" (Josh. 8:3–32, 23:6; Judg. 4:11; 1 Kings 2:3; 2 Kings 14:6; Ezra 3:2). The association of Moses and the law (Torah) continues in the New Testament, where Moses is mentioned around ninety times. There are seven occurrences of the expression "law of Moses" in the New Testament, and around 150 references to "the law."

We now return to the question, how did this giant of biblical and human history vanish? In the early centuries of the Christian era, some gnostic thinkers began to question the role of Moses in the composition of the law.[28] These early critics did not have a serious impact on Christianity or Judaism on this matter; rather, the traditional consensus of Mosaic authorship of the law remained. The Cordovan Ibn Hazam, around A.D. 1000, may have been the first to suggest that Ezra, rather than Moses, was the major individual behind the law. This criticism is interesting for two reasons. First, Ibn Hazam was trying to elevate the Qur'an at the expense of the Bible. The Qur'an, however, emphasizes the role of Moses in the revelation of the law, not Ezra (e.g., surahs 10, 14, 28). Second, the suggestion that Ezra was a central figure in writing (or compiling) the law would become popular in the nineteenth and twentieth centuries. A decade after Ibn Hazam's criticism, Isaac Ibn Yashush thought there were sections of the Pentateuch that did not come from Moses, but this idea was rebutted by the sage Abraham Ibn Ezra who, however, thought there may have been post-Mosaic additions to the Torah.[29]

Seventeenth-century humanist philosophers from Europe, Hobbes and Spinoza, argued that there were episodes written within the Torah that came after the lifetime of Moses.[30] Furthermore, they questioned whether Moses could even write. It must be recalled that these questions were being raised

150 years before the discovery of the Rosetta stone, the decipherment of Egyptian hieroglyphs, and the beginnings of Assyriology. Thus Hobbes's and Spinoza's ignorance of ancient Near Eastern languages and the history of writing is excusable. (I will discuss the question of literacy and the origins of the alphabet in the Bronze Age or the second millennium B.C. below, in chapter 8.)

The driving force behind the critical question about Mosaic authorship was European Enlightenment rationalism and a bias against the Bible because of its claim to be divinely inspired. "The Bible should be treated critically like any other book" was the mantra of many critics. Another factor in shaping the skeptical attitude toward the Bible was an antipathy toward the influence that Protestant state churches had in Germany, Holland, Switzerland, and England since the days of the Reformation. Baruch Halpern's explanation for the zeitgeist of this era is most salutary: "By the eighteenth century, with England on the ascendant and the Protestant upheavals of Cromwell's era subsided, Enlightenment liberals, scientific rationalists, had emancipated themselves from the church's god; they adopted a god, almost a non-god, suited to their program." He notes that Thomas Paine in 1790 attacked the authenticity of the Torah by saying that it was the product of "some very stupid and ignorant pretenders to authorship several hundred years after the death of Moses." Paine's disdain for the Bible is further revealed when he says: "Take away from Genesis the belief that Moses was the author, on which only the strange belief that it is the Word of God has stood, and there remains nothing of Genesis but an anonymous book of stories, fables and traditionary or invented absurdities, or of downright lies." Halpern sees this rationale as purely ideological, claiming it "was no elite theological tract with a readership restricted to seminarians. It was, like Paine's other works, a manifesto for revolution, penned for the advocates of vulgar pluralism, of relativism. If Protestantism had cured Europe of the superstition of tradition, scientific rationalism could exorcise the demon of Scripture."[31]

Source criticism or the documentary hypothesis, the discipline that seeks to separate literary strands of different origin from a piece of literature, is usually traced back to the Swiss medical doctor Jean Astruc, who was the first to suggest that Genesis 1 and 2 preserved two different creation stories—the first story was attributed to the Elohist, on the basis of the use of the name Elohim (God), and the second to the Yahwist, because of the use of God's personal name, Jehovah (YHWH).[32] He believed that what he was doing was identifying sources available to Moses for the writing of Genesis. By the latter third of the nineteenth century, two additional putative sources had been identified, the Priestly (P) and the Deuteronomic (D), but there was little agreement on their dates, especially of P. There were those who actually identified the Priestly material as the earliest source. On another track, scholars such as J. S. Vater thought of these sources as made up of much shorter fragments that derived from forty different sources, and dated the final form of the Torah to the period of the exile.[33] The first three-quarters of the nineteenth century witnessed considerable debate in European academic circles concerning the dating of the various sources. The methodology was supposed to be "scientific" and objective, of course, and thus should guarantee, one would think, a degree of accordance. But there was little agreement, which is why the work of Julius Wellhausen proved to be so important.

With his *Die Composition des Hexateuch* (1877), Wellhausen left an enduring mark on critical Old Testament scholarship, for he brought order out of the dating chaos that had prevailed in the field of Old Testament studies.[34] His approach, like that of many of his predecessors, was to use various literary criteria (divine names, place names, doublets, and so on) to distinguish sources, and then date them largely on assumptions about the point in Israel's religious history that these sources reflect. He was greatly influenced by the ideas of Eduard Reuss and Karl Graf, and in many ways was not so much an innovator as a synthesizer and promoter of earlier ideas.[35] By the final quarter of the nineteenth century, Darwin's evolutionary theory had already begun to penetrate academic fields other than biology. If humans evolved from simple life forms to complex ones, it was reasoned that human culture and institutions, social and religious, must also have evolved from simple to complex forms. Pioneer anthropologists of religion, such as E. B. Tylor (*Primitive Culture*, 1871) and James Frazer (*The Golden Bough*, 1890), studied "primitive cultures" in the nineteenth century. They postulated that religion evolved, following a predictable pattern, that began with animism and totemism, moved on to polytheism, to henotheism or monolatry, and climaxed with monotheism.[36] It was thought that Israel's religion developed accordingly—a development that could be traced in the Bible—and that the religious stages were criteria for dating. This evolutionary model influenced Wellhausen's treatment of the Pentateuchal sources.[37] For him, the decisive moment was when he decided to follow Graf's dating of the law after the prophets. Wellhausen made an astonishing disclosure about how he came to this position: "In the course of a casual visit in Göttingen in the summer in 1867, I learned through Ritschl that Karl Heinrich Graf placed the Law later than the Prophets, and almost without knowing his reasons for the hypothesis, I was prepared to accept it; I readily acknowledged to myself the possibility of understanding Hebrew antiquity without the book of the Torah."[38] It is incredible that one who saw his approach to the Pentateuch as scientific and objective would so quickly accept this radical view without even investigating it! Furthermore, Wellhausen's theory that the law came after the prophets, and that the wilderness tradition derived from the statements in the prophets is peculiar. How could a well-developed narrative spring from passing references and allusions? Logically one would think that a prophet would only need to allude to events or use symbolic language associated with place or action that his audience well understood; otherwise, the allusions would be meaningless.[39] Nevertheless, Wellhausen's evolutionary model and his dating of the Pentateuchal sources soon became the virtually uncontested orthodoxy within biblical scholarship for the next century.

If ever there was an assured conclusion of biblical scholarship, it was that the Hexateuch (Genesis through Joshua, as Wellhausen envisioned it) was a composite document that could be tied to four primary, separate, datable documents: the Jahwist (J) from the ninth century, the Elohist (E) from the eighth century, the Deuteronomist (D) from the seventh century (the Josianic reforms), and the Priestly source (P) from the fifth century, and that these sources were brought together by a redactor (R) in the postexilic period. For nearly a century, Wellhausen's views, (with some minor variations), also known as the documentary hypothesis, dominated Old Testament studies, and, except for some "conservative" Jewish and Christian scholars, these conclusions were uncritically embraced by succeeding generations of scholars. With the emergence of Near Eastern and cognate studies, which investigate comparable biblical and Near Eastern literature, however, a number of scholars began to question the prevailing consensus, although these scholars have generally been viewed with suspicion by the mainstream of biblical scholarship.[40] In recent years, an increasing number of biblical scholars within the guild have begun to distance themselves from the nineteenth-century synthesis. While some are revising conclusions of the last century, others are rejecting them altogether. For instance, Van Seters has argued for down-dating J to the sixth century and the elimination of E as an independent source. For him, D (seventh century) becomes the earliest source that is true history writing.[41]

The traditional fifth-century dating for the P materials has in recent decades been questioned on linguistic grounds. On the basis of the language of P, Avi Hurvitz argues for a late preexilic date.[42] Along similar lines, Robert Polzin addresses the date of P from a grammatical perspective. Based on clearly datable postexilic works, which he calls Late Biblical Hebrew, he observes that sections of the Pentateuch, and P in particular, are written in Classical Biblical Hebrew and notes the late form, which would be expected of a genuinely later work.[43] Z. Zevit suggests a terminus ad quem of 586 B.C. for P on socioreligious grounds.[44] Building on the foundations of these works, Gary Rendsburg has proposed pushing the P materials back to the united monarchy (tenth century); most recently, Friedman has argued persuasively that P should be dated prior to the destruction of Jerusalem in 586 B.C., and that Reuss, Graf, and Wellhausen were "simply wrong" to date P to the Second Temple period.[45]

While some cosmetic changes were being proposed about the dating of J and P, starting in the mid-1980s a number of works appeared that challenged Wellhausen's long-accepted methodology, assumptions, and conclusions. Moshe Weinfeld, on the centenary of Wellhausen's *Prolegomena*, wrote an essay that illustrates the changing mood.[46] Isaac M. Kikawada and Arthur Quinn's book bears a telling subtitle on its cover: "A Provocative Challenge to the Documentary Hypothesis."[47] These professors are from the University of California, Berkeley, and not from a conservative theological college or seminary. No religious or ideological agenda can be assigned to their motives, which is the typical charge leveled against scholars who have dared to question the nineteenth- and twentieth-century scholarship's Tetragrammaton: J E D P.

Kikawada and Quinn compare the structure of early Genesis with that of the Atrahasis epic as the basis for the view that Genesis follows and adapts the structural and thematic features of the Babylonian counterpart. They observe that "the five-part Atrahasis structure is a crucial inheritance of the Hebrew tradition from the ancient Near Eastern civilizations. In a more general sense we have shown that at least one Hebrew author—and a most important one at that—has assumed on the part of the audience a knowledge of this convention." Regarding traditional source criticism, they conclude: "One thing, if anything, we are certain of: the documentary hypothesis at present is woefully overextended."[48]

In 1987, R. N. Whybray offered perhaps the most comprehensive critique of the documentary hypothesis. He poses many tough questions that undermine the theological and stylistic criteria for identifying a certain pericope with a particular source or date.[49] For him, the first ten books in the Hebrew canon are a collection of fragments assembled into its present form in the postexilic period. Although Whybray's penetrating critique of orthodox source criticism is compelling, his proposal represents a return to the old, long-abandoned, fragmentary late eighteenth-century theory advanced by Geddes and Vater, who further developed this hypothesis in an 1805 commentary on the Pentateuch.[50] In the end, Whybray's alternative theory does not advance Pentateuchal studies but sets it back two centuries.[51] Even some of the post-modern minimalists, such as Thompson, are rejecting the old source-critical synthesis. He prefers to see the Pentateuch as comprising literary blocks that he called "narrative chains."[52] He opines that the "affirmation of their existence is a refutation of the documentary hypothesis. The delineation of this narrative level in the Pentateuch offers an incompatible alternative to the hypothesis of sources."[53]

As the documentary hypothesis has lost some of its mastery over Old Testament studies during the past twenty years, tradition history criticism has gained in popularity. Built on the foundation of source criticism and Hermann Gunkel's form criticism, tradition criticism is interested in investigating the prehistory (the traditions) of the text, both oral and written.[54] First Martin Noth and more recently Rolf Rendtorff have championed this approach.[55] This paradigm has been viewed as a serious attack on the old documentary hypothesis in a recent monograph by Nicholson.[56] Indeed, tradition criticism has played a role in the demise of source criticism's preeminent place in Old Testament studies, but Whybray also questions its validity.[57] Although investigating the tradition history of biblical texts has some merit, the amount of subjectivity used in this method poses a serious challenge and, like Wellhausen's source-critical method, certain historical, social, and religious assumptions are made that cannot be convincingly substantiated. Recently, the tradition history approach has been criticized by Van Seters, who points out that it relies too much on assumptions about a preliterate, oral stage of the tradition and how it developed.[58] Naturally, this method, like source criticism, lacks any external controls. It goes without saying that there are no tape recordings of an oral stage of these traditions to test these hypotheses, any more than there are independent surviving manuscripts of J or P that would predate their incorporation into the Torah.

Source criticism and tradition criticism remain pillars in the field of Pentateuchal studies. Their influence, however, seems to have given way to new sociological and literary approaches. The analysis of structure and form of a narrative has shifted from a microscopic study of the Bible, an examination of sources, to a macro or panoramic view of narratives. In order to see the current influence of these literary approaches on the field of biblical studies, one need only consult the program of the annual meetings of the Society of Biblical Literature. Building on the findings of an earlier generation of scholars such as Umberto Cassuto, the "new literary approach" is interested in the broader literary characteristics of a story or passage. The fact that chiasmus operates both on the micro and macro levels, for instance, has resulted in recognizing the literary unity of the flood story.[59] The significance here is that for over a century the flood story, along with the creation narratives, was the starting point for adherents of the documentary hypothesis.[60]

Robert Alter's *The Art of Biblical Literature* has made a significant contribution to new literary readings, and a host of biblical scholars now employs this more comprehensive approach.[61] Such analyses have enabled the reader to see the tapestry of the text, and have shed new light on the rhetorical and thematic dimensions of narratives that have long been overlooked. Scholarly investigation of the past century has been preoccupied with identifying literary threads or strands (that is, sources), thus missing the design of the fabric, which was there all along. To use another metaphor, scholars were so bent on looking at the trees that they missed the forest.

One recent example of this approach is Mary Douglas's *In the Wilderness*.[62] Douglas brilliantly combines her expertise as an anthropologist of religion with a literary reading of the book of Numbers and shows that the book is structured chiastically.

Although literary approaches have provided a breath of fresh air to the now stale, overworked source-critical approaches of the past two centuries, they do pose a problem. Literary readings of the biblical texts often imply a lack of interest in the historical, social, and legal aspects of the narratives, which are the concern of most biblical scholars and historians. For Alter, biblical literature is regarded as "prose fiction."[63] Some postmodern biblical historians have seized upon this point. Philip Davies, for instance, asserts: "All story is fiction, and that must include historiography."[64] On the face of it, this claim is illogical. How can one claim that a work of historiography is fiction? If it is fiction, it can't be historiography. In modern times we have a genre of literature called historical novel in which the author constructs a story using a genuine historical setting and may even weave the story into recognized historical events. But there is no evidence that such a genre was known in the ancient Near East.[65]

Furthermore, Davies declares that "texts cannot reproduce reality except as a textual artifact."[66] If he truly believed this mantra, one wonders why he bothers to write books and articles! For surely, if he is right, Davies can only produce textual artifacts that tell us about him and his worldview, not ancient Israel!

Another example of literary reading of the Bible and regarding it as fiction is found in the more recent writing of Thompson. He claims, "However much archeologists might need a story world to flesh out the bones of their history, or however much they might wish that the Bible's nations were scattered among their potsherds, the wish for the Bible to be history has only confused the discussion about how the Bible relates to the past.... Our question involves more complicated issues of literary historicality and reference, of metaphor and literary postures, evocation and conviction. The Bible doesn't deal with what happened in the past."[67] I contend, however, that using a literary or structural framework that includes such features as chiasm and doublets need not militate against the historicity of the narratives. Let me offer an example of a literary approach that does not jettison history. J. Robin King offers a literary analysis of the stories of Joseph in Genesis and Moses in Exodus that treats the genre of these stories as "a special kind of hero tale," utilizing the ten-step narrative structure found in the Egyptian story of Sinuhe.[68] This Egyptian story originated in the Twelfth Dynasty (ca. 1940 B.C.) and continued to be transmitted down to the Nineteenth Dynasty (ca. thirteenth century B.C.).[69] The ten steps include (1) initial situation, (2) threat, (3) threat realized, (4) exile, (5) success in exile, (6) exilic agon, (7) exilic victory, (8) threat overcome, (9) return and reconciliation, and (10) epilogue.[70] These narrative steps are found in other Near Eastern stories, including those of Idrimi of Alalakh, Hattusilis of Hattusas, Esarhaddon of Assyria, and Nabonidus of Babylon, spanning the second through the mid-first millennia B.C. Their stories are described by King as being "much more historical and lack[ing] the rhetorical polish and romance of the Egyptian story [i.e., Sinuhe]. To be sure, they are all tendentious, but their tendentiousness is expected in the *kind of history writing* they are—dynastic apologetics."[71] Could it be that some aspects of this widely dispersed Near Eastern literary pattern were employed by the Hebrew author(s) to present the biblical stories? In view of the fact that Idrimi, Hattusilis, Esarhaddon, and Nabonidus are well-attested historical rulers, it would seem imprudent to attribute fictional status to the biblical heroes because of the use of this or similar literary structures.[72] On the contrary, if the ten narrative steps of the hero tale are consistently applied to historical personalities, then it should be recognized as a legitimate historiographical technique, as King observes, used by scribes of the ancient Near East, including Hebrew writers.

The use of new literary approaches by biblical scholars has certainly undermined the foundation of the old source-critical consensus. The eighteenth- and nineteenth-century bulwark is now in serious trouble, and the result has been a scramble to determine the dates and reliability of the sources or traditions. As Whybray explains, "With regard to written sources, the rejection of the Documentary Hypothesis simply increases the range of possibilities."[73] The tendency has been to push these sources even later than Wellhausen ever would have imagined.[74] Some of the historical minimalists who have been engaged in the debate over the origins of Israel during the past twenty years have even championed a Hellenistic dating for the composition of various Hebrew books. A recent example of this approach is an edited work entitled *Did Moses Speak Attic? Jewish Historiography and Scripture in the Hellenistic Period.*[75] The thought that the Pentateuch originates in the Hellenistic period cannot be taken seriously, but that is what some of the contributors to this volume advocate. The Hellenistic era (ca. 300–100 B.C.) is the period of the composition of noncanonical or apocryphal works such as Judith and the books of Maccabees. And, not surprisingly, some are written in Greek, not Hebrew, nor even Late Biblical Hebrew, let alone Biblical Hebrew. This is also the period when the Septuagint, the Greek translation of the Hebrew canon, was being made. The Hellenistic period was a time when Greek culture and language were dominating the Mediterranean world; it was not a period known for producing Hebrew literature. Criticism of the radical notion of a Hellenistic-period composition for the biblical books is also offered by Rainer Albertz in *Did Moses Speak Attic?* and by William Dever.[76]

The past twenty years have clearly been tumultuous ones in Pentateuchal studies. The title of Nicholson's recent essay, "The Pentateuch in Recent Research: A Time for Caution," rightly expresses the anxiety of not a few traditional biblicists. To be sure, new literary approaches to Old Testament studies have had their detractors.[77] Many, like Nicholson, John Emerton, Joseph Blenkinsopp, and Friedman, continue to serve as apologists for the flagging documentary hypothesis and its nineteenth-century assumptions, albeit with some modifications.[78] Nevertheless, it is abundantly clear from the foregoing review that "the assured results" of nineteenth-century source criticism no longer have ascendancy in the study of the Hebrew Bible. Sociological and literary methods are enjoying widespread use and could eclipse older approaches.[79] And Nicholson himself is forced to admit that "the

Documentary theory which he [Wellhausen] had so persuasively argued was in the ascendant, commanding ever increasing support, today is in sharp decline—some would say in a state of advanced rigor mortis—and new solutions are being argued and urged in its place."[80]

IV. Historians and the Wilderness Tradition

As the foregoing section illustrates, much of the wilderness tradition has been assigned to P, and therefore, according to Graf, Wellhausen, and many scholars since, it dates to postexilic times (ca. fifth century). There is a tendency among biblical scholars and historians to think that if a narrative derives from a late source, and thus is far removed in time from the event(s) described, that the source cannot be reliable.

The assumption that a historian working with a late source (that is, one separated by considerable time from the events being described) is unreliable for historical study has some merit and in some cases may be true, but is logically flawed. If the issue of how much time separates a historian and his or her data is the deciding factor in one's ability to write an accurate history, then it is utterly futile for any present-day historian to attempt to write history about any earlier period unless there are living and reliable human witnesses to the event in question.

The reality is that critical historians *can* work with sources from very close to the time of the events they investigate and produce works that are spurious because the sources were unreliable even though they were old. On the other hand, one can use more recent sources that are centuries, or even millennia, removed from the events being described, but because they faithfully preserve records of the events, they *can* be relied upon by the modern scholar to write a faithful account of what actually happened in the past. And then too, it is possible for ancient sources to be preserved accurately into later periods, as critical biblical historian Alberto Soggin has acknowledged.[81]

In ancient Egypt, for example, there are religious texts preserved on the walls of Greco-Roman period temples that are based on Middle Egyptian texts from 1,500 to 2,000 years before.[82] Another, perhaps even more relevant illustration is the case of *Aegyptiaca,* Manetho's historical treatise (ca. 290–260 B.C.). Despite the fact that *Aegyptiaca* has not survived, it remains the basis for dynastic sequence (1–30) still used by historians today.[83] Manetho apparently utilized earlier sources such as the Karnak king list (ca. 1450 B.C.), the Turin Canon, and the Abydos and Sakkara king lists (ca. 1300–1270 B.C.), written one thousand years before Manetho's day.[84] Sections of these lists that include the names of kings from Dynasties 1–6, in turn, are based on much earlier texts such as the Palermo stone from the ca. 2300–2400 B.C. Thus, as much as two millennia separate Manetho from the earliest periods about which he writes. *Aegyptiaca*, however, is preserved only in quotations by Josephus in *Contra Apion* (A.D. 90) and in the writings of early Christian writers, Julius Africanus (ca. A.D. 180–250) and Eusebius (ca. A.D. 260–340).[85] Thus when present-day researchers want to consult Manetho, they have to read Josephus, Africanus, and Eusebius, who lived 350 to 600 years after him. And the most reliable and complete version of the *Chronicle* of Africanus survives in an Armenian version that dates between A.D. 1065 and 1306![86] Furthermore, one must realize that Manetho is separated from the sources upon which he relied by one and as many as two thousand years. Today we are around 1,700 years removed from the Christian sources. Despite the great span of time, the transmissions of the texts, and their translations from original Egyptian sources to Greek, historians today take Manetho seriously and follow his dynastic system.

What is incredible about this foregoing illustration is that historians in general and Egyptologists in particular treat Manetho as a partner in the historical enterprise,[87] whereas many critical biblical historians do not extend the same deference to the Bible. So much for treating the Bible like any other book! In the case of the Hebrew scriptures, the time between the period of composition of some books and the oldest extant documents (i.e., the Dead Sea Scrolls, first to second centuries B.C.) represent in some cases only a period of four to six centuries. The important questions, then, are not how much time separates the historian from the sources consulted, but whether they are reliable and whether they are judiciously and critically used by the historian.

It is not clear why there has been a predisposition by many scholars over the past two centuries to date the Pentateuchal materials so late, and then reject evidence that points to an earlier date. My own suspicion is that ideology lies at the root. Either they want the material to be late so as to fit a particular theory or model they advocate, or they want the sources to be late (operating under the assumption that later sources are poor sources) so as to discredit the historical reliability of the Bible. This in turn allows them to reconstruct the history, social framework, and moral or religious traditions in a manner that is more aligned with their own view of things.

I am not alone in suggesting that a biased agenda of some sort is at issue here. Consider the title of Keith Windschuttle's 1996 book, *The Killing of History: How Literary Critics and Social Theorists Are Murdering Our Past*. The author, a modern historian, documents how recent historians are rewriting history by using postmodern methods for reasons of political correctness. Windschuttle gives examples where postmodern historians selectively ignore or include data, thereby distorting evidence so as to obtain the desired end. Although his study is limited to historical events from the time of Columbus to twentieth-century events, his methodological and philosophical observations can be equally applied to biblical scholars who have embraced a postmodern hermeneutic. Some biblical scholars now acknowledge that there is a reductionist or revisionist agenda driving the recent debate, be it positivist or postmodernist. This agenda is reflected in the title of a recent article by Halpern: "Erasing History: The Minimalist Assault on Ancient Israel," and Dever, as mentioned above, has made the connection for us between postmodern hermeneutics and recent biblical minimalism.[88]

Despite these perspectives, not all biblical historians have taken such a dim view of the wilderness tradition. It goes without saying that an earlier generation of scholars, including William F. Albright, G. Ernest Wright, Roland de Vaux, and John Bright, treated the wilderness tradition seriously and believed that it derived from Israel's experiences in Sinai after the exodus from Egypt, even if they were recorded some centuries after the event.[89]

In a new study of Israel's origins, Dever, while somewhat moderating his position, nevertheless refers to the historical value of the wilderness episodes in the Torah as "suspect." And then, concerning the route the Israelites traveled in Sinai as reported in the Pentateuch, Dever states that "after a hundred years of exploration and excavation in the Sinai Desert, archaeologists can say little about the 'route of the Exodus.'" This appears to have influenced his position that Israel is largely an internal development within the Levant, to which may have been added a small Moses group—including the so-called Joseph tribes—that came from Egypt to Canaan.[90]

Among German scholars, Martin Noth recognized the importance of the wilderness tradition and considered it to be one of the blocks of tradition, along with those of the Patriarchs, exodus, and conquest, that made up the Hexateuch. Although he proposed that it was added to the Pentateuchal material "at a relatively late date," the tradition itself, nevertheless, could be traced to "before the beginning of the formation of the Kingdom."[91] By this he means that originally the tradition contained the travel of the Hebrews from the sea crossing directly to Kadesh-Barnea—with no trek to Mt. Sinai for the giving of the law. But at some later date, the Mt. Sinai narratives were inserted into the earlier sequence. This view was shared by Gerhard von Rad, who pointed to the absence of a reference to the wilderness tradition in the creed found in Deuteronomy 26:5–9 as the basis for his opinion.[92] The theory that the wilderness tradition was interpolated between the Exodus-Kadesh narratives at a late date is one reason a number of scholars attach little weight to its historical worth.[93] If we grant Noth and von Rad's view that the wilderness tradition was a late insertion, it does not mean that the narratives themselves are late in origin or fabricated (as Wellhausen maintained). Furthermore, von Rad's reason for late-dating the Sinai episodes because of their absence in the creed of Deuteronomy 26 is an argument from silence. The absence of evidence proves little. It is, in fact, negative evidence. Historian David Hackett Fischer observes that in writing history, "evidence must always be affirmative. Negative evidence is a contradiction in terms—it is not evidence at all." He points out that to write history in this manner is fallacious, that is, it employs the "fallacy of negative proof," which "is an attempt to sustain a factual proposition merely by negative evidence."[94]

In fairness to Noth and his "insertion" theory, it should be said that he nevertheless believed that the central elements of the wilderness tradition, especially the making of the covenant and the giving of the law, "derived from an actual event."[95]

V. How to Read Ancient Texts

At an earlier time it was quite revolutionary to say that one should treat the Bible with the same critical eye as used for any other book. Now, it is interesting to see how many critical scholars, especially those in the minimalist-revisionist camp, do not treat the Bible like any other book. Rather there seems to be a double standard that accepts the claims made in Egyptian or Assyrian texts without external proof, but demands of a biblical witness that it must be corroborated by outside sources. I have pointed out this duplicity in *Israel in Egypt*,[96] and in a more recent essay where I observed, "In the 'origins of Israel' debate of the 1980's and 1990's, many critical scholars rejected the historical value of the Joshua narratives on the grounds that they are tendentious, as well as theological and ideological in nature. These same tendencies permeate the Mernptah Stela. Nevertheless, these same scholars readily accept the historical value of this important text."[97] It is gratifying to see that Dever has also drawn attention to this double standard when he says, "How is it that the biblical texts are always approached with postmodernism's typical 'hermeneutics of suspicion,' but the non-biblical texts are taken at face value? It seems to be that the Bible is automatically held guilty unless proven innocent."[98]

Some of the scholars to whom I am making reference include Giovanni Garbini, Gösta Ahlström, and Niels Peter Lemche.[99] For them no outside verification is required for the Merneptah stela, although these scholars may interpret the reference to "Israel" differently. But when the biblical writers make claims, external proof is a precondition for the assertion to be accepted as historical. In fairness to Thompson, in his more recent work, he transforms even royal monumental inscriptions, like the Mesha stela, into a literary work, so that now the mention of King Omri of Israel in this inscription "is literary, not historical."[100] Consequently, the Mesha stela from ancient Moab cannot be used to confirm the historicity of the Bible's account in 2 Kings 3.

My approach to texts will always attempt to treat texts, be they of Egyptian, Mesopotamian, Canaanite, or Hebrew origin, in the same manner, and follow the admonition of William W. Hallo to "treat the ancient sources critically but without condescension."[101] This naturally raises the larger question of historiography that was treated in some detail in my *Israel in Egypt* (pp. 10–17); only a couple of points will be made here.

I embrace Hallo's understanding of history, that it "begins where writing begins and I see no reason to exempt Israel from this working hypothesis."[102] Important too is Johan Huizinga's understanding that "every civilization creates its own form of history."[103] This means that the present-day scholar should not demand that ancient literature—Egyptian, Assyrian, or Hebrew—must conform to a Western understanding of historiography to be considered historical, and we should not expect to find a one-size-fits-all genre called "historiography," as advocated by Van Seters.[104] George Mendenhall concurs, saying, "Because the Israelites used history-writing conventions different from ours does not mean that they were unable or unwilling to preserve traditions about historical people and events."[105]

If the historian thinks there is a problem with a text's trustworthiness, I maintain, the burden of proof lies with the modern investigator, not the ancient writer who cannot explain himself to the historian. Minimalists who insist that a statement in the Bible be proven by an external source in order to be accepted as reflecting reality are committing the historical fallacy of presumptive proof, which, according to Fischer, "consists in advancing a proposition and shifting the burden of proof or disproof to others."[106]

Kenneth A. Kitchen, an Egyptologist who works expertly with a number of different ancient Near Eastern languages as well as Hebrew, offered a way of looking at texts over thirty years ago that remains germane. He proposed: "It is normal practice to assume the general reliability of statements in our sources, unless there is good, explicit evidence to the contrary. Unreliability, secondary origins, dishonesty of a writer, or tendentious traits—all these must be clearly proved by adduction of tangible evidence, and not merely inferred to support a theory."[107]

The approach utilized in the present volume will follow this principle and will use the "scripture in context," or "contextual approach" of Hallo as the wilderness tradition is investigated.[108] De Vaux similarly described this methodology regarding the early Hebrew history of Israel. Concerning how a historian should treat the Bible, de Vaux declared that "Israel is one of the peoples of the ancient Near East whose place and role he puts in general history. He reconstructs its political and economic history, studies its social, political, and religious institutions and its culture, as he does or would do for any other people. The Bible is for him a document of history which he criticizes, and controls, and supplements by the information which he can obtain outside of the Bible. The result is a history of Israel."[109] This method of investigating biblical texts, then, insists that the linguistic, historical, and social setting of the Hebrew writings be examined in the light of cognate literature of Israel's neighbors.

To summarize, the approach to reading the Bible in this volume will entail

1. treating the Bible and all Near Eastern literature critically, but without condescension. Unfortunately, too many minimalist historians seem to have confused a critical reading with a skeptical reading: the more skeptical, the more objective. I reject this premise.
2. reading the Hebrew Bible contextually, that is, trying to understand and interpret the Bible through the lens of data provided by other ancient texts, archaeological data, geography, and so on. This means being sensitive to ancient literary conventions, which should help prevent a literal reading when a metaphorical reading was intended, and vice versa, and not forcing modern literary conventions on ancient texts.
3. assuming that when a historical claim is made that it was intended to communicate some reality. I will assume the text to be innocent until proven guilty, rather than guilty until proven innocent. If a particular genre is encountered that is known for its use of hyperbole or nonchronological narration, these features will be taken into account before rendering a conclusion.

In this chapter we have largely addressed some fundamental questions about history and the wilderness tradition, but the tradition is not exclusively about history but also about religious laws, rituals, practices, and institutions. As such, the wilderness tradition has also attracted the attention of historians of religion and theologians over the centuries. To this we now turn as we seek to address how religionists have viewed these texts. And in the chapters after that, at the risk of appearing to be an unintelligent archaeologist in Philip Davies's world, we shall take a deeper look at archaeological and linguistic data as a backdrop to studying the wilderness tradition.

2

The Wilderness Tradition and the Historian of Religion

I. Religions of Israel and the Wilderness Tradition

Beginning in the nineteenth century, the *Religionswissenschaft* (the comparative study of religion) approach to the study of Israelite religion thrived in Europe.[1] The idea behind this method was to investigate the religion of Israel in a "scientific" manner by applying the methods of the historian, which were supposedly not tainted by the biases of the theologian. Influenced by the Enlightenment positivism of Auguste Comte (1798–1857), the concerns of the *Religionswissenschaft* approach include[2]

1. treating the religion of Israel comparatively with its other Near Eastern counterparts by examining categories such as deity, cult, temple, sacred writings, and priesthood;
2. being largely descriptive and reducing Israelite religion to its commonality with other religions rather than stressing its differences or uniqueness (this was more the emphasis of theology);
3. inspiring an interest in the religion's historical development and the historical and social contexts out of which these developments occurred;
4. rejecting the concept of revelation;
5. holding evolutionary theory as foundational.

Julius Wellhausen, whose methodology and contributions to the formulation of the documentary hypothesis were discussed in some detail in the previous chapter, had a deep interest in the history of Israel's religion. "Like many other scholars since his time," R. K. Harrison observed, "once Wellhausen had formulated his evolutionary theory to his own satisfaction—based though it was on only a small part of the evidence—he displayed a complete indifference towards subsequent anthropological or archaeological discoveries, even though they demanded a substantial modification of his original position."[3]

Study of Israel's religion has come a long way in the past century.[4] The abundance of data provided by archaeologists in the Near East has offered a more balanced understanding of ancient religions than those reached by anthropologists studying "primitive" cultures in nineteenth-century Africa, Asia, and South America, which influenced nineteenth-century scholars who studied Israelite religion. The discovery of the Ugaritic texts in 1929 at Ras Shamra, for example, has revolutionized the study of Israelite religion vis-à-vis Canaanite religion.[5]

The study of "religions of Israel" from the middle to the end of the twentieth century witnessed the integration of the biblical texts with ancient texts and other archaeological materials, but the Bible served as the primary source. Some representatives of this interdisciplinary approach include William F. Albright, Yehezkel Kaufmann, Roland de Vaux, and Helmer Ringgren.[6] And all of these studies include some treatment of the wilderness tradition and its role in the development of ancient Israel's religion. In fact, the title of one chapter in Ringgren's book, "The Beginnings of Israel's Religion: Moses," acknowledges the centrality of the wilderness tradition to Israel's religion. Operating within the *Religionsgeschichte* (history of religion) method, Georg Fohrer's *History of Israelite Religion* represented something of a departure from earlier German scholarship. He was, for instance, convinced of an Israelite exodus under the leadership of Moses or a Moses host or group, and considered the nomadic period of Israel's history critical to the formation of the religion.[7] A more recent, two-volume study of Israelite religion in the German tradition is that of Rainer Albertz.[8] This scholar follows a tradition history approach to the Pentateuch, while seeking to integrate the methodology of the history of religions and Old Testament theology. Since the nineteenth century, it has been common to separate these two lines of study because they were thought to be incompatible, the former being more scientific and interested in obtaining knowledge, whereas the latter was concerned with issues of faith for the present-day believing community. As far as the wilderness tradition is concerned, Albertz believes that a small, liberated group of Hebrews came out of Egypt and that there was some sort of wilderness experience.[9] He maintains, however, that these traditions are late, postexilic in date. In his own words: "there is a period of a good 800 years between it [the time of writing] and the real historical course of events."[10] For him, the wilderness tradition is largely a theological construct, behind which stands a genuine event.

More recent study of ancient Israel's religion has moved in a slightly different direction, however. Probably owing to the renewed skepticism toward the historicity of the Pentateuch (as noted in chapter 1), and the view that the Bible is elitist and ideological, archaeological remains have replaced the Bible as the primary source of information. Mark Smith's *Early History of God* (1990) and his more recent *The Origins of Biblical Monotheism* (2001) focus primarily on archaeological data, especially Ugaritic texts, to explain the origins of Israel's God.[11] Moses, the exodus, and the wilderness tradition play no role for Smith. Although he never explicitly says so, one gets the impression that his emphasis on "Israel's Canaanite Heritage" derives from a revisionist model that Israel's origins as a people and a religious community are to be found in Canaan rather than Egypt.[12]

Susan Niditch's recent book (1997) promotes the idea that archaeological data offer a more objective way to understand ancient Israel's religion. She avers: "There is, however, a way to explore the Israelite story without using the Hebrew Bible."[13] The archaeological data, she notes, do not portray a religion like that promoted in the Bible itself. And herein lies the tension in pitting archaeology against the Bible, or the Bible against archaeology. A purely artifact-based reconstruction of Israel's religion is destined to reflect almost entirely popular religion, inasmuch as excavation within the Temple Mount in Jerusalem, ancient Israel's (and later Judah's) preeminent religious center, remain off limits to investigators.[14] Fortunately, Niditch does not stop with archaeology but deals with "the experiential," in which she shows appreciation for the contributions of historians of religion.[15]

Two other monographs on Israelite religion from the very end of the twentieth century that warrant mention are those of Othmar Keel and Christoph Uehlinger (1998), and Patrick Miller (2000).[16] The former is a unique contribution to ancient Israelite religion that studies iconographic materials from Canaan and Israel diachronically from the Middle Bronze through the Iron Ages. Drawing on a vast corpus of artifacts, including seals, scarabs, amulets, statues, and molded and painted vessels, Keel and Uehlinger are able to show how religious beliefs developed over the centuries. As important as this study is, it does not treat the wilderness tradition per se. Miller's volume uses a topical approach and traces developments historically. For him, the Bible—following the traditional source-critical approach—is the starting point in the study of religion, but he judiciously integrates it with archaeological material. He does not consider the wilderness tradition to be integral to Israel's religious traditions, although he does allow for the possibility that a "Moses group or Proto-Israel" learned of Yahweh through Jethro the priest of Midian and father-in-law of Moses.[17]

Continuing in the tradition of utilizing archaeological materials as the primary source for studying Israel's religion, Beth Nakhai has authored one of the first works to appear in the new century.[18] Her work considers archaeological materials to be independent witnesses to Canaanite and Israelite religion. Concentrating on sanctuaries and shrines, Nakhai uses sociological and anthropological methods to propose the political and kinship-based relationships that influenced how these religious entities functioned.

Finally, another study of ancient Israel's religion to appear early in the twenty-first century was authored by Ziony Zevit.[19] This massive volume is thoroughly documented, contains a large and helpful bibliography, and critically uses archaeological materials, especially architectural and epigraphic sources from ancient Israel. What makes this book superior to most histories of Israelite religion in recent decades, in my judgment, is that Zevit examines ancient Israel's religion through a phenomenological approach. This method has been widely used by historians of religion in the twentieth century, though most religionists who have studied ancient Israelite religion seem unaware of it. Because the phenomenological approach takes history seriously, Zevit understandably offers a detailed discussion about the different approaches to historiography, and concludes that the study of ancient Israel's religion entails historical research "because it cannot be isolated from the warp and weave of biblical historiography."[20] Zevit, however, concentrates much of his study on ancient epigraphic materials from ancient Israel, and thus the wilderness tradition is passed over.

Thanks to archaeological discoveries of the past fifty years, we know much more about popular religion today than previous generations did. The goddess and her role in Israel has received considerable attention, aided by such titillating discoveries as the Khirbet el-Kom and Kuntillet el-Ajrud inscriptions that mention YHWH and his Asherah.[21] These and other discoveries in Israel over the past thirty years have caused quite a stir, demanding that scholars focus attention on popular religion in ancient Israel.[22] These finds have inspired the writing of numerous monographs and scores of articles.[23] Rather than redefining Israelite religion or demanding that we rethink what was "official" (the dogma that promulgated from the Temple in Jerusalem) at a given period, these discoveries complete the picture of what the prophets so regularly denounced in the name of orthodox Yahwism. Dever puts it this way: "One way to define popular religion would be to look not only at the archaeological evidence, which may differ radically from the official texts, but also to look closely at the condemnation of religious practices in the texts of the Hebrew Bible. In doing so we are making a practical and legitimate assumption, namely that prophets, priests and reformers 'know what they were talking about.' That is, the situation about which they complained was real, not invented by them as a foil for their revisionist message."[24]

Although recent discoveries that have provided new insights into Israelite popular religion are interesting, they do not, in my view, shed any light on Israel's religious origins as portrayed in the wilderness tradition, which is the interest of the present study. The Bible indeed does portray an ongoing tension between Canaanite religion and rituals and Israel's faith. What seems to alarm the Israelite prophets and historians is that elements of Canaanite religion made their way into the official circles of the priesthood and royalty in Jerusalem. For the writers of the Hebrew scriptures, the good kings (such as Jehoshophat, Hezekiah, Josiah) were the reformers who upheld the Torah and attempted to rid the land of the high places, the pillars, the Asherim—whereas the kings who entangled themselves in the cultic practices of Israel's neighbors were viewed as evil. Although it may be true that Yahwistic monotheism became the orthodox position in the Second Temple Period (as most historians of Israelite religion maintain), it will be argued here, following the views of Kaufmann, that the roots of Israelite monotheism derived from the Sinai theophany.[25] Rather than viewing monotheism as the result of an evolutionary process, postexilic orthodoxy should be regarded as a fundamentalist return to original ideals found in the Torah, whose roots go back to the wilderness tradition.

II. The Religionist and the Bible

Many of the scholars who have been engaged in the study of ancient Israel's religion during recent decades have been trained biblical scholars, theologians, and archaeologists. Their works, some of which were mentioned in the previous section, largely ignore or are unfamiliar with the methodologies used by historians of religion who work outside of the field of biblical religion. I point this out because it is largely religionists who come from these academic disciplines who are in the trenches of the methodological debates about how to study modern and ancient religions. The contributions of anthropologists and sociologists of religion, however, have had a greater impact on recent biblical scholars who investigate Israel's religion.

One of the most deleterious approaches to the study of ancient Israel has been Enlightenment rationalism, which still influences biblical scholarship. Enlightenment thinking was reductionistic. Human reason was king and an antisupernatural mindset was the prime minister of this system.[26] Immanuel Kant's dictum "Dare to use your own reason" well reflects the dominant stream of thought among European and North American biblical and religious scholars from the nineteenth century to the present. The philosopher C. Stephen Evans explains what this means: "This is understood as the rejection of all authority; the only authority that exists for the critical historian is the authority that he confers on his sources."[27] In other words, if a historian decides that a written source, be it Herodotus, Manetho, or Genesis, is not a reliable source for history, then it is not history! What a "modern scientific" scholar thinks is believable determines what he or she thinks the faith of an ancient person could be.

Here the perspective of the specialist in religion is helpful. To recognize that different worldviews exist today, and that these are unlike those in ancient times, is an important starting point.[28] Ninian Smart rightly sees the challenge for the present-day scholar who examines ancient texts and traditions.[29] The phenomenological approach, as we shall see, addresses this problem.

The second methodological challenge to the study of the religion of ancient Israel, especially toward the end of the nineteenth and beginning of the twentieth centuries, was evolutionism.[30] As noted above, Wellhausen and many of his contemporaries and followers were influenced by the evolutionary model. Evolutionary theory anticipated how a religion should develop from simple to complex forms, animism to monotheism. This assumption, in turn, influenced how biblical sources were dated and how Israelite religion was reconstructed. The evolutionary model has been jettisoned by religionists working outside of the biblical tradition, but those who still cling to the Graf-Wellhausen synthesis seem unaware of this development. Albrecht Alt's seminal essay of 1929, "Der Gott der Väter," challenged the evolutionary model as the basis by which to understand early Israel's religion.[31] Frank Moore Cross considers this essay to have "repudiated the methods of such earlier scholars as Robertson Smith and Julius Wellhausen, who attempted to reconstruct the pre-Yahwistic stage of the tribal forbears of Israel by sifting Israel's early but fully Yahwistic sources for primitive features, primitive in terms of an *a priori* typology of religious ideas derived largely from nineteenth-century idealism."[32] The evolutionary method was also rejected as untenable by phenomenologists of religion.[33]

The evolutionary model was abandoned as more religious traditions were studied and it became clear that the facts simply did not support the theory. One classic example is the move from polytheism to henotheism or monotheism during the reign of Akhenaten (1352–1336 B.C.). Clearly, no long evolutionary process was involved in this case. This transition took place in a ten- to fifteen-year period, and there was an immediate reversion to traditional polytheism upon the death of the movement's instigator, Akhenaten.

The phenomenology of religion as a distinct methodology grew out of nineteenth- and twentieth-century philosophical circles. Franz Brentano laid the foundation for the phenomenology approach, but it was his student Edmund Husserl (1859–1938) who developed it further through his extensive writings.[34] The aim of phenomenology was "to investigate and become more directly aware of phenomena that appear in immediate experience, and thereby allow the phenomenologist to describe the essential structures of these phenomena."[35] The critical word here is "experience." And this is a critical link to the phenomenology of religion.

Before discussing how the phenomenological approach will be used in this study, it should be pointed out that there are several different ways the term is used by religionists. First, it is used in a general way for investigating the phenomena of religion. Second, it is a system of classification of various religious phenomena and of studying them in a comparative manner; and third, it regards the phenomenology of religion as a branch working within *Religionswissenschaft* (scientific study of religion).[36] It is this third understanding that has been most widely followed, for it utilized many of the critical methods and ways of reading texts, but departed radically from the rationalistic or "scientific" treatments in favor of more sympathetic ones.

A close association with "the holy" or "the sacred" was believed to be the starting point for the study of religion. Rudolf Otto's *Das Heilige* (1917), the English edition of which was published in 1923 as *The Idea of the Holy*, significantly shaped the phenomenology of religion school. In addition to evolutionary theory and Enlightenment rationalism, Freudian psychology had an impact on the study of religion. It sought to reduce religion and religious experience to purely psychological terms. Otto maintained that regardless of the religious tradition, the encounter with divinity, the numinous (the sacred/the holy), was a nonrational (not irrational) or subjective experience.[37] He argued that "the holy" was unique to the realm of religion and defied rational or psychological explanations. In other words, the disciplines of history, science, and psychology simply lacked the necessary tools for assessing religious experience. Otto coined the expression *mysterium tremendum* to define the feeling of fear and awe aroused in the person who encountered the numinous. A related term was *majestas*, that is, the sense of being overpowered. For a person to experience the numinous is to realize "that which is quite beyond the sphere of the usual, the intelligible, and familiar."[38] This state, for Otto, is to experience "the wholly other" (*das ganz andere*). To support his ideas of encountering the holy and the human response to it, Otto cited examples from the Bible, such as Jacob's dream at Bethel and God's appearance to Moses in the burning bush in Sinai. The human responses to these theophanies in the Bible are consistent with those of ancient and modern people. Otto's approach to religion provided a new and fresh way of understanding religion that was diametrically opposed to the mainstream of historians of religion in the early twentieth century.

The Dutch historian of religion and Egyptologist Gerardus van der Leeuw authored a two-volume work that further advanced the phenomenological school. Like Otto, van der Leeuw associated power, awe, and *tabu* with "the sacred." "The sacred" functioned "within boundaries" and was "exceptional." For van der Leeuw, this was the object of religious encounter. The subject, of course, was the recipient of the encounter. Experience of "the sacred" was not something to be investigated in purely subjective terms, but must be studied in concert with historical research. He proposed that investigating phenomenology requires "perpetual correction by the most conscientious philological and archaeological research."[39]

Following in the tradition of van der Leeuw was W. B. Kristensen, whose lectures from the 1930s and 1940s were not published until 1960. Although he believed that a place became sacred by virtue of the presence or revelation of a deity, he took a slightly different tack from Otto. For him, "the starting point of phenomenology is therefore the viewpoint of the believer, and not the concept 'holiness' in its elements or moments."[40] This does not represent a radical departure from Otto's view but rather a difference in perspective, that is, how the phenomenon is perceived.

Building upon the works of these European scholars, Mircea Eliade further advanced the phenomenological approach.[41] His numerous works, especially *The Sacred and the Profane* (1957) and *Patterns in Comparative Religion* (1958), might be considered to be apologetics for Otto's *Das Heilige*. He did this by offering countless examples of theophanies and how sacred space was established and typically protected by walls, and rituals were introduced by which the theophany is renewed (in sacred time) from the ancient Near East, Africa, Oceania, and India. He thereby demonstrated that the encounter with and response to "the holy" was universally experienced at various times in history. He coined the terms "hierophany" (sacred manifestations) and "kratophany" (manifestations of power) to describe the numinous. For him, "every hierophany we look at is also an historical fact. Every manifestation of the scared takes place in some historical situation. Even the most personal and transcendent mystical experiences are affected by the age in which they occur. The Jewish prophets owed a debt to the events of history, which justified them and confirmed their message; and also the religious history of Israel, which made it possible for them to explain what they had experienced."[42]

Herein lies, I believe, one of the greatest strengths of the phenomenological approach, that is, it takes both theophany and history seriously. Unfortunately, as noted above, there has been an unnecessary bifurcation of these two areas for most biblical scholars and some specialists in Israel's religion. What phenomenologists do is to bracket the religious experience under study. This means suspending judgment on the phenomenon in question and examining it empathetically. Biblical scholars with Enlightenment mindsets tend to dismiss a religious phenomenon that cannot be explained empirically.

Hans Frei acknowledged that although biblical narratives appear to describe real events, this does not prove that they are historical, and he noted that the historicity of the narratives was accepted within Judaism and Christianity until only recent centuries. He rightly observed, however, "that modern historians will look with a jaundiced eye on appeal to miracle as an explanatory account of events," even though this was not a problem to earlier generations of readers.[43] Nearly thirty years ago, J. Maxwell Miller spoke for many positivist biblical historians when he declared that a historian is "inclined to disregard the supernatural or miraculous in his treatment of past events."[44] More recently he offered this same assessment in a more nuanced way: "Modern Western historians tend to perceive the world as being more orderly, however, and one of the standard tenets of modern historiography is that natural explanation for a given phenomenon or event is preferable to an explanation that involves overt divine intervention. When speculating about the 'actual historical events' behind the biblical account of Israel's past, therefore, what historians often do, in effect, is bring the biblical story into line with reality as we moderns perceive it."[45] What this position reveals is the inability of the modern historian to do what Smart insists must be done in the study of religion, namely, view the religious phenomenon through its own context and not through the modern (or postmodern) worldview of the critic.

The idea of divine intervention in human history did not create ideological or theological conflicts for peoples of the ancient Near East during the Late Bronze and Iron Ages, the relevant periods to our study. On the contrary, their theistic worldview expected it, and nearly every phenomenon of nature and the events of history were understood to be divinely ordained or orchestrated.[46] When it comes to reports of divine action in human affairs, especially in battle and on various types of campaigns, here too biblical historians of a positivist bent seem to apply a double standard. That is, there is a tendency to accept the historicity of a non-Hebrew story that refers to divine intervention, while dismissing a biblical counterpart, or searching for a natural explanation (as Miller notes). Once again, the much-cited Merneptah stela offers an interesting story. The major portion of the stela contains the report of the king's battle against the Libyans to the west of the Nile Delta. The poetic section that contains the reference to Israel is tucked away at the very end of the inscription. In line 14 of the stela, the scribe recounts how "a great wonder [or miracle] happened" (*biȝt ʿȝt ḫprt*).[47] Somehow the enemy chieftain, Mery, was captured when he apparently took a wrong turn and ended up in or near the Egyptian camp. It is curious that biblical scholars, so quick to spurn stories of divine intervention by Yahweh, the Israelite deity, do not consider the miraculous story of line 14 to militate against the reference to Israel later in the same text. Egyptologists, while recognizing the propagandistic nature of such royal inscriptions, nevertheless accept as factual the Libyan campaign. One scholar who has made a thorough investigation of references of divine intervention (*bȝw*) in Egyptian texts is the Dutch Egyptologist J. F. Borghouts. Two examples he includes are salient to our discussion. One is the occurrence in a battle between Ramesses II and the Hittites, who are overwhelmed by the *bȝw* of Amun and thus defeated. The second reference is the very one we are discussing in the Merneptah stela. He acknowledges that the report contains "propagandistic statements, but that need not prevent them from being taken literally in regard to the purpose intended. . . . In short, like the conflict with the Hittites in the longer run, this Libyan campaign was not fought by military force alone but also by supernatural means. Here, as in the other conflict, the gods took a leading part in the course of history."[48]

It is clear from the way Egyptologists interpret these thirteenth-century B.C. accounts that they do not have the same antireligious bias that positivist historians have against the Bible. On the other hand, when a scholar defends the historicity of a Bible story, the charge is usually made that he or she is a fundamentalist (or neofundamentalist) who is writing for apologetic (theological or political) purposes.[49] In a review of my book *Israel in Egypt*, Philip Davies labels me a credulist.[50] An example of my credulity, Davies claims, is believing that the Joshua military narratives are historical because they are modeled on Assyrian conquest accounts. Evidently he did not read what I said on this subject. In fact, I was critiquing John Van Seters, who proposed that the DtrH borrowed the Neo-Assyrian (seventh-century) literary topos of the conquering king who crosses a river to go to battle. I pointed out that the motif in question is well attested in Mesopotamian texts that can be traced back a thousand years earlier than Van Seters claimed, and thus the Neo-Assyrian material need not serve as the criterion for dating the Joshua narratives. Also, if Davies had indeed read the book he reviewed, he would have known that I was arguing for a Hebrew adaptation of an Egyptian literary form known as the *Tagbuchstil* (daybook style). It seems that some of the revisionist scholars are more eager to hang labels on their critics than to fairly evaluate the argument.

Defending the historicity of events described in Egyptian texts where miracles are reported surely does not make Borghouts's motivations theological in any personal sense. I know the distinguished professor, and he is no devotee of Amun or Amun-Re! But Borghouts does understand the ancient Egyptian worldview, and perhaps he was influenced by the phenomenological school, which had a significant influence on scholarship in Holland.

III. The Phenomenological Approach

My enthusiasm for the phenomenological approach, especially in understanding "the sacred," goes back twenty-five years, and the approach was employed in my dissertation, which was subsequently published as *"Sacred" in the Vocabulary of Ancient Egypt*.[51] I found the methodology to be very helpful in getting at the essence of Egyptian religion without being tainted by my own modern worldview. I maintain that this approach is just as valid at the beginning of the twenty-first century for the study of ancient Israel's religion, as Zevit has also recognized. Furthermore, the phenomenological approach is needed now more than ever because the two dominant paradigms being used today to study ancient Israel's origins as a people and her religious traditions—the rationalistic and the postmodern—are at an impasse. The former seems biased against religious experience and the latter, as argued by scholars like Thompson and Davies, consider the Pentateuchal materials to be fictitious, ideological constructs of the Persian and Hellenistic periods.[52]

Before moving on, let us sum up the main points of the phenomenology of religion as introduced in the foregoing sections.[53]

1. It is descriptive in the sense of being *Religionsgeschichtelich* in approach, but rejects the assumption that only what is rational is real.
2. It is a comparative discipline, employing comparative materials from other religious traditions (van der Leeuw and Eliade are exemplars of this aspect of the phenomenology of religion).
3. It employs bracketing, that is, it requires empathy toward what is investigated and suspends judgment on the phenomenon so as to avoid the bias that might come from one's worldview or the limitations of one's experience.
4. It is empirical in the sense of collecting and examining data without a priori judgments and assumptions.
5. It is intentional, in that it treats acts of "consciousness as consciousness of something."[54] For Otto this meant that there was an intended numinous object.
6. It is historical in that it must be investigated within the context of history (so Eliade) and work alongside historical research, and in many cases be able to clarify problems for the historian.

In this book, an attempt will be made to investigate the religious materials of the wilderness tradition employing the phenomenological approach, and when it comes to historical questions, the principles introduced at the end of the preceding chapter, the contextual approach, will be followed. This combination of approaches will be especially helpful when religious and historical questions collide. The two methods, I believe, will complement each other, and I concur with Paul Ricoeur that "All phenomenology is an explication of evidence and an evidence of explication. An evidence which is explicated, an explication which unfolds evidence: such is the phenomenological experience. It is in this sense that phenomenology can be realised only as hermeneutics."[55] Phenomenology is not only a tool for explicating religious experience but also a means for interpreting texts.

3

Sinai

The Great and Terrible Wilderness

The LORD your God, who brought you out of Egypt, out of the house of slavery, who led you through the great and terrible wilderness, an arid wasteland with poisonous snakes and scorpions. He made water flow for you from flint rock.

—Deut. 8:14b–15

I. Forty Years in the Wilderness

According to biblical tradition, the Israelites spent forty years in Sinai after the exodus and before entering Canaan under the leadership of Joshua. This forty-year period is preserved in a variety of references that represent a range of sources. The forty years is first mentioned as a sentence upon the adult generation that refused to believe that God under the direction of Moses could lead them into the Promised Land (Num. 14:33–34, 32:13). Deuteronomy (2:7; 8:2, 4; 29:5) and Joshua (5:6) recall the forty-year period, as does the eighth-century B.C. prophet Amos (2:10; 5:25), followed by Psalm 95 (v. 10), and Nehemiah (9:21) from the very end of Old Testament history. Here the sources agree, and no alternate figure is offered for the duration of the Sinai wilderness experience.

Although the number forty often appears to be used symbolically in the Bible, here the number actually represents a tallying of the years from the departure from Egypt (first month of the year, day 15; cf. Exod. 12:18–32; Lev. 23:6; Num. 33:3), to the arrival at Mt. Sinai six weeks later (i.e., the third new moon; cf. Exod. 19:1),[1] the eleven months at Mt. Sinai (cf. Num. 10:11), the time to travel from Mt. Sinai to Kadesh-Barnea, and thirty-eight years—the wandering period—in the area of Kadesh-Barnea (Deut. 2:14). These figures add up to a total very close to forty years. One wonders if the symbolic use of the number forty in biblical literature, signifying trial, testing, or punishment, derives from the wilderness tradition.

II. Sinai Yesterday and Today

The Sinai Peninsula today, Egypt's easternmost province, covers 61,000 square kilometers (23,500 square miles), making it comparable in size to the state of West Virginia.[2] The Suez Canal, excavated in the 1850s, now demarcates Africa to the west and Asia to the east. This means that Egypt straddles two continents, and the Suez Canal is the artificial border between them.

The Sinai's eastern border has been marked by the Gaza Strip and Israel since 1948. The Mediterranean Sea coast marks the northern limit of Sinai, and its southern triangular tip, approximately 384 kilometers (240 miles) from the Mediterranean Sea, is embraced by the Red Sea (figure 1). The Gulf of Suez, the western arm, proceeds north to Suez, the entry point for the canal. The eastern arm reaches north to the Israeli port of Elath and the Jordanian port of Aqaba, from which the Gulf derives its name.

Throughout history Sinai's importance has lain in its location as the land bridge between Africa and Asia, Egypt and the Levant. Going back at least 5,000 years, Egyptians and Canaanites trekked across North Sinai for commercial trade, and Egyptian trading posts were established in southern Canaan.[3] Throughout Pharaonic times, this land route was crucial and regularly defended in order to preserve Egypt's vital interest. After the pharaohs, North Sinai flourished as a route for travel and trade well into the Christian era.[4] After the Arab invasion of Egypt and North Africa, the route across central Sinai, known as Darb el-Hajj—the Way of the Pilgrimage—became the principal land route for Muslim pilgrims traveling to Mecca from Egypt.[5]

Sinai was also valued in ancient times for its natural resources. Copper and turquoise were mined in the area of Wadi Maghara and Serabit el-Khadim in south-central Sinai. In these areas, hundreds of Egyptian texts have been found, ranging from simple graffiti to official inscriptions on large stelae, dating from the Third Dynasty (ca. 2650 B.C.) down to the Twentieth Dynasty (ca. 1100 B.C.).[6] The Egyptians, Canaanites, and other Semites worked this region for copper, turquoise, and possibly lapis lazuli.[7] Five of the texts published by Gardiner, Peet, and Černý mention lapis *(ḫsbḏ)* alongside turquoise.[8] Thus, from ca. 2650–1100 B.C., Sinai was a region of vital economic interest to Egypt, the south for mining and the north for travel to the Levant and for defending the Delta.

Sinai, nevertheless, was not considered by the pharaohs to be part of Egypt. Egypt proper, that is, *kmt* or the "Black Land," was made up of the Nile Valley and the Delta,[9] while the desert regions were called "the Red Land" (*dšrt*), which also meant "foreign land." Areas outside of the Nile Valley and the Delta were also known as *ḫ3st*, meaning "foreign land" or desert,[10] written with the foreign land determinative (𓈉) that was usually applied to foreign lands, countries, and city-states."[11]

One of the more important stelae from Serabit el-Khadim, dating to the sixth year of Amenemhet III (ca. 1837 B.C.), contains the report of the expedition leader, Horwerre. He refers to the Serabit el-Khadim area three times as *bi3*: Bia (on Bia, see the following section).[12] He goes on to say that he "came from Egypt" (*iwt ḥr kmt*) and refers to the area as *ḫ3st*, foreign land.[13] This inscription clearly shows that Sinai was considered a foreign land, away from Egypt. This mind-set is still a part of the thinking of modern Egyptians. Recently, while working in Sinai, one of my Egyptian staff was planning on returning to his home in Cairo and asked if he could "go back to Egypt" for the weekend!

Sinai in ancient times was not considered to be Egypt, nor was it Canaan, although Egypt exerted the most influence there. It was home to tribal nomadic people, such as the Shasu of Egyptian texts and/or Amalekites of the Bible. For the biblical writers it was the "wilderness" (מִדְבָּר: *midbār*) par excellence, actually made up of seven smaller wildernesses: Shur, Etham, Sin, Sinai, Paran, Zin, and Kadesh.[14] Yohanan Aharoni proposed that Paran was actually the ancient Hebrew or Semitic name for the whole of the Sinai Peninsula, and that the name Feiran in southern Sinai preserves that ancient name.[15] He bases this on the fact that the name Paran is mentioned by the early second-century A.D. geographer Ptolemaeus for the area today known as Feiran. This means that the name had been preserved and was known prior to the Byzantine period, when Christian monks sought to identify holy sites. Aharoni also points to a number of biblical references to Paran that support his hypothesis, and he suggests that Paran is used of a specific area around Kadesh and for all of Sinai as well.[16] Most pertinent is 1 Kings 11:18, which records the flight of prince Hadad the Edomites from Solomon, stating "They set out from Midian and came to Paran; they took people with them from Paran and came to Egypt, to Pharaoh king of Egypt." According to this reference, Paran was located between Edom/Midian and Egypt. Roland de Vaux likewise wondered if the name for the Sinai during the Old Testament period was not Paran, and "Sinai" merely an area within the southern portion of the peninsula.[17]

III. The Etymology of Sinai and Ancient Names for It

The origin of the name Sinai (סִינַי) remains uncertain, and the Bible also uses the name Horeb (חֹרֵב) for Sinai. Source critics have traditionally regarded the dual usage as indicative of the different sources that stand behind narratives, Sinai being the term used by J and P, whereas E and D prefer Horeb.[18] We shall return to the Sinai-Horeb question in the next chapter.

Sinai is found thirty-five times in the Hebrew scriptures, whereas Horeb occurs but seventeen times. The term Sinai is used three different ways. By far the most frequent usage of Sinai is in combination with הַר (*har* = mountain), which occurs sixteen times, invariably in connection with the location of the giving of the Law.[19] Thirteen times מִדְבַּר סִינָי (wilderness or desert of Sinai) is found,[20] and Sinai stands alone on six occasions, all in poetic materials except Exodus 16:1. The poetic usages mention the theophany at Sinai or apply it as an epithet for God "the one of Sinai" (Deut. 33:2, 16; Judg. 5:5; Ps 68:8, 17). In Exodus 16:1, Sinai is used to indicate the location of the wilderness of Sin (סִין ־מִדְבַּר): "Israel came to the wilderness of Sin." Noth and other scholars think that these terms are related, the one perhaps deriving from the other, Sin being a shortened form of Sinai.[21] This suggestion is unlikely, since Exodus 16:1 locates the wilderness of sin between Elim and Sinai (אֲשֶׁר בֵּין־אֵילִם וּבֵין סִינָי מִדְבַּר־סִין). Furthermore, (the wilderness of) Sinai is not reached by the Israelites until after leaving Rephidim, six weeks after departing Egypt (Exod. 19:1–2; Num. 33:16). This reference means that the wilderness of Sin and the wilderness of Sinai are not one and the same, despite the similarity of the names. Rather, it suggests that Sinai is a more specific area within the present-day Sinai Peninsula.

Another proposed explanation for the origin of the toponym Sinai is that it derives from the bush where God first appeared to Moses (Exod. 3:2).[22] The bush is identified as "the *s*^{e}*neh*" (הַסְּנֶה). This bush is defined as a "multi-coloured bramble . . . (*Cassia obovata*)."[23] Jon Levenson believes that the similarity of the sound between the two words "cannot be coincidental."[24] On the other hand, Umberto Cassuto rejects this explanation, saying it is "dubious if there is any connection between the name of the bush and that of Sinai," because Horeb, not Sinai is the name of the mountain in Exodus 3:2.[25] Given Hebrew writers' penchant for wordplay, one might have expected "Sinai" to be used alongside the *s*^{e}*neh*-bush if there was a linkage between these words, or if the name of the bush is an etiology for the name of the region.

Others have noticed a possible connection between the Hebrew word Sinai and the Egyptian name for the city of Pelusium, Tell Farama in North Sinai. Pelusium is the Greek name, meaning "city of mud," which may have derived from the Egyptian term *sin*, meaning mud of clay.[26] This city is only mentioned twice in the Old Testament, where it is written as סִין (*sin*) in Ezekiel 30:15 and 16, which dates to the early sixth century. Pelusium is also possibly the city mentioned in Assyrian texts as *Sinu* from the time of Ashurbanipal's conquest of Egypt in 667–666 B.C.[27] Given the distance between Pelusium in the northeastmost point of the Delta in the first millennium B.C., and the Bible's location of Sinai as a region that took Israel some time to reach (in the third month after departing Egypt), it seems unlikely that Pelusium (*sin*) gave its name to Sinai, or vice versa.

A final suggestion for the origin of the term Sinai is that it is related to the name of the Mesopotamian moon deity Sin, an Akkadian word.[28] Many years ago, Lina Eckstein argued for close ties between lunar deities and Sinai in a chapter entitled "Sinai a Centre of Moon Cult."[29] She notes that Thoth, who is associated with the moon, is well represented in texts and iconographically in the mining areas of south-central Sinai. However, Raphael Giveon, while agreeing that Thoth is widely mentioned in the texts at Serabit el-Khadim and nearby mining sites, observes that the deity's titles (for example, Lord of nomads [*iwntyw*], Lord of all foreign countries) lead Giveon to the conclusion that Thoth's "early role... was to control the Asiatics of Sinai." Consequently it is "unlikely that Thot represents a local god connected with a presumed moon cult there."[30] And he thinks there is no basis for an "early moon cult."[31] Eckstein also thought that the Akkadian king Naram-Sin may have reached this region. Naram-Sin indeed conquered in Syria (Ebla, for example) and speaks of setting up statues for the god Sin,[32] but there is nothing to suggest that he drove south through Canaan and into Sinai.

None of the theories to explain the origin of the term Sinai presented here has gained widespread support. Furthermore, Sinai is not known in any Egyptian text. In fact, there seems to be no specific Egyptian name to cover the entire peninsula. Sir Alan Gardiner suggested that the term 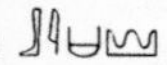 (*biȝ*) that has traditionally been translated as "the mining country," might be the Egyptian term for Sinai.[33] He notes that there are texts that speak of products of Punt and Bia. For him this is critical, since Punt is a specific region where gold, ivory, and other luxury items were obtained. Hence, Bia should be a similar region. He concludes: "If Bia is not the Egyptian name for Sinai it may safely be declared that no name for the peninsula occurs on the monuments, which would be an astounding fact, unless Sinai was merely considered a part of some larger geographical area."[34]

A group of recently discovered texts at Ain Sukhna, situated on the western coast of the Red Sea about forty kilometers (twenty-four miles) south of Suez, offer further support for Gardiner's explanation.[35] The inscriptions were recorded by mining expeditions apparently going to Serabit el-Khadim. One, dated to the first year of the last monarch of the Eleventh Dynasty, Montuhotep IV, records that the expedition came "in order to bring turquoise... of the highlands (*ḫȝst*)," but no specific name is used.[36] A second text, probably from the reign of Senusert I about forty years later, mentions *biȝ* (written with the foreign-land determinative).[37] Although Gardiner's points are well taken, Bia may only apply to the south-central area of Sinai where the turquoise and copper mining occurred, and not the entire peninsula. Certainly, Bia was not applied to what we today call north Sinai. Rather that was known as the "Ways of Horus," referring either to the route traveled across Sinai to Canaan, or the name of the region in the vicinity of Tjaru, Egypt's frontier town and fort.[38]

The usage in the Pentateuch suggests that the name Sinai applied to a limited area, and not the entire peninsula. How and exactly when Sinai became the name for the entire region is unknown. In the writings of Herodotus and other classical writers, Arabia is the name given to Sinai.[39] When Herodotus recounts Cambyses's conquest of Egypt (525 B.C.), he speaks of Arabia and Arabians as situated between Palestine and Egypt.[40] The reason for this development is that Sinai is geographically connected to Arabia, and during the first millennium, migrations from southern Arabia brought Arab tribes, such as the Qedrites, to the areas east of Israel.[41] The first mention of Arabs in Near Eastern texts is in the Kurkh monolith of Shalmaneser III. It reports that one thousand camels of Gindibu of Arabia were contributed to the Battle of Qarqar, Syria, in 853 B.C.[42] During the Persian period (sixth and fifth centuries B.C.), Arabs are mentioned in inscriptions, indicating that they had moved into the areas of southern Palestine and Transjordan, and Sinai.[43] During the Hellenistic period, the Septuagint translators of Genesis 46:34 added a note that the land of Goshen was "of Arabia" (γῆ Γεσεμ Ἀραβίᾳ), showing that they understood that the northeastern delta where Goshen was situated was beside Arabia, which can only be Sinai.

Possibly during the Byzantine period, when Christian pilgrims began visiting holy sites in the Holy Lands, the biblical name Sinai replaced Arabia and was extended to the entire peninsula.

IV. The Physical Geography of the Sinai Peninsula

Deuteronomy offers a fitting description of Sinai as "the great and terrible wilderness, an arid wasteland with poisonous snakes and scorpions" (Deut. 8:15): בַּמִּדְבָּר הַגָּדֹל וְהַנּוֹרָא נָחָשׁ שָׂרָף וְעַקְרָב וְצִמָּאוֹן אֲשֶׁר אֵין־מָיִם. The peninsula is often divided into three geographical zones: the north (the Dune Sheet), central (the Tih Plateau), and the south (the Sinai Massif).[44] Sinai was shaped by tectonic forces associated with the Red Sea Rift. Rising plumes of magma deep in the crust caused the region to be uplifted into a dome structure. Erosion of the dome exposed Precambrian granites and metamorphic rocks in the center, surrounded by tilted sedimentary rocks that were deposited on the Precambrian stratum. The sedimentary sequence includes Nubian sandstones, Cenomanean-Turonian limestones and Dolomites, Senonian chalk, and Eocene chalk.[45] Fracture systems in the deformed strata resulted in the formation of the dividing valleys (wadis) that are so important to travel, vegetation, and agriculture in Sinai.

The Mediterranean coast of Sinai is influenced by a tectonic feature known as the Pelusium line.[46] It is probably the surface expression of a deep fault, the line of which can be seen in space imagery. The east side of Sinai was formed by the Red Sea Rift, which runs down the Jordan Valley, through the Arabah, the Gulf of Aqaba, on through the Red Sea, and into Africa.[47] The Gulf of Suez is an extension of this fault line that runs north into the Isthmus of Suez. The tearing activity along this line also created the depressions that make up the sequence of lakes along this line (see below).

North Sinai

Because of the long tradition of association with the events of Exodus 19–Numbers 10 (that is, the giving of the law at Mt. Sinai), southern Sinai has been studied in more detail than the other two sections of Sinai. But, in recent years, geological and archaeological research has begun in earnest in North Sinai.[48] The northern sector, as mentioned above, served as the strategic land bridge between Egypt and the Levant. It is covered by sandy dunes, making travel difficult. On a recent trip between Qantara and el-Arish (eastern North Sinai) during the Khamisin (sandstorm) season, a section of the paved road on which I had traveled the previous day was completely covered by sand upon our return the following day, and a front-end loader was attempting to clear the road like a snow plow. It is along this route, close to the Mediterranean, that the Egyptians traveled to Canaan for trade and military purposes. During the New Kingdom (ca. 1540–1100 B.C.), a chain of Egyptian forts guarded this route; more about these in chapter 5.[49] This route is best known from the famous relief of Seti I at Karnak Temple, which contains a pictorial map of this route, with forts and their accompanying wells, all of which are named (figure 2). The first Egyptian fort in the sequence is Tjaru (Sile), and the final one in Canaan is Raphia.[50] Interestingly, the town of Raphia today is the border town between Egypt and Israel for those driving to either country across North Sinai.

Along the northern coast of Sinai is Lake Bardawil, or Serbonis, as it was known in Greco-Roman times (figure 1). This lagoon, which begins just east of Pelusium (Tell el-Farama) and stretches east to Ostrakina, was present in ancient times. The barrier island that separates the lagoon from the Mediterranean was used as a route of travel during Persian and Greek times.[51] The absence of archaeological evidence prior to this time indicates that this route was not used earlier,[52] probably because the barrier island was still forming and did not connect to the mainland until some time during the first millennium B.C.[53] The lagoon itself is very old, as confirmed by radiocarbon dates of shells, ranging from 35,500 to 2,800 years B.P.[54] Similar lagunal lakes still exist to the west: Manzelah east of Tanis and Mariyut near Alexandria.

Of special interest to this book and the investigation of the geography of the exodus (see chapters 4 and 5) was the discovery of another lagoon just east of the Suez Canal, near Qantara East and Pelusium, which now appears to be a desert or *sabkah* (mud flat). Manfred Bietak's geoarchaeological map of the eastern Delta and North Sinai, published in 1975 and updated in 1996, identified this large paleolagoon and showed the parameters for the el-Ballah lake system to the south. His work illustrates how different the region was in Pharaonic times from what it is today (figure 3).[55] Now the entire area east of the Suez Canal is covered by aeolian sands, even where there were lakes in earlier times. During the Israeli occupation of Sinai after 1967, teams from the Israel Geological Survey explored the area between the Suez Canal and Pelusium, and their map also shows the remains of this ancient lagoon, as well as traces of the Pelusiac branch of the Nile, which ran east of Pelusium. Furthermore, they discovered the remains of an ancient canal that ran east of Qantara.[56] The implications of this canal have been discussed in detail by this writer and treated below in chapter 5.[57]

During the early 1990s, a study of this area by the Italian geomorphologist Bruno Marcolongo provided more information on this lagoon.[58] As revealed by the map shown in figure 4, the Geographical Survey of Egypt from the 1940s shows that this lagunal area was in modern times flooded during the rainy season.

In 1995, the author visited North Sinai to study the ancient lagoon that was situated between the archaeological sites of Hebua I and Hebua II. We drilled a series of auger probes through the ten to twenty centimeters of surface sand and down into the underlying deposit of sandy mud and shells. The shells are mostly fresh- to brackish-water mollusks (*cerastoderma*) in sediment that is consistent with riverine deposition—possibly an ancient Nile distributary that emptied into the lagoon.[59]

After obtaining recently declassified Corona satellite images from the U.S. Geological Survey, which date from the 1960s, I returned to Sinai for further study of this region in 1998, accompanied by geologist Stephen O. Moshier.[60] On this occasion, however, we concentrated our investigation on the so-called Eastern Frontier Canal discovered by Sneh and Weissbrod in the early 1970s.[61] In 1999 we continued our archaeological and geological survey work in this area. The rapid development of the as-Salam irrigation project in the Qantara-Baluza region, although damaging to archaeological sites, provided scores of kilometers of excavated canals that exposed the underlying stratigraphy to a depth of two and three meters. Fortuitously, this enabled Moshier and our geological team to obtain subsurface data that allowed us to make a regional map of what the area was like in the ancient past. Although this aspect of our investigation is ongoing, a preliminary map is now available (figure 5).

We were convinced that the distinct line running in an east-west direction on the Corona satellite image was an earlier coastline—actually part of the Pelusium line (figure 6). This barrier island, made up of a highly eroded *kukar* sandstone ridge, separated the lagoon from the Mediterranean Sea. Since the ancient site of Tell Hebua was situated on it, and it has New Kingdom and

Second Intermediate Period remains, we surmised that this barrier island may have marked the coast during the second millennium B.C.[62] This ancient barrier island, or dune ridge, is also clearly visible on the above-mentioned 1940s Geographical Survey map and in Bietak's reconstruction of the region. Our hypothesis was confirmed by the publication of important research by coastal geologists D. J. Stanley and G. A. Goodfriend, who dated this coastal ridge to 4,000 years B.P.[63]

During the 2001 season, Moshier and his associates discovered an early distributary of the Pelusiac Nile that ran parallel to the coastline and emptied into the eastern end of the paleolagoon (figure 5). In time this branch of the Nile migrated north, which allowed the Delta to expand north. This means that during the first millennium B.C. the Delta actually extended approximately thirty kilometers (nineteen miles) east of the line of the Suez Canal to the ancient site of Pelusium, although during the second millennium most of this area was covered by waters of the Mediterranean Sea.

South of the eastern lagoon were the northern limits of the above-mentioned el-Ballah Lake system. This marshy area was drained of its water during the excavation of the Suez Canal in the nineteenth century, but much of its outline can be delineated from topographic maps and satellite images (figure 6). The historical identification of this lake will be offered in chapter 5.

At the end of the Wadi Tumilat, which runs east from the mid-point of the eastern Delta, lies yet another body of water, Lake Timsah. This wadi has been described as "a natural valley approximately fifty-two kilometers (thirty-one miles) long with a present width ranging between two and nine kilometers."[64] It was apparently formed by a now-defunct river branch in the Pleistocene epoch.[65] During Pharaonic times, and even in recent history, the wadi has served as an overflow channel for the Nile during the inundation season. In 1800 A.D., a particularly high flood filled the Wadi Tumilat and brought so much water to Lake Timsah that it in turn overflowed its banks, so that water poured south to the Bitter Lakes, around fifteen kilometers (nine miles) away.[66] The Great and Small Bitter Lakes, which are connected, stretch nearly thirty-five kilometers (twenty-two miles) in length, after which one must go another twenty kilometers (twelve and a half miles) before reaching the northern tip of the Red Sea (that is, the Gulf of Suez). Today, the Suez Canal runs from the Gulf of Suez through the Bitter Lakes and Lake Timsah, and proceeds north for another eighty kilometers (fifty miles) before reaching the Mediterranean Sea.

These lakes along the Isthmus of Suez constitute a natural barrier for would-be invaders. Sneh and Weissbrod, who discovered the ancient canal traces in North Sinai, argue that the ancient canal dates to the early second millennium B.C.,[67] and that it also flowed between Lake Timsah and the el-Ballah Lakes. If their scenario is correct, then Egyptians themselves added to the defense of the eastern frontier, which in turn would have created a clear border between Egypt and Sinai.

Central Sinai

East of the Wadi Tumilat is the biblical "Way of Shur," a route that crossed between the desert of North Sinai and the plateau to its south (figure 1). It turned north toward the Negev, passing through Beersheba and Hebron, and through the hill country of Canaan/Israel. It is likely that the wilderness of Shur *(midbār šûr)*, located just east of the Wadi Tumilat, gave its name to this route, or possibly the route gave rise to the name of the wilderness. Moving south from the desert environs of North Sinai, the central section of Sinai is increasingly complex geologically. It begins with a series of limestone massifs that mark the beginning of the Tih Plateau, which covers 20,000 square kilometers (ca. 13,2000 square miles).[68] The limestone cuestas or escarpments in this region include Gebel Helal (892 meters/2,900 feet), Gebel Yeleq (1,094 meters/3,556 feet), and Gebel (Har) Karkom (847 meters/2,753 feet) on the east side of Sinai.[69]

The Tih Plateau is a desolate area. The Arabic word *tih* means "wandering," leading some scholars to associate at least part of this region with the area where the Israelites spent the majority of their wandering period, as described in the book of Numbers.[70] The wilderness of Paran, some think, lies in the eastern side of this plateau.[71] One of the most important hydrological features of the Tih Plateau is the el-Arish basin. An incredible network of wadis, constituting about 28 percent of Sinai,[72] collects the limited amount of rain that falls in the area (twenty-five to fifty millimeters per year), from which it flows north toward the Mediterranean and the present-day town of el-Arish. The northern end of the wadi is a very fertile area and now, with the aid of water pumps, it produces much of Egypt's fruits and vegetables.

On the northwestern side of the Tih Plateau, near Wadi Sudr—which leads into the Red Sea coastal town of Ras el-Sudr—is Gebel Sin Bishr (618 meters/ 2,009 feet). The limestone Tih Plateau continues its incline as it proceeds south, reaching its maximum height at Gebel Igmah (1,626 meters/2,602 feet). The chalky plateaus of the Tih are separated from the granite Sinai Massif by a system of valleys that range between twenty and thirty kilometers (twelve and a half to nineteen miles) in width.[73] Some of the important areas within this region are the mountains and valleys around Serabit el-Khadim and Wadi Feiran.

South Sinai

Even from satellite images, the ruggedness and beauty of the pink granite peaks of South Sinai are striking in their beauty. These granites are occasionally criss-crossed by narrow dikes of black basalt. Forming the oldest rock formations in Sinai, these granites correspond to the Red Sea granites across the Gulf of Suez in African Egypt, and date from the end of the Precambrian period, 600 million years ago.[74] The gorgeous mountains in this region include Gebel Katarina, the highest peak in Sinai, which rises 2,637 meters (8,550 feet) above sea level, the traditional site of Mt. Sinai; Gebel Musa (Mt. Moses), which stands at 2,285 meters (7,345 feet); and Gebel Serbal at 2,070 meters (6,727 feet). This southern mountainous region receives more rainfall than any other area of Sinai, about 50–75 millimeters (1/4–3/8 inch) per year, and in the winter it can snow at the higher elevations. Bedouin plant crops and gardens in the valleys to catch the rainwater that flows over impermeable granite bedrock down to the wadis. They also build small dams in the valleys to trap water, which can be slowly released for irrigation purposes.

Environmental Considerations in Sinai

Rainfall in Sinai is limited, as has been noted. However, local thunderstorms can unleash torrents of water running through the wadis. Henry Spencer Palmer, a nineteenth-century explorer of Sinai, reports that water charging through the wadis can rise as high as three to ten meters (ca. ten to thirty-three feet). He comments on the devastating results of one such a storm that struck on December 3, 1867, describing it as "the worst which has happened within living memory, thirty persons perished thus, besides scores of sheep, goats, camels, and donkeys; in fact, an entire Arab encampment, which had been pitched in the mouth of a small valley on the north side of Jebel Serbal."[75] I have personally seen large stones and boulders that have been moved by such torrents in Wadi Feiran. The power of such floods can be truly awesome. Unfortunately, such flooding is of little value to farming efforts.

The deserts, chalk cliffs, sandstone mountains, and granite peaks, combined with the diminutive amount of rain in Sinai, may create the impression that little vegetation can grow in this "great and terrible wilderness." For the most part, this impression is valid. Nevertheless, when the limited rains do come, a variety of desert plants spring up, virtually overnight. Surprisingly, 180 different plant specimens were identified during the nineteenth century and were registered at the Kew Royal Herbarium.[76] Small bushes and shrubs abound, on which sheep, goats, and camels feed. Palm trees require more water, and tend to be limited to wadis, oasis areas, or nearby springs and wells. The oases of Ayun Musa and Wadi Feiran abound with palm tress, especially the latter, which has groves of date palms (figure 7). The hardy acacia tree (*Acacia raddiana*) that is found scattered about Sinai is valued for the shade it provides, and its leaves and twigs are eaten by camels and goats that actually climb up into the tree. With trees so few in number, the acacia was (and is) cut down for wood for making utilitarian objects and to burn for fuel. Its sap is a resinous gum (*gum Arabica*) that was used for medicinal purposes.[77] Acacia trees are found here and there, sometimes only few in number, and in better-watered areas like wadis they are found by the dozens (figure 8). In recent years, a grove of juniper trees was documented near Gebel Halel.[78]

Trees are sparse in Sinai. Consequently, they were (and are) exploited for every possible purpose. They are so prized that Beduoin sheiks (tribal chieftains) and saints were often buried near trees, which thus became places of pilgrimage. Trees still serve as landmarks. In 1998 I was given directions to an archaeological site: I was to drive along the el-Arish road toward Baluza (in North Sinai). When I saw a tree off to the left side of the road, I was to turn left and drive three kilometers to the site!

The weather is another dynamic factor for one traveling through or living in Sinai. In July the mean temperature in North Sinai is in the range of 26–28°C (78–82°F); it is 23–25°C (72–78°F) in Central Sinai, and in the higher elevations of South Sinai, 15–20°C (60–69°F). In January, the mean temperatures for these three regions are, respectively, 12–14°C (54–59°F), 7–10°C (42–50°F), and 0–2°C (32–36°F).[79] However, these temperatures, registered in the shade, are often difficult to find. In May 1998, while surveying in the open sun of North Sinai, we recorded a temperature of 48°C (120°F). In 1995, when climbing Gebel Musa in mid-May at around 7:00 A.M., a rain shower moved in, the winds picked up, and the temperature plummeted to 7–8°C (44–46°F). I had never been so cold in my life. A few hours later, as we departed the St. Catherine's area and exited the Wadi Feiran, I noticed the temperature was 40°C (104°F)! Clearly the temperatures in Sinai vary considerably, depending on one's location. The sudden changes in temperature make life a challenge indeed.

What we have presented here is a brief description of the Sinai Peninsula and its history. Within the borders of this intriguing land, the Bible claims the Israelites camped and traveled. But before we consider this chapter of biblical history, we want to attempt to trace the departure of the Hebrews from Egypt and their movements until they crossed the sea and entered Sinai.

4

The Geography of the Exodus

Ramesses to the Sea

These are the stages by which the Israelites went out of the land of Egypt in military formation under the leadership of Moses and Aaron. Moses wrote down their starting points, stage by stage, by command of the LORD; these are their stages according to their starting places.

—Num. 33:1–2

I. Mythology, History, and Geography

Mythology is a type of literature that has fascinated people in every generation. The second half of the twentieth century and the early part of the twenty-first century are no exception. Adults and children alike have been captivated by C. S. Lewis's *Narnia Chronicles,* George Lucas's *Star Wars* saga, and J. R. R. Tolkien's *Lord of the Rings.* In these masterful stories the reader (or viewer of the movies) is introduced to solar systems, worlds, and geographic regions that derive from the creative genius of the authors. So vivid and realistic is the world created by Tolkien that one writer has produced the *Atlas of Middle Earth: A Geographic Guide to J. R. R. Tolkien's Writings.* This interesting book notwithstanding, readers of Tolkien understand that his world is imaginary, and there are no archaeologists searching for Middle Earth or philologists trying to determine the etymologies of the toponyms. It is evident to the reader that there is no correlation between Middle Earth or Narnia and any geographic reality on earth. This is the expectation when one reads mythological literature.

Bernard Batto and the late Gösta Ahlström are among the scholars who in recent years have argued that the exodus story and the trek to and through the Re(e)d Sea (Exod. 13–15) is mythological in nature, or is historicized mythology.[1] This suggestion is not really a new one, but marks a return to views advanced by earlier scholars.[2] Other scholars have recognized a possible link between the Egyptian Field (*sḫt*) or Lake (*ŝ*) of Reeds or Rushes (*i3rw*) from the Egyptian Pyramid Texts (2500–2200 B.C.), Coffin Texts (2100–1700 B.C.), and the Book of the Dead (1500 B.C. to Greco-Roman times), in which the deceased passes through these waters and thus is purified and able to proceed into the heavenly realm of the gods.[3]

A mythological approach assumes that originally the story was not historical but "timeless" and thus geographically nebulous, but that at a later date for some reason—for Bernard Batto it is P's contribution—the story is historicized.[4] In other words, there is an attempt to transform the story into something that looks historiographic. But what evidence is there for this transmogrification? Is the use of mythic language in the Song of the Sea in Exodus 15 sufficient to explain that the mythic tradition was metamorphized into the historiographic narrative in Exodus 14? The suggestion of historization is not particularly convincing. This is probably why even Donald Redford, usually a sharp critic of the Bible, has rejected this explanation. He observes: "This is a curious resort, for the text does not look like mythology (at least on the definition of the latter as a timeless event set in the world of the gods). The Biblical writer certainly thinks he is writing datable history."[5]

It should be noted that the Egyptians could use mythic language to describe actual events. The Poetic stela of Thutmose III, for example, tells of the king's stunning victories over neighboring lands with the help of Amun-Re, who declares: "I set your might, your fear in every country, the dread of you as far as heaven's four supports. . . . my serpent on your brow consumed them."[6] Here, clear mythic language is employed, followed by heaped-up hyperbole to describe the king's triumphs in Asia and Nubia. Is the use of this mythic language and elevated speech an indicator that these campaigns are purely myth (that is, a reference to timeless actions of the gods)? Not at all. Thanks to the same king's annals, the Gebel Barkel stela, the Armant stela, and other texts, we know about Thutmose's campaigns in great detail.[7] The Poetic stela is simply a summation of the king's deeds that uses mythic language and hyperbole to explain how the deity made it all possible. No Egyptologist would suggest that the annals, for instance, are historicized from the mythic Poetic stela. This Egyptian evidence demonstrates that poetic and historiographic works about the same events exist as parallel, contemporaneous traditions. I see no reason for denying the same possibility to Exodus 14 and 15.

A slightly different approach to interpreting the geography of the exodus is to regard the route as ideological and theological in nature. Hence, William Johnstone opines, "it is again futile, therefore, to attempt to locate this theological affirmation in geographical detail."[8]

Fortunately, these extreme views are not widely held, as more than a century of research from biblical scholars, historical geographers, and archaeologists attests. Inasmuch as the exodus begins in Egypt, and the Bible lists several toponyms prior to reaching Sinai, Egyptologists have also played a central role in the investigation of the route of the exodus. The reason most scholars have researched the toponyms is that it seems logical that if the story of the trek from Egypt to Mt. Sinai and on to Kadesh-Barnea (as presented in Exodus and Numbers) was historical rather than mythical, the geographic descriptions offer an empirical test. Not only could geographic terms and place names help demonstrate the authenticity of the setting of a report, it might offer clues to the date of the story or when it was written. On this final point, scholars with minimalist leanings have tried to use the toponyms to argue for a seventh- to sixth-century date for the origin of the biblical story.[9] The fact that such a line of research has been pursued suggests that these scholars also believe that the geography of the exodus serves as a clue to either the authenticity or fabrication of the text, and that the toponyms are diagnostic for dating purposes.

A detailed study of the toponymy in the book of Exodus 1–14 was offered in my *Israel in Egypt* (chapters 5, 7, 8), and thus we do not need to reiterate all this material here. Only a brief review will be offered of those conclusions, as well as interaction with some of the literature on the topic that has appeared since 1996. Furthermore, when *Israel in Egypt* was written, the work of the East Frontier Archaeological Project, which I direct, had only conducted archaeological and geological survey seasons in 1994 and 1995. But in 1998, archeological and paleoenvironmental study of the Qantara-Baluza region began and has continued, and archeological excavations at Tell el-Borg commenced in 1999. As of this writing, four seasons of work have concluded, and a fifth is planned for spring 2005. Although this work is still at a preliminary stage, and our conclusions are tentative, the discoveries made in this short period have provided some significant data for understanding the military and geographic history of this region. As a consequence of the new evidence, I am happy to revise some of the proposals I made in *Israel in Egypt*. The very purpose of archaeological research is to put forward ideas based upon the data available. When new information appears, old theories need to be altered in the light of the new material.

The intent of this chapter is to raise several important questions. Do the geographic data recorded in Exodus and Numbers, when studied alongside archaeological and geographic information provided in this chapter, read like myth (like *Lord of the Rings*, for example) or do they appear to describe a real geographic picture? And does the geographic information fit a New Kingdom or Late Bronze Age picture or a seventh- to sixth-century scenario?

II. The Biblical Sources

The toponymy of the exodus story is found in narratives such as Exodus 1:8–11, in which the forced labor of the Hebrews results in the building of the store-cities of Rameses and Pithom. The passage in which these names occur is believed to be from J, although E is suggested by other source critics.[10] According to Exodus 13:17, supposedly E's version of events, the Israelites did not depart by the expected route to Canaan from the eastern Delta, that is, "the Way of the land of the Philistines." This route was the same one that the influential Egyptologist Sir Alan Gardiner called "the ancient military road between Egypt and Palestine."[11] From Ramesside-era texts, which will be discussed in detail below, it is known that the road was guarded by a series of forts. This may explain why this route was avoided, a point that concurs with the explanation offered in verse 17: "If the people face war, they may change their minds and return to Egypt." For this reason, the text informs us that the Hebrews went "by the roundabout way of the wilderness toward the Red Sea" (*yām sûp̱*; Exod. 13:18). Exodus 12:37 claims they journeyed from Rameses to Succoth, a passage assigned to J or P, depending on the scholar.[12] From Succoth, they camped at Etham, which is described as being situated "at the edge of the wilderness" (בִּקְצֵה הַמִּדְבָּר). At this juncture, the Israelites "turn back and camp in front of Pi-hahiroth, between Migdol and the sea, in front of Baal-Zephon" (Exod. 14: 1–2). This segment of the itinerary is thought to derive from the P source, although John Van Seters argues that P is actually using J's itinerary.[13]

A final source that deals with the route of the exodus from the departure from Egypt to the arrival at Moab in the Transjordan is the itinerary recorded in Numbers 33. The relevant section for the route from Egypt to the sea is 33:2–10:

> They set out from Rameses in the first month, on the fifteenth day of the first month; on the day after the passover the Israelites went out boldly in the sight of all the Egyptians, while the Egyptians were burying all their firstborn, whom the Lord had struck down among them. The Lord executed judgments even against their gods. So the Israelites set out from Rameses, and camped at Succoth. They set out from Succoth, and camped at Etham, which is on the edge of the wilderness. They set out from Etham, and turned back to Pi-hahiroth, which faces Baal-zephon; and they camped before Migdol. They set out from Pi-hahiroth, passed through the sea into the wilderness.

The wilderness itinerary in Numbers 33 has been the subject of considerable discussion in recent years. Because it appears to be a tedious list, source critics consistently assign this chapter to P.[14] Martin Noth believed that this Priestly list was based upon an old document, quite independent of J or E, and might have derived from a pilgrim list from travel from Israel to Sinai.[15]

The literary form of this material is generally understood to be an itinerary, although Benjamin Scolnic has proposed a slight variation, to wit, that the genre of Numbers 33 is a list used by P that could be quite ancient.[16] The toponym list or itinerary as presented in Numbers 33 shares a number of features with Egyptian toponym lists, or itineraries, found on New Kingdom monuments.[17] In fact, Charles Krahmalkov has recently noted that the Egyptian lists are "maps of Late Bronze Age Palestine," and believes he has correlated some of the place names in the Egyptian sources with those found in Numbers. This correspondence, given that there is no dispute concerning the fourteenth-century B.C. date of the Egyptian toponym lists, leads him to conclude that "the account sounds credible enough, even authoritative, as if based on real and reliable sources. It certainly creates in the mind of even the most critical reader the impression of historical fact. After all, the historian is absolute and specific: He describes the Tran-Jordanian route he took in quite remarkable detail. . . . On the face of it, this passage [Numbers 33:45b–50] is an impressive and credible piece of ancient historical writing."[18]

This understanding of the Numbers itinerary is at odds with the view of many biblical scholars who consider the wilderness itinerary to be the work of P, and that it must be late in origin, or at least late in its placement into the WT.[19] The reality is that for over a century scholars have wrestled with the question of sources in the exodus narratives, and, as we have seen, there is little consensus on the dating of the sources or, in some cases, what source stands behind a pericope. Nearly forty years ago, Lewis Hay recognized this dilemma, which still holds today, opining, "The literary critics, despite the air of assurance with which they individually proceed, have been unable to convince one another of the precise, or even approximate, limits of the major constituent strata in the narrative."[20] Consequently, the approach followed here will be to treat the geography of the exodus narratives as reflecting a unified itinerary rather than one that reflects different and conflicting traditions, and one that at least in the early stages makes sense on a map of ancient Egypt and Sinai. In a sense, this approach to the geography is not dissimilar to Jean Louis Ska's treatment of Exodus 14, in which he assumes the use of a variety of sources in this chapter, and yet sees a unity and coherence in the final form of the narrative.[21]

III. Early Egyptologists and the Geography of the Exodus

The Egypt Exploration Fund (now Society), which publishes *the Journal of Egyptian Archaeology*, was founded in 1882 by, among others, Amelia Edwards, a Victorian-era writer and traveler to Egypt. Her book, *A Thousand*

Miles up the Nile, first published in 1877, is a classic that remains in print. Under her energetic leadership, the Egypt Exploration Fund (EEF, later the EES) began with goals of surveying and recording monuments in Egypt, with the Bible playing a central role. Because of the prominence of the Delta in the Pentateuchal stories, it was the focus of some of the early excavations. Two of the pioneer Egyptologists to excavate under the auspices of the EEF were Sir William Mathew Flinders Petrie and Edouard Naville. Naville was a Swiss professor from the University of Geneva.[22] Their interest in the Bible is reflected in the titles of some of the publications of their excavations. Two of Naville's earliest excavation reports were *The Store-City of Pithom and the Route of the Exodus* (1885) and *The Shrine of Saft El Henneh and the Land of Goshen* (1887). The latter excavations were undertaken in 1885 in Saft el Henneh, Khataanah-Kantir, and Tell Rotab (Retabeh), located in the eastern Delta and the Wadi Tumilat.[23] Meanwhile, Petrie's early work took him to San el-Hagar (Tanis), Tell el-Yehudiah, and Tell Retabeh (twenty years after Naville).[24] His interest in biblical history is reflected in the title of one of his publications, *Hyksos and Israelite Cities.*[25] In 1922, Sir Alan Gardiner wrote a very sharply worded critique of Naville and others whom he thought were naïvely using the Bible to find the Delta sites associated with the exodus story; this was followed by another in 1924 that was a response to an article by Naville.[26] T. E. Peet likewise rebuked Egyptologists whom he accused of being unduly influenced by the Bible in their Egyptological research. Naville took umbrage at Peet's charge that his suggestion that Tell el-Maskhuta was Pithom was the result of "guesses of early explorers, bent on finding biblical sites at any cost."[27]

With the work of these early Egyptologists, the search for the biblical cities associated with the exodus was on. But it seems that Gardiner's strong condemnation of those whom we might call biblical Egyptologists, continues to cast a pall over serious investigation of biblical history with the aid of Egyptology. Since the 1930s there have been only a few Egyptologists who have integrated their work with biblical studies, in particular as it relates to the exodus tradition. One notable exception to this trend was a small book written by Alfred Lucas in 1938 called *The Route of the Exodus of the Israelites from Egypt.* Lucas is best known for his classic book *Ancient Egyptian Materials and Industries* (1926), which is still available in print in the fourth edition (including some revisions by J. R. Harris in 1962 and 1989). Although he spent most of his career analyzing artifacts and the materials from which they were made, Lucas suggested that his forty years in Egypt gave him some basis to offer some insights into the biblical exodus story. Quite aware of the harsh tone of the debate about the location of the cities of the Exodus, Lucas pledged to follow the dictum of the chemist Robert Boyle, who said: "A man may be a champion for truth without being an enemy of civility: and may confute an opinion without railing at them that hold it."[28] Some of his ideas will be discussed in subsequent chapters.

It seems that the heated debate of the 1920s has been ignited once again in the past few decades, as more recent archaeological discoveries are being scrutinized in view of a renewed skepticism about the Bible. Like Lucas, it is my desire to contribute to the debate in a civil manner.

Before undertaking a careful study of the toponyms associated with the Israelite sojourn and exodus, some comments regarding the nature of geographical names are in order. The place names found in the wilderness tradition fall into four different categories:[29]

1. names of Egyptian etymology that reflect actual Egyptian toponyms (e.g., Rameses, Pithom, *yām sûp̱*)
2. Hebrew descriptive terms that explain the feature (e.g., Pi-hahiroth, Marah)
3. Semitic names or loanwords in the Egyptian vernacular (e.g., Baal Zephon, Migdol)
4. aetiological names given by the Hebrews to explain an event that occurred at a certain location (e.g., Meribah)

As the geographical terms are examined in the following pages, we shall attempt to identify the name type, and propose locations.

IV. Rameses, Starting Point of the Exodus

Exodus 1:11 names Pithom and Rameses as the two cities connected with the oppression of the Hebrews and their brickmaking tasks.[30] In 1918, Gardiner made an exhaustive text-based study of all available inscriptions in order to identify the Delta Ramesside capital, Pi-Ramesses, the full name of which is "House of Ramesses Beloved of Amun, Great of Victories" (*pr-r^{c} mss sw mry imn ^{c}3 nḫtw*).[31] After reviewing scores of texts, he concluded that "whether or no [*sic!*] the Bible narrative be strict history, there is not the least reason for assuming that any other city of Ramesses existed in the Delta besides those elicited from the Egyptian monuments. In other words, the Biblical Raamses-Rameses is identical with the Residence-city of Pi-Ra^{c}messe."[32] At this date, Gardiner speculated that Pi-Ramesses was located "near Pelusium," that is, Tell Farama on the Mediterranean coast, east of the present-day Suez Canal in Sinai. Locating Pi-Ramesses at or near Pelusium had been proposed in 1888 by Max Müller.[33] In holding this location for Pi-Ramesses, Gardiner differed with Petrie and Naville, who had worked in the Wadi Tumilat (which they thought was the Land of Goshen), and proposed that Tell Retabeh was Pi-Ramesses and Tell el-Maskhuta was Pithom.[34]

Both locations for Pi-Ramesses were abandoned in the 1930s when the French under the direction of Pierre Montet began excavations at San el-Hagar, starting in 1928. In 1933 Montet published an important article in which he proposed that his excavations at San el-Hagar had yielded the city of Avaris, the old Hyksos capital, Pi-Ramesses, and Tanis (Zoan of the Bible).[35] In the same year, Gardiner printed a hasty retraction of his earlier views, and embraced the interpretation of Montet and Brugsch that San el-Hagar is Tanis. No one doubted that San el-Hagar was Zoan/Tanis because the Arabic name *ṣan* linguistically corresponds to Hebrew צֹעַן: *ṣōᶜan*. The presence of hundreds of inscribed Ramesside blocks, statues, stelae, and obelisks led to the obvious conclusion that San el-Hagar was Pi-Ramesses and Tanis. As late as his *Egypt of the Pharaohs* (1962), Gardiner still held that Tanis was Pi-Ramesses, despite acknowledging that Labib Habachi was then making a strong case that the site of Qantir was Pi-Ramesses.[36] Only recently have Habachi's discoveries at Qantir been fully published, nearly two decades after his death. Before his death in 1984, Habachi was convinced that Qantir was the Ramesside royal residence and that it was the Rameses of the biblical narratives.[37] After Habachi's work in the Qantir area, Manfred Bietak of the University of Vienna has been meticulously excavating at Tell el-Dabᶜa since 1966, while at nearby Qantir, Edgar Pusch of the German Institute, in cooperation with Bietak, has been uncovering the ancient Ramesside capital. The consensus is that these adjoining sites were Avaris and Pi-Ramesses, respectively, and that the blocks discovered at Tanis (around twenty kilometers/twelve miles north of Qantir), as well as some from Tell Basta, were taken from the Qantir-Dabᶜa area (mostly Pi-Ramesses) for reuse by the Twenty-first Dynasty builders starting around 1069 B.C., the accession date for Smendes, the builder of Tanis.[38] Some of the Ramesside blocks and statues, however, did originate at Tell Basta itself, as can be seen by two stela dedicated to Bast, the patron deity.[39]

Despite the abundance of textual and archaeological evidence produced over the past forty to fifty years that locates biblical Rameses at Qantir, there are a few naysayers. Some years ago Donald Redford, a leading Egyptologist, suggested that there are two linguistic or scribal problems in the Hebrew writing of Rameses. First, he thought that the omission of the element *pi* (for Egyptian *pr*, meaning house or residence) meant that the Ramesside city Pi-Ramesses was not intended. Second, he claimed that the Egyptian *ss* in Pi-Ramesses should appear in Hebrew as *shins* and not *sameks*.[40] From these two problems, Redford concluded that these vocalizations reflect later (ca. sixth-century) writings for the names. The questions raised by Redford were thoroughly answered by Wolfgang Helck, who was able to cite cases where the city of Ramesses was written without the prefix *pi*, and showed that Redford's objection to the precise correlation of the sibilants was unwarranted.[41] Furthermore, the second place name mentioned along with Rameses is Pithom, the etymology of which is universally accepted to be the Hebrew writing of *pr-itm*, house or temple of Atum, a point Redford acknowledges.[42] So it is inconsistent to say that the Hebrew author should retain the *pi* element in the one case but not the other.

The normal writing of the Egyptian *s* in Hebrew is *samek*, not *shin*, as shown by the following examples of Egyptian names written with s that appear in Hebrew with a *samek*:

pr bstt (Bubastis) appears in Ezekiel 30:17 as פִּי־בֶסֶת (Pi-beseth);
p3 nḥsy appears in Exodus 6:25 and Numbers 25:7, 11 as פִּינְחָס (Phineas);
t3 ḥ(mt) p3 nsw appears in 1 Kings 11:19 as תַּחְפְּנֵיס (Tehpenes);
t3 ḥ(wt) p3 nḥsi appears in Jeremiah 2:16, 43:7–9; 44:1, 14 as תַּחְפַּנְחֵס (Tahpanhes); and
p3 t3 rsy, meaning Upper Egypt, appears in Isaiah 11:11; Jeremiah 44:1, 15 and Ezekiel פַּתְרוֹס (Pathros).

These examples suffice to show that when an Egyptian name or word written with an *s* was rendered in Hebrew, the *samek* was the appropriate sibilant, and this has been reconfirmed recently in a comprehensive study of Egyptian terms in Hebrew by Yoshiyuki Muchiki.[43] Consequently, the writing of Rameses in Hebrew as רַעְמְסֵס is precisely as it should be.[44]

As already noted, Redford has dismissed the suggestion that the exodus geography is historicized myth on the basis that the biblical material looks historiographic, but he surmised that the toponymy in Exodus and Numbers reflects the facts on the ground of sixth-century Egypt during the Saite Twenty-sixth Dynasty.[45] A lengthy article on the geography of the exodus recently published by Van Seters is largely a defense of Redford's position that the geographical terms reflect the sixth century.[46] The results of Redford's 1987 study[47] were warmly received by Israel Finkelstein and Neil Silberman in their new minimalist manifesto, *The Bible Unearthed* (2001).[48] Interestingly, these writers accept Redford's argument but entirely ignore Helck's authoritative refutation of Redford's study, not to mention my critique in *Israel in Egypt* from 1997. Niels Peter Lemche also has tried to make the case that the use of Rameses and Pithom do not reflect second-millennium history, but are anachronistic references by the Jewish writers in their "fictitious picture of the sojourn."[49] Lemche's Egyptological authority for the lateness of these names is not Bietak or Redford (he does not even cite the 1987 study!); rather it is Edward Wente, who wrote a brief dictionary entry on biblical Rameses.[50]

Wente and Redford point out that there were first-millennium cults of the gods of Ramesses (the king or the city) that sprang up elsewhere in the Delta, probably because of the relocation of the statues and shrines from Pi-Ramesses to Tanis and Bubastis. Wente and Redford, in turn, seem to draw their conclusion on the basis of observations of Bietak on the survival of minor cult centers from Pi-Ramesses in later times.[51] It is clear, however, that Bietak does not attribute to these the origin of the name Rameses in the Bible, rather linking the name directly to Pi-Ramesses during the Twentieth Dynasty (early twelfth century).[52] Thus Rameses of the exodus narratives refers not to the Delta residence but to these shrines. Hence, Lemche opines: "Ramses may in Exod. 1.11 refer to Tanis." Although this suggestion is interesting, it is seriously flawed.

If Tanis were the intended location of the writer(s) of the exodus story, it would surely have been known to Israelite scribes any time during the first millennium. Tanis was occupied continuously from the eleventh century B.C. down to Greco-Roman times, and was the principal city of the northeastern Delta.[53] The biblical evidence is clear: Israelite scribes did know about Tanis and mentioned it by name. In the late eighth century B.C., the prophet Isaiah knew that Zoan or Tanis (צֹעַן) was a Delta capital (Isa. 19:11, 13; 30:4), and so did Ezekiel in the sixth century (Ezek. 30:14). More important, when Psalm 78 was written it referred to the events of the exodus occurring in the "Fields of Zoan" (vv. 12, 43), and not in Rameses.[54] Clearly this first-millennium B.C. Psalmist knew of and used the name Tanis/Zoan as the location of the miraculous events of the exodus because it was the major city of the northeastern Delta and was situated in the biblical Land of Goshen. He did not use Rameses.

Why then would the author(s) who was (were) writing about the starting point of the exodus in Exodus and Numbers not follow the thinking of the Psalmist, if their works are roughly contemporaneous? This is what one would expect, following Van Seter's position that the names in the itinerary reflect the period of writing: "the geographic background of the exodus story is Egypt in the time of the writer."[55] Furthermore, it is hard to believe that the small first-millennium Delta cults of Ramesses would have made such an impression on the writing of the exodus story, as Wente and Redford maintain, but not on the writer of Psalm 78. Another problem, if we assume that seventh- and sixth-century Judean travelers brought the name Rameses back to Judah, is that these foreigners would not have been permitted to enter Egyptian temple precincts, where they would have seen these old relics. The biblical prohibition against foreigners entering the temple because they were thought to be defiling is well known (cf. Deut. 23:3; Neh. 13:1; Acts 21:28–30). The same was true in Egypt, which is why massive temenos walls were built around temples, and why only the initiated priests and royalty, when acting in a priestly capacity, could enter.[56] The priest-king Menkheperre of the Twenty-first Dynasty (1035–986 B.C.) left an inscription at Karnak Temple in Thebes in which he reports building a great wall around the complex.[57] Prior to this he had to remove Egyptian squatters. He states that the reason for his building was "to conceal the temple of his father Amun-[Re, to clean]se (it) of the people, after he had found it built with houses belonging to Egyptians which remained in the court of the House of Amun. . . . The Thebans were escorted out of the gate of the temple of his father Amun."[58] A few centuries later, during the Persian period, a text reports how Cambyses dealt with foreign squatters in the temple of Neith: "His majesty commanded the driving out of all the foreigners [who] were squatting in the temple of Neith, the demolition of their houses and all their damage that was in this temple. They carried out [all their things] themselves to the gate of the wall of the temple."[59] These texts demonstrate that Egyptians in general and foreigners in particular were prohibited from entering temples. Consequently, Hebrew visitors or biblical writers would not have had direct access to the so-called Ramesses cult centers of the late first millennium. It seems far more likely that if the exodus story indeed reflected sixth-century geography, Tanis would have been named in Exodus and Numbers as the starting point of the exodus and Egypt's capital at that time.

Pi-Ramesses was one of the greatest cities in antiquity. In the early 1980s, Eric Uphill pointed out that it "was probably the vastest and most costly royal residence ever erected by the hand of man. As can now be seen its known palace and official center covered an area of at least four square miles, and its temples were in scale with this, a colossal assemblage forming perhaps the largest collection of chapels built in the pre-classical world by a single rule at one time."[60] The ongoing work of Edgar Pusch at Qantir has confirmed the massive size of the city that had been projected on the basis of ancient texts. Extensive magnetometer surveying has showed that Pi-Ramesses was larger than thought, occupying ten square kilometers, or six square miles.[61]

What happened to this ancient megalopolis named for its builder, Ramesses II (1279–1212 B.C.), is important for the issue at hand. Before the Twentieth Dynasty ended (ca. 1069 B.C.), the city had been abandoned, and the remaining Ramesside kings moved to Memphis. The city became a ghost town because the Pelusiac branch of the Nile that passed by the city had migrated so far away that the city had been cut off from its transportation artery. The founder of the Twenty-first Dynasty, Smendes, that is, Nesu-ba-neb-djed of the Tale of Wen-Amun, is thought to be the builder of royal Tanis.[62] The name Zoan (Eg. *ḏᶜn*), however, is attested in Egyptian texts during the reign of Ramesses II, where it is actually *sḫt ḏᶜn*, the Field(s) of Zoan, just as it is written in Psalm 78.[63] This area is thought to have referred to the Tanis area and the nearby Lake Manzeleh.[64] So the region of Zoan was known in New Kingdom Egypt, but it apparently only became a city of any importance beginning in the Third Intermediate Period (eleventh century B.C.).[65]

This evidence suggests that the occurrence of Ramesses in the exodus narratives points to the city of Pi-Ramesses, which flourished for only 150 years (ca. 1270–1120 B.C.). Tanis soon replaced it as the dominant city of the northeast Delta, beginning in the eleventh century, for the next thousand years. The identification of Rameses in Exodus 1:11, 12:37, and Numbers 33:3 makes best sense as Pi-Ramesses. Furthermore, the appearance of Rameses in the exodus story suggests that either the memory was preserved to later times, when the city no longer existed, or that the actual writing took place when the city still flourished. Had the biblical writer(s), as Lemche has imagined, been creating a "fictitious picture" five to six hundred years after the purported event, then an amazing coincidence occurred. They blindly got the name right!

It seem obvious to me that the recent problems raised concerning the writing of Rameses in the Bible, the dredging up of late obscure cults of Pi-Ramesses, and the proposal that the biblical writer actually meant Tanis are pure obfuscation. Eighty years after Peet and Gardiner's debate with Naville and Petrie, we have come full circle, but now it seems that those who oppose this rather obvious correlation between Rameses of the Bible and Pi-Ramesses of Ramesside Egypt are bent on denying credibility to the biblical narratives at any cost.

V. Pithom

This site is mentioned just once in the Pentateuch, in Exodus 1:11. It plays no role in the exodus itinerary, however. Rather it is mentioned only in connection with the Israelites' brickmaking and forced labor. It is identified along with Rameses as עָרֵי מִסְכְּנוֹת: *ᶜārê miskᵉnôt* = store-cities. There is no disputing the etymology of פִּתֹם: Pithom, and here Egyptologists agree that it is the Hebrew writing for *pr-itm*, the house or temple of Atum.[66] The location and the nature of the site remain controversial, nevertheless.

The search for Pithom, like that of Rameses, has had a long history, but unlike Rameses, its location has not been established with absolute certainty. From the early excavations of Naville and Petrie in the Wadi Tumilat, this region was thought to be the biblical Land of Goshen.[67] This narrow strip of arable land was a well-established access route to Egypt that connected with the route across Sinai to Canaan known as the Way of Shur in the Bible.[68] Beginning in 1883, Naville excavated at Tell Retabeh,[69] followed by Petrie in 1905. Because it had produced Ramesside-era remains, they concluded that it was Pi-Ramesses (that is, Rameses of the Bible).[70] Meanwhile, the earlier work of Naville at Tell Maskhuta, located fourteen kilometers (ca. eight miles) east of Tell Retabeh in the Wadi Tumilat, led him to think that it was Pithom. And Petrie and Naville agreed with each other's identifications.

In the previous section, the debate over the location of Pi-Ramesses between Gardiner and Naville was discussed. Naturally, it had obvious implications for the identification of Tell el-Maskhuta as Pithom. From the 1930s till the 1960s and 1970s, Tanis was widely believed to be Pi-Ramesses (Rameses). The reference to Pithom and Rameses together suggests to some scholars that these two toponyms may have been fairly close to each other, although there is no proof of that. But, with the northeast Delta location of Pi-Ramesses/Rameses almost certainly at Tanis or Qantir, problems were raised for Maskhuta as the site of Pithom. (The connection of Pithom with Succoth will be taken up in the next section.) Because Retabeh is the only Wadi Tumilat site to have produced in situ Ramesside remains,[71] Bietak and Kenneth Kitchen think that this site might be the elusive Pithom.[72]

After a long hiatus in excavations at Tell Maskhuta, a team directed by John S. Holladay of the University of Toronto commenced investigating it in the 1970s.[73] His work helped clarify the occupational history of this strategic site. A settlement of the Second Intermediate Period/Middle Bronze IIB (eighteenth to seventeenth centuries B.C.) was documented, followed by a long break until the late seventh century, when apparently Neco II rebuilt the site in connection with the Red Sea canal project that was eventually completed by Darius.[74] On the basis of an inscription found on a Twenty-second Dynasty statue discovered by Naville, and some Hellenistic-period sources, Holladay thinks that Maskhuta is actually Pithom, which in turn was inserted into the biblical text, and hence is anachronistic. This conclusion is unwarranted because, as Holladay recognizes, earlier texts mention *pr-itm* that predates what he calls "the new Per-Atum" from 610 B.C. onward, which is located at Maskhuta.[75]

Lemche has picked up on Holladay's conclusions as evidence for a late, and hence fictitious, origin of the exodus story. Now Van Seters champions Holladay's and Redford's view of identifying biblical Pithom with Tell el-Maskhuta and dating the biblical itinerary to the Saite period.[76] He is clearly eager to show that the Yahwist's (J) portion of the exodus itinerary dates to the sixth century, not the tenth, as is traditionally held by source critics.[77] Central to Van Seters's argument is that Tjeku (Succoth) in the Ramesside period was a region and not a city, because writings of Tjeku in Egyptian texts from this period are not written with the city determinative. Since the recent Toronto excavations at Maskhuta show a hiatus in the stratigraphy between the early second millennium and the seventh century B.C., he concludes: "This means that references to these places in the biblical record could only reflect the geography of a mid-first millennium BCE dating at the earliest."[78]

It is remarkable that a scholar of Van Seters's erudition could come to such a dogmatic conclusion on the basis of so little evidence, and in the process ignore important data that in fact militate against that conclusion. Let me enumerate several of these points.

First, the references to Succoth in Exodus 12:37; 18:18, and Numbers 33:5–6 do not identify what kind of place it is—city, village, fort, or region. What makes Van Seters think it is a city?

As it turns out, Van Seters is quite wrong to say in his article of 2001 that Tjeku in Egyptian texts "only receives the town determinative, signifying the name of the principal town of the region, in the late [Saite] period."[79] In 1938, Georges Posener published a hieratic ostracon from Deir el-Medineh (1076) that included a writing of Tjeku with the city sign (⊗).[80] No translation was offered by Posener, however. In 1979, Kitchen collated this text for his *Ramesside Inscriptions* II and brought it to the attention of the scholarly world at a conference in Memphis, Tennessee, in 1987, and again a decade later at a symposium organized by Eliezer Oren, the proceedings of which were published in 1998.[81] Kitchen kindly allowed me to refer to his text and to use his translation in my *Israel in Egypt* in 1997 (p. 180). So this important datum about the nature of Tjeku in the Ramesside period, so crucial to Van Seters's argument, has been available for some time.

Not only are the recent Canadian excavations at Maskhuta, in which Van Seters participated, critical to his identification of the site with Pithom of the Bible but this also prompts him to reject the view of many that nearby Tell el-Retabeh is Pithom of the New Kingdom. Van Seters asserts that "Gardiner's identification of Pithom with Tell er-Rataba is not possible because—on the basis of the Wadi Tumilat expedition's ceramic survey of the site in 1977 and all the published materials to date—Tell er-Rataba was largely unoccupied from the Saite to Roman times, precisely the time when the monuments attest the existence of the *town* of Pithom."[82] Van Seters fails to mention that Hans Goedicke of Johns Hopkins University directed investigations at Retabeh in 1977–1978, and although he has yet to fully publish his finds, two articles by Goedicke have appeared that address the identity of Pithom. He argues that because of the New Kingdom remains at his site, and the absence of Eighteenth- to Twentieth-Dynasty levels at Maskhuta, that *pr-itm* of Pap. Anastasi VI, 55 and the Bible can only be Retabeh and not Maskhuta.[83] Besides Goedicke's articles, a complete study of the stratigraphy of the 1978 season at Retabeh was undertaken by Michael Fuller, who was the project's geoarchaeologist and architect.[84] Although the work at Retabeh was limited in scope, a good stratigraphical sequence was nevertheless established. Fuller dates the eleven strata as follows:[85]

1	End of Dynasty 25 and into 26
2–3	Dynasties 20–23
4	Nineteenth Dynasty (major rebuilding)
5–7	Late Eighteenth Dynasty (decline in population)
8–10	Early Eighteenth Dynasty
11	Second Intermediate Period

The fact that eight of the eleven strata are from the New Kingdom demonstrates that Tell el-Retabeh was the major Empire-period site in the Wadi Tumilat. The Hopkins survey and excavations of the 1970s identified no material from the Greco-Roman period, indicating that the site was probably abandoned about the time Tell el-Maskhuta was rebuilt.[86] Fuller also argues that the large mud-brick structure that Petrie thought was a temple is really a military structure.[87]

Holladay's work at Maskhuta showed that the reoccupation began during the reign of Neco II (610–595 B.C.).[88] Consequently, it seems logical to conclude that the inscribed blocks, statues, and stela uncovered at Tell el-Maskhuta that date to before the end of the seventh century came from another site. Recognizing that Retabeh is the only major site in the area that could have produced such material, it seems to be the best candidate as the source for the inscribed materials at Tell el-Maskhuta.[89] In fact, after studying the Maskhuta naos of Ramesses II, Karol Myśliwiec has suggested that Retabeh is the most likely source for this object and the other Ramesside materials.[90]

Let us turn to the textual evidence used to support equating Pithom with Tell el-Maskhuta, used by Redford, Holladay, and Van Seters. All cite the so-called Pithom stela discovered by Naville at Maskhuta as providing evidence for locating Pithom at Tell el-Maskhuta.[91] The inscription belongs to Ptolemy II Philadelphos (282–246 B.C.). It actually contains more references to Tjeku (12) than to *Pr-itm* (2). One of the deities depicted on the right side of the lunette is Atum, who is called: *itm ʿꜣ nṯr ṯkw* = "Atum, the great god of Tjeku."[92] Tjeku is written here, and in two other instances (lines 25 and 28), with both city and foreign land determinatives, while in other writings in the stela it is either written with the city sign or no determinative at all. Variations on this initial epithet are repeated many times throughout the stela. The most frequently occurring epithet is *it.f itm ʿꜣ nṯr ʿnḫ n ṯkw*, "his father [i.e., the king's] Atum the great and living god of Tjeku" (lines 2, twice in 7,[93] 14, 16, 19, 21, 25, 28). Line 3 names another important deity who is associated with Tjeku: *ḥr smꜣ tꜣwy ʿꜣ nṯr ḥry-tp ṯkw*, "Horus, Uniter of the Two Lands, the great god who is chief of Tjeku." The second time Tjeku is written in line 7 is significant: *is spr.n ḥm.f r ḥwt n(y)t pr-krth s??t ḥwt n(y)t it.f itm ʿꜣ ʿnḫ nṯr ṯkw*, "Now his majesty came to the temple of Pr-Kereteh ??? the temple of his father Atum, the great god of Tjeku." Here it is clear that the temple at Tjeku is identified as a *ḥwt*, not a *pr*, and certainly, not *pr-itm*. The final line (28) of this inscription refers to the place where the stela itself was set up: *ḫft-ḥr n it.f itm ʿꜣ nṯr ʿnḫ ṯkw*, "before[94] his father Atum, the great and living god of Tjeku." The reference in line 13 has received the most attention because it is written in combination with *pr-itm*, Pithom. It refers to the *nṯrw pr-itm ṯkw*, "the gods of Pithom and Tjeku," or "the gods of Pithom of Tjeku." Both names use the city determinative. On the basis of this text, one might think that two different cities are in view. A second occurrence of *pr-itm* is in line 10, but adds nothing to the identity of the site, any more than does the epithet of Atum Lord of Heliopolis in line 2.

On the basis of these two somewhat obscure references to *pr-itm* or Pithom, Naville came to the conclusion that Tell el-Maskhuta was Pithom of the exodus narratives and that Tjeku (Succoth) was the surrounding area.[95] It must also be recalled that in the late nineteenth century, he, Petrie, and others believed that nearby Tell el-Retabeh was Rameses of the Bible, and thus Rameses and Pithom of Exodus 1:11 where accounted for.

Despite the ambiguous evidence from the Ptolemy II ("Pithom") stela, I see no reason not to deny that Pithom was the name of the settlement at Tell el-Maskhuta from the late seventh century B.C. down to Greco-Roman times. But since Holladay has shown that Maskhuta was not occupied during the entirety of the New Kingdom (1540–1069 B.C.) and for 350 years of the Third Intermediate Period, then it must be concluded that the earlier inscribed materials found at Maskhuta should have originated elsewhere and were moved there at the end of the seventh century B.C.

Pap. Anastasi V, 51–61, describes permitting Edomite bedouin to water their flocks at "the Fortress of Merneptah-hetephirma'at, Life, Prosperity, and Health, to the pools (*brkt*) of *pr-itm* of Merneptah-hetephirma'at which belongs to (*nty*) Tjeku."[96] Bietak, based upon his paleoenvironmental study of the eastern Delta, suggests that these pools were a part of a lake system that was situated at the western end of the Wadi Tumilat, its eastern end being close to Tell el-Retabeh.[97] For Bietak, this lake system and the reference to the "pools of *pr-itm*" from the Nineteenth Dynasty, suggest to him that Retabeh is Pithom.[98]

Also at Tell el-Maskhuta, Naville discovered a statue of an official named Ankh-Renp-nefer[99] who served under Osorkon II (ca. 860 B.C.). Interestingly, this statue contains important data and mentions Pithom. The owner bears the titles *idnw n ṯkw* (lieutenant of Tjeku) and *ḥry n pr-ᶜ3* (commander of Pharaoh).[100] The former is apparently a military title, which would be in keeping with the military presence in the Wadi Tumilat, that is, Tjeku.[101] *Pr-itm* occurs twice on this statue.[102]

In the light of the clarification of the stratigraphy at Maskhuta, and the fact that this statue dates to 250 years before the rebuilding under Neco II (ca. 610 B.C.), Holladay comes to the obvious conclusion that this statue originated elsewhere.[103] Consequently, it must have been brought to the site in the Saite period, and cannot be used to identify the name of the site prior to the time of Neco. It also shows that there was a site of some sort (e.g., temple, town, temple estate) known as Pithom prior to its relocation to Tell el-Makshuta.

Naville also discovered an inscribed fragment bearing the cartouches of Sheshonk I (Shishak of 1 Kings 14:25) at Maskhuta.[104] So other Twenty-second Dynasty evidence is present that does not belong at Maskhuta. These objects, if they came from Retabeh, correspond to level 3.

After a thorough examination of all the inscriptions from the Wadi Tumilat, Kitchen observes: "We possess not one single scrap of hieroglyphic evidence to prove that Pithom was ever the proper name of a settlement of Tell el-Maskhuta."[105] It is true that the name Patumus is mentioned as a site along the course of the Red Sea canal that went through the Wadi Tumilat in Herodotus (II, 158).[106] A. B. Lloyd believes that Patumus is the Greek writing for *Pr-itm* and that it is to be found at Tell el-Maskhuta.[107] The problem with locating Pithom at a specific site in the Wadi Tumilat is that this entire region was associated with the god Atum. At different times and in more than one location in the area there were probably temples or shrines of Atum. In fact, the Arabic name Tumilat preserves the name of Atum in the first syllable of the name. Atum is widely attested in documents relating to this region,[108] and is depicted on a block found by Petrie at Retabeh, coupled with the epithet "Atum Lord of Tje(k)u."[109] This block was from a temple wall at the site, undoubtedly one belonging to Atum himself. Tjeku, as will be demonstrated in the following section, is the New Kingdom name for the Wadi Tumilat. At the same time, as suggested by the Deirel-Medineh ostracon introduced above, Tjeku could also have referred to a more specific location within the region.

A different location for Pithom of Exodus 1:11 has been offered by Uphill. He speculates that Pithom might be the biblical name for Heliopolis.[110] Heliopolis is located in the shadow of present-day Cairo. As the name suggests, this city was a main cult center of Atum, whose usual epithet is *nb iwnw*, "Lord of Heliopolis." Uphill points to the massive building projects at the site during the reigns of Seti I and Ramesses II. A great number of storage facilities and a large enclosure wall measuring fifteen meters in thickness are included in this building project.[111] In support of Uphill's theses, the Septuagint of Exodus 1:11 mentions the building of Pitho(m) and Rameses but, interestingly, adds "and On, which is Heliopolis." Associating Pithom with the cult center of Atum at On is intriguing, but is not without problems. Chiefly, the name of the cult center of On is *ḥwt bnbn*, "the Mansion of the Ben-Ben" and not *pr-itm*. Thus Uphill's association of Pithom with On/Heliopolis seems most unlikely.

A final possibility needs to be considered. It should be noted that Pithom and Rameses, based upon the Bible's description of them, should be understood to be storage facilities and not cities or settlements per se. By this I mean that Pithom might not be a name of a city. Like the Iron Age "store-cities" discovered as Megiddo, Hazor, and Gezer, and mentioned in 1 Kings 9:19 and 2 Chronicles 8:4 and 6—called עָרֵי מִסְכְּנוֹת,—such facilities would typically be connected to either palace, administrative, or temple institutions.[112] This is also true in Egypt, where a network of storage facilities are made up of rows of long, narrow mud-brick chambers that were constructed adjacent to temples and palaces. Large mud-brick enclosure walls surrounded these complexes. Funerary temples, like those of Ramesses II and III in western Thebes, contain scores of such well-preserved storage chambers,[113] and New Kingdom palaces at Malkata and Deir el-Ballas were entirely constructed of mud brick, as were their storage facilities.[114] Thus it might be suggested that the reference to the store-cities of Pithom and Rameses in Exodus 1:11 points to the vast storage facilities of a temple of Atum and the palace at Rameses or of Rameses (i.e., the king). Consequently, the search for a city by the name of Pithom that corresponds to the Bible might indeed be futile. Thus although Tell el-Retabeh may be the site described in Exodus 1:11, alternatively, the "store cities" might only be the storage complexes attached to a temple of Atum (in Pi-Ramesses, Heliopolis, or elsewhere) and for the palace or some administrative institution at Pi-Ramesses.

After examining all the material concerning the possible location of Pithom, it seems, on the basis of the Egyptian textual evidence, that Pithom—the house or domain of Atum—was located within the region called Tjeku (Succoth). Whatever *pr-itm* was, it left its imprint in the region, which is why the name of Atum has even survived into the Arabic name, Wadi Tumilat. The archaeological work from a quarter century ago at Tell el-Maskhuta and Retabeh has shown that *pr-itm* can be found at both sites. The conclusion seems obvious. The name Pithom was initially associated with Tell el-Retabeh of the New Kingdom to Dynasties 22 and 23 (ca. tenth through seventh centuries). The establishment of the site at Makshuta during the reign of Necho II (ca. 610 B.C.), apparently because of its location in relation to the Red Sea canal that was being excavated, led to the abandonment of old Pithom. The transportation of the inscribed blocks, statues, and other materials, I propose, was not just a case of pragmatic recycling of building materials but was rather an intentional incorporation of objects from old Pithom into the new Pithom for purposes of establishing continuity of the name and the sacred (especially of temples).[115]

In the following chapter, it will be shown that the ancient site of Tjaru/Sile moved from Tell Hebua to Tell Abu Sefêh, which is why for over seventy-five years the latter site was thought to be Tjaru of New Kingdom times. One of the reasons Abu Sefêh was thought to be Egypt's frontier town through which the pharaohs of the New Kingdom passed on their military campaigns to the Levant was the presence of Ramesside blocks.[116] Could it be that these blocks were intentionally moved from old Tjaru/Sile to serve as a way of Christening new Sile? Likewise, it is shown in the next chapter that the toponym Migdol can be associated with three different sites, dating to the New Kingdom, Persian-Saite, and Greco-Roman periods. Some reason, probably changing environmental factors, led to the relocation of strategic defensive sites on Egypt's eastern frontier.

The foregoing discussion regarding Pithom in Egyptian texts, the archaeological evidence from Tell el-Maskhuta and Tell Retabeh, and Exodus 1:11 indicate that Pithom was probably identified with the former site from the late seventh century through Roman times, and at the latter site from the early seventh century B.C. and back to the New Kingdom. Redford is right to say that reference to *pr-itm* in Pap. Anastasi V, 51–61, does not prove that it corresponds to Tell Retabeh,[117] but when we take into account the other references to Pithom (such as the statue of Ankh-Renp-nefer), and the stratigraphical sequence at Retabeh, a compelling case can be made that it is the name of the site, a temple within it, or temple estate associated with Tell el-Retabeh and its immediate vicinity. This means that those, like Holladay and Van Seters, who argue that Pithom in the Bible derives from Maskhuta may be right. However, it is just as likely that it points to Retabeh during the New Kingdom.

If Pithom were the only toponym available in the Torah to date the narrative, one would have to conclude that a range of dates from ca. 300 B.C. to 1300 B.C. is possible. However, when we consider the other toponyms (such as Rameses and others, treated in the following chapter), an earlier date is more likely.

VI. Succoth

Both Exodus 12:37 and Numbers 33:3 agree that the Israelite departure from Egypt started at Ramesses.[118] Exodus 13:17 reports that they did not go by the northern route, called the Way (or road) of the land of the Philistines, which was the guarded military route to Canaan that the Egyptians called the Ways of Horus.[119] As will be detailed in the next chapter, the Fortress Tjaru, which guarded the beginning of this route, was discovered during the 1980s.[120] Its immense size and location on a narrow strip of land, with water on two sides, made it an ominous obstacle to invaders from the east and unauthorized parties trying to leave Egypt (see figure 5). Instead of going via the Ways of Horus, Exodus 13:18 indicates that the route was taken "by the roundabout way of the wilderness toward the Red Sea" (*yām sûp̱*). The mention of Succoth (סֻכּוֹת) in 13:20 shows that the route followed moved in a southeasterly direction. For well over a century, Egyptologists have recognized that Hebrew סֻכּוֹת corresponds to the Egyptian toponym *ṯkw* (Tjeku).[121] On linguistic grounds, it appears that the root is Semitic and was borrowed into Egyptian, where it first appears in texts during the reign of Ramesses II.[122] It means "covering," hence booth or hut.[123] The name probably reflects the fact that since early times Semitic-speaking people, desert clans or merchant traders, camped along the Wadi Tumilat on their way into Egypt. This picture squares with Holladay's discovery of evidence of seasonal dwellings at Tell el-Maskuta from the Second Intermediate Period (ca. 1750–1600 B.C.) of Asiatics, to judge from their material culture.[124] The fact that the Arabic name Maskhuta preserves that ancient pharaonic name Tjeku creates a serious problem for those who wish to identify Tell el-Maskhuta with Pithom.

Tjeku is generally taken to refer to the Wadi Tumilat itself. The reason for this is that most writings of the word occur with the throwing stick (𓌙) and foreign land (𓈉) determinatives. Together, they point either to the foreign name (as suggested above), or to the fact that this area was on Egypt's frontier.[125] Recently Kitchen published a study that brought together all known references to Tjeku in Egyptian texts. Although most use the foreign land sign, indicating a district, the aforementioned hieratic letter from Deir el-Medineh refers to the gods of Tjeku—but in this case, the city sign is used.[126] In Pap. Anastasi V (18.6–19.2), an officer instructs a subordinate to bring the Medjai militia (Nubian paramilitaries) to him at Tjeku. This statement would only be meaningful to the recipient of this order if a specific location in Tjeku were understood. Kitchen posits that these two references show that Tjeku also could refer to a specific location, such as the keep (*sgr*) of Tjeku mentioned in Pap. Anastasi V, 19.7–8, or the Fort of Merneptah Hetephirma'at (Life, Prosperity and Health-L.P.H.), which is in Tjeku (*ḫtm mr-n-ptḥ ḥtp ḥr m3ʿt, ʿnḫ wḏ3 snb nty* <*m*> *ṯkw*) of Pap. Anastasi VI, 54–61.[127] Consequently, in Nineteenth-Dynasty Egypt, Tjeku (Succoth) could refer to a region (the Wadi Tumilat) or a specific location within the region.[128] In drawing this conclusion, Kitchen is in agreement with the earlier findings of Wolfgang Helck.[129] The point is that Tjeku in Egyptian texts could refer to either a region or a specific location—probably a fort—by the same name, which means that biblical reference to Succoth likewise could be understood in the same manner.

Pap. Anastasi V, 19.2–20.6, reports on the travel of the troop commander (*ḥry pḏt*) Ka-Kem-Wer in pursuit of two runaway servants or workers. He says: "I was sent from the broad-halls of the king's house (*pr nsw*) L.P.H, on 3 Harvest 9, at the time of evening, after those two workers. When I reached the fortress (*sgr*) of Tjeku, on 3 Harvest 10, they told me: 'They are reporting from the south that they passed on 3 Harvest 10.' When I reached the fort (*p3 ḫtm*) they told me: 'The groom has come from the desert (*ḫ3st*), saying: "They have passed the wall of the Tower (*mktr*) of Sety Merneptah."' "[130]

A number of valuable nuggets of information can be mined from this text.

1. It is clear that the *sgr* and the *ḫtm* were two different military installations in the Wadi Tumilat during the Nineteenth Dynasty.
2. It shows that there was a direct route of travel from the palace (the broad halls of the king's house) at Pi-Ramesses to the Tjeku region (i.e., Rameses to Succoth).
3. The area outside of the Delta and the Wadi Tumilat was called *ḫ3st*, that is, desert, or what the Bible would call *miḏbār*.
4. Perhaps the most important point is that these runaways, who are thought to be Canaanite or Syrian, were trying to flee Egypt and did not follow the most direct route, that is, the northern, military road (Ways of Horus), which the Bible calls the Way or road of the land of the Philistines.
5. Equally significant is the fact that on Ka-Kem-Wer's first stop at the *sgr*, the soldiers on duty had seen the runaways, but because they had not received orders to detain them, had allowed them to pass by unmolested.
6. The internal dating indicates that the troop commander and his unit were apparently able to trek from Pi-Ramesses through a stretch of desert to the *sgr* in a day's time. If the *sgr* was at Tell el-Retabeh, this was a distance of just under thirty kilometers (ca. eighteen and a half miles).[131] The fact that he was dispatched in the evening may suggest that he made the trip through the night, with only a little rest. The text, unfortunately, tells us nothing about the mode of transportation—whether on foot or by chariot.[132]

7. He reached the next military installation, the *ḫtm*, without reference to the amount of time involved. Since this installation is called the Fort (*p3 ḫtm*, using the direct article), it would seem that this is a reference to the Fort (*ḫtm*) of Merneptah Hetephirma'at (L.P.H.), which is in Tjeku of Pap. Anastasi VI, 55.[133]
8. The soldiers at the Fort apparently had not seen the runaways, but a groom who had returned from the desert (*ḫ3st*) had, and knew the direction they were heading: namely north.
9. They were heading toward *t3 inbt mḥty n p3 mktr n sty mr n ptḥ*, which I translate as "the northern wall of the Fort (or Tower) of Sety-Merneptah."[134] Apparently before actually reaching the Fortress (*p3 ḫtm*) itself, the runaways turned north, as suggested by the use of the word *mḥty*, but they had crossed paths with the groom, who was coming south. It appears that rather than having to face the Fort and the other military installations south of Lake Timsah, they turned north. An alternative interpretation of *p3 ḫtm* was offered by Gardiner, who thought it referred to the Fortress Ṯjaru (*ḫtm n ṯ3rw*) because of the juxtaposition of the reference to the Migdol of Seti-Merneptah, which he knew to be on the Ways of Horus.[135] But this suggestion was rejected by Ricardo Caminos and Edward Bleiberg on the grounds that Tjaru is too far away to be considered Ka-Kem-wer's next stop after the *sgr* in Tjeku, and that his movements go from north to south.[136] These concerns not withstanding, I am inclined to agree with Gardiner in the light of more recent archaeological work in North Sinai and the recent comprehensive study of Ellen Morris, which will be treated below.

In a recent study, Kitchen shows that the defenses in the Wadi Tumilat were a part of a larger network of forts that marked a route from Pi-Ramesses, via Bubastis (Zagazig), Pi-Sopd (Seft el-Henneh), Tell Samad (at the western entrance of the Wadi Tumilat), Tell el-Retabeh, and Tell el-Maskhuta; then, upon reaching Lake Timsah, the route continued south, where more sites have been identified.[137] This means that throughout the Wadi Tumilat and then south to the northern end of the Gulf of Suez there was a chain of forts, in addition to the Bitter Lakes, which would have guarded the southeast sector.[138] The prospects of encountering additional forts after the *sgr* of Tjeku may explain why the two runaways turned north, hoping to find a less well-guarded way to freedom.

The data one can glean from Pap. Anastasi V, 19.2–20.6, shed considerable light on the first section of the Israelite departure from the Delta capital. First, a trek in a direct line from Pi-Ramesses (Rameses) to the Tjeku area was possible, especially if the travelers were in a hurry, as was the case with both runaways and the fleeing Israelites. The normal route would be to follow the southeast sector line via Bubastis and Saft el-Henneh, as proposed by Kitchen. But this route was longer, and, for the two runaways and the Israelites, it would have meant passing by a number of forts. Hence the direct route was preferable in both cases. Second, the two runaways probably took the southern route rather than the northern military road for the same reasons as the Israelites, to avoid this heavily fortified route, especially given the impressive size of the fortress (*ḫtm*) of Tjaru. The presence of the fort (*pȝ ḫtm*) somewhere in the Wadi Tumilat was especially foreboding to both sets of escapees, because a *ḫtm*-fort was not just a military installation (like the *sgr*). Rather, it had specific duties to monitor movements of people. It should be recalled that in Pap. Anastasi VI the Bedouin tribe was permitted to enter Egypt by the military stationed at the *ḫtm*-fort Merneptah Hetephirma'at.

An inscribed stone doorpost of the Middle Kingdom has recently been found at Hebua I (Tjaru). Although it only contains an offering formula, it belonged to an important official: "the hereditary prince and governor (*r-p*^{c}*t ḥȝty-*^{c}), the seal bearer (*sḏȝw bity*) king of Lower Egypt, unique friend, overseer of the seal (*imy (r) ḫtm*), Aper-Ba'al-ni."[139] It is of some significance that a man with a Semitic name is bearer of the royal seal (*ḫtm*) at this frontier site. *Ḫtm* derives from a Semitic root, meaning to seal or affix a seal.[140] It appears that the border official's duties to inspect travelers and to seal documents stands behind the term *ḫtm* meaning "fort": for example, *ḫtm n ṯȝrw* (the Fortress of Tjaru) or the Fort of Merneptah Hetephirma'at (L.P.H.) in Tjeku (*ḫtm mr-n-ptḥ ḥtp ḥr mȝ*^{c}*t,* ^{c}*nḫ wḏȝ snb, nty* <*m*> *ṯkw*) of Pap. Anastasi VI, 54–61.

In a recently defended dissertation from the University of Pennsylvania, Ellen Morris points out that a *ḫtm*-fortress derives its name from its function, namely, monitoring movements of people and blocking strategic entry points.[141] Sealing documents, thereby granting permits to enter Egypt, may also have been a function of a *ḫtm*-fort. Further, a *ḫtm*-fort was supervised by an overseer of the fort (*imy-r ḫtm*) or a troop commander (*ḥry pḏt*). Evidently, *imy-r ḫtm* stamped documents, thereby granting permission for people to enter or depart Egypt. This is analogous to the modern practice of stamping a passport with a visa when the bearer enters or departs a country. Recognizing the function of a *ḫtm*-fort may explain why the two runaways avoided the *ḫtm* in Tjeku and turned north. It seems logical to think that the same reasoning might be involved when the Israelites turned away from the *ḫtm*-fort at the end of the Wadi Tumilat, and why both wanted to stay clear of the *ḫtm*-fort in Tjaru.

VII. Etham

The next leg of the journey is reported as follows: "They set out from Succoth and camped at Etham (אֵתָם), which is on the edge of the wilderness" (Exod. 13:20).

Source critics are in a state of disarray when it comes to identifying the source at work here. Some attribute this verse to J.[142] Van Seters maintains that geographical information is a part of J's historiography, which he dates to the sixth century B.C.[143] Taking a different tack, Brevard Childs thought that P had appropriated this verse from E.[144] Meanwhile, William Propp has recently endorsed the theory of Richard E. Freidman that this verse should be assigned to the final redactor of the book (R), who was active after P's contribution to the Pentateuch.[145] It is evident that source criticism simply is ill equipped to answer the question of the origin of this verse. The meaning of the toponym Etham also presents a challenge.

There are those who have suggested that Etham refers to one of the forts in the Wadi Tumilat area, hence a writing for *ḫtm*.[146] On linguistic grounds, the identification of *ḫtm* with *'tm* is highly problematic.[147] Regarding the association with *'tm*, Muchiki declares: "Though often proposed, *ḫtm* is impossible phonetically."[148] Following the view of P. Weimer, who believes that a late editor simply did not really know the geography of the east Delta, Manfred Görg proposed that Etham represents a shortened writing for Pithom, and that the writing actually reflects a Twenty-first Dynasty writing of the Egyptian deity, Atum.[149] This suggestion, while intriguing, is problematic because Pithom is spelled appropriately in Exodus 1:11. So why would Exodus 13:20 get it wrong? Furthermore, if the omission of the initial element *pi* is indicative of the lateness of composition (as Redford suggested was the case in the writing of Pi-Ramesses and Rameses), then why does the sixth-century prophet Ezekiel refer to the east Delta city Bubastis as Pi-beseth (House of [the cat-goddess] Bastet)—פִּי־בֶ֫סֶת (Ezk. 30:17)? Clearly the absence of *pi* in the writing of Etham (and also Rameses) cannot be used as a criterion for the lateness of a toponym.

As mentioned in the previous section, the region of Tjeku in New Kingdom times was associated with the god Atum, and the epithet, "Atum, Lord of Tjeku" is attested. A testimony to Atum's influence on the area is the fact that the modern Arabic name of this area is Wadi Tumilat, which, as mentioned above, preserves the name of this deity. Görg might be partially correct when he proposed that Etham is a writing for Atum. The association is certainly possible on linguistic grounds. In his thorough investigation of Egyptian words in Semitic texts, Muchiki refers to Exodus 13:20 and Numbers 33:6, 7, and 8, where this toponym occurs, and observes: "Phonetically the most natural correspondence is (Egyptian) *itm* 'Atum.' "[150] Kitchen agrees, positing that Etham may be a writing for *i(w) itm*, the Isle of Atum.[151] This suggestion is certainly worthy of consideration, since there is a site located to the north in the Lake Manzelah region known as *p3 iw n imn*, "The Isle of Amun," modern Tell Balamun.[152] In the story of Sinuhe, he reports leaving Egypt through the *Km wr*, or Bitter Lakes region, and resting at the "Isle of Snefru" (*iw snfrw*). The name *i(w) itm* supports the idea of a toponym that connects a feature called a *iw* with the name of a deity.[153] Given that there is no known Hebrew etymology for this word,[154] an Egyptian origin seems plausible, and connecting it with the deity Atum, who was sovereign of the Tjeku/Succoth region, might be the best working hypothesis that can be offered presently. If this hypothesis is accepted, then one would expect it to be somewhere toward the end of the Wadi Tumilat, perhaps in the Lake Timsah area. It would certainly have been not too far from the *ḫtm*-fortress mentioned in Pap. Anastasi V, which we here propose was the type of fort that the Israelites, like the two runaway slaves, were trying to avoid. The additional note in Exodus 13:20 that Etham was located at the edge of the wilderness suggests that it was probably just outside of the Wadi Tumilat (Succoth) proper.

In addition to a number of forts, including the *ḫtm*-fort of Merneptah Hetephirma'at in the region, there is reason to believe that an ancient canal may have run through the Wadi Tumilat. As mentioned above, the Red Sea canal, apparently started by Necho II (610–595 B.C.), was completed by the Persian Emperor, Darius I (521–486 B.C.). Its exact route remains a subject of investigation, but it either cut across or ran through part of the Wadi Tumilat before it merged with the easternmost Nile branch.[155] But there is reason to believe that an earlier canal may also have existed in this area. Members of the Geological Survey of Israel discovered traces of canals in Sinai and along the Isthmus of Suez during the occupation of Egyptian Sinai after 1967 and before the implementation of the Camp David accords in the early 1980s.[156] They postulated that the canal might have been connected to the Wadi Tumilat, because of their belief that water ran through it "continuously since Pharaonic time," fed from the southern end of the Bubastite branch of the Nile.[157] This interpretation, however, has been challenged by others. Without offering any evidence, Karl Butzer claims that the "obvious" head of the canal was the Pelusiac near Tell Defeneh.[158] Oren and Holladay, who have conducted archaeological survey work in North Sinai and the Wadi Tumilat, respectively, concur with Butzer.[159] However, Herodotus, who visited Egypt within decades of the completion of the Red Sea canal, gives the following description of its course: "Psammetichus had a son Necos, who became king of Egypt. It was he who began the making of the canal into the Red Sea, which was finished by Darius the Persian." He further describes it as: "four days' journey voyage in length, and it was dug wide enough for two triremes to move in it rowed abreast. It is fed by the Nile, and is carried from a little above Bubastis by the Arabian town of Patumus; it issues into the Red Sea."[160] Patumus, as mentioned above, is thought to be Tell el-Maskhutta by Holladay, although Tell el-Retabeh could also be a candidate. If either identification is correct, then the Saite-Persian–period canal passed through a portion of the Wadi Tumilat. However, Herodotus's description that Patumus is "a little above Bubastis" might be more appropriate for a location further west in the Wadi Tumilat than Maskhuta, which is toward the eastern end. Naville apparently found traces of an ancient canal in the Wadi.[161] Furthermore,

Pierre Montet believed that a stela of Ramesses II found in the Wadi Tumilat marked the line of a canal that existed during the Nineteenth Dynasty.[162] Traces of at least two defunct canals through the Wadi Tumilat have been identified, and one still flows through it.[163] Dating these waterways is difficult indeed. Nevertheless, it is clear that the Wadi Tumilat has enjoyed a long history of canal activity, and in prehistoric times apparently had a branch of the Nile flowing through it.[164] In her detailed study and survey of the Wadi Tumilat, Carol Redmount investigated the history of the canals. She notes that the later traditions in Classical sources refer to the canal activities of Sesostris (Greek for Senusert). If these preserve accurately an ancient memory, they could point to the Twelfth Dynasty, when three Pharaohs bear the name Senusert (ca. 1943–1843 B.C.), although Herodotus often conflated these names with Ramesses II. During the Twelfth Dynasty, Redmount argues, Egypt's political and economic strength was such that a canal could be excavated and maintained. The Ramesside period, she observes, would also be a time when major canal activities could have been sustained.[165]

It is also possible that canals from an earlier period that had silted up and were abandoned could have been subsequently reopened and maintained. It would certainly be easier to reuse an older canal than to make one de novo. Georges Posener considered this scenario a possibility with a New Kingdom–period canal and the later Persian-Hellenistic–period Red Sea canal.[166] In fact, Tuvia Weissbrod believes that sections of the Neco-Darius canal were from an earlier system, and that the difficulty Neco had in excavating the Red Sea canal was due to tectonic activity along the Isthmus of Suez that had elevated the ground since the canal's earlier usage.[167]

Thus there is evidence to suggest that there was a canal in the Wadi Tumilat prior to the Necho-Darius canal, which, in part, may have been a reopening of an earlier canal. If this scenario is correct, then, assuming a Ramesside-period exodus date, a functioning canal in the Wadi Tumilat would have presented an additional obstacle for the departing Israelites when they reached Succoth/Tjeku.

VIII. "Tell the Israelites to Turn Back"

Following the encampment at Etham in the Wadi Tumilat region, the text of Exodus reports: "Tell the Israelites to turn back and camp in front of Pi-hahiroth, between Migdol and the sea, in front of Baal-zephon; you shall camp opposite it, by the sea." The critical verb is וְיָשֻׁבוּ which means "turn back, return."[168] Previously I argued that there is some ambiguity in how to interpret this verb, leading me to propose that the Israelites continued in a southerly direction from the eastern end of the Wadi Tumilat.[169] The meaning of "turn back" is clear enough, as Scolnic has recently argued.[170] It would mean that the trek from Rameses to Succoth was heading in a south-southeasterly direction, and then turned north toward the military highway and the fort (*ḫtm*) of Tjaru. Given the statement in Exodus 13:17, that they avoided the "Way of the land of the Philistines" (i.e., the military highway), and that in the 1980s the massive fortress of Tjaru was discovered, it seemed illogical to me that the Israelites would initially avoid the northern route, only to turn back to that very region. Despite these objections, the text clearly indicates that this was the case, and most exegetes recognize this. Umberto Cassuto understood this text to mean: "let them turn round and not continue to travel in a south-easterly direction."[171] Simons, a Hebrew scholar and an historical geographer, explains the text as meaning, "The verb used means not only a change of direction but more particularly a change involving a setback, in this sense namely that by this maneuver the Israelites moved somewhat away from their immediate goal—the crossing of the border of Egypt."[172]

The logical question that might be asked is, could the Israelites not simply go north and circle east around Lake Timsah and be safely in Sinai? Once again we return to the canal traces discovered along the Isthmus of Suez. The Neco-Darius canal, as noted above, may have partially passed through the Wadi Tumilat before turning north to meet the Bubastite branch of the Nile (see Herodotus, *Histories* II, 158). In the nineteenth century, Linant de Bellefonds discovered traces of an ancient canal that ran from Lake Timsah north, where it emptied into the el-Balah Lake.[173] He thought this was a section of the Saite-Persiant–period canal. This canal trace can still be seen in aerial photographs,[174] as well as in recent satellite images (figures 5–6). The location of this segment in no way matches the geographical description offered by Herodotus of the canal he may actually have witnessed in the Persian period when he visited Egypt, only several decades after the completion of the canal by Darius. Sneh and Weissbrod are of the opinion that this particular canal was a part of a much earlier system that harks back to the Twelfth Dynasty, which if it had been maintained during the New Kingdom may explain why the Israelites, and the two runaway slaves in Pap. Anastasi V, moved northward looking for another way out. The canal trace between the two lakes, Weissbrod and Sneh argue, was a part of the "East Frontier canal" that was discovered in North Sinai in the Qantara-Baluza region.[175] This northern section of the canal was discussed in some detail in *Israel in Egypt* (chapter 7) and was the subject of my own investigations in 1995 and 1998. There is more on this in the next chapter.

Because the text of Exodus 14:1–2 insists that from the area at the east end of the Wadi Tumilat (Succoth/Tjeku region) the Israelites turned back and headed north, and because of the discovery of new data from recent archaeological and paleoenvironmental research in North Sinai, I am happily forced to revise the working hypothesis presented in *Israel in Egypt*. The reconstruction proposed here does not represent an acceptance of the old northern route theory that was propounded in the early 1930s by Otto Eissfeldt and C. S. Jarvis, and followed by some more recent investigators.[176] In this scenario, the Israelites would have left the east Delta and followed a route along the coast and traveled over the thin strip of land that separated the Mediterranean from Lake Bardawil or Sirbonis of Greco-Roman times (figure 1). This theory actually made more sense when Tanis was thought to be Pi-Ramesses, as it was the northernmost major city in the eastern Delta. One of the main pieces of evidence for this proposed route is the association Eissfeldt made between the Greco-Roman shrine of Zeus Casius and the toponym Baal Zephon in Exodus 14:2.

But, as I have pointed out, this reconstruction fails because recent geological work shows that the barrier island, upon which the Israelites would have traveled according to this theory, did not fully extend to the east and connect with mainland until perhaps a thousand years later.[177] Consequently, it could not have been part of the Via Maris in the New Kingdom or Late Bronze Age, and this is supported by Oren's survey that failed to identify a single site from the second millennium B.C. on this barrier island (figure 1).[178] Textual evidence garnered by Pau Figueras in a new study suggests that even in when Cambyses invaded Egypt in 525 B.C. this route was not taken, and that it was not until the period of Alexander the Great and his successors that this route was regularly traveled as an alternative to the old military highway or Via Maris.[179] Consequently, the shrine of Zeus Casius could only date to the Greco-Roman period. This also means that any possible association with the Canaanite deity Baal-Zephon is no longer possible, and this route for the exodus will have to be abandoned. Graham Davies, who has published widely on the subject of the wilderness itineraries and the route of the exodus, immediately recognized the implications of the geological and archaeological evidence for Eissfelt's widely accepted theory.[180] He maintains that this theory must now be abandoned. I agree.

A trek north from the Lake Timsah region and around the western side of the el-Ballah Lake system to its northern end would take one to the present-day Qantara region, a distance of around fifty kilometers (thirty-one miles). This could place the ancient Israelites in the vicinity of the toponyms recorded in Exodus 14:2, that is, Pi-hahiroth, Migdol, Baal-zephon, and the sea through which they would pass. Until recently, little could be said about these locations, but now, in the light of new archaeological data, a new hypothesis can be advanced.

5

The Location of the Re(e)d Sea

Tell the Israelites to turn back and camp in front of Pi-hahiroth, between Migdol and the sea, in front of Baal Zephon; you shall camp opposite it, by the sea.

—Exod. 14:2

I. Phenomonology and the Re(e)d Sea Crossing

The flight of the Israelites from Egypt and the crossing of the sea is undoubtedly one of the most memorable stories in the Torah.[1] At the end of Exodus 14, we are told the outcome of the sea-crossing episode was that the Israelites "feared the LORD and believed in the LORD and in his servant Moses" (14:31). This event was viewed as a theophany, a divine manifestation, because "the LORD drove the sea back by a strong east wind all night, and turned the sea into dry land; and the waters were divided. The Israelites went into the sea on dry ground" (Exod. 14:21–22a). Consequently, the sea crossing is also remembered in later historical retrospectives. Prior to his death and at the end of the wilderness period, Moses is recorded as saying:

> Remember today that it was not your children (who have not known or seen the discipline of the LORD your God), but it is you who must acknowledge his greatness, his mighty hand and his outstretched arm, his signs and his deed that he did in Egypt to Pharaoh, the king of Egypt, and to all his land; what he did to the Egyptian army, to their horses

> and chariots, how he made the water of the Red Sea (*yām sûp̱*) flow over them as they pursued you so that the LORD has destroyed them to this day. (Deut. 11:2–4)

Rahab of Jericho confesses:

> I know that the LORD has given you the land, and that dread of you has fallen on us, and that all the inhabitants of the land melt in fear before you. For we have heard how the LORD dried up the water of the Red Sea (*yām sûp̱*) before you when you came out of Egypt, and what you did to the two kings of the Amorites that were beyond the Jordan, to Sihon and Og, whom you utterly destroyed. As soon as we heard it, our hearts melted, and there was no courage left in any of us because of you. The LORD your God is indeed God in heaven above and on earth below. (Josh. 2:9–11)

Joshua, Israel's military leader, makes the analogy that the Israelites who were about to cross the Jordan River to enter Canaan would cross the river in the same miraculous way as the previous generation had come out of Egypt through the sea:

> For the LORD your God dried up the waters of the Jordan for you until you crossed over, as the LORD your God did to the Red Sea (*yām sûp̱*) which he dried up for us until we crossed over, so that all the peoples of the earth may know that the hand of the LORD is mighty, and so that you may fear the LORD your God forever. (Josh. 4:23–24)

Examples of the sea-crossing episode from the prophetic corpus are found in Isaiah. The prophet uses the sea crossing in such a way as to make it clear that it was a well-known motif in the late eighth through earlier seventh centuries.[2]

> The LORD of hosts will wield a whip against them, as when he struck Midian at the rock of Oreb; his staff will be over the seas, and he will lift it as he did in Egypt. (Isa. 10:26)

> And the LORD will utterly destroy the tongue of Egypt; and will wave his hand over the river with his scorching wind; and will split it into seven channels, and make a way to cross on foot; so there shall be a highway from Assyria for the remnant that is left of his people. As there was for Israel when they came up from the land of Egypt. (Isa. 11:15–16)

> Then they remembered the days of old, of Moses his servant. Where is the one who brought them out of the sea and with the shepherds of his flock? (Isa. 63:11)

Furthermore, the sea crossing was the subject of Israelite liturgies over the centuries. In fact, Psalm 66:5–6 combines the two crossings mentioned in Joshua 4:23–24:

> Come and see what God has done: he is awesome in his deeds among mortals. He turned the sea into dry land; they passed through the river on foot. There we rejoiced in him who rules by his might forever.

Psalm 78 is the longest psalm to deal with the exodus and Sinai experience. Concerning the sea crossing it states:

> He divided the sea and let them pass through it and made the waters stand like a heap. (78:13)
>
> Then he led them in safety, so that they were not afraid; but the sea overwhelmed their enemies. (78:52–53)

Exodus 14:10–18 describes that when apparently trapped by the approaching Egyptian army behind them and the sea before them, the Israelites broke faith with God out of fear and complained to Moses about their fate. This incident is recalled in Psalm 106:7–9:

> Our ancestors, when they were in Egypt, did not consider your wonderful works; they did not remember the abundance of your steadfast love, but they rebelled against the Most High at the Red Sea (*yām sûp̱*). Yet he saved them for his name's sake, so that he might make known his mighty power. He rebuked the Red Sea (*yām sûp̱*), and it became dry; he led them through the deep as through a desert.

Psalm 136:11–15 offers thanks to God for delivering Israel from Egypt: "and brought Israel out from among them, . . . with a strong hand and outstretched arm, . . . who divided the Red Sea (*yām sûp̱*) in two, . . . and made Israel pass through the midst of it, . . . but overthrew Pharaoh and his army in the Red Sea (*yām sûp̱*)."

The greatest song celebrating the sea crossing is the so-called Song of the Sea or Song of Miriam found in Exodus 15. Despite the attempts of several recent scholars to date this song to the sixth or fifth century (with the implication is of little historical value), there is general agreement among specialists in Hebrew poetry—particularly those who compare Ugaritic poetry with Hebrew, such as Frank M. Cross and David N. Freedman—that this song is one of the oldest in the Hebrew canon, and not dependent on J, E, or P.[3] Georg Fohrer went so far as to say that the song "certainly dates from the same period as the events themselves."[4] John Towers thought that "it is not unlikely that the author of the original portions would be conversant with the theological terminology of ancient Egypt."[5] If this assessment is correct, then the song is the earliest surviving witness to the sea crossing.

These biblical references suggest that this event was viewed as genuine by later generations of Israelites, and therefore should not be summarily dismissed as unhistorical in nature. To do so is to assume the condescending view that today one knows more about the events the ancient authors wrote about than they did. William Hallo's sage advice, "treat the ancient sources critically but without condescension," is appropriate here. His corollary to this principle is, "we should not expect to know more than the ancient sources knew."[6] I heartily endorse both principles; they certainly apply to the Reed Sea story.

Another noteworthy point is that a number of the references quoted here mention the strong hand (*yāḏ ḥ^{a}zāqāh*) and outstretched arm (*z^{e}rôa^{c} n^{e}tûyâ*) in connection with the sea crossing, and these expressions or variations on them are found in Exodus 15:6, 12, and 16. I have demonstrated that this language originated in the exodus narratives (cf. Exod. 3:19; 6:6; 13:3, 14, 16; 32:11), and that it was used as a deliberate play on the Egyptian concept of the victorious pharaoh who conquered his enemies with his powerful arm (*ḫpš*) and outstretched hand (*pr-^{c}*).[7] Rather than Pharaoh defeating his enemies with his powerful arm, it was the God of Israel whose arm triumphed. The metaphorical use of the Egyptian language shows further the writer's familiarity with royal ideology, just as Towers argued was the case for Exodus 15. It is this language and ideology that reached its zenith in New Kingdom times in Egypt, which is used polemically against the pharaoh of the exodus.[8]

At the outset of the previous chapter, it was pointed out that there are some scholars who wish to view the story of Israel's departure from Egypt as mythology and hence deal with a story that is "timeless" and set in the world of the gods. Unfortunately, biblical scholars who are not trained in the methodologies of the historian of religion use the term "mythology" in ways quite different from the way it is used by the phenomenologist of religion. Now postmodern approaches to myth are further muddying the interpretive waters. Richard Walsh, for example, understands myth to require a diversity of meanings that include the fictitious, romantic, and sociological.[9] This approach, with its preoccupation with the reader's world rather that the context of the author or his audience, misses the sense of reality and history associated with myth in the ancient Near East. A preferable way of interpretating texts is the classic understanding of Mircea Eliade. He spoke of "revelations [that] occurred in mythical time" that are associated with cosmogony; Eliade noted, however, that "the situation is altogether different in the case of the monotheistic revelation. This takes place in time, in historical duration: Moses receives the Law at a certain place and at a certain date."[10] For Eliade, myth does not mean that what is being described is ahistorical, nonhistorical, or metahistorical. Rather he detects in the biblical stories of the Old Testament, as do other phenomenologists, a keen awareness of history and location of theophany. He goes on to say, "Of course, here too archetypes are involved, in the sense that these events, raised to the rank of examples, will be repeated; but they will not be repeated until the times are accomplished, that is, in a new *illud tempus*." The example he uses to support his claim is the Red Sea crossing in the book of Exodus: "as Isaiah (11:15–16) prophesies, the miraculous passages of the Red Sea and the Jordan will be repeated 'in that day.' Nevertheless, the moment of revelation made to Moses by God remains a limited moment, definitely situated in time. And, since it also represents theophany, it thus acquires a new dimension: it becomes precious inasmuch as it is no longer reversible, as it is historical event."[11] In this passage from Isaiah, the oracle anticipates a day when God will send a scorching wind to dry up the Nile so that his remnant can leave the land "as there was for Israel when they came up from the land of Egypt" (v. 16b). It will be recalled in connection with the sea-crossing episode of Exodus 14 that it was believed that a strong east wind, a wind directed by God, drove back the waters. Once again the Re(e)d Sea story is the archetypal event for the crossing of the Jordan River by the Israelites when entering Canaan in Joshua 4:23.

The salient point here is that for the phenomenologist of religion, mythology is not the opposite of history; rather it is at its very essence dealing with historical events. And subsequent use of archetypal language is rooted in belief in the historical reality of the archetypal event. This discussion well illustrates why I think a phenomenological approach to biblical stories in general, but the exodus events in particular, is so important, for it frees one from both the positivist's shackles and the revisionism of postmodern readings, which treats such a story as ideological fiction. To be sure, because of their theistic worldview, the biblical writers interpreted the events they experienced or heard about in a theological manner for didactic or liturgical reasons. This approach to interpreting history is common in the ancient world. In fact, Bertil Albrektson has argued for a close connection between history and divine revelation on the basis of his study of many texts from across the ancient Near East.[12] There is a report in 1 Samuel 7:10–14 of a battle between Israel and Philistia in which the LORD "thundered a mighty voice that day against the Philistines and threw them into confusion" (v. 10), resulting in a rout of the Philistines. Thunder, a naturally occurring phenomenon, is viewed as coming from YHWH, which caused panic in the Philistine ranks and led to their defeat.

The Egyptians wrote history and understood events in the light of divine planning and intervention. Ramesses II (1279–1213 B.C.) described himself in battle against the Hittites in the following manner: "Now His Majesty was after them like a griffon [a mythological creature], I slaughtered among them, without letting up. I raised my voice to call out to my troops, saying: 'Stand firm, be bold-hearted, my troops, see my triumph, [all] on my own, with only

Amun to be my protector, his hand with me.'"[13] Earlier on, Thutmose III (1479–1425 B.C.) described a battle in which a shooting star disturbed the enemy, causing their chariot horses to bolt out of fear. This event was described as "the miracle (*bi3t*) of Amun-Re . . . who had ordained the victories."[14]

The Hittite king Mursili II in his Ten Year Annals reports of his victories during the span of his first decade as king. Throughout, victory is attributed to the sun goddess of Arinna as the result of answered prayers. He asks her: "'Stand by me. . . . Destroy those enemy foreign lands before me. After I sat down on my father's throne, in ten years I vanquished these enemy foreign lands and destroyed them."[15]

Several studies have been made of Mesopotamian literature to show that there was a relationship between history and divine involvement in human affairs. This is especially true in the annalistic reports of the kings of Assyria and Babylon.[16] The Weidner Chronicle, perhaps originating in the second millennium B.C., offers a theological interpretation of history in which military failures are attributed to the impious or unjust acts of a king (e.g., Naram Sin), while the fidelity of Sargon to Marduk's temple, Esagila, is linked to his successful empire building.[17]

In the Bible itself there are cases of non-Israelites explaining events and phenomena of nature as divinely orchestrated. This mindset is evident in the case of Rahab of Jericho, in the passage quote above. She and her fellow Canaanites had heard of what Yahweh had done and they were fearful. This is the expected response to a mysterium tremendum, in Eliade's words. These observations from Israel's neighbors all reveal the same theistic worldview. From a modern or scientific worldview, some of these phenomena might be easily explained as a passing comet or meteor, thunder, earthquakes, shifting tides, and the like, or merely the good fortune of a successful warrior-king, whereas the peoples of Egypt, Anatolia, Mesopotamia, and Canaan/Israel saw the hand of deity in the planning and execution of these events. These events, and here I would include Israel's sea crossing, are understood to have occurred at certain times and specific locations, and were understood by people of the ancient Near East to have been the result of theophany. None of the events described in these ancient texts should be relegated to the category of myth, that is, timeless events in the realm of the gods.

Since a phenomenological approach to interpreting the Exodus 14 narrative assumes a real event, and does not pass judgment on or try to explain how the phenomenon occurred, it means that the historian and archaeologist is not on a fool's errand when investigating historical, archaeological, and geographical questions related to this episode, although there are no guarantees of success. Theoretically, then, there ought to be (or have been) a real body of water that the Bible's authors had in mind, and that location is associated with three other toponyms that will be considered below in §IV.

II. Red Sea or Reed Sea?

Readers of the Bible may be confused when it comes to understanding the name of the body of water to which the exodus story refers.[18] First, some passages call the sea in question simply "the sea" (*hayyām*) (Exod. 14:2, 9, 16, 21, 23; 15:1–4; Num. 33:8; Ps. 78:13). In other texts, *yām sûp̱* is used in the Hebrew (MT) of Exodus 13:18; 15:4b, 22; Joshua 2:10; 4:23; Psalm 136:13, 15. *Sûp̱* clearly means reeds or rushes,[19] as can be seen in Exodus 2:3 when the mother of Moses places him in a basket among the reeds (*sûp̱*) on the Nile's shore. Isaiah 19:6 also mentions reeds (*sûp̱*) in the Nile. In the Septuagint, the Greek translations of the Hebrew Bible, *sûp̱* is rendered as ερυθρα, "red,"[20] and this is the tradition followed in the Latin Vulgate, where the sea is called *mari Rubro*. Most English translations have followed this translation tradition (e.g., KJV, AV, RSV, NRSV, NASB, NIV), but a few have followed the Hebrew reading (e.g., JB, NJPS). There is no convincing explanation for why the Greek translators did not literally translate *sûp̱*, although it might have been their aim to locate the sea at the place they thought the text was indicating, that is, the Red Sea, the present-day Gulf of Suez.

Despite the uncertainties surrounding the reasons for the Septuagint's translation of *sûp̱*, and the inability of scholars to explain why the Gulf of Aqaba should be called *yām sûp̱* (e.g. Deut. 1:40, 2:1; 1 Kings 9:26), one thing is certain: that the word *sûp̱* derives from the Egyptian word *ṯwf* or *ṯwfy*. This was recognized initially by H. Brugsch in 1868 and accepted by other linguists and Egyptologists since Max Müller, and confirmed by more recent etymological studies.[21] Even though he was always very careful about associating Egyptian and biblical matters, Sir Alan Gardiner was emphatic about associating these two words, asserting that the connection was "beyond dispute."[22] What is equally important is that there is a geographical term known in Ramesside period texts called *p3 ṯwfy*, which is thought to have been somewhere in the northeastern Delta or the Isthmus of Suez area.[23] Because the element *p3* is the definite article in Late Egyptian (from the late fourteenth century onward), a specific location is probable.[24]

Lately, however, Marc Vervenne has argued against connected Egyptian *p3 ṯwfy* with *yām sûp̱* of the exodus narratives.[25] He offers a helpful and exhaustive history of the association of the Egyptian and Hebrew expressions, and rightly ponders whether the word *ṯwfy* is a Semitic loanword into Egyptian. In the end Vervenne determines that "the Egyptian sources themselves would not allow us to identify the territory of *p3 ṯwf* with *yām sûp̱*."[26] What is surprising about this outcome is that he reaches it without considering seriously the Egyptian texts that mention *ṯwfy*, and proclaims that Manfred Bietak "wrongly transfers the correspondence of *ṯwf*='reed' to the Hebrew expression with *yām sûp̱*."[27] His conclusions rely heavily on Henri Cazelles's observation that, in Vervenne's own words, "*p3 ṯwf(y)* does not refer to an expanse of water ('Reed Sea') but rather indicates a region ('Reed Land') were both papyrus grows and pasture land and farms are to be found."[28] In a token gesture to Egyptology, he points out that the expression *p3 ṯwf(y)* is not written with a "water" determinative. Vervenne is clearly an able comparative Semitist, as his study shows, but apparently lacks training in Egyptology, which is probably why he devoted only one short paragraph (out of a study of twenty-seven pages) to a couple of Egyptian texts that mention *p3 ṯwf(y)*.[29] Hence his conclusions should not go unchallenged, because a careful study of *all* the texts that include *p3 ṯwf(y)* suggest otherwise.

If *p3 ṯwfy* were just a fertile region in which papyrus grows and not a *yām* (a body of water) per se, then one might expect a land or region determinative to be used, but this is not the case. The most common determinative used in the writing of *ṯwfy* is Gardiner's sign M–2, which is used with the words for reeds and rushes,[30] but M–15 is also attested,[31] which is used of "papyrus and watery regions."[32] The city determinative is actually written with *ṯwfy* in a few cases, which is curious indeed, as no city is connected to this toponym (see below). Consequently three different determinatives are used for exactly the same feature. This means that the determinatives are not particularly helpful in describing the nature of the *ṯwfy*, although the use of M–15 demonstrates that a swampy region existed in part of this region.

Three other considerations militate against Vervenne's rejection of the correlation of *p3 ṯwfy* and *yām sûp̱*.

(1) Etymological considerations: The linguistic relationship between the two words is significant, and even Vervenne acknowledges that Hebrew *sûp̱* in Exodus 2:3, 5 and Isaiah 19:6 "appears to be a transcription of the Egyptian *ṯwf*."[33] However, for reasons that are unclear to me, he is unwilling to extend this meaning to *sûp̱* in the case of *yām sûp̱*.

(2) Geographical considerations: Occurrences of *p3 ṯwfy* in Egyptian texts located it generally in the northeastern Delta, as we have suggested. On the basis of our reading of Exodus 14:2 (see chapter 4, §VIII), *yām sûp̱* is situated in the northeastern Delta. Further support for this location is found in the eighth plague of Exodus 10. Locusts infest the land and are only removed when a strong wind from the west drove the hordes of locusts into *yām sûp̱* (Exod. 10:19). As is widely recognized, the starting point of the exodus and the epicenter of the plagues was in the region of Pi-Ramesses/Avaris (cf. chapter 4, §IV). So when the Bible describes the wind from the west driving the locusts east toward the Sea of Reeds, that is, *yāmmâ sûp̱*,[34] it is referring to the only major body of water east of the Ramesses region, the el-Ballah Lakes, which is located forty kilometers directly to the east.

(3) Chronological considerations: *P3 ṯwfy* occurs in texts primarily from the Nineteenth and Twentieth Dynasties, the period to which many scholars date the exodus event. Not attested in texts prior to the thirteenth century B.C.,

p3 ṯwfy is only found in a few texts after the New Kingdom.[35] This means that later Hebrew writers may not have come across the toponym *p3 ṯwfy* in the seventh through fifth centuries.[36]

These considerations make it clear that connection between *p3 ṯwfy* and *yām sûp̱* is not only plausible but also highly likely, especially when they are considered along with the other geographical terms in Exodus that will be discussed below.

Vervenne's idea drew a quick rejoinder from Galit Dayan, who politely pointed out that he had ignored a section from the Petubastis Cycle, a late-period Demotic text, which in her opinion may contain an allusion to the exodus.[37] She believes, on the basis of internal evidence, that elements of the narrative originally date to the New Kingdom. It speaks of thirteen infiltrating Asiatics (*ᶜ3mw*) in the *p3-ṯwf* region. Dayan's suggestion that the number thirteen is symbolic for the Israelite tribes and their departure through the *p3-ṯwf* region is interesting, but far from compelling.[38] However, the reference does point to this region on Egypt's northeast frontier, precisely where *p3 ṯwfy* is located on the basis of other evidence. As we shall see below, there is a convergence of data that ties *p3 ṯwfy* to the area of the northeastern Delta, some of which is in present-day North Sinai, that Vervenne did not consider.

Sarah Groll has also written recently and extensively on *p3 ṯwfy* and the exodus in a series of articles that drew upon texts in Pap. Anastasi VIII.[39] She notes that this is an actual letter, and not a scribal copy, written in nonliterary Late Egyptian that dates to the middle years of Ramesses II.[40] The letter, from the hand of the scribe Ramose, describes troubled times in the land, and not in a literary manner in the tradition of Egyptian didactic literature. He asks for confirmation of a rumor that a certain crewman, Any, and his children have died, and mentions the death of other crewmen (*iswt*).[41] Then he speaks despairingly of traveling to Pi-Ramesses, "if we are alive" (*ir ᶜnḫ.n*).[42] Furthermore, there is a report of ecological conditions in the *p3 ṯwfy* region that resulted in the lack of tamarisks and reeds (*ṯwfy*) for shipment to the capital.[43] Worse yet, the shipment of fish from this region is negligible, he observes: ". . . fish is the total that you have this year, which is fitting that you ship in a single day."[44] Clearly the normal bounty of fish that came to *p3 ṯwfy* was reduced to a token amount. Groll attributes the ecological disaster to a drought (low Nile).[45] The combination of the death of groups of people in Egypt and the dry conditions in *p3 ṯwfy* lead her to propose associating these circumstances from the middle years of Ramesses II's reign to the Hebrew exodus story, opining, "It is conceivable that precisely under these circumstances a group of "hard laboured" slaves of Pharaoh undertook the crossing of the now dry 'sea.' "[46]

Although Groll's careful study of Pap. Anastasi VIII may provide information about the ecological conditions in the Delta during the troubled days of the plagues and exodus, what is important for the current discussion is that *p3 ṯwfy* is recognized as being located in an area east of Pi-Ramesses that under normal conditions had abundant reeds and rushes. Toward the end of his lengthy study of the relationship between *p3 ṯwfy* and *yām sûp̱*, Vervenne praises Bernard Batto's study that associated *yām sûp̱* with mythological language, and not a geographical reality.[47] One wonders if these sympathies led Vervenne to reject the connection between *p3 ṯwfy* and *yām sûp̱*. Certainly the Egyptian evidence does not support his position.

The solid linguistic connection between Egyptian *ṯwf*, and the fact that there is a swampy lake known in New Kingdom Egypt as *p3 ṯwfy* notwithstanding, Batto in 1983 suggested that *yām sûp̱* was only interpreted as "reed" sea in the light of modern Egyptological research.[48] He prefers to read *sûp̱* as *sôp̱*, which would mean "end," and hence have mythological overtones—the "sea of the end."[49] I have offered an extensive critique of Batto's studies, and have shown that Hebrew literature occasionally used mythological language to describe historical events.[50] Hans Goedicke has also demurred at Batto, noting that "In the fashionable desire to remove the Exodus narrative from any physical implication he envisages 'that P consciously intended to historicize and localize the sea miracle at the Red Sea.' From attributing motives to P without explaining their desirability at the time P is dated, he turns to the Song of the Sea (Ex. 15:4–5) where *yām sûp̱* is also mentioned as the place where the Pharaonic troops perished. What would seem to be a confirmation of the historic tradition about the location of the Miracle of the Sea he takes as the starting point for a mythological tour de force."[51]

Unfortunately for Batto's proposal that attaching the meaning "Sea of Reeds" to *yām sûp̱* is the result of erroneous Egyptian linguistic scholarly work, it was apparently reached without careful consideration of earlier sources. If Batto were correct, then there should be no translator or commentator of Exodus prior to the late nineteenth century to render *yām sûp̱* as Reed Sea or Sea of Rushes. But, as it turns out, this is not the case. In fact, early exegetes and commentators of the book of Exodus did suggest this meaning for the Hebrew *sûp̱* without knowledge of ancient Egyptian. Included here would be Christian scholars such as John Calvin and Martin Luther, as well as such Jewish sages as Jonathan Ben Uzziel and Rashi.[52] Even earlier evidence for understanding *yām sûp̱* as meaning "Sea of Reeds" is found in the Bohairic (Northern) Coptic translation of Exodus. The sea is rendered as *pyom n ša(i)ri*. This writing may derive from the Egyptian *š i3rw*, lake or reeds or rushes that is known from the Pyramid texts (2500–2300 B.C.), the Coffin Texts (ca. 2200–1700 B.C.), and the Book of the Dead (fifteenth century B.C. through the Greco-Roman period).[53] Tower saw a symbolic connection between the Egyptian mythic Lake of Rushes or Reeds and the Israelite sea crossing. In Egyptian funerary literature, the deceased enters the Seas of Reeds where he or she is purified and reborn.[54] For him, the Hebrew borrows this understanding—the Israelites are born as a people when they pass through *yām sûp̱*.

Clearly the modern discovery of the Egyptian word *ṯwfy* is not the only reason modern scholars translate *yām sûp̱* as "sea of reeds." There is a long history of rendering the Hebrew in this manner. The realization that Hebrew *sûp̱* is the proper writing for the Egyptian term *ṯwf*—regardless of whether it is originally a Semitic loanword into Egyptian—simply confirms the translation, and adds an important Egyptian background element to the story. More significant, it is unlikely that a sixth- to fifth-century B.C. writer would have known the Egyptian term. If he knew the Egyptian word, it probably would not have been written in Hebrew as *sûp̱*. By the late period, the Egypt letter *ṯ* was pronounced as *ṯ* or *ḏ*, and thus would not have been written by Hebrew *samek*.[55] Consequently this factor suggests that use of *yām sûp̱* reflects the antiquity of the inclusion of the toponym in the exodus tradition, and it also adds to the authenticity of the geography because *p3 ṯwfy* was known as a specific lake or swampy region in Egyptian texts of the New Kingdom.[56]

III. The Location of *p3 ṯwfy*

Two possible understandings of *yām sûp̱* in the Bible might be suggested: first, that Hebrew *yām sûp̱* refers to a specific body of water known as *p3 ṯwfy* in Egyptian texts; second, that the name is generic—that it is a Hebrew description of a body of water with reeds or rushes. This second possibility would make it harder to locate, as it could apply to a number of bodies of water in the east Delta-Sinai region. Today, even though salt water from the Red and Mediterranean seas flow through the Suez Canal and fill Lake Timsah, one can see inlets and bays around the lake where rushes grow four and five meters (twelve to fifteen feet) high. In addition to Lake Timsah, the other lakes in the region include the present-day Lake Manzelah, the Balah system, and the Bitter Lakes. However, the present-day lakes do not always correspond to their size of three and four thousand years ago, as much desiccation of the region has occurred since the Pelusiac branch of the Nile dried up in North Sinai between A.D. 1000 and 500.[57] In fact, there is yet another lake or lagoon (the eastern lagoon) situated north of the Ballah Lakes (figures 3 and 5). What remained of the Ballah Lakes was drained in the nineteenth century, when the Suez Canal was excavated, but parts of its ancient configuration can be partially seen in satellite images (figures 5 and 6), and marshy patches still exist on the west side of the Suez Canal.[58] Finally, as coastal geologists have recently proved (see chapter 3 above), the Mediterranean coastline was located well south of where it is today. All these factors have to be born in mind when attempting to study the ancient topography of the east Delta and Isthmus of Suez areas.

In my earlier study of the location of *yām sûp̱*, I realized that, on the basis of the evidence available at that time, it was impossible to determine the particular lake mentioned in Exodus 14 and 15. Consequently, I offered different scenarios in which any one of these lakes (except Manzelah and Lake Barawil) could be *yām sûp̱*. Because I did not take *šûḇ* in Exodus 14:2 verbatim, I provisionally suggested that Lake Timsah might have been *yām sûp̱*.[59] But, as I pointed out above (see the discussion in chapter 4, §VIII), Exodus 14:2 demands a turn away from the Tjeku (Succoth) and Lake Timsah areas, and requires a movement north, which should eliminate both Lake Timsah and the Bitter Lakes from being candidates for the sea of crossing. This does not, however, preclude the Hebrews from using *yām sûp̱* as a descriptive term to identify these two lakes, since they all probably looked very similar in Pharaonic times. The Egyptian name for the Timsah and Bitter Lakes was *km wr*, the Great Black.[60] Based upon the available Egyptian texts, these lakes appear to be separate from *p3 ṯwfy*, which appears to lie north of *km wr*.[61]

Unfortunately, most of the references to *p3 ṯwfy* in Egyptian texts do not help determine its location with any precision, although they tell of the fertility of the region. Pap. Sallier I 4, 9, for instance, reports that horses (at Pi-Ramesses?) are fed on the "best grass from the papyrus marshes" (*p3 ṯwfy*), which tells us only that the area was verdant.[62] An occurrence in the Blinding of Truth (Pap. Chester Beatty II, 9.2)[63] locates *p3 ṯwfy* in an interesting, but not particularly helpful, way. In this story, Falsehood has taken Truth's ox. Truth, who is portrayed as a blind boy, finds Falsehood's herds and asks the herdsmen about his missing ox. He describes its fantastic size by saying: "Is there an ox as large as my own ox? If it should stand on The Island of Amon, the tip of its tail would be lying upon the Papyrus Marshes (*p3 ṯwfy*), while one of its horns would be on the Western Mountain and the other on the Eastern Mountain, and the Great River would be its spot for lying down."[64] Although the location of the Island of Amun is thought to be at Diospolis Inferior (Tell el-Balamun),[65] the mention of the ox's tail falling on *p3 ṯwfy*, while not specific, does place it in the northeastern delta. In his study of the toponyms in the Onomasticon of Amenope, which also mentions both the Island of Amun (no. 413) and *p3 ṯwfy* (no. 418), Gardiner suggested that *p3 ṯwfy* "evidently refers to the swamps between that northern town and the sea."[66] Having reviewed the references to *p3 ṯwfy*, Goedicke believed that Lake Manzelah was intended.[67] Unfortunately, there are other possibilities for this location, as Truth's scale of the ox is not precise enough to fix the location, although the swampy region from Lake Manzelah to the el-Ballah Lakes is surely the general area in view. Gardiner was certainly unaware in his day of the proximity of the Mediterranean coastline to this area, nor was he aware of the other lakes in North Sinai that more recent geological study of the region has shown did exist in ancient times. And Goedicke apparently made his suggestion without taking into account Bietak's proposed location for *p3 ṯwfy*. Bietak's theory is based upon his important paleoenvironmental study, which succeeded in providing a more accurate picture of the east Delta and North Sinai in ancient times than had been available previously.[68]

A more helpful reference is found in Pap. Anastasi III, for it provides other geographical data, found in a letter dated to the third regnal year of Merneptah (ca. 1210 B.C.) by the scribe Pabes who has reached Pi-Ramesses, the capital, and then praises the bounty of its fields and orchards as well as its fish-filled waterways.[69] Then he adds that the abundance of the areas east of the capital comes to Pi-Ramesses for festive occasions: "*p3 ṯwfy* comes to it with rushes (*mnḥw*) and the Lake of Horus (*p3 š ḥr*) with reeds (*isyw*)."[70]

Mention is also made of the reeds, rushes, and fish that came from the area of *p3 ṯwfy* in Pap. Anastasi VIII (see above, §II). One of the officials mentioned within the communiqués is the unnamed *p3 imy-r ḫtm*—the commander of the fortress (VIII, r I, lines 2, 8).[71] The contents of the letters suggest that this official had some role in the shipment of goods to the capital, Pi-Ramesses (especially section 6). Groll believes that the *imy-r ḫtm* was situated in the capital.[72] This seems unlikely, however, inasmuch as there is nothing within Pap. Anastasi VIII to support this, nor is there any evidence that a *ḫtm*-fort existed within the Delta itself. Rather, *ḫtm*-fortresses, as Ellen Morris has recently shown, had a very specific function, that is, the term "designat[es] a border-fortress or a fortress specifically designed to regulate movement in or out of a particular area."[73] Only two *ḫtm*-fortresses are known in the eastern frontier, that of Tjaru and the other in the Wadi Tumilat/Tjeku region (see chapter 4, §VI). The references in Pap. Anastasi VIII to *p3 ṯwfy* (VIII, r II, line 4) and products made of reeds (*b3kw n ṯwfw*) may indicate that the *ḫtm* in mind is the one at Tjaru, which was known to have been administered by an *imy-r ḫtm.*[74] If the commander of the *ḫtm*-fortress in Pap. Anastasi VIII is in fact stationed at Tjaru (that is, Hebua I), then one might expect to find *p3 ṯwfy* in the same region.

The proximity of Tjaru and *p3 ṯwfy* is further supported in the Onomasticon of Amenemope, a text that dates to the Twentieth Dynasty (ca. 1150–1100 B.C.).[75] Entries no. 314–420 are a geographical list of the cities (*dmi*) of Egypt.[76] The list goes from south to north, beginning with Biggah (no. 314), an island in the First Cataract just south of Aswan, followed by Elephantine Island (no. 315) and continuing northward. Memphis (*mn-nfr*) is no. 394, and no. 400 is Heliopolis (*iwnw*),[77] indicating that the list has advanced into the Delta. The Ramesside capital city is no. 410, while no. 417 is Tanis, placing this section of the list in the eastern Delta. The last two in this geographical list are *p3 ṯwfy* (no. 418) and Tjaru/Sile (no. 419), which represent Egypt's easternmost frontier.[78] Here the immediacy of these two toponyms is evident. The numerical order suggests that *p3 ṯwfy* is south of Tjaru.

As mentioned above, *p3 ṯwfy* is written with the city determinative in this onomasticon. The peculiarity of this usage with this toponym prompted Gardiner to explain: "it does not seem likely that any instance a definite town was meant, though the inclusion in the On(omastica) of Am(enemope) points clearly to a circumscribed area."[79] This understanding of *p3 ṯwfy* is completely the opposite of Vervenne's recent claim: "the use of the expression *p3 ṯwf* in these and other Egyptian documents reveals that the term refers to more than one particular place in the region of the Eastern delta where there was a luxuriant papyrus growth. We are not, therefore, dealing with one particular and well defined location."[80] The Onomastica reference, which Vervenne does not consider, shows that his understanding of this toponym is wrong.

With the location of Tjaru and its fortress now known to be at Tell Hebua in North Sinai (see below, §IV), *p3 ṯwfy* was evidently close by. On the basis of a thorough study of relevant Egyptian texts, archaeological data, and geological considerations, Bietak proposed that Lake Manzelah was *sẖt-ḏ*ᶜ,[81] and that the eastern lagoon was *p3 š-ḥr*, that is, Shi-hor of the Bible (cf. Josh. 13:3; Isa. 23:3; 1 Chron. 13:5).[82] The Ballah Lakes he identified with *p3 ṯwfy*, largely on the basis of the occurrence in Pap. Anastasi III. He noted that *p3 ṯwfy* and *p3 š-ḥr* appeared in a parallel relationship in the text, which pointed to the proximity of the two bodies of water to each other.[83] He suggested that *p3 ṯwfy* corresponded to *yām sûp̱* of the Exodus tradition. He reaffirmed this interpretation in a recently published map, maintaining that *p3 ṯwfy* is to be identified with the Ballah Lakes.[84] Here I would like to introduce some new linguistic evidence that would support Bietak's theory, which generations of scholars apparently have overlooked.

Today, the Ballah Lakes are gone, and desert sands, especially in the area east of the Suez Canal, cover its ancient depression. But its ancient name may have been preserved in the name of Tell Abu Sefêh, the site that was probably Greco-Roman Sile, an important frontier town of Egypt in the Persian through Roman periods.[85] Present-day (Arabic) names for ancient cities often preserve (with some variation) the ancient namesake. But this does not seem to be the case with Tell Abu Sefêh and Sile. I am not aware of any scholar who has suggested it, because there is no linguistic basis for doing so. Could the name Abu Sefêh (pronounced sè-fee in Arabic), on the other hand, preserve the name of the ancient lake adjacent to it?

Beginning in 1995, excavations at this site uncovered the remains of a harbor with quays where boats docked, and a stone corniche that marked the water's edge. These discoveries demonstrate that two thousand years ago a lake large enough to handle trading vessels flourished (figure 3).[86] The geological research of the East Frontier Archaeological Project in 2001 produced evidence to show that the lake probably extended six to eight kilometers to the north and east of Tell Abu Sefêh during the second millennium B.C. (figure 5).[87] Hence it may be significant that this site was situated on the north end of a lake whose ancient name might have been *p3 ṯwfy*.

Ba, bu, or *abu* is actually how the Arabic preserves the writing of Egyptian *pi* (from *pr*) or *p3*. The linguistic reason for this is that there is no *p* in Arabic, and, in some cases the Egyptian *p* was pronounced as *b* in Greek, as can be seen in some Greco-Roman–period texts. Indeed, a number of Egyptian toponyms written with the letter *p* that become *b* in Greek and Arabic can be cited. For instance, Pi-baste(t), Pi-Beseth of the Bible (Ezek. 30:17), becomes Βουβαστος (Bubastis) in Greek (cf. Diodorus I, 27.5). Today the site is known in Arabic as Tell Basta. The aforementioned Tell Balamun is the writing for the Egyptian name *p3 iw n Imn* (that is, the Island of Amun).[88] More significant, there are a number of Pharaonic toponyms that begin with the element *pi* or *p3* that survive in Arabic as *abu*. Some examples include *p3 šnᶜ*, which in Coptic is written as ΠΟΘΙΚΗ (*potheke*), but in Arabic becomes Abu *tîg*;[89] *pi-wsir* in Greek is written as Βουσιρις (Bousiris), and becomes Abu sir in Arabic;[90] and *pi-djodj* survives in the name of the village Abu-tist.[91] The important Delta city of Buto (Tell el-Fara'in) was named *pi-w3d̲yt* in Egyptian, in Greek was pronounced Βουτω, and it survives in the Arabic name of the village near the tell called Abtou.[92] So, clearly, the Arabic elements *abu, ab*, and *bu* do represent the ancient Egyptian writing of *p3* or *pi*. And just as Hebrew *sûp̱* corresponds to Egyptian *t̲wf*, so does the Arabic *suf*.[93] Thus the name *abu sefêh* appears, on solid linguistic grounds, to preserve the ancient Egyptian name *p3 t̲wfy*, and thus it points to the name of the ancient lake on whose shores it was situated, el-Ballah Lake.

If Bietak is correct in thinking that *p3 t̲wfy* is the ancient name for the el-Ballah Lake system, then the linguistic evidence presented here supports his theory. Furthermore, this body of water may well be the biblical *yām sûp̱*. But an important question needs to be asked: Is there archaeological evidence to show that the toponyms Pi-hahiroth, Migdol, and Baal-Zephon, all mentioned in Exodus 14:2 as being in the vicinity of "the sea," existed in the same area? If any one of these three place names could be identified, that would go a long way to confirming el-Ballah Lake as the sea that the exodus narratives have in view. The problem has been that up until now, all proposed identifications for these locations have been speculation without the benefit of archaeological evidence, but the picture has now changed and new opportunities present themselves to offer a solution.

IV. Archaeological Exploration in North Sinai: 1970s to the Present

In recent decades, there has been a flurry of archaeological investigation in North Sinai after a long hiatus. Because of the hostilities that existed in the region between World Wars I and II, and the more recent Arab-Israeli conflict, virtually no archaeological work was undertaken in North Sinai during this period. During the Israeli occupation of Sinai after the 1967 war, Eliezer Oren conducted a systematic archaeological survey across North Sinai between 1972 and 1982. He identified over a hundred New Kingdom sites of varying sizes between the Suez Canal and Gaza.[94] His excavations of New Kingdom sites were in central and eastern Sinai, that is, Bir el-ᶜAbd (site BEA 10) and Haruba (sites A–289 and A–345) situated between el-Arish and Rafa.[95]

The aftermath of the Camp David accords and the return of Sinai to Egyptian control witnessed a renaissance of archaeological exploration in North Sinai. Mohamed Abd el-Maksoud in 1981 began to investigate various archaeological sites in North Sinai, many of which had been occupied by Israeli and then Egyptian armies and had suffered some damage as a result. Among his interests was determining the location of key New Kingdom sites on the Ways of Horus and, in particular, the discovery of Sile/Tjaru, Egypt's frontier town and strategic defensive fort. Another factor that has accelerated exploration in North Sinai is a new effort to reclaim vast tracks of desert for agricultural purposes. This has required bringing fresh water from the Nile across to Sinai and the construction of a system of irrigation canals, pipelines, pumping stations, and open drainage canals. Known as the as-Salam Canal Project, work began in the early 1990s. Some sites have been salvaged and others completely lost. Nevertheless, the archaeological data and historical information that has been extracted from this region over the past twenty years has filled tremendous gaps in our knowledge of the region and will permit the writing of new chapters in Egyptian history. Inasmuch as Egyptian and biblical history do intersect at some point during the New Kingdom (1550–1100 B.C.), according to the book of Exodus, this new information will advance our understanding of the geography of the exodus, and clarify some of the longstanding difficulties in interpreting these narratives.

Tjaru/Sile

Egyptologists have long wished to know the location for the frontier town of Tjaru/Sile and its fort (*ḫtm*) because of its importance over many centuries. In 1888, Müller rightly observed that "no town of the eastern Delta frontier has greater importance than Tharu, which was not only its largest town, but also the principal point for the defense of the entrance to Egypt, therefore also for the military and mercantile roads to the East." He went on to propose that Tjaru was linguistically equivalent to Hebrew Shur mentioned in Exodus 15:22 just after the sea crossing.[96] However, he did not suggest a location for this important site. Müller's proposed correlation between Tjaru (Tharu) and Shur can no longer be sustained; as Egypto-Semitic studies developed, scholars came to realize that if Tjaru were a name of Semitic origin then the Egyptian *ṯ* would have been written with a *samek*, not *shin*. The name may derive from the Akkadian word *sulu*, meaning "highway."[97] From the same root comes the noun *sôlalâ*, which in Hebrew means "siege and assault rampart."[98] Certainly Sile/Tjaru guarded the highway to the Levant, and possibly as early as the Middle Kingdom it had some military architecture that would be associated with the second meaning.

Tjaru, as many Egyptologists pronounce the name of this important frontier town, is also called Sile by scholars.[99] In an Amarna letter (EA 288) from the fourteenth century B.C., this town is called *sillu*,[100] revealing the Egyptian pronunciation of Tjaru—notice that it is not written with a *shin*.[101] This name appears to be the same one mentioned in the Antonine Itinerary, which located Sile south of Pelusium (Tell Farama), on the road to Serapeum and Clysma (Suez) in Roman times.[102]

The earliest attestation of Tjaru/Sile in an Egyptian text is the "Satire of the Trades," a didactic piece dating to the Middle Kingdom, in which the sage is introduced as "the man of Tjaru, named Dua-Khety" who instructs his son Pepi.[103] But it is chiefly known for its role in military history. The Rhind Mathematical Papyrus contains a daybook entry associated with Ahmose's campaign against the Hyksos in which the king seizes control of Tjaru.[104] The annals of Thutmose III contain the first reference to the fortress of (*ḫtm n*) Tjaru, where it serves as the launching point of his campaign to Megiddo.[105] In Seti I's battle reliefs at Karnak, *p3 ḫtm n ṯ3rw* is the point where the king approaches Egypt with his prisoners of war from his razzia in North Sinai (and possibly the Negev), where he rounds up troublesome Shasu Bedouin (figure 2).[106] It is also the starting point of Ramesses II's march to Kadesh for his famous battle with the Hittites.[107] That Tjaru marked the beginning of the route to Canaan is further acknowledged in the claim of the scribe in Pap. Anastasi I.[108] Here the scribe brags of his knowledge of the route to take from Egypt to Canaan, stating "head toward (?) the fortress (*ḫtm*) of the Way[s of Horus],"[109] with Gaza being the destination, or end point. This usage suggests that at least during the New Kingdom, *ḫtm n ṯ3rw* and *w3wt ḥr* were used interchangeably.

Although it is not mentioned as a geographical term in Exodus (unless Müller is right), Tjaru's location has been recognized as a possible reason why Exodus 13:17 explicitly states that the Israelites did not depart Egypt by the coastal highway, or the "Way of the land of the Philistines." Roland de Vaux, for instance, cites the presence of Sile as the reason this route was not taken.[110] Likewise, Nahum Sarna recognized the military nature of this route as being a factor for its avoidance, declaring that "it is quite clear that it was the better part of wisdom for the Israelites to have avoided the 'ways of the land of the Philistines.' They thereby avoided having to contend with the strongly entrenched Egyptian forces on what would have been hopelessly unequal terms."[111]

Since the early part of the twentieth century, Tell Abu Sefêh, located three kilometers east of the Suez Canal at Qantara East, was thought to be the location of Tjaru, or Sile.[112] This identification was championed by Gardiner, beginning with his seminal study of 1920 on the military road to Palestine. There he said, "Today, at all events, the question is finally settled; for in 1911 Dr. C. Küthmann produced convincing evidence that Thel (Tjaru), known from the hieroglyphs to have been the starting-point on the Egyptian frontier, was situated at Tell Abu Séfeh."[113] Gardiner continued to defend this identification throughout his career, and no challenge to his theory was put forward until recently.[114]

In the 1880s, F. L. Griffith discovered some inscribed blocks of Seti I and Ramesses II at Tell Abu Sefêh, which contributed to the belief that it was Sile (Tjaru).[115] He also reported on a few trenches he dug that revealed only Roman-period remains,[116] a factor that unfortunately was not taken seriously by subsequent generations of scholars. Beyond this brief investigation, little archaeological work was undertaken in this area in the next century, due largely to the regular military activity in Sinai since World War I.[117]

While working in Sinai between 1972 and 1982, Oren visited Tell Abu Sefêh and collected pottery from the surface, and made some soundings. The earliest materials encountered were Persian and "a few specimens of the Saite period."[118] I visited the site in 1994, still believing that it might be Tjaru, but full-scale excavations began later that year and have continued periodically ever since by members of the Supreme Council for Antiquities (SCA) of Egypt. Mostly Greco-Roman–period materials were uncovered, including an impressive harbor and two different Roman-period forts, and possibly some Persian-period remains.[119] This probably means that Tell Abu Sefêh can no longer be identified with Tjaru, a point some scholars had begun to recognize even before these excavations began.[120]

Alessandra Nibbi and Claude Vanderslayen have argued against equating Tell Abu Sefêh with Tjaru, but for entirely different reasons. They want to locate Tjaru near the base of the Delta.[121] Vanderslayen points to Pap. Rhind, which shows the line of march of Ahmose, during his wars of liberation against the Hyksos, as proceeding from Helioplis to Tjaru and then to Avaris.[122] This suggests to him that Tjaru is located between these two sites. However, he failed to consider that Ahmose's strategy was to cut off the exit route to Canaan prior to attacking the Hyksos capital.[123] Nibbi is right to question the traditional identification of Tell Abu Sefêh with Tjaru of the New Kingdom, and to suggest that it might be Sile of Roman times.[124] Her reason for wanting to locate New Kingdom Tjaru in the southern Delta is to support her bizarre theory that Canaan is in the northeastern Delta.[125] Her Canaan-in-the-Delta theory is simply untenable. She places Canaan in the northeastern Delta, in the very area that geologists now say was covered by Lake Manzelah and the Mediterranean during the second millennium (see chapter 3)! As for her proposed south Delta location for Tjaru, the excavations at Hebua in North Sinai, which were at their early stages when she wrote in 1989, and of which she was aware, have settled the issue once and for all, thus repudiating her theory.[126]

Shortly after Egypt regained control of the Sinai, Mohamed Abd el-Maksoud of the SCA began surveying sites and excavating some in North Sinai. Early on he investigated a series of four closely related sites called

Hebua I–IV, starting in 1981 (figure 6). He began to uncover a massive fort at Hebua I when excavations began there in 1985; these continue to the present. Still thinking that Tell Abu Sefêh was Tjaru/Sile, he initially thought that Hebua was the Dwelling of the Lion, the second fort on the military road that Gardiner had studied, on the basis of the reliefs of Seti I at Karnak and Pap. Anastasi I.[127] But as the New Kingdom fort grew in size with further excavations, and at the same time as the excavations at Tell Abu Sefêh were producing no New Kingdom remains, Abd el-Maksoud began to change his mind, believing instead that Hebua was ancient Tjaru, and that the fort at Hebua I was the Fortress (*ḫtm*) of Tjaru.[128] In 1997 I too expressed my belief that Tjaru was to be found at Hebua; certainly all the evidence was pointing in that direction.[129] Proof of this identification came with the discovery of a Ramesside-period votive statue found in a New Kingdom temple at Hebua I. Fortunately for me, I was in North Sinai on the very day it was uncovered in May 1999, and Abd el-Maksoud and I were able to read the name Tjaru on the statue.[130] Since the statue was found in a New Kingdom setting, it could not have been transported there at a later date, as after the New Kingdom the site appears to have been abandoned. Only some scattered tombs of the Greco-Roman period represent the late period.[131] Consequently, we can be fairly certain that the ancient town-site of Tjaru was located at Hebua, and the fortress mentioned in New Kingdom military contexts is the one uncovered at Hebua I.

What this discovery shows is that de Vaux's instinct was right that Sile/Tjaru was a formidable obstacle to the departing Israelites. Tjaru had an enormous fort, the outside wall of which measures 800 by 400 meters and dates to the New Kingdom (figure 9).[132] But perhaps even more significant, it was located on a narrow strip of land, perhaps less than a kilometer across, with water on either side (figures 5 and 6). Exiting Egypt by this route would have been a disaster for a force being pursued, and gaining entry to Egypt via this route by an enemy would have been a monumental challenge. The geological evidence for understanding the nature of Egypt's New Kingdom frontier has only recently become available. Coastal geologists from the Smithsonian Institution, Daniel Stanley, Vincent Coutellier, and Glenn Goodfriend, conducted research on history of the northern Delta and western North Sinai in the late 1980s and into the 1990s.[133] Their data were obtained by boring at strategic points in the region. They conclude that this coastal ridge was actually the Mediterranean coastline before the Middle Kingdom, and probably during the New Kingdom too (figures 5 and 6). The geologist of the East Frontier Archaeological project, Stephen Moshier, had suggested this scenario to me in 1997–1998 based upon his study of satellite images.[134] South of Hebua was either a narrow lagoon (west lagoon) or a branch of the Nile, and the large lake (or lagoon) east of Hebua was probably an estuary of that branch of the Nile.[135] The French team of scholars who have worked tirelessly in North Sinai ever since the 1980s differentiated these two bodies of water as the west lagoon (west of Hebua) and the east lagoon (east of Hebua) (figures 5 and 6).[136]

No additional New Kingdom sites have been identified on the coastal ridge east of Hebua I by either Oren or Abd el-Maksoud. This is probably because the coastal ridge was punctuated with wide openings that allowed water to pass back and forth between the Mediterranean and the lagoon (figures 5 and 6). This means that my earlier proposal that the military road went east from Hebua I across the coastal ridge must now be abandoned.[137] In 1998 Donald Redford had also proposed that the route went this direction, but then he did not have the benefit of Goodfriend and Stanley's study, and the excavations at Tell el-Borg that began in 2000.[138]

Probably by the first millennium B.C. some desiccation of the lagoon had begun as the Mediterranean coastline and the Nile Delta moved north, and the Pelusiac branch of the Nile likewise migrated north. Possibly during Saite and Persian times one could travel across the ancient barrier island to Tell Qedua (Oren's T–21) and east to the Levant, although the eastern lagoon (Shihor) was still filled with water during Greco-Roman times.[139] But this was impossible during New Kingdom times. So where did the military road go and where are the subsequent forts?

Gardiner made the first serious attempt to trace this route by linking the sequence of toponyms on the so-called Ways of Horus from the battle reliefs of Seti I at Karnak and the itinerary outlined by the scribe in Pap. Anastasi I[140] with the known tells in North Sinai.[141] Gardiner proposed that the first in the sequence, Tjaru or Sile, the key frontier town and fort of Egypt, was at Tell Abu Sefêh, that the Dwelling of the Lion (or Sese) was possibly at Tell Habwe (not Tell Hebua, located seven kilometers north–northeast of Tell Abu Sefêh, but rather a site also called Tell Ahmar),[142] and that the third in the sequence, Migdol (e.g., *mktr*) of Menmaatre (Seti I), was at Tell el-Herr (figure 10). Over the decades, Gardiner's reconstruction was widely accepted because little archaeological work took place in North Sinai after his study of 1920 against which to test his text-based reconstruction.

The questions that now must be asked are, which way does the Ways of Horus or the way of the land of the Philistines lead after Tjaru, and where are the subsequent forts in the sequence?

V. Migdol, Pi-ha-hiroth, and Baal-zephon

Migdol

The third fort in the Karnak sequence is the Migdol of Menmaatre.[143] It might be the place mentioned in Amarna Letter (EA 234), which is referred to as "Magdalu in Egypt," likening it to Akka (Acco) in Canaan, but the reason for the comparison is unclear and the reference tells us nothing about its location.[144] However, if Magdalu of EA 234 is the same fort mentioned in the Seti Karnak relief, it is the earliest attestation of this toponym. Could this Migdol on the Ways of Horus be the elusive Migdol of the exodus narratives? Gardiner himself thought the Migdol mentioned in Jeremiah 44:1 and 46:14 and Ezekiel 29:10 and 30:6 was the same one mentioned in Exodus 14:2 and Numbers 33:7, which in turn is to be equated with the Migdol of Menmaatre.[145] He reiterated this view a few years later, and the equation between Migdol of the exodus story and fort of Seti I and Ramesses II with the same name has been accepted by many other scholars since.[146] T. E. Peet, for example, agrees that biblical Migdol is "identical with the Migdol of Menmare [King Seti I] shown in the Karnak sculptures."[147] Henri Cazelles questioned this association, but believed that Migdol of Exodus 14 and the prophets were one and the same.[148] More recently, Siegfried Herrmann and Benjamin Scolnic have accepted the connection between the two Migdols.[149]

The references in the Hebrew prophets make it clear that Migdol was also the frontier town or fort (as the name suggests) in the sixth century B.C. The correlation between the Migdol of the prophets and the exodus narratives had been accepted by a number of scholars over the years, although de Vaux thought it might be located closer to the Wadi Tumilat (and thus would not be the same as Migdol of the prophets).[150] J. Simons, on the other hand, saw no reason for connecting Migdol of the prophets and the exodus.[151] Like Gardiner, he proposed that Migdol was located at Tell el-Herr on the east side of the large lagoon mentioned above (figures 5, 6, and 10).

Thanks to the recent archaeological work in North Sinai, the picture is becoming clearer. One of the sites Oren excavated during the 1970s was T–21 (Tell Qedua). It had Saite and early Persian remains (seventh to sixth centuries B.C.), which led him to propose that it was Migdol of the Hebrew prophets, as the title of his preliminary report suggests: "Migdol: A New Fortress on the Edge of the Eastern Nile Delta." The absence of New Kingdom remains, however, forced him to conclude that New Kingdom Migdol must be located elsewhere.[152] Those who believe that the geographical references in Exodus and Numbers were written in the mid-point of the first millennium B.C. point to Oren's discovery as proof that the author used the geography of his time. Dever, for example, has said, "that would explain why the biblical editors knew where the site of 'Migdol' actually was, although they did not know that it lacked any earlier history."[153]

Redford worked at Qedua during the 1990s and has only confirmed Oren's dating—still no New Kingdom remains. After two seasons, Redford has determined that "the time represented by the occupation of Tell Qedwa was not long and was confined to a single period," the "last third of the 7th century B.C.," and "appears not to have survived into the 5th century B.C."[154]

Because Tell Qedua's occupation does not last into later Persian and Greco-Roman periods, Oren does not think it can be Magdolo of classical times.[155] He theorizes that during this period, the name was transferred to the fort at Tell el-Herr (which his survey suggested likewise did not have New Kingdom–period or Late Bronze Age remains), located about six kilometers south of Qedua. This development, in addition to the results of his survey at Tell Abu Sefêh, led Oren in 1984 to conclude that "T–21 has nothing to do with the Exodus episode or with the Egyptian New Kingdom period" and that "the location of New Kingdom Thel (Sile), like that of Migdol, remains hypothetical and must await further study."[156]

Tell el-Herr was first excavated by early in the twentieth century by Jean Clédat, who uncovered remains that he dated to the seventh and sixth centuries.[157] This early date, however, has not been substantiated by more recent work at the site. Abd el-Maksoud also investigated Tell el-Herr in the early 1980s and discovered a fortified site of the Persian to Roman periods.[158] With his work expanding at Hebua, he handed over the excavations at Tell el-Herr to Dominque Valbelle, who in 2004 completed her nineteenth year of work there, and still no remains earlier than the Persian period have been uncovered. Early and later Persian forts have been discovered, but nothing from the early part of the first or second millennia have come to light.[159] This means that Tell el-Herr could not have been Migdol of the prophets, let alone the New Kingdom fort associated with Seti I.

The excavations of the past twenty years at Tell Qedua and Tell el-Herr make it clear that the former could be Migdol of the biblical prophets, and perhaps the place with the same name mentioned in Esarhaddon's annals when he recounts his invasion of Egypt, but not Magdalos or Magdolum of the Classical period.[160] On the other hand, Tell el-Herr, six kilometers south of Qedua, seems to fit with the location of the later site, as it remains the only late Persian to Greco-Roman–period fort between Pelusium (Tell Farama) and Sile (Tell Abu-Sefêh). Finally, the work at these two tells also eliminate them from being the thirteenth-century fortress, the Migdol of Menmaatre; as Kenneth Kitchen observes, "The New Kingdom 'Migdol' of Sethos I is identical with neither of these sites, but remains to be discovered somewhere in the vicinity."[161]

The East Frontier Archaeological Project has been conducting archaeological survey work in the Qantara-Baluza region since 1994, with the main objective being to identify the route of the Ways of Horus and its accompanying forts. Combining the archaeological and geomorphological data now available, it is now clear that the ancient military highway could not go north or due east of Hebua, leaving only a southern direction around the eastern lagoon to investigate. Working with satellite images, and being aware of the locations of the ancient lakes and lagoons, we investigated the area between the northern end of the el-Ballah Lakes and the eastern lagoon, believing that for strategic reasons a fort ought to be located in this area.

Just over a kilometer southeast of Hebua I is the site of Hebua II (figure 6), thought by Abd el-Maksoud to be connected to Hebua I (Tjaru) because of its proximity. Between the two sites there was either a branch of the Nile (depending upon the period) or a paleolagoon (figures 5 and 6).[162] While conducting an archaeological survey at Hebua II in 1992, a French team encountered New Kingdom materials on the surface, including part of an octagonal pillar with a partially preserved inscription that read: *sty [mr]n [ptḥ] di ʿnḫ mi rʿ*, "Seti [beloved] of [Ptah], granted life like Re."[163] A brief season of excavations by the SCA there in 1999 revealed a New Kingdom complex of buildings with Nineteenth-Dynasty pottery and other remains, including a door lintel or cornice with the cartouches of Seti I on it.[164] So, clearly, Hebua II is a New Kingdom site, and its location suggests to me that the direction of the route from Hebua I was toward the southeast. Because it is so close to the fort at Hebua I, Hebua II appears to be a part of Tjaru complex rather than being the second fort in the Seti I map. Further excavations at the site, however, may clarify this question. For information concerning the identity of Hebua II, see below.

Around four kilometers southeast of Hebua II is a site called Tell el-Borg. As best can be determined, Tell el-Borg was first documented in the archaeological literature when Jean Clédat made a brief visit to the site in 1909, but only cursory notes were taken then.[165] It was subsequently catalogued by Oren as T–108 and 109 (figure 10), and he identified it as a site with New Kingdom remains on the basis of surface finds.[166] Mohamed Abd el-Maksoud, then the SCA director for North Sinai, asked me to investigate this site because it was being destroyed by the as-Salam irrigation project. In May 1999 I visited the site with a small team only to find out that it had already been severed by a drainage canal, several roads had been laid over the site, and pipelines had been dug for water. The surface finds, indeed, supported earlier observations that it was a New Kingdom site. Datable fourteenth- to thirteenth-century sherds were found, including Egyptian blue-painted (Amarna) ware, Cypriote (white slip) milk bowl sherds dating to the Late Bronze II period, and Canaanite "pilgrim flasks" (figure 11). To our surprise, no sherds from the first millennium B.C. were found. Cleary this was an important site that needed to be salvaged before further damage was done to it, and the SCA was extremely helpful in expediting matters, allowing excavations to begin in 2000; three more seasons followed in 2001, 2002, and 2004. A minor report on this salvage operation appeared in *Egyptian Archaeology* in 2002, and a more detailed preliminary report has been published in *Journal of Egyptian Archaeology* by Abd el-Maksoud and this author.[167]

Some of the finds from the first seasons of excavations include limestone blocks probably of a temple of Ramesses II, showing a deity (Amun-Re or

Atum) (figure 12), part of a battle scene that depicts the king in his chariot, a partial chariot wheel, and what appears to be foreigners fleeing from the pharaoh (figure 13). The battle motif is rather common beginning with New Kingdom, and there are many surviving parallels from the battle reliefs of Seti I, Ramesses II, Merneptah, and Ramesses III.[168] Although the hairstyling and facial features of the enemy show that the people on this block are foreigners (figure 14), they do not quite match features typical of the Shasu Bedouin against whom Seti I fought on the Karnak reliefs (figure 2), although they probably are Shasu.[169] The same type of duck-bill axe, however, is carried by the warriors on our block as is shown in the hands of some of Shasu in the Karnak Seti I relief.[170]

Another limestone block fragment was found with the cartouche of Thut[mose] partially preserved on it. It probably belongs to Thutmose III and is inscribed in a different style from the texts on the Ramesside-period blocks, showing that it came originally from a different structure.[171] Tombs from the late Eighteenth to early Nineteenth Dynasties (Late Bronze II) were uncovered that were rich with Cypriote vessels and blue-painted Egyptian wares. The military nature of the site, which we had expected from the outset, received some support with the discovery of a small inscription on a limestone fragment (13.5 × 11 × 5 centimeters) that contained the name of a military officer named Khay. He was a weapons bearer (*ṯ3i ḫ*^{c}*w*) who was a part of the military division (*s3*) of "Amun is glorious and victorious" during the reign of Ramesses II. An *s3* was a unit of 250 troops plus three senior officers.[172]

Beginning in 2000, the remains of two forts were discovered (for site map, see figure 15). The main feature of the later fort is a mud-brick wall that measures 3.8 meters (12 feet 4 inches) wide, though only one to three courses of brick in thickness were preserved (figure 16). Measuring about 80 meters (260 feet) on a side, nearly half of the fort was demolished when a recent irrigation canal was excavated through the site. Ceramic and stratigraphic evidence indicates that this fort functioned throughout the thirteenth century B.C., and probably into the twelfth century. In the gate area, around a half dozen inscribed fragments were uncovered containing the cartouche of Ramesses II.

A unique moat or fosse is the principal structure discovered from the earlier fort. To our great surprise, the top of the walls of this moat, which were made of mud brick, were constructed on a foundation of fired brick (figure 17). Red brick is typically found in Roman-period buildings, although limited use of fired brick has been documented in prior centuries.[173] The foundation of the Tell el-Borg moat is nine to fourteen layers high, making this a major use of fired brick, the like of which has not been documented in Egyptian archaeology for such an early period. There is no doubt of the New Kingdom date of the moat for several reasons:

1. only New Kingdom pottery, including one sherd of the early to mid-Eighteenth Dynasty, was recovered from within the moat;
2. in one square cut into the moat, a jar handle was discovered with the cartouche of the ephemeral successor of Pharaoh Akhenaten, 'Ankh-kheper-re [w' en]-r', whom some equate with Smenkhkare (1338–1336 B.C.); and
3. the moat was intentionally filled in order to build the later fort, and the wall of the second fort was constructed over the filled moat in Field IV. This latter point is proven by a square that we cut through Wall C, which showed the outside moat wall turning west under that wall and reappearing west of the corner where Walls C and D meet (figure 18).

We provisionally have dated the moat to the mid-fifteenth century and suggest that it was built by Thutmose III; the second fort we date to the late fourteenth to early thirteenth centuries B.C.[174]

It might be tempting to identify Tell el-Borg with the Migdol of Menmaatre because the name *borg* is the Arabic for tower, just as *migdol* means tower in Hebrew, and *migdol* is recognized as a Semitic loanword into Egyptian.[175] How early this name was attached to this tell is difficult to say. As mentioned above, the name was known to Clédat when he visited the site in 1909. There is also a Bir el-Borg (that is, the well of the tower) located about six kilometers south of Tell el-Borg, which is documented on the 1945 Survey of Egypt map. Nonetheless, the distance between the two makes it doubtful that either one was responsible for the name of the other site.

One scholar, Giacomo Cavillier, has lately proposed identifying Tell el-Borg with Seti I's Migdol,[176] but we are not convinced of this proposal, principally because he did not consider Hebua II and its role in the sequence of sites. This site may hold the key to clarifying the identity of Tell el-Borg. However, because Hebua II is situated so close to the fort at Hebua I, as stated already, we believe that it is part of Tjaru and not the next fort in the succession. The discovery of a text at either Hebua II or Tell el-Borg, naming the site, would obviously settle the matter. In the absence of such evidence, however, what makes the best sense of archaeological, textual, and paleoenvironmental evidence we do have?

The Seti I relief shows the monarch returning from his military campaign against the Shasu, heading toward Egypt's border (figure 2). The movement, then, is from east to west, the sequence being: 4. the Migdol of Menmaatre; 3. the Dwelling of the Lion; 2. the fortress (*ḫtm*) Tjaru; 1. *t3 dnit,* (the canal or the dividing waters).[177] The final scene (1), *t3 dnit,* shows a bridge (or dyke) connecting Tjaru to a larger building complex on the west side of the scenes (and hence to the west or north of 2. Gardiner described this part of the scene as follows: "the fortress is depicted as a rectangular space contained on each flank by the three buildings with doors. The entrance was through a large portal on the Egyptian side, and on reaching the canal one passed through a second portal on to a bridge, the desert side of which ends in a third portal."[178] The Epigraphic Survey of the Oriental Institute offers a similar explanation: "A compound on the Asiatic side is apparently a parade ground, having a gate and (east and west) also a reviewing stand. More extensive buildings can be seen on the Egyptian side across the bridge."[179]

It might be appealing to associate *tꜣ dnit* with the East Frontier Canal discovered by members of the Israel Geological Survey in the early 1970s (figure 19).[180] This identification would have made sense if Tell Abu Sefêh were home to the New Kingdom fortress of Tjaru, but it is not. The reconstruction of Sneh and Weissbrod shows a canal passing just south of Tell Abu Sefêh, where it connects to a surviving trace, after which it makes a sharp turn north passing west of Tell el-Herr, where the restored portion meets with a north-south segment that proceeds north to Pelusium (Tell el-Farama). However, our subsequent work in North Sinai leads us to question this reconstruction. In 1998, Moshier and I were able to walk the course of the easternmost section of the canal with the aid of Corona satellite images from the 1960s and early 1970s (figures 5 and 6). These images are especially valuable because they were taken from a higher altitude than the Israeli pictures that were taken from planes; consequently the Corona images allow one to study the region at different times of the year and under different climatic conditions, allowing features on the ground to be seen more clearly. What these images reveal is that the east-west trace discovered by Sneh and Weissbrod (east of Tell Abu Sefêh) does not turn north (figure 19), but continues due east about ten kilometers, where it comes to an end in what today is a kilometer-long oasis (figures 5 and 6). Thus it is impossible for this segment of the canal to have joined up with the northern one. The north-south canal trace, it appears, is a first-millennium canal that ran from the eastern lagoon north to Pelusium, and had nothing to do with the east-west trace.[181]

What this means is that neither of these canals is close enough to Hebua I to be the water feature called *tꜣ dnit*. Another scenario might be proposed: namely that *tꜣ dnit* is the "dividing waters"—as Gardiner translated it—that separated the entry point of Tjaru (Hebua II) and the main fortress of Tjaru (Hebua I). This suggestion is supported by two pieces of evidence: first, the label Tjaru is on the building on the east side of *tꜣ dnit*, suggesting that Hebua II represents that structure which served as the entrance to Tjaru; and second, Hebua II is built on a peninsula that extends into the lagoon waters, thus shortening the distance across the water that the bridge or dyke had to span. This peninsula was still visible in the 1945 Survey of Egypt map (figure 4), and the French archaeological survey map clearly shows this detail, as does Manfred Bietak's regional map (figure 3).[182] Thus, the bridge across *tꜣ dnit*, it might be suggested, was located at the narrowest portion of the lagoon that separates Hebua I and II. According to the Seti I relief, reeds grew on the banks and the water was filled with crocodiles. Now lost, but visible to earlier epigraphers, was a larger body of water teeming with fish that was situated beneath the feet of the captured Shasu (figure 2).[183] This feature extends east toward the next fort, the Dwelling of the Lion (figure 2). One wonders if this does not represent the eastern end of the lagoon (Shihor), which our geological investigations have shown to have extended south to within a kilometer of Tell el-Borg (figures 5 and 10). Morris, alternatively, speculates that the body of water with the fish might be the Mediterranean Sea.[184] She, however, was influenced by Redford's theory that the route went due east of Hebua I and that the Dwelling of the Lion was near Tell Qedua, in which case the Mediterranean would have been close by.

Working with the evidence now available, our provisional hypothesis is that Tell el-Borg is the Dwelling of the Lion for the following reasons: first, its location in the sequence after Hebua I and II, Tjaru/Sile; second, Pap. Anastasi I agrees with the Seti I relief that "the Dwelling of Sese" (i.e., Ramesses, the fort's name during his reign) is the fort after Tjaru;[185] and third, Pap. Anastasi V, 24[186] reports three stelae that were transported by boat "from the place where the King is" (i.e., the capital, Pi-Ramesses) via Tjaru and on to the Dwelling of Ramesses-Beloved of Amun[187] for offloading. This reference indicates that Tjaru and the Dwelling could both be reached by water, a point recognized by Gardiner and Kitchen.[188] Fortunately, our work at Tell el-Borg during the 2001 season may have provided the evidence for how a boat could travel from Pi-Ramesses to Tjaru, and end up at the Dwelling. First, it was noticed that between the main tell area at Borg and Field IV, where the forts were uncovered, there was a low-lying trough running in an easterly direction about 100 to 150 meters across. This feature is also discernible on the Corona satellite images (figures 5 and 6) and can be seen on our contour map of the site (figure 15). While excavating in Field II, which is on the south side of the tell and on the edge of the trough, black Nilotic silt was reached, which proved to be the water's edge of a distributary of the Nile.[189] It was approximately 100 meters wide and was rather shallow, so could apparently be forded.[190] Thus it appears that one could travel by boat directly from Pi-Ramesses to Tell el-Borg on this branch of the Pelusiac. Since the particular shipment described in Anastasi V, 24 first docked by Tjaru, it may have returned west to where the Pelusiac forks (perhaps near the Suez Canal?), and then east to the Dwelling, or the ship might have fared east from Tjaru to the western part of the lagoon and then proceeded west along the newly discovered branch before docking at the Dwelling. In either case, there is now evidence that Tell el-Borg was accessible by water.

A fourth reason to identify Tell el-Borg with the Dwelling of the Lion is that the discovery of the forts at Tell el-Borg also shows that the New Kingdom military highway or Ways of Horus went southeast from Hebua I and Hebua II

(Tjaru's entry point), past Tell el-Borg, on around the southern end of the eastern lagoon, and then north toward the Mediterranean coast (figures 6 and 10).

For all these reasons, we provisionally propose that Tell el-Borg is the Dwelling of the Lion/Ramesses/Sese, and not the Migdol of Menmaatre. Nevertheless, because we now know the route of the military highway from Tjaru, the location of the third fort in the New Kingdom sequence, Migdol, should be located around five kilometers southeast of Tell el-Borg, most likely near the southern end of the eastern lagoon. A New Kingdom site in this area was identified by Oren as T-78 (figures 5 and 10). This site may be where the Migdol of Menmaatre was located, although we are uncertain about whether it survived the recent canal development, as the area on the south side of the paleo-(eastern) lagoon was developed extensively during the 1990s. For strategic reasons it seems essential to have had some sort of military installation at the southern end of the lagoon, lest a hostile force proceed directly east past the southern end of the lagoon in a straight line toward the Delta.

In April 2002, a small survey team under my direction visited another site on the east side of the eastern lagoon called Tell el-Ebedah, which is adjacent to the Bedouin village of Gilbana. The name of the tell means "white"—the site is covered with shells from decomposed brick. This site is possibly T-116 in Oren's survey of New Kingdom sites, and we identified New Kingdom sherds, with no late-period ones in evidence.[191] This site could be the fourth fort in the sequence, Edjo (i.e., Buto) of Seti Merneptah according to the Seti relief, which in Pap. Anastasi I replaces Seti with the name of his son, Ramesses, that is, Sese.[192]

Many years ago, Gardiner documented four other place names in the Delta that included the Semitic word *migdol* toponym. But as Morris has noted, these toponyms date to the first millennium and are located within the Delta, and thus do not assist us with locating the New Kingdom fort on the Ways of Horus. In her recent study on the role of fortresses and administrative headquarters in New Kingdom foreign policy, a 1,200-page dissertation completed in 2001, Morris observed that "as far as can be determined from an examination of the evidence, however, migdol-forts had a very limited distribution in the New Kingdom. Outside Egypt itself they are only found in northern Sinai. One or possibly two *mkdr* were situated along the Ways of Horus." Her study also reveals that the Semitic term *mkdr/mktr* (*migdol*) is only used for forts outside of Egypt's borders in the Nineteenth Dynasty.[193] This means that at the end of the second millennium B.C. (Late Bronze II), there was only one toponym, or possibly two, and that it (or they) would be found east of Tjaru, and not west of it (i.e., in the Delta). This location is significant for Migdol of Exodus, because it is encountered after departing the Delta (i.e., Rameses or the Land of Goshen) and they are on the edge of the desert (*miḏbār*; Exod. 13:20) just before coming to the location described in Exodus 14:2. This means that both the Bible and the Egyptian sources locate Migdol outside of the Delta proper.

References to Migdol are attested only from a few texts. The occurrence in the Seti I Karnak relief has already been discussed. But it also is actually depicted in the Seti I relief, where it is shown between the hind legs and the tail of the horses (figure 2). Its minute size should be attributed to its placement in the scene. That is, in order to make it fit behind the horse, the fort was scaled down to accommodate the available space.[194] In front of the Migdol of Menmaatre a circular-shaped pool of water is shown. By way of comparison, a rectangular-shaped pool with a pair of adjacent trees is portrayed in front of the Dwelling of the Lion. The pool at Migdol is named *t3 ẖnm ḥpn*. In Pap. Anastasi I, this same well is written differently, as *ḥṯyn*. Long ago Gardiner pointed out that the difference lies in the misreading of the bird sign:[195] the Karnak writing has the *p3*–bird (G–41 in Gardiner's sign list), whereas in Pap. Anastasi I, the *ṯ3*–bird is recorded (G–47 in Gardiner's sign list).[196] The two signs are easily confused. Unfortunately, a third witness to this well does not exist to help with the writing, although there seems to be a consensus now that the intended word is *ḥṯyn*, in which case it is an Egyptian writing for a Semitic word *ḥsyn* meaning "little stronghold."[197] Kitchen, on the other hand, notes that the idea of a fortified well beside a fort makes little sense and therefore proposes a different Semitic root meaning "wealth, abundance" *ḥṯyn*, which would make better sense in reference to a well in a desert setting.[198] Both interpretations have linguistic support. It should be noted that the picture clearly shows a feature of some sort (a wall?) wrapped around the water, shaped like a horseshoe, and opened at the top. I am at a loss to explain this feature, although it looks similar to the way how moats from Levantine fortifications are depicted in New Kingdom reliefs.[199] What is certain is that this fort also had a body of water or man-made pool associated with it. If the former is intended, it might be illustrating this fort's proximity to the nearby eastern lagoon.

Pap. Anastasi V, which contains the report of the runaway slaves, provides another reference, but here it is the Migdol of Seti-Merneptah, possibly a variation on the Migdol of Menmaatre in which the nomen of the pharaoh is used instead of the prenomen. Alternatively, Seti Merneptah could refer to Seti II, in which case, the practice of changing the name of the fort to reflect the reigning monarch is again attested.[200] In either case, it appears that this fort is the third fort in the Karnak itinerary. This passage was already discussed in some detail (chapter 4, §VI). There it was argued that the escapees, like the Israelites, traveled from Pi-Ramesses south toward the Wadi Tumilat, but then turned north where "they passed by the northern walls of the Migdol of Seti-Merneptah."[201] This text does not help us with the location of the fort, but, as Morris points out, since Kakemwer was directing his letter to two different troop commanders (*ḥry pḏt*), one of them would have been the commandant of Migdol of Menmaatre. A *pḏt* was probably a military unit larger than 250.[202] This suggests that this fort was rather substantial in size and had a large number of troops stationed there. At Tell el-Borg, as noted above, a division (*s3*) of 250 soldiers was stationed; whereas Migdol, if Morris is correct, had in excess of 250 soldiers because its commander was a *ḥry pḏt*.

A final New Kingdom mention of a border fort named Migdol in Egyptian sources dates to the reign of Ramesses III (1184–1153 B.C.) from his funerary temple at Medinet Habu. In the aftermath of a naval battle with the Sea Peoples, the pharaoh returned to the Migdol of Ramesses, ruler of Heliopolis, to celebrate his victory and tally the number of fallen enemies. Migdol is portrayed as a fort with crenellations on the walls, like those shown in the Karnak reliefs of Seti I.[203] Given the findings of Morris that just one and at most two forts use the element "Migdol" in their name during New Kingdom times, and that it (they) is (are) restricted to North Sinai, it seems safe to conclude that Ramesses III's fort, Ramesses Ruler of Heliopolis, is the Twentieth-Dynasty name of the Migdol of Menmaatre. The same conclusion has been reached recently by David O'Connor and Donald Redford.[204] Changing the name of a fort to fit the reigning pharaoh was seen in the case of the Dwelling of Menmaatre, which became the Dwelling of Sese under Ramesses II.

Redford suggests that the land battle with the Sea Peoples would have taken place close to this fort and that the naval battle may have occurred nearby. He, however, thought that Migdol was located somewhere in the vicinity of present-day Baluza, near ancient Pelusium, where the Nile debouched.[205] In view of the paleoenvironmental data presented above (and in chapter 3), we now know that the Pelusiac did not enter the Mediterranean at Pelusium during the second millennium B.C., as it did between 700 and 1,000 years later. However, Redford's thought that the two battles occurred close to each other make very good sense in the light of the new data. If Migdol is located near the south shore of the eastern lagoon (Shihor), as we believe, it would have been the fort that would have guarded the strategic area between the aforementioned lagoon and the north end of the el-Ballah Lakes (*p3 ṯwfy* = *yām sûp̱*), and the sea battle, thought to have occurred in the mouth of the Nile, could have taken place in the lagoon into which the two branches of the Nile emptied. Another consideration is the role that the East Frontier Canal may have played in these events. Satellite images clearly show the canal passing near our suggested location for the Migdol of Menmaatre, and extending five kilometers east, where it apparently ends in an oasis (figures 5 and 6). If the canal was functioning during the New Kingdom,[206] then the open land between the fort (and the lagoon to its north) was restricted to no more than a few hundred meters.

This scenario makes good sense of the pictorial, textual, archaeological, and paleoenvironmental evidence and, it might be suggested, the Egyptian army and navy chose this location to face the invading Sea Peoples because it played into Egypt's hands. The narrow strip of land where the invading coalition would have to pass was easy to defend with a nearby fort (Migdol), with other forts to the east. In terms of the naval battle, an Egyptian armada was surely docked at Tjaru and would have had easy access to the lagoon, and then too, there is the new Nile channel that passed by Tell el-Borg (Dwelling of the Lion) on which boats could travel to face the Sea Peoples' navy, as well as supply Migdol and the front lines of the land battle.

The foregoing data suggest that the Egyptian New Kingdom fort Migdol, associated with Seti I, Ramesses II, Seti II (possibly), and Ramesses III, is located southeast of Tell el-Borg, near the south end of the paleolagoon. We have good reason to think that this is also Migdol of Exodus 14:2, and this case can be made stronger when the other toponyms of this verse are examined.

Pi-hahiroth and Baal-Zephon

The Bible specifically places the Israelites "in front of Pi-hahiroth, between Migdol and the sea, in front of Baal-Zephon" (Exod 14:2). The etymology of Pi-hahiroth has long been discussed, because both Egyptian and Semitic etymologies have been proposed.[207] Redford is certain that this name "is obviously closely related to *Ḥnt t3 Ḥ3-r-ti* of Demotic, which is plausibly located in the vicinity of Lake Timsah."[208] Of course, if this correlation is correct it might support a late dating of the geography, which Redford favors—although it should be noted that the occurrence of a name in a later text does not mean that the place did not exist earlier on. Many other interpretations of this toponym, however, have been offered. In my earlier study of this toponym, I agreed with several earlier scholars who suggested that this name derived from either a genuine Semitic expression or a Semitic popular etymology of an Egyptian toponym meaning "the mouth of the canal."[209] In the latter case this would mean that an Egyptian toponym that sounded close to *pi-ha-hiroth* existed and the Hebrews transformed the term to fit a meaning that made sense to them and that also sounded like the Egyptian term.

Associating this understanding with a canal was made far more possible with the discovery of what members of the Israel Geological Survey called the Eastern Frontier Canal in the early 1970s. They too thought that Pi-hahiroth meant "the opening or mouth of the canal(s)," and associated it with their discovery.[210] I accepted this interpretation and pointed out that the word *ḫarāru* is attested in Akkadian going back to the Old Babylonian period, and that in the Kassite period in Babylon (1600–1200 B.C.), *ḫerūtu* is a noun whose meaning is applied to canals and ditches.[211] One problem I noted with attempting to locate this toponym precisely is that if it referred to the mouth of a canal, that is, where a canal opened into another body of water, there were a number of candidates. This is because canal traces have been found between the north side of Lake Timsah running up to the southern end of el Ballah, as well as on the northeast side of the same lake (figure 19). Now that a more certain location for Migdol has been advanced, the intersection between the canal and the Ballah lake seems the most likely candidate among the several options, and if a corresponding Egyptian toponym could be found in this area of North Sinai, the case would be strengthened.

Nearly fifty years ago, Cazelles drew attention to the toponyms in Pap. Anastasi III 2.8–12 that all began with *ḫ* or *ḥ* in Egyptian (which would correspond to Hebrew ח), which might be behind the name in Exodus 14:2.[212] It is this text, which was discussed above (§III), that led Bietak to suggest that *p3 ṯwfy* and *p3 š-ḥr* were located close to each other, and corresponded to the Ballah Lake system and the large lagoon that stretched east of Hebua all the way to Tell el-Herr (figure 3). In this passage the scribe describes the lush conditions of the east Delta region from Pi-Ramesses all the way to the lake region of the eastern frontier. In line III 2.8, he mentions the "*ᶜd*-fish of the *ḫ*/// waters of the waters of Baal." A break in the text, unfortunately, prevents us from reading the word that begins with *ḫ*, although enough of the determinatives are preserved that a probable reading can be ascertained for them. The top of the three running water signs is present (Gardiner's sign list N–35) and beside it the top of the channel or water canal sign (N–36). During the New Kingdom, the combination of these signs are written as determinatives for "names of rivers, lakes and seas."[213] Thus although the name of this body of water is uncertain, but begins with *ḫ*, it is closely associated with "the waters of Baal." The mention of the Canaanite storm god in connection with a body of water within the general area where *p3 š-ḥr* and *p3 ṯwfy* are located presents itself as a candidate for Baal-Zephon (Baal of the North) of Exodus 14:2. Given the lacustrine nature of the eastern Delta, present-day North Sinai, the understanding of this toponym provided by Pap. Anastasi III makes good sense. It is certainly preferable to an association with the east Delta city of *t3-ḥwt-p3 nḥsy*. Many years ago Noël Aimé-Giron pointed to a sixth- to fifth-century B.C. papyrus written in Phoenician that names Baal Zaphon as the patron of the city.[214] This led him to propose that the name of this deity stands behind the toponym of Exodus. The problem with this suggestion is that the name of the city is known to Jeremiah, the sixth-century prophet of Judah, as Tahpanhes (Jer. 2:16; 43:7–9, 13; 44:1; 46:14), not Baal-Zephon.

It was also noted earlier (chapter IV, §VIII) that Eissfeldt's theory that Baal-Zephon was associated with Mt. Casius on the barrier island of Lake Serbonis (Bardawil) must be abandoned because of the geological evidence, which now shows that this land bridge on the eastern end did not connect to the mainland. Thus the reference to the waters of Baal in North Sinai, dating to the thirteenth century B.C., is highly significant, especially since *p3 ṯwfy* (Ballah Lake) and *p3 š-ḥr* (the eastern lagoon) are in the vicinity. The former is said to have papyrus plants (*mnḥw*)[215] and the latter reeds or rushes (*isw*)[216] (l. 2, 12–13).

The salient line, however, for the identification of Pi-hahiroth is 2.9, which says: "The lake of Horus (*p3 š-ḥr*) contains salt, and *p3 ḥrw* contains natron, [its] ships sail and dock." Caminos was at a loss to know how to translate the second body of water and so rendered it as "the *p3-ḥr* waters."[217] He apparently did not recognize that the word *ḥr(w)* might be Semitic. In his substantial study of Semitic words in Egyptian texts, James Hoch identifies the word *ḥrw* in this text as deriving from the Semitic root *ḫarra*, meaning canal.[218] In a translation of Pap. Anastasi III published in 2002, James Allen offers the following translation: "The Lake of Horus has salt, the Canal has natron. Its ships set out and dock. . . ."[219] He further characterizes *p3-ḥr* by saying it is the "name of a navigable, brackish body of water in the eastern Egyptian Delta, perhaps joining an arm of the Nile to the Lake of Horus."[220] What is uncanny about Allen's interpretation of this line is that the scenario he envisions is plausible in the light of our discovery of a branch of the Nile that runs through Tell el-Borg and empties into the eastern lagoon or *p3 š-ḥr*. A study of satellite images suggests that the canal trace discovered in the 1970s may have intersected with this Nile branch, in which case it served as the water source for the canal (figures 5 and 6).

If *p3 ḥr* is the Egyptian name for the East Frontier Canal, then Pap. Anastasi III demonstrates that this canal was functioning during the New Kingdom. Furthermore, if *p3 ḥr* is the feature behind Pi-hahiroth, then the Hebrew *pi*, instead of being the construct form of *peh* (mouth), would be the writing of the Egyptian definite article *p3*.

This analysis of Pap. Anastasi III 2.8–12 indicates that there may be a connection with three of the toponyms found in Exodus 14:2. Baal, *p3-ḥr*, and *p3 ṯwfy*, all associated with bodies of water, we propose correspond to Baal-Zephon, Pi-hahiroth, and *Yām sûp̱*. The fourth toponym, Migdol, as the evidence presented here suggests, was a frontier fort of the Nineteenth and Twentieth Dynasties, which spanned at least from the reign of Seti I to Ramesses III (ca. 1294–1153 B.C.), a period of 140 years. This period could be extended if Magdalu of EA 234 is the same site. The excavations at Tell el-Borg have shown the direction the military highway took from Tjaru/Sile to Canaan during New Kingdom (Late Bronze I and II). If Borg is not the Migdol of Menmaatre, then this Migdol is likely to be found around five to eight kilometers (three to five miles) to its southeast, perhaps another New Kingdom site like those documented by Oren, such as T–78 or T–116.

The possible convergence of three of the Exodus 14:2 toponyms situated in the eastern frontier in a single text, Pap. Anastasi III, and dated to the thirteenth century B.C. is highly significant. No first-millennium Egyptian text mentions these names together in a single document. Groll likewise considers this convergence to be important, stating, "One should note, moreover, that although such toponyms also appear in later texts, it is to the best of my knowledge only in texts from the time of Ramesses II and Merneptah that several appear together in the same context."[221] Additionally, the fact that new archaeological investigation also places a New Kingdom fort that incorporates the name Migdol in the same vicinity cannot be a coincidence. Clearly the thirteenth-century Egyptian texts place these four names together in the very same area of the ancient eastern Delta, present-day North Sinai, where the Bible places Migdol, Pi-hahiroth, Baal-Zephon, and *yām sûp̱*.

VI. Conclusion

What this investigation of *p3 ṯwfy* (*yām sûp̱*) and the place names associated with it in Exodus 14:2 demonstrates is that the author has a specific location in mind and that the terms correspond best to Egyptian toponyms of the thirteenth century B.C. Consequently, they cannot be attributed to an onomasticon derived from mythology. Redford's conclusion drawn in 1987, that the toponyms of the exodus story reflect the geographic realities of the sixth century, when the narratives were written, seemed plausible before the archaeological discoveries of the past fifteen years in North Sinai. Although an argument still might be made that the toponyms of the exodus story could have derived from later times, it would be because of the continuity of names from the second millennium into the first millennium. Here the case of Migdol/Magdalu is germane. It is attested in several thirteenth- and twelfth-century B.C. Egyptian sources, in the Hebrew prophets (sixth century), and in Greco-Roman–period texts. It was also noted that in these three periods, three different sites apparently bore the name Migdol.

The toponyms of Exodus 14:2 have a specificity that was certainly not necessary for a writer inventing the story or drawing on his creative imagination. The names themselves seem to serve no theological or aetiological agenda, and they are not contrived and garbled. If P were historicizing an original mythic version of the sea-crossing episode, he did a remarkable job of identifying toponyms known in New Kingdom Egypt, and they fit into a geographical zone that accords well into the generally wet paleoenvironmental situation of the late second millennium B.C. I conclude, therefore, in the light of the new archaeological and paleoenvironmental data presented here, that the geographical setting of Exodus 14 is the area between the north side of the el-Ballah Lake system and the southern tip of the eastern lagoon (i.e., the proposed location of Migdol). By P's day (fifth century B.C.), this area had radically changed. The Pelusiac had migrated fifteen to twenty kilometers to the north, meaning that the Qantara region began to dry up, resulting in dessication of the East Frontier Canal.

From a phenomenological perspective, the evidence adduced here demonstrates that the theophany of the sea crossing occurred in a specific geographical location and at a particular time in history. Neither the phenomenologist of religion, nor anyone else for that matter, is equipped to explain how the event happened or what might be the source behind it.

Here people are welcomed to speculate. However, I do not think they are free to banish the event from the realm of history because the nature of the event cannot be explained to fit a modern or postmodern worldview. For the Israelites, as the Song of the Sea suggests, it marked the end of the oppression of Egypt, and it permitted them to go to the Mountain of the God to serve Yahweh, as Moses had been directed to do in Exodus 3:12.

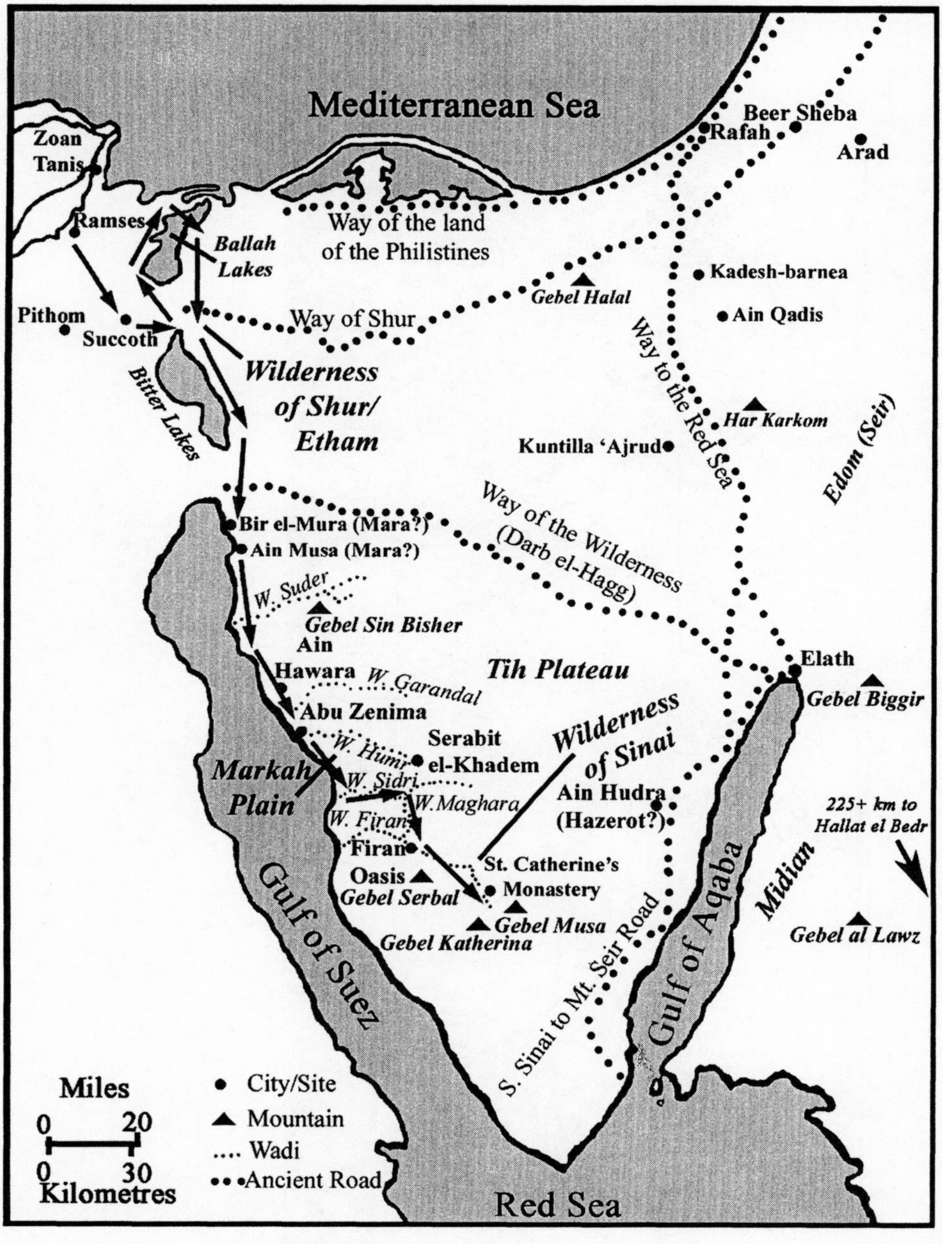

Figure 1. Map of Sinai (created by Jessica T. Hoffmeier)

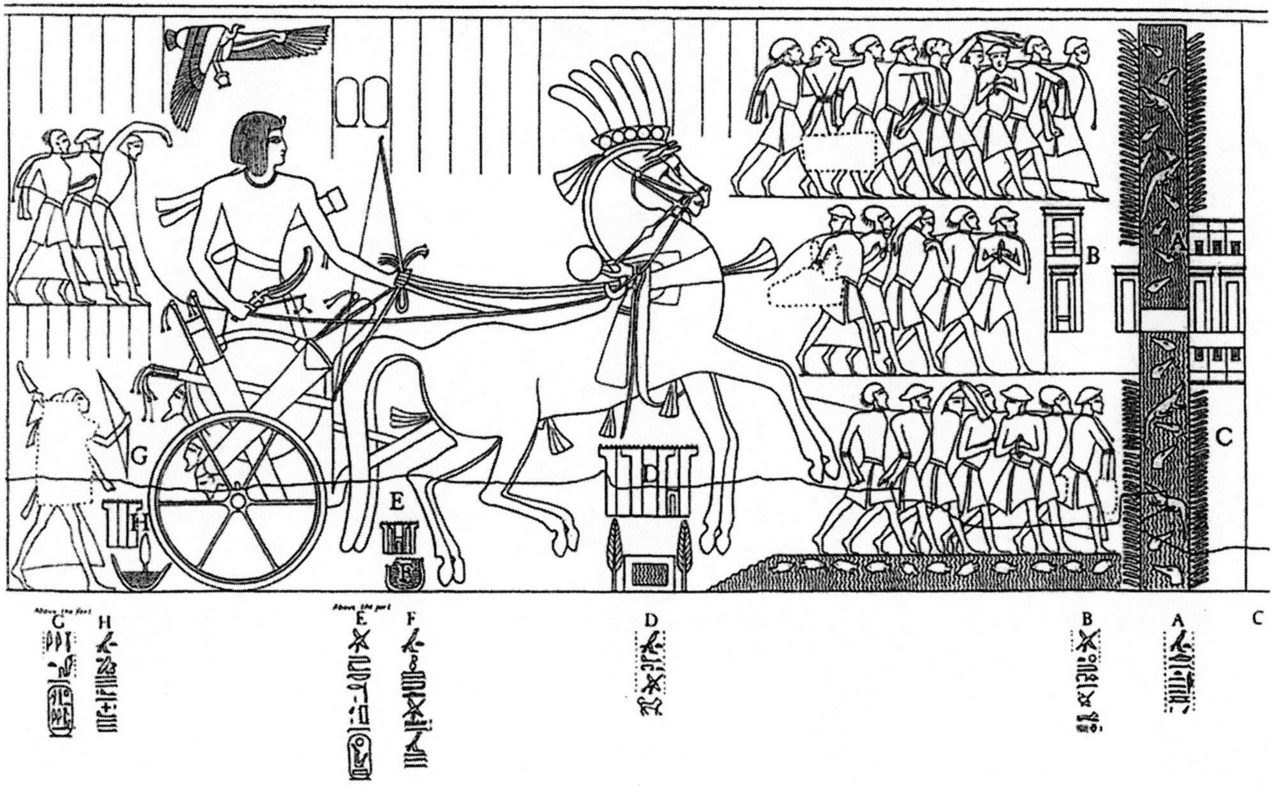

Figure 2. Seti I Relief at Karnak (from Gardiner, *JEA* 6 [1920], plate XI)

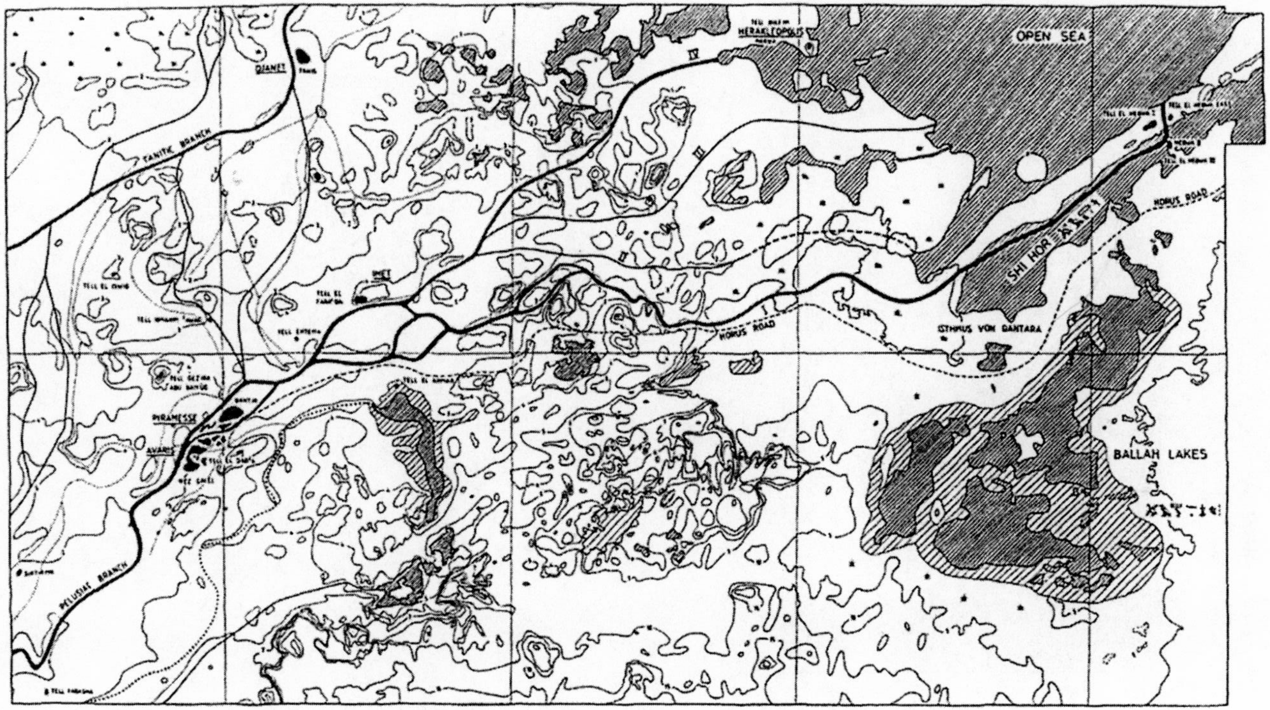

Figure 3. Bietak's map of East Delta and North Sinai (from M. Bietak, *Avaris: The Capital of the Hyksos* [London: British Museum, 1996], Fig. 1; with permission of the author)

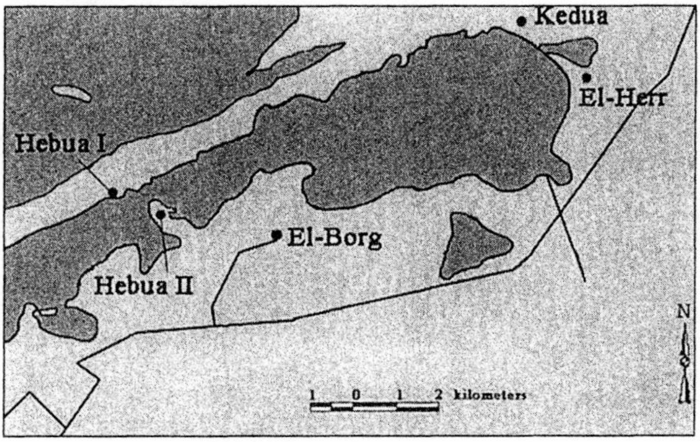

Figure 4. Map of Qantara region (based on Geographical Survey of Egypt, 1945, created by Jessica T. Hoffmeier)

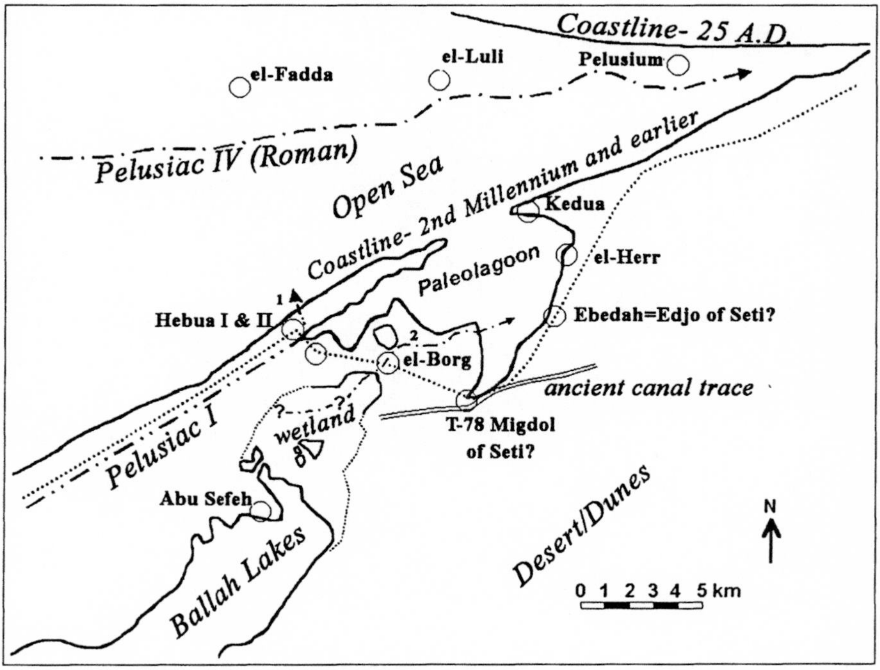

Figure 5. Map of Qantara-Pelusium area (created by Stephen Moshier, 2002)

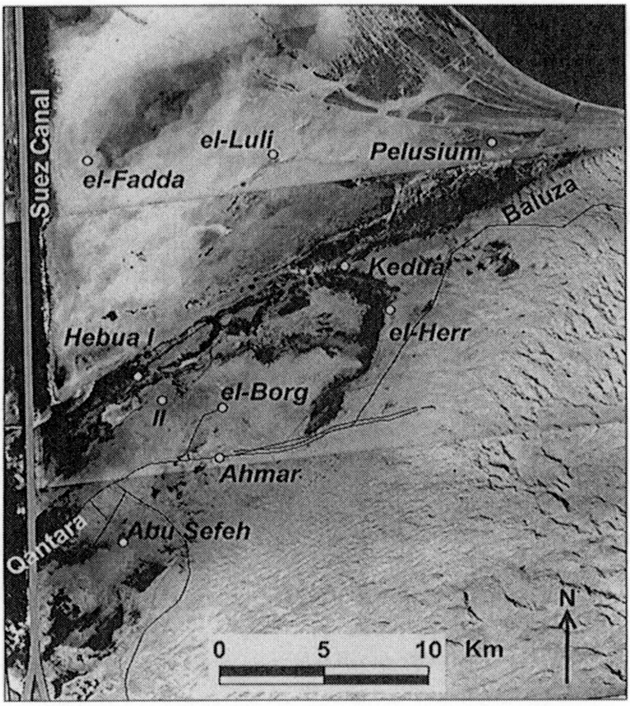

Figure 6. Corona satellite image with new geological data
(created by Stephen Moshier, 2002)

Figure 7. Wadi Feiran (photograph by James K. Hoffmeier)

Figure 8. Acacia of Sinai (photograph by James K. Hoffmeier)

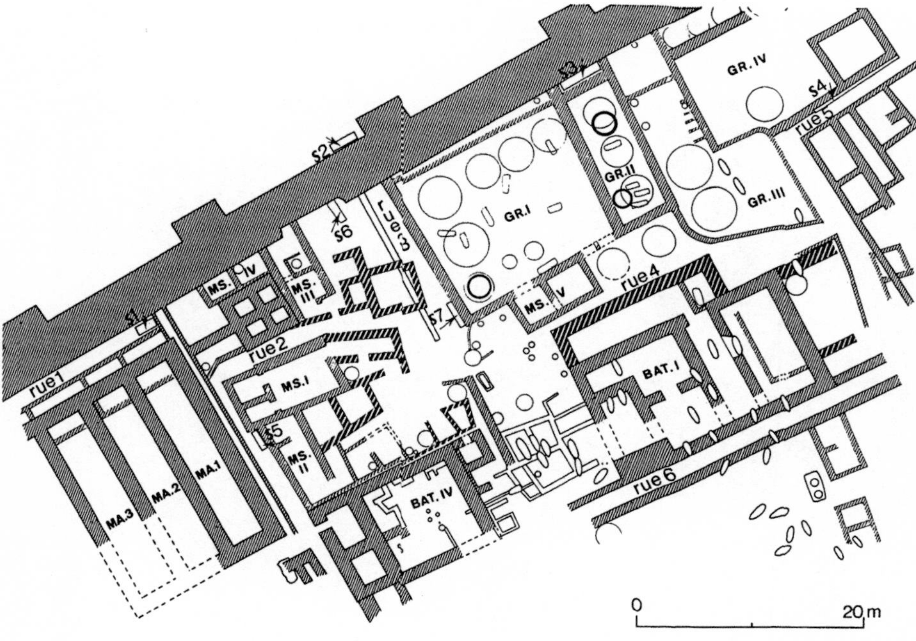

Figure 9. Plan of Hebua I (from Mohamed Abd el-Maksoud, *Tell Hebua* (1981–1991), Fig. 1; with permission of the author)

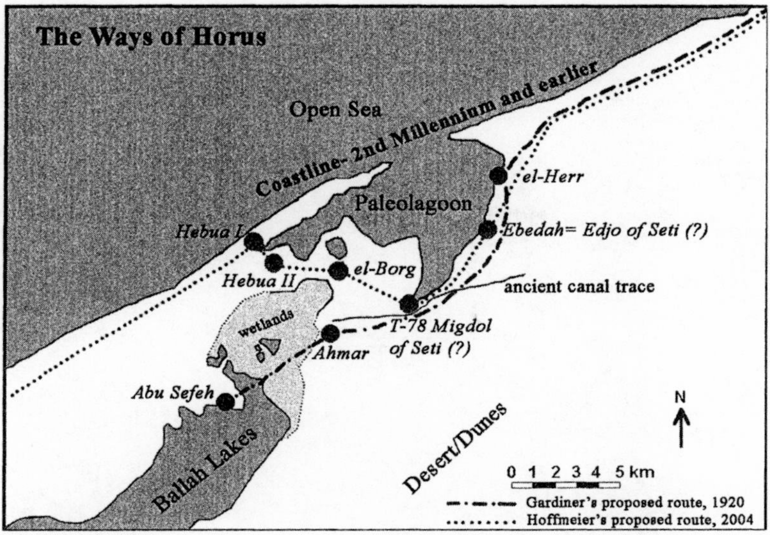

Figure 10. Map showing "Ways of Horus" routes of Gardiner and Hoffmeier (created by Jessica T. Hoffmeier)

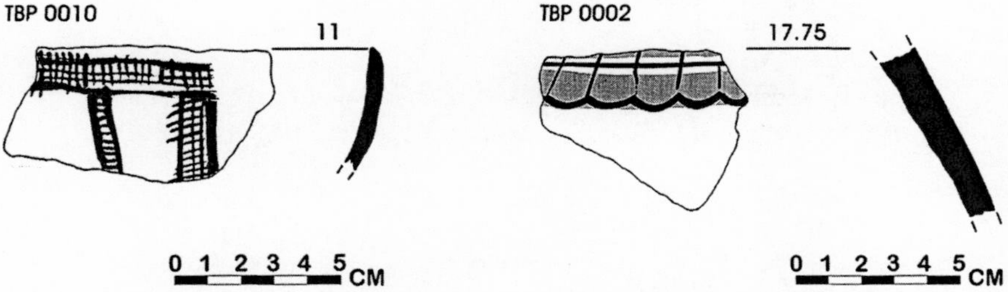

Figure 11. Potsherds from surface survey at Tell el-Borg, May 1999 (drawings by Lyla Pinch Brock)

Figure 12. Relief of deity from Tell el-Borg (drawings by Lyla Pinch Brock)

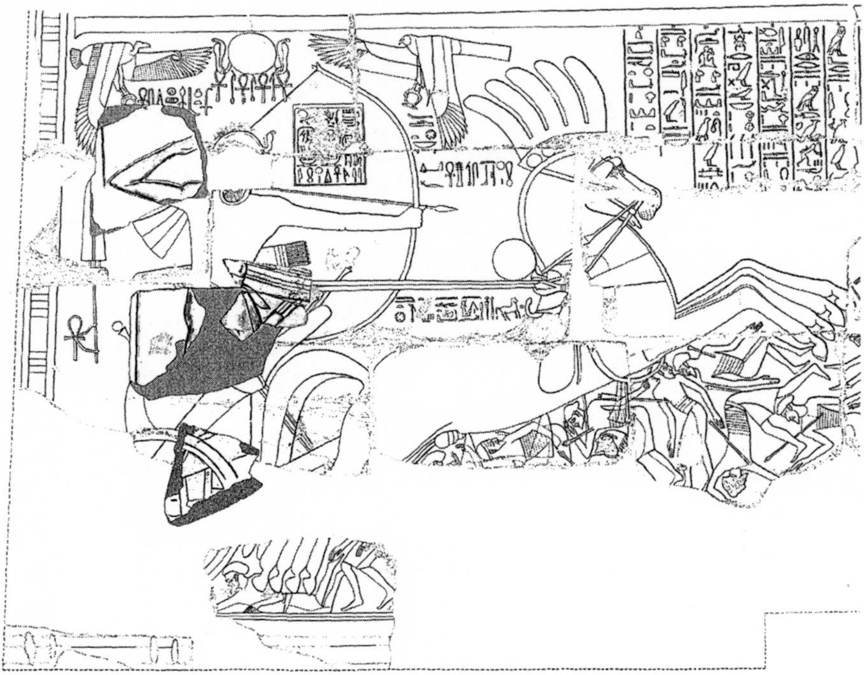

Figure 13. Reconstruction of Tell el-Borg reliefs, superimposed on relief of Seti I from Karnak (drawing and reconstruction by Lyla Pinch Brock)

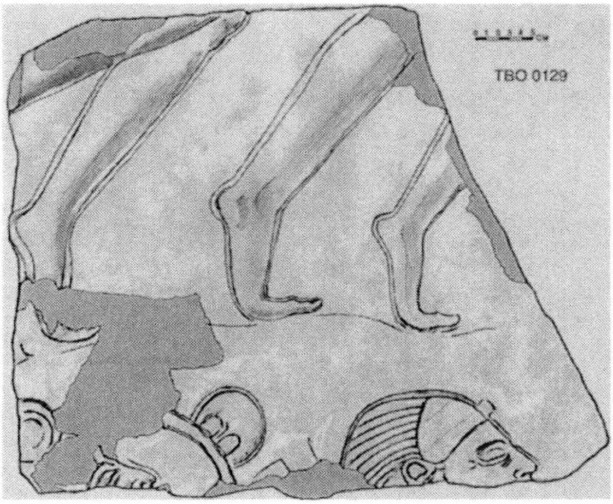

Figure 14. Relief of fleeing enemies from Tell el-Borg (drawings by Lyla Pinch Brock)

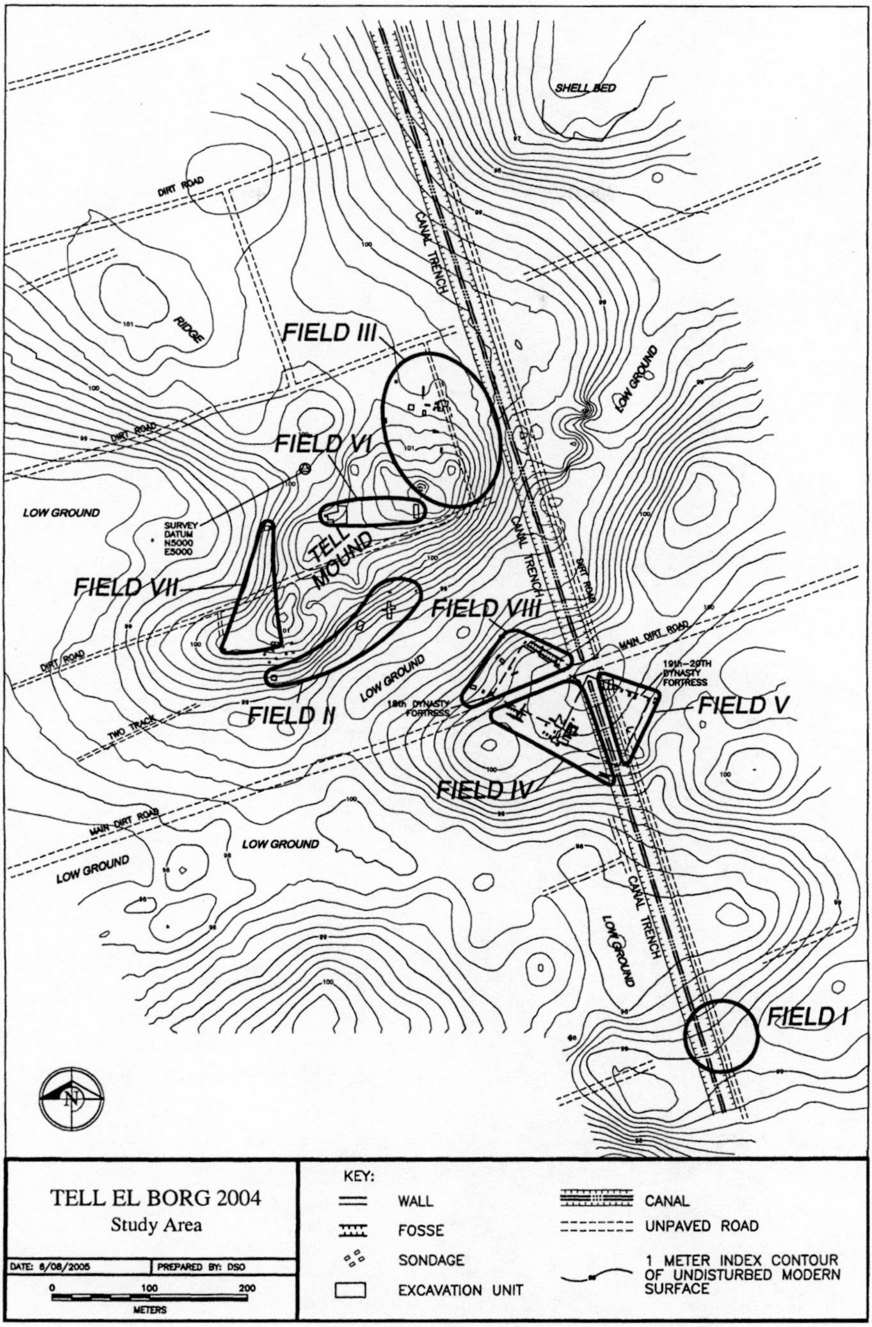

Figure 15. Site plan of Tell el-Borg

Figure 16. Ramesside-period fort wall at Tell el-Borg, Field IV (2004; photograph by Heather Alexander)

Figure 17. Moat of Eighteenth Dynasty fort at Tell el-Borg, Field IV (2002; photograph by Heather Alexander)

Figure 18. Outer corner of moat under Ramesside-period fort wall, Field IV (2001; photograph by Heather Alexander)

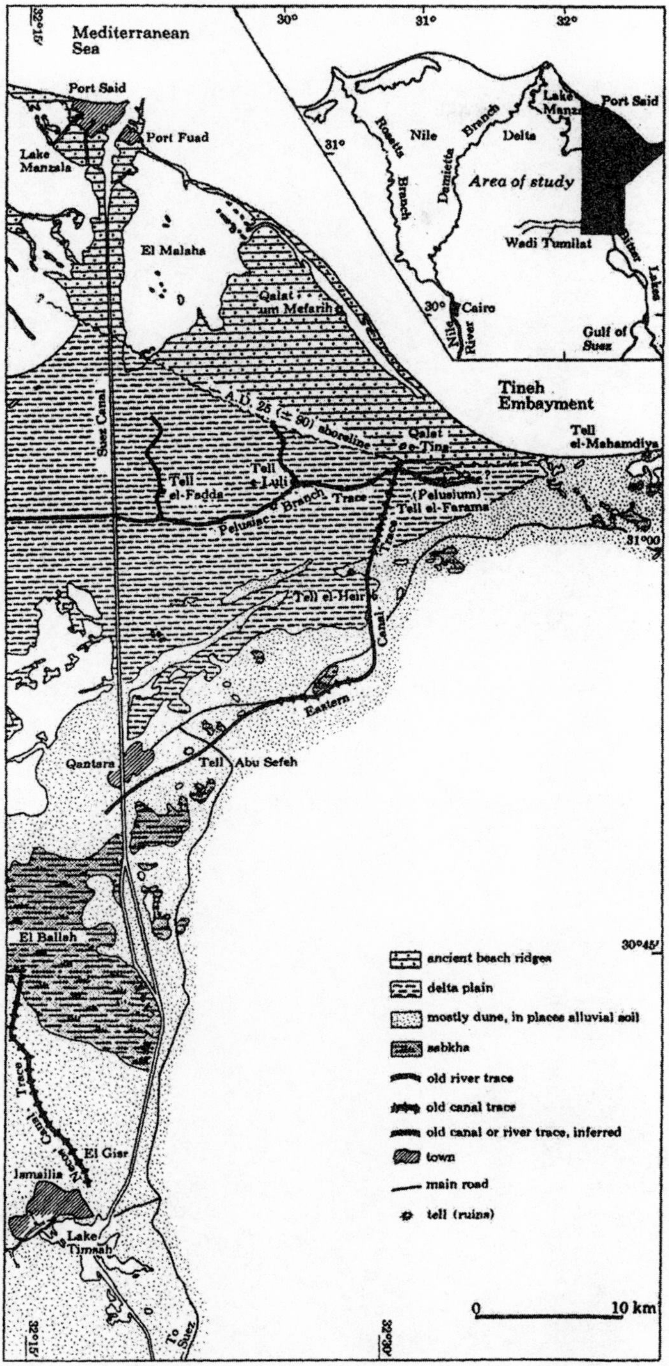

Figure 19. Map showing route of ancient canals in North Sinai (from A. Sneh, T. Wessbrod, and I. Perath, in *Scientific American* 63 [1975]: 543; with the permission of the authors)

Figure 20. ‘Ain Qudeirat, Sinai (2001; photograph by James K. Hoffmeier)

Figure 21. Gebel Sin Bishr, Sinai (2004; photograph by James K. Hoffmeier)

Figure 22. "Pillars" from Hazor (photograph courtesy of the Seltz Foundation Hazor Excavations in Memory of Yigael Yadin)

Figure 23. Burning bush beside chapel at St. Catherine's Monastery (photograph by James K. Hoffmeier)

Figure 24. St. Catherine's Monastery (photograph by James K. Hoffmeier)

Figure 25. Gebel Musa (photograph by James K. Hoffmeier)

Figure 26. Gebel Safsafa (photograph by James K. Hoffmeier)

Figure 27. The Rahah Plain (photograph by James K. Hoffmeier)

Figure 28. Gebel Serbal (photograph by James K. Hoffmeier)

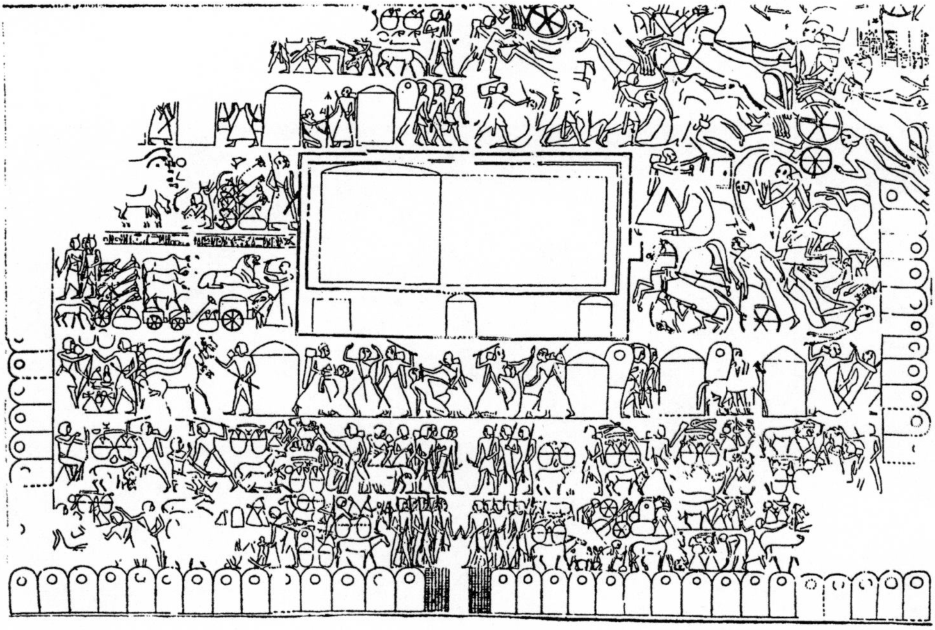

Figure 29. Ramesses II's tent camp at Kadesh (from Hoffmeier, "Tents in Egypt and the Ancient Near East," *JSSEA* VII, no. 3 [1977])

Figure 30. Asian man from the tomb of Khnumhotep at Beni Hasan (from Percy Newberry, *Beni Hasan*, vol. 1 [London: Kegan Paul, 1893], plate 31)

Figure 31. Well in Wadi Humr (photograph by James K. Hoffmeier)

Figure 32. Serabit el-Khadim Temple (photograph by James K. Hoffmeier)

Figure 33. Mine M text at Serabit el-Khadim (photograph by James K. Hoffmeier)

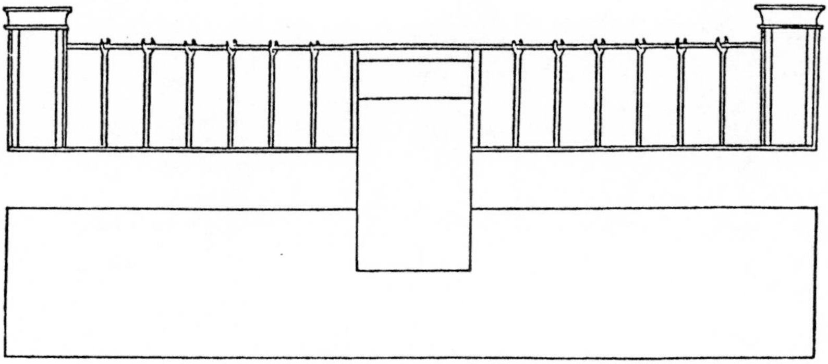

Figure 34. Tent of purification from the tomb of Pepi Ankh at Meir (from Hoffmeier, "The Origins of the Tent of Purification," *SAK* 9 [1981]: 168)

Figure 35. Royal tent of Ramesses II from Abu Simbel Temple
(photograph by James K. Hoffmeier)

Figure 36. Camp of Ashurbanipal, British Museum
(photograph by Jessica T. Hoffmeier)

Figure 37. Gold shrine from tomb of Tutankhamun in Cairo Museum (photograph by James K. Hoffmeier)

Figure 38. Hathshepsut and Thutmose III behind the bark of Amun-re at Karnak Temple (photograph by James K. Hoffmeier)

Figure 39. Seti I's portable shrine for Amun and Re at Karnak Temple (photograph by James K. Hoffmeier)

Figure 40. Ramesses III at Medinet Habu (photograph by James K. Hoffmeier)

Figure 41. Soldiers and trumpeter from Deir el-Bahri Temple of Hatshepsut (from E. Naville, *The Temple of Deir el-Bahri VI* [London: EES, 1908], plate CLV)

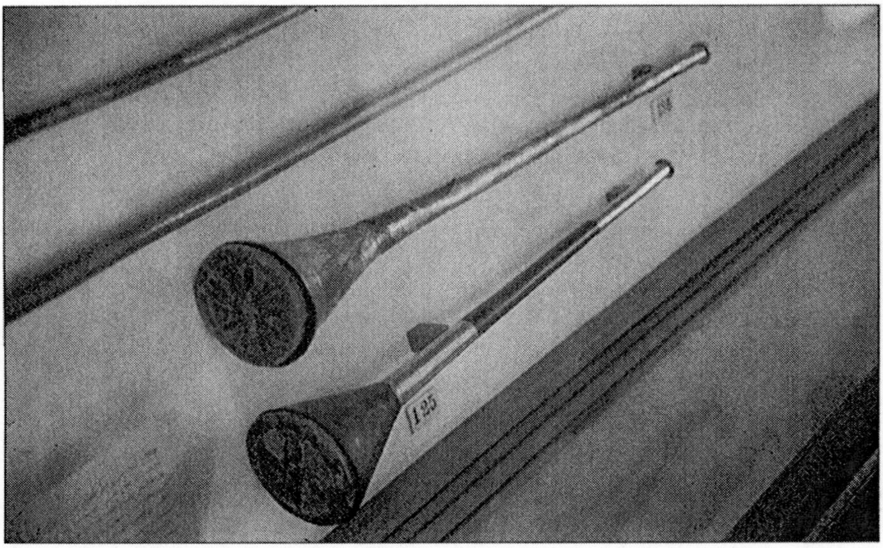

Figure 42. Trumpets of Tutankhamun, Cairo Museum (photograph by James K. Hoffmeier)

Figure 43. Oxcarts from Akhenaten's temple at Karnak
(from Donald Redford, ed., *The Akhenaten Temple Project*, Vol. 2
[Toronto: University of Toronto, 1988], plate 31; with permission of the author)

Figure 44. Seti I battle against Shasu Bedouin from Karnak Temple
(photograph by James K. Hoffmeier)

Figure 45. Merneptah scene of Canaanites/Israelites (?)
(photograph by James K. Hoffmeier)

Figure 46. Merneptah scene of Shasu/Israelites (?)
(photograph by James K. Hoffmeier)

6

The Mountain of God

Now Mount Sinai was wrapped in smoke, because the LORD had descended upon it in fire; the smoke went up like the smoke of a kiln, while the whole mountain shook violently.

—Exod. 19:17

Great things are done when men and mountains meet.

—William Blake

I. Sacred Mountains: Phenomenological Considerations

The phenomenological approach to the study of religion was introduced in some detail above (chapter 2, §II). There it was shown that sacred space was established as a result of a human encounter with the numinous, the divine. Phenomenologists have long recognized the central role played by mountains in theophanies throughout the ancient Near East, and in the Bible as well. Often sacred mountains are called "cosmic mountains," from the German *Weltberg.*[1] Because of their physical elevations, mountains are often viewed as a meeting place between the heavens and the earth, a link from the mundane to the sublime. W. B. Kristensen and Gerardus van der Leeuw both recognized that the mountains were viewed as the source of life in many religious traditions.[2] Mircea Eliade made three cogent observations concerning sacred mountains, which he identified with the Cosmic Center:

1. the Sacred Mountain—where heaven and earth meet—is situated at the center of the world;

2. every temple or palace—and, by extension, every sacred city or royal residence—is a Sacred Mountain, thus becoming a Center;
3. being an *axis mundi*, the sacred city or temple is regarded as the meeting point of heaven, earth, and hell.[3]

Significantly, Eliade further recognized that sacred mountains "are the especial domain of all hierophanies of atmosphere, and therefore the dwelling of the gods. Every mythology has its sacred mountain, some more or less famous variation on the Greek Olympus."[4] The Ugaritic pantheon, for instance, resided on Mt. Saphon, which is likened to Olympus in Greece, and is thought of as "the mountain of the gods."[5] On the northern border of ancient Israel with Phoenicia stands Mt. Hermon, a massif that is approximately fifty kilometers (thirty-six miles) long and twenty-five kilometers (eighteen miles) at its widest, and its highest summit is 2,814 meters (9,145 feet). On its major peaks and surrounding the mountain more than twenty temples have been identified, clearly indicating the sacred nature of this mountain.[6] These finds confirm what the name Hermon suggests. A widely attested Semitic word, חרם *(ḥrm)* means "to dedicate," "forbidden because sacred," and "sacred precinct."[7] Mount Hermon, הַר חֶרְמוֹן, has been rendered "sacred mountain."[8] This same root stands behind the Arabic name for the Temple Mount in Jerusalem, Harem el-Sharif, "the noble sanctuary."[9]

The Canaanite and Mesopotamian idea of sacred mountain has been studied in some detail,[10] and there is some evidence that the Sumerian ziggurat was intended to represent a cosmic mountain, symbolizing the link between heaven and earth.[11] Because the Tigris-Euphrates Valley is such a flat plain, the ziggurat seems to be an architectural representation of a mountain that was absent in the natural terrain.

As in ancient Sumer, mountains do not dominate the terrain of the Nile Valley. Nevertheless, the cosmic hill is well represented in the religious traditions of Egypt. The primeval hill where creation occurred is associated with two words in Egyptian, *i3t* with the determinative  and *ḫʿ* plus .[12] Both show a mound or hill, with the latter showing the sun rising over it. Such elevated spots, where the sun (Re) shone after the floodwaters subsided, is where creation occurred, and these in turn became the spots on which temples were built, and in particular where the *st ḏsrt*, the "sacred place" or holy of holies, was located.[13]

Furthermore, various deities and their theophanies are associated with mountains. Min is associated with the mountainous region near the Red Sea. On an Eleventh-Dynasty stela in the Wadi Hammamat, Min bears the epithet "lord of highlands (*ḫ3swt*), at this august mountain (*ḏw*)."[14] Gebel Barkal in Nubia, beginning in the Eighteenth Dynasty, became the center of the worship of Amun-Re. Six temples, spanning from the fifteenth century B.C. down to Roman times, are built around the foot of the mountain.[15] According to

Thutmose III's Gebel Barkal stela, the mountain's name is *p3 ḏw wʿb*, "the pure mountain."[16] Timothy Kendall, who directs the current excavations there, observes that "from at least the 18th Dynasty, Gebel Barkal was identified as a sacred hill."[17] The impressive limestone cliffs of western Thebes are the setting for the famous funerary temple of Hatshepsut at Deir el-Bahri. Texts refer to this mountain as "that holiest (*ḏsry*)[18] mountain," and Hatshepsut's temple is called *ḏsr ḏsrw*, "holy of holies."[19] The theophany that gave rise to the name and sacred character of this spot is a manifestation of the goddess Hathor, whose chapel is situated behind the funerary temple.[20]

Because across the Near East, even where mountains play little or no role in the geography, sacred mountains are closely associated with theophanies, cosmology, mythology, and temples, it is not surprising that the same is true in ancient Israel. Furthermore, the mountains associated with theophanies and the dwellings of deity, be they Olympus, Zaphon, Zion, Barkal, or the peaks of Hammamat, are located in geographical space as we know it. They are not mythological in the sense of belonging to the world of the gods but are present and visible to humans. One would thus expect that Mt. Sinai would also be a mountain in a specific area that the ancient Israelites could have identified. Certainly from a phenomenological perspective the mountain of God should be so understood, as it was the place of ancient Israel's ultimate theophany.

The Torah describes the theophany at Mt. Sinai as including fire, smoke, and quaking of the land (Exod. 19:16–20). This indeed is the language of kratophany, an overwhelming encounter with the other. In anticipation of the theophany, Moses is instructed to do the following: "You shall set limits for the people all around, saying, 'Be careful not to go up the mountain or to touch the edge of it. Any who touch the mountain shall be put to death' " (Exod. 19:12). The principle of protecting the sacred from the profane is obvious. The people of Israel were overwhelmed, experiencing what Otto called the *majestas*, which prompted them to request that they stay away from the mountain and allow Moses to act as their mediator during future oracles (Exod. 20:18–20). It is little wonder that Mt. Sinai/Horeb is called the mountain of God. The importance of mountains in the Bible extends beyond Sinai.

When Jacob had his dream and theophany, he responded by saying "Surely the LORD is in this place—and I did not know it!" (Gen. 28:16). And he was afraid, and said, "How awesome is this place! This is none other than the house of God, and this is the gate of heaven," and he erected a pillar (*maṣṣebâ*) and poured a libation and named the place Bethel, "house of God" (Gen. 28:16–18). Jacob's reaction reflects the typical human response to an encounter with the sacred. Subsequently when God appeared to Jacob in Haran, he introduced himself, saying "I am the God of Bethel" (Gen. 31:13). Upon his return to Canaan, Jacob returns to the holy spot at Bethel and erects an altar (מִזְבֵּחַ: *mizbbēah*) to God (Gen. 35:1–15). Significantly, Bethel is located in the mountainous (הָר: *har*) country of Ephraim, and in later history, because of Jacob's theophany it served as an important cultic center during the period of the Judges (Judg. 20:18, 26; 21:2; 1 Sam. 10:3); from the time of Jereboam I it became the preeminent cult center in the southern part of the Northern Kingdom (cf. 1 Kings 12:29–30; Amos 3:14; 7:10–13).

Jerusalem was also located in the mountainous region of Judah, and the mountain on which Solomon's temple was built was called Mt. Zion (e.g., 2 Kings 19:31; Ps. 2:6; Ps. 48:2, 11; Ps. 74:2; 78:68; 125:1; Isa 4:5; 8:18; 10:12; 18:7; 24:23; 29:8). Its sanctity was established by the theophany at the end of David's reign (2 Sam. 24:14–25). After its destruction in 586 B.C., the second temple was built in its place between 520 and 515 B.C. (Ezra 6:1–15), and then Herod's temple, built largely between 19 B.C. and 9 B.C., superseded it and continued until its destruction in A.D. 70.[21] And today, the Western (or Wailing) Wall remains the holiest place for worship in the Jewish tradition.

How is such a tradition sustained? In part, the idea of the continuity of the sacred is pivotal. But this raises a more complex question: How did knowledge of the whereabouts of Mt. Sinai fade from memory so that no one today can be certain of its location, even though it is arguably the most important sacred spot for ancient Israel's religious history? Why was Mt. Sinai not a place of regular pilgrimage and a cult center throughout ancient Israel's history? An explanation for this problem will be approached in chapter 8.

II. Mt. Sinai or Mt. Horeb?

The Torah associates the theophany in the Sinai wilderness with a mountain. As was noted above in chapter 3, the central and southern regions of Sinai have many mountains. There is some understandable confusion concerning the name of the mountain, since it is associated with both Sinai (סִינָי) and Horeb (חוֹרֵב). Biblical scholars who adhere to the documentary hypothesis typically regard the dual usage as indication of the different sources that stand behind narratives. Sinai is the name used by J and P, whereas E and D opt for Horeb.[22] For those who believe that Horeb is the Deuteronomist's mountain, the appearance of Sinai in the Blessing of Moses in Deuteronomy 33:2 is hard to explain. The term Sinai is applied to a wilderness (*mi<u>d</u>bār*), and mount (*har*) Sinai occurs sixteen times (Exod. 19:18, 20, 23; 24:16; 31:18; 34:2, 4, 27, 32; Lev. 7:38; 25:1; 26:46; 27:34; Num. 31; 28:6; Neh. 9:13). The term Horeb is written seventeen times in the Hebrew Scriptures (Exod. 3:1; 17:6; 33:6; Deut. 1:2, 6, 19; 4:10, 15; 5:2; 9:8; 18:16; 29:1; 1 Kings 8:9; 19:8; 2 Chron. 5:10; Psa. 106:19; Mal. 4:4). Only once is "Mount Horeb" used, in Exodus 33:6. This lone reference might not actually name the mountain, but *har ḥôrē<u>b</u>* in this case might be a genitive of association, which could be translated "mountain of Horeb," that is, a mountain located in Horeb, rather than a mountain named Horeb.[23] Exodus 3:1 states that Moses "came to Horeb, the mountain of God," and Deuteronomy 1:6 declares: "The LORD our God spoke to us at Horeb, saying, 'You have stayed long enough at this mountain.'" All other references use Horeb as a regional name. So it is hardly the case that two different names are found in the Bible for the mountain of revelation. These references indicate that the sacred mountain is located within Horeb. Although it was noted in chapter 3, §III, that the origin and the derivation of the word Sinai is unclear, Horeb's meaning is certain—a dry wasteland and devastation—and is cognate with Akkadian *ḫurbu* and *ḫuribtu*, which mean "desert."[24] Interestingly, never does the expression "wilderness of Horeb" occur, perhaps because that would be redundant.

A. D. H Mayes offers two scenarios to explain the origin of these terms: "They may have been originally two distinct mountains, or, more likely, Horeb was originally the designation of a region in which Sinai lay, and gradually it came to be understood as simply synonymous with Sinai."[25] Based upon Exodus 17:1–7, Nahum Sarna proposes that Horeb might have been a larger geographical region because Rephidim is situated in Horeb, before the Israelites arrived at Sinai in Exodus 19:2.[26] This is a reasonable suggestion. As noted previously, the meaning and origin of the name Sinai is uncertain. Could it be the name given by local tribes such as Amalekites or Midianites who frequented the peninsula? It is obvious that the term Horeb is descriptive, reflective of the terrain, and was possibly given by the Israelites. Consequently, these two different names could be used interchangeably in the Bible.

III. Where Is Mt. Sinai?

The location of Mt. Sinai, the mountain of God, has never been identified with certainty. Many candidates for Mt. Sinai, however, have been proposed by earlier Christian-era pilgrims and monks, as well as nineteenth-century explorers and biblical scholars. More recent suggestions have proposed locating this mountain in north-central, central, and southern Sinai, as well as in Edom and Arabia. None, however, has any convincing archaeological evidence to support the identification. This is surprising, given the importance of this mountain to the origins of Israel's religion as presented in the Torah. One would think that with the details offered on the route to Mt. Sinai from Egypt in the Numbers 33 itinerary and the details provided in Exodus 15:22–19:2, following the trail to Mt. Sinai should be relatively easy. The fact that all scholars who have tried to locate Mt. Sinai over the past 1,500 years have used the Bible as the primary source for their investigation shows that such an endeavor is no simple exercise, or there would be a consensus on the identity of the mountain. For some recent writers in the minimalist mold, the lack of certainty about the location and archaeological support means that the Bible is not speaking of real events that occurred in a specific area.[27] The phenomenological approach to religion insists that the scores of references in the Bible to the revelation at Sinai must be considered as evidence that something occurred to give rise to the tradition.

Let us now consider the biblical evidence.

The Wilderness Itineraries

Before proceeding and examining several crucial texts that bear on the location of Mt. Sinai, the so-called wilderness itinerary needs to be considered for what it can tell us about the location. The term "itinerary" has been applied to the literature that deals with Israel's travels in Sinai by many scholars in recent decades, and this has been recognized as a particular genre.[28] Biblical scholars are inclined to consider the itineraries, be they in Exodus or Numbers, to be derived from the P source because of its terse and formulaic style.[29] Noth, on the other hand, spoke of the itinerary as being formed from a collation of sources.[30]

Fortunately, ancient itineraries from the first and second millennia have survived from Mesopotamian and Egyptian sources. Graham Davies has analyzed some of these texts and compared them with the itineraries in the Torah. He determined that the "wilderness itineraries are not isolated, but belong to a widely-attested literary genre."[31] Furthermore, he noted that most ancient itineraries derive from military campaigns, and hence it is appropriate to consider the biblical portrayal of the events of the exodus and wilderness as a military expedition.[32]

Egyptian toponym lists from New Kingdom temples were in some cases, as Donald Redford has demonstrated, composed from actual itineraries, which in turn drew from the daybook of the king's house.[33] Rather than simply being a list of toponyms, the Thutmose III itinerary provides additional data, as Redford's study demonstrates. He observed "the combination of settlement names with geographical terms. In fact, the same genres are represented: mountain (*d̲w*), valley (*šdrt*), stream (*ḫd*), spring (*'ynn*). These are clearly markers for the traveler, indicating major geographical features he will have to negotiate."[34] The Hebrew wilderness itineraries include similar geographical features that are found in the section of Thutmose III's itinerary from the Transjordan. For instance, Exodus 14:2–3 mentions "the sea" (*hayyām*) and "the wilderness" (*hammid̲bār*), and that "at Elim there were twelve springs and seventy palm trees." Subsequently various mountains are named (i.e., Mount Shepher and Mount Hor: Num. 33:23–24, 37).

Charles Krahmalkov has recently described the Egyptian toponym lists as "Egyptian maps of the Late Bronze Age Palestine."[35] Furthermore, he has identified parallel sequences of some of the Transjordanian toponyms in Egyptian itineraries and those in the book of Numbers. These observations led him to conclude that the Hebrew itineraries are very old, originating in the Late Bronze Age. Krahmalkov offers a very positive assessment of the historical worth of the biblical itineraries: "The account sounds credible enough, even authoritative, as if based on real and reliable sources. It certainly creates in the mind of even the most critical reader the impression of historical fact. After all, the historian is absolute and specific: He describes the Transjordanian route the invaders took in quite remarkable detail. . . . On the face of it, this passage [Num. 33:45b–50] is an impressive and credible piece of ancient historical writing."[36]

When these Egyptian itineraries are examined, they compare very favorably to those in the Pentateuch.[37] Pap. Anastasi I, dating to the reign of Ramesses II, contains the words of a bragging scribe to his colleague about his knowledge of travel to and in different parts of the Levant.[38] He describes travel routes, names of forts, cities, water sources, the challenges of finding enough water, and the trials of having to deal with the Shasu-Bedouin. This is not unlike the accounts in the Israelite wilderness travels that identify sites, oases, wells, lack of water, and a hostile clash with Amalekites. The similarities between the two suggest that the "itinerary" genre and the nature of travel accounts, not the canons of the Priestly school, explain the style of the wilderness itineraries in the Pentateuch.

The following chart compares the Exodus and Numbers itineraries. For the following geographical discussions, see figure 1.

Exodus Itinerary	*Numbers Itinerary*
Departed Rameses month one, day fifteen (12:18, 29 ff.)	Departed from Rameses, month one, day fifteen (33:3, 5)
To Succoth (12:37; 13:20)	Camped at Succoth (33:5)
Camped at Etham at edge of wilderness (13:20)	Camped at Etham at edge of wilderness (33:6)
Turned back to the sea in front of Pi-hahiroth, between Migdol and the sea, in front of Baal-zephon (14:2)	Turned back to Pi-hahiroth in front of Baal-Zephon, camped in front of Migdol (33:7)
Passed through the sea (14:26–39)	Crossed the sea into the wilderness (33:8a)
	Set out from Hahiroth (33:8b)
From the *yām sûp̱*, they went into the wilderness of Shur (15:22)	
Three days in the wilderness (of Shur)	Three-day journey in the wilderness of Etham (33:8a)
Came to Marah (15:22b–23a)	Camped at Marah (33:8b)
Came to Elim—twelve springs and seventy palms (15:27)	Camped at Elim: twelve springs and seventy palms (33:9)

Set out from Elim (16:1)	Set out from Elim and camped by *yām sûp̱* (33:10)
Came to the wilderness of Sin (16:1a) which is between Elim and Sinai; on the fifteenth day of the second month	Camped in wilderness of Sin (33:11)
Moved on through the wilderness of Sin by stages	Camped at Dophkah (33:12) Camped at Alush (33:13)
Camped at Rephidim, no water (17:1)	Camped at Rephidim, no water (33:14)
Third new moon, arrived at wilderness of Sinai (19:1)	
Set out from Rephidim and came into and camped in the wilderness of Sinai and camped before the mountain (19:2)	Set out from Rephidim Camped in wilderness of Sinai (33:15)

There is considerable agreement between the two lists, although some variants exist. Both agree that:

1. the departure date from Egypt is the fifteenth day of the first month;
2. the third campsite is by the sea of passage, which was reached after turning back from the second site, Etham;
3. a three-day journey into the wilderness followed the crossing of the sea;
4. the distance traveled after crossing the sea to Mt. Sinai is greater than the distance from Rameses to *yām sûp̱*. Seven toponyms are named in Exodus, while nine are listed in Numbers 33, of places where the Israelites camped (וַיַּחֲנוּ). Dophkah and Alush are mentioned after the departure from Elim in Numbers 33:12–13, whereas Exodus 17:1 generically states: "From the wilderness of Sin the whole congregation of the Israelites journeyed by stages." The Numbers itinerary, apparently, offers the names of two of the stages. The word for stage (מסע) has been understood to mean "a day's journey."[39]

Exodus 16:1 reports that they arrived at the Wilderness of Sin on the fifteenth day of the second month, that is, a month after departing Rameses. The next important chronological note indicates the date of the arrival in the vicinity of Mt. Sinai: "On the third new moon after the Israelites had gone out of the land of Egypt, on that very day, they came into the wilderness of Sinai" (Exod. 19:1). The inclusion of the phrase "on that very day" (בַּיּוֹם הַזֶּה), suggests that this was the first day of the following month, or two weeks after the date provided by Exodus 16:1.[40] If this interpretation of these passages is correct, a period of six weeks passed from the departure from Egypt until the arrival at Mt. Sinai. Certainly this block of time does not represent how much time was actually required to cover the distance, as the Exodus or Numbers itineraries never record how much time was spent at each campsite, or how much time it took to travel between encampments. This means that the Torah is interested both in dates of departure and arrival at key locations, and distances traveled, but these are not one and the same.

Determining the exact number of campsites between *yām sûp* and Mt. Sinai presents a challenge. After departing from the sea-crossing, Numbers 33:8a reports "a three-day journey into the wilderness of Etham," but no campsites are mentioned until Marah in 33:8b. It is unclear whether the three-day journey should be added to the eight named encampments that follow (Num. 33:8b–15), or if the three campsites after the statement about the three-day journey in 33:8a are incorporated into the three-day journey. In the latter scenario, eight days of travel represented the distance from the sea, whereas in the former, eleven days are intended. Exegetes and geographers do not agree on which is the correct interpretation. Simons, for example, speaks of "the three days' march between the time of their escape across the Sea of Reeds and the arrival at Marah."[41] Cassuto, likewise, argued that they came to Marah "after the period [three days] mentioned."[42] This view is supported by the fact that during the three days they found no water; when the Israelites arrived at Marah water was available, but because it was bitter, it could not be drunk (cf. Exod. 15:22–23).

In the event that eleven days' distance is the correct interpretation, then it might represent a symmetrical pattern: eleven days from the sea to Mt. Sinai, and an eleven-day journey from Mt. Sinai/Horeb to Kadesh-Barnea, as reported in Deuteronomy 1:2. Assuming this scenario as the correct understanding of Numbers 33:8–13, it would mean that the distance between the sea crossing and Mt. Sinai, and between Mt. Sinai and Kadesh-Barnea, should be approximately the same. Interestingly, in 1819 John Burkhardt traveled by camel—at a human's walking pace—from Cairo to Gebel Musa in eleven days. He departed from Cairo on the evening of April 20 and arrived at St. Catherine's Monastery on May 1.[43] Several decades late, Robinson described the pace of travel of his caravan and their Beduoin who accompanied them as follows: "They walked lightly and gaily by our side; often outstripping the camels for a time, and then often lagging behind; they seldom seemed tired at night."[44] He typically traveled ten to twelve hours, at a pace of about two miles per hour.[45]

Travel in the Bible and in other Near Eastern texts is measured in terms of the number of days of travel required to cover the distance (cf. Gen. 30:36; Exod. 3:18, 5:3, 8:27; Num. 10:33, 11:31, 33:8; Deut. 1:2; 1 Kings 19:4; Jon. 3:3–4). Nineteenth-century explorers who traveled—typically on camels—in the desert terrain of Sinai and adjacent territories, attempted to determine the distance one could travel in a day. One such investigator, H. Clay Trumbull, calculated that fifteen to eighteen miles (twenty-four to twenty-nine kilometers) approximates the distance.[46] A more recent study based on texts from across the ancient Near East from the second and first millenniums was made by the historical geographer Barry Beitzel, who makes the following observation: "The evidence is generally uniform and mutually corroborating that one day's journey in the ancient world incorporated between 17 and 23 miles" (twenty-seven to thirty-seven kilometers).[47] A thorough study by Graham Davies shows that that these figures are probable, although he cautions that the data were not consistent about the distance traveled in a day's time, as circumstances could vary considerably.[48] An early second-millennium text from Mari, for instance, suggests that a caravan could move around twenty-two miles (thirty-five kilometers) per day in desert environs.[49] This figure accords well with ethnographic evidence gathered from camel and donkey caravans, which travel between sixteen and twenty-three miles (about twenty-six to thirty-seven kilometers) per day.[50] Davies believes that the measure of a day's travel originated in the distance a caravan could travel.[51] The pace of a donkey and/or camel caravan would not be greater than that of a human, because the pack animals were carrying trade goods, and the caravaneers would walk alongside the animals or lead them. This means that if a day's journey is based on the distance traveled by a caravan, then it also represents a distance that humans could cover in a day of walking.

The salient point is that a day's journey represents a fixed and understood distance, despite our inability to determine the amount precisely. This distance, however, could vary somewhat depending on the terrain. Thus when the wilderness itineraries mentioned a three-day journey (Exod. 15:22; Num. 33:8) or an eleven-day journey (Deut. 1:2), a specific distance was intended. Such a datum does not mean that a three-day journey indicated that the Israelites took only three days to get from point A to point B. Given the fact that they were traveling with flocks and herds (Exod. 12:38), one might expect a slower pace. Nevertheless, this factor does not change what the Bible meant by a day's journey. For the purpose of our investigation, the distances represented by a day's journey, or between campsites, provide us with valuable information for establishing plausible locations for some of the toponyms mentioned in the itinerary.

If we allow for a minimum of one day's travel between campsites, and assign twenty-four kilometers (fifteen miles)—a rather low figure on the basis of the above-mentioned studies—this would suggest that the trek from Rameses to Pi-hahiroth and Migdol, which is by the Sea of Reeds (and the third campsite) is about seventy-two kilometers (forty-five miles), and it is 265 kilometers (165 miles) from the sea to Mt. Sinai, if we allow for eleven campsites. Should we use the higher figure of thirty-two kilometers (twenty miles), the distance traveled before reaching *yām sûp̱* would be ninety-six kilometers (sixty miles), and from the sea to Mt. Sinai would be 352 kilometers (220 miles).

The itineraries in Exodus and Numbers concur that the distance from Rameses to the sea was relatively short, just three stops, which covered seventy-two to ninety-six kilometers (forty-five to sixty miles), whereas the march from the sea to Mt. Sinai was a much longer journey, spanning 265–352 kilometers (165–220 miles).

Exodus 3:1

When Moses fled from Pharaoh after inadvertently killing an Egyptian official, we are informed that he fled to the land of Midian (Exod. 2:11–15). There he met Jethro the priest of Midian, was hospitably taken in, and married Jethro's daughter, Zipporah. After this brief biographical note, Exodus 3:1 reports:

וּמֹשֶׁה הָיָה רֹעֶה אֶת־צֹאן יִתְרוֹ חֹתְנוֹ כֹּהֵן מִדְיָן וַיִּנְהַג אֶת־הַצֹּאן אַחַר הַמִּדְבָּר
וַיָּבֹא אֶל־הַר הָאֱלֹהִים חֹרֵבָה

"Moses was keeping the flock of his father-in-law Jethro, the priest of Midian; he led his flock beyond the wilderness, and came to Horeb, the mountain of God." A more literal reading of the last phrase should be rendered, "he came to the mountain of God, toward Horeb." Horeb is written with a directional *he* (חֹרֵבָה).[52] Exodus 3:12 makes it clear that it was this same mountain of God that Moses was to return to with the liberated Hebrews: it states, "when you have brought the people out of Egypt, you shall worship God on this mountain."

This is the first reference to the mountain where God would give the law to Moses. For some, this reference suggests that Mt. Horeb/Sinai should be found in Midian. Historical geographers generally agree that the land of Midian occupies the area of northern Arabia opposite the Gulf of Aqaba from the Sinai Peninsula.[53] It cannot be ruled out that Midianites, a pastoral-nomadic people, would have grazed their flocks in nearby Sinai. By way of analogy, the patriarch Jacob dispatched his son Joseph to check on his brothers who were tending their flocks. Genesis 37:14 reports that Joseph went from "the valley of Hebron" to Shechem, some ninty kilometers (fifty-six miles) to the north. But his brothers had already moved further north to Dothan, yet another twenty-five kilometers (fifteen and a half miles) away (Gen. 37:17). This means that the grazing of flocks took the sons of Jacob 115 kilometers (71.5 miles) from home. Consequently it might be concluded that the Midianites had a specific territory, the land of Midian, but that they could range some distance away. This interpretation is further supported by the phrase אַחַר הַמִּדְבָּר in Exodus 3:1. This could be rendered "to the west of the wilderness,"[54] that is west of Midian, hence the Sinai Peninsula.

There is also evidence within the Pentateuch that Midianites were not restricted to "the land of Midian." Prior to the entry into Canaan, when the Israelites are positioned in the plains of Moab opposite Jericho, the local Moabite king Balak had allied himself with Midianites in Numbers 22:4–7:

> Moab was in great dread of the people, because they were so numerous; Moab was overcome with fear of the people of Israel. And Moab said to the elders of Midian, "This horde will now lick up all that is around us, as an ox licks up the grass of the field." Now Balak son of Zippor was king of Moab at that time. He sent messengers to Balaam son of Beor at Pethor, which is on the Euphrates,

> in the land of Amaw, to summon him, saying, "A people has come out of Egypt; they have spread over the face of the earth, and they have settled next to me. Come now, curse this people for me, since they are stronger than I; perhaps I shall be able to defeat them and drive them from the land; for I know that whomever you bless is blessed, and whomever you curse is cursed." So the elders of Moab and the elders of Midian departed with the fees for divination in their hand; and they came to Balaam, and gave him Balak's message.

Furthermore, Cozbi, the daughter of Zur, a Midianite chieftain, was sexually involved with an Israelite in a pagan rite within the Israelite camp (Num. 25:6–15). Then in Numbers 31, we find the Israelites doing battle against the Midianites in the Plains of Moab. Specific reference is made to their towns and settlements (Num. 31:10).[55] Evidently the Midianites were not restricted to a section of northern Arabia opposite the Sinai Peninsula, but their presence is also documented in Sinai, the Arabah, and the southern Transjordan. In the latter region, archaeological surveys by Garth Bawden of Harvard University in southern Jordan have identified "Midianite" pottery from the final centuries of the second millennium B.C. (i.e., Late Bronze Age).[56] "Midianite" pottery has also been documented in the Timna shrine, likewise dating to the Late Bronze Age.[57]

Further evidence that the land of Midian was not in the Sinai Peninsula is that Exodus 3:1 does not locate Horeb in Midian. Then too we are informed in Exodus 4:18 that after the theophany, "Moses went back to his father-in-law Jethro." The phrase וַיֵּלֶךְ מֹשֶׁה וַיָּשָׁב אֶל־יֶתֶר can be translated "went and returned," that is, "went back."[58] This statement is followed by the Lord instructing Moses "in Midian" to go back to Egypt (Exod. 4:19). These data suggest that Moses was in Horeb when he was encountered at the burning bush; he then returned to Midian, and there received further divine instruction to return to Egypt.

Before departing from Mt. Sinai, Moses urged his brother-in-law, Hobab (son of Jethro/Reuel the Midianite), to join the Israelites and act as a guide during their travels to Canaan (Num. 10:29–32). Hobab was reluctant to accept Moses's offer, and declared: "I will not go, but I will go back to my own land and to my kindred" (וַיֹּאמֶר אֵלָיו לֹא אֵלֵךְ כִּי אִם־אֶל־אַרְצִי וְאֶל־מוֹלַדְתִּי אֵלֵךְ; Num. 10:30). From these texts we gather that Midian and Sinai were distinct but adjacent territories, a conclusion also reached by Manashe Har-el and Jon Levenson.[59] Recognizing this distinction is essential because there are a number of scholars who believe that the Bible locates Mt. Sinai in Midian or Edom to its north (see below, §IV B).[60]

Deuteronomy 1:2

Deuteronomy 1:2 provides cogent information regarding the location of Mt. Horeb/Sinai, stating: אַחַד עָשָׂר יוֹם מֵחֹרֵב דֶּרֶךְ הַר־שֵׂעִיר עַד קָדֵשׁ בַּרְנֵעַ, "By the way of

Mount Seir it takes eleven days to reach Kadesh-Barnea from Horeb." At the turn of the nineteenth century, S. R. Driver regarded this reference as describing "an approximate idea of the distance from Ḥoreb, the scene of the delivery of the Law, to Ḳadesh-Barnea."[61] He thought that this was indeed a meaningful datum, pointing to Edward Robinson's trek in 1838 from Gebel Musa in southern Sinai to 'Ain Qadis—a suggested location for Kadesh—a distance of around 160 miles (256 kilometers) that took precisely eleven days.[62] J. A. Thompson likewise sees this verse as referring to an "approximately correct" distance, whereas Graham Davies refers to this statement as "important and quite precise."[63] One reason that this figure is taken seriously is that the number eleven has no particularly symbolic or theological value, as numbers such as seven or twelve would have.

The reason for including this intriguing datum in the opening verses of Deuteronomy ultimately may be literary or theological. J. G. Millar has recently proposed that because Deuteronomy 1–3 is set in Moab, when the new generation of Israel had the opportunity to obey God's commandments, "The purpose of v. 2 is to bring the national failure at Kadesh Barnea to the forefront of the listener's or reader's mind, in contrast to the response demanded of Israel at Horeb."[64] This may be the case, but, as many commentators have noted, the reference to the eleven-day journey is a valuable datum.

This being the case, and using the formula offered above for a day's journey, an eleven-day journey might range between 265 and 350 kilometers (165–220 miles). Davies allows for a range of 180–250 miles (288–400 kilometers).[65] Because the identity of Kadesh-Barnea is fairly certain, Deuteronomy 1:2 becomes a useful reference for providing some range within which the biblical writers would situate Mt. Sinai.

Two oases standing less than ten kilometers (six miles) apart in northeastern Sinai, 'Ain Qudeirat and 'Ain Qadis, have both been identified as Kadesh-Barnea of the wilderness tradition. The latter was proposed by Trumbull, largely on the basis of the Arabic name, Qadis, which appears to preserve the Hebrew קָדֵשׁ בַּרְנֵעַ, Kadesh-Barnea.[66] In more recent times, Martin Noth also equated 'Ain Qadis with Kadesh-Barnea.[67] The Arabic and Hebrew words mean holy or sacred, but the meaning of בַּרְנֵעַ being uncertain, although the meaning "sanctuary at the place of conflict" has been proposed by Noth.[68] The geographer Manashe Har-el also considers 'Ain Qadis to be biblical Kadesh-Barnea.[69] Shortly after the 1956 Suez crisis, Beno Rothenberg and Yohanan Aharoni visited a number of sites in Sinai, including 'Ain Qadis. They reported the discovery of an elliptically shaped fort (40 × 30 meters/130 × 98 feet) from the early Iron Age. They were able to find ceramic evidence for a firm date "which cannot possibly be later than the tenth century and may well be earlier," and they found some Negev-Sinai wares that are notoriously hard to date, which are attributed to the local population.[70] Unfortunately, this evidence neither proves or disproves that 'Ain Qadis is biblical Kadesh, but certainly this site—especially because of the name—should not be ruled out.

Alternatively, 'Ain Qudeirat was identified with biblical Kadesh-Barnea by Sir Leonard Woolley and T. E. Lawrence (a.k.a. Lawrence of Arabia).[71] Further investigations of this site were made in the 1950s and 1970s, and now by Egyptian archaeologists with the Supreme Council for Antiquities. This oasis enjoyed human occupation very early, going back to Paleolithic through Neolithic times (60,000–7000 B.C.).[72] Early Bronze Age materials have also been found in the wadi area, but none have thus far been identified for the Late Bronze period, when the Israelites are thought to have been in the area.[73] This very early occupation around the spring shows that it has been a steady source of water from earliest times down to the present. Water from the spring overflows through the wadi, making it a lush strip of land in an otherwise barren region (figure 20).

An Israelite-period fort, from three different building periods, was excavated in modern times, first by Moshe Dothan in 1965 and subsequently by Rudolph Cohen between 1976 and 1982. The lower fort dates to the tenth century; the middle fort was built in the eighth century B.C., after the earlier one was destroyed and abandoned; and the upper fort was built on the ruins of the previous fort during the second half of the seventh century, but did not survive the Babylonian conquest of Judea in 586 B.C.[74]

Because the two candidates for Kadesh-Barnea are so close to each other, for the purpose establishing general coordinates for Sinai geography it matters little which it is. Perhaps Kadesh-Barnea of the Pentateuch referred to this oasis region in northeast Sinai, rather than one specific spot. Based upon the range established in our investigation, the distance from Mt. Sinai to Kadesh-Barnea via Mt. Seir (i.e., Ezion-geber, according to Num. 33:36) should be between about 265 and 350 kilometers (165–220 miles).

IV. Proposed Locations for Mt. Sinai

As some of the various candidates for the mountain of God are considered here, the following biblically based criteria will guide our investigation.

(1) Despite the inability of generations of scholars to locate a Mt. Sinai around which a consensus has occurred, the Torah offers sufficient details to allow an approximate region to be determined in which that mountain might be found. In other words, the information provided by the Exodus and Numbers itineraries gives the impression that Mt. Sinai has a definite location that could be traced if some of the key toponyms could be located.

(2) Our analysis of the wilderness itineraries in Exodus and Numbers in the previous section suggests that a distance of approximately 240 to 320 kilometers (150–200 miles) should separate *yām sûp̱* from Mt. Sinai.

(3) Deuteronomy 1:2 records an eleven-day journey between Mt. Sinai and Kadesh-Barnea. This distance should be around 265 to 350 kilometers (165–220 miles). Assuming that Kadesh-Barnea is in the 'Ain Qudeirat-'Ain Qadis region,

an important coordinate is established from which to measure the distance provided by the "eleven-day journey."

A. North and Central Sinai

GEBEL HELAL. Scholars such as Otto Eissfeldt and William F. Albright, as well as Major C. S. Jarvis (the British governor of Sinai in the 1920s) theorized that the exodus route saw the Israelites depart via the northeast, traveling on the barrier island that separates the Mediterranean from Lake Bardawil (Serbonis) (figure 1).[75] This lake would have been *yām sûp̱*. The route would have then gone southeast to Gebel Helal, located about forty-five kilometers (thirty miles) directly south of el-Arish; it stands 892 meters (2,900 feet) high. The data provided by the itinerary and Deuteronomy 1:2 would preclude this mountain from being a contender for the biblical Mt. Sinai. The distance from the crossing point to Gebel Helal—about sixty-three kilometers or forty miles—would not accommodate the eleven campsites prescribed by the Numbers 33:1–7 itinerary, nor the eleven-day journey to Kadesh-Barnea, as it is less than fifty kilometers (thirty-one miles) from Gebel Helal. Consequently, this mountain does not meet the geographical specifications of the wilderness itineraries.

HAR KARKOM. Located about fifty-five kilometers (thirty-four miles) in a straight line southeast of 'Ain Qudeirat, and ten kilometers (six miles) inside Israel's present border with Egypt, is Har Karkom (figure 1). The Italian prehistorian Emmanuel Anati has spent the better part of twenty years surveying and excavating at Har Karkom and the surrounding area, beginning in the 1950s up until 1999.[76] Like Gebel Helal, this mountain is associated with the limestone edge of the beginning of the el-Tih plateau. It stands 847 meters (2,753 feet) above sea level. Anati and his team have identified about 1,200 archaeological sites around this mountain, including campsites, huts, tumuli, and small circular cultic installations with standing pillars—all made of local stone, and spanning forty millennia. Some of the standing pillars are carved to represent human figures. Scores of rock carvings and petroglyphs have also been recorded.[77] Analysis of flint implements, carbon 14 analysis, and other artifacts have led the Italian team to date the periods of occupation around Har Karkom as follows: Paleolithic through Chalcolithic periods (40,000–3400 B.C.); the Early through Middle Bronze I ages (3400–2000 B.C.); followed by a hiatus from around 2000 B.C. through 900 B.C., and abundant evidence for occupation during the Roman and Byzantine periods.[78] There is no evidence of a human presence in the Late Bronze through Iron I periods, when most scholars would expect to find the Israelites at Har Karkom should they have visited this site.

This absence notwithstanding, Anati proposes a major revision to biblical chronology, pushing the exodus to the late third millennium B.C., so that his site accords with the Bible. He points to what he believes is the base of an altar and to twelve stones or pillars standing nearby as evidence of the altar and twelve pillars Moses erected in Exodus 24:4: מִזְבֵּחַ תַּחַת הָהָר וּשְׁתֵּים עֶשְׂרֵה מַצֵּבָה לִשְׁנֵים עָשָׂר שִׁבְטֵי יִשְׂרָאֵל, "[he . . . built] an altar at the foot of the mountain, and set up twelve pillars, corresponding to the twelve tribes of Israel." An interesting rock drawing discovered by Anati leads him to believe that it represents the "Tablets of the Law" because it has "a dual rounded top and ten partitions."[79]

Scholars have reacted with either indifference or antagonism to Anati's revisionist theory. Revisionist chronologies are not new but have been roundly rejected by trained historians, biblical scholars, and archaeologists.[80] One early critic was Israel Finkelstein, who penned a devastating review.[81] He rightly rejects Anati's conclusions, because the type of Early Bronze Age cultic installations discovered at Har Karkom have also been found in significant numbers in the southern desert, Negev, and Sinai—so Anati's finds are not unique, and Finkelstein is appalled by Anati's chronological revisionism.[82] He also finds the location so close to Kadesh and the Negev problematic, especially since a few years earlier he had argued for a south Sinai location for the mountain of God on the basis of ecological factors.[83] Another problem for Anati's theory is that if this mountain marks the place where Israel received the tablets with the ten commandments, in what language would they have been written between 2200 and 2000 B.C.? The Canaanite alphabetic script, from which the Hebrew script was borrowed, was still developing around 1800 B.C.[84]

Because of the reference to the eleven-day journey from Mt. Sinai to Kadesh-Barnea ('Ain Qudeirat) in Deuteronomy 1:2, Anati realizes he has a problem, since the distance between his Mt. Sinai and 'Ain Qudeirat is less than fifty kilometers (thirty-two miles). Hence he posits that a circuitous route through eleven stations was taken by the Israelites—but this measures only 124 kilometers (77.5 miles).[85] As we have shown, this distance should be around 265–350 kilometers (165–220 miles). Because of this, and all the problems for the Har Karkom theory noted by Finkelstein, this possible Mt. Sinai seems highly doubtful.

GEBEL SIN BISHR. This mountain is located by the Wadi Sudr, just under thirty kilometers (nineteen miles) northeast of Ras el-Sudr, which is on the coast of the Gulf of Suez (figure 1). Standing 618 meters (2,009 feet) in height, this mountain was connected to Mt. Sinai by the historical geographer Manashe Har-el.[86] He traces the route of the exodus from the northeastern Delta down to the Bitter Lakes, which he proposes the Israelites would have crossed, escaping Pharaoh's army.[87] Turning south, the Israelites first stopped at Marah, where the water was bitter (Exod. 15:22–23), which is what מָרָה (*mārâ*) means. Har-el links the biblical site with Bir el-Mura, which means "bitter well" in Arabic; Elim, the next campsite, he thinks is 'Ayun Musa (the Springs of Moses).[88] From this point, the Israelites would have traveled south about thirty-eight kilometers (twenty-four miles) before turning to the northeast to follow the Wadi Sudr. In support of this location for Mt. Sinai, Har-el observes that the name Sin Bishr in Arabic means "the reporting of the law, or the Laws of man," thus preserving the memory of the events of Mt. Sinai, and he concludes that "this is the only mountain in the Sinai Peninsula, Midian and Edom where the name Sinai has been preserved in the form 'Sin.'"[89]

If the linguistic argument could stand up to scrutiny, this would be a critical piece of evidence in favor of this identification. Although Har-el's proposal is intriguing, it is unfortunately not totally convincing. *Sin* also is the Arabic word for tooth, and is related to the same root that Har-el suggests has to do with giving law; *bishr* can mean man or human.[90] Thus the meaning "human tooth" might be implied. This interpretation becomes more likely when one looks at a picture of the peak of this mountain (figure 21). In fact, Har-el includes a picture that shows the peak of this mountain, with the caption "Sin Bisher mountains—tooth shaped."[91] If the meaning "tooth" stands behind the name of this mountain, then the Hebrew name would be *šen* (שֵׁן), which is cognate with Akkadian *šinnu* and Arabic *sin*.[92] The fact that in Hebrew Sinai is written with a *samek* (סִינָי) makes it unlikely that the Arabic name of this mountain preserves the name Sinai.[93] The name Sin Bishr is probably the local Arabic name, based on the similarity of the shape of the mountain to a human tooth. Clinton Bailey's valuable study on Bedouin place-names in Sinai has identified the types of place-names given by the Arab Beduoin who came to Sinai during the fourteenth through sixteenth centuries A.D.[94] He explains that names are sometimes given that reflect "features of the landscape."[95] It seems to me that it is the shape of this peak that stands behind the name Sin Bishr.

Another obstacle Har-el has to overcome for locating Mt. Sinai at Gebel Sin Bishr is that it is a relatively short distance between the sea-crossing point, which for him is the Bitter Lakes, and Mt. Sinai. He rightly sees an apparent conflict with the data provided by the Exodus and Numbers itineraries, that is, that there were at least eight and possibly eleven campsites between the sea crossing and Mt. Sinai. Consequently, he has to dismiss these data. Har-el's solution is to appeal to the request of Moses to Pharaoh to allow the Israelites to depart on a three-day journey to worship YHWH in the wilderness (Exod. 3:18; 5:3; 8:27).[96] It must be noted, however, that the three times this request is made, never does Moses indicate that the destination is Mt. Sinai. The three-day request, therefore, cannot be used as a datum to determine the distance to Mt. Sinai from Rameses, and the other campsites mentioned between the sea crossing and Mt. Sinai should not be dismissed because they pose a problem for one's candidate for the mountain of God.

In addition to the fact that the distance from the sea crossing proposed by Har-el (the Bitter Lakes) to Gebel Sin Bishr is too short, so too is the space from Sin Bishr to Kadesh-Barnea (ca. 220 kilometers or 137 miles). Davies likewise sees the distance between these locations as militating against Gebel Sin Bishr being Mt. Sinai.[97] According to the data we have gathered here, however, the distance between these two sites is about 265–350 kilometers (165–220 miles). Consequently, as appealing as Gebel Sin Bishr may be as a contender for Mt. Sinai, serious obstacles make the identification unlikely.

B. Mt. Sinai outside of the Sinai Peninsula

EDOM. Locations for Mt. Sinai have also been proposed in Edom/Mt. Seir, that is, the area east of the Arabah, between the Dead Sea and the Gulf of Aqaba, and in Midian, that is, northern Arabia inland from the Gulf of Aqaba. Edom and Midian are recognized to be adjoining territories.[98]

Recent biblical scholars such as Gösta Ahlström and Frank Moore Cross have noted the prominence given to places in Midian/Edom in some Israelite poetry when it is describing the Sinai theophany.[99] Several texts are usually cited to support this view:

> The LORD came from Sinai,
> and dawned from Seir upon us;
> he shone forth from Mount Paran.
> With him were myriads of holy ones;
> at his right, a host of his own (Deut. 33:2)
>
> LORD, when you went out from Seir,
> when you marched from the region of Edom,
> the earth trembled,
> and the heavens poured,
> the clouds indeed poured water.
> The mountains quaked before the LORD, the One of Sinai,
> before the LORD, the God of Israel (Judg. 5:4–5)
>
> God came from Teman,
> the Holy One from Mount Paran. *Selah*
> His glory covered the heavens,
> and the earth was full of his praise (Hab. 3:3)

Deuteronomy 33:2, the blessing of Moses, and the Song of Deborah (Judg. 5) have been identified as early pieces of Hebrew Yahwistic poetry by Cross and Freedman, who note that the former "antedate(s) the eleventh century in all probability, and may be considerably older," whereas the latter they date to ca. 1100 B.C.[100] All three passages appear to be referring to the theophany of YHWH, and they mention Edom, Seir, and Teman. The latter two terms are understood to be either synonyms for Edom or regions within it.[101] The connection with YHWH and Teman has been recently reinforced with the discovery of an ostracon and a plaster wall fragment at Kuntillet ʿAjrud in northeastern Sinai. They bear the epithet, "YHWH of Teman," and date to ca. 800 B.C.[102]

Such evidence is used to suggest not only that Mt. Sinai is in Edom but also that YHWH may originally have come to Israel via the Edomites,[103] and that YHWH's name is perhaps derived from the name of a Kenite town by the name YHWH.[104] In my view, it is quite a stretch of the evidence to believe that these poetic references to YHWH and Edom trump all the references in the Bible to the mountain of God as being in the wilderness of Sinai and Horeb. Furthermore, never does the Bible explicitly situate Mt. Sinai in Edom, nor is Sinai ever used in parallelism with Midian to suggest the two are synonymous. So how should we understand Deuteronomy 33:2, Judges 5:4–5, and Habakkuk 3:3?

If Cross and Freedman are correct in assigning a late second-millennium date to the Blessing of Moses and the Song of Deborah, it should be noted that both mention Sinai. The opening line of the Blessing declares: "The LORD came from Sinai, and dawned from Seir upon us" (מִסִּינַי בָּא וְזָרַח מִשֵּׂעִיר לָמוֹ יְהוָה). This statement manifestly shows a movement of YHWH that begins at Sinai and moves toward Seir. The verb translated "dawned" or "shine" (זָרַח) is used in Ugaritic texts in military contexts.[105] The martial nature of the Song of Deborah is quite apparent in the light of the battle described in the preceding chapter, and by the use of terminology such as "march" in 5:4. And, as Davies has shown, the wilderness itineraries likewise have military dimensions.[106] Hence the poem offers a dramatic picture of YHWH departing Sinai, the place of theophany, and his march to claim territory, tracing the route followed by the Israelites (cf. Num. 10:11–21:35).

In a recent study of these texts along with the song in Habakkuk 3, Nili Shupak has shown that these poems utilize the language of Egyptian solar imagery.[107] She further observes that "in Habakkuk the names Teman and Mount Paran indicate the stations in God's passage in his travel from the south." Regarding the Kuntillet ʿAjrud references to YHWH of Teman, she notes that this epithet "appears several times, and in one of them the verb *zrḥ* is used to describe the appearance of God, exactly as in Deuteronomy 33 . . . meaning, 'when God shines forth . . . mountains melt,' as in the biblical passages dealing with the theophany, the phrase YHWH *Tmn* should also be understood here as a reference to God's arrival from the south, and not as an indication of a local god."[108] I find that Shupak's observations do make sense of both the geographical questions and the sense of movement on a campaign. I would suggest, however, that the mention of Mt. Paran in the Deuteronomy and Habakkuk passages, if Aharoni is correct in thinking that Paran is the original name of Sinai (see chapter 3, §II)—as well as the wilderness around Kadesh-Barnea—is used here synonymously with Sinai.[109]

Consequently, the references to Edom, Seir, and Teman in these paeans only mean that YHWH's campaigns that began at Sinai and moved north and his theophany (that is, his glory in the tabernacle) passed through the region of Edom, just as the narratives in Numbers 10:11–21:35 report. In fact, Numbers 10:33–34 speaks of the theophany leading Israel, and verses 35–36 illustrate the military results:

> So they set out from the mount of the LORD three days' journey with the ark of the covenant of the LORD going before them three days' journey, to seek out a resting place for them, the cloud of the LORD being over them by day when they set out from the camp.
> Whenever the ark set out, Moses would say,
> "Arise, O LORD, let your enemies be scattered,
> and your foes flee before you."
> And whenever it came to rest, he would say,
> "Return, O LORD of the ten thousand thousands of Israel."

Consequently, the three passages under consideration tell us nothing about the origin of YHWH, nor can they be used to locate Mt. Sinai in Edom, and never is Midian mentioned at all. This latter point is significant, since scholars over the centuries have attempted to locate Mt. Sinai in Midian.

MIDIAN-ARABIA. One of the early proponents for locating Mt. Sinai in Arabia or Midian was Charles Beke, who in 1878 identified it with Mt. Biggir, located around fifteen kilometers (nine miles) east of Elath/Ezion-geber (figure 1).[110] This placement would have been in the very northern part of the Land of Midian. For him, *yām sûp̱* is identified with the Gulf of Suez, on the basis of the reference to Solomon's fleet docked there (1 Kings 9:26), which meant that the escaping Israelites crossed the Gulf of Suez. The declaration by St. Paul in Galatians 4:25 ("Now Hagar is Mount Sinai in Arabia and corresponds to the present Jerusalem"), he believed supported his theory.[111] Given the allegorical nature of Paul's statement, one might be inclined not to put too much geographical weight on such a statement. But more problematic is the assumption that first-century A.D. geographical terminology applies to the second millennium B.C. As we observed above (chapter 3, §III), the term Arabia as used in Greco-Roman times included Sinai. This is proven in the translation of the Septuagint of Genesis 46:34, which locates the Land of Goshen beside or in Arabia (i.e., Sinai). The Hebrew of Genesis 46:34 does not include this explanatory note, clearly because the association of Sinai with Arabia only begins in the Persian period. The MT version evidently predates this correlation. Hence, Paul is plainly using the geographical term that was understood in his day to refer to Sinai. Those who appeal to Galatians 4:25 err by interpreting this verse through the lens of twentieth-century international borders, and not from a first-century A.D. geopolitical map, which would have included Sinai within Arabia.

There is a serious problem for those who build on Beke's Midian hypothesis (see the positions of Cornuke and Humphreys below). He maintained the absurd notion that the Israelites did not sojourn in Egypt in Africa as we know it today.[112] He places Mizraim of the Bible in the area of Philistia, the Negev, and south into mid- to eastern Sinai. Now that Rameses is known to be located at Qantir in the Sharkiya province of the east Delta, this means that Beke's proposed site of Rameses—east of the Wadi el-Arish—is approximately 180 kilometers (113 miles) east of the ancient Ramesside capital.[113] Beginning his geographical study so far off the mark means that there is little likelihood that any of his following reconstruction can be taken seriously. Unbelievably, many of those who appeal to Beke's work as an authority on the geography of the wilderness period conveniently ignore this blunder.

In addition to this fatal flaw in Beke's theory, there is the problem of the proximity of Mt. Biggir to Kadesh-Barnea. Depending on the route taken, a distance of less than 150 kilometers (90 miles) separates Kadesh-Barnea from Mt. Biggir. This distance can hardly be described as an eleven-day journey (265–350 kilometers or 165–220 miles). Finally, it is difficult to believe that if Mt. Biggir were the Israelites' destination when they departed Egypt that they would not have taken the Way of the Wilderness or Darb el-Hagg across central Sinai toward Ezion-geber/Eloth, rather than crossing the Gulf of Aqaba (figure 1). It is worth noting that only on the return trip from Mt. Sinai is Seir mentioned (i.e., Edom = Ezion-geber) (Deut. 1:2), but not on the way to Mt. Sinai. Beke's location for Mt. Sinai was accepted by Alfred Lucas, although he realized that the beginning point was within the Delta.[114]

A number of other scholars have also suggested that various mountains in Midian are Mt. Sinai. In addition to the early work of Beke, Alois Musil visited northern Midian in 1910 and published his study fifteen years later. He influenced many later biblical scholars such as E. Meyer, Hermann Gunkel, Hugo Gressman, Martin Noth and Jean Koenig.[115] They all thought that the biblical descriptions of the theophany at Mt. Sinai described volcanic activity, and since there was no evidence of volcanoes in Sinai, that northern Arabia was the more likely venue for the events of Exodus 20. Musil, Noth, and later Koenig were able to point to a number of Arabic toponyms that seemed to reflect the names found in the wilderness itineraries (such as Ayla = Elim, 'Ayn Marra = Marah, Horb = Horeb),[116] leading to the proposal that al-Jaw or Hala el-Badr, a volcanic peak, was Mt. Sinai (figure 1). It stands around 1,692 meters (5,500 feet) above sea level, with the cone of Badr reaching 154 meters (500 feet) above the surrounding mountain table, which was formed by lava flows and volcanic debris.

One archaeologist and biblical scholar who critiqued the Midian–Mt. Badr location was Roland de Vaux. He declared the specific identification of Mt. Sinai with Badr to be "quite arbitrary" but conceded that it is possible that the Bible is describing a volcano, in which case northern Arabia could be a possible location for it.[117] He concludes, however, that somewhere within the Sinai Peninsula is still the most likely location for the mountain of God. The most compelling part of de Vaux's argument against the Midianite location is that the biblical references frequently cited to support this location (Deut. 33:1–2, Judges 5:4–5, Hab. 3:3), about which we have already commented, never mention Midian. Rather they refer to locations in Edom, well north of Midian. Additionally, he points out that the Jewish population of northern Arabia from the fifth century B.C. onward may be responsible for bringing traditions about "Sinai and the memories of Moses that are found in Arab folklore into this region."[118] This would not be unlike the Pilgrims and early Christian settlers who came to North America and used biblical names for their settlements (such as Salem, Bethlehem, Zion, Hebron).

Consequently, the Arabic names that appear to be like the toponyms in the wilderness itineraries were probably assigned in more recent times and thus may be false leads. This is also true of those in Sinai. In his study of Arabic place-names in Sinai, Bailey has shown that the Arab Bedouin who came to Sinai between the fourteenth and sixteenth centuries A.D. were interested in the biblical and Quranic traditions about Moses and the Hebrews in Sinai, and they too assigned names like 'Ayun Musa (Springs of Moses), Gebel Musa (Mt. Moses), and Badyat at-Tih (the Desert of Wandering) to sites in Sinai.[119] This is particularly significant, since these Bedouin would have migrated through the Hijaz, and thus passed through places in Midian that were associated with Muslim traditions about Moses. This notwithstanding, they applied names reflecting biblical memories to locations in Sinai.

Bailey also discovered that water sources in Sinai were often named to reflect the quality of the water. Hence the names 'Ain Mura (bitter) or Malha (salty) are widely attested in Sinai, and this probably accounts for similar names in northern Arabia. As a consequence of these factors, the use of Arabic toponyms in Sinai or Arabia to identify biblical place names should not be accepted uncritically and should probably only be considered seriously when there is other compelling evidence to support this association. Such evidence might be archaeological and/or inscriptional data, or an Arabic toponym that preserves the ancient name, such as Paran > Feiran, and Kadesh > Qadis, which are not descriptive names like Mura and Malha. These types occur too frequently to be helpful.

The Israeli occupation of the Sinai Peninsula from 1967 to 1982 afforded the opportunity for unprecedented investigation of Sinai.[120] But in the absence of new archaeological evidence to shed light on the location of Mt. Sinai in the peninsula, renewed interest in a location in Arabia has recently been reignited. A group of amateur biblical archaeologists inspired by the explorations of the late Jim Irwin (the Apollo 15 astronaut), called the Bible Archaeology Search and Explorations Institute (BASE), now directed by Bob Cornuke, has been involved in investigating a site in northern Arabia, or Midian, called Gebel el-Lawz (figure 1). Lawz means "almonds," and the mountain is located around 120 kilometers (75 miles) south of Eloth/Ezion-geber. The adventures of Cornuke (a former Los Angeles SWAT policeman and more recently a real estate agent) and his team have been heralded to popular audiences and church groups, and have been widely publicized in television programs, videos, on an Internet site (www.baseinstitute.org), and in popular books, best known of which is probably *The Gold of the Exodus*, and more recently, *In Search of the Mountain of God: The Discovery of the Real Mt. Sinai*.[121]

It would be easy to simply ignore the fanciful theory of these dilettantes, because scholars typically ignore popular works that lack academic credibility. However, given the frequency with which I am asked about the views of BASE by students and laypeople, I feel constrained to point out some monumental blunders to which Cornuke and his colleagues have succumbed that trained archaeologists and biblical scholars would not make. The following points explain their approach, some of their finds, and conclusions.

1. They affirm that the Bible can only be interpreted literally.[122] This affects the next two points.
2. Paul's statement in Galatians 4:25 that Mt. Sinai is in Arabia means present-day Saudi Arabia.[123]
3. The crossing of *yām sûp̱* must be the Gulf of Aqaba because of the statement in 1 Kings 9:26.[124] This means that the Israelites departed Egypt and traveled south along the western coast of Sinai, and then crossed the Gulf of Aqaba from the southern tip of Sinai.
4. The top of Gebel el-Lawz, a granite mountain in northern Arabia, has been blackened. They believe that this phenomenon was caused by the fiery theophany as described in Exodus 19.[125]
5. They found pillars and an altar, which they identify with those described in Exodus 24:4.

I offer the following criticism of the five points identified here of the BASE Institute's Gebel el-Lawz theory:

(1) BASE's unswerving literal interpretation of the biblical text actually creates serious problems for their theory. The reality is that they are reading English translations of the Bible, and not the Hebrew text itself. An example of their literalist approach is that they attempt to find campsites large enough to accommodate more than a million people. (The question of the number of Israelites in the wilderness will be addressed in the following chapter.) But the reality is that they don't take every text literally at critical points when these texts interfere with their theory. For instance, the information provided by the Exodus and Numbers itineraries shows that only three stops are recorded from the departure from Rameses in the eastern Delta until the arrival at Migdol and Pi-hahiroth, which was beside the sea (see figure 10). This distance, the evidence suggests, should range between seventy-two and ninety-six kilometers (forty-five and sixty miles). The trek from Rameses to their proposed crossing point at the southern tip of Sinai at the Straits of Tiran, however, is around 515 kilometers (322 miles). From that point to Gebel el-Lawz is less than one

hundred kilometers (sixty-three miles). Within this short space, according to the biblical itineraries, there should be at least ten campsites, and based upon our analysis above, an approximate distance of 265–352 kilometers (165–220 miles) would be required. Clearly, if Gebel el-Lawz is biblical Mt. Sinai, then the Exodus and Numbers itineraries cannot be read literally. In fact, the line of march proposed by Cornuke and his associates is precisely the opposite of what the wilderness itineraries stipulate, should a literal reading be made!

(2) Enough has been said already in this chapter and in chapter 3 (§III) regarding the use of the term Arabia in Greco-Roman times. To cite Galatians 4:25 as the sole basis for locating Mt. Sinai in present-day Arabia, while ignoring all else stated in the Torah, is a fallacy, the fallacy of the lonely fact.[126] This means that too large a conclusion is drawn from too little evidence. Again it needs to be stressed that never does the Old Testament locate Mt. Sinai in Midian specifically or Arabia generally.

(3) There is no doubt 1 Kings 9:26 is referring to the Gulf of Aqaba and that *yām sûp̱* is the name used for the northwestern branch of the Red Sea in the days of King Solomon (or the DtrH). Why *yām sûp̱* is used in this text is uncertain,[127] but what is evident is that in the context of the exodus story, the use of *sûp̱* must be understood in the light of Exodus 2:3 in which baby Moses is placed in a basket among the reeds (*sûp̱*). Also, Exodus 10:19 must be taken into account; there we are told that a westerly wind drove the plague of locusts from the Delta east into *yām sûp̱*. And, as was shown in chapter 5, Egyptian textual evidence connects *sûp̱* with Egyptian *p3 ṯwfy*, which was located on the eastern frontier. We may never know why the Gulf of Aqaba is called *yām sûp̱* in 1 Kings, but this lone reference is insufficient evidence to relocate *yām sûp̱* or *p3 ṯwfy* to the opposite side of the peninsula. If *yām sûp̱* was located in the Isthmus of Suez, then the Exodus itinerary makes sense, especially of Exodus 12–14.

(4) The blackened color of the top of Gebel el-Lawz is explained by geologists as a phenomenon known as desert varnish, which is "a black-to-brown coating of iron, manganese, and clay, [that] commonly forms on exposed rock and artifact surfaces embedded in desert pavements, and it also forms in arid regions as a result of organic microbial activity on the rock surface which fixes the iron and manganese."[128] The BASE Institute's explanation is that it was caused by the theophany. This, however, is contrary to the biblical description of the fiery bush theophany. We are plainly told that it did not burn up the bush (Exod. 3:2). Are we to believe that the intense heat of the fire on the mountain was such that igneous rock would be discolored, and yet Moses could be on the mountain, but did not have a hair on his head singed (Exod. 19:20–25; 20:22)? Clearly, Cornuke's metaphysical explanation for the blackened peak is unnecessary on both geological and biblical grounds.

(5) The altar that the BASE Institute team associates with the one built by Moses lacks any parallel in the ancient Near East. Cornuke describes this

feature rather unscientifically (with no measurements), stating: "I inspected the size and configuration of the rocks. From every angle it remains an altar, unnaturally arranged, thick and imposing at the bottom, flat and smooth on top. To heft its large and unwieldy boulders into place would have required thousands of skilled, able-bodied workers."[129] Plainly, this structure, whatever it is, does not meet a literal reading of Exodus 24:4, which specifies that Moses "built an altar at the foot of the mountain." Nowhere does the text even hint that "thousands of skilled, able-bodied workers" were required to build the altar. During a second visit to the site, Cornuke and his colleague, Larry Williams (a commodities trader), described the altar as "shaped like a giant V, it resembled an airliner, wings spread and ready for takeoff." And it measures "a third of a football field in length," which I take to be around seventy meters long.[130]

Then, demonstrating total ignorance of the archaeological evidence of stone altars in the region, Cornuke declares that stone altars are not known to be found "in the middle of a desert."[131] He apparently knew nothing of the stone altars discovered by Anati at Har-Karkom, or the sanctuary at Timna in the Arabah, or those found in Israelite contexts at Beersheba and Arad.[132] These are not giant V-shaped altars!

As for the pillars Cornuke and Williams found, they are described as being "smooth to the touch, hand chiseled, like polished marble," measuring "eighteen inches in diameter and twenty-two inches tall."[133] These pillars look nothing like what is meant by the Hebrew word מַצֵּבָה (*maṣṣēbâ*). Such pillars are ubiquitous in the Levant, and whether they come from Canaanite or Israelite sites, they look the same. Uzi Avner, who has recently been compiling the known examples of archaeological sites with pillars in the Negev and Sinai, has documented 142 examples.[134] Most "pillars" are not carved at all, while some are (see above concerning those at Har-Karkom). At Timna, some of the pillars that stand near the altar have the head of the Egyptian goddess Hathor on them.[135] Canaanite "pillars" discovered at Hazor are roughly hewn and some have iconographic images (figure 22), and to those discovered decades ago by Yadin, a new collection of more than twenty can be added from the current excavations at the site by Amnon Ben-Tor. These pillars, beside which are offering tables, date to the Late Bronze Age, and are possibly associated with the approach to the palace.[136] Israelite-period "pillars" have also been discovered within the temple at Arad, and recently within the gateway at Dan.

Unfortunately, Cornuke seems unaware of these and allows the English word "pillar" (typically smoothly shaped and cylindrical, in a shaped column) to influence his understanding of the artifacts he discovered. These smooth pillars seem more likely to be objects from Nabatean to Roman times. Pottery, so critical to dating anepigraphic structures and associated artifacts, receives no mention whatsoever in the BASE reports. I suspect that this is because they did not know how to read pottery.

In my view none of the archaeological evidence proffered by the BASE Institute team points to pillars or altars of the second millennium B.C. Because of the foregoing criticism, there is neither biblical nor archaeological evidence to support associating Gebel el-Lawz with Mt. Sinai. I concur with Gordon Franz's devastating critique of Cornuke's theory and his conclusions that "Mt. Sinai should be located in the Sinai Peninsula right where the Bible places it, not in Saudi Arabia."[137]

As I was in the final stages of preparing this book, a book was published in 2003 by Colin Humphreys, a distinguished physicist and material scientist from Cambridge University.[138] Admitting not to be an archaeologist or a biblical scholar or to be trained in any ancient Near Eastern languages, Humphreys works with the English text of the Bible and examines the evidence through the "lens of science." It is apparent that he has read a good deal of literature on the history of the debate and has a high regard for the Bible as a reliable source for determining the location of Mt. Sinai; he frequently cites information he has obtained from personal conversations with authorities in the field of Near Eastern studies, such as Alan Millard and Kenneth Kitchen.[139] Despite these factors, this book merely demonstrates that a natural scientist, no matter how brilliant, lacks the tools essential for this type of research—although when Humphreys uses his mathematical knowledge for investigating the meaning of large numbers in the Bible, such as the censuses in Numbers 1 and 26, he submits some helpful insights.[140]

Humphreys believes that Mt. Badr (or Hala el-Badr) in Hegaz, northern Arabia (Midian), is biblical Mt. Sinai (figure 1). He starts with his scientific reasons for locating Mt. Sinai in Arabia, that is, that the biblical description of the theophany can only be explained as a volcano.[141] After reviewing a book on volcanoes, he discovered that there were only three that had been active within the past 10,000 years within a range that could possibly fit the biblical setting, and these are located between Aqaba and Medineh. After coming to this conclusion, Humphreys seeks to analyze the biblical itineraries to show that they lead to Mt. Badr. Here is where the flaws are so serious so as to invalidate his "scientific" approach. Only some of my major objections are presented here.

(1) He argues that the pillar of cloud by day and fire by night, which led the Israelites from Egypt to Mt. Sinai, fits the description of an erupting volcano.[142] On the basis of the distance from which the eruption of Mt. Saint Helens was seen, he argues that the Israelites would have seen this phenomenon in the sky when departing Egypt. This theory has, admittedly, some attractive elements, but two serious problems present themselves. First, if this phenomenon were guiding the Israelites to the erupting mountain, then it would be more likely that the Israelites would have traveled south along the western coast of Sinai to its southern tip, and the crossing of *yām sûp̱* would have been in the area of the Straits of Tiran, where Cornuke would place it.

Humphreys, rather, has the Israelites cross Sinai in an easterly direction along the Darb el-Hagg toward Elath-Aqaba, and has the "crossing" occur at the northern tip of the Gulf of Aqaba.[143] This scenario would hardly mean that the Israelites were guided to the mountain by the phenomenon of a volcanic pillar as they would have been traveling east across Sinai. The second problem for Humphreys' volcano hypothesis is that if he were correct, then this phenomenon should not play a role in the movement of the Israelites after leaving north Arabia, because in traveling toward Kadesh-Barnea and the Land of Canaan, the pillar, if the volcano was still active, would be behind them. However, we are informed that the cloud of the LORD directed them toward the Promised Land when they left Mt. Sinai (Num. 10:34). This theophany is described as a feature that made Israel unique. Moses refers to this ongoing theophany when interceding with God on Israel's behalf after the people broke faith with YHWH at Kadesh-Barnea:

> But Moses said to the LORD, "Then the Egyptians will hear of it, for in your might you brought up this people from among them, and they will tell the inhabitants of this land. They have heard that you, O LORD, are in the midst of this people; for you, O LORD, are seen face to face, and your cloud stands over them and you go in front of them, in a pillar of cloud by day and in a pillar of fire by night. Now if you kill this people all at one time, then the nations who have heard about you will say, "It is because the LORD was not able to bring this people into the land he swore to give them that he has slaughtered them in the wilderness." (Num. 14:13–16)

In fact the word "cloud" (הֶעָנָן) or "pillar of cloud" (עַמּוּד עָנָן) occurs frequently in the book of Numbers, and the cloud that covered the mountain, the place of theophany, covers the tabernacle once it is erected (Num. 9:19, 20, 21, 22; 10:11, 12, 34; 12:10; 14:14; 16:42), and in later history, it occupies the holy of holies in Solomon's temple (1 Kings 8:10–11; Isa. 4:5). Numbers 12:5 specifically refers to God coming down in a pillar of cloud to denounce Miriam's charges against Moses after departing the mountain of God. So clearly, the phenomenon Humphreys considers to match an erupting volcano in northern Arabia is not restricted to Mt. Sinai in the Pentateuch. Fire and cloud are understood to be vehicles of theophany.

(2) Humphreys' use of the itinerary is problematic because he has to force the data to fit his location, rather than allowing the itinerary to lead us to the mountain. He follows the Egyptian evidence that begins the exodus from Rameses, which he accepts as the Ramesside capital at Qantir, followed by a stop at Succoth, which he takes to be the Wadi Tumilat area, as is commonly accepted.[144] So far so good. But the troubles begin with Exodus 13:20, which states: "They set out from Succoth, and camped at Etham, on the edge of the

wilderness." As has been shown above, the distance between encampments is taken to be a day's journey (twenty-four to thirty-two kilometers or fifteen to twenty miles). The inability of others to precisely locate Etham leads Humphreys to think it can be located at a stop that fits his theory. He triumphantly announces his discovery of Etham: it is established from the name of a mountain and wadi named Yitm located near Aqaba on Richard Burton's 1879 map, Yitm = Etham.[145] This name is actually an alternative to Mt. Biggir, Beke's Mt. Sinai. If this identification is correct, the Exodus and Numbers itineraries make little sense, for this would mean that the distance traveled between Succoth and this Etham is 180 miles (288 kilometers) according to Humphreys, which he estimates was traveled in six and a half days, requiring the travelers to cover twenty-eight miles (forty-five kilometers) per day.[146] If one were to follow Humphreys' methodology of looking at a map and identifying the biblical site on the basis of an Arabic name, then we could likewise locate Mt. Sinai on the basis of the Arabic name Gebel Musa in southern Sinai. This is patently an unscientific approach. Furthermore, Humphreys is unable to present a compelling case for locating the three toponyms by the sea, Migdol, Pi-hahiroh, and Baal-Zephon (Exod. 14:2) in the southern Arabah, the area between the Dead Sea and the Gulf of Aqaba. As he well knows, because he frequently cites my *Israel in Egypt*, these sites have all been provisionally located in the Isthmus of Suez. Never has anyone suggested locating these sites in the southern Arabah. Pi-hahiroth, Humphreys proposes, might be identified with the mining area at Timna and its shrine devoted to the deity Hathor. The name of this temple or site, accordingly, derives from the Egyptian *pr-ḥ(w)t ḥr*, the House or Temple of Hathor. Here the author's unfamiliarity with Egyptology is evident. The cultic installation at Timna is small, originally measuring only 7 × 9 meters but was subsequently enlarged slightly to be 9 × 10 meters.[147] Consequently, Alan Schulman observes that this structure would not have been called a temple in Egyptian terminology, that is, *pr*, *'(w)t*, or *r'-pr*, any of which would require a pillared hall forecourt in front of the sanctuary.[148] A small structure such as the Timna shrine, on the other hand, would be called an *itrt* or *k3ri*.[149] Therefore, despite the role of Hathor at the Timna shrine, it would not have been known to the Egyptians as Pi-Hathor. It might also be added that the association of Pi-hahiroth with Pi-Hathor is incompatible linguistically. So locating Pi-hahiroth at Timnah simply will not work.

(3) Another complication for the Israelites traveling from Succoth in Egypt across the central part of Sinai to Aqaba (288 kilometers or 180 miles) is the practical challenge for Egyptian chariots. Humphreys reasons that the Israelites covered twenty-eight miles (forty-five kilometers) per day, and that it took six and a half days to trek across Sinai to the northern end of the Gulf of Aqaba. It is highly unlikely that Egyptian chariots could travel across the rough Darb el-Hagg or Way of the Wilderness. The thin wheels of the chariots could not take the type of beating this route would have delivered to these

lightweight vehicles. The same argument holds for the Egyptian chariots chasing the Israelites down the western coast of Sinai, according to Cornuke's theory. The inscriptions at Serabit el-Khadim in South Central Sinai never mention chariots being used on the mining expeditions in Sinai. Rather, donkeys were the beasts of burden used to transport food, supplies, and equipment to the mining area, and they were in turn used to carry the precious commodities back to be shipped across the Red Sea. From Middle Kingdom stelae, as many as five and six hundred donkeys are recorded as supporting the expedition, while smaller expeditions had two hundred or as low a figure as fifty or twenty donkeys.[150] The only route in Sinai for which there is evidence that chariots ever traveled is the military highway also known as the Ways of Horus or the Via Maris, that is, the coastal route across northern Sinai that ran between Tjaru and Canaan. Thutmose III took this route, according to his annals, leading his army by chariot from Tjaru to Gaza in ten days.[151] The distance between these points is around 240 kilometers (150 miles), meaning that this force traveled at a rate of twenty-four kilometers (fifteen miles) per day, and it should be noted that Thutmose traveled with a sense of urgency to deal with a rebellion at Megiddo. Interestingly, this average distance matches the lower figure we have used to fix a day's journey. Concerning the rapidity of the movement of this military force, Yohanan Aharoni wrote: "This is an appreciable speed which was achieved only by virtue of the route's perfect organization."[152] He is referring, of course, to the system of forts and wells along this much-traveled route to Canaan. New information can now be added to indicate why chariot travel along this route was made possible. A section of the road that apparently led from the Delta has been identified on the east side of the Suez Canal that leads to Hebua I (Tjaru). Crushed limestone powder now covers the road, which would help mark it, but also this surface was probably intended to enable wheeled vehicles to travel without getting stuck in the sand.[153] If Humphreys' projected pace for the Israelites at twenty-eight miles (forty-five kilometers) per day reflects reality, the Egyptian chariots going at the pace of twenty-four kilometers (fifteen miles) per day never would have caught up to the escaping Hebrews!

(4) Then too, there is the problem of the eleven-day journey from Mt. Sinai to Kadesh-Barnea. In order to make this datum fit the Arabian location, Humphreys has to adjust the distance of a day's journey from the figure he used earlier (twenty-eight miles or forty-five kilometers per day) to an excessive sixty kilometers (or almost thirty-eight miles) per day.[154] He justifies this extension by appealing to Musil's earlier study that examined the distance traveled by Muslim pilgrims passing through the Hegaz on their way to Mecca, and to the fact that the distance between water sources was greater in that area. With this expanded figure, Mt. Badr is well within a distance of 412 miles "as the crow flies" from Kadesh-Barnea.[155] In my view, the distance represented by a day's journey is not an accordion that can be stretched or

compressed to fit a desired theory. Nor was distance measured in the biblical world "as the crow flies." In his seminal study of the wilderness itineraries published twenty-five years ago, Graham Davies rejected locating Mt. Sinai in the Hegaz because "the distance from Kadesh of some 350 miles (560 kilometers) can only be reconciled with the 'eleven days' journey' of Dt. 1:2 by assuming an improbably high rate of travel."[156] This is precisely what Humphreys does in order to make the biblical data comport with his reconstruction.

To summarize, the reasons for rejecting the arguments of Humphreys for locating Mt. Sinai in the volcanic regions of northern Arabia are as follows: a volcano is not necessarily the best explanation for the phenomenon of the theophany at Mt. Sinai, which is why he looks to Mt. Badr; the distance between the second and third stops on the itinerary, Succoth and Etham, 180 miles (288 kilometers), renders the itinerary meaningless; locating Etham near the northern end of the Gulf of Aqaba on the basis of an Arabic name on a nineteenth-century map is not convincing; the distance from Succoth (i.e., the end of Wadi Tumilat) to Mt. Badr is too far to fit the Exodus and Numbers itinerary, which we estimate to be 265 kilometers (165 miles) to 352 kilometers (220 miles), whereas according to Humphreys' reckoning, the distance from Succoth to Mt. Badr is 380 miles (608 kilometers); and finally, the distance between Kadesh-Barnea and Mt. Badr far exceeds the eleven-day journey as prescribed by Deuteronomy 1:2. For these reasons, the distant volcanic peaks of the Hegaz ought not to be considered viable candidates for the biblical Mt. Sinai.

C. Southern Sinai

Finally we come to the last region for consideration, southern Sinai, where early Christian traditions locate the mountain of God. My inclination at the outset of this study was to discard the traditional locations a priori just because the tradition is relatively recent (fourth century A.D.), and because of my predisposition to reject traditions that are driven by ecclesiastical interests. Early Christian-era cartographers, such as Eusebius, sought to confirm church dogma about holy sites.[157] Hence a certain degree of skepticism regarding "traditional" sites is in order. One should not, however, summarily reject a theory or an interpretation of data because of the traditions associated with it; neither should one be accepted uncritically because it stands in a long tradition. If, however, other evidence, biblical and/or archaeological, can be adduced to support a site, that should be the determining factor. Three areas of evidence compel me to consider seriously locating Mt. Sinai in the southern part of the peninsula.

A question must be asked regarding the location of Mt. Sinai in the southern Sinai massif: What was the basis for the tradition? Five different early Christian monastic communities and churches were located in southern Sinai, at Gebel Musa, Gebel Serbal, Gebel Umm Shomer, Wadi Feiran

(Pharan), and et-Tur. Edward Robinson, one of the earliest explorers in Sinai in modern times (1838), points to a statement by Dionysius of Alexandra from about A.D. 250 that persecuted Egyptian Christians fled to south Sinai for safety.[158] Could they possibly have chosen this area because they believed it was biblical Sinai/Horeb and, like the persecuted prophet Elijah (1 Kings. 19:3–8), went there for safety and in hopes of rekindling the theophany, as the prophet experienced? By the early fourth century, Christian monks began taking up the hermetic lifestyle in the area, and by A.D. 360 a Syrian monk named Julianus Sabus and his followers built a chapel at the summit of Gebel Musa.[159] Visitors to the area of Gebel Musa reported a settlement of monks at the foot of the mountain by the late fourth century. It is thought that under the sponsorship of Helena in about A.D. 330 a chapel was built to the Virgin Mary at the supposed site of the burning bush (figure 23).[160] Between A.D. 381 and 384, the Christian traveler Egeria made her pilgrimage through the Holy Land, Egypt, and Sinai. She went to Gebel Musa, and throughout that region there were monks and chapels commemorating nearly every event associated with the Israelites' stay at Mt. Sinai as reported in Exodus.[161] The famous St. Catherine's Monastery with its fortress, which still stands, was built with the support of the Roman emperor Justinian in the sixth century (figure 24).

The early Christian tradition is not based on local legends alone. Aharoni maintained that the biblical evidence pointed toward south Sinai, and this may have led the third- and fourth-century clerics and pilgrims to this area in search of sites associated with wilderness stories in the law.[162] G. E. Wright believed that the Numbers 33 itinerary might in part have been composed of early pilgrim routes, like that taken by the prophet Elijah who came to the mountain of God, Horeb (1 Kings 19:1–8).[163] The fact that Elijah is reported as traveling to Horeb suggests that during the Iron II period, Israelites knew of the location and how to get there. Wright also made a compelling point in support of the early Christian traditions regarding southern Sinai when he observed that "it is extremely difficult to understand why the early Church would have located the sacred spot in the most inaccessible and dangerous area imaginable for pilgrims, especially at a time when the tendency was to do just the opposite, unless the tradition was so old and firmly fixed that no debate was permitted about it."[164] Thus although the tradition of locating Mt. Sinai in southern Sinai can only be traced back with certainty to the early Christian era, it has been an enduring one that has led generations of Bible scholars to embrace it, and it may be built upon even older biblical traditions.

Recently another important factor has been advanced to support the southern location for Mt. Sinai. Aviram Perevolotsky and Israel Finkelstein find the ecology of the region (which I shall discuss shortly) to have been an important factor in the spread of early Christian communities in southern Sinai.[165] Itzhaq Beit-Arieh has argued along similar lines after spending the better part of fifteen years surveying and excavating in Sinai from the late

1960s to the early 1980s.[166] Even before the considerations of these contemporary archaeologists, Burkhardt, who conducted extensive research on the Beduoin of Sinai during the early nineteenth century, observed that during the dry and hot summer months the Bedouin moved to the higher elevations where foliage and water could be found long after plants had dried up in the lower regions.[167] His findings may also explain why Moses would be grazing his father-in-law's flocks in the area of the mountain of God (Exod. 3:1). The dwellers of Sinai in recent times, like their ancient counterparts, evidently understood the environmental advantages of occupying the higher elevations of southern Sinai during the summer months.

The ecological-geographical argument is based further on the fact that the mountainous region of the south is ecologically favorable for a larger group of people to have lived for eleven months (see chapter 3, §I). Greater quantities of water, the most essential commodity for survival in arid locations, are available in the south because the granitic mountains cannot absorb the rain. Rather, the water runs off into wadis, collects in pools, and can be dammed up. Beit-Arieh pointed out that "water accumulated in these pools can be drawn on for many months of the year."[168] He has identified more than forty small settlements from the Early Bronze II period (2850–2650 B.C.). Each settlement was made up of five to twenty stone huts that were partially sunk into the ground. These early residents raised goats and mined and processed copper, leading Beit-Arieh to conclude that the area of south Sinai could support small populations on a continuous basis.[169] Ofer Bar-Yosef has documented even earlier, pre-Neolithic circular installations in south Sinai, which included flint tools and grindstones.[170]

Returning to ecological considerations, Perevolotsky and Finkelstein's ethnoarchaeological research led them to believe that a southern location for the Israelites made sense because of the ability of the region to produce food. They determined that "the wadis of the red granite area enjoy an actual water economy equivalent to approximately 15 inches (37.5 cm), while only about two inches fall directly on the rock surfaces. Good alluvial soil is also deposited in these areas. As a result we find in this region a particular type of agriculture, orchards, which are not feasible in other desert areas. These orchards can support a considerable sedentary population."[171] Furthermore, they studied small present-day Bedouin orchards, some of which actually occupy earlier Byzantine-period farms, and determined that a wadi orchard covering only 600 square feet with fifty-one trees produced 1,623 pounds (738 kilograms) of fruit per season. The fruits included grapes, almonds, apples, pears, apricots, pomegranates, figs, plums, quinces, and peaches.[172]

Ecological considerations must be taken seriously, as the Israelites stayed in this region for nearly a year. This would not be long enough to produce fruits and vines, but it illustrates that water was available to people in the area. Beit-Arieh's investigations have shown that from earliest times down to recent centuries, southern Sinai had "the largest concentration of ancient settlements," and that around 10,000 Bedouin resided in this region during the period of his investigations.[173] Thus, according to Beit-Arieh as well as Perevolotsky and Finkelstein, south Sinai's geography and climate best lent itself to the Israelite sojourn at Mt. Sinai as described in Exodus 20–Numbers 10. The only other area in Sinai where a larger group of people could have stayed for a protracted period of time was the Kadesh-Barnea area with its steady water source, and it is precisely in this area that the Bible reports the Israelites spent the longest block of time (Numbers 13–20).

The first two points, while circumstantial, are supported by a third, that is, the travel distances as indicated by the wilderness itineraries in Exodus and Numbers; the reference in Deuteronomy 1:2 also best fits a locale in southern Sinai. Not only does Deuteronomy 1:2 provide the distance between Horeb to Kadesh-Barnea but it also adds another detail about the route: that it was via Mt. Seir. It was observed above that Mt. Seir corresponds to Edom, and was not mentioned enroute to Mt. Sinai, but only on Israel's journey from Horeb to Kadesh-Barnea. The inclusion of the detail about traveling via Mt. Seir probably means that there was more than one road that could have been taken to reach Kadesh-Barnea. Davies argues that the inclusion of the words concerning the way of Mt. Seir "surely imply that there was more than one possible route form Horeb to Kadesh, and that the covering of the distance between them in eleven days (rather than, say, nine or twelve) was conditional upon the use of a particular route."[174] In an attempt to identify this particular route, Davies cautiously points out that the exact extent of the territory of Mt. Seir is a problem. Nevertheless, he opines that "the choice would appear to be the road that ran south-east from Kadesh to the head of the Gulf of Akaba (the Arabic *darb el-'azza*), which would be a route that went 'via Mt. Seir.'"[175] The Arabic *darb el-'azza*, the Gaza Road, was mapped and studied by Zeev Meshel to determine its history and published only in 2000 (figure 1).[176] The route is marked by piles of stones, and nearby remains from Roman times all the way back to the Early Bronze age are attested along its length, which leads Meshel to date the origin of the road to the end of the third millennium B.C.[177] The route, going south, ran from Gaza, passed near 'Ain Qudeirat, 'Ain Qadis, and Kuntilla, to the northern end of the Gulf of Aqaba. Just before reaching that end point, another road turns off and heads toward south Sinai (figure 1). This is the route that Davis and Meshel propose was intended by Deuteronomy 1:2, and might have been taken by the Israelites when traveling from Mt. Sinai to Kadesh-Barnea.

Modern roads in the ancient Near East often are constructed near and sometimes over their ancient counterparts because the ancient routes typically followed the natural roads provided by wadis. Meshel's survey indeed shows this is true for the *Darb el-'azza*. Following modern-day roads from the Gebel Musa region to the eastern coast of Sinai, and north to near Eilat, where this road would meet *Darb el-'azza*, and then north to Kadesh-Barnea, covers approximately 320 kilometers (200 miles). Breaking this figure into eleven travel segments would mean an average distance of twenty-nine kilometers (eighteen miles) per day. This figure precisely lies between the twenty-four and thirty-two kilometers (fifteen and twenty miles) per day that was reckoned based on comparative travel distances derived from ancient texts. Traveling, then, from the region of south Sinai to Kadesh-Barnea via Mt. Sinai fits admirably the prescription of Deuteronomy 1:2, as the other locations scholars usually propose do not.

Let us turn to consider some of the candidates for Mt. Sinai in south Sinai.

GEBEL MUSA/RAS SAFSAFAH. This rugged mountain, the top of which houses a stone church built by the monks of St. Catherine's Monastery, reaches a height of 2,285 meters (7,345 feet) (figure 25). This peak stands at the southeast end of a granite range that is around three and a half kilometers (just over two miles) long. The summit of Gebel Musa is actually not visible from the valley below, where St. Catherine's Monastery is situated, nor can it be seen from er-Rahah plain, thought by many to be the campsite of the Israelites. At the northwestern side of this range is Gebel or Ras Safsafah (2,168 meters / 7,046 feet), which may actually be a more plausible site for Mount Sinai (figure 26) because er-Rahah plain begins at the northwestern side of Ras Safsafah, and extends, according to Robinson's 1838 survey, "7000 feet, or 2333 yards" (2,154 meters) in length, and occupies approximately one square mile (just over 1.6 square kilometers) (figure 27).[178] This plain is widely thought to be the location of the Israelite camp. Some of the monks believed that Gebel Musa is Mt. Sinai and Gebel Safsafeh is Mt. Horeb, a position some nineteenth-century travelers to south Sinai entertained.

Many of the early explorers, however, were not captivated by traditional sites associated with the wilderness experiences of the Israelites. Furthermore, they were not as interested in confirming traditions as they were to determine locations, using the Bible as their guide. Along these lines, Robinson opined: "Scriptural narrative and monkish tradition are very different things; and while the former has a distinctness and definiteness, which through all our journeyings rendered the Bible our best guide-book, we found the latter not less usually and almost regularly to be but a baseless fabric."[179] Arthur Stanley, who visited Sinai in 1852–1853, was likewise not sympathetic toward either the Greek monastic traditions or those of the local Bedouin. He cautioned that "if the monks of the convent have been able so completely to stamp the name of St. Catherine on one of their peaks, there is no reason to doubt that they may have been equally able to stamp the name of Moses on the other. But secondly, the moment the Arab traditions of Moses are examined in detail, they are too fantastic to be treated seriously."[180]

It is not surprising, then, that many early explorers reacted with skepticism, even disappointment, when first encountering Gebel Musa. Robinson admits: "My first and predominant feeling while upon this summit, was that of disappointment. Although from our examination of the plain er-Râhah below, and its correspondence to the scriptural narrative, we had arrived at the general conviction that the people of Israel must have been collected on it to receive the law."[181] Stanley also demurred at the tradition of equating Mt. Sinai with Gebel Musa, and declared, "The peak of Gebel Mousa, now pointed out by them [monks] as the scene of the giving of the Law, fails to meet the most pressing requirements of the narrative."[182] He further opined: "But the mountain never descends upon the plain. No! If we are to have a mountain without a wide amphitheatre at its base, let us have Serbâl; but if otherwise, I am sure that if the monks of Justinian had fixed the traditional scene on the Râs Sasâfeh, no one would for an instant have doubted that this only could be the spot."[183]

The Reverend D. A. Randall, who traveled the Holy Lands in 1862, was likewise impressed with er-Rahah plain and Ras Safsafeh, stating, "The bold and frowning front of Horeb was directly before us, rising up from the plain in an almost perpendicular wall from two to three thousand feet into the air. The site was grand and majestic beyond description."[184] He also noticed that there was a (seasonal) water source located at Gebel Safsafeh, just a ten-minute walk from the monastery, which would have been important to any people staying in the area. He described it in the following manner: "A few rods from us, flowing directly from a crevice in the granite rock of the mountain was a copious stream of pure sweet water. How refreshing, after the stale water we had so long drank!"[185] Associated with the Palestine Exploration Fund, E. H. Palmer spent nearly two months in 1868–1869 exploring this area. He rightly saw that Gebel Musa was rather isolated behind this large range, and could not even be seen from er-Rahah plain where he, Randall, Stanley, and Robinson proposed locating the Israelite camp.[186] In fact, Randall was so convinced that er-Rahah plain was the campsite of the Israelites that he included in his book a detailed drawing of this plain with the Israelite camp and the tabernacle at its center. In the spring of 1882, Dr. Henry Fields traveled to southern Sinai. Like Robinson and others before him, he believed that Gebel Musa was an unlikely choice for the mountain of God. He climbed Ras-Safsafeh and was immediately converted. He said: "when I reached the summit and looked down into the plain of Er-Rahah, I saw the conditions were met, and no longer doubted that I was standing on the holy mount."[187]

What troubled all these early investigators was that Gebel Musa lacked an appropriate place for the Israelites' camp as described in Exodus 19:2, which is quite specific in describing the juxtaposition of the encampment and Mt. Sinai: "They had journeyed from Rephidim, entered the wilderness of Sinai, and camped in the wilderness; Israel camped there in front of the mountain":

וַיִּסְעוּ מֵרְפִידִים וַיָּבֹאוּ מִדְבַּר סִינַי וַיַּחֲנוּ בַּמִּדְבָּר וַיִּחַן־שָׁם יִשְׂרָאֵל נֶגֶד הָהָר. The meaning of נֶגֶד (*neged*) is "in front of, before" or "immediately in front of."[188] Clearly there is no suitably sized wadi or plain adjacent to Gebel Musa to fit this description. This factor troubled me the three times I have stood atop Gebel Musa and studied the surroundings. I do, however, resonate with the reaction of these nineteenth-century explorers when viewing Ras-Safsafeh from er-Rahah plain (figure 26). It is a spectacular sight, and the association between the plain and the mountain makes Gebel Safsafeh a plausible candidate for the biblical Mt. Sinai. Today, unfortunately, the area west of Mt. Safsafeh is occupied by the burgeoning village of Katarina, a tourist village with hotels being added regularly to cope with the hundreds, if not thousands, of pilgrims and tourists who visit the area on a daily basis.

Although the Gebel Musa/Ras Safsafeh massif is widely believed to be Mt. Sinai by those who accept a south Sinai location, other peaks in the area have also been proposed to be the mountain of God in the area.

GEBEL SERBAL. Gebel Serbal (figure 28) is made up of a series of jagged peaks that stand 2,070 meters (6,727 feet) high; it stands a short distance from Wadi Feiran (figures 1 and 7). All of the nineteenth-century investigators cited above visited this mountain, located south of the eastern end of Wadi Feiran. All were impressed with it, and those who climbed it found it so exhausting because of its steep slopes that they had difficulty believing Moses would climb it. Henry Field reported the following: "The ascent of Serbal nearly finished me. It took about as long to descend as to ascend, and the descent was hardly less fatiguing."[189]

One of the earliest nineteenth-century explorers of Sinai was Burkhardt, whose book was published in 1822; he espoused the association of Serbal with Mt. Sinai because inscriptions (Amenian and Nabatean) show that it was a place of pilgrimage, whereas no such texts are found at Gebel Musa or Safsafeh.[190] Eighty-five years later, Flinders Petrie, after conducting extensive archaeological surveys and some excavations in Sinai, likewise thought that this mountain should be linked to the mountain of God of Exodus.[191]

There is an early Christian tradition represented in this area, as there is at Gebel Musa. The ruins of at least four churches from the fourth through sixth centuries have been identified in Wadi Feiran and recently studied by Peter Grossman.[192] When the pious pilgrim Egeria visited Pharan at the end of the fourth century, she records being taken to a church on a mountain (Gebel Tahuna), which she was told commemorated the stop where Moses raised his rod during the battle against the Amalekites.[193] Predating the presence of Christians, there are hundreds of Nabatean inscriptions in the Wadi and among the rocks of Gebel Serbal. The inscriptions suggest that the mount was held to be sacred prior to the arrival of Christians in search of holy sites. Ceramic evidence suggests that the Nabateans may have been in south Sinai as early as the second century B.C., and at Tell Feiran there is evidence of a settlement going back at least to the Iron II period (seventh century B.C.).[194] Additionally, owing to the height of Serbal and its proximity to the Mediterranean, snow and rain make this area "the richest water source in the whole of southern Sinai," according to Har-el. Water, of course, is an important consideration for the location of a site where the Israelites would have spent nearly one year.

Gebel Serbal has certainly not held the attention of investigators as much as has Gebel Musa/Safsafeh, perhaps because shortly after the Arab conquests of Sinai and Egypt, the Christian community at Pharan was scattered, with some of the survivors joining the monastery at St. Catherine's located about fifty kilometers (thirty-one miles) to the east.[195] Prior to this time, Pharan was the seat of the Episcopal center of south Sinai and was headed by a bishop. Sometime early in the second millennium A.D., the seat was moved to St. Catherine's.[196] The fact that for several centuries Pharan was the seat of the bishop indicates the importance of this region. I am not convinced, as some have suggested, that Serbal represents a rival tradition to that at Gebel Musa, the former being revered within the Coptic (Egyptian) orthodoxy while the latter was preferred in the Byzantine (Greek) church.[197]

Like Gebel Musa/Safsafeh, Gebel Serbal lacks any archaeological evidence to support its association with the events described in Exodus 20 through Numbers 10, but it nevertheless fits within the general parameters provided by the wilderness itineraries and the eleven-day journey of Deuteronomy 1:2. Furthermore, it is suitable on ecological grounds. Thus I maintain that there is no reason for excluding it from consideration. Furthermore, it is quite isolated from the surrounding mountain range and has areas for the Israelite encampment. Dewey Beegle speaks for many of his contemporaries in the 1960s and 1970s, such as Simons and Wright in preferring the Musa/Safsafeh massif, when he says, "In spite of the good water supply and the popularity of the region, it is doubtful that Jebel Serbal is the mountain of God. The plain in Wadi Feiran is quite small and the big valley leading up to the Serbal range is quite steep; thus there is hardly enough camping space. Since Jebel Musa fits the biblical description of the mountain of God much more closely than Jebel Serbal, it is still the preferable location."[198]

The proximity of the oasis of Wadi Feiran—thought by many to be Rephidim—to Gebel Serbal is considered as support for the theory that these peaks are Mt. Sinai. It should be noted, however, that between Rephidim and Mt. Sinai there appears to be an encampment in the wilderness of Sinai, mentioned prior to the encampment before Mt. Sinai, according to Exodus 19:2, which states: "They had journeyed from Rephidim, entered the wilderness of Sinai, and camped in the wilderness; Israel camped there in front of the mountain." Cassuto thought that the twofold reference to "camp" in this verse might be redundant, but perhaps it should be taken seriously.[199] If

Rephidim is the Feiran oasis, and the data furnished from the itineraries are taken into account, then it appears that Gebel Serbal, less than 10 kilometers away, is too close to require a campsite between the two. However, given the uncertainty of how to interpret the double mention of "camped" in Exodus 19:2, Serbal should not be eliminated as a possible Mt. Sinai.

GEBEL KATARINA. Named after the martyred saint whose name is associated with the famous monastery, Gebel Katarina is the highest mountain in the entire peninsula, reaching a height of 2,637 meters (8,570 feet). According to the tradition of the monks at St. Catherine's, Catherine was executed for her faith in Alexandria and her body was carried to Sinai by angels, who placed her remains on this peak.[200] No local tradition associates this peak with Mt. Sinai, nor do any of the many explorers and Bible scholars claim it to be the mountain of God. Located about 3.5 kilometers to the south-southeast of Gebel Musa, Gebel Katarina is approached by Wadi Arba'in, the "Wadi of the Forty," named for forty martyrs who were killed in Cappadocia.[201] A monastery, no longer occupied by monks, stands in this wadi and, like St. Catherine's, is situated to accommodate pilgrims traveling to the mountain. Only a reference in Josephus (stated twice) that Mt. Sinai "was the highest of the mountains in those regions"[202] might lead one to consider this mountain, but beyond this claim, there is no reason to consider Gebel Katarina as biblical Mt. Sinai. In fact, Josephus seems to locate Mt. Sinai in Midian, which would rule out Mt. Katarina as the mountain he had in mind.

Conclusions

When all the biblical data are considered, along with the ecological factors introduced above, southern Sinai seems the most likely region in which Mt. Sinai of the Torah is located. Which peak the tradition has in mind may never be proven, but Gebel Safsafeh and Gebel Serbal (despite some problems) are viable candidates. Proposed mountains in ancient Midian (Arabia), although they have attracted support from some eminent scholars, do not fit the distances or the geographic and toponymic data. Simply put, never does the Bible place Mt. Sinai/Horeb in Midian.

In chapter 9, where Israel's desert sanctuary (the tabernacle) is treated, an intriguing suggestion will be made for why the importance of Mt. Sinai faded and its location lost from memory, which has made tracing its identity a challenge.

7

From Egypt to Mt. Sinai

Traveling and Living in the Wilderness

He said, "I will be with you; and this shall be the sign for you that it is I who sent you: when you have brought the people out of Egypt, you shall worship God on this mountain."

—Exod. 3:12

I. Archaeology and Travel

In the foregoing chapter, I argued that there is ample archaeological evidence for human occupation throughout Sinai in ancient times. In southern Sinai, where I believe biblical Mt. Sinai was located, there is also evidence for seasonal presence in the Late Bronze Age sites such as Serabit el-Khadim and Wadi Maghara. These data raise a vital question: Why is there evidence of people living in the area from the second through sixth millennia B.C., but no specific archaeological evidence of the Israelite presence in Sinai? It is unfortunate that the Israelites did not live in stone structures that would have left a permanent archaeological record of their habitats, like many of the ancient residents of Sinai.

Itzhaq Beit-Arieh recognized this problem and allows that "presumably the Israelite dwellings and artifacts consisted only of perishable materials."[1] He does not, however, elaborate on this point. The Bible indeed does report explicitly that they lived in tents (אֹהָלִים) during this period (e.g., Exod. 16:16; Num. 1:52; 9:17, 18, 20, 22, 23; 16:27; 24:2, 5; Deut. 1:27, 33; 5:30; 11:6), and even during the early period in the Land of Canaan (Josh. 7:22–24; 22:6). We learn, not surprisingly, that Jethro the Midianite lived in a tent (Exod. 18:7), apparently not too far from Mt. Sinai. When leaving that area, Moses prevails upon his brother-in-law Hobab, according to Numbers 10:29–32, to come along as a guide or scout for the Israelites, because "you know where we should camp in the wilderness, and you will serve as eyes for us" (v. 31). Judges 1:16 informs us that the Kenites, a clan whose ancestry is traced to the father-in-law of Moses, associated with the tribe of Judah and lived in the Negev.[2] Later in the book of Judges, a group of Kenites, including the heroine Jael, is portrayed as living in tents in northern Israel centuries after the wilderness period (Judg. 4:11–22; Judg. 5:24–26). Early in the sixth century B.C., when Nebuchadnezzar's troops were campaigning in Judah, the book of Jeremiah records that the Rechabites, a conservative sect, wished to preserve the traditional ways from the wilderness by living the old life style: "We have obeyed the charge of our ancestor Jonadab son of Rechab in all that he commanded us, to drink no wine all our days, ourselves, our wives, our sons, or our daughters, and not to build houses to live in. We have no vineyard or field or seed; but we have lived in tents, and have obeyed and done all that our ancestor Jonadab commanded us" (Jer. 35:6–8). This episode illustrates that there were those in Israel who, centuries after the wilderness experience, still preferred to live in tents and to refrain from engaging in agriculture and viticulture. Furthermore, it reminds us that the Israelites during the wilderness period lived a nomadic, tent-dwelling lifestyle. This conclusion is further supported by the verb "to camp" that is used in the Numbers itinerary; וַיַּחֲנוּ (they camped) derives from the root חנה, and is attested at Mari as a term used of the nomadic element.[3] It is related to the Arabic word *ḵan* (caravansary).[4]

One might logically think that tents would leave little or no trace in the terrain of Sinai and Kadesh-Barnea, and we would not expect nomadic peoples who only occupy a particular spot for a short period of time to leave tangible evidence of their presence. In fact there has been a rather energetic debate about this matter in recent years.[5] Of special interest to the current study is the question of whether nomads are discernible in the archaeological record. Finkelstein and Perevolotsky, who were engaged in considerable survey work in the Negev and Sinai, argue for only negligible evidence, if any, which is true not only of ancient desert dwellers but even of nineteenth-century Bedouin, whose traces are "difficult to identify."[6] They further observe that "nomadic societies do not establish permanent houses, and the constant migration permits them to move only minimal belongings. Moreover, their limited resources do not facilitate the creation of a flourishing material culture that could leave rich archaeological finds."[7] They acknowledge, however, that nomadic people do leave such evidence of their presence as cemeteries, desert kites (for hunting), cult places, and rock drawings.[8] But for the most part, they speak of the "nomadic lifestyle" as "archaeologically 'invisible,'" one that does not leave an "archaeological footprint."[9] Their study is not primarily aimed at tracing nomadic peoples in the archaeological record, but at explaining what happened at different periods in the Early Bronze Age when certain urban centers in southern Canaan were abandoned. They rightly want to explain how sites vanish and then reappear. They offer a model of nomadization followed by sedentarization, caused by shifting economic factors.[10]

Subsequently, Steven Rosen offered a critique of the nomadization-sedentarization theory, based primarily upon his ability to point to some (albeit scant) evidence for nomads.[11] He is especially critical of Finkelstein and Perevolotsky's nomadization-sedentarization theory, preferring not to see populations that shift between these two modes of existence. Finkelstein responded forcefully to Rosen with a more detailed study in a monograph, reiterating and expanding upon his earlier arguments.[12] He argues that the scanty evidence Rosen points to does not account for the disappearance of the large urban centers and thus rejects the notion that the absence of archaeological evidence means that the Negev and Sinai were devoid of people. Curiously, when it comes to the Israelites in Sinai, Finkelstein is quite adamant that "some archaeological traces of their generation-long wandering in the Sinai should be apparent."[13] Apparently Finkelstein applies a different set of criteria when the question of nomadism applies to the early Israelites.

In his monograph of 2003, William Dever has added his voice to the chorus of those objecting to Finkelstein's theory.[14] He particularly challenges the view that the earlier Israelite so-called four-room house developed from a Bedouin tent. Rather, he points to other possible explanations, such as that this house plan can be traced to the lowland farmhouses, or developed from the Egyptian villa-style house of the Late Bronze age.[15] Then there is the view of Lawrence Stager, that this early Israelite house simply adapted to the demands of agricultural life and "changes in family structure," and was not the result of "desert nostalgia," that is, replicating in stone or brick Israel's tent habitat from the wilderness period.[16]

Although these considerations must be borne in mind, I find Finkelstein's argument regarding the problem of detecting nomadic peoples in the archaeological record to be quite plausible and think it may explain why there is no clear evidence for the presence of the Israelites in Sinai. In a new monograph on tents in the Bible and the ancient Near East, Michael Homan came to the same conclusion as did Finkelstein and Perevolotsky, that "tents by their nature leave very little for the archaeological record."[17]

By way of analogy, the annals of Thutmose III and the Kadesh inscriptions of Ramesses II report the pitching of Egyptian camps on these respective campaigns.[18] From the Gebel Barkal stela, we learn that Thutmose's siege of Megiddo lasted seven months.[19] In the case of Ramesses II, we have several portrayals of his tent camp (figure 29). Even given the prolonged period of the Egyptian siege at Megiddo, with thousands of soldiers and hundreds of horses from the chariots present, no archaeological evidence of this camp has been discovered, despite a century of excavations and exploration at Megiddo. The same is true at Tell Nebi Mend (Kadesh), where a Roman-period encampment has been found, but no evidence of Ramesses II's encampment.[20]

The same problem is evident in recent cases. In May 1999, when I first visited Tell el-Borg in North Sinai, the site that I am currently excavating, there were several tents pitched at the edge of the site where workers lived during the construction of the nearby canal and a bridge. When I returned eight months later, the tents were gone, and no traces of the tents were visible. Blowing sand had even covered the places where they had made their fires. During our four seasons of excavations at Tell el-Borg, we employ more than a dozen Bedouin men. I have noticed that when they daily make fires for boiling water for tea and baking bread, they rarely use the same spot twice.[21] In fact, in one area where a group made fires, I noticed six spots, the precise number of days worked in the week. For some reason, the workers prefer to move their fire holes, and they do not regularly use stones to establish a fireplace. Such fire holes do not leave large amounts of ash, as would be the case if they used the same spot day after day. These conditions and practices may explain why there is little archaeological evidence for desert dwellers in earlier eras. Hence, it is not surprising that archaeological evidence of the tent-dwelling Israelites in Sinai has not been identified.

Additionally, people traveling in the Near East used skins rather than pottery vessels to transport liquids. Pottery is heavy, and thus not very useful for people traveling in the desert. The Bible clearly reflects the practice of using skins in tent-dwelling or traveling contexts. When Abraham, whom the Bible portrays as living in a tent, dismissed Hagar and Ishmael, he gave them a skin of water as they headed off into the wilderness of Beersheba (Gen. 21:14-14, 19). When Sisera fled from the battle with the Israelites in Judges 4, he took sanctuary in the tent of Heber the Kenite (v. 17). The thirsty general was given a drink of milk from a skin by Jael (v. 19). Likewise, Samuel's mother Hannah is reported as taking a skin of wine when she traveled to Shiloh for a pilgrimage (1 Sam. 1:24). Three men on a pilgrimage to Bethel in 1 Samuel 10:3 carried a skin of wine, and when Jesse sent young David from Bethlehem to the battlefront in the Valley of Elah, a skin of wine was included among his rations (1 Sam. 16:20). These examples demonstrate that people traveling typically carried liquids in skins. This practice is illustrated pictorially in the famous painting of the traveling Asiatics from the tomb of Khnumhotep at Beni Hasan. The minstrel who plays a lyre is also shown with a skin (canteen) strapped over his shoulder (figure 30). The text of Genesis 21:14 explicitly states that Hagar placed the skin on her shoulder (עַל-שִׁכְמָהּ שָׂם). This is precisely the practice the Beni Hasan scene depicts.

The use of waterskins for travelers and Bedouin in desert regions continued into modern times. John Burkhardt, the early nineteenth-century traveler, reported that the Beduoin of Sinai used animal skins for water, as did he during his treks through Sinai in 1816.[22] Similarly, Edwin Robinson tells of his use of waterskins in his journeys in Sinai and the Holy Land in the 1830s. Recounting the preparations for his trip through Sinai, Robinson states: "A tent was to be purchased and fitted up; water-skins were to be procured and kept full of water, which was to be changed every day in order to extract the strong taste of the leather."[23] The practice of living in tents and using waterskins by those living and traveling in the desert areas of the Near East, including Sinai, has indeed had a long history.

The point of the foregoing discussion on tents and skin canteens is that such objects would not leave their mark on the archaeological record in Sinai or anywhere else. Stone and ceramic vessels would have been used on a limited basis by travelers like the Israelites. So it is not surprising that no clear archaeological evidence for the Israelites in Sinai has been found. To expect otherwise is unrealistic.

II. How Many Israelites?

One of the great interpretive and logistical dilemmas of the Exodus and wilderness tradition is the number of Israelites who departed Egypt and were numbered in the censuses in Sinai. Exodus 12:37 states: "The Israelites journeyed from Rameses to Succoth, about six hundred thousand men on foot, besides children." Because the number is actually written out in Hebrew (*šēš me'ôṯ 'elep̱* = שֵׁשׁ־מֵאוֹת אֶלֶף), this extremely large figure cannot be explained as a textual error of adding an extra zero or two. The book of Numbers contains the results of two censuses. Numbers 1:1–3 records that during the second year after the exodus, while still at Mt. Sinai, a census was taken of men "from twenty years old and upward, everyone in Israel able to go to war" (כָּל־יֹצֵא צָבָא בְּיִשְׂרָאֵל מִבֶּן עֶשְׂרִים שָׁנָה וָמַעְלָה). The total is given in 1:46: "their whole number was six hundred three thousand five hundred fifty." It might be thought that the figure in Exodus 12:37 is simply a rounding off of the total given in the survey of Numbers 1:46. The proximity of the two figures is hardly coincidental.

If there were actually 600,000 fighting men, to which women, children, older men, and the Levite tribe (which are reckoned separately in Numbers 3–4) should be added, a total of 3–4 million is likely. Three million alone results from adding a wife and three children per family. Three children might actually be a conservative number, but that is the number of children attributed to Amram and Jochebed in Exodus 6:20, that is, Aaron, Miriam, and Moses.[24] Modern scholarship is nearly unanimous in recognizing that several million is an unrealistic figure. Nahum Sarna rightly observes that this number "poses intractable problems."[25] Not only would there be serious logistical problems for millions of people camping and moving about in Sinai, but such a horde would have created a demographic disaster departing Egypt and arriving in Canaan.

The problems begin when it is realized that the entire population of Egypt during the Ramesside period is estimated to be only about 3.5 million.[26] It is true that the pharaoh of Exodus 1 is worried about the burgeoning population of Hebrews; it is, however, inconceivable that 3 to 4 million Hebrews (and other non-Egyptians from the "mixed-multitude" of Exod. 12:38) could have lived within the restricted area of the northeastern Delta. Certainly, the results of the excavations at Tell el-Dab'a and Qantir, along with the thorough magnetometer survey of this region, do not allow for such a massive population of non-Egyptians in the region that everyone now agrees was the Land of Goshen or Land of Rameses of the Bible.[27] Surely if there were 600,000 able-bodied Hebrew men, they could have walked away from their bondage at any time they chose, as they would have simply overwhelmed their taskmasters!

Then, too, the pharaoh who dispatched 600 chariots to round up and return the escaping Israelites could not possibly have believed he could be successful against 600,000 fighting men, plus the several million other individuals![28] The figure of 600 chariots does not appear to be an exaggeration. In recent excavations at Qantir/Pi-Ramesses, the German archaeologists have uncovered horse stables that are estimated to have had room for 460 horses.[29] There were certainly other stables in and around the capital and other strategic military sites such as Tjaru, Egypt's frontier town. The size of the Hittite chariot force is reported to be 2,500 by Ramesses II in the Battle of Kadesh.[30] It might be logical to assume that the Egyptian chariot corps was of comparable size. The point is that Pharaoh could well have dispatched more chariots than he did. The number of chariots sent, one might deduce, was thought to be sufficient to track down and apprehend the fleeing Hebrews.

Based on a careful study of ranks, titles, and organization of the Egyptian army during the New Kingdom, Alan Schulman determined that the army during the height of the empire was 20,000 strong, and no larger than 25,000.[31] Never would the entire army have been concentrated in one location (such as the capital), even on a major military expedition during the New Kingdom period, as there would have been troops permanently stationed in garrisons in Canaan, the dozen or so forts that stretched across North Sinai, those in the Wadi Tumilat Corridor, and in the forts in Nubia. Evidence is now emerging that during the Ramesside era a line of forts extended from the western Delta all the way to near the present-day Libyan border, much as there was a line of forts from the eastern Delta across Sinai and into southern Canaan. One of these forts is currently being excavated by Steven Snape at Zawiyet Umm el-Rakham, a site located along the Mediterranean coast toward the present-day border with Libya.[32] These considerations mean that an even smaller number of troops would have been stationed in Pi-Ramesses during the Nineteenth Dynasty. Once the size and distribution of the Egyptian army is understood, it further illustrates that 600,000 for the number of Israelite men of military age is impossible.

The size of armies elsewhere in the ancient Near East indicates that fighting forces of the time are minuscule when compared to 600,000. For instance, in the battle of Qarqar, Shalmaneser III (853 B.C.) documents the names of the nations and city-states that marshaled troops against him. Eleven kings contributed forces in what was one of the largest battles in ancient history. According to the Kurkh monolith, there were 3,940 chariots, 2,900 cavalry and camels, and around 53,000 troops amassed against the Assyrians.[33] This total number of troops is small indeed compared to the gigantic figure of 600,000 Israelite fighting men.

Further testimony that suggests the Israelites did not number in the millions is found elsewhere in the Old Testament. Regardless of when one might date the exodus and nature of the entry of the Israelites into Canaan during the Late Bronze Age,[34] if millions of people had arrived the archaeological record would surely attest to such an influx.

Over the past twenty-five years a number of studies have been undertaken to learn the population of Canaan and Israel at different periods. The results are based upon decades of archaeological work and extensive regional surveys from the 1970s and 1980s. During the Early Bronze Age (ca. 2600 B.C.), the maximum population of the region is thought to be around 150,000.[35] In the Middle Bronze II period (ca. 2000–1500 B.C.), the population appears to have dipped slightly, there being an estimated 140,000 people dwelling in Canaan.[36] In Iron Age II Israel, it appears that the population of the Northern and Southern Kingdoms swelled to between 750,000 and 900,000.[37] Another study of the Iron II period, however, offers a significantly lower figure: 460,000 for the two kingdoms.[38] One may question the accuracy of the population figures that have emerged from this recent research, but even if the projected totals were doubled, which is a highly unlikely total, several million Israelites would simply have overwhelmed the peoples of Canaan in the Late Bronze Age.

It appears from various texts that Israel did not see itself as matching or exceeding the indigenous population of Canaan. Exodus 23:30, for instance, reports God as saying: "Little by little I will drive them out from before you, until you have increased and possess the land." It is clear that the spies who reported to Moses in Numbers believed that Israel did not have the needed strength to take the land. The spies complained: "We came to the land to which you sent us; it flows with milk and honey, and this is its fruit. Yet the people who live in the land are strong, and the towns are fortified and very large" וְהֶעָרִים בְּצֻרוֹת גְּדֹלֹת מְאֹד (Num. 13:27–28). When we consider the size of the cities the Israelites are said to have taken in Canaan, one wonders why the Israelites with an army of 600,000 would have been pessimistic about their ability to conquer these very large cities. Jericho, the first city attacked by the Israelites (Josh. 6), at its maximal size measured only 300 by 140 meters, or approximately the size of seven football fields. Hazor, recognized by archaeologists to be the largest city in all of Canaan, occupied 210 acres (both upper and lower tell), according to Amnon Ben-Tor, the current excavator.[39] The massive size of this ancient city is acknowledged in Joshua 11:10. The estimated population of Middle Bronze Age Hazor is 33,000–42,000, and it apparently was somewhat smaller in the Late Bronze Age.[40] While Hazor was formidable and Jericho quite small by Levantine standards, fortified cities like these should not have been a serious challenge to an army of 600,000. In fact, an army of that size could fight on many fronts at the same time, rather than fighting in a united manner (i.e., "all Israel"), taking on one city at a time.[41] The biblical references cited here, along with the data regarding the demography and size of fortified cities in Canaan, indicate that Israelites felt outnumbered and overmatched.

Finally, during the battle against Ai (Josh. 7:2–5), Joshua is reported to have dispatched just three thousand (כִּשְׁלֹשֶׁת אֲלָפִים אִישׁ) Israelites to take this site "since they are so few" (v. 3). In this attack, thirty-six of their troops were killed, and this was regarded as a major defeat. In reality, this loss is negligible out of 3,000 troops (if three *^{a}lāp̱îm* be taken as 3,000), representing less than 1.5 percent, let alone out of 600,000. So why was this event viewed as such a setback by the Israelites that it resulted in communitywide mourning (cf. Josh. 7:6–9)?

One can only conclude that the 600,000 has been misunderstood by translators and commentators until more recent times, when other historical records and archaeological data offer a clearer picture about the sizes of armies and the realities of populations in Egypt and the Levant during the second millennium B.C.

Because the figures in Exodus 12:37 and the census of Numbers 1 are in general agreement, it is suggested here that the problem does not lie with the text but in how one translates the word *'elep̱* (אֶלֶף). Although it can be rendered "thousand," it can also be translated as "clan" and "military unit."[42] Clan is clearly understood in a statement made by the judge Gideon: "How can I deliver Israel? My clan is the weakest in Manasseh, and I am the least in my family" (Judges 6:15) (אוֹשִׁיעַ אֶת־יִשְׂרָאֵל הִנֵּה אַלְפִּי הַדַּל בִּמְנַשֶּׁה וְאָנֹכִי הַצָּעִיר בְּבֵית אָבִי בַּמָּה). Most modern translations of this verse recognize that *'elep̱* refers to a subsection of a tribe; for example, RSV, NRSV, NKJV, JPS, NEB, NASB, and NIV. Consequently, 600 clans is a possible translation of *elep̱*, but in the case of Exodus 12:36 this translation seems unlikely because 600 *'elep̱* is applied to *hagg^{e}bārîm* (הַגְּבָרִים), which is typically translated "men," but could be rendered warriors or heroes.[43] In 2 Samuel 23:8, a list of David's *hagg^{e}bārîm* (הַגִּבֹּרִים) recounts the military prowess and heroic deeds of his elite fighters. A number of English translations render this word as "mighty men" (KJV, ASV, RSV, NIV), while others offer the meaning as "warriors" (NAB, JPS, NRSV). Consequently, the translation "clan" is inappropriate in this case.

The translation "military unit" for *'elep̱* is another option. In 1 Samuel 17:18, for instance, Jesse directed his son David to present a gift "to the commander of the *'elep̱*" (לְשַׂר־הָאָלֶף); "the commander of their thousand" is the literal translation (cf. KJV, RSV, NRSV, JPS), but some recognize the meaning to be a title, that is, "commanding officer" (cf. JB, NEB), and others understand *'elep̱* as referring to a unit (NIV).[44] Somewhat related to this interpretation is the proposal to repoint the Massoretic text to read *'allûp̱*, meaning tribal chief,[45] or "fully armed man."[46]

With these possibilities for translating *'elep̱*, let us turn to how scholars have interpreted the 600 *'elep̱* of Exodus 12:37. There are those who take the reference to mean 600,000, but these are divided into two camps. First, there are the traditionalists who believe that there were literally several million involved, a view that I have argued is implausible. Many of the nineteenth-century explorers of Sinai unquestioningly accepted the high totals, and this view is maintained by some present-day literalists such as Walter Kaiser and Robert Cornuke.[47] The large number is viewed by some commentators to be an intentional exaggeration for theological purposes, to elevate the greatness of YHWH's saving acts.[48] Others consider the inflated figure as reflecting P's belief that such a figure represented historical reality.[49] Along similar lines, Daniel Fouts has argued that the massive numbers were intended for hyperbolic purposes.[50] It is true that in some cases, the hyperbolic use of numbers, especially in military settings, is well attested. One apparent example in the Bible is 2 Chronicles 14:9, where the army led by Zerah the Cushite is said to be one million.[51] Assyrian annals often contain very large numbers in military contexts, and exaggeration or hyperbole may be the intention.[52] Egyptian military texts also use numbers such as thousands (*ḏbᶜw*), tens of thousands (*ḫ3w*), or hundreds of thousands (*ḥfnw*) hyperbolically.[53] However, these numbers are not usually modified by a numeral like six or seven (i.e., 600,000 or 700,000).

Thus on comparative grounds, the use of 600 *'elep̱* in Exodus 12:37 as an intentionally exaggerated figure is a plausible explanation, but the number does not compare favorably with the hyperbolic use of numbers in the available corpus of ancient Near Eastern literature. Furthermore, since this number is referring to the size of Israel's potential fighting force, one might expect the number to be reduced to make God's intervention more impressive. The reduction of an army to a small fighting force so as to credit God with the victory clearly stands behind the story of Gideon's band of 300 (Judges 7). Another way of regarding the 600 *'elep̱* is to interpret it sexagesimally.[54] The base 6 numbering system was known in early Sumer, but it apparently did not spread through the Near East, which militates against this suggestion.

One of the first scholars of the early twentieth century to wrestle with the question of the number of Israelites involved in the exodus and wilderness narratives was Flinders Petrie.[55] Many scholars since have sought to unravel the problem of the number of Israelites, but not all can be treated here.[56]

On the basis of his analysis of the Numbers 1 itinerary, Petrie proposed understanding *'elep* as "tent groups," and that the hundreds figure represents the actual number of men in the *'elep*. According to his theory, the 600 figure represents the total number of *'eleps* (units) in the census figures. He then added the hundreds column, which he believed would produce the actual number of fighting men, viz. 5,500.[57] This figure certainly accords better with the comparative numbers of armies, and would mean that although a sizeable force, it would not vastly outnumber the Egyptian army.

Perhaps the most thorough and enduring study of the Numbers 1 census is that of George Mendenhall, from 1958.[58] He built on Petrie's conclusions and accepted the meaning of *'elep* as "some subsection of a tribe."[59] I concur with his observation that, because of the military nature, the census of Numbers 1 had to be precise for organizing Israel's military force. Therefore, it seems unlikely that the totals would be artificially inflated for either theological reasons or as a hyperbolic device. Working within Martin Noth's amphictyonic tribal system and considering other sociological factors, Mendenhall argued that the census reveals the contribution of each tribe to the army. He regarded the census as "an authentic list from the period of the Federation which reflects this sort of military organization and mobilization, probably coming from specific occasions when the Federation army had to be mobilized to meet the common peril."[60] The number of men per tribal unit varied considerably, ranging between five and fourteen. On the basis of these figures, Mendenhall declared that they are "so random that no pattern can be seen underlying them—historical reality is the best foundation for their interpretation."[61] He concluded that the system of tallying forces used by the Priestly writer derived from earlier sources that were influenced by the type of military reckoning found on texts from Alalakh and Mari.[62] Although Petrie believed that the censuses originated in the Mosaic period, Mendenhall considered the tribal system in place in Numbers 1 and 26 to reflect what he calls the period of Federation, that is, from the time of Joshua-Judges. By the period of the early monarchy, Mendenhall noted, the traditional tribal organization system was deteriorating.[63] He also thought it possible that later in Israelite history it became difficult for different authors and copyists to understand how to interpret *'elep*, which led to confusion and ambiguity that resulted in thinking that hundreds of thousands or millions of Israelites were involved in the exodus and wilderness episodes.[64]

Nearly twenty years after his seminal study, Mendenhall took up the question of Israel's system of tribal organization and modified his earlier conclusion. He now believes the origin of the census should be moved down to the period of the United Monarchy.[65] The corvée labor system in which each tribe was responsible to conscript laborers for Solomon's building projects, he proposes, stands behind the census that P projected back onto the Mosaic period in Numbers 1 and 26. It is unclear to me why Mendenhall changed his interpretation of 1958, since no new data were offered to support the revision. It appears that he has simply been swept up in the metachronistic tendencies that have characterized much of biblical scholarship since the 1970s.[66]

Mendenhall's view that an *'elep̱* is a clan-based military unit has been accepted by other scholars who also utilize sociological approaches to the Hebrew scriptures. One of these is Norman Gottwald, who further suggests that *'elep̱* occasionally was used as a synonym with *mišpaḥâ*, the usual word for clan.[67] J. David Schloen, in his recent and groundbreaking study of the *bêt 'ab* ("house of the father," i.e., household), likewise concurs with Mendenhall, agreeing that the typical *'elep̱* consisted of nine to ten men, and that a *mišpaḥâ* was composed of one to two dozen households.[68] Although some recent studies have challenged Mendenhall on his lowering the date of the censuses, there is still agreement that his analysis is on the right track in his understanding of *'elep̱*.[69] Colin Humphreys, a Cambridge University mathematician, through his mathematical analysis of the numbers determines that the number of Israelites included in the exodus was around 20,000.[70]

The evidence offered here, along with the thoughtful studies of the problem of the size of the Israelite exodus, leaves little doubt that the number of individuals would have been in the thousands, maybe a few tens of thousands, but certainly not hundreds of thousands, let alone millions.

III. The Route to Mt. Sinai

The route from the crossing of the Sea of Reeds to Mt. Sinai has been the subject of continued debate for centuries. The main reason for the lack of a consensus is, as was discussed in the previous chapter, that numerous candidates have been advanced for Mt. Sinai. This factor naturally has a bearing on how the route the Bible describes is interpreted. Those who locate Mt. Sinai in the southern sector of the peninsula do concur that a route along the western coast of Sinai was taken and at some point, the Israelites would have turned east toward the central mountainous region. This tradition can be traced as early as the itinerary of Egeria (A.D. 381–384), and was followed by most of the nineteenth-century explorers such as Burkhardt, Robinson, and Palmer.

The following is a review of the key toponyms furnished by the Exodus and Numbers itineraries with an attempt to place these locations, based largely upon the research of earlier generations of scholarship. It must be recognized that the following reconstruction is tentative, but in my view it is plausible.

Wilderness of Shur/Etham

Exodus 15:22a reports that immediately upon departing *yām sûp̱*, "they went into the wilderness of Shur" (וַיֵּצְאוּ אֶל־מִדְבַּר־שׁוּר). In addition to this reference to Shur, there are five others in the Bible, and these show plainly that it is located adjacent to Egypt in Sinai. Genesis 20:1 states: "From there Abraham journeyed toward the region of the Negeb, and settled between Kadesh and Shur." While not so precise, this reference places Abraham in the Negeb between Kadesh (i.e., 'Ain Qadis or Qudeirat) and Shur, which is apparently located west of Kadesh. The Ishmaelites are said to have "settled from Havilah to Shur, which is opposite Egypt" (אֲשֶׁר עַל־פְּנֵי מִצְרַיִם; Gen. 25:18). King Saul, when fighting the Amalekites of the Negev, pursued them "as far as Shur, which is east of [lit. opposite] Egypt" (אֲשֶׁר עַל־פְּנֵי מִצְרָיִם; 1 Sam. 15:7), and subsequently, David conducted raids against the Amalekites in "Shur and on to the land of Egypt" (וְעַד־אֶרֶץ מִצְרָיִם; 1 Sam. 27:8). In Genesis 16:7 there is a reference to "the way of Shur" (דֶּרֶךְ שׁוּר), indicating that there was a route from the Negev to Shur, which is before (in front of) Egypt.

These references demonstrate that Shur is located in the Sinai, between the Negev and Egypt, or between Kadesh (a specific spot within the southern Negev) and Egypt. The "Way of Shur" is widely accepted to be the route that leads from the hill country of Ephraim and Judah, which passes by Bethel, Jerusalem, and Beersheba, from which it turns west toward Egypt approximately in the Lake Timsah region.[71] Furthermore, these references ought to eliminate Edom or Midian as a location for Mt. Sinai. Crossing the Gulf of Aqaba and into northern Arabia would not land one in the wilderness of Shur. David and Saul's campaigns against the Amalekites in the Negev would not have led them to the Hejaz area of Arabia, but to Sinai, in the direction of Egypt.

As for the meaning of Shur (שׁוּר), it is thought to be related to a Semitic word for wall.[72] Some have suggested that it alludes to the Egyptian "Walls of the Ruler," that is, the series of forts across North Sinai.[73] This interpretation seems unlikely, since the Bible refers to this northern road as the "Way of the land of the Philistines" (Exod. 13:17). Given that the way of Shur (from the perspective of Canaan/Israel) runs parallel to, but south of the Way of the land of the Philistines (i.e., the Egyptian Ways of Horus), a more plausible explanation for the name Shur is the mountainous ridge that runs east-west, which marks the beginning of the Tih Plateau, and specifically Gebel er-Raha, as Graham Davies has argued (see chapter 3, §IV).[74]

The Numbers itinerary identifies the name of the desert encountered after leaving the sea as Etham (33:8a) rather than Shur. There is little doubt that this variant is intended to apply to the same desert, as both passages mention a three-day journey until the arrival at Marah (cf. Exod. 15:22; Num. 33:8). Etham, as was suggested (chapter 4, §7), is probably of Egyptian etymology, whereas Shur is clearly a Semitic term. Hence it appears that Exodus 15:22 used the Semitic name for this desert area, whereas Numbers opts for the Egyptian counterpart. If Numbers 33 is P's late itinerary, it is curious that the Egyptian name, which would have little or no significance to a postexilic audience, is used.

The proximity of Etham to Egypt is undeniable, as it was a toponym encountered prior to reaching *yām sûp̱*, and was reported to be "on the edge of the wilderness" (Exod 13:20; Num. 33:6). The fact that the itinerary included Etham both before and after the crossing of the sea shows that a circuitous route was taken, which brought Israelites back to the general area of Succoth and Etham (figure 1). In other words, when Israel turned back at Etham (Exod. 13:20, 14:2) they headed northward away from the Lake Timsah region where they encountered *yām sûp̱*, that is, the Ballah Lakes, according to our reconstruction (see chapter 4, §VIII). Once they crossed it from its northern side, the Israelites would have traveled south, which would allow them to once again be in the wilderness of Etham. This reconstruction, as it turns out, is precisely like that of the *Oxford Bible Atlas* (2nd edition) and the revised *Macmillan Bible Atlas.*[75] The reference to Shur in Exodus 15:22 reinforces this interpretation because of the consensus opinion that it lies in the vicinity of Lake Timsah, where the way of Shur terminated. Thus the reference to Shur and Etham place the Israelites in approximately the same place, that is, east of the lakes of the Isthmus of Suez, evidently traveling in a southerly direction.

Marah and Elim

As the text of Exodus 15:23 states, Marah derives its name from the bitter water reached after traveling three days through the desert of Shur without finding water (15:22). As travelers have attested, brackish water is found in many of the wells and springs in Sinai. The Israelites would have traveled south from the crossing area on the northern portion of the Ballah Lakes. Using thirty-two kilometers (twenty miles) as the approximate distance for the average day's journey (see chapter 6, §III), they would have traveled past the Bitter Lakes, approximately ninety-six kilometers (sixty miles), which would land them in the area of present-day Suez, that is, the northern end of the Gulf of Suez. The lack of drinking water along the Isthmus of Suez is likewise reported in the Egyptian story of Sinuhe. During his flight to Canaan, Sinuhe passed by the Bitter Lakes (*km wr*) and claims: "An attack of thirst overcame me; I being parched, my throat being dry, and I thought, 'this is the taste of death.'"[76] The story of Sinhue shows that early in the second millennium B.C. sweet water was lacking in the area opposite the Bitter Lakes. Conditions were no different toward the end the same millennium, when the Israelites traveled three days through the desert of Shur and could find no water.

On the basis of his explorations in Sinai in 1816, Burkhardt identified Marah with 'Ain Hawara, which is located just over two days' travel south of Suez.[77] Robinson, who was influenced considerably by Burkhardt, concurred with this identification. He too journeyed from Suez to 'Ain Hawara in two days and several hours on the third day, and described the water as "unpleasant, saltish, and somewhat bitter."[78] Other nineteenth-century investigators, such as Arthur Stanley and E. H. Palmer, accepted this identification, as have some more recent commentators.[79] This location made sense because they thought that the sea crossing occurred at the very north end of the Gulf of Suez (i.e., the Red Sea), and 'Ain Hawara was reached on the third day of travel from Suez by both Burkhardt and Robinson.

The problem with equating 'Ain Hawara with Marah is that it only works if the sea crossing took place near Suez. Moreover, Burkhardt, Robinson, and others suggested that nearby Wadi Gharandel is Elim, the next stop on the itinerary.[80] Burkhardt traveled from 'Ain Hawara to Wadi Gharandel in three hours, whereas Robinson made it in just two and a half hours. This short distance means either that 'Ain Hawara cannot be Marah or Wadi Gharandel cannot be Elim, as there was no reason to camp at Marah with its bitter water when Gharandel (Elim) lies only a few hours away and the water was good. This short distance can hardly be construed as a day's journey. The latter site, Robinson learned from local Bedouin, is "still one of the chief watering-places of the Arabs."[81]

Alternatively, some more recent scholars, such as Manashe Har-el and George Kelm, propose Bir el-Mura as biblical Marah.[82] The Arabic name *murr* is cognate with Hebrew Marah, and means bitter.[83] Clinton Bailey has shown that the Bedouin of Sinai frequently name a well or spring on the basis of the quality of the water, and *murr* is one such name.[84] If this water source was bitter in ancient times, there is little likelihood that its quality has changed. The water is not described as salty, in which case the Hebrew word *mlḥ* would be used.[85] Interestingly, the Arabic word *maliḥ* or *malḥa* is found in geographical terms in Sinai.[86] Bitter water in some areas of Sinai, and in 'Ayun Musa in particular, is due to the presence of magnesium sulfate.[87] It would appear that the presence of such minerals in the water gave rise to the name Marah. Thus a connection between the site named in Exodus 15:23 and the present day Bir el-Mura is certainly plausible, and it would fit within the distance of a three days' journey or approximately ninety-six kilometers/sixty miles from our proposed crossing point on the south side of the el-Balah Lake (figure 1).

Another possibility is to locate Marah at 'Ayun Musa, as Simons and the hydrologist Arie Issar have done.[88] 'Ayun Musa, meaning "springs of Moses" in Arabic, is surrounded by palm trees and has a number of springs. Burkhardt described the water as "copious," but only one of the springs produces "sweet water."[89] When Robinson visited this site in 1838, he counted seven springs, and noticed that local Bedouin channeled the overflow toward small plots where barley and cabbage grew.[90]

The next campsite, according to both Exodus 15:27 and Numbers 33:9, is Elim (אֵילִם). The meaning of this word is unclear, and it is only attested in the Exodus and Numbers itineraries.[91] It is described in both books as having twelve springs and seventy palms, making it a natural place to stop. Nineteenth-century investigators identified Elim with Wadi Gharandel.[92] This wadi, like many others, has acacia, tamarisk, and palm trees growing in the mouth of its wadi bed. Robinson recorded that "the Arabs procured water... from fountains with a running brook. It was brackish.... When the rains fail for two or three years, the brook ceases to flow; but water is always to be found by digging a little below the surface."[93]

Manashe Har-el, on the other hand, has proposed that 'Ayun Musa is Elim, largely because he needs to place it after Bir el-Mura (his Marah), which is only twelve kilometers (seven miles) away and before the Wadi Sudr, located approximately thirty-eight kilometers (twenty-four miles) to the south. He considers the opening of this wadi to be Rephadim of Exodus 17:1 and Numbers 33:14.[94] Har-el's theory, in my opinion, fails on several points. First, Bir el-Mura and 'Ayun Musa are too close to each other to stand a day's journey apart. Second, for Wadi Sudr to be equated with Rephadim, Har-el has to either compress the next four campsites of the Numbers itinerary (33:10–13) into just thirty-eight kilometers (twenty-four miles) or eliminate them. Third, he wants to locate Mt. Sinai at Gebel Sin Bishr, which as has been shown, places it too close to both the sea crossing and the eleven-day journey from Mt. Sinai to Kadesh, as required by Deuteronomy 1:2 (cf. chapter 6, §IV).

The nature of the itineraries is such, I maintain, that some of the actual campsites may have been omitted, perhaps for literary or structural reasons. An example of this would be the next names in the Numbers sequence, which read, *yām sûp̱*, the wilderness of Sin, Dophkah, and Alush. Exodus 16, which contains this segment of the itinerary, does not include *yām sûp̱*, Dophkah, and Alush. It seems unlikely to me that toponyms were artificially added to Numbers 33 to embellish the list. I can see no rational explanation for expanding an itinerary. Consequently, the distance from Rameses to Mt. Sinai may have included more campsites than are recorded in the itineraries of the Torah, but it is not likely that the number of sites were reduced. To do so is arbitrary and only serves the purpose of the modern scholar who wishes to make the itinerary fit his or her reconstruction. In this study, I will limit myself to working with the data supplied by the Pentateuch.

Yām Sûp̱ and the Wilderness of Sin

Following Elim, the itinerary has the Israelites camping at *yām sûp̱* (Num. 33:10). I have argued in some detail in chapter 5 that this term applied to the area covered by the el-Balah Lake system east of the Delta, and that *yām sûp̱* corresponded to the Egyptian toponym *p3 ṯwfy*. How then do we encounter this same name at least six days of travel after crossing *yām sûp̱*? There can be little doubt that here, as in 1 Kings 9:26, the Red Sea was intended. In the Kings passage, the Gulf of Aqaba is in view, whereas here in Numbers the Gulf of Suez is intended. This is how most commentators understand this occurrence.[95] Some critics, such as Bernard Batto, argue that since this usage of *yām sûp̱* is unquestionably the Red Sea, it therefore cannot refer to the Sea of Reeds, that is, one of the marshy lakes in the Isthmus of Suez.[96] Prior to this study, I had argued that in the Bible *yām sûp̱* is applied to all three of the above-mentioned bodies of water, and that in the mind of the ancient Hebrew geographers, the gulfs of Suez and Aqaba were viewed as an extension of the sea of crossing.[97] The name *yām sûp̱*, however, derives from the first body of water encountered and was subsequently applied to the Red Sea.

One implication of the location of this campsite is that prior to this point, the route took the Israelites slightly inland from the sea. Why no other name is associated with this campsite is unclear. It could be that the earlier water sources were closer to the wadis and foothills of west-central Sinai. Another consideration is that after passing Wadi Gharandel, the Gebel Hammam Pharaon comes right down to the sea, and is known for its hot sulfur springs. This water is exceptionally putrid in smell and repulsive to drink.[98] There is only a narrow section of beach between the mountain and the sea, and here the extremely hot water oozes out of the sand and runs into the sea; the entire area reeks of sulfur. The geographical obstruction caused by Gebel Hammam Pharaon would have forced the Israelites to go around it to the east, just as the asphalt road does today. In fact, the road skirts around the mountain and continues south out of view of the sea for a distance of twenty-six kilometers (about sixteen miles) until it once again comes to the coast. At this point is the present-day town of Abu Zenimah.

Going closer to the sea would afford the opportunity for fishing, a source of protein the Israelites had enjoyed in Egypt that would have been denied them throughout most of the wilderness period. That the Israelites missed fish in Sinai is plainly seen in the complaint in Numbers 11:5: "We remember the fish we used to eat in Egypt for nothing." The Nile and its canals and swampy inlets, especially in the Delta, were ideal spawning grounds for many kinds of fish. Fish, unlike other sources of meat, was freely available for anyone willing to fish with a hook and line or net. Consequently, fish was a favorite source of protein among poorer people, but it was also the food of royalty and was offered to deities. The abundance of fish in Egypt is illustrated by the donation lists of Ramesses III, who over a period of thirty-one years recorded that nearly a half million fish were donated to various temples for various festivals.[99]

One might not be inclined to think that by going close to the sea, drinking water could be obtained naturally. But Burkhardt learned that there were places along the coast in Sinai within fifty yards of the sea where he witnessed drinkable water being obtained by "digging a hole about three feet deep and one foot in diameter, it filled in half an hour with very tolerable water." Petrie and Currelly also offer testimony for this practice from their explorations in Sinai.[100] This intriguing method for finding water may explain why the Israelites camped by the sea at this juncture.

The Markha Plain has been suggested to be the area where the Israelite campsite simply called *yām sûp̱* was located.[101] Other researchers have suggested that the Markha Plain is within the sphere of the wilderness of Sin, the next campsite, which Exodus 16:1 places between Elim and Sinai (for further discussion about the wilderness of Sin, see chapter 3, §III).[102] A spring in el-Markha produces water that is described as tasting bad, and yet it remains the main source of water for that area after Wadi Gharandel to its north.[103] A team associated with the University of California Expedition in Africa, headed by Wendell Phillips, explored parts of Sinai in 1947. W. F. Albright was brought along as a consultant. They investigated the Markha Plain near Abu Zenimah and discovered a port used by Egyptian miners in the New Kingdom.[104] A new archaeological survey of the Markha Plain is now being conducted by Gregory Mumford of the University of Toronto. Thus far Mumford's team has confirmed Albright's observation that this site was seasonally occupied by miners during the New Kingdom, and that there is evidence that some of the copper smelting occurred near the harbor.[105]

A final proposal for the location of the *yām sûp̱* campsite has been made by Graham Davies, who has suggested the mouth of Wadi Tayibah, situated almost twenty-six kilometers (sixteen miles) south of Wadi Gharandel.[106] But he admits that this spot, like the others that have been suggested, is not certain.

Dophkah and Serabit el-Khadim

Since we have concluded that Mt. Sinai is located somewhere in south-central Sinai, the route would have to turn east at some point through one of several wadis, where the remaining campsites would be found. There are three wadis that serve as roads to the interior, all of which lead to the mountainous area of Serbal and Safsafeh-Musa. The northernmost of these is Wadi Humr, followed by Wadi Sidri and Wadi Feiran (figure 1).[107] Wadi Humr was the route taken by Robinson on his way to the St. Catherine's area. From his entry into the wadi by the coast, it was a full day's travel to Serabit el-Khadim.[108] I have driven through this wadi to Serabit; it is broad and very accessible for travel. Wadi Humr is the probable route taken by the Egyptian mining expeditions in Pharaonic times. Wells are found through this wadi, which would have facilitated travel through it (figure 31). Inscriptions of miners heading for Serabit from Egypt have recently been discovered at Ain Sukhnah on the Red Sea coast of Egypt, about forty kilometers (twenty-five miles) south of Suez. A text dated to the first year of Montuhotep IV of the Eleventh Dynasty (ca. 1970–1963 B.C.) states that an expedition of 3,000 men were on their way to bring turquoise, probably from Serabit.[109] A decade later, another inscription dating to the sixth year of Amenemhet I, the founder of the Twelfth Dynasty, records that a troop of 4,000 men passed through the same location. Undoubtedly, these large expeditions would have traveled through the Wadi

Humr to get to the turquoise mines of Serabit el-Khadim. Whether or not the Israelites would have entered central Sinai via this route, these newly found texts show that large numbers of troops could have traveled through this wadi.

Over the years, some have suggested that Dophkah (דָּפְקָה) of Numbers 33:12 might be located in the area of Serabit el-Khadim, principally because of the similarity of the Egyptian word, *mfk't*, turquoise.[110] A number of historical geographers actually trace the route to Mt. Sinai as passing by Serabit, with Dophkah being written with or without a question mark.[111] Lina Eckenstein went so far as to think that biblical Mt. Sinai or Horeb was located at Serabit.[112] This view, however, has not been taken seriously.

Those who associate Serabit with Dophkah recognize the linguistic problem of the Egyptian *m* appearing in Hebrew as *d*.[113] The Septuagint's reading of Raphaka (Rafaka) is no help, and probably does not preserve the original reading. Rather it seems that the Greek translators misread the Hebrew ד (*daled*) as a ר (*resh*), a common scribal error. Graham Davies rejects the association of Hebrew Dopkhah with the Egyptian *mfk't* as "misguided."[114] Although he does not elaborate on this point, I suspect that he and others who reject this identification do so for two reasons: linguistic problems and the fact that it is thought that *mfk't* is not used as a geographical term. It is certainly true that in scores of texts from Serabit, *mfk't* is never used as the name for the site. *Mfk't* is generally used in two different ways at Serabit: First, as the principal commodity that the miners were there to uncover, that is, turquoise; and second, as a part of the epithet for the Hathor Lady of Turquoise (*nbt mfk't*), the patron of the region and the deity to whom the grand temple at Serabit is dedicated (figure 32).[115] There are, however, writings of *mfk't* with the foreign or mountainous region determinative (𓈉), but they are found at Wadi Maghara. Wadi Maghara, situated about twenty kilometers (twelve miles) directly south of Serabit, had been another Egyptian mining center since the third dynasty (ca. 2700 B.C.). Concerning this writing of *mfk't*, Gardiner noted that it "seems to indicate that *mfk't* was occasionally interpreted not as the name of a mineral but as that of a country." Gardiner also points to an interesting statement recorded at Luxor temple that refers to turquoise from *ḏw n mfk't*, "the mountain of turquoise."[116] Could this expression stand behind the Hebrew name Dophkah? There remain some linguistic problems with this proposal, one being the Egyptian *k* written as *ḳ*. However, the Egyptian *ḏ* appearing as *d* is not a problem in New Kingdom, because at this time the Egyptians actually vocalized the *ḏ* as *d*.[117]

Then too there is the expression *ḫtyw mfk't*, "terraces of turquoise," which also refers to the Maghara area.[118] Thus it is evident that the word *mfk't* did indeed play a role in several geographical terms found at Wadi Maghara. Consequently, we cannot rule out the possibility that Dophkah represents a garbled writing for the name given to the mining district of Wadi Maghara, but not Serabit el-Khadim.

It might be natural to think that, because of the presence of Egyptians in the mining regions of Serabit el-Khadim and Wadi Maghara, the Israelites would want to avoid these locations. We know from the inscriptions at Serabit that mining expeditions typically came early in winter so they could complete their mission and return to Egypt before the searing heat of summer settled in. Text 90, a large stela dated to year six of Amenemhet III (ca. 1837 B.C.), contains the instructive account of an expedition led by Harwerre. He complains that his mission occurred out of season: "This country was reached in the third month of winter, though it was not the season for coming to this mining district. This god's treasurer [i.e., Harwerre] says to the officials who shall come to this mining district at this season: Do not be downcast because of it. . . . Hard was it in my opinion to find the [right] colour when the foreign country was hot in summer. . . . Then when I reached this land, I began the work, at a favorable moment. My expedition returned complete in its entirety, no loss had ever occurred among it. . . . I broke off in the first month of summer."[119] What we learn from Harwerre's disclosure is that his expedition arrived in Sinai late in winter (third month of winter; *3bd 3 3ḫt*), long after the time when expeditions were generally sent, due to the change of seasons. His operation came to a successful end in the first month of summer (*tpy šmmw*). At one point he refers to the season of his work as "this evil season of summer" (*ḳsn n šmmw*). There is no doubt that the Egyptian miners would not normally have been on mining expeditions during the period of May through September. The period when the Israelites would have passed through the mining regions, if indeed this was the route taken, would have likely been in May–June, when Egyptians were not at work in the mines.[120]

Wadi Maghara is located about twenty kilometers (twelve miles) inland from the Gulf of Suez. Its mines were worked regularly from around 2700 B.C. onward, though during the New Kingdom there was apparently only limited exploitation of the mines, to judge from the number of inscriptions from that period.[121] If I am correct in suggesting that Mt. Sinai is somewhere in the granite massif of south-central Sinai, it is noteworthy that Wadi Maghara is only about a three days' journey away from Gebel Musa and just two from Gebel Serbal. The proximity of Mt. Sinai to the mining district may account for the use of turquoise in the priestly breastpiece that held the Urim and Thummim. The word written in Exodus 28:18 and 39:11 is *nopek̲* (נֹפֶךְ) and is recognized as being etymologically related to the Egyptian word *mfk't*, turquoise.[122] The interchange between the *m* and the *n* poses no linguistic problem, leading Yoshiyuki Muchiki to determine confidently that "there is little doubt that נפך originated from Eg. *mfk'.t*."[123] Over the years most English translations of the Bible have not recognized the correct meaning of *nopek*, but several have recently adopted "turquoise" as the translation (cf. NIV, JPS, NRSV).

In the light of this evidence, one has to ask whether it is just a coincidence that the only references to turquoise (*nopek̲*) in the Torah occur in a geographical setting (Mt. Sinai) so close to the major source for turquoise in the region, and that the Egyptian word for turquoise should appear in Exodus as a loanword. The other known sources for turquoise are a great distance away in the Libyan massif and Persia.[124] The references in Exodus 28:18 and 39:11 are assigned to P by source critics, and hence date to the fifth century B.C.[125] How did the putative Priestly writer(s) know about turquoise and why was the Egyptian word used in Hebrew? (There are other gemstones of Egyptian origin in the priestly breastpiece, which will be discussed in a subsequent chapter.) The only other occurrences of *nopek* in the Old Testament are found in Ezekiel 27:16 and 28:13, which indicate that the word was known in the sixth century as well. In the first instance, turquoise is mentioned as a trade commodity of the Edomites. This is not surprising, given the proximity of Edom to Sinai and given that the territory of Edom occupied a strategic place on the trade route or king's highway between the Red Sea and Damascus in the north.[126] In the second occurrence in Hebrew text (MT) of Ezekiel, it is mentioned in a list of nine gemstones associated with the king of Tyre and his symbolic association with the Garden of Eden. As it turns out, all nine are found among the twelve gems in the priest's breastpiece of Exodus 28:17–20. The fact that three of the gems on the priestly breastplate are absent in Ezekiel's list suggests that the prophet probably borrowed the gem list from the Exodus passage, and not the other way around. John Wevers speculated that "the list of nine stones is a much later insertion taken from the list of Exod. 28:17–20."[127] Daniel Block, in his monumental commentary on Ezekiel, suggests that the list of gems in Ezekiel 28:13 was "inspired by" the priestly breastplate.[128] The difference in sequence may be attributed to Ezekiel's desire to have a different color sequence.[129] Interestingly, the Septuagint actually records all twelve stones, which leads Moshe Greenberg to suggest that the omission of the three stones in the MT was a scribal error in transmission.[130]

The point is that the Exodus references to the priestly breastplate lie behind Ezekiel's later usage. The rarity of the word *nopek̲* in the Hebrew scriptures, coupled with the knowledge that the main source of turquoise in the second millennium B.C. in Egypt and Canaan was south Sinai, and that the Egyptian word for turquoise is used for the priest's breastpiece in Exodus, can hardly be coincidental. It might be logical to conclude, then, that the Israelites passed within range of the turquoise-mining region of Serabit el-Khadim or Wadi Maghara on their way to Mt. Sinai, whence turquoise was obtained. Finally, Dophkah, the otherwise unattested toponym of Numbers 33:12, may derive from the Egyptian word *mfk't*, although linguistic problems remain. If Dophkah is connected with the Egyptian word for turquoise, then it would more likely be associated with Wadi Maghara than with Serabit el-Khadim.

Another possible meaning for Dophkah would relate it to the root דפך, which means "beat or knock."[131] Unfortunately, it occurs only a few times in the Bible. In Genesis 33:13 it applies to driving flocks, and in Song of Solomon 5:2

and Judges 19:22 it is used for knocking on a door. How this meaning could stand behind the campsite in Sinai is unclear.

Alush and Rephidim

From Dophkah, the Israelites proceeded to Alush (אָלוּשׁ), according to Numbers 33:14. This site is not mentioned in Exodus 17 as a stopover prior to Rephidim, a toponym which both itineraries agree was the final campsite before arriving at Mt. Sinai.

Burkhardt reported that he camped at Wadi 'esh, where he found "a well of sweet water." Interestingly, he camped there on April 29 and arrived at St. Catherine's Monastery on May 1. He observed that rainwater from this area runs through wadis to nearby Wadi Feiran.[132] He advanced from this point to Wadi el-Sheikh and then to St. Catherine's, whereas twenty-two years later, Robinson at this point split off via Wadi el-Akhdar (i.e., green wadi), which leads to Wadi Feiran.[133] Robinson noted that from the juncture of the wadis 'esh and Akhdar, both Gebel Musa and Gebel Serbal were visible. Neither of these explorers linked Wadi 'esh with Alush. Rather it was later scholars, such as J. Simons and Dewey Beegle, who proposed associating Alush with Wadi 'esh, which is located between the turquoise-mining area and Wadi el-Sheikh.[134] Some see philological problems with this identification, however,[135] while others prefer to consider Alush as still "unidentified."[136]

If we accept the reconstruction advanced here, then Wadi 'esh is a plausible campsite because of its position between Wadi Maghara and Wadi Feiran. The latter has long been accepted as Rephidim of Exodus 17:2 and Numbers 33:14. Christian activity is documented in this area as early as the third century A.D., apparently because it was believed to be Rephidim, the place of the battle with the Amalekites (cf. chapter 6, §III). And many scholars of the nineteenth century (e.g., Robinson, Stanley, and Palmer)[137] and twentieth century (e.g., Aharoni, Beegle, and Perevolotsky and Finkelstein)[138] agree on the identification of Wadi Feiran/Paran with Rephidim (figure 7).

The text plainly tells us that there was once again a problem with water: "The people quarreled with Moses, and said, 'Give us water to drink.' Moses said to them, 'Why do you quarrel with me? Why do you test the LORD?' But the people thirsted there for water; and the people complained against Moses and said, 'Why did you bring us out of Egypt, to kill us and our children and livestock with thirst?' " (Exod. 17:2–3). One gets the impression from this description that the Israelites expected to find water at this location. Wadi Feiran, as noted early, is an oasis rich with hundreds of palm trees, and water at 'Ayan Feiran is plentiful. Conceivably the water had run dry, as Cassuto proposed, but why would the Amalekites stay if there had been no water?[139] The following episode—the battle with the Amalekites—it has been suggested, was the consequence of the Israelites being denied access to the major water sources.[140]

The word Rephidim (רְפִידִים) appears to derive from the root *rpd*, which means help, support, aid, and which, it has been suggested, reflects the divine assistance required to defeat the Amalekites.[141] Although this is an intriguing suggestion, it is not without its problems. If an etiology stands behind the name, no explanation for it is offered in the text. On the other hand, the names Massah or Meribah in the preceding episode are aetiological, and reflect circumstances associated with the stopover at Rephidim.[142] In the episode contained within this chapter, the people complained and tested God (Exod. 17:3–7). Exodus 17:7 concludes, "He called the place Massah and Meribah, because the Israelites quarreled and tested the LORD" (וַיִּקְרָא שֵׁם הַמָּקוֹם מַסָּה וּמְרִיבָה עַל־רִיב בְּנֵי יִשְׂרָאֵל וְעַל נַסֹּתָם אֶת־יְהוָה). This statement suggests that Rephidim was already the name of the site when the Israelites arrived, but owing to the story of Israel's actions, Massah and Meribah were attached to the site.[143]

The name Rephidim has also been connected by some modern scholars with another valley in the area called Wadi Refayid.[144] Simons agreed with this identification, and pointed out that within the wadi is an oasis and mountain called Refayid.[145] In this case, the Arabic name appears to preserve Rephidim remarkably well. Graham Davies considered the equation between these two names to be a plausible example of the Arabic name preserving an earlier Semitic toponym.[146]

The sensational element of this story is that Moses, at God's command, produces water from a rock. " 'I will be standing there in front of you on the rock at Horeb. Strike the rock, and water will come out of it, so that the people may drink.' Moses did so, in the sight of the elders of Israel" (17:6). First we note that this occurs "at Horeb," which supports the view of a number of scholars that Horeb was an area within which Mt. Sinai was located.

The phenomenon of water being obtained from a rock when struck, as described in Exodus 17:5–6, has been witnessed in modern times. The British governor of Sinai during the 1920s, Colonel Jarvis, author of *Yesterday and Today in Sinai* (1933), was an authority on Sinai who frequently drew connections between experiences he had or phenomena he witnessed in Sinai and those reported in the pages of Exodus and Numbers. He observed men of the camel corps digging in limestone rock that had small amounts of water oozing from it. At one point in the digging, the trickle suddenly because a gush of water.

The hydrologist Philip LaMoreaux explains that in igneous formations, such as those in the Wadi Feiran, dykes can create "the hydrogeological setting for the accumulation of shallow ground water." He continues, "The black, near vertical bands, mark the spots where water is present below found in shallow beds of sand." He learned that the Bedouin know how to tap water from such rock formations, the same practice that he attributes to Moses in Exodus 17.[147] This may explain how water sprang from a rock when struck in

Exodus 17. Certainly Jarvis's experience has convinced scholars such as G. Ernest Wright and Dewey Beegle that this is a plausible explanation for the phenomenon attributed to Moses,[148] whereas LaMoreaux's theory would make better sense in southern Sinai, the area where I believe Rephidim was located.

Exodus 19:1–2 offers the final datum related to the itinerary to Mt. Sinai: "On the third new moon after the Israelites had gone out of the land of Egypt, on that very day, they came into the wilderness of Sinai. They had journeyed from Rephidim, entered the wilderness of Sinai, and camped in the wilderness; Israel camped there in front of the mountain." Since Israel departed Egypt on the fifteenth of Abib (Exod. 12:18; 13:4), the first day of the third new moon would be six weeks later.[149] Abib falls in the months of March and April, meaning that six weeks would take one into May and June.[150] As we have seen in chapter 3, §IV, southern Sinai is more temperate during the summer months than north and central Sinai, and water is more available. These ecological considerations made south Sinai more attractive to the seminomadic population of the peninsula during the summer months.[151] This factor may account for the presence at Rephidim of the Amalekites, who are known to be at home in the Negev and northern Sinai in other Bible references (cf. Num. 13:29; 1 Sam. 15:7, 1 Sam. 27:8).

IV. Culinary Considerations

Manna

Along the way from Egypt to Mt. Sinai, two sources of food are mentioned in Exodus 16, manna and quail. Both are mentioned in Psalms 105:40, where the psalmist recalls the divine provision. Manna served as a type of bread. Exodus 16:14–15 describes the phenomenon in the following way: "When the layer of dew lifted, there on the surface of the wilderness was a fine flaky substance, as fine as frost on the ground. When the Israelites saw it, they said to one another, 'What is it?' For they did not know what it was. Moses said to them, 'It is the bread that the LORD has given you to eat.'" Numbers 11:7 offers a more detailed description of this edible substance: "Now the manna was like coriander seed, and its color was like the color of gum resin." The Hebrew writing for manna is מָן הוּא, literally, "what is it?" as the text observes. This expression is an example of popular etymology for this substance. An explanatory note follows Exodus 16:14 to clarify this mysterious grain: "a fine flaky substance" (*daq mᵉḥuspās*: דַּק מְחֻסְפָּס). In the absence of a clear Hebrew etymology for *mᵉḥuspās* (מְחֻסְפָּס), Manfred Görg has proposed that it derives from the combination of two Egyptian words, *mḥw.s*, "grain from Lower Egypt," and *psy*, "to dry, to bake."[152] *Dq* is an Egyptian word meaning "thin."[153] It is noteworthy both that grain of the Delta is the word used, since the Land of Ramesses or Goshen is clearly located in the northeastern Delta, and that Egyptian terms should be used to explain this mysterious substance. If Görg's proposed etymology is correct, then it is difficult to explain as a late gloss, since the use of the Egyptian terms would have little impact upon a first-millennium audience, not to mention being alien to the writer. Consequently, the use of *daq mᵉḥuspās*, it might be suggested, illustrates the antiquity of this statement.

Considerable scholarly discussion has occurred over the years seeking to explain the phenomenon of the appearance of manna in Sinai. When Robinson visited St. Catherine's Monastery in 1838, he learned that the monks gathered what they called manna and that it was highly valued. In fact, the abbott of the monastery promised to give Robinson some. The American explorer recounts the following:

> In accordance with a former promise, the old man likewise put into our hands a small quantity of the manna of the peninsula, famous at least as being the successor of the Israelitish manna, though not to be regarded as the same substance. . . . It is found in the form of shining drops on the twigs and branches (not upon the leaves) of the Turfa, *Tamarix Gallic mannifera* of Ehrenberg, from which it exudes in consequence of the puncture of an insect of the coccus kind, *Coccus manniparus* of the same naturalist. . . . It has the appearance of gum, is of sweetish taste, and melts when exposed to the sun or to a fire. The Arabs consider it as a great delicacy, and pilgrims prize it highly.[154]

An alternative explanation is that manna is a lichen (*Lecanora esculenta*) that grows on rocks and produces pea-size sweet pellets, but this phenomenon has been rejected by F. S. Bodenheimer, who observed that this particular substance has not been documented in Sinai. He prefers the explanation of Ehrenberg that Robinson accepted, namely, that manna is produced by the excretion of certain insects. He notes that this phenomenon occurs annually in June, and he observed it himself during a visit to Sinai in June 1927. He also noted that it was during the period of May–June that the Israelites would have reached the area where tamarisk manna occurs. This concurs with the dating observed in the previous section, based upon chronological data provided by the Torah. Bodenheimer discovered that in northern Iraq, the Kurds collect "thousands of kilograms every year in June and July." This observation demonstrates that the volume of manna required to feed a large group of people can indeed be produced, leading him to conclude: "We have seen that all the eye-witness reports of the Bible can be taken as literal descriptions of the tamarisk manna of Sinai."[155] Although we cannot be certain that tamarisk manna is the mysterious food that sustained the Israelites during their sojourn in Sinai, it is certainly a plausible explanation.

Another element in the manna episode requires treatment. Prohibitions are given against gathering manna on the Sabbath (Exod. 16:5, 22). This inclusion is peculiar because it is not until the Israelites receive the law at Mt. Sinai in Exodus 20 that the commandment regarding Sabbath observance is made. Source critics identify the first occurrence as belonging to J and the second to P.[156] William Propp, however, has recently questioned this understanding by declaring, "Unaware of the Documentary Hypothesis, we would probably not suspect multiple hands in chap. 16."[157] Cassuto observed that the name Sabbath was already known from Mesopotamia, although it is very different in application.[158]

What is known is that in Egypt the concept of the seven-day week was completely absent. The Egyptian year was divided into three four-month seasons, and each month had thirty days; five days were added to allow for the difference between the lunar and solar calendars.[159] In New Kingdom Egypt, the week was based on a ten-day work cycle, of which eight days were given to work.[160] Therefore, there would be three Egyptian weeks in a month. Fresh from a long stay in Egypt under the Egyptian work system, it would appear that the Hebrews were free to abandon the Egyptian week in favor of the Hebrew six-work-day system, followed by a day of rest, that was rooted in creation (Genesis 2:1–3). It may be, then, that the difference between the Egyptian and Hebrew work systems is the reason for the Sabbath instruction in Exodus 16 just after the departure from Egypt.

Quail

Quail is mentioned as a source of meat for the Israelites in Exodus 16:13: "In the evening quails came up and covered the camp; and in the morning there was a layer of dew around the camp." A second time in the wilderness tradition, shortly after departing Mt. Sinai and before reaching Kadesh-Barnea, the Israelites are visited by quail (שְׂלָו; Num. 11:31–32). Those familiar with Egypt and Sinai know that they are on the seasonal migratory path of birds that fly between Europe and Africa, and that the quail is one of these birds, along with cranes and storks. The common quail (*Coturnix coturnix*) is portrayed in Egyptian tomb scenes as early as the Old Kingdom, and the quail chick is used as a hieroglyph (𓅱), with the phonetic value of *w*.[161] In both Old and New Kingdom scenes, quail are shown being captured by net-wielding farmers in a field.[162] In the autumn months, flocks of quail arrive along the Mediterranean coast. Until recent times, Egyptian hunters were known to greet the quail with long nets that were secured to poles. The birds, exhausted from their long flight across the Mediterranean would be trapped in the nets and then eaten as a delicacy. From his years in Sinai, Colonel Jarvis observed that the arrival of the quail from Europe, as if "obeying some instinct, arrange their flight so that their arrival on the opposite side of the Mediterranean coincides with the dawn." Even when not netted, he reported that "the quail when he lands is so completely exhausted that he staggers into the first bit of cover he sees and remains there for some hours, sometimes a whole day, resting." Thus the birds are easily grabbed or netted by hunters. Back in the 1920s, because so many quail were being captured, the Egyptian government set restrictions upon the placement and use of the large nets. Today the practice is banned altogether. Jarvis further disclosed that it was not uncommon for 50,000 quail a day to be exported from Sinai![163]

Because of this migratory pattern and the abundance of quail in Sinai, Jarvis astutely connected this phenomenon to the quail episode in Exodus 16, and it was critical to his argument for his northern route theory.[164] Although I accept the main points of his theory, there are a couple of problems. First, as we have noted, on the basis of the chronological data provided by Exodus, the departure from Egypt occurred in March–April, and the arrival at Mt. Sinai was approximately six weeks later. March–April is the period when the migrating birds return north and fly over Sinai. I have personally witnessed migrating cranes and storks in North Sinai in late March, and they do not normally touch down on the Mediterranean coast. Thus it seems to me that the time of year suggested for the Israelites encountering quail better fits the return migration, and geographically, a location along the western coast makes better sense. After flying across the Gulf of Suez, the quail land on Sinai, much as they do in autumn along the northern coast of Sinai. R. K. Harrison recognized this factor some years ago, stating: "Quails only land on the Mediterranean coast of the Sinai peninsula from Europe in the autumn and at dawn. By contrast, the hungry Israelites encountered them in spring, in the evening, and during the month of March."[165] In the first century B.C., Josephus commented on the migrating quail in his *Jewish Antiquities* (Book III, 5.22), reporting: "Accordingly a little after came a vast number of quails, which is a bird more plentiful in this Arabian gulf than anywhere else, flying over the seas, and hovered over them, till wearied with their laborious flight, and, indeed, as usual, flying near to the earth, they fell down upon the Hebrews, who caught them and satisfied their hunger with them."[166]

A second challenge to Jarvis's application of the quail migration to Exodus 16 is that during the southerly migration the quail reach the Mediterranean coast of Egypt in September at dawn. Exodus 16:13 explicitly places the time of the arrival of the quail in the evening (וַיְהִי בָעֶרֶב), as Harrison observed. The reference to evening should not be dismissed as a meaningless detail. In their study of birds in ancient Egypt, Steven Goodman and Patrick Houlihan included a discussion of the common quail. The quail's return migration in March coincides with the harvest of grain in the Nile Valley, and it is in the harvest setting that the quail-netting scenes are shown.[167] The quail stop in Egypt to feed and fortify themselves for the long flight back to Europe. Based on his analysis of the tomb scenes, along with ethnographic evidence, Houlihan notes that the capture of the quail occurs in the grain fields and "usually takes place at night."[168]

The Lack of Vegetables

Numbers 11:5, a portion of which was discussed above, mentions the Israelite complaint that they did not have fish to eat in the wilderness, as they had in Egypt. This verse also contains the protest about the absence of "the cucumbers, the melons, the leeks, the onions, and the garlic" (אֵת הַקִּשֻּׁאִים וְאֵת הָאֲבַטִּחִים וְאֶת־הֶחָצִיר וְאֶת־הַבְּצָלִים וְאֶת־הַשּׁוּמִים). Many recent commentators on this verse have recognized that this list of vegetables and fruit looks authentically Egyptian. Philip Budd, for example, notes: "The fruit, fish and vegetables mentioned here reflect a genuine familiarity with Egyptian diet."[169] Baruch Levine describes this verse as being "strikingly realistic."[170] The foods mentioned here are typically associated with the common folk in Egypt, both in Pharoanic and modern times. Hermann Kees noted that "among vegetables onions and leeks served as food for the common people, as is the case today."[171] Referring to the poorer people in Egypt, Barbara Mertz observes that "they ate onions and leeks . . . the villagers may have eaten fish."[172] One should not get the impression that only the peasantry consumed these food items, for they are often depicted on funerary stelae and on false doors of tombs, and on vignettes from the Book of the Dead papyri. Such scenes are found from the Old Kingdom through the Greco-Roman periods. On these tableaus, the deceased (or his or her Ka) sits before a sumptuous feast of a variety of foods, often with onions or leeks on the top of the pile.[173] Typically only higher-class Egyptians could afford such funerary equipment, which means that people at all levels of society, then, ate cucumbers, melons, leeks, onions, and garlic.

These five food items, interestingly, occur only in this passage.[174] Thus while they may have been known in the Levant, they do not occur in the Bible among the many references to food. The people's complaint about the lack of vegetables and fruits in the wilderness appears to be an authentic one of a people accustomed to such food in Egypt, which obviously were not available in Sinai. These five food items seem out of place in Canaan or Israel and hardly seem to reflect the dietary passions of an exilic or postexilic community.

With manna and quail, not to mention milk products from their flocks as sources of food, the Israelites made their way down the western coast of Sinai—so I have argued here—and at some point turned east, possibly into Wadi Sidr, to reach Mt. Sinai, where the mountain theophany and the giving of the law would occur.

8

The Sinai Legislation

Then God spoke all these words: "I am the LORD your God, who brought you out of the land of Egypt, out of the house of slavery."
—Exodus 20:1–2

I. Moses and the Law

According to Exodus 20–24, Israel's covenant was drafted at Sinai, Moses being the recipient of the laws on Mt. Sinai. Regardless of the question of the Pentateuchal sources and the complex history of transmission, the prior question must be raised: could Moses or any Hebrew scribe of the Late Bronze Age have written the laws of Sinai? This question was actually raised early in the Enlightenment period, when skepticism toward the Bible began. Some scholars denied Mosaic authorship of the Pentateuch because, they reasoned, writing was not sufficiently developed when Moses lived (see chapter 1, §III). This was a legitimate question. By the nineteenth century, of course, linguists had deciphered many of the scripts and languages from the ancient Near East. As will be clear from the following discussion of the development of the Semitic alphabet, there is no reason to deny that the heart of Sinai legislation could have originated in the Late Bronze Age.

II. The Origins of the Semitic Alphabet

The history of Canaanite/Hebrew alphabetic script has become clearer over the past century. Since this particular writing system is pertinent to the question of the origins of the Sinai covenant, it needs to be explored in some detail.

The famous inscriptions usually called Proto-Sinaitic were first noticed in Sinai at Wadi Maghara by E. H. Palmer in 1868 during his exploration of Sinai.[1] Subsequently, in 1905, Flinders Petrie excavated the Pharaonic copper and turquoise mining site at Serabit el-Khadim. Mining at Serabit may go back to the reign of Sneferu of the Fourth Dynasty, judging from inscriptional evidence, although at nearby Wadi Maghara a relief of the Third Dynasty king Sekhemkhet is inscribed on a rock face, where he is depicted smashing the head of a local desert dweller.[2] In his 1906 publication of his work in Sinai, Petrie offered some of the first pictures of the Proto-Sinaitic inscriptions. It is clear that at this early date, Petrie did not understand these texts, but he did recognize that they were "a definite writing system, and not merely ignorant scribbling." In mine L, which contains one of the longest texts, Petrie discovered pottery that he dated to the reign of Thutmose III. He also pointed to a statue with Proto-Sinaitic writing on it that was associated with a shrine built by Hatshepsut, and to a sandstone sphinx of Thutmose III that also had this peculiar script on it. Although he was not a specialist in languages, Petrie proposed a date in the Eighteenth Dynasty for these enigmatic texts.[3]

The publication of the Proto-Sinaitic inscriptions, along with the hieroglyphic texts at Serabit and Wadi Maghara, was handed by Petrie to a young and then little-known Egyptologist, Alan Gardiner.[4] Not until 1955 did the full publication of the inscriptions appear, with the collaboration of T. E. Peet and Jaroslav Černý.[5] In 1916, however, Gardiner did publish some early reflections on the texts in which he determined that the signs were alphabetic and that the language was Semitic.[6] He demurred from Petrie's opinion that all the Proto-Sinaitic texts were from the Eighteenth Dynasty. Gardiner suggested that some of the texts could date to the Twelfth Dynasty, because a stela of Amenemhet III contained the ox-head (aleph) sign, and the shrine of Sopdu that Petrie attributed to Hatshepsut actually originated in the Twelfth Dynasty; Gardiner thus concluded that the script dates back to the nineteenth century B.C.[7]

William F. Albright wrote a small monograph that further investigated the Proto-Sinaitic script comparatively, with numerous examples of the script found at various tells in Canaan/Israel. Three signs on a sherd from a Middle Bronze II-period (ca. 1800–1630 B.C.) cultic vessel discovered at Gezer, and a dagger blade from Lachish dating to the Middle Bronze III period (ca. 1600–1550 B.C.) indicate that the Semitic alphabetic writing system was known in Syria-Canaan prior to the Late Bronze Age.[8] On the basis of the Levantine evidence, Albright concluded that "the Proto-Sinaitic texts, which had been rather isolated, were joined by early alphabetic scripts from Syria-Palestine, which were clearly earlier or later than the Proto-Sinaitic forms."[9] When he studied them alongside examples of the alphabetic scripts from Western Asia, Albright believed that an evolution of the signs could be detected, which suggested to him that the Eighteenth Dynasty date is most likely for the Sinai texts.[10]

Interestingly, at Serabit el-Khadim (mine M), one of the most intriguing inscriptions was found, which reads: *ʾl ʿlm*, "god the eternal" (figure 33). Frank Moore Cross was the first to recognize the reading of this text, and his reading was subsequently accepted by Albright and others.[11] This same epithet for God is also found in the Abraham narratives (אֵל עוֹלָם; Gen. 21:33).

Because a corpus of Middle Bronze and Late Bronze texts from Canaan have been identified, scholars now refer to this script as Proto-Canaanite, and its evolution has been studied thoroughly by Cross.[12] More recent study of the history of the alphabet by Joseph Naveh concurs with Cross's views and with the dating of the development of the Semitic-alphabetic script and the dating of the Sinai corpus to the fifteenth century.[13] The earlier date of some of the texts found within ancient Canaan suggests that this script originated in Canaan and not Sinai, as some scholars had thought.

The recent discoveries by John Darnell at Wadi el-Hôl in the western desert of Egypt have revealed a collection of rock drawings and inscriptions, including a couple of early Semitic-alphabetic texts.[14] Although they are still being studied, preliminary reports indicate that these texts may be the oldest West Semitic alphabetic writing known. The team of scholars who are examining these texts provisionally believe, based upon the orthographic comparison with Egyptian hieratic signs from First Intermediate Period texts, that the Wadi el-Hôl script dates to ca. 2100 B.C.[15] This new evidence might indicate that the Semitic alphabetic script was actually invented in Egypt by Semites at the end of the third millennium, rather than in Canaan or Sinai, a date much earlier than Semitists had thought.

The importance of Darnell's discovery is that the Semitic alphabet originated several centuries earlier than previously thought. Furthermore, this early date allows for additional time for this script to have developed to a level that Moses could have had a hand in recording the law in Sinai. It was noted in chapter 1, §III, that some early critics of the Bible denied Moses a role in authoring the Pentateuch because they thought that writing was not sufficiently developed in his day. If we place Moses in the thirteenth century, then more than a half millennium separates him from the earliest known Semitic alphabetic writing.

In the seventeenth and eighteenth centuries, when firsthand knowledge of ancient scripts and writing systems was negligible, scholars might be pardoned for raising questions about their availability in the second millennium B.C. But in the intervening centuries, with the decipherment of the cuneiform scripts of Mesopotamia, Syria, and Anatolia, as well as hieroglyphic and hieratic texts in

Egypt, it is recognized by all linguists that writing originated toward the end of the fourth millennium B.C., and now it appears that we can possibly place the Semitic alphabet at the very end of the third millennium B.C.[16]

I have previously pointed out that the Torah's claim that Moses was raised in Pharaoh's court (Exod. 2:10) resonates with the Egyptian royal educational institution known as the *k3p*, or royal nursery, where royal children were reared and educated. Egyptian textual evidence shows that for the first time, during the New Kingdom foreign princes were trained in the *k3p* and took the title *ẖrd n k3p*, "child of the nursery."[17] Moses's education in the *k3p* may stand behind the first-century A.D. tradition that "Moses was instructed in all the wisdom of the Egyptians."[18]

In 1977 an important ostracon was published by Moshe Kochavi, which had been discovered at 'Izbet Sartah in Israel/Canaan about twenty-five kilometers (about sixteen miles) west of Shiloh.[19] The Paleo-Hebrew script appears to be an abecedary, the practice text of a scribe who was working on the alphabetical order. It contains a number of mistakes that Cross attributes to scribal error. He also thought the inscription could be dated to the first half of the twelfth century B.C. on paleographic grounds.[20] The fact that this marginal site has yielded such an important text from this early date—Kochavi assigned it to the "Judges period"—indicates that writing was not restricted to major urban administrative centers.[21] Israel Finkelstein, one of the excavators of 'Izbet Sartah, has argued that this site is an example of an early Israelite settlement from the Late Bronze–Iron Age transition (stratum III dates to the end of the thirteenth century).[22] He too saw the significance of this ostracon for the question of literacy, noting that it "provides important evidence of literacy among the inhabitants of the hill country during the period of Israelite Settlement and the Judges."[23] William Dever has recently commented on the significance of this text as it relates to literacy in early Israel. Because it is recognized as a schoolboy's practice text, he states that it cannot be "an isolated item" and points at least to the "beginnings of functional literacy."[24]

From Canaan at the end of the second millennium B.C., the Semitic alphabet spread to Arabia. In the 1920s a tablet written in the Ugaritic-cuneiform script was found at Beth-Shemesh, but only recently was it shown to be written in Old South Arabian.[25] Kenneth Kitchen, a specialist in south Arabian history, says of this find that "it reflects contact between Canaan and Saba in the field of writing at about 1200 B.C." He adds that this discovery demonstrates that the "South-Arabian script originated as a conscious adaptation of the Late-Bronze Age Canaanite alphabetic linear script of the 13th/12th centuries B.C."[26] If the Sabeans from distant southern Arabia had borrowed the alphabetic script from Ugarit in the Late Bronze II period, there is no reason to deny that the Israelites could have borrowed the Canaanite alphabet during the same period.

The 'Izbet Sartah abecedary indeed demonstrates that during the settlement period, the Israelites may have already adapted the Proto-Canaanite script. Because of this, and since the Proto-Canaanite script was apparently originated in Egypt by Canaanites who were familiar with the Egyptian writing system at the end of the third millennium, and the script is attested in Egypt, Sinai, and Canaan throughout the second millennium B.C., there is no objective reason to deny Moses the ability to use the Proto-Canaanite script and record laws, itineraries, and historical observations.

There are numerous references in the Torah to Moses writing. Exodus 17:14 reports his recording the events of the battle with Amalek, while Exodus 24:4 and 12, and 34:27–28 refer to Moses writing laws; in Numbers 17:2 Moses is instructed to write the name of each priest on his rod, and Numbers 33:2 plainly states that Moses wrote the stages of the Egypt-to-Moab itinerary. Moses is also credited with writing "the Book of the Law" in Deuteronomy 31:24, and many other references could be cited. Enough evidence has been marshaled to show that there is no doubt that Moses played a crucial role in the recording of the Torah, if its own testimony is to be believed. But this testimony is often rejected by biblicists who follow Wellhausen's dictum that the law came after the prophets, and hence was a rather late development in Israel's religious history rather than the foundation for it.[27]

Other critical scholars, however, have at least credited Moses with a minimal role in the recording of the Ten Commandments. In 1971, J. P. Hyatt, a strong advocate of the documentary hypothesis, observed that since around 1930 a growing number of scholars have been willing to consider crediting Moses with the decalogue, based upon some unknown "pre-prophetic document." I concur with his conclusion that the "ethical Decalogue, in a brief and succinct form, *could* have originated with Moses," and he reasons: "there is nothing in the Ten Commandments which could not have originated with Moses."[28]

Those who deny a role to Moses in the recording of the Torah have to dismiss cavalierly the Bible's own testimony, as well as the available and unambiguous evidence for the early development of the Semitic alphabet. Instead they adhere to eighteenth- and nineteenth-century theoretical literary reconstructions of the Torah that were spawned in the dark age of biblical scholarship, when little was known of the Near Eastern context of the Bible, and were built upon the flawed foundation of belief that writing was not sufficiently developed in Moses's day to account for the writing of the Torah. Now, comparisons with ancient Near Eastern treaties can bolster an even stronger argument for the antiquity of the Sinaitic legislation.

III. The Sinai Legislation

Literary critics have long been at odds when it comes to explaining the sources behind Exodus 20–24, which recount the covenant ceremony at Mt. Sinai. A thorough review of the history of this debate could easily occupy a large monograph, and this has admirably been done recently by John Van Seters.[29] Consequently, we need only address some of the views about the origin of what biblical scholars call "the book of the covenant" (סֵפֶר הַבְּרִית). This name derives from Exodus 24:7, which reports that Moses "took the book of the covenant, and read it in the hearing of the people." The problem of identifying the sources (typically J, E, and P) behind the book of the covenant prompted B. S. Childs to describe the challenge that has faced source critics as the "extreme difficulty of analyzing the Sinai pericope."[30] Welhausen maintained that Exodus 20–23 was the Yahwist's (J) legislation.[31] Martin Noth believed that P, E, and J are all found in Exodus 19, and that chapter 20 contained E and J materials.[32] For him, "the book of the covenant was limited to 20:22–23:33 and represents a "self-contained entity" inserted into the Pentateuch.[33] Other scholars maintained that different sources were at work in the book of Exodus, such as a Kenite source (K) that Morgenstern believed was behind Exodus 33 and 34, and that in turn J and E borrowed from K in Exodus 20.[34] Robert Pfeiffer, on the other hand, proposed that there was a source originating in Seir (i.e., Edom) which he dubbed "S."[35] Meanwhile, Georg Fohrer spoke of an "N" (nomadic) source that originated during the wilderness period. More specifically, he labeled the "Covenant Code" of 20:22–23:33 "C," while assigning the Decalogue to J.[36]

Clearly there is no end to the different scenarios advanced by source critics to explain the origin and development of the book of the covenant. Consequently, there is no broad consensus on the matter. Sounding a note of despair, John Durham declares: "Though many helpful observations may be harvested from the critical work of more than a century, the sum total of that work is a clear assertion that no literary solution to this complex narrative has been found, with more than a hint that none is likely to be found."[37] Although Van Seters acknowledges that Exodus 19–24 "has been one of the most difficult and controversial problems of Pentateuchal Studies," his solution is to reject E as a source and to attribute any editorial work to the Deuteronomist.[38] He then reduces the entirety of the pericope to a compilation of P and J materials.[39] Van Seters's date for J is the sixth century B.C. rather than the traditional date of the tenth or ninth century. In his most recent treatment of the problem, Van Seters has elaborated on his argument to deprive E of any role in the Book of the Law.[40] Alternatively, Richard Elliot Friedman avers that the Decalogue is from P, and the balance of the book of the covenant is the work of E.[41]

After nearly two centuries of source analysis, critics are unable to concur, even though its adherents consider it to be an "objective" and "scientific" method for analyzing the Torah. The problem lies, in my opinion, with source criticism as it has been practiced. It is simply a flawed approach, and a number of mainline biblical scholars are now rejecting source criticism as the means for critical study of the Bible.[42]

The introduction of new literary approaches to the study of the Torah in recent years has resulted in some seeing a literary unity to the book of the covenant. It was observed independently by D. Patrick and G. C. Chirichigno that the speeches in Exodus 19–24:2 use a common narrative framework.[43] Building on the idea of common narrative framework, Joe Sprinkle uses a synchronic, discourse method to investigate Exodus 19–24.[44] What these scholars have observed is that these chapters consist of narrative (*haggaḏah*) and regulation (*halaḵah*). Sprinkle demonstrates that the sequence of laws—at times appearing odd to source critics and indicative to them of later insertions—is arranged chiastically.[45] The realization that such a sophisticated literary structure shapes Exodus 20–24 makes a strong case for the literary unity of the passage. It certainly renders problematic the argument that various passages were inserted by later redactors. Even if one were to argue that the redactor was responsible for the chiastic structure and the blending of the various sources or traditions, it seems that they become so blurred by the structuring process that they are no longer distinguishable. In my view, this may explain why source critics over the decades have had such varying opinions about the Sinai pericope.

T. D. Alexander has recently examined the introduction to the speeches in Exodus 19–24, and concludes: "Although minor variations in wording exist, the strong similarities between the narrative frameworks and the introductory words of the divine speeches in Ex. xix 3–6 and Ex. xx 22–xxiv 2 suggest common authorship."[46] He also argues that Exodus 19–24:11 shows no sign of a Deuteronomistic redaction (contra Nicholson and Van Seters), rather that this passage "already existed before the book of Deuteronomy and that it could have been penned as early as the pre-monarchic period."[47]

Literary approaches have certainly advanced our understanding of the structure of Exodus 19–24 and have suggested that this important passage may represent a literary nit, and not a patchwork of sources awkwardly lumped together by a crude editor. The use of a common literary framework and chiastic pattern demonstrate that a brilliant author or editor stands behind this material. If the latter used earlier and divergent sources, then his skill at weaving the material together is so effective that sources have become blurred, preventing critics from successfully delineating the sources behind the pericope.

Although new literary approaches to Exodus 19–24 are welcome indeed, the literary structure can now be studied comparatively with ancient Near Eastern literature.

IV. Ancient Near Eastern Treaties and the Sinai Legislation

The word *b^eriṯ* (בְּרִית) occurs more than thirty times in the book of Exodus. Julius Wellhausen was of the opinion that the idea of covenant developed relatively late in Israelite history. He points to late preexilic and exilic prophets (i.e., Jeremiah, Deutero-Isaiah, Ezekiel) and the covenant ceremony in Josiah's time (2 Kings 22; 2 Chron. 34) as evidence for his position. In the nearly 125 years since he articulated this position, an abundance of texts from across the world of the Old Testament show that covenants or treaties were widely known from Mesopotamia to the Nile Valley as early as the third millennium B.C. Wellhausen was correct in associating the word *bᵉrîṯ* (בְּרִית) with the concept of treaty making.[48] But little did he know that during the second millennium B.C. it was an important Semitic word used in international diplomacy in Mesopotamia, Syria-Palestine, and even in Egypt, where it is found as a loanword.[49] The Amarna letters, discovered in 1887 in Egypt, are diplomatic correspondence between kings of the Near East and the pharaohs Amenhotep III and Akhenaten.[50] These texts offer marvelous insights into the treaty relationships between Egypt's equals and subjects.[51]

In addition, one of the expressions in the Old Testament for making a covenant or treaty is כרת ברית (e.g., Gen. 15:18; 21:27, 32; 26:28; 31:4; Exod. 23:32; Deut. 7:2; 29:13), which literally means "cut a covenant."[52] Early on in the study of the Qatna texts of the mid-second millennium B.C., W. F. Albright noticed that these texts used the Akkadian idiom TAR *be-ri-ti*, meaning "to cut a covenant." This clear parallel suggested to him that these two expressions were related conceptions.[53] The cutting probably refers to the sacrifice of animals that commonly occurred in the treaty ceremony. Animal sacrifice and/or a fellowship meal is frequently mentioned when treaties are made in the Bible, apparently signifying the communion between the parties, such as God and Noah (Gen. 8:20), God and Abraham (Gen. 15:9), Abraham and Abimelech (Gen. 21:27–28), Isaac and Abimelech (Gen. 26:30), Jacob and Laban (Gen. 31:54).[54] Such sacrifices are also attested elsewhere in the Near East where, as in the Bible, the sacrifice is associated with the oath.[55] At Mari during the early second millennium B.C., donkeys and lambs are mentioned in this connection. The sacrificial meal was also practiced in the ancient Near East and among modern Bedouin.[56]

The evidence from ancient Near Eastern treaties tends to discredit Wellhausen's evolutionary model for interpreting Israel's social and religious development. It further illustrates the limitations of methods of analyzing texts for their date and origin that ignore or trivialize comparative materials.[57]

In 1931, Viktor Korošec, a specialist in ancient Near Eastern law, published an early analysis of Hittite treaty texts.[58] They were largely treaties with the vassals of Hatti, and they date from the fourteenth and thirteenth centuries B.C. He recognized that they have a distinctive six-part formula. The treaties shared common features, although variations did exist. In fact, Mendenhall has pointed out that the six parts of the treaty formula "will almost always be found in the Hittite treaty texts, but it must be emphasized that the form is not an extremely rigid one."[59] In his recent translation and discussion of the Hittite treaties of the second millennium B.C., Gary Beckman has similarly observed that "with some omissions and a certain variation in the order of components, most of these treaties follow a similar pattern."[60] The pattern or structural form (*Gattung*) of these treaties, as recognized by these and other scholars, is presented here.[61] Bearing in mind what Mendenhall and Beckman have observed, that there is some variation between treaties (that is, the order of points may differ or some may be omitted) and that some treaty texts have lacunae, the following is compiled from several documents.

(1) Preamble/Title: Here the names of the parties involved in the treaty are introduced; for example, "Thus says My Majesty Suppiluliuma, Great King, King of Hatti, Hero."[62] Another begins with the following: "[Thus says] My majesty, Mursili, [Great King, King of Hatti], Hero, Beloved of the Storm-god; [son of] Suppiluliuma, [Great King, King of Hatti, Hero]."[63]

(2) Historical Prologue: Prior relations with the parties are reviewed, and these typically provide the reason(s) why the vassal is obliged to the Hittite king; for example, "When the king of the land of Mittanni sought to kill Sharrupshi, and the king of the land of Mittanni entered the land of Nuhashshi together with his infantry levies and his chariotry, and when he oppressed (?) him, Sharrupshi sent his messenger to the King of Hatti, saying: 'I am the subject of the King of Hatti, Save me!' And I, My Majesty, sent infantry and chariotry to his aid, and they drove the king of the land of Mittanni, together with his troops and his chariotry out of the land of Nuhashshi."[64]

(3) Stipulations: The tribute, terms, or laws that the vassals are expected to meet are detailed; for example,

> [... shekels of gold(?)] shall be his yearly tribute. It shall be weighed out with the weights of the merchants of Hatti. Tette[65] shall come yearly to My Majesty, his lord, in Hatti. He shall be at peace with my friend and hostile to my enemy. If the King of Hatti goes against the land of Hurri, or Egypt ... when I the King of Hatti, go forth to attack, if Tette does not mobilize <whole> heartedly, he will transgress the oath.... If someone incites Tette to evil [matters], whether [a Hittite or] his own subject, and Tette [does not seize him] and send him [to the King] of Hatti, he will transgress [the oath].[66]

(4) Deposition of Text and Public Reading: The text of the treaty was to be recorded and placed in the temples of the respective parties, and the text was to be periodically read publicly as a reminder to the vassal of its commitments to its overlord; for example:

Deposition: "A duplicate of this tablet is deposited before the Sun-goddess of Arinna, since the Sun-goddess of Arinna governs kingship and queenship. And in the land of Mittanni a duplicate is deposited before the Storm-god, Lord of the *kurinnu* of Kahat."[67]

Public Reading: "It shall be read repeatedly, forever and ever, before the king of the land of Mittanni."[68] Another one stipulates: "Furthermore, this tablet which I have made for you, Alaksandu, shall be read out before you three times yearly, and you Alaksandu, shall know it."[69]

(5) Witnesses Summoned: Like any legal document, the treaty had to be witnessed. In the case of treaties, the gods of the parties were listed, or features from nature could serve as witnesses; for example, "The Storm-god, Lord of Heaven and Earth, the Moon-god and the Sun-god, the Moon-god of Harran, heaven and earth, the Storm-god, the Lord of the *kurrianu* of Kahat, the Deity of Herds of Kurta, the Storm-god, Lord of Uhushuma, Ea-sharri, Lord of Wisdom, Anu, Antu, Enlil, Ninlil, the Mitra-gods, the Varuna-gods, Indra. . . ."[70] Another one invokes: "The mountains, the rivers, the springs, the great sea, heaven and earth, the winds, and the clouds. They shall be witnesses to this treaty and oath."[71]

(6) Curses and Blessings: The treaty concludes with a list of curses and blessings that would be administered by the deities who had acted as witnesses. The curses and blessings are the consequences of upholding or violating the stipulations. Of the twenty-two treaties included in Beckman's edition, the order of curses followed by blessings is without exception, and typically the curses are longer.[72] For example:

Curses: "If Tette does not observe these words of the treaty and oath, but transgresses the oath, then these oath gods shall destroy Tette [together with his person], his wives, his sons, his grandsons, his household, his city, his land, together with his possessions."

Blessings: "But if Tette observes [these] words [of the treaty] and oath which [are written] on [this tablet, these oath gods shall protect] Tette, together with his person, his wives [his sons, his grandsons], his family [household], his city, his land [together with his possessions]."[73]

Nearly a quarter century passed before the connection between this covenant form and that of Exodus 20–24 was made, thanks to the perspicacity of Mendenhall. His study, entitled "Covenant Forms in Israelite Tradition,"[74] is truly groundbreaking, and no serious investigation of the Sinaitic covenant can be made without considering the form-critical implications. The significance of connecting the two lies in the fact that most of nineteenth- and early twentieth-century biblical criticism—in particular source criticism—was theory-driven and lacked objective controls that could evaluate the conclusions. Mendenhall recognized this dilemma, declaring that "some external criterion is necessary for the historian to check his theories."[75] In the second-millennium treaty texts from the Near East he saw the possibility of introducing such controls on the Sinai pericope. He applied the covenant form only in a general way to the Exodus 20–24, and also to Joshua 24, which contains a covenant renewal ceremony in Canaan at the end of Joshua's life.[76] Because of the similarity of the six points of the Hittite treaties with those in Exodus and Joshua, Mendenhall concluded: "It is very difficult to escape the conclusion that this narrative rests upon traditions which go back to the period when the treaty form was still living."[77] Surprisingly, Mendenhall did not actually align the six parts of Near Eastern covenant formula with the text of Exodus 20–24, nor did he realize that Leviticus is presented as a part of the covenant. It was left to others to show that the book of Deuteronomy also shared the same structural pattern.

The 1960s and 1970s saw the appearance of a plethora of studies that correlated the biblical texts to the covenant form and examined the implications for the date and sources associated with Exodus and Joshua, and Deuteronomy too.[78] The features of the Late Bronze Age treaty form and the Sinaitic covenant are as follows:

1. Preamble/title	Exod. 20:1, 2a	"Then God spoke all these words: 'I am the LORD your God'"
2. Historical prologue	Exod. 20:2b	"who brought you out of the land of Egypt, out of the house of slavery."
3. Stipulations	Exod. 20:3–17, 22–26; 21:1–23:33; 25–31; (Lev. 1–25)	"You shall have no other gods before me." Other laws that follow . . .
4. Deposition of text and	Exod. 25:16	"You shall put into the ark the covenant that I shall give you."
public reading	Exod. 24:7	"Then he took the book of the covenant, and read it in the hearing of the people; and they said, 'All that the LORD has spoken we will do, and we will be obedient.'"
5. Witnesses	Exod. 24:4	"He [Moses] rose early in the morning, and built an altar at the foot of the mountain, and set up twelve pillars, corresponding to the twelve tribes of Israel."
6. Blessings	Lev. 26:3–13	"If you follow my statutes and keep my commandments and observe them faithfully, I will give you your rains in their season, and the land shall yield its produce, and the trees of the field shall yield their fruit. Your threshing shall overtake the vintage, and the vintage shall overtake the sowing; you shall eat your bread to the full, and live securely in your land. And I will grant peace in the land."

Curses	Lev. 26:14–33	"But if you will not obey me, and do not observe all these commandments, if you spurn my statutes, and abhor my ordinances, so that you will not observe all my commandments, and you break my covenant, I in turn will do this to you: I will bring terror on you; consumption and fever that waste the eyes and cause life to pine away. You shall sow your seed in vain, for your enemies shall eat it. I will set my face against you, and you shall be struck down by your enemies; your foes shall rule over you, and you shall flee though no one pursues you."

From the foregoing we can clearly see that the maker of the treaty/covenant in the case of Exodus 20:1–2a is YHWH, the God of Israel, and it is a suzerainty/vassal type. In a parity treaty (that is, between rulers of equal standing), both parties are introduced by name in the preamble, as in the case between Ramesses II and Hattusilis III.[79]

The purpose of the historical prologue is to establish the basis for the treaty and why the vassal is beholden to the suzerain.[80] Korošec recognized this in his original study of Hittite treaties. He observed that "what the description amounts to is this, that the vassal is obligated to perpetual gratitude toward the great king because of the benevolence, consideration, and favor which he has already received. Immediately following this, the devotion of the vassal to the great king is expressed as a logical consequence."[81]

In the case of the historical prologue of Suppililiuma and Tette, a portion of which is quoted above, the Hittite king had rescued Tette, who had called for help when the Mittannians invaded. The intervention obligated the kingdom of Nuhashshi to submit to the Hittite treaty and its stipulations. In the same way, in Exodus 20:2b it is because of YHWH's deliverance of Israel from the bondage of Egypt that Israel is duty-bound to God. Because the historical prologue plays such a vital important role in establishing the basis for the treaty, one might logically conclude that a genuine historical event or events stand behind the prologue. This is why, Delbert Hillers argued, the historical prologue section of the ancient Near Eastern treaties did not employ a stereotyped text inserted into the treaty structure; as it provided the rationale for the obligation, "it had to be substantially accurate."[82]

The implications of Hillers's stance are highly significant for the Sinai covenant and Israel's origins. First, it makes it difficult to deny the historicity of the exodus from Egypt, since it was this event that established the obligation for Israel. Furthermore, this observation presents a problem for those who in recent years have theorized that Israel never was in Egypt and was purely an indigenous development within Canaan.[83] Second, it illustrates that the relationship between the exodus narratives and the wilderness tradition are closely connected. This of course challenges Noth's and von Rad's view that the Sinai pericope is a late insertion into the wilderness narrative (see the discussion in chapter 1, §IV). D. J. McCarthy likewise recognized the problem that this historical prologue makes for their idea. He declares: "The Decalogue with its designation of Yahweh as the God of the Exodus, is thus ancient and an essential part of the Sinai complex. In this way one of the most striking propositions of modern scholarship, von Rad's hypothesis that Sinai traditions and the Exodus traditions were originally separate, can be denied."[84]

The view taken here follows that of Kitchen, that is, that the stipulations are not limited to the laws in Exodus but also include the ceremonial and ritual laws in Leviticus.[85] The concluding verse of Leviticus (27:34) supports this proposal: "These are the commandments that the LORD gave to Moses for the people of Israel on Mount Sinai." Including Leviticus in the Sinai covenant of Exodus 20ff. may explain why the blessings and curses components of the covenant formula are located in Leviticus 26. Hillers has shown that the material in Leviticus is clearly a list of blessings and curses.[86] If the blessings and curses of the Sinai covenant are those enumerated in Leviticus 26, it does present an interesting problem. Invariably in Near Eastern treaties of the latter half of the second millennium B.C., the curses precede the blessings. In Leviticus 26, the order is reversed, as it is in Deuteronomy 28. Why the reversal? The Code of Hammurabi concludes with a statement about erecting the stela, followed by a series of blessings and curses, just as we have in Leviticus 26! This suggests to Kitchen that the Sinaitic covenant may have been influenced by both the treaty formula and the structure of Mesopotamian law codes. He sees in the Sinaitic covenant a "confluence" of the treaty formula of the second millennium B.C. and the early second-millennium Mesopotamian law code tradition.[87]

The deposition of the text of the treaty, the fourth point of the formula, presented a dilemma for Israel in Sinai, because it had no sanctuary in which to deposit the copy of the text. This may explain why immediately after the covenant ceremony (Exod. 24), in which the oath is taken, the animal is sacrificed, and the covenant meal is eaten, instructions for constructing the ark of the testimony/covenant, the altar, the tabernacle, and all its trappings follow (Exod. 25–31). These instructions, in turn, are followed by narratives that describe how these features were made by the artisans (Exod. 36–40).

The witnesses in Near Eastern treaties, as documented above, are typically the principal deities of the treaty partners. In the case of the Sinaitic treaty,

God and Israel are the two parties, and given the monotheistic nature of the Torah—and the first two commandments in particular—no other deities could be introduced. Elsewhere in the Bible, stones or pillars (small monoliths) served as witnesses to a treaty or to memorialize an event (e.g., Gen. 31:45–48; Josh. 4:19–23; 22:26–27; 24:26–27; 1 Sam. 7:12). In Deuteronomy (4:26; 31:28; 32:1), heaven and earth are named as witnesses, which is strikingly similar to what we find in the treaty between Suppiluliumas I and Tette ("The mountains, the rivers, the springs, the great sea, heaven and earth, the winds, and the clouds"), which dates to the period 1350–1325 B.C.

The similarity of the form of the "Hittite" type of treaty with the structure of Exodus 24–Leviticus, Deuteronomy, and Joshua 24 directly bears on the question of the dating of these narratives. Many scholars acknowledge the antiquity of these biblical treaty-texts because of the similar structure of the six points of the Hittite treaties. Mendenhall, for example, concluded: "It is very difficult to escape the conclusion that this narrative rests upon traditions which go back to the period when the treaty form was still living." Klaus Baltzer maintained that "it remains, however, a striking and historically unexplained fact that the Old Testament texts resemble most closely the highly developed formulary of the Hittite treaties." Kitchen determined that "if we take the nature and order of nearly all the elements in the Old Testament Sinai covenant and its renewals [i.e., Deuteronomy and Joshua 24] . . . it is strikingly evident that the Sinai covenant and its renewals *must* be classed with the late-second-millennium covenants."[88]

To be sure, there were scholars who sought to downplay the relationship between the second-millennium treaties and the Sinai covenant. D. J. McCarthy sought to minimize the structural similarities between the second-millennium treaties and the material in Exodus and Deuteronomy. John Thompson and others, while recognizing the parallels, tried to direct attention to treaties of the first millennium.[89] Eberhard Gerstenberger took a slightly different approach, that of, proposing the reduction of the treaty formula from the six parts recognized by Korošec, Mendenhall, Kitchen, and most scholars who have critically examined the ancient Near Eastern treaties, to just three points.[90] These features are mutual agreement, stipulations, and curses. This truncated formula, conveniently for Gerstenberger, is close to the Neo-Assyrian treaty structure (see below)!

Moshe Weinfeld also concluded that Deuteronomy was significantly influenced by first-millennium Assyrian treaties.[91] He compared the curses of Deuteronomy 28 with those of Esarhaddon vassal treaties. Although he admits that some of the same parallels can be found in the curses in the Code of Hammurabi, he opts for "direct Deuteronomic borrowing from Assyrian treaty documents."[92] Hillers rejected the idea of an Israelite borrowing of the curses in Leviticus and Deuteronomy from the Assyrian treaties, considering it to be naive supposition.[93] One wonders to what extent Weinfeld's decision to embrace the first-millennium link is because of his prior commitment to the popular view that Deuteronomy originated during the reforms of Josiah (621 B.C.) rather than in the time of Moses, as the book itself claims.[94]

A decade after his classical study, McCarthy revisited the treaty formula question, and showed no departure from his earlier conclusions, claiming, "We have already noted some of the cautions raised against the too ready acceptance of the covenant-treaty parallel, particularly in regard to the historical conclusions attached to it."[95] His reference to "historical conclusions" is telling. Clearly he realizes that if the structure of the second-millennium B.C. ancient Near Eastern treaties stand behind Exodus 20ff., then the long-cherished source critical assumptions fall apart.

Thirty years later, Van Seters echoes this sentiment, completely jettisons the early material, and favors a late-J source (not E) as largely standing behind Exodus 20 and following. He finds elements of the first-millennium treaties to be more closely aligned with Deuteronomy than with the covenant code of Exodus. As a consequence, Van Seters argues that the Deuteronomic code (late seventh century) predates Exodus 20ff., which is based upon his idiosyncratic and ultra-late J, sixth century.[96]

Given the fact that a number of distinguished scholars have been persuaded by the Neo-Assyrian connection to the Sinai and Deuteronomy treaty texts, a closer examination of these important documents is required. During the excavations of Sir Max Mallowan at Nimrud (Calah) in 1955, over 350 fragments of cuneiform tablets were uncovered in the throne room of the palace and in an adjacent room to the north. When carefully pieced together, they proved to be at least eight treaties of Esarhaddon (681–669 B.C.). These were published in detail by the staff Assyriologist, Donald J. Wiseman. He immediately noticed that they were "stylistically closest" to the Aramaic treaty texts from Sefire from the eighth century B.C., but also he recognized "affinities with treaties of the second millennium B.C., especially those made by the Hittite kings."[97] In other words, Wiseman found both similarities and differences between the Esarhaddon treaties and those of the second millennium. Consequently, the curses used by Esarhaddon may be based on earlier models. A further indication of the connection of the Neo-Assyrian treaties with the past is that they had the impressions of three large older cylinder seals on them. These include one belonging to Sennacherib, Essarhaddon's father, another with the figure of the god Assur that dates to the Old Assyrian Period (ca. eighteenth century), and a final one of Middle Assyrian times (thirteenth–twelfth century).[98] Wiseman called these dynastic seals.

Before proceeding further, let us examine the structure of the Aramean and Assyrian treaties. They contain four main features in the following order:[99]

Aramean	*Assyrian*
1. Preamble	1. Preamble
2. Witnesses	2. Witnesses

3. Stipulations	3. Curses
4. Curses	4. Stipulations

Although these two treaty types are separated by less than a century, they contain the same elements, with the stipulation and curse clauses reversed. When compared with the content and structure of the so-called Hittite-type treaties, radical differences are evident. The first-millennium treaties lack a historical prologue, and the deposition/reading provision is absent.[100] Furthermore, the witnesses stand early in this period, whereas they are fifth in the second-millennium formula, and there are no blessings. As a consequence of these omissions and differences in order, it is illogical to believe that the six-point structure of the Sinai and Deuteronomy treaty texts originated from the four-point treaty formula of the first millennium. The absence of the historical prologue from the late-period treaties, and their presence in the second-millennium texts convinced Baltzer of the early date of the biblical treaties. Kitchen likewise points to these differences in the Syrian and Aramean treaties and the closer parallels between the second-millennium treaties and those in the Torah as the reason for dating the biblical treaties to the Late Bronze Age.[101]

The other approach to explain the origin of the Sinai and Deuteronomy covenants was to argue that they developed in later history from statements gleaned from prophetic literature.[102] This approach was refuted by Hillers in his published dissertation from Johns Hopkins University. He exposed this method by saying: "One can hardly escape the conclusion that this treatment of the evidence is in each case due to the need to make the facts fit a preconceived notion."[103] His criticism equally applies to those who ignore or reject the obvious differences between the Neo-Assyrian and Aramean treaty structure and the biblical treaties, but claim that these serve as the inspiration for the Sinai and Deuteronomy covenants. The preconceived notions of source critics who date Pentateuchal sources to the first millennium make them unwilling to abandon their theories in favor of more objective criteria.

Dating the Sinai covenant to this early date is important because it supports the view of Kauffman and Fohrer that Mosaic Yahwism (i.e., monotheism), as exemplified by the first commandment, "you shall have no other gods before me" (Exod. 20:3), had its origin in Sinai.[104] It also logically follows that Israel's covenant document was to be deposited in a sanctuary. But the tribes of Israel did not have a temple. This may explain why the instructions for the tabernacle begin in Exodus 25, immediately after the conclusion of the covenant ceremony in Exodus 24. One might be inclined to think that in the wilderness, a portable structure was essential. In the following chapter we will examine the history of scholarship on the tabernacle and possible models for Israel's tent-shrine.

9

Israel's Desert Sanctuary

Then you shall erect the tabernacle according to the plan for it that you were shown on the mountain.

—Exod 26:30

I. The Tabernacle: Israel's First Sanctuary

The deposition of the covenant document in the sanctuary of both parties is called for in the fourth clause of the covenant formula.[1] But after the exodus, while in the wilderness, Israel had no sanctuary. It is not surprising, then, that immediately following the covenant ceremony of Exodus 24, Exodus 25–30 records the instructions and plans for Israel's desert sanctuary and all its cultic and priestly utensils. The sanctuary is first introduced as the tabernacle in Exodus 25:9, but its design is elaborated upon in Exodus 26. Interestingly, however, Exodus 25:10–22 begins by describing the objects that would be placed within the holy of holies—the ark (אֲרוֹן), or—the repository for the text of the covenant. It then moves on to describe the table for the bread of presence (Exod. 25:23–30), and the lampstand or "menorah" (Exod. 25:31–40). For the purpose of our discussion here, we shall treat the tabernacle first.

For Wellhausen, the tabernacle was not the architectural prototype for Solomon's temple, but the other way around.[2] The tabernacle, he believed, was the invention of the Priestly writer, who could not imagine Israel without a sanctuary in their early history. Parenthetically, one might at least credit Wellhausen with affirming that Israel did have an early history in the wilderness, unlike many current critical scholars. Consequently, for him, "the tabernacle is the copy, not the prototype, of the temple at Jerusalem" and "in fact a projection of the later temple."[3] The Priestly Code's tabernacle, in Wellhausen's view, belonged to Ezra's world (fifth century B.C.). He asserted that "it was according to the model furnished by it that the Jews under Ezra ordered their sacred community, and upon it are formed our conceptions of the Mosaic theocracy, with the tabernacle at its centre."[4] For nearly three-quarters of a century, this view dominated the thinking of Old Testament scholarship. In fact, in a study from the mid-1970s, Bernhard Pelzl offered some support of Wellhausen's theory by arguing that the tabernacle of Torah was based on the temple, which had derived from a tent shrine, but not the one described in Exodus 26.[5] Rather he proposed that the tabernacle of Exodus was a shrine intended to replace the temple during the Babylonian captivity. This highly speculative suggestion, while interesting, lacks evidence. One might think that the prophet Ezekiel, a man of priestly stock (Ezek. 1:1–3) who was active in the exile between 592 and 571 B.C., would have mentioned the existence of such a cultic tent in Babylon, but he does not.[6] Is it far-fetched to suppose that if Israel had as a part of her history a period in the wilderness of Sinai and in the Transjordan prior to the settlement in Canaan, a mobile and portable sanctuary would be a logical cultic installation? This question will be addressed in the following section, but first, let us examine the terminology used for the wilderness sanctuary.

Two principal expressions are used in Hebrew for Israel's tent-sanctuary, *miškān* (מִשְׁכָּן) usually rendered "tabernacle" and *'ohel môēd̲* (אֹהֶל מוֹעֵד), "tent of meeting." The former derives from the root *škn*, meaning "to dwell, settle down," and is widely attested in Semitic languages, including Ugaritic.[7] The idea that this structure is a dwelling place for the deity is clearly indicated in Exodus 25:8, a verse that Brevard Childs considered as expressing the purpose of the tabernacle.[8] It states: "Have them make me a sanctuary (מִקְדָּשׁ: *miqdāš*), so that I may dwell (*šakāntî*) among them." The idea, then, is for God's presence to reside in the tabernacle to be with his people, but also so that God can witness the provisions of the treaty, as Deuteronomy 31:26 declares: "Take this book of the law and put it beside the ark of the covenant of the LORD your God; let it remain there as a witness against you." This dimension of the tabernacle is well reflected in the use of the expression "tabernacle of the covenant" (*miškan hā'ēdut̲:* מִשְׁכַּן הָעֵדֻת) in Exodus 38:21 and Numbers 1:50, 53 and and 10:11.

There are 94 occurrences of *miškan* in the Pentateuch, whereas *'ohel mô'ēd̲* is used 129 times. There are many cases when *miškan* occurs with *'ōhel mô'ēd̲* or *'ohel* in the same verse (e.g., Exod. 26:12, 13; 36:14; 39:32, 33, 40; 40:2, 19, 22, 24, 29, 34, 35; Lev. 17:4; Num. 3:7, 8, 25, 38; 4:25; 9:15). The "tent of meeting," according to Menaham Haran, may point to the place where God appeared and prophetic activity occurred, that is, the place where God meets his people.[9] *Mô'ēḏ* means "place for meeting, assembly point."[10] The dual use of *miškan* and *'ohel mô'ēḏ* continues to baffle investigators, but it appears not to be attributable to different sources.

Complex literary reasons may account for their appearance in the Pentateuch, as Ralph Hendrix has recently argued.[11] After careful analysis of each occurrence, he determined that their usages are "discrete and specific; they are not interchangeable," and that the literary context determines which word is selected.[12] Although both terms apply to the abode of God, *miškan* appears to be used in Exodus 25–40 in the context of construction, whereas, *'ohel mô'ēḏ*, Hendrix proposes, occurs where cultic matters are addressed. He concludes: "Within Exodus 25–49 the biblical writer has masterfully controlled the use of *miškan* and *'ohel mô'ēḏ* in order to clarify the dual nature of YHWH's habitation. That habitation was to be understood as a transient dwelling place, such as was consistent with the dwelling places of nomadic peoples; therefore the choice of *miškan*. But yet, that habitation also had the continuing function of fostering the cultic relationship, and this aspect was best expressed by the choice of *'ohel mô'ēḏ*."[13]

This suggestion has some merit, and Hendrix may be on to something, but even he has to admit that there were "exceptions" to the use of *miškan* in a purely constructional setting. In Exodus 39:32 and 39:40 we find the following expression: "In this way all the work of the tabernacle of the tent of meeting was finished; the Israelites had done everything just as the LORD had commanded Moses." The combination "tabernacle of the tent of meeting" (מִשְׁכַּן אֹהֶל מוֹעֵד) minimally shows how closely related they are, as the two terms are used as direct genitive. Umberto Cassuto thought that the juxtaposition of the "synonymous expressions" was to "stress the formal solemnity" of the fact that the work on the sanctuary was complete.[14] Again in Exodus 39:40 the two expressions are juxtaposed: "all the utensils for the service of the tabernacle, for the tent of meeting" (כָּל־כְּלֵי עֲבֹדַת הַמִּשְׁכָּן לְאֹהֶל מוֹעֵד). Here the preposition *lamed* (ל) separates them, probably used as an apposition[15]—the tabernacle, that is, the tent of meeting. The appositional usage demonstrates that they were one and the same structure.

Particularly instructive is Exodus 26, containing instructions for the tabernacle that include details on the three layers of coverings that rested on the wooden framed structure. In Exodus 26:7 (cf. also 36:14 and 40:19) there is another interesting collocation of "tent" and "tabernacle." It states, "You shall also make curtains of goats' hair for a tent over the tabernacle; you shall make eleven curtains" (תַּעֲשֶׂה אֹתָם וְעָשִׂיתָ יְרִיעֹת עִזִּים לְאֹהֶל עַל־הַמִּשְׁכָּן עַשְׁתֵּי־עֶשְׂרֵה יְרִיעֹת). Here one gets the impression that "tent" is being used to describe the cover that fits on the wooden structure of the *miškan*. This may be because tents were made of fabric, typically goats' hair. The third or outer layer is described as follows: "You shall make for the tent a covering of red-dyed ramskins, and covering of *tᵉḥašîm* skin over it" (עֹרֹת אֵילִם מְאָדָּמִים וּמִכְסֵה עֹרֹת תְּחָשִׁים מִלְמָעְלָה וְעָשִׂיתָ מִכְסֶה לָאֹהֶל).[16] This outer layer appears to be made of a substance that offered better protection than the linen and ramskin layers. Regardless of how the terms for tent and tabernacle originated, they clearly refer to Israel's tent shrine.

II. Tents in Egypt and the Near East

The word *'ohel* is the most common Hebrew word for tent, be it the desert sanctuary or the dwelling place of nomadic people, whether the Genesis patriarchs (e.g., Gen. 12:8; 13:3, 12, etc.), the Midianite Jethro (Exod. 18:7), or the Kenites in Canaan (Judges 4:18–22). It is also widely found in military contexts to describe the abode of soldiers (e.g., 1 Sam. 17:54; Judges 7:13; 2 Kings 7:8).

In his attempt to lower the date of the composition of Abrahamic narratives in Genesis, John Van Seters argued that tents were indicators of a later development, reflecting Arab migrations of the first millennium B.C.[17] A number of scholars, including Kenneth Kitchen, Donald Wiseman, and me, recognized that this suggestion was not only illogical, given the simplicity of tents, but simply was not supported by textual or iconographic evidence.[18] Wiseman, an Assyriologist, examined Mesopotamian sources and showed that tents were well known in second-millennium sources.[19] The Assyrian King List, in fact, refers to the early rulers as living in tents.[20]

My studies and those of Kitchen, which were completely independent of each other, were both published in 1977. I assembled a body of textual and pictorial evidence from Egyptian sources spanning from the eighth century B.C. back to the Middle Kingdom (twentieth century B.C.) which demonstrated that the Egyptians used tents (*imw*) on military and trade campaigns, as well as for religious purposes.[21] When Thutmose III defeated the Canaanite coalition at Megiddo, he took away as booty the tent poles—ornamented with silver—of the enemy kings.[22] This text clearly shows that tents were used in the Levant. One text that is particularly damaging to Van Seters's position is found in the Admonitions of Ipuwer, the dating of which is disputed, but which certainly predates the sixteenth century B.C.[23] Dates vary from the Middle Kingdom down to the early Eighteenth Dynasty (sixteenth century B.C.). Interestingly, Van Seters, just a decade prior to the publication of his book on Abraham, had argued that Ipuwer reflected on the Hyksos period.[24] The line in question speaks of the troubles within Egypt and how people who had owned houses now were forced to live in tents. Ipuwer laments: "It is tents that they have pitched, just like the Bedouin *(ḫ3styw)*."[25] Van Seters in an earlier study believed that reference to *ḫ3styw* (i.e., "foreigners") pointed to the Hyksos period. If his dating is correct, then the Egyptians during the seventeenth to sixteenth centuries B.C. knew that the Bedouin of the Levant lived in tents. Consequently, the inescapable conclusion is that the Egyptians recognized that there were tent-dwelling people living in the Levant during the second millennium B.C. This point is further supported by references to tents in the Sinuhe story in which he is described as living in a tent (*im*) while staying in the Levant. After defeating his opponent in a duel, Sinuhe "seized what was in his tent."[26] So there is no doubt that tents were used in Canaan and Syria during the second millennium B.C., but all these references use the Egyptian word for tent.

There are, however, examples in Egyptian texts where the Semitic word *'ohel* is written as a loanword in group writing, the typical way of rendering foreign words in Egyptian hieroglyphs.[27] In the Great Harris Papyrus, Ramesses III (twelfth century B.C.) reports on a campaign against the Shasu Bedouin, probably in Sinai or the Negev, in which he claims, "I destroyed their tents (*ihꜣrw*)."[28] From the reign of Merneptah (1213–1204 B.C.) comes an earlier example of the writing of *'ohel*, but here it is found in connection with the king's battle with the Libyans to the west. The word "tents" is modified by the word *h̲n*, leather.[29] Because the word *'ohel* is the habitat of nomadic people in these texts, the *Wörterbuch* understands this term as "Zelt der Nomaden," that is, tent of nomads.[30]

In addition to the use of *'ohel* in Egyptian sources, it is attested in Ugaritic texts of the fourteenth to thirteenth centuries. The significance of the occurrences in the Ugaritic is that they are associated with the abode of the deity El, which illustrates that this term could also be associated with the shrine of a deity. Examples of the use of *'ohel* as a dwelling of deity were noted by Richard Clifford.[31] In one case, *'ohel* and *miškan* are used in parallelism, suggesting that the two terms were probably synonymous at Ugarit:

> The gods bless, they go,
> The gods go to their tents (*'ahalima*)
> The circle of El to their tabernacles (*miškanatihumu*).[32]

Moreover, the word *mô'idi* is used alongside *puḫuru*, the Akkadian word for "assembly," and together they mean "the meeting of the (divine) assembly."[33] Additionally, the use of *mô'idi/mô'ēḏ* occurs in the Egyptian story of Wen-Amon, as John Wilson noted, where it means "assembly."[34] In this case, Zakar Baal, the king of Byblos (south of Ugarit) called together his *m'd* to hear the case of Wen-Amon. The combination of Ugaritic and Egyptian references makes it clear that this word for assembly was well known in the Levant during the Late Bronze period. Furthermore, the parallel or synonymous use of these words at Ugarit means that they could also be employed interchangeably in the Torah and may have nothing to do with different sources or traditions, as some source critics believe.

One of the reasons given by Van Seters for his dismissal of the use of tents in the second millennium "Patriarchal" period in Genesis is that tents are rarely mentioned in Near Eastern texts and "not mentioned in the Mari archives at all."[35] As it turns out, Van Seters's rush to judgment on the matter was premature. Renewed investigation of the Mari texts since the 1980s has determined that earlier generations of scholars misunderstood the words *ḫa-na* and *ḫanûm*, thinking that they were tribal names. Collaborating in Paris with the new Mari text team—headed by Jean-Marie Durand and Dominique Charpin—Daniel Fleming has been engaged in the study of these important texts.[36] These scholars have shown that the terms *ḫa-na* and *ḫanûm* should be rendered "tent-dwellers," and Fleming reports that these words are "ubiquitous" in the Mari archive.[37] This same root is found in the Hebrew verb חנה, which means to camp or encamp, that is, set up tents.[38] It occurs nearly eighty times in the books of Exodus and Numbers, usually referring to Israel's travels in Sinai and camping at a certain site (e.g., Exod. 13:30; 14:2, 9; 15:27; Num. 1:50, 53; over forty times in Num. 33).

The foregoing references demonstrate that tents were widely used in the ancient Near East during the second millennium as the dwelling for nomadic and traveling folk, in military and trade missions, and most important for this chapter, as a shrine.

III. The Tabernacle and the Phenomenology of Religion

Richard E. Friedman has likewise distanced himself from Wellhausen's late dating of the tabernacle in a pair of somewhat overlapping studies.[39] He attempted to determine the precise size of the tabernacle; this represents an important breakthrough because it had always been assumed that the structure measured 10 by 30 cubits (ca. 5.25 × 15.75 meters / ca. 17 × 51 feet), on the basis of the length of the covers and the frames. Although he rightly observes that the Pentateuch never does disclose the dimensions of the tabernacle itself, they have been deduced by adding the number of frames on a side (20) by their width (1.5 cubits). Friedman proposes that the frames (הַקְּרָשִׁים: *haq-q^erāšîm*) actually overlapped each other by a half cubit, meaning the tabernacle was just 20 cubits long (10.5 meters) and 6 to 8 meters wide.[40] The 28-cubit-long coverings (Exod. 26:2) would precisely cover the structure, but not the ends: 10 cubits on each side (on the basis of the length of the frames; Exod. 26:16) and 8 cubits across the top. The 20-cubit length is further supported by the width of the curtains, 4 cubits, and five of them are to be joined together, according to Exodus 26:2–3: "The length of each curtain shall be twenty-eight cubits, and the width of each curtain four cubits; all the curtains shall be of the same size. Five curtains shall be joined to one another; and the other five curtains shall be joined to one another." The veil (הַפָּרֹכֶת) of Exodus 40:3, Friedman thinks, functioned to cover the front and rear of the structure. Subsequently, he learned that these dimensions corresponded to those of the Arad sanctuary.[41] Earlier on, Yohanan Aharoni had suggested that the tenth-century Arad sanctuary, which he discovered, was patterned after the tabernacle. If this scenario is correct, the tabernacle is very small indeed, hardly a magnificent structure, as some biblical scholars have thought.[42]

Additionally, Friedman believes that the old tabernacle was actually housed within the holy of holies in Solomon's temple.[43] He points to a number of biblical texts to support this hypothesis. At the dedication of Solomon's temple, 1 Kings 8:4 and 2 Chronicles 5:5 report: "So they brought up the ark of the LORD, the tent of meeting, and all the holy vessels that were in the tent; the priests and the Levites brought them up." Prior to the building of the temple, we learn from 1 Kings 3:4–5 that Solomon had gone to nearby Gibeon to make sacrifices to YHWH, who appeared to him there. The significance of this cultic center is elucidated in several statements made by the Chronicler:

> For the tabernacle of the LORD, which Moses had made in the wilderness, and the altar of burnt offering were at that time in the high place at Gibeon. (1 Chron 21:29)
>
> Then Solomon, and the whole assembly with him, went to the high place that was at Gibeon; for God's tent of meeting, which Moses the servant of the LORD had made in the wilderness, was there. (2 Chron. 1:3)
>
> So Solomon came from the high place at Gibeon, from the tent of meeting, to Jerusalem. (2 Chron. 1:13)

Evidently, when the ark of the covenant was taken by the Philistines (2 Sam. 5), the tabernacle was taken from Shiloh, and it was abandoned as a cultic center (Jer. 7:12–15; 26:4–9), and subsequently the sacred tent ended up at Gibeon. Clearly the tent that David made for the ark was not the one from the wilderness period. David's tent is never called "tent of meeting" or "tabernacle" (2 Sam. 6:17; 7:6).

Friedman also pointed to a number of psalms that demonstrate that the earlier tent-shrine was in the holy of holies of Solomon's temple.[44] Consider the following:

> O LORD, I love the house in which you dwell (מִשְׁכַּן), and the place where your glory abides. (Ps. 26:8)
>
> One thing I asked of the LORD, that will I seek after: to live in the house of the LORD all the days of my life, to behold the beauty of the LORD, and to inquire in his temple.
>
> For he will hide me in his shelter in the day of trouble; he will conceal me under the cover of his tent. (Ps. 27:4–5)
>
> Let me dwell in thy tent forever! Oh to be safe under the shelter of thy wings! (RSV, Ps. 61:4)

The tabernacle is mentioned in Psalm 74:7, which appears to lament the destruction of the temple in 586 B.C.: "They set your sanctuary on fire; they desecrated the dwelling place (מִשְׁכַּן) of your name, bringing it to the ground."

The use of both *'ohel* and *miškan* in these psalms certainly could support Friedman's theory that the old tabernacle was actually erected in the holy of holies (הַדְּבִיר) of the first temple, although the use of *miškan* in these psalms could refer to the temple as God's dwelling place and not be an allusion to the old tabernacle.

Friedman's intriguing theory, questioned by some reviewers, has been harshly attacked by V. A. Hurowitz, who found problems with Friedman's interpretation of the nature of the construction and questioned the overlapping alignment of the frames (*qᵉrašim*) that would make the structure smaller.[45] Hurowitz charges Friedman with starting from the premise that the old tabernacle stood beneath the cherubim in Solomon's temple, and hence had to reduce its size to make it fit within this space. Although he raises some valid questions about Friedman's reconstruction, Hurowitz likewise starts with unfounded assumptions. For instance, he correctly admits that the Bible does not furnish a description of the tabernacle "in its final, assembled form," and yet can say that "according to Exodus 25–40 . . . when assembled, the tabernacle measured thirty cubits in length, ten cubits in width, and ten cubits in height." The reality is that he too has to speculate about certain features that are not delineated clearly in Exodus, such as the manner in which the corners of the frame are constructed, in order to come to the dimensions he proposes. He declares, "they may have been isosceles trapezoids," for which there is absolutely no evidence. Hurowitz demurs from Friedman's reliance upon the Chronicler's descriptions of the tabernacle, which are highly theologized, and using psalms (some of which are cited above) that he believes should be understood symbolically. He then charges that, "It is curious that not a shred of evidence comes from the older Book of Kings."[46] Here Hurowitz is simply wrong, on two counts. First, 1 Kings 8:4 does mention the ark and the tent of meeting being taken to the new temple at its dedication (see above where this verse is quoted), and second, he fails to acknowledge that Friedman discusses this verse on the first page of his groundbreaking article in *Biblical Archaeologist*.[47] We can only wonder how Hurowitz could have overlooked 1 Kings 8:4 and the fact that Friedman did cite it.

In a monograph published in 2002, which was originally a dissertation supervised by Friedman, Michael Homan offered a spirited defense of his mentor's theory. Among other arguments presented, Homan too notes Hurowitz's erroneous claim that the book of Kings contains no evidence to support Friedman's theory regarding the placement of the old tabernacle in the holy of holies in Solomon's temple.[48]

Hurowitz may be right to question the size of the tabernacle and whether it could have fit between the cherubim, but the tent need not actually have been set up in the holy of holies in Solomon's temple for it to have had great religious significance. It may have been placed somewhere within the temple, which would have been sufficient to establish a connection between the wilderness tabernacle and the new temple. Hurowitz's criticism notwithstanding, Friedman's proposal that the old tent was placed in Solomon's temple has merit from a phenomenological perspective. Historians of religion recognize that it was vital for a sanctuary to maintain the continuity of theophany or hierophany, thereby preserving or reestablishing sacred space (see chapter 2, §II). In the case of Jerusalem, more was at stake, that is, establishing the temple as the continuity of the Sinai theophany.

The principle of perpetuating sacred space is seen in the practice of shrines and temples being retained and rebuilt over the centuries on the same spot. The ziggurat of Ur, for instance, was built over a platform temple that originated in the Uruk period (ca. 3200–3000 B.C.), and that precinct continued in use to the Neo-Babylonian period (sixth century B.C.).[49] In Egypt, temples also enjoyed long histories through Pharaonic times into Greco-Roman times, and in the Christian era were used as temples or monasteries. Luxor temple, for instance, was first built around 1400 B.C., and was expanded and inscriptions added to the end of Pharaonic times. Alexander the Great added a shrine in the holy of holies, and a chapel for Serapis was added by Trajan (A.D. 98–117). The precinct served as a church for Christians and then, after Islam reached Egypt, the mosque that still occupies the Pharaonic precinct was built inside of the pylon of Ramesses II. It is dedicated to the local saint, Abu el-Haggag, whose birthday is annually observed with great celebrations.[50] The Temple Mount in Jerusalem offers yet another example of the continuity of sacred space. Solomon's Temple was replaced by the second temple that was built after the Babylonian exile by Zerubbabel, which in turn was replaced by Herod's magnificent temple; when it was destroyed, Islamic and then Christian (Crusader) ecclesiastical structures were erected over what was believed to be an earlier holy spot.[51]

How do we account for such continuity in various regions of the Near East, over the millennia, and across different religious traditions? It seems that once a spot was deemed sacred because it was believed that a theophany had occurred, it was thought to retain the sanctity even by adherents of different faiths, because, as Eliade explained, "the hierophany repeats itself" and "the continuity of hierophanies is what explains the permanence of these consecrated spots."[52] Tradition alone does not explain the perpetual rebuilding of sanctuaries on the same spot over centuries of time, but continuity based upon a believed hierophany does.

In this regard, Israel had a problem. The Sinai theophany occurred in a remote region, and its surrounding area was not intended to be their home. How would Mt. Sinai retain its sanctity in the absence of a cult to perpetuate it? And how could its holiness be transferred to Israel's new home in Canaan?

The tabernacle, it might be suggested, served as the vehicle of ongoing manifestation after they departed from Horeb, thereby creating the nexus between Sinai and Jerusalem. The glory (כָּבוֹד: *k^{e}ḇôḏ*) of YHWH, it is reported, appeared on Mt. Sinai during the covenant ceremony: "The glory of the Lord settled on Mount Sinai, and the cloud covered it for six days; on the seventh day he called to Moses out of the cloud. Now the appearance of the glory of the Lord was like a devouring fire on the top of the mountain in the sight of the people of Israel" (Exod. 24:16–17).

The link between this theophany and the function of the tabernacle itself is obvious in 24:16 with the phrase: "the glory of the Lord settled on Mount Sinai" (וַיִּשְׁכֹּן כְּבוֹד־יְהוָה עַל־הַר סִינַי). The use of the verb *wayyiškōn* (וַיִּשְׁכֹּן) from the root *škn*, "settled" or "abode" (NJPS), just as in *miškan*, "tabernacle," in the final pericope of Exodus 24, can hardly be coincidental, since the instructions for the tabernacle (*hammiškān*) is the subject of the following chapters (Exod. 25ff.). The connection between YHWH's glory settling on the mountain and the tabernacle was recognized by Cassuto, who declared: "The initial word *wayyiškōn* ['and dwelt'] gives here, at the end of the section, a preliminary inkling of the subject of the next section, to wit, the work of the *miškan* ['the dwelling-place (of God)'], tabernacle, and a nexus is thereby formed between the two sections."[53] Brevard Childs likewise recognized this connection when he stated: "The final verses in the chapter furnish the context from which the instructions regarding the tabernacle are given."[54] The link between the end of chapter 24 and the beginning of 25 goes beyond a literary association; rather it goes to the heart of connecting the Sinai theophany to the tabernacle. When the tabernacle is completed and erected at the very end of the book of Exodus (40:34), the text states: "Then the cloud covered the tent of meeting, and the glory of the Lord filled the tabernacle" (וַיְכַס הֶעָנָן אֶת־אֹהֶל מוֹעֵד וּכְבוֹד יְהוָה מָלֵא אֶת־הַמִּשְׁכָּן). Here once again we find the parallel use of "tent of meeting" and "the tabernacle."

In his recent study of the tabernacle, Myung Soo Suh considers the tent to be the new place of divine communication, which explains the prophetic role played by the tent of meeting, as Haran believed.[55] Once the tabernacle was erected, Moses never again ascended the slopes of Sinai to communicate with God. Clearly, the tent had replaced the mountaintop. I concur, therefore, with Suh when he observes: "Yahweh no longer calls Moses from Mt. Sinai but now from the tabernacle. Obviously Yahweh has moved from the mountain to the tabernacle."[56]

At the dedication of Solomon's temple in 1 Kings 8, as mentioned above, verse 4 reports that "the tent of meeting" was brought to the new temple (v. 4), as was the ark of the covenant.[57] Concerning the latter, 1 Kings 8:9 declares: "There was nothing in the ark except the two tablets of stone that Moses had placed there at Horeb, where the Lord made a covenant with the Israelites, when they came out of the land of Egypt." One should note here the clear association between the ark and Horeb/Sinai. In the following verses we fined that YHWH's glory now filled the temple: "And when the priests came out of the holy place, a cloud filled the house of the LORD, so that the priests could not stand to minister because of the cloud; for the glory of the LORD filled the house of the LORD" (1 Kings 8:10–11).

By placing the original Sinai tent in Solomon's temple, as suggested by 1 Kings 8:4 and 2 Chronicles 5:5, the archetypal theophany is transferred to the new temple.[58] On the basis of statements in Psalm 97 that associates YHWH's theophany with Mt. Zion (i.e., Jerusalem), Jon Levenson cogently observed that "Sinai is not the focus, but the new mountain, Mount Zion (v. 8). The traditions of YHWH's theophany, his earthshattering apparition to man . . . [has] been transferred from Sinai to Zion. In short, Sinai has not so much been forgotten as absorbed."[59] This transferral, via the medium of the tabernacle, in my view, may explain why the location of Mt. Sinai faded from memory—because the theophany was ongoing in Solomon's temple—and why locating it in modern times has been a challenge. Although Horeb was the place where the Torah located the revelation of the law, it was superseded by the new Mt. Sinai that contained the original tent and still functioned as the dwelling place of the deity.

The idea of transferring the holiness of one sanctuary to another is well known in Egyptian temple-building practices. The classic example of this is attested at Karnak Temple. When Amenhotep III built the third pylon, he incorporated into it a number of earlier altars and shrines, including the "White Chapel" of Senusert I in its entirety, believed to be the earliest structure built at Karnak.[60] A text on the "White Chapel" explains the rationale for the original building of this shrine: "His majesty made [it] as a monument for his father, Amun-Re, erecting his place of manifestation anew" (*ir.n.f m mnw.f n it.f Imn-rʿ sʿḥʿ n.f st.f nt ḫʿwt m mȝwt*).[61] The word *ḫʿwt* is typically used for the appearance of the sun, or the coronation of Pharaoh when he "appears" as the Son of Re.[62] Thus the original temple was built at the place of Amun-Re's theophany, and the blocks of that original chapel were incorporated into Amenhotep III's pylon some five hundred years later, thereby shifting the sanctity of the original place of the theophany to the new structure.

IV. The Tabernacle and Near Eastern Analogues

Not everyone was convinced by Wellhausen's theoretical reconstruction concerning the origins of Israel's tabernacle. In his 1913 book, Hugo Gressman cited the tent camp of Ramesses II at Kadesh, which is also depicted on the pylon of Luxor Temple, the funerary temple of Ramesses II (i.e., the Ramesseum) and inside the magnificent temple of Abu Simbel (Figures 29 and 35).[63] The striking comparison he noted between the tent of Ramesses and the tabernacle is that they are both located in the center of the camp. In the ninety years since Gressman pointed to the reliefs of Ramesses II, other scholars have questioned Wellhausen's fifth-century dating of the wilderness tabernacle.

In 1947, Frank Moore Cross, while accepting that Exodus 26–40 belong to the Priestly tradition, claimed that "they must be deemed an important historical witness to the Mosaic age."[64] He further disclosed his belief "that Moses instituted the aniconic tradition of Israel as argued persuasively by Wright and Albright, so that we may assume that the Ark, understood as the throne of an invisible God, was instituted in the days of Moses." He suggested that the "Egyptian backgound" of the tabernacle was continued in Shiloh, as evidenced by the Egyptian names of Eli's sons, Hophni and Phineas (more on these names below).[65] His observations on the antiquity of the tabernacle were based on the presence of terminology in the Exodus narratives that are attested in Ugaritic, and he also collected numerous examples of tent-shrines from Islamic and pre-Islamic times in the Middle East.[66] More recently, Cross appears to have backed away from his earlier support for a Mosaic-period prototype behind P's tabernacle. Rather he now considers David's tent for the ark in Jerusalem (2 Sam. 6:17), and not the Shiloh sanctuary, as some have averred, as the inspiration for the description found in Exodus 25ff.[67] Although he refers to "new data" that have prompted him to revise his earlier views, he produces little to support this shift. As an expert in Northwest Semitic languages, he is influenced by the Ugaritic materials bearing on El and his tent as presented in Clifford's study. In the end, it seems that what drives Cross to this new position is that the tabernacle as portrayed in Exodus 25ff., with its "richness and sophistication," does not fit the picture of a wilderness tent, but would confirm to the wealth and opulence of David's Jerusalem.[68] The issue of "riches and sophistication" strikes me as being too Wellhausenian.

Mark Smith is likewise influenced by the Ugaritic material, asserting that "the 'tent of meeting' derived from Canaanite prototypes."[69] He indeed acknowledges that parallels in language do not necessarily translate to "parallels in a cultural setting," but because Israel "drew heavily" from many aspects of Canaanite culture, the tent of meeting was probably another example. If one were to look only at the Ugaritic corpus of texts, then Smith has come to a reasonable conclusion. He completely ignores, however, all the Egyptian data presented here, most of which has been known from earlier studies, and thus in my opinion has limited his options.

Let us return to the view of Cross that the tabernacle of Exodus is based on David's tent. There are a number of problems with this. First, the Bible is very clear in calling David's tent neither the tabernacle nor the tent of meeting, nor does it provide any description of its layout or the materials from which it was made (cf. 2 Sam. 6–7). In fact, one might even conclude that the tent David made was rather mundane, because he observes to Nathan the prophet that while he lived in a cedar palace, "the ark of God dwells in a tent." Plainly a contrast between David's and YHWH's dwelling is intended by the king's comment.[70] In 7:2, where the contrasting statement is made, David is quoted as referring to the abode of the ark as הַיְרִיעָה (lit. curtain) and not an אֹהֶל (tent), as it is in 2 Samuel 6:17 and 7:6. Some translations recognize that although "tent" may be intended, nevertheless the use of הַיְרִיעָה leads them to render this word as "curtains" (KJV), "tent curtains"(NASB), "housed in curtains" (NEB), and "awnings" (NJB).[71] The use of the word "curtain" suggests that David was in fact accentuating the difference between his palace and God's tent. It is doubtful, on the basis of the lone description in the Bible of this structure, that it was a highly decorated tent that inspired the tabernacle as detailed in Exodus 25ff. Consequently, it seems unlikely that David's tent could be the prototype for the "Priestly tabernacle" of the Torah, as Cross believes.

In the study that so influenced Cross, Richard Clifford noted that the chief deity of the Canaanite pantheon, El, dwelt in a tent, rather than a temple or palace, as did Baal.[72] He suggested that the absence of any temple of El in the archaeological record in the Levant might be because his earthly sanctuary was a tent-shrine.[73] In addition to the tent-tabernacle terminology found in Ugartic texts, Clifford agreed with the earlier study of Frank M. Cross that the term for the tent-frames, *haqq*ᵉ*rāšim*, in the Torah is an exact parallel to the Ugaritic term.[74] When all this material is considered, Clifford determines that "it appears likely, then, that the Israelite Tent of Meeting is one more instance of the Israelites confronting and appropriating the religious and cultural institutions of Canaan."[75] If indeed the Israelites appropriated a northern Canaanite tent-shrine the like of which is attested in Ugaritic texts, then it rests on a Late Bronze Age, not Iron II or later model.

Recently, Daniel Fleming has shown that some of the same tabernacle terminology used in the Torah and in Ugaritic texts is also found in documents from Mari that date to approximately five hundred years earlier.[76] The text in question (Mari 6873) describes a large tent *(ḫu-ur-pa-tum)* that required sixteen men to carry and was made of ten frames called *qé-er-su*, cognate with Hebrew *q*ᵉ*rāšim*. Other men were assigned to carry various components of this tent, including a fence. In all, forty-three men were required to transport this large tent structure.[77] Obviously, large and transportable tents like Israel's tent-shrine were known in the Near East during the second millennium B.C. The use of the word *q*ᵉ*rāšim* as a part of the architecture of a tent at Mari, Ugarit, and the Torah illustrates that this word was a common term known throughout in the Levant and in Mesopotamia in the second millennium B.C.

Shrines made of perishable materials are well known from Egypt going back to the fourth millennium B.C. Some of the First Dynasty (ca. 3200–3000 B.C.) ivory labels show religious ceremonies occurring in or before such shrines.[78] Excavations at Hierakonpolis, ancient Nekhen, have recently uncovered the postholes that supported the reed shrine.[79] With the development of stone architecture in the Third Dynasty in the Djoser pyramid complex, the shrines in the Heb-Sed court are clearly replicas of the earlier reed prototypes.[80] The Pyramid texts of the Old Kingdom (2500–2350 B.C.) refer to many of the reed shrines, in particular the tent of purification used in the funerary ritual.[81] The illustrations of the tent of purification (*ibw*) in private tombs of the Old Kingdom show that these structures were made of woven reed mats (as in the case of the Fifth Dynasty tomb of Kar at Giza),[82] and were supported by a network of poles (clearly visible in the example in the tomb of Pepi-ankh at Meir) (figure 34).[83] An actual canopy frame belonging to Queen Hetepheres, the mother of Khufu, builder of the great pyramid at Giza, was discovered near the great pyramid.[84] This bedroom canopy, which is presently displayed in the Cairo museum, was covered with linen. The poles are elegantly decorated with gold foil and were set into sockets on a base and ceiling beams, thus constituting a frame. This discovery, along with the illustrations of purification tents from Meir and Giza, demonstrate that the technical knowledge to construct booths or tentlike structures, like the Israelite tabernacle, was known in Egypt over a thousand years before the exodus and the wilderness period.

As early as 1960, and regularly ever since, Kitchen has pointed to these Egyptian structures to show that the technology required to construct the Israelite tabernacle had long been available in the Nile Valley.[85] Like Gressmann early in the twentieth century, Kitchen and now Michael Homan are all struck by the similarity in the structure and layout of the tabernacle to Ramesses II's camp at Kadesh as portrayed on this monarch's temples.[86] For the purpose of our investigation, the examples from the pylon of Luxor Temple (figure 29) and within the great temple at Abu Simbel (figure 35) will be considered. An outer wall is shown, which surrounds some smaller tents, horses, chariots, and soldiers busy in their duties; standing in the center of the camp is a second enclosure. Within it is the royal tent, besides which are three smaller tents that most likely belonged to the princes who had accompanied Ramesses on this campaign. No depiction of the tent encampment of other earlier pharaohs is presently known. The annals of Thutmose III, however, do provide some terminology related to the camp that suggests it had a similar configuration. The term *iḥy/w* is used for the camp itself, and the expression *w3ḥ iḥy* means "set up camp." The annals also refer to the king resting in the *ᶜᶜny*, which is best translated as "enclosure," and probably refers to the area in the center of the camp in which the king's tent was situated.[87] The verbal description provided by the annals accords well with the military camp of Ramesses II as portrayed in his temples, suggesting that this had been used in the previous dynasty, as well.

It is unclear from the Egyptian representations of Ramesses's tents whether they were sustained by poles or by some type of wooden frame.

A prefabricated frame structure was found in the tomb of Tutankhamun, within the gilded shrines that covered the sarcophagus and coffin of the monarch. Between the first and largest of the shrines and the second one was a light wooden frame over which a linen pall was spread. Why this odd frame is included with the elegantly carved and molded shrines is unclear, but it does offer another model for the tabernacle—a wooden frame covered by linen. The shape of this framework is unlike that of any of the other shrines in the set, suggesting that it originally had a different function. It measures 4.32 × 2.93 meters (14' 2" × 9' 7¾") and reaches a maximum height of 2.78 meters at the peak of the gable; the four legs of the frame were supported by feet so that it could stand alone. The linen pall, which measured 5.5 × 4.4 meters (18' 1½" × 14' 5¼"), according to Nicholas Reeves, was made of several widths of cloth that had been sewn together to provide the width needed.[88] Here we observe the same technique used in making large linen sheets by joining narrow strips to cover the tabernacle. As we have seen, Exodus 26:2–3 records that "The length of each curtain shall be twenty-eight cubits, and the width of each curtain four cubits; all the curtains shall be of the same size. Five curtains shall be joined to one another; and the other five curtains shall be joined to one another."

The outer wall of the Ramesside camp is made of what appears to be a series of interlinking shields (figure 29). Painted details on the Abu Simbel version suggests that the shields were made of cowhide, which is typical of Egyptian shields in most periods in Pharaonic times.[89] Large leather shields that exceed the height of a warrior, like those used in the Nineteenth Dynasty encampments, are known from the Twelfth Dynasty.[90]

The Israelite wilderness tabernacle also had an outer wall, thus forming a court (חָצֵר) within which cultic activity was to occur (Exod. 27:9–19). Based upon the 100-cubit length given for the linen (שֵׁשׁ) that was draped over the twenty standing supports (עַמֻּדִים), it appears that the court could be no longer than 100 cubits; the width was 50 cubits and consisted of ten pillars (Exod. 27:9–13). Thus the ratio of width to the length was 2 to 1. Homan points out that this is the same ratio as Ramesses II's camp. The width and length of the king's tent and the tabernacle, he observes, also correspond to each other—the ratio being 3 to 1.[91] Homan shows that the two tents share common features. Ramesses's tent, for example, had appended to it a structure. In my study of 1977, I suggested that this feature was an awning, meaning that the tent required seven poles to support it: four for each corner, one to hold up its center, and two to sustain the awing.[92] This proposal, in my view, was supported by the fact that when the tent of the king of Kadesh was seized as booty by Thutmose III, according to his annals, seven silver decorated tent poles were also taken.[93] Homan thinks that the feature attached to the tent is a "reception tent" that he compares to the holy place, the king's tent being parallel to the holy of holies of the tabernacle.[94] The Abu Simbel relief shows five kneeling and adoring foreigners, whose upraised hands are directed toward the royal tent (figure 35). For Homan, this detail is suggestive of a reception tent where dignitaries could meet the king. His theory certainly has merit, and he may be correct. The problem is that Egyptian artistic conventions make it impossible to determine whether the feature attached to the tent is an awning or the sides of a tent, as Homan suggests. Either interpretation of this scene is possible. Regardless of which is correct, it offers a close parallel with the bipartite structure of the tabernacle with its surrounding court.

Another compelling piece of evidence for connecting the two tents is found at Abu Simbel. The focus of adoring foreigners is the king himself in the tent, here represented by the cartouche of the king, which contains his prenomen (User-maat-re Setep-en-re) (figure 35). On either side of the cartouche are falcons with their wings extended to protect the royal presence. Here the comparison with winged cherubim protecting the divine presence over the ark of the covenant within the holiest place of the tabernacle is striking indeed.[95]

The plan of Ramesses II's camp, which unquestionably dates to the mid-thirteenth century, is the closest analogue to the wilderness tabernacle as described in Exodus 25ff. When the military camps of Assyrian kings such as Sennacherib and Ashurbanipal are depicted in the seventh-century B.C. reliefs, they are arranged in a circular or elliptical configuration, and not rectangular (figure 36). Given the lateness usually assigned to the Priestly writer's period of activity, one might expect that the wilderness tabernacle would have followed the plan attested in the first millennium B.C., but this is not the case. Homan argues persuasively for the Egyptian influence on the tabernacle and for the antiquity of the tradition. When he attempts to deal with the apparent contradiction between the theory of the traditional dating of P and the obvious early Egyptian influences that would not have been known during the middle of the first millennium B.C., his explanation languishes. He proposes that "P is not basing the tabernacle's disposition on an Egyptian model knowingly. Rather, P is reconstructing based on historical records in his possession that pictorially or verbally describe an earlier Israelite tent-shrine."[96] Here Homan wants it both ways, that is, to continue to adhere to the late date of P while embracing the second-millennium B.C. Egyptian influences. Kitchen, on the other hand, prefers to see the tabernacle's design and construction as being based on Egyptian technology that naturally points to the Late Bronze Age rather than the exilic period for its origin.[97]

I believe that this is a sound conclusion, one supported by other Egyptian elements associated with the tabernacle and associated terminology of Egyptian etymology (not taken into account by Homan), some of which are examined in the following section. Methodologically, I maintain that one should determine the date and origin of a text on the basis of the internal elements rather than being influenced by a theory about the date, origin, and setting of the text that was developed prior to the availability of the comparative material.

V. Egyptian Elements in Israel's Wilderness Sanctuary

Acacia Wood

Šiṭṭāh (שִׁטָּה) or *šiṭṭîm* (pl., שִׁטִּים) is the word used for the acacia tree and is certainly a loanword from Egypt, *šnḏ.t.*[98] It is evident that this word entered the Canaanite/Hebrew language at an early date, because the Egyptian feminine ending (*t*) had dropped out before the *d* became *t* in the New Kingdom.[99] One of the few types of trees found in dry climates such as the Negev, the Arabah, and Sinai suitable for making wooden furniture and instruments is the acacia. Regarding the acacia of Sinai, Henry Spencer Palmer in 1892 observed: "Of native trees there are very few varieties. The most valuable for economic purposes are the date-palm, the acacia, and the tamarisk."[100] Palmer further reported that acacia trees were overly exploited in the nineteenth century and in earlier times they were probably more plentiful, observing that "these trees have been cut down unsparingly by the Bedawin, and turned into charcoal for exportation to Egypt."[101] Despite this exploitation, acacia trees are found in Sinai today, and they are most prominent in wadis where there is more moisture (figure 8).

Given the prominence of these trees in Sinai, it is not surprising, then, that acacia is the principal word used in the construction of the tabernacle (Exod. 26:15, 26, 32), the screen for the door (Exod. 26:37), the ark of the covenant (Exod. 25: 10) and its poles (Exod. 25:13), the table for the presentation of bread (Exod. 25: 23), the altar (Exod. 27:1)[102] and its poles (Exod. 27:6), and the incense altar (Exod. 30:1) and its poles (Exod. 30:5). In fact, of the twenty-eight occurrences of *šiṭṭîm* in the Old Testament, twenty-six are found in Exodus and one is found in Deuteronomy (10:3), where Moses recalls making an ark out of acacia. The lone reference to acacia outside of the Pentateuch is in Isaiah 41:19, but even here it is located "in the wilderness."

The facts that *šiṭṭîm* is a word of Egyptian origin and that this tree provides the only suitable wood for construction use, lend authenticity of this element of the wilderness tradition. This view, however, has been questioned in a recent study by Z. Zevit.[103] He rightly notes that the tabernacle is not a copy of Solomon's temple, at least as far as the timber is concerned, since the latter employed cedar, whereas the tabernacle used acacia.[104] Most kinds of acacia are short and tend to be twisted, and do not provide suitable planks or long pieces of wood. Those that commonly grow in Sinai today are of this variety. In order to produce planks or poles to construct ten-cubit-high poles needed for the tabernacle (cf. Exod. 26:26), Zevit reasons, the species *Acacia albida*—because of its height—would be required to produce this length.[105] This species, however, is not found in Sinai but is found in the land of Israel north of the Negev. This circumstance leads Zevit to ask, "given the details of the blueprints [of the tabernacle], why did the literary architect insist that the framing of the tabernacle be accomplished with a commodity not available in Sinai?"[106] His answer is that the author "was unfamiliar with the *realia* of Sinai." He continues that the tabernacle tradition reflects the milieu of northern Israel where the *Acacia albida* was available, and then rashly concludes that "no historicity can be assigned to the tabernacle as described in Exodus as a structure constructed by any group in Sinai."[107]

It is incredible that on the basis of this single datum that appears to Zevit to be out of line, he would dismiss the Sinai context and the historicity of the tabernacle tradition. David Hackett Fischer has labeled a historical conclusion that relies on a single piece of evidence as "the fallacy of the lonely fact."[108] It would be as if an anthropologist in the future were to determine that Chinese men at the beginning of the twenty-first century were extremely tall because he or she discovered the skeletal remains of Yao Ming, the 7' 6" Chinese basketball player. Zevit does not discuss any of the Egyptian features of the tabernacle reviewed here which suggest the antiquity of the tradition and the genuinely Sinaitic elements.

There are other problems, too, with Zevit's understanding of the acacia used to build the tabernacle. The first is that he believes that Exodus 26:15 describes the taller acacia. The text reads: אֶת־הַקְּרָשִׁים לַמִּשְׁכָּן עֲצֵי שִׁטִּים עֹמְדִים וְעָשִׂיתָ. He renders the end of this verse as "erect *šittîm* trees," following the interpretation of Y. Feliks, namely, that עֹמְדִים (*'om^{e}d̲îm:* standing) modifies שִׁטִּים (*šittîm:* acacia) rather than הַקְּרָשִׁים (*haqq^{e}rāšîm:* frames), as most translators and commentators have understood this phrase.[109] Here are some of the standard translations of this verse:

> And you shall make *upright frames* for the tabernacle of acacia wood (RSV).
> You shall make *upright frames* of acacia wood for the tabernacle (NRSV).
> For the tabernacle you shall make the boards of acacia wood, *standing upright* (NKJV).
> You shall make boards of acacia wood as walls for the Dwelling (NAB).
> You are to make frames of acacia wood for the tabernacle, these to *stand upright* (JB).
> For the Dwelling you will make *vertical frames* of acacia wood (NJB).
> You shall make the planks for the Tabernacle of acacia wood, upright (NJPS).
> Make *upright frames* of acacia wood for the tabernacle (NIV).
> You shall make the boards for the tabernacle of acacia wood, *standing upright* (NASB).
> Make for the Tabernacle planks of acacia-woods as uprights (NEB).

All ten translations treat *^{c}om^{e}d̲îm* as modifying the board or frames (*haqqerāšîm*). The Septuagint goes in an entirely different direction, rendering this verse as "And thou shalt make the posts of the tabernacle of incorruptible (ασηπτων) wood." Many commentators on the book of Exodus also believe that the frames are being modified; for example, Keil and Delitzsch, Cassuto, Hyatt, Cole, Durham, and Houtman.[110] Thus while the translation "erect acacia trees," as advocated by Zevit, is possible syntactically, it has little support.

A second problem with Zevit's conclusion is that he assumes that the ten-cubit-high frames required ten-cubit-long planks (ca. five meters or sixteen feet), thus requiring a type of tree not present in Sinai. Here the text is silent, and it is more likely that the frames were constructed in such a way as not to require lengthy pieces of wood. From earliest times, the Egyptians had mastered making wooden boats, shrines, and coffins of shorter pieces of wood. The solar bark of Khufu at Giza (ca. 2650 B.C.), for instance, is 43.6 meters (143 feet) long and is made of planks that are lashed together with rope or leather thongs.[111] Following Zevit's logic, Khufu's boat should be made of boards equaling the length of the vessel! Furthermore, laminating woods was known in Egypt, as the composite bows of Tutankhamun illustrate.

Third, Zevit assumes that only the species of acacia present in Sinai today were available thousands of years ago, and that those in northern Israel now were standing in the second millennium. It is widely believed that there has been considerable deforestation of ancient Palestine, some of it owing to human activity as recently as the Ottoman period.[112] The growth in population of Israel during the Iron Age contributed to the exploitation of wood for a host of applications.[113] And, as noted above, Palmer was aware of the tremendous exploitation of acacia in the nineteenth century by the Bedouin for making charcoal for sale in Egypt. In ancient times, Egyptians and Canaanites alike would have used large amounts of wood in central Sinai for smelting copper ore. Thus although it may be true that the flora present in Sinai today is the same as centuries or millennia ago, it is entirely possible that some species died out, especially one that was overused by humans.

It seems to me, then, that Zevit's conclusion that the acacia wood used in the construction of the tabernacle as reported in the book of Exodus has to reflect a later (northern) Israelite tradition is unwarranted. The facts that *šittîm* is a loanword from Egypt and that acacia is known to be indigenous to Sinai, along with the other Egyptian terms and features found in the construction of the tabernacle narratives in Exodus, there is no need to dismiss this detail as coming from a later, uninformed writer.

Gold Overlay

Most of the wooden furnishings and objects associated with the tabernacle were overlaid with gold. *Paḥ* (פַּח) refers to thinly pounded gold plates and is found only in Exodus 39:3 and Numbers 16:38 (Heb. 17:3). In the latter reference, pounded gold foil was to cover the incense altar. In fact, all the wooden furniture mentioned that was made of acacia was overlaid with gold foil (Exod. 25:11, 13, 24; 26:32). The Egyptians were highly skilled in covering wooden objects with gold foil, as in the case of the burial and cultic shrines of King Tutankhamun (figure 37). The Hebrew word *paḥ* (פַּח) is an Egyptian loanword into Hebrew, coming from the word *pḫ(3)*.[114] Since Exodus describes the gilding technology that the Egyptians had mastered, and because the Egyptian word to describe this process is written, I believe that the tabernacle was constructed under Egyptian influence.

Linen

Among the materials used in the construction of the tabernacle was linen (e.g., Exod. 26:1, 31, 36; 27:9, 16, 18), and it is also mentioned as the material from which the priestly garments were made (e.g., Exod. 39:27, 28, 29). The word *šēš* (שֵׁשׁ) occurs just over thirty times in the Old Testament, and all but two occurrences are found in the Torah. Its Egyptian etymology is widely recognized; it comes from the Egyptian word šś.[115] Interestingly, the first occurrence of this word is in the Joseph story in Genesis (41:42) where Pharaoh rewards the young Hebrew with a gold chain and linen garments.[116] Linen is found in Egypt as early as ca. 4000 B.C. and "was especially known for its high quality and sharp, white color."[117] Avi Hurvitz has pointed out that the use of *šēš* clearly reflects a preexilic usage, because in postexilic sources, *bûṣ* occurs.[118] For instance, 2 Chronicles 3:14, which is a quote of Exodus 36:35, replaces *šēš* with *bûṣ*. On the other hand, *bûṣ* is not found in the Torah. It is, however, attested in Aramaic and Akkadian sources. These factors lead Hurvitz to conclude that "the distribution of *šēš* and *bûṣ* in the Bible should be explained in both chronological [preexilic/postexilic] and geographical [Egypt/Mesopotamia-Syria] terms."[119] The use of this Egyptian word for the tabernacle and priestly garments suggests to Hurvitz that these narratives are of an "early origin."[120]

Leather Covering for the Tabernacle

The third layer covering the tabernacle is made of an obscure material called *tᵉḥāšîm* (תְּחָשִׁים; e.g., Exod. 25:5; 26:14; 35:7, 23) that has been variously translated as "badgers' skins" (KJV), "fine leather" (JB, NJB, NRSV), "goatskins" (RSV) "porpoise-hides" (NEB), "dolphin skins" (NJPS), and "hide of sea cows" (NIV). Following the suggestion of W. F. Albright, Cross thought that *tᵉḥāšîm* might be related to the Egyptian expression *ṯḥś*, which has to do with stretching leather.[121] Subsequently, Cross changed his mind, suggesting that *tᵉḥāšîm* in the Torah is a Semitic word based on the Arabic cognate *tuḫaš*, meaning dolphin or porpoise.[122] Given that dolphins do inhabit the Red Sea waters around the Sinai Peninsula, this suggestion has influenced some recent translations (e.g., NJPS, NEB).[123] To Cross, the use of dolphin skins in the construction of the tabernacle has a ring of authenticity to it; he declares, "I must say that I find it hard to believe that priests bent on producing a fraudulent description of Moses' tabernacle would have chosen dolphin skin for outer curtains."[124] He associates the use of dolphin skins with El's marine abode, despite the fact that dolphins are never mentioned in the Ugaritic texts in question.

Of the fourteen references of *tᵉḥāšîm* in the Old Testament, thirteen are in Exodus and Numbers and refer to the material covering the tabernacle. The term occurs once more in Ezekiel 16:10, where it applies to the sandals of a bride. Interestingly, during his travels in Sinai, Robinson discovered that Bedouin made sandals of "the thick skin of a fish which is caught in the Red Sea."[125] He goes on to state: "The skin is clumsy and coarse, and might answer very well for the external covering of the tabernacle, which was constructed at Sinai."[126] Koehler and Baumgartner thought it unlikely that dolphin skins fit the context of Ezekiel 16—apparently unaware of Robinson's discovery—and proposed that *tᵉḥašîm* referred to fine leather imported from Egypt.[127]

Thus although different etymologies for this skin or leather are possible, they nevertheless point to a Sinaitic or Egyptian origin.

Ark of the Covenant

The ark of the covenant is the central furnishing of the tabernacle and is made of acacia wood and overlaid in gold. It is designed to be transported by acacia poles that passed through four golden rings, one on each corner (Exod. 25:10–13) and shares some features that can be traced to Egyptian portable shrines that are widely depicted on Egyptian temple reliefs of the New Kingdom. The "Red Chapel" of Hatshepsut and Thutmose III at Karnak Temple (1479–1469 B.C.), for example, shows the two monarchs following a procession of priests who are carrying the bark of Amun (figure 38). A pair of poles lie under the boat and rest on the shoulders of the nine priests. In the center of the boat is a wooden shrine that contains the statue of the deity.

The Nineteenth and Twentieth Dynasties offer numerous depictions of portable shrines being carried by priests. In the Hypostyle Hall at Karnak, a relief of Seti I shows a phyle of priests transporting a shrine by its poles in a religious procession (figure 39). A striking detail is included that is not shown in the Eighteenth-Dynasty scenes: statues of Amun and Re are shown in the shrine, with a pair of goddesses extending their wings to protect the deities. At Medinet Habu, the funerary temple of Ramesses III, the king himself is portrayed seated on a throne within a shrine that is borne, in this instance, by a group of his sons (figure 40). Behind the king is a pair of deities with their wings extended to protect him.

Wings are a well-known symbol of divine protection that probably originated in Egypt and spread throughout the Near East.[128] Winged figures appear in the art of the Levant and Mesopotamia, such as ivories of Nimrud and

Samaria, which display an unmistakably Egyptian style, complete with Egyptian winged goddesses.[129] Ancient Israel also adopted this motif of divine protection, as is known in many of the Psalms (e.g., 17:8; 36:7; 57:1; 61:4; 91:4), and it is found on stamp seals and seal impressions from Israel and Judah,[130] as well as the cherubim of the ark. Exodus 25:18–20 offers the following description of the pair of winged figures on the ark: "You shall make two cherubim of gold; you shall make them of hammered work, at the two ends of the mercy seat. Make one cherub at the one end, and one cherub at the other; of one piece with the mercy seat you shall make the cherubim at its two ends. The cherubim shall spread out their wings above, overshadowing the mercy seat with their wings. They shall face one to another; the faces of the cherubim shall be turned toward the mercy seat."

A portable shrine with carrying poles was discovered in the tomb of Tutankhamun, upon which was a wooden statue of the god Anubis. The shrine measures 95 × 37 centimeters and was 54.3 centimeters high (3' 2⅛" × 1' 2⅝" × 1' 9⅜"), and the carrying poles were 273.5 centimeters (8' 11⅜") long.[131] The shrine was made of gilded wood. According to Exodus 25:10, the ark measured two and a half cubits in length, and one and a half cubits in width and height. Based upon the reckoning that the cubit in the Bible was 45 centimeters long (ca. 18"),[132] the ark was 112 × 67 × 67 centimeters (3' 9" × 2' 3" × 2' 3"). Although the length of the poles of the ark is not given, they were to be overlaid with gold (Exod. 25:13), just as were those of the shrine from Tutankhamun's tomb. The ark of the covenant, then, was just slightly larger than the Anubis shrine from the tomb of Tutankhamun.

Thus in the ark of the covenant we have a portable shrine that was made mobile by carrying poles. And priests—just as was prescribed for the sons of Aaron in Numbers 4—were responsible for its care and transport. It had a pair of winged cherubim to protect the divine presence. As we have seen here, all these features, including the gilded wood, are found in Egypt. It seems quite possible that standing behind the technical and artistic features of the Israel ark was Egyptian influence.

The Lampstand

The seven-branch lamp, widely known by its Hebrew name menorah (מְנֹרַה), is described in detail in Exodus 25:31–39. One feature of the lamp is the oil-holding "cups" (גְּבִעִים; vv. 33–34), a term thought to be an Egyptian loanword, *ḳbḥ*.[133] This word is typically written with a determinative () showing that it was a water vessel.[134] In her authoritative study of the menorah thirty years ago, Carol Meyers examined ancient Israel's lampstand in the light of different Near Eastern artistic motifs and goldsmith technology, and in her view Egypt had some influence.[135] She maintains that the origin of the tabernacle, along with the menorah, has its roots in the Sinai, and concluded, "its authentic place in the traditions of the wilderness period has been assumed in this study because the archaeological data that have been adduced in preceding chapters cannot allow us to do otherwise."[136] For those who would question that such an elegant lampstand could have been produced by the early Israelites in the wilderness, Meyers correctly points out that some nomadic people did specialize in metallurgy—like those depicted in the Tomb of Khnumhotep at Beni Hasan[137]—and that during the sojourn in Egypt, some Israelites in service to Pharaoh's building projects could have been "involved in technological labor." She showed that the technological and artistic attributes of the menorah were well known in the Late Bronze Age and states: "In so far as this coincides with the Exodus-Wilderness period of at least some portion of the Israelite tribes, the very period to which tradition ascribes the inception of the tabernacle/tent as an Israelite institution, the traditions concerning the fabrication of the menorah within that sanctuary must be seen as an authentic part of the Exodus narratives."[138]

The Altar

The altar (הַמִּזְבֵּחַ) was a portable device made of acacia wood and covered with bronze (Exod. 27:1–4), and the top was a bronze grate or grill (מִכְבָּר). This word only occurs in Exodus (27:4; 35:15; 38:4, 5, 30; 39:39). Although it has been associated with the Hebrew root *kbr*, meaning "weave," Manfred Görg has questioned this interpretation and proposed that an Egyptian compound expression stands behind *miḵbbār: mk* + *biꜣ rwḏ*.[139] The former means "covering," and the latter literally means "strong or hard copper."[140] The combination *biꜣ rwḏ* is attested as early as the Middle Kingdom, and stands behind the Coptic word Βαρωτ, which means bronze.[141] The reduction of the *ḏ* to *t* is the result of a shift in vocalization of *ḏ* > *d* > *t* which occurred during the second millennium because of the "devoicing of the dentals."[142] Görg explains the omission of the *ot* as the result of the Hebrews treating it as a plural feminine ending, making *miḵbbār* the singular form.[143] If Görg's interpretation of this word is correct, then we have another technical word associated with the tabernacle's furnishings that is of Egyptian origin.

Incense Dish

At the dedication of the tabernacle in Numbers 7, a representative of each of the twelve tribes offered a "golden dish weighing ten shekels, full of incense" (כַּף אַחַת עֲשָׂרָה זָהָב מְלֵאָה קְטֹרֶת; Num. 7:14, 20, 26, 32, 38, 44, 50, 56, 62, 68, 74, 80). This utensil is found elsewhere in the Torah in connection with other cultic paraphernalia (Exod. 25:29; 37:16; Num. 4:7; 7:86), and it is mentioned as among the objects in Solomon's temple (1 Kings 5:50), which were carried off in 586 B.C. when Nebuchadnezzar plundered the temple (2 Kings 25:14). As for the Numbers 7 passage, Baruch Levine has shown, on the basis of comparative study with other Near Eastern lists of cultic offerings, that it describes an ancient practice.[144] His observations find further support in that the word *kap̱*, incense dish, has a striking counterpart in Egypt. *Kap̱* in Hebrew means "hand,"[145] and so-called arm vessels have been found in the Levant and Anatolia. In her study of the arm-shaped vessel, Ruth Amiran argued against connecting these to the Egyptian arm-shaped incense utensil.[146] Rather she showed that those found in ancient Israel were for anointing or libations and not for incense. However, the Egyptian word *k3p* means "to burn incense."[147] And it specifically applies to burning incense to the gods as early as the Old Kingdom Pyramid Texts.[148] There were two basic types of censers in Pharaonic Egypt. One type was made up of a pair of bowls, the one being the base and the other the lid, which had a stemlike handle.[149] It is this brazier that serves as the determinative for the word *k3p*. The second type is fashioned like an extended arm, at the end of which a carved hand holds a bowl.[150] Perhaps the Israelite incense bowl (*kap̱*) derived its function and name from the Egyptian incense brazier.

Another Type of Censer or Tray

The term *maḥtāh* (מַחְתָּה) is sometimes rendered censer (Lev. 10:1, 12; Num. 16:6, 17, 18), or firepan or tray (Exod. 25:38; 37:23; Num. 4:9); it is usually made of bronze (Exod. 38:3; Num. 16:39), but sometimes of gold (Exod. 37:23). Interestingly, Koehler and Baumgartner offer no Semitic cognates for this word.[151] In the absence of a clear Semitic etymology, I should like to propose that it is possibly related to the Egyptian root *ẖt*, which can mean fire, or, with a different determinative, it is a word for offering.[152] The initial *mem* could be a preformative that occurs regularly in Egyptian and Semitic languages with nominal forms.[153] Although this proposal is by no means certain, it at least affords a possible etymology for this otherwise obscure word.

Priestly Girdle or Sash

Among the priestly regalia in Exodus 28:4, 39, 40; 29:9 and Leviticus 8:7, 13; 16:4 is a sash worn around the waist.[154] It is called *'āḇnēt* (אַבְנֵט) and this word derives from the Egyptian verb *bnd*, which means "wrap up."[155] In Egypt, this word is first attested in Egyptian texts of the New Kingdom.[156]

Head Opening in Priestly Robe

Exodus 28:32 offers a description of the robe of the priestly ephod and describes the opening for the head as being "like the opening in a coat of mail (תַחְרָא), so that it may not be torn." *Taḥrā'*—a rather obscure word—occurs only one other time in the Old Testament, in Exodus 39:23, and it is used in the same way. The lexicographers Koehler and Baumgartner declared the word to be of uncertain origin,[157] but the meaning "coat of mail" is accepted by some more recent translations (NJPS, NKJV, NJB). Nahum Sarna sees this type of armor being worn by Canaanite charioteers on the relief on the chariot body of Thutmose IV (1410–1400 B.C.).[158] The coat of mail used in the New Kingdom was a leather jacket or vest onto which small bronze or copper plates were sewn, to judge from a scene in the tomb of Ken-Amun and from a portion of such a coat found at the palace of Amenhotep III at Malqata.[159]

The significance of this suggestion lies in the possible etymological relationship between *taḥra'* and the Egyptian word *dḥr*, which means "leather" or "animal hide."[160] It is written with the leather sign (𓄛 or 𓄜), as is the word for mail armor (*mśś*).[161] Although there are some linguistic problems with this identification, the relationship between leather and mail armor is not insignificant. If *taḥrā'* means leather and refers to the leather jacket for mail armor, the point of its use in this text is that the opening of the linen robe probably had a leather collar like that of a coat of armor. Thus there is reason to believe that there may be a relationship between Egyptian *dḥr* and Hebrew *taḥra'*.

Undergarments of the Priest

The undergarments (מִכְנְסֵי: *mik̲nᵉsê*) of the priest are made of linen (*šēš*), which is clearly an Egyptian word, as we have seen, and occurs just four times in the Torah (Exod 28:42; 39:28; Lev. 6:3; 16:4), and only once elsewhere.[162] It is commonly thought that this word derives from the root כנס, which means "gather."[163] Exodus 28:42 offers the best description of this garment: "You shall make for them linen undergarments to cover their naked flesh; they shall reach from the hips to the thighs." One scholar has recently argued, in support of the traditional view that P dates to the fifth century, that pants or trousers are only attested beginning in the Persian period.[164] First, the absence of earlier examples may in part be due to the fact that one would not expect to see undergarments on statues or in relief at any period. Second, actual linen garments are not likely to survive in most areas of the Levant, although they have in the desert climes of Egypt. In fact, linen undergarments have been found among the clothes of Tutankhamun.[165] Similarly, the tomb of Kha from Deir el-Medineh included all the linen garments of a gentleman from New Kingdom Egypt.[166] Also, in response to Sperling's charge that the reference to priestly trousers in the Torah reflects the *realia* of the Persian period, Zevit has pointed out that he failed to take into account the pictorial representations of Judean officials wearing pants like pedal pushers on the Lachish reliefs of Sennacherib (701 B.C.).[167] Sperling came to the wrong conclusion concerning the biblical data because he was apparently unaware that different types of men's pants are attested prior to the Persian period in Israel, and from the second millennium in Egypt.

The description of the pants in Exodus 28:42 suggests that the purpose of this garment was to cover the sexual organs. Zevit understands the garment to have this purpose, suggesting that it functioned like a jockstrap.[168] Cassuto is surely correct to connect the reason for protective pants described in Exodus 28:42 with the reference in 20:26 that offers the prohibition: "You shall not go up by steps to my altar, so that your nakedness may not be exposed on it." He maintained that modesty among the priests was valued in ancient Israel.[169] If this idea is valid, then it is further supported by a possible Egyptian root that stands behind the obscure Hebrew word *mik̲nᵉsê*. *Kns* refers to the sexual area or pubic region.[170] Since we do not know the Egyptian word for a man's underpants, one wonders if *mkns* might not have been that word for the royal linen drawers of Tutankhamun.

Gemstones on the Priest's Breastplate

(1) Turquoise. *Nop̱ek* (נֹפֶךְ; Exod. 28:18; 39:11) is clearly the Egyptian word for turquoise (*mfk't*) and was fully discussed in chapter 7 §III, in the section on Dophkah. A number of recent English translations now recognize that *nop̱ek* is the Hebrew word for turquoise (NRSV, NIV, NJPS).

(2) Amethyst. *'Aḥālāmâ* (אַחְלָמָה) occurs in two passages in Exod. 28:19; 39:12 and is recognized to be the writing of the Egyptian word *ḫnm(t)*.[171] The use of *n* in the Egyptian word and *l* in the Hebrew is found in many instances, and is due to the fact that in some cases the Egyptian *n* was actually vocalized as an *l*, and there was no *l* in the Egyptian language.[172] The fact that the Hebrew word is written with the *l* demonstrates that the word did not come into Hebrew in written form, but from hearing the word being vocalized. J. R. Harris thought it was red jasper.[173] Lucas and Harris observed that although jasper comes in different colors, red was the favorite in Egypt, and that it was used "chiefly for beads and amulets, though sometimes as inlay for jewelry."[174]

(3) Jacinth. *Lešem* (לֶשֶׁם; Exod. 28:19; 39:12), another gem in the breastplate, is of Egyptian etymology: *nšm(t)*.[175] In the absence of any Semitic cognate, Muchiki believes that *lešem* is "most likely" an Egyptian loanword.[176] Harris identifies it as a green feldspar that was one of the most widely used semiprecious stones in Egypt.[177]

Weights and Measures

(1) Hin (הִין) is a liquid measure that occurs frequently in the Pentateuch (e.g., Exod. 29:40; Lev. 23:13; Num. 15:4) and is the writing for Egyptian *hn.w*.[178] The early influence of this Egyptian measure in the Levant is demonstrated by its appearance in Ugaritic (thirteenth century) and in the Amarna letters (fourteenth century).[179] A hin-jar in Egypt held around .50 liter (a pint), whereas in Israel it was approximately 3.65 liters (just under a gallon).[180]

(2) Ephah (אֵיפָה) is a dry measure that derives from the Egyptian measure *ip(t)*.[181] The *ip(t)* was a quarter of a *ḥkt*, which was 4.8 liters or 5 quarts.[182] In the Torah it is used to measure grain as food or for offerings (Exod. 16:36; Lev. 5:11; 6:20; 19:36; Num. 5:15; 28:5). Although the Hebrews borrowed the Egyptian name of the measurement, the size was different, being equal to about 7.3 liters (just under 2 gallons).[183]

Linear Measures

The system for measuring lengths in Israel has an Egyptian stamp on it. Both systems used the cubit (אַמָּה; *'emmāh*; Eg. *mḥ*), which is based upon the length of an arm from the finger tip to the elbow. In fact, the Egyptian word for cubit is written with the arm (𓂝) as a determinative, or it can stand alone as an ideogram, meaning cubit.[184] There were actually several different Egyptian cubits in New Kingdom times. A number of actual cubit sticks have been discovered over the years in Egypt. A pair of cubit sticks, one of wood and the other of stone, was discovered in the 1980s in the tomb of Aper-el from the late Eighteenth Dynasty at Saqqara.[185] The following observations are based on the stone cubit, although the two are nearly identical. The cubit is divided into seven palms. Moving from right to left, four fingers or digits (*ḏbꜥ*) made a palm (*šsp*), and the second four make the second palm. The third is labeled "small span" (*ḏrt nḏs(t)* = 26.14 cm), while the fourth palm is divided in half with a vertical line and is called the "great" (*'3*) span, which is also a half (royal) cubit. The fourth palm includes the sign 𓂦 (*ḏsr*), meaning holy or sacred.[186] It is not altogether clear what this usage signifies. The fifth palm contains the sign of the forearm with palm turned down (𓂢, *rmn* = 37.35 cm). The sixth palm formed the "large cubit" (*mḥ wr*, 44.82 centimeters / ca. 18 inches), and the seventh formed the "royal cubit" (*mḥ-nsw*, 52.3 centimeters / ca. 21 inches). The seven-palm cubit was the standard cubit used for measurement in New Kingdom Egypt for architecture.[187]

The length of the cubit in Israel is based largely on data from the Iron II period and is thought to be shorter than the Egyptian cubit, or 44.45 centimeters = 17.5 inches.[188] But the length of the Israelite cubit in the Late Bronze/ Iron I period is not certain. There are some indications in some biblical texts to show that there were differences. For instance, Deuteronomy 3:11 reports on the size of King Og's iron bed that was seized by the Israelites, and its measurements are given in "common cubits" (lit. cubit of a man: בְּאַמַּת־אִישׁ). Jeffrey Tigay understands this reference to indicate a different measure from the standard cubit, which was possibly the royal cubit.[189] In Judges 3:16, the length of Ehud's dagger is reported to be a *gōmeḏ* long. This measurement does not occur elsewhere in the Hebrew Bible. As a consequence, the intended length and the origin of this word are unknown. Then too there is an allusion to the royal cubit in Ezekiel 40:5, where the measuring stick is "a cubit and a handbreadth in length." As we noted in the Egyptian system, the large cubit is made up of six palms, while the royal cubit adds a seventh, or to use Ezekiel's terminology, a cubit plus a handbreadth. These three references, from three different periods, hint that there was not a standard length for the cubit in all periods, otherwise these additional comments would not have been required.

As we have seen already, Egyptian dry and liquid measures are found in the Pentateuch within the wilderness tradition, so it is not surprising that the Egyptian linear measures also influenced early Israel. The cubit and its component parts—fingers, palms, and spans—are found in the Bible, and some of the terminology is Egyptian.

Span (זֶרֶת: *zereṯ*) is the measurement used in Exodus 28:16; 39:9 to describe the size of the priestly breastplate. This word appears to have developed from the Egyptian word for hand or span, *ḏrt*.[190] Because the Hebrew is written with a *zayin*, Lambdin believed the word must have been borrowed into Semitic early in the second millennium.[191] It is attested as *drt* in Ugaritic (before 1200 B.C.). Despite some linguistic problems, the absence of a Semitic etymology indicates that an Egyptian origin is certainly a possibility.[192]

The word "finger" is never found in the Old Testament to indicate a length. The Hebrew word for finger, אֶצְבַּע (*'eṣbba'*), is a common Semitic word for finger (e.g., Ugaritic, Akkadian, Arabic).[193] The Egyptian word for finger, both the digit and the measurement, is *ḏb'*.[194] Its use in Egypt as early as the Old Kingdom indicates that this word has a very early history and may be a proto-Semitic word that is common to both Egyptian and Semitic. Thus we cannot be certain what the Hebrew word for the finger measurement was, but it seems probable that it would have been this common word for finger (אֶצְבַּע), which may have come to Hebrew from the Egyptian word *ḏb'*.

The cubit used by the Hebrews in the wilderness narratives in connection with building the tabernacle may well have been the Egyptian cubit, given the fact that the cubit, span, palm, and finger system was used in Israel, and that some of the terminology from Egypt appears to be used in Hebrew.

Silver Trumpets

Numbers 10:2 contains the following instructions: "Make two silver trumpets (חֲצוֹצְרֹת כֶּסֶף); you shall make them of hammered work; and you shall use them for summoning the congregation, and for breaking camp." Some commentators, such as E. W. Davies and Philip Budd, regard this reference to be a late alternative to the earlier use of the ram's horn (הַיֹּבֵל or שֹׁפָר).[195] Part of their thinking is that because Numbers 10 derives from P, it must be late (i.e., fifth century). These scholars then point to illustrations of such trumpets on the Arch of Titus in Rome and on Jewish coins of the first century A.D. While also citing the Titus relief, Jacob Milgrom remarks that in Egypt trumpets were used for religious and military purposes.[196] He acknowledges the classical study by H. Hickman on the trumpet in ancient Egypt.[197] Apparently Budd and

Davies were unaware of Hickman's work from 1946 and the implications for the history of the metal trumpet. Among the earliest reliefs showing the use of trumpets is one from the grand funerary temple of Hatshepsut at Deir el-Bahri, where soldiers are being rallied (figure 41). Trumpets are also shown in military scenes throughout the New Kingdom, including the Amarna period.[198] Also from the Eighteenth Dynasty, trumpets are shown in religious contexts, such as at the Opet festival at Luxor temple (figure 42). In a block from Tell el-Amarna, an officer blasts his trumpet, apparently to announce the approach of an important individual.[199] Proof that the trumpets known from artistic representations were made of metal came with the discovery of Tutankhamun's tomb (ca. 1325 B.C.). It yielded two trumpets and their wooden cores. Although one was made of a copper alloy, the other was fashioned from silver. Consequently, there is no basis for understanding the references to the silver trumpets of Numbers 10:2 as a late-period fabrication. Thus we see that in New Kingdom Egypt, copper and silver trumpets were used in religious ceremonies and in military settings, just as they were according to Numbers 7:1–10.

Ox Carts

To carry the tabernacle and its furnishings, ox carts or wagons were prescribed to transport the sanctuary through the wilderness (Num. 7:3, 6–8). Ox carts were known during the latter part of the second millennium B.C. Perhaps the best-known example is found on the "Sea People" reliefs at Medinet Habu. Ramesses III's artists included a land force approaching Egypt that included carts drawn by oxen, carrying women and children. New evidence for the use of a heavy-duty cart has come to light, in this case in a cultic context. Among the talatat-blocks pieced together by the Akhenaten Temple Project in the 1980s, there is a procession of huge carts with solid wooden wheels (figure 43).[200] In this case, the carts haul mammoth bulls that probably had been fattened for offerings. So heavy is the load that three axles and six wheels are required to sustain cargo, and, rather humorously, twelve to fifteen men are shown straining to pull the wagons. Clearly, the use of ox-drawn carts by the Israelites poses no technical problem. In addition, the Semitic word for cart (*'egᵉlōṯ*) in the Torah references is attested in Egyptian texts of the late New Kingdom. A text from the desert region of Wadi Hammamat illustrates that the carts were used by miners.[201] This text shows that ox carts were used in Egypt and in Sinai by the Israelites under identical conditions.

VI. Conclusion

In this section, we have seen that a significant number of words connected to the tabernacle, the priestly garments and breastplate, and cultic utensils have an Egyptian etymology, and that some of the artists' motifs appear to be connected with Egyptian prototypes; many of the technological aspects of the construction of the tabernacle find parallels in Egypt during the second millennium, and in some cases earlier. Over twenty years have passed since Meyers offered the following assessment of the tabernacle: "Archaeologically, linguistically, and historically, many of the features of the movable shrine can be shown to have been rooted in the Near Eastern culture of the end of the Late Bronze Age and the early Iron age, the period of Moses, Joshua and the Judges."[202] She too spoke of "Egyptian technology and design" that influenced the elements of the tabernacle, and then she concluded: "parallels to Near Eastern ritual practices of the Late Bronze and early Iron Age can be detected. In particular an Egyptian influence, such as could have been affected only during an immediate post-Exodus period, can be discerned in the configuration and identity of certain cultic acts and personnel."[203] Here we have shown far more linguistic evidence than Meyers considered, which I believe strengthens her claims. To the data presented here, we can also add the personal names of some of the priestly family and other individuals, but these will be treated in the following chapter.

10

Egyptian Personal Names and Other Egyptian Elements in the Exodus-Wilderness Narratives

When the child grew up, she brought him to Pharaoh's daughter, and she took him as her son. She named him Moses, because she said, "I drew him out of the water."

—Exod. 2:10

I. Personal Names in the Torah

In the 1930s, Theophile Meek pointed to a number of personal names of Egyptian etymology in the Torah, especially among the Levitical tribe, as clear evidence that at least some Israelites had been in Egypt. He was responding to some critics who had challenged the biblical sojourn tradition. To the six names whose etymologies were, in his words, "unquestionably Egyptian" (Moses, Assir, Pashḥur, Hophni, Phineas, and Merari),[1] a number of other names can be adduced. The following is a list, including these six, with a discussion of the Egyptian roots behind the name.

Aaron (אַהֲרֹן: *'ah^{a}ron*): The elder brother of Moses and Israel's first priest. The origin of this name is uncertain and, in the absence of any obvious Semitic derivation, Martin Noth over seventy-five years ago thought it might be Egyptian.[2] More recently, John Spencer posits an Egyptian origin without suggesting a stem.[3] One Egyptian explanation for the name of Aaron is that it derives from the word "overseer."[4] Michael Homan has reviewed many of the proposed roots behind the name of Aaron, and then proposed that, as keeper of Israel's Tent of Meeting, the origin of the name might be found in the Hebrew word "tent" (אֹהֶל: *'ohel*).[5] He suggests that that Hebrew *'ahᵃron* is an "Egyptianized form of Semitic אֹהֶל."[6] This explanation accounts for the use of *resh* in the Hebrew writing, as there was no *lamed* in Egyptian. When a Semitic word with an *l* is written in Egyptian, *r* is used (as in the case of Israel in the Merneptah stela which is written, *ysr'ir*). Homan recognizes the problem posed by his theory, that is, that there is no other example of a Semitic word in the Bible that has been altered under the influence of another language that then "reentered the original language as a borrowing."[7] The addition of the concluding adjectival element *on* would make the name mean something like "tent-man" or "he who is of the tent." A similar name (*'aharaya*) is found in Egypt during the Eighteenth to Nineteenth Dynasties.[8] Although scholars are unable to come to a consensus on the origin of the name Aaron, there is general agreement that it is probably Egyptian.

Ahira (אֲחִירַע: *'ᵃḥîra'*): Ahira is a leader from the tribe of Naphtali, mentioned in the wilderness census recorded in Numbers 1:15; 2:29; 7:78, 83; 10:27. Some commentators have glossed over this name, declaring that its "meaning [is] uncertain," while others suggest that it means "my brother is a friend," to which Koehler and Baumgartner add a question mark because this etymology is so unclear.[9] The fact that this name does not occur again in the Hebrew scriptures seems to militate against it being a solely Hebrew fraternal-type name, since such names were very common in ancient Israel.[10] Another possibility is that it is a hybrid name that combines Egyptian and Hebrew elements: *'ᵃḥî* + *ra'*, meaning "brother (Heb.) of Re (Eg.)," that is, brother of (the sun-god) Re.[11] This interpretation of the name was entertained by Noth.[12] Egypto-Semitic hybrid names are attested from ancient times in Egypt and the Levant (e.g., Abd-osir = Servant of Osiris,[13] Ahimoth = Brother of (the goddess) Mut,[14] Asarel = Osiris is god,[15] Abd-hor = "Servant of Horus"[16]), and might indicate a bilingual or bicultural influence on the naming process.[17]

Assir (אַסִּיר: *'assîr*): A son of Korah (Exod. 6:24) who was the nemesis of Moses and Aaron in Numbers 16, and part of the cabal that complained of being brought from Egypt, "a land flowing with milk and honey, to kill us in the wilderness." Koehler and Baumgartner follow a suggestion by Martin Noth that the name derives from the Egyptian deity Osiris (*wsir*).[18] Muchiki agrees with this possibility, pointing out that Osiris is found as a personal name in the New Kingdom but suggests another viable option, Egyptian *isr*, for the tamarisk tree, which also occurs as a personal name in Egypt.[19] He also observes that the Assir of Exodus 6:24, as the text presents it, was "probably born in Egypt."[20]

Hori (חוֹרִי: *ḥorî*): This name occurs but once in the Bible, at Numbers 13:5. Ernst Axel Knauf believes that this name occurs in a list by P that actually came from Genesis 36:20 and 22, which mentions one חֹרִי (*ḥōrî*) who is of Edomite stock. This leads him to believe that the Hori of the spy list of Numbers 13 to be the result of speculation, and thus it is "doubtful whether a biblical personal name 'Hori' ever existed."[21] Knauf's conjecture is interesting, but a simpler explanation, which he did not entertain, must be considered. The name Hori is well known in Egypt and derives from the name of the deity Horus (see next entry) and means "He of Horus."[22] Given the fact that Hori is one of the twelve spies dispatched to reconnoiter in Canaan for Moses, he may have been born in Egypt or was named by parents who had lived in Egypt. Consequently, an Egyptian name for this intelligence officer is probable.

Hur (חוּר: *ḥûr*): A leader who, along with Aaron, stood with Moses during Israel's battle with Amalek (Exod. 17:10, 12), and is mentioned again as a leader who would serve as a stand-in for Moses when he went up Mt. Sinai with Joshua (Exod. 24:24). It is not certain, though certainly possible, that he is the grandfather of the chief artisan of the tabernacle, Bezalel (Exod. 31:2; 35:30; 38:22).[23] Hur, the grandfather of Bezalel, is reported to be from the tribe of Judah (Exod. 31:2). If two different men named Hur are intended, then they would have both been born in Egypt. It is quite likely that this name represents a transliteration of the Egyptian sky god, Horus (*ḥr*).[24] Moreover, Pharaoh was considered to be the incarnation of the god Horus, hence the usual title for the king, "Living Horus" (*ʿnḫ ḥr*).[25]

Merari (מְרָרִי: *mᵉrārî*): This name first occurs as the name of the son of Levi who emigrated to Egypt with Jacob in Genesis 46:11. Subsequently, this name became a tribal subdivision or family name of those who had the responsibility of transporting the frames and pillars of the tabernacle (cf. Num. 3:17, 20, 33, 35, 36). There are proposed Semitic roots, Hebrew and Arabic, for this name,[26] but in response to these, Meek opined that they are "most unlikely and far fetched when we have the common Middle Egyptian personal name *Mrry*."[27] Muchiki likewise considers the Egyptian connection with Merari to be a factor in determining the origin. If Merari derives from a Semitic root, then one might expect to find this name elsewhere in the Bible and the Levant, but this is not the case. Consequently, the Egyptian root appears preferable.

Miriam (מִרְיָם: *maryām*): The sister of Moses and a prophetess, like her brother, appears to have an Egyptian name. Although there are different linguistic explanations for the second *mem*, there is agreement that *mary* is the writing of the root *mry*, meaning "love" or "beloved,"[28] just as was proposed with Miriam's ancestor, Merari. This is behind the name Mary in the New Testament, and of course continues to be used in the twenty-first century. Alan Gardiner considered this to be one of several ancient Egyptian names that has survived into English.[29]

Moses (מֹשֶׁה: *mošeh*): The name of Israel's great leader occurs more than 700 times in the Hebrew Bible and around 150 times in the New Testament. Standing behind this name is thought to be the Egyptian root *msi*, so that even some scholars who question the historicity of Moses have to admit the Egyptian origin of the name.[30] *Msi* or *ms*-type names, such as Amenmose, Thutmose, Ramose, and even Mes and Mesu, were very popular in the New Kingdom.[31] There is, however, a problem with the Egyptian *s* appearing in Hebrew as *š*. For an extensive linguistic discussion of this problem, see the treatment offered in *Israel in Egypt*.[32]

Phineas (פִּינְחָס: *pîneḥās*): He was an Israelite priest of the wilderness period, and grandson of Aaron, whose father-in-law was Putiel (see Exod. 6:25, and last entry here). There is no disputing that this word derives from an Egyptian name *p3 nḥsy*, which means "the Nubian."[33] It is not an indicator of ethnicity, but could have been used of a boy of darker complexion.[34] As a name, Nehsy (*nḥsy*) is found in Egypt as early as the Fourteenth Dynasty Delta king. In the New Kingdom, the definite article *p3* is added to the name.[35] This explains the initial element *pî* in the Hebrew writing. The name of this priest was used centuries later in the priestly family of Eli (cf. 1 Sam. 1:3; 2:34; 4:4, 11, 17).

Puah (פּוּעָה: *pû'â*): The name of one of the Hebrew midwives in Egypt when the oppression of the Israelites began (Exod. 1:15). Two possible roots have been proffered for this name: a Ugaritic word *pgy*,[36] and the Egyptian word *p3c3*, "The Great."[37] Because this woman was born in Egypt, one might expect a local influence on the name. Because she is a woman, the feminine for *t3́3* might be expected.

Putiel (פּוּטִיאֵל: *pûtî'ēl*): Only attested in Exodus 6:25, Putiel was the father-in-law of Phineas, and would have been born in Egypt as he would have been of the same generation as Aaron. Putiel is a hybrid name, according to Noth and others, which combines Egyptian *p3-di* and the Hebrew *'ēl*, god, and would mean "He whom god has given."[38] The *p3-di* type names are attested in Egypt beginning in the New Kingdom.[39]

II. Personal Names outside the Pentateuch

A number of names with Egyptian origins are found outside the Pentateuch. These fall into two categories: those in genealogical lists that may include individuals from the exodus and wilderness periods, and hence are relevant to this discussion,[40] and names associated with the priesthood. Meek was of the impression that the continued use of Egyptian names centuries after the Egypt-Sinai narratives was evidence that the tribe of Levi has definitely been in Egypt.[41]

Ahimoth (אֲחִימוֹת: *'aḥîmôṯ*): This name occurs but once in a genealogical list of Levites via Kohath (1 Chron. 6:25). Ahimoth could be a Semitic theophore, "Brother of Mot (or death)."[42] The Hebrew *môṯ* could be a writing for the Egyptian goddess Mut, who was very important in the New Kingdom and a member of the Amun-re/Mut/Khonsu triad from Thebes.[43] In this case, Ahimoth could be "Brother of Mut" or "Mut Is Glorious."[44] The second option understands the initial element to be *ꜣḫ*, meaning glory or glorious.[45] Akh-mut is found in Egypt as a personal name.[46] Undoubtedly the most famous example of the Akh-type name in Egypt is Pharaoh Akhenaten. Dating Ahimoth is problematic, though Muchiki does place him in the generation of the exodus.[47] It is worth noting that two different near relatives are named Assir (1 Chron 6:22–23), which as we have seen above is an Egyptian name given to the son of Korah (Exod. 6:24).

Harnepher (חַרְנֶפֶר: *ḥarneper*): This name occurs only in 1 Chronicles 7:36 in a genealogical list; it falls sixth after the tribal ancestor, Asher. Asher, Beriah, and Heber represent a sequence found in a genealogical list in Genesis 46:17, and are probably clan names that appear again in the military census of Numbers 26:44–47.[48] It is thus difficult to determine precisely when Harnepher would have lived, but the generation of the exodus-wilderness period is possible. A clear Egyptian etymology stands behind this name: *ḥr nfr*, "Horus Is Good" or "Beautiful," and is attested as a personal name in Egypt beginning in the Middle Kingdom (ca. 2000 B.C. onward).[49] This etymology is also recognized by Diana Edelman, who explains that this Egyptian name might have entered Judean archives during the period of Egyptian influence on Judah in the Saite period (late seventh and early sixth centuries B.C.).[50] It is hard to believe that the Judaeans would welcome this Egyptian name during the period in which Necho II killed king Josiah, deported his successor to Egypt, and set up Jehoiakim as his puppet (2 Chron. 35:20–22; 36:4).

Hophni (חָפְנִי: *ḥapnî*): The son of Eli, the priest of Shiloh (1 Sam. 1:3; 2:34; 4:4, 11, 17). The Egyptian origin of this name has been recognized for decades.[51] It is the Egyptian word for "tadpole" (*ḥfn(r)*), and was used in Egypt as a personal name as early as the Middle Kingdom.[52] It is significant that Hophni's brother is Phineas (1 Sam. 1:3; 2:34; 4:4, 11, 17), an Egyptian name given to Aaron's grandson (see above).

Jarha (יַרְחָע: *yarḥā'*): Mentioned twice in a geneology of Hezron, a descendent of Judah, and described as an Egyptian slave of Sheshan (see below). C. F. Keil showed that Ahlai, Sheshan's father, was the tenth generation from Judah, making Sheshan the eleventh (just as Joshua is from Ephraim, cf. 1 Chron 7: 20–27); this means that he had lived in Egypt.[53] This would account for an Egyptian slave in his possession. Jarha may represent the Egyptian expression *ir(t)-ḥ'(i)*, "Eye of Rejoicing," the eye being that of Horus.[54] This name, however, has not yet been documented in Egypt, but the name "Eye of Horus" (*ir(t) ḥr*) occurs as early as the Middle Kingdom.[55]

Jeremoth (יְרִימוֹת/יְרֵמוֹת: *yrēmôṯ* / *yrîmôṯ*): According to a genealogical list in 1 Chronicles 7:7–8, Jeremoth/Jerimoth was a grandson of Benjamin, in which case he was born in Egypt. Muchiki has suggested that it derives from the name type *iri* + divine name, with the second element being the Egyptian goddess Mut, as in the case of Ahimoth (see above).[56] Others have argued that this name is based on the Hebrew root *yrm*, meaning exalted, which John Wright claims was a popular name in Judah in the fifth to fourth centuries B.C.[57] However, appearance of the second *yod* in the name poses a problem for the stem *yrm* being the basis for the name.[58] A third option should be considered: that this name is completely Egyptian. I concur with Muchiki that *môṯ* might correspond to the deity Mut but wonder if Hebrew *yri* is the writing for the Egyptian verb *iri*, which means "begat."[59] In other words, the name would mean "begotten of Mut."

Pashhur (פַּשְׁחוּר: *pašḥûr*): The name of a priest in Jerusalem who arrested Jeremiah the prophet. This name is widely recognized as being Egyptian, but two etymologies are possible. One, *p(s)š-ḥr*, means "Share (or division) of Horus."[60] Alternatively it might mean "The Son of Horus" (*p3 šri n ḥr*), a name that is documented in Egypt.[61] The etymology of the latter is somewhat problematic, as we can offer no explanation for the omission of the *n*, which is preserved in Greek writings of this name in Egypt, showing that it continued to be vocalized.[62] Hence the first proposal is preferred.

Sheshan (שֵׁשָׁן: *šēšān*): The owner of the Egyptian slave Jarha introduced above, who is mentioned in the genealogical list in 1 Chronicles 2:31–35. It has long been recognized as being the writing for *ššn*, the Egyptian word for water lily. These flowers were ubiquitous in the Nile, canals, and swampy areas of Egypt, especially in the Delta. Indeed, it was a name in Egypt.[63] In the Chronicler it represents the name of a man, whereas it survives into the New Testament (Luke 8:3) as Susanna, and into English as Susan.

III. What's in a Name?

After reviewing a number of names that are of certain or probable Egyptian etymology, one cannot help but see validity to Meek's observation of seventy-five years ago that the use of Egyptian names, especially among the Levites, is evidence that this tribe had been in Egypt. The continued use of Egyptian names in later centuries in Israel is puzzling indeed. Rather than being an indication of a secret propensity toward Egyptian religion in the kingdom of Judah, it might be simply due to the conservatism that accompanies clergy. By way of analogy, Christian clerics today wear gowns that go back to European traditions centuries earlier, and monastic orders wear types of garments that their predecessors wore over a thousand years ago. Similarly, priests and clergy in the Roman Catholic and Orthodox (Greek, Russian, and Egyptian) traditions take the names of long-departed saints and church fathers, such as Justin, Athanasius, Cyril, and Shenoute.[64] The phenomenon of connecting a priestly office with one's forbears may account for the Egyptian names in Israel's later priesthood, but another question needs to be raised. That is, How much influence did Egyptian religion have on early Israel? The fact is that we do not know to what extent their religion was syncretistic. The appearance of theophoric names among the exodus generation (e.g., Ahimoth, Ahira, Assir, Harnepher, Hori, Hur) might indicate some adherence to Egyptian deities. In the previous chapter, an abundance of evidence was produced to demonstrate that the tabernacle and some of its cultic equipment, both in terminology and technology, were Egyptian. Could it be that they even had developed a priesthood prior to that of Aaron?

The episode of the rebellion of Korah in Numbers 16–17 is thought by source critics to represent a composite of rebellion traditions that the Priestly writer used to legitimize the Aaronic priesthood.[65] The unanswered question is, why Korah? Why should he be a ringleader? The text reports that he is a Levite through the priestly family of Kohath (Num. 16:1). Although one might get the impression from his statement in 16:3—that all Israel is holy—that he was advocating the abolition of particular priesthood and promoting everyone to be priests, it seems unlikely that as a Levite he would want to forego his own status. We are informed in 16:17–18 that Korah and his associates had censers and incense, suggesting that they exercised some priestly service.

The question has been raised as to whether there was among the Israelites some sort of priesthood already established in Egypt, in which case, could Korah have been one such cleric? Korah (קֹרַח) means "bald head" or "shaved head."[66] This name could point to a trait of Egyptian *w'b* -priests. The Egyptian word *w'b* means "pure."[67] Purification was achieved by ablutions or incense fumigation. A text in the tomb of the Eighteenth Dynasty vizier Ramose states: "Using incense, pouring libations, purifying the way (*sw'b*) to the necropolis."[68]

These *w'b*-priests, Denise Doxey notes, were "a lower-ranked class of priests" that assisted the *ḥm nṯr* or priest who attended the cult image in the sanctuary, although the *w'b*-priest could not enter the holy of holies. She further observes that they did "handle sacred objects and cult instruments. They were therefore required to observe strict rules of purity, and they can be identified in some representations by their shaved heads."[69] In his classic study of priests in ancient Egypt, Serge Sauneron likewise described the hallmark of the *w'b*-priests as being "their perfectly smooth heads." Significantly, circumcision was also a custom practiced by the priests.[70] These are the priests who are shown carrying shrines of deities in New Kingdom scenes, often depicted with clean-shaven heads (figures 38 and 39). One cannot help but wonder if Korah might not have been a priest in the tradition of the *w'b*-priest and is pressing Aaron for a promotion that would give him the status of a *ḥm nṯr*-priest (*kohēn* in Hebrew) and direct access to the holy place. Another point that might further support this hypothesis is that one of Korah's collaborators in Numbers 16:1 is On. The name On (אוֹן: *'ôn*) is the same as the Egyptian city located at the base of the Delta. The cult center of the sun god Re or Atum was located there—hence from Hellenistic times it was called Heliopolis. It might be recalled that Joseph's wife Asenath was the daughter of the Priest of On (Gen. 41:45, 50; 46:20). This, then, represents a direct connection between the Hebrews and the cult center at On and may explain why a man with the same name who was not a Levite would join a conspiracy against Aaron the priest.

IV. Miscellaneous Laws

There are a number of laws that point to Israel's sojourn in Egypt.

Prohibition against Eating Pork

Pigs are banned from Israel's diet by prohibitions in Leviticus and Deuteronomy:

> The pig, for even though it has divided hoofs and is cleft-footed, it does not chew the cud; it is unclean for you. (Lev. 11:7)
>
> And the pig, because it divides the hoof but does not chew the cud, is unclean for you. You shall not eat their meat, and you shall not touch their carcasses. (Deut. 14:8)

Over the centuries, many interpreters have sought to explain why this prohibition should have been introduced. This is not the place to review the history of interpretation,[71] but I believe that Mary Douglas, the anthropologist of religion, is probably correct in thinking the taxonomy has to do with the Israelite idea of holiness, cleanliness, wholeness, and normality.[72] The dietary laws were intended to reinforce this idea. Douglas puts it this way: "To be holy is to be whole, to be one, holiness is unity, integrity, perfection of the individual and of the kind. The dietary laws merely develop the metaphor of holiness on the same lines."[73] Less than a decade later, she modified her view in the light of what she believed was valid criticism of her taxonomic approach as being too narrow to explain "the multiple dimensions of thought and activity" of the Israelites.[74] One of her critics, Ralph Bulmer, on the basis of his ethnographic study in New Guinea, argued that there "were probably multiple reasons for avoiding" foods, and that it is just as likely that the pig was a taxonomic anomaly because it was viewed as unclean.[75] Douglas retained her taxonomic approach, that is, that the pig does not fall into a classification, but allows that the fact that the pig eats carrion and that it was eaten by non-Israelites contributed to the dietary taboo.[76]

A number of Old Testament scholars have voiced their approval of Douglas's earlier understanding. Gordon Wenham, for example, considers her approach to avoid the dangers of "total subjectivity" so common to many exegetes attempting to explain the dietary prohibitions in Leviticus, and he goes on to say: "The strongest argument in favor of Douglas' interpretation of the food laws is its comprehensiveness and coherence."[77]

In his recent review of different theories to explain Israel's pork prohibition, Edwin Firmage finds the view of Frederick Simoons to have merit.[78] First published in 1961, but updated and republished in 1994, Simoons links the ban on eating pork to a bias of sheep and goat pastoralists, for whom swine were alien.[79] Given the emphasis on sheep and goats in Israel's cult—various sacrifices, Passover, and so on—this view is quite plausible. I see no reason to consider Douglas's and Simoons's views as incompatible. Douglas's theory offers a religio-anthropological rationale, whereas Simoons's explanation presents a social and logical outcome of the former.

Pigs are known to have been domesticated as early as the ninth millennium B.C. in Anatolia. Swine bones have been found in the renowned Neolithic village of Jarmo in northern Iraq in the seventh millennium B.C., and they are attested in the Levant from ca. 6000 B.C.[80] The limited number of depictions of pigs, especially of the domesticated variety, in Egyptian tombs and temples led earlier generations of Egyptologists to think that pigs were rare. Then, too, a taboo is attached to the pig because of the mythological perspective presented in the Coffin Texts (spell 157) of the early second millennium B.C. and the Book of the Dead (chapter 112) of the New Kingdom. There the god Seth transformed himself into a pig when he attacked his brother Horus. Because of this desecration, an explanatory gloss offered in both manuscript traditions declares: "That is how the detestation (*bw*) of the pig came about for Horus's sake by the gods who are in the suite."[81] The word *bw*, as a verb, means "detest" or "abominate," and as a noun (*bwt*) means "abomination."[82] Then too, the foraging and mud-wallowing habits of swine were obviously seen as characteristics that offended the fastidious upper-class Egyptian. This attitude can be seen in the "Satire of the Trades," a Middle Kingdom literary work that in mocking fashion criticizes various occupations. "The potter," it bemoans, "is under the soil, though as yet among the living; He grubs in the mud more than a pig."[83] Perhaps these considerations influenced Herodotus's observations from the fifth century B.C. that "swine are held by the Egyptians to be unclean beasts."[84]

Whether such defamatory attitudes toward the pig in Egypt in any way influenced ancient Israel is impossible to say. It was noted earlier in this book that among the Semitic population at Tell el-Dab'a there appears to have been a religious taboo against pigs, as their bones have not been found among temple refuse that included bovines and sheep. Then, too, there is textual and archaeological evidence to suggest that the pig was rather common in Egypt.[85] The early Eighteenth Dynasty mayor of Nekhbet (near modern el-Kab), Reneny, who was also the "Overseer of Priests" (*imy-r ḥmw nṯrw*), claims that among his herds and cattle were 1,500 pigs.[86] Later in the Eighteenth Dynasty, during the reign of Amenhotep III, we find that herds of pigs numbering around 2,000 were maintained on the fields of the Temple of Ptah in Memphis.[87] The same is true for the Nineteenth Dynasty, when pigs are mentioned as part of the inventory of temple estates.[88]

Recent archaeological investigations, especially by zooarchaeologists, show that pig remains have been documented throughout Egypt from earliest times and down into the New Kingdom.[89] Pig bones are well represented in the Delta region from prehistoric times, although apparently in no greater numbers than elsewhere in Egypt.[90] Skeletal remains of *Sus domesticus* have been identified at Tell el-Dab'a from the early second millennium B.C.[91] We have uncovered remains of swine among the faunal remains at Tell el-Borg. After three seasons of excavations, 107 (8.7 percent of bones documented) pieces of pig bone have been identified, compared with 182 (14.8 percent) of cattle and 98 (8.0 percent) of sheep and goats.[92] Clearly pork was a significant part of the diet of the soldiers and support staff at Tell el-Borg. The distribution of pig remains—such as at the workmen's village at Tell el-Amarna[93]—indicate that although pork was widely consumed, it was primarily the food of the "poorer classes," according to Hecker.[94] It is noteworthy that in Islam eating of pig is prohibited, but in the 1980s in Egypt more pigs than cattle were butchered for meat.[95] The high cost of beef, combined with the inexpensiveness of pork, has made forbidden meat attractive, the religious taboo notwithstanding.

It appears, then, that in ancient Egypt, there were, in Patrick Houlihan's words, "deeply ambivalent feelings about the pig." Although the pig was valuable for food, because of mythological themes, it was also "a powerful symbol of evil."[96]

Swine were of little economic value. Unlike sheep and goats, the milk, hair, and hides of pigs were not utilized by humans. So its meat is the only practical reason to raise pigs. Domesticated pigs by nature prefer to live and forage in forested areas and near water sources. They cool themselves by wallowing in mud and shallow pools. Hot, dry, and desert environments are inhospitable to swine. In fact, it has been observed that "the pig is the least tolerant of arid conditions,"[97] and pigs are not easily herded like sheep, goats, and cattle. These practical considerations tend to support the biblical tradition that Israel had spent time in the wilderness of the Sinai prior to entering the land of Canaan. On this point, the anthropologist Marvin Harris has commented: "For pastoral nomadic people like the Israelites during their years of wandering in search of lands . . . swineherding was out of the question."[98] Given the presence of pig bones in Bronze Age Canaan and especially in the Philistine territory in the twelfth century, their absence in areas thought to be occupied by Israelites is significant.[99] Brian Hesse and Paula Wapnish do caution against rushing to conclude that ethnicity or religious or dietary prohibitions are behind the dearth of pig bones in an area, as there are other factors that must be weighed.[100] They do admit that in the Byzantine period, in the Galilee region Christian sites have bones, whereas known Jewish sites do not, and therefore the absence of pig bones may be an indicator of "social identity."[101] William Dever sees the absence of pig bones in Iron I hill country settlements as germane to locating early Israel, since pork consumption "was relatively common" in Bronze Age Canaan. In fact, he declares that "the presence or absence of pig bones may thus be our best archaeological indicator of the much-debated 'ethnic boundaries' " of early Israel.[102]

Ancient Israel's dietary injunction against eating pork is hard to explain if Israel originated as a people in Canaan and evolved from the Canaanites. In other words, there was no social or religious rationale to reject pork if they had simply emerged from Canaanite culture. On the other hand if, as the Bible reports, Israel migrated from Egypt—where pork consumption was considerable despite the pig's theological unpopularity—and spent several decades in the wildernesses of Sinai and Transjordan, this provides a reasonable background for explaining the absence of pig bones at Israelite sites and the dietary prohibitions of the Torah.

Leviticus 14:37

This text deals with the problem of the priest diagnosing an anomaly on the wall of a house. The text reads: "He shall examine the disease; if the disease is in the walls of the house with greenish or reddish spots (שְׁקַעֲרוּרֹת), and if it appears to be deeper than the surface." The interpretation of the word *šᵉqaʿᵃrûṯ* has posed a challenge to commentators. In his recent commentary on Leviticus, Jacob Milgrom, who renders the word "eruptions," declares that "interpretations of word are legion."[103] The reason for this is that it occurs only here in the entire Hebrew corpus. Görg has suggested that *šᵉqaʿᵃrûṯ* is a writing for the Egyptian expression *sḳr r rwti*, which means "strike [from the inside] to the outside."[104] What makes this theory so attractive is that it is a linguistically sound association, and this expression is found in Egyptian medical texts to diagnose disorders. Görg understands the idiom *sḳr r rwti* to mean "a kind of exudation or eruption," which means that semantically this word fits the context of Leviticus 14:37.

The Priestly Blessing

One of the better-known passages in the book of Numbers is the "high priestly prayer." The tricolon benediction reads as follows:

> Speak to Aaron and his sons, saying, Thus you shall bless the Israelites:
> You shall say to them,
> The LORD bless you and keep you;
> the LORD make his face to shine upon you, and be gracious to you;
> the LORD lift up his countenance upon you, and give you peace.
> (Num. 6:23–26)

The sensational discovery of this text inscribed on a silver amulet in 1978 in a tomb outside of the old city of Jerusalem in the Hinnom Valley has elicited considerable enthusiasm among biblical scholars.[105] Presently, it is the oldest surviving text from the Bible, dating to the end of the seventh century B.C.

Literary parallels for this text have been proposed in Akkadian literary finds.[106] Sharon Keller argues that although lexical similarities and the tricolon structure are present in the Mesopotamian examples, these do not entirely match the prayer in the Torah.[107] A better parallel, she concludes, is found in a prayer in a Letter to the Dead papyrus from the First Intermediate Period (the end of the third millennium B.C.). The Egyptian prayer exclaims:

> The Great One shall Praise you
> The face of the Great God will be Gracious over you
> He will give you pure bread with his two hands.[108]

Not only is this a tricolon like the prayer of Numbers, but has the same progression in the number of words per line 3 > 5 > 7, leading Keller to believe that "this progression, found both in the Hebrew and Egyptian forms, is too precise to be arbitrary or coincidental."[109] Although they have different functions (a Letter to the Dead was a communication between a living individual and a family member who had died), it is germane to point out that both were found in a tomb, and that the silver amulet had a protective or magical function.[110] If indeed the high priestly prayer dates back to the wilderness period—David Noel Freedman dates it to ca. 1200 B.C.[111]—then it is not inconceivable that the prayer's pattern may have been influenced by Egyptian prototypes.

II

The Wilderness Tradition and the Origin of Israel

Moses sent messengers from Kadesh to the king of Edom, "Thus says your brother Israel: You know all the adversity that has befallen us: how our ancestors went down to Egypt, and we lived in Egypt a long time; and the Egyptians oppressed us and our ancestors; and when we cried to the LORD, he heard our voice, and sent an angel and brought us out of Egypt; and here we are in Kadesh, a town on the edge of your territory."

—Num. 20:14–17

The nature of Israel's origins has been the subject of considerable scholarly discussion over the past two decades. Although there are a number of different theories about who early Israel was and where they came from, the theories fall into three groups: first, those that believe that Israel entered Canaan from the outside (either as invaders or peacefully infiltrating emigrants); second, those that maintain that Israel was an indigenous development within Canaan; and third, those that advocate some sort of combination of the two.[1]

The material present in this study tends to support the first model, while casting serious doubt on the indigenous development theory. To conclude this study, we now turn to a number of other considerations that support this thesis.

I. The Origins of Israel's God

The encounter between God and Moses at the burning bush in Sinai is thought to be the occasion when the divine name was revealed. During the burning-bush theophany, Exodus 3:13–15 records the following dialogue:

> But Moses said to God, "If I come to the Israelites and say to them, 'The God of your ancestors has sent me to you,' and they ask me, 'What is his name?' what shall I say to them?"
>
> God said to Moses, "I AM WHO I AM." He said further, "Thus you shall say to the Israelites, 'I AM has sent me to you.' "
>
> God also said to Moses, "Thus you shall say to the Israelites, 'The Lord, the God of your ancestors, the God of Abraham, the God of Isaac, and the God of Jacob, has sent me to you':
>
> This is my name forever,
> and this my title for all generations."

Scholars remain divided as to whether this passage signals the first time the divine name was revealed (which might be supported by Exod. 6:3—"I appeared to Abraham, Isaac, and Jacob as God Almighty, but by my name 'The Lord' I did not make myself known to them"), or whether its history can be traced back to the patriarchal era. Although the latter view has few supporters today, J. P. Hyatt, for example, advocated this view, believing that the name Yahweh was originally Amorite and is attested in personal names in the early second millennium B.C. by the element *Yahwi*.[2] Indeed, there are names at Mari, an Amorite kingdom, that apparently utilized the root from which the divine name Yahweh came (i.e., *haya*), that may offer clues to the process for the development of new divine names.[3] According to those who see a Syro-Mesopotamian connection, the name came via Mesopotamia and was "the god of one of the ancestors of Moses."[4] In the name Jochebed, the mother of Moses, the element *yo* might be the shortened form of the name, which to Hyatt is evidence that the name was known prior to the theophany of Exodus 3.[5] Childs considers the possibility that although the name may have earlier antecedents, it is presented in Exodus 3 with a "totally new meaning."[6]

One of the most influential theories to explain the origin of the name of Yahweh is that Moses actually learned of this deity in Midian, perhaps through his Midianite father-in-law. After all, he was a priest (Exod. 2:16), and in Exodus 3:1, where Moses encounters God, Horeb bears the epithet "mountain of God," suggesting to some that this was a recognized holy site by the Midianites. Finally, the Midianites are descendents of Abraham's second wife, Keturah (Gen. 25:1–2), meaning that they were distant kin who may have preserved something of Abraham's faith that the Israelites had forgotten during their sojourn in Egypt. This view is closely tied with the theory that

Mount Sinai was in Midian/Arabia, which goes back to the end of the nineteenth century (cf. chapter 6). A number of distinguished scholars from the 1950s to 1960s advocated this view, including H. H. Rowley, Martin Noth, W. F. Albright, and Helmer Ringgren.[7] George Mendenhall considers the fact that Moses married a Midianite woman to be an authentic element of the story, given the later antipathy for Midianites (cf. Num. 33:4–18; 31:3–9; Judg. 6:1–2).[8] Why make Moses look bad in later tradition by creating such a fictional account, one might ask? Consequently, Patrick Miller agrees that this scenario "provides a plausible point of contact between the cult of Yahweh in the South and the Moses group or Proto-Israel."[9]

Another possible salient point of contact with the Midianites is that there is ceramic evidence for their presence at the copper-mining site of Timna, and, it is posited, they used a tent-shrine there. After the Egyptians abandoned the site around 1150 B.C., Midianites (who probably had worked with or for them) stayed on and probably continued mining enterprises.[10] They altered the Hathor temple and established a tent-shrine. Proof of this came from the discovery of a "large amount of heavy red and yellow cloth," which, along with the pottery, was "clear archaeological evidence for attributing this tented sanctuary to the Midianites."[11]

Others find support for the Midianite link to Israel's religion—bearing in mind that Midian is located in northern Arabia and that Midianites are found further north up into the Transjordan—from Bible references like Habakkuk 3:3 (i.e., "God came from Teman") and Deuteronomy 33:2, which mentions Yahweh in Seir (i.e., Edom) and Mount Paran, thought to be in the southern Transjordan, as well as Judges 5:4–5. These passages were all discussed already in chapter 6, §IVB. It was shown there that these passages do not imply that Israel's God originated at these locations, merely that he passed through them in military fashion on his way from Sinai to Canaan. There well may have been later sanctuaries or shrines of Yahweh in these southerly regions, as inscriptions from Kuntillet ʿAjrud in northeastern Sinai suggest. They include the epithet, "YHWH of Teman," and date to ca. 800 B.C.[12] The reference to Teman is evidence of some sort of worship of Yahweh in or near this location, but ought not be used to indicate that this is where his name and cult originated. On one of the famous *pithoi* from Kuntillet ʿAjrud, the God of Israel is called "Yahweh of Samaria." No one would cite this text as evidence that he originated in Samaria. It only means that there was a shrine to him there. Both epithets should, indeed, be treated in the same manner.[13]

One positive thing that can be said about the Midianite connection is that it takes seriously the origin of Israel's deity in the wilderness. However, Kaufmann pointed out many years ago that there is nothing in the exodus narratives to suggest that Moses actually learned about Yahweh and his cult from the Midianite priest.[14] On the contrary, it is only after the marvelous exodus from Egypt that Jethro offers praise for Yahweh, as if it was through these events that he came to believe in the God of Israel:

> Moses went out to meet his father-in-law, and did obeisance and kissed him; and they asked each other of their welfare, and went into the tent. Then Moses told his father-in-law all that the LORD had done to Pharaoh and to the Egyptians for Israel's sake, all the hardship that had come upon them in the way, and how the LORD had delivered them. And Jethro rejoiced for all the good which the LORD had done to Israel, in that he had delivered them out of the hand of the Egyptians. And Jethro said, "Blessed be the LORD, who has delivered you out of the hand of the Egyptians and out of the hand of Pharaoh. *Now I know that the LORD is greater than all gods,* because he delivered the people from under the hand of the Egyptians, when they dealt arrogantly with them." (Exod. 18:7–11)

Rowley believed, this statement notwithstanding, that Jethro and the Midianites were devotees of Yahweh and so dismissed this text, declaring it to be "scarcely cogent."[15] When, however, we consider this statement in combination with several facts it seems unlikely that Jethro introduced Moses to Yahweh. First, not until this confession do we have the Midianite priest mentioning Yahweh; second, he is never called "Priest of Yahweh"; third, the mountain where Moses encounters God (if indeed it had been a holy mountain to the Midianites) is called the mountain of God (הַר הָאֱלֹהִים) and not mountain of Yahweh; and fourth, a second name by which Jethro is known is Reuel (רְעוּאֵל: *re'û'ēl*), which means "friend of god," using *'ēl* and not *yah* or *yo* (typical abbreviated forms for the divine name).[16] On the contrary, based on the biblical evidence, it appears that Jethro learned of Yahweh through Moses.

Mendenhall, followed by Norman Gottwald, initiated the so-called peasant-revolt model to explain Israel's origin, sometimes wrongly called an indigenous development model.[17] For Mendenhall, the Israelites were Apiru slaves who fled Egypt and were part of a mixed rabble of whom Moses was the leader.[18] Gottwald likewise maintains that there was a Moses group of freed slaves that came from Egypt who were worshippers of Yahweh. Then he offers a rather bizarre twist: this group was not Israelite, but only later became identified with Israel when it linked up with other groups such as a Kadesh-Sinai group that may have had some ideas about a covenant with God.[19] These groups associated with other lower classes and displaced people (like the Apiru), who in turn fomented a peasant (Marxist) revolt against the urban elite power brokers, and under the banner of Yahwism became Israel.[20]

The Mendenhall-Gottwald hypothesis, despite the many objections that may be made to it, recognizes that ancient Israel cannot be explained without Yahweh, and that this deity was brought with them either from Egypt or by contact with Midianites/Kenites in the wilderness. Those who advocate a purely indigenous origin for Israel from within Canaanite culture, like Ahlström and Lemche, can offer no satisfactory explanation for the roots of the religion of Yahweh.[21] Canaanite religion and the highly informative religious texts from Ugarit have failed to produce the God of Israel. Mark Smith has offered a creative way for an indigenous Israel to have been introduced to Yahweh by Midianites. He builds on the thoughtful study of J. David Schloen, who explains the social and trade dynamics involved in the background of the Song of Deborah in Judges 5.[22] Smith wonders if the Midianite traders might not have been the link between Midian and Israel during the Judges period.[23] Although this is an intriguing explanation, it seems a bit farfetched to think of the Midianites as early missionaries spreading their gospel of Yahwism around! Furthermore, there are textual problems with Judges 5:10 and 14, which are critical points for the theory to be correct. So this seems like an unlikely theory for explaining how the god Yahweh was introduced to Israel.

The pantheon of Egypt with its hundreds of deities has likewise failed to produce the God of Israel. True, there are those who have sought to link the monotheism of Akhenaten with the monotheism of Moses, but too many problems exist for this connection.[24] Even if we allow that there was some sort of influence on the Hebrews, the actual name YHWH in no way can be connected with the Amarna heresy, which lasted no more than fifteen years. It was James Henry Breasted in his *History of Egypt* in 1905 who first drew attention to similarities between the Great Hymn to Aten and Psalm 104 in the Bible. There has been some debate whether the similarities reflect direct or indirect borrowing. An entire monograph could be devoted to dealing with problems of the relationship between these two great pieces of literature. But for the purposes of this section, it must suffice to make a few comments. In a forthcoming study, I have shown that the solar language in the Aten hymn has precursors in the earlier Coffin texts and Pyramid texts, so that this hymn does not constitute a radical new theology; and second, the same type of language is found in late Egyptian hymns and within the Book of the Dead.[25] As for the Aten hymns, there are no later versions found either on ostraca or papyrus, indicating that it was not a classical text that later generations of scribes transmitted. Given that these hymns are found only on the walls of tombs at Amarna, around 300 kilometers (185 miles) away from the "Land of Rameses" where the Israelites would have been, it is unlikely that "the Israelite poet who composed Psalm 104 borrowed directly from the sublime Egyptian 'Hymn to the Aten'," as Stager has recently claimed.[26]

After reviewing the current theories about the origin of the divine name, Childs offered what to many scholars might sound like a radical departure from recent trends: "take seriously Israel's own tradition."[27] And that tradition squarely places the defining encounter between God and Moses in the Sinai wilderness. From the phenomenological perspective introduced in chapter 6 §I, associating a theophany with a mountain, as the Bible suggests, makes sense.

II. The Israelites as Shasu?

The Torah portrays the Israelites departing Egypt and spending decades in the Sinai and then some years in the Transjordan (lands of Edom and Moab); this perspective is strongly supported in the later presentation of Israel's origins by the prophets of Israel and Judah (cf. chapter 1). Is there any tangible evidence from Egyptian sources that might support this perspective?

Egyptologists and biblical scholars have long recognized that the term *š3św* was the Egyptian designation for desert dwellers, which occurs first in the early Eighteenth Dynasty. It was used by the Egyptians in a generic way, and was not applied to any particular ethnic group, thus making it comparable to the word Bedouin, a word of Arabic derivation.[28] This word derives from a verb *š3ś*, which means "go" or "pass through,"[29] clearly referring to the mobile lifestyle associated with desert dwellers. Undoubtedly because nomads were viewed as marauders and thieves, it is believed that the Canaanite word *šasah* can be traced to the Shasu; it means "to plunder."[30] The Egyptian antipathy toward such people is well known. No better place is this witnessed than in Pap. Anastasi I, where the scribe describes the dangers for Egyptians traveling through Shasu country: "Lions are more abundant than leopards and bears, while it is hemmed in on all sides by Shasu-Beduin. . . . He has . . . joined up with those who are wicked. He consorts with Shasu-Beduin. . . . The narrow pass is dangerous, having Shasu-Beduin concealed beneath the bushes. [They] have fierce faces. They are unfriendly."[31] Surely this disdain is reflected in Joseph's counsel to his brothers, should the Pharaoh inquire about their profession:

> Joseph said to his brothers and to his father's household, "I will go up and tell Pharaoh, and will say to him, 'My brothers and my father's household, who were in the land of Canaan, have come to me; and the men are shepherds, for they have been keepers of cattle; and they have brought their flocks, and their herds, and all that they have.' When Pharaoh calls you, and says, 'What is your occupation?' you shall say, 'Your servants have been keepers of cattle from our youth even until now, both we and our fathers,' in order that you may dwell in the land of Goshen; for every shepherd is an abomination to the Egyptians." (RSV, Gen. 46:31–34)

The Shasu are often the object of Egyptian military action in northern Sinai and the Negev.[32] The classic example of that are the famous battle reliefs of Seti I at Karnak. These are the scenes that show the series of forts across North Sinai, between Tjaru/Sile and Gaza, the entry point of Canaan.[33] Seti's first military campaign was apparently triggered by internecine conflict between tribes along the strategic route from Egypt to Canaan. The opening text records: "The Shasu enemies are plotting rebellion! Their tribal leaders are gathered in one place, standing on the foothills of Khor, and they are engaged in turmoil and uproar. Each of them is killing his fellow. They do not consider the laws of the palace." The zone of this upheaval is further delineated by the statement: "the devas[-tation] which the energetic Pharaoh . . . made against the Shasu enemies, from the fortress Tcharu (i.e., Sile) to Canaan."[34] The late William Murnane is surely correct in thinking that the Shasu were no threat to Egypt's power but they were irritants, and the turmoil they spawned could disrupt communication and travel between Egypt and Canaan.[35] No doubt the type of problems in travel reflected in Anastasi I—which date to the reign of Ramesses II—were the sort that prompted Seti's actions. The reliefs show a detailed battle with the Shasu, and some of them are the POWs marching before the king's chariot as he returned to Egypt (figure 2).

The exquisite details in the battle scene provide the best picture available of these desert people (figure 44). The men wore pointy beards and floppy caps, while the caps of others have short tassels on the back, and the warriors wear some sort of garment wrapped around their torsos. Could it be leather strips intended to afford some protection against the Egyptian arrows? Concerning the different caps, one wonders if they might point to different clans or tribes of Shasu. They fight with spears and small duckbill axes. They are shown running for higher ground, apparently hoping to evade the Egyptian chariots.

Fortuitously, our excavations at Tell el-Borg have recently added a new relief to the discussion (figure 45). It was discovered in 2002 in the canal debris that was churned up when the canal was excavated in the late 1990s. Unfortunately, only one block of a larger scene has been discovered thus far, but it shows that there were at least two lines of fleeing enemies. The legs of the upper group are visible, running over hilly terrain, and the heads of two men are shown on the lower register. One has the duckbill axe, and they wear caps, but they look different from those on the Seti I Karnak reliefs. Further study of this piece is required before final conclusions are drawn, but clearly these figures do represent a desert-people enemy of the pharaoh, in this case probably Ramesses II.[36]

The textual evidence has revealed that occasionally the term Shasu is conjoined with a second name, perhaps indicating a geographical region or tribal name. Pap. Anastasi VI, 55–56, introduced in chapter 4 §V, refers to the Shasu of Edom (*š3św n idwm*) who were permitted to water their herds in the waters of Pithom (*pr itm*).[37] This Edom is no doubt the same one known in the Bible as the brother of Jacob (Gen. 25:29–34; 36). At the end of the wilderness period, Moses attempted to lead the Israelites through Edomite territory in order to reach Moab. He requests safe passage through Edom by saying:

> Moses sent messengers from Kadesh to the king of Edom, "Thus says your brother Israel: You know all the adversity that has befallen us:

> how our ancestors went down to Egypt, and we lived in Egypt a long time; and the Egyptians oppressed us and our ancestors; and when we cried to the LORD, he heard our voice, and sent an angel and brought us out of Egypt; and here we are in Kadesh, a town on the edge of your territory. Now let us pass through your land. We will not pass through field or vineyard, or drink water from any well; we will go along the King's Highway, not turning aside to the right hand or to the left until we have passed through your territory." (Num. 20:14–17)

Here Edom has a clear territory and is addressed as the brother of Israel. This means that the name is understood to be both a region and the ancestral name of the tribe. The ʿAmarah list (no. 93) records the name *t3 š3św śe-ʿ-r-er,* which has been associated with Seir of the Bible.[38] Genesis 32:3 suggests that this territory is one and the same as Edom or is some part of it or adjacent to it: "Jacob sent messengers before him to his brother Esau in the land of Seir, the country of Edom." Other passages in Genesis demonstrate the correlation of the two: "So Esau settled in the hill country of Seir; Esau is Edom. These are the descendants of Esau, ancestor of the Edomites, in the hill country of Seir" (Exod 36:8–9).

Of particular interest is the Shasu name that has attached to it the element 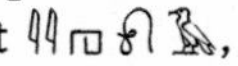, which reads *yhw3*. Because this linguistically corresponds to Hebrew YHWH, it was quickly associated with the personal name of the God of Israel. These texts were recorded by a Liverpool University Egyptologist, Herbert Fairman, and preliminarily reported in 1940.[39] It was recognized that this name list from a temple of Ramesses II actually represents a copy from the earlier temple of Amenhotep III (1390–1353 B.C.) at nearby Soleb.[40] When the two lists are placed side by side, the sequence of numbers 95 to 98 at ʿAmrah, which include the *yhw3* names, match the order in the Soleb list, showing the antiquity of the list.[41] The initial response to the occurrence of the toponym "Shasu land of Yahwa" led many scholars to conclude that this name points to a geographical territory where a cult for Yahwa existed in the fourteenth century B.C.[42] This interpretation is strengthened by the proximity of Seir in the same list. Thus it has been thought that "the Shasu land of Yahwa" was in the same region as the Shasu land of Seir (i.e., Edom). This connection, if correct, would support the position that Yahweh may have had his origin in the area of northeastern Sinai or the Arabah. This area, in turn, is associated with the home of the Kenites, who are associated with the in-laws of Moses (Judg. 1:16).[43]

Thus this Egyptian evidence seems to support the theory that Israel spent time in the very region the Bible suggests. More recent studies of the ʿAmrah lists have pointed to a number of problems. First it was noted by Michael Astour that *śe-ʿ-r-er* has two *r*'s, whereas Seir has only one, and the name as it stands can be associated with a toponym in the Lebanon-Syria region.[44] Unless we allow that Seir is inaccurately recorded, then the equation of this toponym with Sier of the Bible presents a challenge. If Astour is correct, the toponym containing the supposed divine name is placed hundreds of miles north, and thus either is not YHWH or is too far removed to have had any influence on Israel. This also means that Shasu, in addition to living a nomadic existence in Sinai, the Negev, and the Transjordan, also traversed lands far to the north.

The problems Astour raised for identifying and locating the Shasu land of Yahwa has not prevented Shmuel Ahituv from identifying it as the region where the "worshipers of Yahu, the God of Isreal" wandered, and it is probably found in northeastern Sinai, around Kadesh-Barnea.[45] Redford too accepts the connection between the *yhw3* of the Amrah/Soleb lists and the God of Israel, believing that this toponym points to the regions where Yahweh originated, and that these Shasu somehow figured into the "later amalgam that constituted Israel."[46]

The peaceful migration theory advanced by Alt in 1925 maintained that Israelite tribes infiltrated Canaan from the Transjordan at the end of the Late Bronze Age.[47] In the 1970s, Manfred Weippert continued to champion Alt's old thesis, and tied the Israelites to the Shasu of Edom and Moab.[48] As enticing as this theory may be, Merneptah on his stela did not connect the two, calling them Shasu of Israel. The other question is, would the Israelites in the course of just two generations in Sinai be transformed from Hebrews (as they were known in Egypt, cf. Gen. 39:14, 17; 41:12; Exod. 1:15, 16, 19; 2:7) to Shasu? Manfred Bietak's excavations at Tell el-Dab'a in the northeastern Delta since the late 1960s have shown that in time the second millennium B.C. Asiatic population became Egyptianized, displaying both Egyptian and Canaanite elements in their cultural remains. By the late seventeenth and early sixteenth centuries B.C., we even find the Hyksos leaving inscriptions written in Egyptian hieroglyphs and employing traditional pharaonic titles.[49] In essence they were bicultural. This model also works for the Israelites of the exodus-wilderness period. According to Genesis, three generations of Hebrews lived in Canaan prior to emigrating to Egypt for two to four centuries, and yet they were called Hebrews. These considerations suggest that early Israel was a culturally complex entity that in the course of one to two generations would not have been transformed into Shasu.

Certainly if ancient Israel were originally Shasu, the case I am trying to make to show the significance of Israel's wilderness experience would be strengthened. Despite this favorable consideration, I am not convinced that the ancient textual evidence supports this connection, so it must remain an open question. However, for those who advocate a connection between early Israel and the Shasu, the debate has been renewed with a sensational discovery in Egypt: a relief that might represent early Israel.

III. Israelites Depicted in Egypt?

In the late 1970s, a young Egyptology graduate student, Frank Yurco—whose untimely death in 2003 will deprive us of his considerable scholarly contributions—made a breakthrough discovery at Karnak Temple.[50] In the so-called "Cour de la Cachette," on the wall that runs perpendicular to the Bubastite-Sheshonk reliefs, Yurco discovered that the inscriptions and scenes belonged to King Merneptah.[51] The problem is that Seti II (1200–1194 B.C.) had usurped the original cartouches with his name. But thanks to Yurco's careful study of the wall, he was able to detect the name of Merneptah beneath Seti II's name.[52] The scenes themselves show a series of battles, although most of the upper portion of the wall is, regrettably, missing. The names of Ashkelon and Yenoam occur here, and they also appear on the famous Merneptah stela. Since they are rarely attested in Egyptian records, Yurco thought their presence in both the wall and the stela could not be coincidental. Through meticulous examination of the texts and reliefs, Yurco demonstrated that the scenes on the walls at Karnak were a pictorial version of the Asiatic campaign of Merneptah in 1208–1209. Egyptologists were quick to concur with Yurco's new interpretation of these scenes, including the most revered Ramesside-period scholar, Kenneth Kitchen.[53]

Yurco attempted to harmonize scenes with the sequence of place names of Merneptah's campaign. In so doing, he proposed that in scene 4—the top portion of which is completely missing and thus the texts that might identify the enemy are not available—the enemies depicted are portrayed as Canaanites (figure 45). The reason he gave for this identification is that, unlike the other scenes that show fortified cities under attack, scene 4 lacks a city, but portrays a battle on open land.[54] Since the writing of Israel in the Merneptah stela lacks a city or state determinative, but is written as a people,[55] Yurco maintained that this portrayal corresponded well with early Israel's geopolitical reality, which scene 4 depicts.

His interpretation was challenged by several scholars, the most forceful being Anson Rainey. Although agreeing with Yurco's reading of the usurped cartouches, Rainey diverged on how the sequence of scenes should be understood. He particularly differed with Yurco's assumption that the scene should be read in clockwise order.[56] Rainey further argued that the Israelites would not have been shown with a chariot, as are the figures in scene 4, and thus believed the order in which the scenes were interpreted by Yurco was off. The Canaanites shown in Yurco's scene 4, Rainey insists, are in fact Canaanites who are mentioned before Ashkelon in the Merneptah stela.[57] According to Rainey's reconstruction of the scene sequence, he believes that Yurco's scene 7 should be the Israelite scene. Here Shasu prisoners are shown (figure 46). Although the scene is poorly preserved, they are called Shasu in the text.[58] A problem for Rainey's interpretation is the fact that the Shasu are not mentioned in the stela, but are portrayed in the battle scenes.[59] If indeed the scene was meant to correspond to the stela, as Yurco and Rainey both agree, who then are these Shasu? Rainey proposes that in the absence of any other candidates from the list of peoples and cities attacked in Merneptah's campaign, that they may well be the Israelites. Yurco responded that since they are called Shasu in the scene itself, Merneptah's scribes would not have confused them with the Israelites name on the stela.[60] It should be noted that Stager has also questioned the association of the Israelites with the Shasu on this scene because the stela refers to Israel by name and they are not called Shasu.[61]

The dilemma of identifying the Israelites among the peoples depicted on the reliefs of Merneptah will, unfortunately, go on because the scene is incomplete. The worst way to resolve the proper reading of these scenes is to start with an assumption that the Israelites were Canaanites or Shasu and arrange the sequence to fit one's theory. I knew Frank Yurco personally and had conversations with him over the years about the Merneptah scenes, and am satisfied that he did not come to his understanding of the sequence of scenes on the basis of presuppositions about Israel's origins. He was not out to prove that they were Canaanites or Shasu. Rather he relied on Egyptian artistic canons for organizing military scenes (such as the Seti I battle reliefs on the northern wall of the hypostyle hall).

In the end, both Yurco and Rainey could be wrong and the Israelites may have been recorded on a panel now lost altogether. It must be admitted that both Yurco and Rainey have made compelling cases for their positions. Until the portion that named Israel is found—and that may never happen—we will never know for sure. But in summing up his position, Rainey makes a good point. Because of the unanimity of the biblical tradition that Jacob and his descendents were pastoralist, he asks "is it not more reasonable to conclude that there is probably some relationship between these pastoralists on Merneptah's wall reliefs and the tribal/ethnic group called Israel in the victory poem on the stele?"[62] We must also bear in mind that the Torah places Abraham and his descendents in Canaan for three generations before they immigrate to Egypt, after which they spent two generations in Sinai before entering Canaan. Thus, they had been in the desert, but not of the desert. It could be argued, then, that the Israelites would be portrayed as Canaanites, just as the Hyksos were in the recently discovered reliefs in the funerary temple of Ahmose at Abydos.[63]

IV. "You Shall Not Make for Yourself an Idol"

The second commandment of the Decalogue prohibited the making of images, human or animal, for the purpose of worship (Exod. 20:4–5). This law naturally posed problems for the Israelites, since the peoples of the Near East all used various iconographic techniques to represent their deities. Israel's struggle with local pagan elements, both in Canaan and Egypt (assuming they were there) left an imprint in the Bible and in the archaeological record. First, the Torah records a specific ban against Egyptian and Canaanite practices: "You shall not do as they do in the land of Egypt, where you lived, and you shall not do as they do in the land of Canaan, to which I am bringing you. You shall not follow their statutes" (Lev. 18:3). Second, there are the numerous episodes recorded in the Bible that describe the influence of Baal and Asherah worship, beginning in the Transjordan and throughout the periods of the Judges and monarch in Israel (e.g., Num. 25:1ff.; Josh. 24:14–15; Judg. 2:11–15; 6:25–32; 1 Kings 11:1–8; 14:22–24; 16:30–32; 2 Kings 1:2–4; 16:2–4, 10–16; 21:3–9). There is an increasing body of archaeological evidence to support the syncretistic tendencies of Israel as presented in the Bible.[64] For some, this evidence is used to support the view that Israel originated in Canaan. Mark Smith, for example, rejects the idea of syncretism altogether, believing that the biblical and archaeological data, rather, point to Israel's "Canaanite heritage."[65] In his two-hundred-page study, only a few references are made in passing to Egypt, and even the Red Sea crossing is interpreted through the lens of Ugaritic mythology.[66]

Whether or not Israel's religion in the "Promised Land" was syncretistic or merely an expression of Israel's Canaanite roots cannot be fully debated here. There are able scholars who hold both positions. My interest here is to deal with the implications of Israel's aniconism, that is, the absence of images or the presence of abstract motifs of God, rather than animal or anthropomorphic representations. This subject has spawned considerable discussions in the past decades that make use of comparative iconography.[67] Israel's classic aniconic image would be the empty space above the ark of the covenant and cherubim. Traditionally, it has been thought that this void represented the throne of the invisible deity or illustrated Yahweh's transcendence.[68] Such theological reflection as the basis for aniconism has been rejected by some scholars.[69] Ronald Hendel, for instance, has sought a social rationale, suggesting that the Bible's early antipathy toward kingship was behind the practice with regard to the ark, since in Levantine iconography human kings are depicted enthroned, surrounded by cherubim.[70] Officially, such imagery would be reserved for Israel's God who was their king (cf. Deut. 33:5; Judges 8:23; Ps. 10:16; 43:15).

Earlier on, Othmar Keel had attributed the aniconic tradition to Israel's "nomadic heritage" and their rejection of "kingship and other institutions of the settled people."[71] This suggestion is intriguing, especially when one considers the origins of the standing pillars (מַצֵּבוֹת: *maṣṣēbôṯ*).[72] These cultic objects are well known in the Levant and in Israel (figure 22). Although the Torah prohibits the usage of the *maṣṣēbôṯ* (Lev. 26:1; Deut. 7:5; 16:21–22), they are embraced and not condemned in the Patriarchal narratives (Gen. 28:18–19; 31:43–45; 35:13–14), and even Moses set up twelve *maṣṣēbôṯ* in connection with the covenant ceremony at Mt. Sinai (Exod. 24:4). Uzi Avner, who for the past twenty years has investigated *maṣṣēbôṯ*-shrines in the Negev and Sinai, has shown that the Bible refers to *maṣṣēbôṯ* in three ways: negatively, neutrally, and in positive ways.[73] This is not the place to sort out fully the reason for these apparent discrepancies. The origins and history of *maṣṣēbôṯ* are our concern, and answers may be forthcoming.

Avner has documented 142 different sites with standing pillars in eastern Sinai and the southern Negev, and has shown that they can have a single standing stone, or more—two, three, and groups of as many as five, seven, and nine.[74] The earliest examples date to the eleventh and tenth millennia B.C. and are found in the Negev and southern deserts of Jordan, and continue through the centuries into the biblical period, with a significant increase in such cultic installations in the second millennium B.C.[75] On the basis of extrabiblical and biblical texts, such stones appear to have been associated with ancestral spirits and were believed to be the dwelling of a deity. On the latter point, consider Jacob's statement in Genesis 28 when he sets up a *maṣṣēbâ* (v. 18) and calls the place Beth-el or "House of God" (v. 22).

It is worth noting that in Exodus 24:4, the twelve pillars are not associated with either of these interpretations. Rather, they appear to serve as witnesses to the covenant ceremony (see discussion above in chapter 8 §IV), as they are in other narratives in the Old Testament (e.g., Gen. 31:45–48; Josh. 4:19–23; 22:26–27; 24:26–27; 1 Sam. 7:12). Thus it could be that, at least in the case of the early use of pillars, their function was different. It appears from the references cited here that the stones served as witnesses or memorial stones. This suggests that the particular function of the *maṣṣēbôṯ* was at issue in their assessment by the biblical authors. The three prohibitions to the use of *maṣṣēbôṯ* cited here are all associated with other clearly Canaanite pagan practices (such as carved images, Asherah).

Avner is of the opinion, and the data certainly supports it, that *maṣṣēbôṯ* originated in the deserts of Sinai and the Negev, and Israel's usage of them "was not because of Canaanite influence, but rather because of the common desert origin of both."[76] The fact that Moses sets up pillars in Sinai (Exod. 24:4) plainly connects the practice to Sinai, the very region where *maṣṣēbôṯ* abound. The strong desert influence of the *maṣṣēbôṯ* tradition can be seen on Egyptian stelae found at Serabit el-Khadim in south-central Sinai, especially the great freestanding inscribed stelae in the Temple of Hathor. These are tall and unusually slender stelae, measuring as tall as 2.40 meters (8 feet), and have a height-to-width ratio of about 5 or 4 to 1.[77] Stelae from Egypt more typically have a height-to-width ratio of around 2 to 1.[78] Why are these Sinai stelae so unlike those from the same time period, made by the same artisans in the Nile Valley? I believe that these Egyptian sculptors were influenced by the shape of the *maṣṣēbôṯ* of the region. If the Egyptians, who had well-established artistic canons, were so influenced by this local tradition, it seems quite likely that the ancient Israelites could have been similarly influenced during their experience in Sinai.

In the end, Avner thinks that the *maṣṣēbôṯ* are "abstract representation of gods, directly associated with aniconic theology," and then concluded that "the ancient desert origin of Israelite religion may explain why the *masseboth* played such an integral part in the Israelite cult."[79]

V. Conclusion

At the outset of this book, it was shown that the Torah presents a case for the tribes of Israel having been in Egypt, and after enduring a long period of oppression, escaped Egypt under the leadership of Moses. In the Sinai Peninsula, they spent nearly two generations; there they entered into a covenant relationship with God, their laws originated, and their cultic practices and the tabernacle were birthed before they traveled through the Transjordan and entered Canaan. This picture, we observed, is affirmed in the prophetic corpus.

In recent decades some scholars have questioned or rejected much of the biblical witness to Israel's origins, preferring to use sociological and anthropological models to account for early Israel. Often those who appeal to the Bible take obscure and isolated statements to create Israel as they would like it to be. In so doing, the wilderness tradition is typically marginalized. What this study attempts to do is to draw attention to the wilderness episodes in the light of archaeological evidence, textual materials, geography, toponymy, and personal names. What we have shown is that the geography of the exodus itself has been clarified, thanks to new data from North Sinai. The details of travel and life in Sinai as the Torah presents them square well with what is known about Sinai. The tabernacle makes sense as a mobile sanctuary for a people on the move, and prototypes from Egypt closely parallel to the tent-shrine of Exodus. In the structure of the covenant, literary parallels with treaty documents from the second half of the second millennium B.C. best correlate with Exodus 24ff. and Deuteronomy; first-millennium treaty documents are entirely different and cannot account for the pattern used in the Torah. It was also demonstrated that a surprising number of words used to describe objects in the tabernacle and garments worn by the priests were of Egyptian etymology. Similarly, a surprising number of individuals of the exodus and following generations had Egyptian names. If the Israelites had not been in Egypt, how do we account for these elements? Surely a writer from the mid-first millennium B.C. in Judah or Babylon would not have known these Egyptian terms, let alone refer to Egyptian cities (i.e., Rameses) that had been abandoned centuries earlier. It seems doubtful that a late-period writer would have been interested in researching historical and cultural details simply to make the account look authentic to an audience who would not know the difference!

It seems to me easier to believe that the Bible accurately preserves an authentic picture of the travels and life in the Sinai wilderness than to suppose that authors six to seven hundred years later, writing in ignorance of the past and using creative imagination, got so much certifiably correct as this investigation has demonstrated. In his recent book on the historical credibility of the Old Testament, *What Did the Biblical Writers Know & When Did They Know It?*, William Dever determined that "they knew a lot; and they knew it early, based on older and genuinely historical accounts, both oral and written. One simply cannot force all the biblical texts down into the Persian, much less the Hellenistic, period."[80] Not only do I concur with Dever but I also believe that the same is true of the earlier wilderness tradition. It is hoped that the evidence marshaled here and the ideas advanced will further support the view that "they knew a lot; and they knew it early." If one jettisons the wilderness tradition, as some have done, we are left with too many unanswered questions about ancient Israel's origin, her religion, the covenant, and most significantly about the divine name Yahweh.

Notes

CHAPTER I

1. For the past century, most biblical scholars who subscribe to the so-called documentary hypothesis would assign these books to the work of the Deuteronomic historian (Dtr H) who wrote in the late seventh century. This view is not unanimously held, however. Recently, Yairah Amit proposes dating Judges to the eighth century, *History and Ideology: An Introduction to Historiography in the Hebrew Bible* (Sheffield: Sheffield Academic Press, 1999), 34–410.

2. D. N. Freedman and F. M. Cross, *Studies in Ancient Yahwistic Poetry*, SBL Dissertation Series 21 (Missoula, Mont.: Society of Biblical Literature, 1975), 3–4; Robert D. Boling, *Judges*, ABC6A (1974). Recently Jean Bottéro reiterated his view from forty years ago that the Song of Deborah is a very old poem in Bottéro, *The Birth of God: The Bible and the Historian*, trans. Kees Bolle (University Park: Pennsylvania State University Press, 2000).

3. Why the Philistines should place the plagues in the wilderness is curious indeed. Perhaps they had garbled the tradition.

4. I reject the view of some who have recently argued against a kingdom of David and Solomon in Jerusalem in favor of the view that the first state to be established in Israel was that of Omri and Ahab at Samaria. One of the advocates of this revisionist history is Niels Peter Lemche, *The Israelites in History and Tradition*, ed. Douglas A. Knight, Library of Ancient Israel (Louisville, Ky.: Westminster/John Knox Press, 1998). William G. Dever provides a thorough critique of this position in *What Did the Biblical Writers Know & When Did They Know It? What Archaeology Can Tell Us about the Reality of Ancient Egypt* (Grand Rapids, Mich.: Eerdmans, 2001), 124–157. See also Kenneth Kitchen, "How We Know When Solomon Ruled," *BAR* 27, no. 4 (2001), 32–37, 58. Especially helpful is Kitchen's treatment of the geopolitical

realities of the Near East around 1000 B.C. There were no major imperial powers to stop David and Solomon from establishing a moderate-size empire at this time. Egypt, Assyria, the Hittites, and other former world powers where either in a period of military, economic, and political weakness, or no longer existed. To argue, as Lemche does, from the basis of Assyrian texts in the ninth and eighth centuries, which speak of Israel and not Judah, as evidence that Judah did not become a state or kingdom until toward the end of the eighth century is flawed. First, the argument from silence is the basis of his case. To follow this logic would mean that Egypt was not a kingdom either, because Egypt plays no role in the same Assyrian texts. The reason that Israel is mentioned by the early Assyrian kings such as Shalmaneser III when he was campaigning in Syria-Lebanon in the ninth century is that Israel, as a near neighbor, realized that it was in its best interest to join coalitions against the advancing Assyrians or to pay tribute. Once the Assyrians had moved further south in the Levant, not unexpectedly, Judah's monarchs are named.

5. Amos 1:1 clearly dates the prophet's proclamation to the reigns of Jeroboam II of Israel and Uzziah of Judah, usually thought to be around 760 B.C. (see Bruce Willoughby, "Amos," *ABD* 1: 203–205).

6. Gerhard Maier, "Truth and Reality in the Historical Understanding of the Old Testament," in *Israel's Past in Present Research: Essays on Ancient Israelite Historiography*, ed. V. Philips Long (Winona Lake, Ind.: Eisenbrauns, 1993; reprint, 1999), 204.

7. Some commentators now suggest that a garment was not taken as collateral per se, but that it would be taken when a debt was defaulted; cf. Shalom Paul, *A Commentary on the Book of Amos* (Minneapolis: Fortress, 1991), 83.

8. Maier, "Truth and Reality in the Historical Understanding of the Old Testament," 204.

9. J. Maxwell Miller and John H. Hayes, *A History of Ancient Israel and Judah* (Philadelphia: Westminster, 1986), 78.

10. Thomas L. Thompson, *The Mythic Past: Biblical Archaeology and the Myth of Israel* (London: Basic Books, 1999), 78.

11. Philip Davies, "The Intellectual, the Archaeologist and the Bible," in *The Land I Will Show You: Essays in Honour of J. Maxwell Miller*, ed. J. A. Dearman and M. P. Graham (Sheffield: JSOT Press, 2001), 247.

12. Siegfried Herrmann, "The Devaluation of the Old Testament as a Historical Source," in *Israel's Past in Present Research: Essays on Ancient Israelite Historiography*, ed. V. Philips Long (Winona Lake, Ind.: Eisenbrauns, 1993; reprint, 1999), 346–355.

13. New York: Oxford University Press, 1997. For a very recent summary and assessment of the debate, see Ziony Zevit, "Three Debates about Bible and Archaeology," *Biblica* 83, no. 1 (2002): 1–27.

14. See chapters 1–3. See my favorable review of Dever's book in *Hebrew Studies* 43 (2002): 247–249.

15. Dever, *What Did the Biblical Writers Know?*, chapter 2.

16. See for example William G. Dever, "The Impact of the 'New Archaeology,'" in *Benchmarks in Time and Culture: An Introduction to Palestinian Archaeology*, ed. Joel F. Drinkard, Jr., Gerald L. Mattingly, and J. Maxwell Miller (Atlanta: Scholars Press, 1988), 337–352; and Dever, "Biblical Archaeology: Death and Rebirth," in *Biblical*

Archaeology Today, 1988, ed. A. Biran and J. Aviram (Jerusalem: Israel Exploration Society, 1993), 706–722.

17. *What Did the Biblical Writers Know?*, 44.

18. This term could apply to either a postmodern or a positivist hermeneutic.

19. New York: Free Press, 2001.

20. This book also received considerable press attention. I have received more letters, e-mails and calls from students and the general public asking for my reaction to this book than to any other book to appear in the past twenty years.

21. Finkelstein and Silberman, *Bible Unearthed*, 1.

22. Richard Elliott Friedman, *Who Wrote the Bible?* (San Francisco: Harper, 1987).

23. Some of the proponents of the theory that Israel originated indigenously are Niels Peter Lemche, *Early Israel: Anthropological and Historical Studies on the Israelite Society before the Monarchy* (Leiden: Brill, 1985); Gösta W. Ahlström, *Who Were the Israelites?* (Winona Lake, Ind.: Eisenbrauns, 1986), and Israel Finkelstein, *The Archaeology of the Israelite Settlement* (Jerusalem: Israel Exploration Society, 1988). For a discussion and critique of these views, see Hoffmeier, *Israel in Egypt*, chapter 2.

24. They were influenced by the views of Eduard Reuss, which were presented in a lecture in 1833 but not published until 1879 (cf. Friedman, *Who Wrote the Bible?*, 162–163).

25. On his indebtedness to Graf, see Julius Wellhausen, *Prolegomena to the History of Ancient Israel* (Gloucester, Mass.: Peter Smith, 1878; reprint 1973), 3–4.

26. "Moses," in *The Encyclopedia of Religion*, ed. Mircea Eliade (New York: Macmillan, 1987), 10: 116.

27. It has been pointed out that ספר is the Biblical Hebrew word for scroll, and that in Late Biblical Hebrew the term used for scroll is אגרת; see Avi Hurwitz, "The Historical Quest for 'Ancient Israel' and the Linguistic Evidence of the Hebrew Bible: Some Methodological Observations," *VT* 47 (1997): 301–315. Interestingly, אגרת is a word attested in Akkadian, which might mean that it entered the Hebrew lexicon during the Babylonian captivity (KB 11).

28. R. K. Harrison, *Introduction to the Old Testament* (Grand Rapids, Mich.: Eerdmans, 1969), 3–5.

29. See Friedman, *Who Wrote the Bible?*, 17–21.

30. R. E. Friedman, "Torah (Pentateuch)," *ABD* 6: 618.

31. *The First Historians: The Hebrew Bible and History* (San Francisco: Harper and Row, 1988), 17.

32. For a history of biblical criticism, see John Barton's *Reading the Old Testament: Method in Biblical Study*, 2nd ed. (Philadelphia: Westminster, 1997).

33. Harrison, *Introduction to the Old Testament*, 14–15.

34. Ernest Nicholson, *The Pentateuch in the Twentieth Century: The Legacy of Julius Wellhausen* (Oxford: Clarendon, 1998).

35. Friedman, *Who Wrote the Bible?*, 25–27.

36. James Waller and Mary Edwardsen, "Evolutionism," in *The Encyclopedia of Religion*, 214–218.

37. Harrison, *Introduction to the Old Testament*, 19–22.

38. Wellhausen, *Prolegomena to the History of Ancient Israel*, 3–4.

39. See notes 5 and 6 above.

40. For example, Umberto Cassuto, *The Documentary Hypothesis* (Jerusalem: Central Press, 1941; English translation by I. Abrahams, 1961); Cyrus H. Gordon, *The Ancient Near East*, 3rd ed. (New York: W. W. Norton, 1964); Kenneth A. Kitchen, *Ancient Orient and Old Testament* (Downers Grove, Ill.: Intervarsity Press, 1966), see chapters 1 and 6.

41. John Van Seters, *Abraham in History and Tradition* (New Haven: Yale University Press, 1977); *In Search of History: Historiography in the Ancient World and the Origins of Biblical History* (New Haven: Yale University Press, 1983); further developed in his more recent monographs, *Prologue to History: The Yahwist as Historian in Genesis* (Louisville, Ky.: Westminster/John Knox Press, 1992), and *The Life of Moses: The Yahwist as Historian in Exodus–Numbers* (Knoxville, Tenn.: Westminster/John Knox Press, 1994).

42. Avi Hurvitz, "The Evidence of Language in Dating the Priestly Code—A Linguistic Study in Technical Idioms and Terminology," *RB* 81 (1974): 24–36; and *A Linguistic Study of the Relationship between the Priestly Source and the Book of Ezekiel*, Cahiers de la Revue Biblique 20 (Paris: J. Gabalda, 1982). It should be noted that Philip Davies has recently challenged Hurwitz's approach because his conclusions are based on the unfounded assumption that Ezekiel is dated to the sixth century; Philip Davies, *In Search of "Ancient Israel"* (Sheffield: JSOT Press, 1992), 102. That Davies should question the sixth-century dating of Ezekiel simply reflects the metachronistic tendencies seen throughout his work. It was pointed out around twenty-five years ago that the chronological data interspersed throughout the book of Ezekiel makes it one of the most securely dated books in the Hebrew canon; see K. S. Freedy and D. B. Redford, "The Dates in Ezekiel in Relation to Biblical, Babylonian and Egyptian Sources," *JAOS* 90 (1970): 462–485. For Hurvitz's response to Davies, see Hurvitz, "The Historical Quest for 'Ancient Israel' and the Linguistic Evidence of the Hebrew Bible: Some Methodological Observations," *VT* 47 (1997): 301–315.

43. Robert Polzin, *Late Biblical Hebrew: Toward an Historical Typology of Biblical Hebrew Prose* (Decatur, Ga.: Scholar's Press, 1976).

44. Ziony Zevit, "Converging Lines of the Evidence Bearing on the Date of 'P'," *ZAW* 94, no. 94 (1982): 481–511.

45. Gary Rendsburg, "Late Biblical Hebrew and the Date of 'P,'" *JANES* 12 (1980): 65–80; Rendsburg, "A New Look at Pentateuchal *HW*,'" *Biblica* 63 (1982): 351–369; and Rendsburg, *The Redaction of Genesis* (Winona Lake, Ind.: Eisenbrauns, 1986), chapter 7. See more recently Rendsburg, "Reading David in Genesis: How We Know the Torah Was Written in the Tenth Century BCE," *BR* 17:1 (February 2001): 20–33, 46–47; Friedman, *Who Wrote the Bible?*, 161–172.

46. Moshe Weinfeld, *Getting at the Roots of Wellhausen's Understanding of the Law of Israel on the 100th Anniversary of the Prolegomena* (Jerusalem: Hebrew University of Jerusalem, 1979).

47. Isaac Kikawada and Arthur Quinn, *Before Abraham Was: A Provocative Challenge to the Documentary Hypothesis* (Nashville, Tenn.: Abingdon, 1985). Kitchen had argued along similar lines nearly a decade earlier; see Kenneth Kitchen, *The Bible in Its World: Archaeology and the Bible Today* (Exeter: Paternoster Press, 1977), 31–34; Kikawada and Quinn's study makes no mention of Kitchen's comparison of the thematic structure of Atrahasis and Genesis.

48. Kitchen, *Bible in Its World*, 124, 125.

49. R. N. Whybray, *The Making of the Pentateuch: A Methodological Study*, *JSOT* Supplement Series 53 (Sheffield: JSOT Press, 1987).

50. For a discussion of these works, see R. K. Harrison, *Old Testament Times* (Grand Rapids, Mich.: Eerdmans, 1970), 14–15.

51. E. W. Nicholson offers a number of criticisms of Whybray's work in "The Pentateuch in Recent Research: A Time for Caution," *VTS* 43 (1991): 10–21.

52. Thomas L. Thompson, *The Origin Tradition of Ancient Israel: The Literary Formation of Genesis and Exodus 1–23*, *JSOT* Supplement Series 55 (Sheffield: JSOT Press, 1987), 63–64.

53. Thompson, *Origin Tradition*, 63–64.

54. Douglas Knight, "Tradition History," in *ABD* 6: 633–638.

55. Martin Noth, *The Deuteronomistic History*, translated by Jane Doull from *Uberlieferungsgesichtliche Studien* (Sheffield: JSOT Press, 1981). Rolf Rendtorff, *Das Uberlieferungsgesichichtliche Problem des Pentateuch*, *BZAW* 147 (Berlin: de Gruyter, 1977); Rendtorff, *The Old Testament: An Introduction* (Philadelphia: Fortress, 1979).

56. Nicholson, *Pentateuch in the Twentieth Century*, chapter 4. This chapter is entitled "The Theory under Attack: Rolf Rendtorff's New Paradigm of the Origin of the Pentateuch."

57. Whybray, *Making of the Pentateuch*, 133–219.

58. John Van Seters, *The Pentateuch: A Social-Science Commentary*, ed. Diana J. V. Edelman and Brian B. Schmidt, vol. 1, *Trajectories* (Sheffield: Sheffield Academic Press J, 1999), 63–64.

59. Chiasmus derives from the Greek letter χ, *chi*; it means that a literary structure follows a pattern of movement that repeats itself: A B C C′ B′ A′, like the letter X.

60. Gordon J. Wenham, "The Coherence of the Flood Narrative," *VT* (1978): 336–348, repeated in his *Genesis 1–15*, Word Biblical Commentary 1 (Waco, Tex.: Word, 1987), 155–169. Wenham's chiastic analysis was subsequently accepted by Kikawada and Quinn (*Before Abraham Was*, 103–104).

61. Robert Alter, "A Literary Approach to the Bible," *Commentary* 60, no. 6 (1975): 70–77; and *The Art of Biblical Narrative* (New York: Basic Books, 1981). The following works represent a range of literary approaches: Michael Fishbane, *Text and Texture: Close Readings of Selected Biblical Texts* (New York: Schocken, 1979), and Fishbane, "I Samuel 3: Historical Narrative and Narrative Poetics," in *Literary Interpretations of Biblical Narratives*, ed. Kenneth R. R. Gros Louis (Nashville, Tenn., Abingdon, 1982), 191–203; Jack Sasson, "The 'Tower of Babel' as a Clue to the Redactional Structuring of the Primeval History (Gen. 1–11:19)" in *The Bible World: Essays in Honor of Cyrus H. Gordon*, ed. Gary Rendsburg et al. (New York: Ktav, 1980), 211–219; Kenneth R. R. Gros Louis, ed., *Literary Interpretations of Biblical Narratives*, vol. 2 (Nashville, Tenn.: Abingdon, 1982); David W. Baker, "Diversity and Unity in the Literary Structure of Genesis," in *Essays on the Patriarchal Narratives*, ed. A. R. Millard and D. J. Wiseman (Winona Lake, Ind.: Eisenbrauns, 1983), 197–215; Kikawada and Quinn, *Before Abraham Was*; Joel Rosenberg, *King and Kin: Political Allegory in the Hebrew Bible* (Bloomington: Indiana University Press, 1986); Gary A. Rendsburg, *The Redaction of Genesis* (Winona Lake, Ind.: Eisenbrauns, 1986); David Damrosch, *The*

Narrative Covenant: Transformations of Genre in the Growth of Biblical Literature (San Francisco: Harper and Row, 1987); Regina Schwartz, ed., *The Book and the Text: The Bible and Literary Theory* (Oxford: Blackwell, 1990); Leland Ryken and Tremper Longman III, eds., *A Complete Literary Guide to the Bible* (Grand Rapids, Mich.: Zondervan, 1993); and D. F. Watson and A. J. Hauser, *Rhetorical Criticism of the Bible: A Comprehensive Bibliography with Notes on History and Method* (Leiden: Brill, 1994). I am using the expression "literary approaches" in a rather broad sense, as some of the above works indicate.

62. Mary Douglas, *In the Wilderness: The Doctrine of Defilement in the Book of Numbers* (Oxford: Oxford University Press, 2001).

63. *Art of Biblical Narrative*, 23–46.

64. Davies, *In Search of "Ancient Israel,"* 13.

65. In the recently published three volumes of *Context of Scripture (COS)* there is no category "historical novel." A genre of fictional autobiography has been proposed for Akkadian literature: see Tremper Longman III, *Fictional Akkadian Autobiography* (Winona Lake, Ind.: Eisenbrauns, 1991).

66. Davies, *In Search of "Ancient Israel,"* 15.

67. Thompson, *Mythic Past*, 34.

68. J. Robin King, "The Joseph Story and Divine Politics: A Comparative Study of a Biographic Formula from the Ancient Near East," *JBL* 106 (1987): 577–584.

69. Miriam Lichtheim, "Sinuhe," in *COS* 1: 77.

70. King, "Joseph Story and Divine Politics," 584.

71. Ibid., 581. The emphasis is my own, to show that King understands this type of genre to be historiographical.

72. The matter of the historicity of Sinuhe remains a debated point among Egyptologists. He could have been the invention of the writer for purely propagandistic ends. On the other hand, Sinuhe might have been a historical figure around whom the story was embellished. Unfortunately, the preserved story cannot be used to prove or disprove his existence. Recently it has been argued on the basis of comparing the story of Sinuhe with other Egyptian literature that it best conforms to the characteristics of an Egyptian autobiography; cf. Kenneth Kitchen, "Sinuhe: Scholarly Method versus Trendy Fashion," *Bulletin of the Australian Centre for Egyptology* 7 (1996): 55–63.

73. Whybray, *Making of the Pentateuch*, 236.

74. Philip Davies's recent monograph argues that the biblical works dealing with early Israel date to the sixth through third century, with his inclination being toward the latter end of that horizon (*In Search of "Ancient Israel,"* see chapters 6–9).

75. Lester Grabbe, ed., *Did Moses Speak Attic? Jewish Historiography and Scripture in the Hellenistic Period*, European Seminar in Historical Methodology (Sheffield: Sheffield Academic Press, 2001).

76. Rainer Albertz, "An End to the Confusion? Why the Old Testament Cannot Be a Hellenistic Book!" in *Did Moses Speak Attic?* 30–46; Dever, *What Did the Biblical Writers Know?*, 275–277.

77. For example, John Emerton, "An Examination of Some Attempts to Defend the Unity of the Flood Narrative in Genesis, Part I," *VT* 37 (1987): 401–420, and Emerton, "An Examination of Some Attempts to Defend the Unity of the Flood Narrative in Genesis, Part II," *VT* 38 (1988), 1–21.

78. Nicholson, *Pentateuch in the Twentieth Century* and "The Pentateuch in Recent Research"; Emerton, "An Examination," Parts I and II; Joseph Blenkinsopp, "An Assessment of the Alleged Pre-Exilic Date of the Priestly Material in the Pentateuch," *ZAW* 108 (1996): 495–518; and, for example, Friedman, *Who Wrote the Bible?*

79. Sociological approaches have not had a serious impact on source criticism, the way literary readings of biblical texts have. By their nature, sociological investigations are not particularly interested in literary and compositional questions. Hence a discussion of the contribution of sociological investigations of the Old Testament has not been considered here. Some representative works, however, include Robert R. Wilson's *Sociological Approaches to the Old Testament* (Philadelphia: Fortress, 1984) and Norman Gottwald's *The Hebrew Bible: A Socio-Literary Introduction* (Philadelphia: Fortress, 1985). See also an important collection of essays: Charles Carter and Carol Meyers, *Ancient Israel among the Nations: Social Scientific Approaches to the Hebrew Bible*, Sources for Biblical and Theological Study (Winona Lake, Ind.: Eisenbrauns, 1996).

80. *Pentateuch in the Twentieth Century*, 96.

81. J. Alberto Soggin, *A History of Ancient Israel from the Beginnings to the Bar Kochba Revolt, A.D. 135*, trans. John Bowden (Philadephia: Westminster, 1984), 19–20.

82. L. V. Zabkar, "The Adaptation of Ancient Egyptian Texts to the Temple Ritual at Philae," *JEA* 66 (1980): 127–136.

83. Donald Redford, "Manetho," in *The Oxford Encyclopedia of Ancient Egypt*, ed. Donald B. Redford (New York: Oxford University Press, 2001), 336–337.

84. James K. Hoffmeier, "King Lists," in COS 1: 68–73; Donald Redford, *Pharaonic King-Lists, Annals and Day-Books: A Contribution to the Study of the Egyptian Sense of History*, SSEA Publications 4 (Mississauga, Ont.: Benben Publications, 1986).

85. Compare W. G. Waddell, *Manetho*, Loeb Classical Library (Cambridge: Harvard University Press, 1940); Redford, "Manetho," 336–337.

86. Waddell, *Manetho*.

87. This is not to say that Egyptologists blindly accept everything Manetho claims. It is widely acknowledged that names are garbled and that some of the dynasties are not sequential but contemporaneous, and that there are clearly legendary stories preserved (see Redford, *Pharaonic King-Lists, Annals and Day-Books*, chapters 7–9). Nevertheless, Manetho is taken seriously in historical studies.

88. Baruch Halpern, "Erasing History: The Minimalist Assault on Ancient Israel," *BR* 11:6 (December 1995): 46–47; Dever, *What Did the Biblical Writers Know?*, 23–27.

89. William F. Albright, *From Stone Age to Christianity: Monotheism and the Historical Process* (Baltimore: Johns Hopkins University Press, 1946); G. Ernest Wright, *Biblical Archaeology* (Philadelphia: Westminster, 1957); Roland de Vaux, *The Early History of Israel*, trans. David Smith (Philadelphia: Westminster, 1978); John Bright, *A History of Israel*, 3rd ed. (Philadelphia: Westminster, 1981).

90. William G. Dever, *Who Were the Early Israelites and Where Did They Come From?* (Grand Rapids, Mich.: Eerdmans, 2003), 18, 20, 229–237.

91. Martin Noth, *The History of Israel* (London: Adam and Charles Black, 1960), 127.

92. Gerhard von Rad, "The Form-Critical Problem of the Hexateuch," in his *The Problem of the Hexateuch and Other Essays* (Edinburgh: Oliver and Boyd, 1966), 3–8.

93. For example, Soggin, *History of Ancient Israel*, 128–129; Ernest Nicholson, *Exodus and Sinai in History and Tradition* (Richmond, Va.: John Knox Press, 1973), 1–32.

94. David Hackett Fischer, *Historians' Fallacies: Toward a Logic of Historical Thought* (New York: Harper and Row, 1970), 47, 62.

95. Noth, *History of Israel*, 128.

96. Especially in chapters 1 and 2.

97. Hoffmeier, "The (Israel) Stela of Merneptah," in COS 2: 41. See also my discussion in "Understanding Hebrew and Egyptian Military Texts: A Contextual Approach," in COS 3: xxi–xxvii.

98. Dever, *What Did the Biblical Writers Know?*, 128.

99. Giovanni Garbini, *History and Ideology in Ancient Israel* (New York: Crossroads, 1988); Ahström, *Who Were the Israelites?*, chapter 4, for example; Lemche, *Israelites in History and Tradition*.

100. Thompson, *Mythic Past*, 13.

101. William W. Hallo, "The Limits of Skepticism," *JAOS* 110, no. 2 (1990): 189.

102. William W. Hallo, "Biblical History in Its Near Eastern Setting: The Contextual Approach," in *Scripture in Context: Essays on the Comparative Method*, ed. W. W. Hallo, C. D. Evans, and J. B. White (Pittsburgh: Pickwick, 1980), 1–26.

103. Johan Huizinga, "A Definition of the Concept of History," in *Philosophy and History: Essays Presented to Ernst Cassirer*, ed. R. Kiblansky & H. J. Paton (Oxford: Clarendon, 1936; reprint, New York: Harper, 1963), 1–10.

104. John Van Seters, *In Search of History: Historiography in the Ancient World and the Origins of Biblical History* (New Haven: Yale University Press, 1983), chapters 1 and 7.

105. George E. Mendenhall, *Ancient Israel's Faith and History: An Introduction to the Bible in Context* (Louisville, Ky.: Westminster/John Knox Press, 2001), 43.

106. Fischer, *Historians' Fallacies*, 48.

107. Kitchen, *Ancient Orient and Old Testament*, 29.

108. Hallo, "Biblical History in Its Near Eastern Setting."

109. "Method in the Study of Early Hebrew History," in *The 100th Meeting of the Society of Biblical Literature, December 1964*, ed. J. P. Hyatt (Nashville, Tenn.: Abingdon, 1965), 15.

CHAPTER 2

1. Helpful surveys are available in R. K. Harrison, *Introduction to the Old Testament* (Grand Rapids, Mich: Eerdmans, 1969), 351–414; Rainer Albertz, *A History of Israelite Religion in the Old Testament Period*, trans. John Bowden, vol. 1, *From the Beginnings to the End of the Monarchy* (Louisville, Ky.: Westminster/John Knox Press, 1994), 3–17.

2. Kurt Rudolf, "Comparative Religion," in *The Encyclopedia of Religion*, ed. Mircea Eliade (New York: Macmillan, 1987), vol. 3, 578–580.

3. Harrison, *Introduction to the Old Testament*, 355.

4. For a helpful survey of the study of Israelite religion from its development as an academic discipline to the 1990s, see Bill T. Arnold, "Religion in Ancient Israel," in

The Face of Old Testament Studies, ed. D. W. Baker and B. T. Arnold (Grand Rapids, Mich.: Baker Book House, 1999), 391–420.

5. Although many scholars could be cited here, the works of Frank Moore Cross stand out as having influenced the discipline for the past four decades; see Cross, *Canaanite Myth and Hebrew Epic* (Cambridge: Harvard University Press, 1973). Some of his earlier ideas are updated and discussed afresh in Cross, *From Epic to Canon: History and Literature in Ancient Israel* (Baltimore: Johns Hopkins University Press, 1998).

6. William F. Albright, *Yahweh and the Gods of Canaan* (Winona Lake, Ind.: Eisenbrauns, 1968); Yehezkel Kaufmann, *The Religion of Israel: From Its Beginnings to the Babylonian Exile*, trans. Moshe Greenberg (New York: Schocken, 1972); Roland de Vaux, *Ancient Israel*, vol. 2 (New York: McGraw-Hill, 1962); and Helmer Ringgren, *Israelite Religion*, trans. David E. Green (Philadelphia: Fortress, 1966).

7. Georg Fohrer, *History of Israelite Religion*, trans. David Green (Nashville, Tenn.: Abingdon, 1972).

8. Albertz, *History of Israelite Religion in the Old Testament Period.*

9. Ibid., chapter 2.

10. Ibid., 23. The evidence for the lateness of the wilderness tradition, according to Albertz, is the absence of references to the Sinai theophany in the early prophets. I would disagree and point to Hosea 13:5: "It was I who knew you in the wilderness." The reference of "know" (ידע) refers to the intimate relationship God established with Israel by means of the Sinai covenant. This idea is developed in more detail in Hosea 2:14–20, in which Israel's covenant relationship with God will be reestablished by YHWH, who will bring Israel to the wilderness (*miḏbār*). Similarly, Amos (3:1–2) uses the word "know" in the same manner as Hosea.

11. His more recent book is very similar in its approach to dealing with the monotheism in Israel: Mark S. Smith, *The Origins of Biblical Monotheism: Israel's Polytheistic Background and the Ugaritic Texts* (Oxford: Oxford University Press, 2001).

12. Mark S. Smith, *The Early History of God: Yahweh and the Other Deities in Ancient Israel* (San Francisco: Harper and Row, 1990), 1–40.

13. Susan Niditch, *Ancient Israelite Religion* (New York: Oxford University Press, 1997), 9.

14. The only surviving artifact from the first temple is believed to be the eighth-century pomegranate-scepter head with its inscription: "belonging to the hou[se of . . .]. A holy thing of the priests." Cf. P. Kyle McCarter, *Ancient Inscriptions: Voices from the Biblical World* (Washington, D.C.: Biblical Archaeology Society, 1996), 89.

15. Niditch, *Ancient Israelite Religion*, chapter 2.

16. Othmar Keel and Christoph Uehlinger, *Gods, Goddesses, and Images of God in Ancient Israel*, trans. Thomas H. Trapp (Minneapolis: Fortress, 1998); Patrick D. Miller, *The Religion of Ancient Israel*, ed. Douglas A. Knight, Library of Ancient Israel (Louisville, Ky.: Westminster/John Knox Press, 2000).

17. Miller, *Religion of Ancient Israel*, 1.

18. Beth Alpert Nakhai, *Archaeology and the Religions of Canaan and Israel*, vol. 7 (Boston: ASOR Books, 2001).

19. Ziony Zevit, *The Religions of Ancient Israel: A Synthesis of Parallactic Approaches* (London: Continuum, 2001).

20. Ibid., 79.

21. McCarter, *Ancient Inscriptions*, 106–110.

22. For example, Susan Ackerman, *Under Every Green Tree: Popular Religion in Sixth-Century Judah*, Harvard Semitic Monographs 46 (Atlanta: Scholars Press, 1992); William G. Dever, "The Contribution of Archaeology to the Study of Canaanite and Early Israelite Religion," in *Ancient Israelite Religion: Essays in Honor of Frank Moore Cross*, ed. P. D. Miller et al. (Philadelphia: Fortress, 1987), 209–247.

23. For a recent review of the material and a discussion of its impact, see William G. Dever, "Archaeology and the Ancient Israelite Cult: How the Kh. el-Qom and Kuntillet Ajrud 'Asherah' Texts Have Changed the Picture," *EI* 26 (1999): 9–22; see also Zevit, *The Religions of Ancient Israel*.

24. *What Did the Biblical Writers Know & When Did They Know It? What Archaeology Can Tell Us about the Reality of Ancient Israel* (Grand Rapids, Mich.: Eerdmans, 2001), 195.

25. Kaufmann, *The Religion of Israel*.

26. Allen W. Wood, "The Enlightenment," in *The Encyclopedia of Religion*, ed. Mircea Eliade (New York: Macmillan, 1987), vol. 5, 109–113.

27. C. Stephen Evans, "Critical Historical Judgment and Biblical Faith," in *History and the Christian Historian*, ed. R. A. Wells (Grand Rapids, Mich.: Eerdmans, 1998), 48.

28. See, for example, Ninian Smart, *Worldviews: Cross-Cultural Explorations of Human Beliefs* (New York: Scribner, 1983).

29. Ninian Smart, *The Phenomenon of Religion* (New York: Herder and Herder, 1973).

30. Evolutionism originated in the field of anthropology and then moved into other disciplines, including biblical studies; see James Waller and Mary Edwardsen, "Evolutionism," in *The Encyclopedia of Religion*, ed. Mircea Eliade (New York: Macmillan, 1987), vol. 5, 214–218.

31. Albrecht Alt, *Essays on Old Testament History and Religion*, trans. R. A. Wilson (Garden City, N.Y.: Doubleday, 1966).

32. Cross, *Canaanite Myth and Hebrew Epic*, 3.

33. Mircea Eliade, *Patterns in Comparative Religion*, trans. Rosemary Sheed (New York: New American Library, 1958), 4–7.

34. Dagfinn Føllesdal, "Edmund Husserl," in *Routledge Encyclopedia of Philosophy*, ed. Edward Craig (London: Routledge, 1998), vol. 5, 574–588.

35. Douglas Allen, "Phenomenology of Religion," in *The Encyclopedia of Religion*, ed. Mircea Eliade (New York: Macmillan, 1987), 11, 272–285.

36. Ibid., 273.

37. Rudolf Otto, *The Idea of the Holy*, trans. J. W. Harvey (London: Oxford University Press, 1946), 6–7.

38. Ibid., 5, 12–14, 19, 26.

39. Gerardus van der Leeuw, *Religion in Essence and Manifestation*, trans. J. E. Turner (Gloucester, Mass.: Peter Smith, 1967), 47, 677.

40. W. B. Kristensen, *The Meaning of Religion*, trans. J. B. Carman (The Hague: M. Nijhoff, 1960), 18, 358.

41. Eliade was a Romanian who spent many years in Paris before coming to the United States, where he was professor of religion at the University of Chicago. Thus he stands very much in the European tradition.

42. Eliade, *Patterns in Comparative Religion.*

43. Hans Frei, *The Eclipse of Biblical Narrative: A Study in Eighteenth and Nineteenth Century Hermeneutics* (New Haven: Yale University Press, 1974), 14.

44. J. Maxwell Miller, *The Old Testament and the Historian* (Philadelphia: Fortress, 1976), 11–28.

45. J. Maxwell Miller, "Reading the Bible Historically: The Historian's Approach," in *To Each Its Own Meaning: An Introduction to Biblical Criticisms and Their Application*, ed. S. R. Haynes and S. L. McKenzie (Louisville, Ky.: Westminster/John Knox, 1993), 12.

46. A number of studies have addressed this issue, and although there may be different perspectives about how Israel's view may be similar to or different from those of her neighbors, it is clear from the studies cited here that all peoples of the ancient Near East subscribed to a theisitic worldview. See Bertil Albrektson, *History and the Gods: An Essay on the Idea of Historical Events as Divine Manifestations in the Ancient Near East and Israel* (Lund: Gleerup, 1967); H. W. F. Saggs, *The Encounter with the Divine in Mesopotamia and Israel* (London: Athlone, 1978); J. F. Borghouts, "Divine Intervention in Ancient Egypt and Its Manifestation (*B3w*)," in *Gleanings from Deir el-Medîna*, ed. R. J. Demarée and J. J. Janssen (Leiden: Netherlands Institute for Near Eastern Studies, 1982), 1–70.

47. Text in KRI 4: 19.4–5.

48. Borghouts, "Divine Intervention in Ancient Egypt and Its Manifestation (*B3w*)," 28.

49. For examples of such charges, see Niels Peter Lemche, "Response to William G. Dever: Revisionist Israel Revisited," *Currents in Research: Biblical Studies* 5 (1997): 9–14; and Thomas L. Thompson, "A Neo-Albrightean School in History and Biblical Scholarship?" *JBL* 114, no. 4 (1995): 638–705.

50. Philip R. Davies, "Israel in Egypt: A Review," *Theology* 103 (July–August 2000): 285–286.

51. James K. Hoffmeier, *"Sacred" in the Vocabulary of Ancient Egypt*, Orbis Biblicus et Orientalis 59 (Fribourg: University of Fribourg, 1985). I acknowledge with gratitude how much I was influenced by Willard G. Oxtoby, who was the director of the Centre for Religious Studies (University of Toronto), and who taught the year-long religious studies method course I took in 1977–1978. His article "The Sacred, the Holy" in the *Dictionary of the History of Ideas* got me started in the phenomenology of religion and inspired me to pursue a study of the "Sacred" in ancient Egyptian, which subsequently developed into my dissertation.

52. Philip Davies, *In Search of "Ancient Israel"* (Sheffield: JSOT Press, 1992).

53. These points can be seen in some form in the following studies: Zevit, *Religions of Ancient Israel;* Thomas Ryba, *The Essence of Phenomenology and Its Meaning for the Scientific Study of Religion*, ed. Donald Wiebe, Toronto Studies in Religion 7 (Frankfurt: Peter Lang, 1991); Allen, "Phenomenology of Religion," 272–285.

54. Allen, "Phenomenology of Religion," 281.

55. Paul Ricoeur, "Phenomenology and Hermeneutics," in *Hermeneutics and the Human Sciences*, ed. John B. Thompson (Cambridge: Cambridge University Press, 1981), 128.

CHAPTER 3

1. For the six weeks that passed and the possible significance of six weeks of travel followed by a seventh of rest at Mt. Sinai, see Umberto Cassuto, *A Commentary on the Book of Exodus*, trans. I. Abrahams (Jerusalem: Magnes Press, 1951), 224.

2. Joseph J. Hobbs, *Mount Sinai* (Austin: University of Texas Press, 1995), 5.

3. Ram Gophna, "Egyptian Trading Posts in Southern Canaan at the Dawn of the Archaic Period," in *Egypt, Israel, Sinai: Archaeological and Historical Relationships in the Biblical Period*, ed. Anson Rainey (Tel Aviv: Tel Aviv University Press, 1987), 13–21.

4. Pau Figueras, *From Gaza to Pelusium: Materials for the Historical Geography of North Sinai and Southwestern Palestine (332 BCE–640 CE)*, Beer-Sheva Studies by the Department of Bible and Ancient Near East 14 (Beer-Sheva: Ben-Gurion University of the Negev Press, 2000).

5. Barry Beitzel, *The Moody Bible Atlas* (Chicago: Moody Press, 1985), 86–87.

6. Alan H. Gardiner, T. Eric Peet, and Jaroslav Černý, *The Inscriptions of Sinai* (London: EES, 1955).

7. Itzhak Beit-Arieh, "New Discoveries at Serabit el-Khadim," *BA* 45 (1982): 13–18; Beit-Arieh, "Canaanites and Egyptians at Serabit el-Khadim," in *Egypt, Israel, and Sinai: Archaeological and Historical Relationships in the Biblical Period*, ed. Anson Rainey (Jerusalem: Tel Aviv University Press, 1987): 57–67; Beit-Arieh, "Fifteen Years in Sinai," *BAR* 10 (1984): 26–54; Beit-Arieh, "Serabît èl-Khâdim: New Metallurgical and Chronological Aspects," *Levant* 17 (1985): 89–116.

8. Gardiner, Peet, and Černý, *Inscriptions of Sinai*, 9.

9. *Wb* 5: 126; *Wb* 5: 494 offers the translations of *dšrt* as "das rote Land" (red land), "die Wüste" (the desert), and "das Ausland" (foreign land).

10. *Wb* 3: 234.

11. Alan H. Gardiner, *Egyptian Grammar: Being an Introduction to the Study of Hieroglyphs*, 3rd ed. (London: Oxford University Press, 1957), 288.

12. Gardiner, Peet, and Černý, *Inscriptions of Sinai*. Plate XXVI contains the texts. The three references to Bia are in lines 2 and 3. For translation, see p. 97.

13. Ibid., lines 5 and 7.

14. David Seely, "Wilderness of Sin," in *ABD* 6, 47.

15. Yohanan Aharoni, "Kadesh-Barnea and Mount Sinai," in *God's Wilderness: Discoveries in Sinai*, ed. Beno Rothenberg (New York: Thomas Nelson, 1961), 167–169.

16. Ibid., 168–169.

17. Roland de Vaux, *The Early History of Israel*, trans. David Smith (Philadelphia: Westminster, 1978), 431.

18. J. Philip Hyatt, *Exodus* (London: Marshall, Morgan, and Scott, 1971), 71; Robert North, "Perspective of the Exodus Author(s)," *ZAW* 113 (2001): 497–499.

19. Exod. 19:18, 20, 23; 24:16; 31:18; 34:2, 4, 27, 32; Lev. 7:38; 25:1; 26:46; 27:34; Num. 31; 28:6; Neh. 9:13.

20. Exod. 19:1, 2; Lev. 7:38; Num 1:1, 19; 3:4, 14; 9:1, 5; Num. 10:12; 26:64; 33:15, 16.

21. Martin Noth, *History of Pentateuchal Traditions* (Englewood Cliffs, N.J.: Prentice Hall, 1972), 133; William H. C. Propp, *Exodus 1–18*, ABC 2 (1999): 592; Seely, "Wilderness of Sin," 47.

22. Dewey M. Beegle, *Moses, the Servant of Yahweh* (Grand Rapids, Mich.: Eerdmans, 1972), 63.

23. KB 760.

24. Jon D. Levenson, *Sinai & Zion: An Entry into the Jewish Bible* (San Francisco: Harper and Row, 1985), 20.

25. Cassuto, *A Commentary on the Book of Exodus*, 31.

26. Alan H. Gardiner, "The Residence of the Ramessides," *JEA* 5 (1918): 253–254. For a more recent discussion, see Edmund S. Meltzer, "Pelusium," in *ABD* 5, 221–222; Wendy Cheshire, "Remarks on the Names of Pelusium," *GM* 84 (1985): 19–24; Yoshiyuki Muchiki, *Egyptian Proper Names and Loanwords in North-West Semitic*, ed. Michael Fox, SBL Dissertation Series 173 (Atlanta: Society of Biblical Literature, 1999), 232. For an exhaustive treatment of Pelusium in ancient texts, see Jean-Yves Carrez-Maratray, *Pelusé et l'angle oriental du delta égyptien aux époques greque, romaine et byzantine*, Bibliothèque d'Études 124 (1999), 3–32.

27. Kenneth Kitchen, *The Third Intermediate Period in Egypt (1100–650 B.C.)*, 3rd ed. (Warminster: Aris and Phillips, 1986), §353. Herodotus is the first to mention Pelusium, and speaks of it as an entrance to Egypt where Assyrian armies camped; cf. Figueras, *From Gaza to Pelusium*, 36.

28. KB 751.

29. Lina Eckenstein, *A History of Sinai* (London: Society for Promoting Christian Knowledge, 1921), 8–16.

30. Raphael Giveon, "Inscriptions of Sahure and Sesostoris I from Wadi Kharig (Sinai)," *BASOR* 226 (1977): 61–62.

31. Ibid., 62.

32. *COS* 2: 244–245.

33. Gardiner, Peet, and Černý, *Inscriptions of Sinai*, 1–2. See also *Wb* 1: 438.

34. Gardiner, Peet, and Černý, *Inscriptions of Sinai*, 2.

35. Mahmoud Abd el-Raziq, Georges Caster, Pierre Tallet, and Victor Ghica, *Les inscriptions d'Ayn Soukhna*, MIFAO 122 (Cairo: IFAO, 2002).

36. My own translation based on the text ibid., 40.

37. Mahmoud Abd el-Raziq, Georges Caster, Pierre Tallet, and Victor Ghica, *Inscriptions d'Ayn Soukhna*, 57.

38. Eliezer Oren, "Northern Sinai," in *The New Encyclopedia of Archaeological Excavations in the Holy Land*, ed. Ephraim Stern (Jerusalem: Israel Exploration Society and New York: Simon and Schuster, 1993), 1386–1396; Oren, "The 'Ways of Horus' in North Sinai," in *Egypt, Israel, Sinai: Archaeological and Historical Relationships in the Biblical Period*, ed. A. F. Rainey (Tel Aviv: Tel Aviv University Press, 1987), 69–119; Dominique Valbelle, "La (Les) route(s)-d'Horus," in *Hommages à Jean Leclant*, Bibliothèque d'Études 106 (Cairo: IFAO, 1994), 379–386.

39. A. D. Godley, *Herodotus I–IV* (London: William Heinemann, 1931), Book II, 8, 12, 15, 19. For references to other classical writers, see H. G. Liddell, R. Scott, and H. S. Jones, *A Greek-English Lexicon* (Oxford: Clarendon, 1996), 233.

40. Godley, *Herodotus I–IV*, Book III, 4–9.

41. Kedar is mentioned with some frequency in the prophets, indicating their presence in the region: cf. Isa. 21:16–17, 42:11, 60:7; Jer. 2:10, 49:28; Ezek. 27:21.

42. *COS* 2: 263–264.

43. M. C. A. Macdonald, "North Arabia in the First Millennium BCE," in *Civilizations of the Ancient Near East*, ed. Jack M. Sasson (New York: Charles Scribner and Sons, 1995), 1355, 1367–1368.

44. Ned H. Greenwood, *The Sinai: A Physical Geography* (Austin: University of Texas Press, 1997), chapters 2–3.

45. Ibid., 16–17, 36.

46. N. Bakler, D. Neev, and K. O. Emery, *Mediterranean Coasts of Israel and Sinai: Holocene Tectonism from Geology, Geophysics, and Archaeology* (New York: Taylor and Francis, 1987), 82–90.

47. Greenwood, *Sinai*, 16–19.

48. On the geology of the coastal area of North Sinai, see Bakler, Neev, and Emery, *Mediterranean Coasts of Israel and Sinai*. In chapters 4 and 5 below, a detailed discussion of recent archaeological work in North Sinai will be introduced.

49. Alan H. Gardiner, "The Ancient Military Road between Egypt and Palestine," *JEA* 6 (1920): 99–116; Ellen Morris, "The Architecture of Imperialism: An Investigation into the Role of Fortresses and Administrative Headquarters in New Kingdom Foreign Policy," (Ph.D. dissertation, University of Pennsylvania, 2001); Oren, "Northern Sinai" and "'Ways of Horus' in North Sinai."

50. Gardiner, "Ancient Military Road between Egypt and Palestine."

51. Figueras, *From Gaza to Pelusium*, 7–11.

52. Eliezer Oren, who directed the archaeological survey along this land bridge, has told me that he carefully surveyed this area and did not find a single potsherd that dated to the second millennium.

53. For a translation of D. Neev's preliminary report in Hebrew, in which he drew this conclusion, see Graham I. Davies, "The Wilderness Itineraries and Recent Archaeological Research," *VTS* 41 (1990): 164–165.

54. Bakler, Neev, and Emery, *Mediterranean Coasts of Israel and Sinai*, 19.

55. Manfred Bietak, *Tell el-Dab'a* (Vienna: Österreichischen Akademie der Wissenschaften Wien, 1975), 2: 136–137.

56. Amihai Sneh, Tuvia Weissbrod, and Itamar Perath, "Evidence for an Ancient Egyptian Frontier Canal," *American Scientist* 63 (1975): 542–548.

57. James K. Hoffmeier, *Israel in Egypt: The Evidence for the Authenticity of the Exodus Tradition* (New York: Oxford University Press, 1997), chapter 7.

58. Bruno Marcolongo, "Évolution du paléo-environnement dans la partie orientale du delta du Nil depuis la transgression flandrienne (8000 B.P.)," *CRIPEL* 14 (1992): 23–31.

59. I reported on this work in *Israel in Egypt*, 186–187.

60. Dr. Moshier is associate professor of geology at Wheaton College, Illinois. He directs the paleoenvironmental research for the East Frontier Archaeological project. For further details about the 1998 season, see below, chapter 5, §V.

61. Sneh, Weissbrod, and Perath, "Evidence for an Ancient Egyptian Frontier Canal."

62. Mohamed Abd el-Maksoud, *Tell Hebuoa (1981–1991)* (Paris: Éditions Recherche sur les Civilisations, 1998); Abd el-Maksoud, "Tjarou, porte de l'orient," in *Le Sinaï durant l'antiquité et le moyen age*, ed. Charles Bonnet and Dominique Valbelle (Paris: Errance, 1998), 61–65; Abd el-Maksoud, "Une nouvelle forteresse sur la route d'Horus: Tell Heboua 1986 (Nord Sinaï)," *CRIPEL* 9 (1987): 13–16.

63. G. A. Goodfriend and D. J. Stanley, "Rapid Strandplain Accretion in the Northern Nile Delta in the Nile Delta in the 9th Century AD, and the Demise of the Port of Pelusium," *Geology* 27, no. 2 (1999): 147–150.

64. Carol Redmount, "On an Egyptian/Asiatic Frontier: An Archaeological History of the Wadi Tumilat" (Ph.D. dissertation, University of Chicago, 1989), 18.

65. John S. Holladay, "Wadi Tumilat," in *Encyclopedia of the Archaeology of Ancient Egypt*, ed. Kathryn Bard (New York: Routledge, 1999), 878.

66. Redmount, "On an Egyptian/Asiatic Frontier," 39–40.

67. Sneh, Weissbrod, and Perath, "Evidence for an Ancient Egyptian Frontier Canal," 546–548.

68. Manashe Har-el, *The Sinai Journeys: The Route of the Exodus* (San Diego: Ridgefield, 1983), 29.

69. *Gebel* or *jebel* is the Arabic word for mountain, while *har* is Hebrew for mountain.

70. Arthur Penrhyn Stanley, *Sinai and Palestine in Connection with Their History* (London: John Murray, 1856), 7; Clinton Bailey, "Bedouin Place-Names in Sinai," *PEQ* 116 (1984): 44.

71. Beitzel, *Moody Bible Atlas*, 86–87.

72. Greenwood, *Sinai*, 31.

73. Ibid., 33–34.

74. For a complete study of the Red Sea granites, see Jeffrey Greenburg, "Characteristics and Origin of Egyptian Younger Granites," *Geological Society of American Bulletin* 92, no. 5 (1981): 749–840.

75. Henry Spencer Palmer, *Sinai: From the Fourth Egyptian Dynasty to the Present Day* (London: Society for Promoting Christian Knowledge, 1892), 33.

76. Ibid., 45–46.

77. Irene Jacob and Walter Jacob, "Flora," in *ABD* 2, 804.

78. Har-el, *Sinai Journeys*, 55.

79. Greenwood, *Sinai*, 54–55.

CHAPTER 4

1. Bernard Batto, "The Reed Sea: *Requiscat in Pace*," *JBL* 102 (1983), 27–35; Gösta W. Ahlström, *Who Were the Israelites?* (Winona Lake, Ind.: Eisenbrauns, 1986); Bernard Batto, *Slaying the Dragon: Mythmaking in Biblical Tradition* (Louisville, Ky.: Westminster/John Knox Press, 1992).

2. Some examples include Maurice Copisarow, "The Ancient Egyptian, Greek and Hebrew Concept of the Red Sea," *VT* 12 (1962): 1–13; Norman Snaith, "Yam Suph: The Sea of Reeds: The Red Sea," *VT* 15 (1965): 295–298; Robert Luyster, "Myth and History in the Book of Exodus," *Religion* 8, no. 1 (1978): 155–169.

3. G. R. H. Wright, "The Passage of the Sea," *GM* 33 (1979): 55–68.

4. Batto, "Reed Sea: *Requiscat in Pace*," 29–30.

5. Donald Redford, *Egypt, Canaan, and Israel in Ancient Times* (Princeton: Princeton University Press, 1992), 409.

6. Miriam Lichtheim, *Ancient Egyptian Literature* (Berkeley: University of California Press, 1976), 2:36.

7. For a recent translation of these three texts, and a discussion of some historiographic implications, see Hoffmeier, *COS* 2:5–19. For more detailed discussion about the composition of the annals and the problem of history, see Hoffmeier, "The Problem of 'History' in Egyptian Royal Inscriptions," in *VI Congresso Internazionale de Egittologi Atti*, ed. Silvio Curto (Turin, 1992); and Hoffmeier, "The Structure of Joshua 1–11 and the Annals of Thutmose III," in *Faith, Tradition, and History: Old Testament Historiography in Its Near Eastern Context*, ed. A. R. Millard, J. K. Hoffmeier, and D. W. Baker (Winona Lake, Ind.: Eisenbrauns, 1994).

8. William Johnstone, *Exodus*, Old Testament Guides (Sheffield: JSOT Press, 1990).

9. Donald Redford, "An Egyptological Perspective on the Exodus Narrative," in *Egypt, Israel, Sinai: Archaeological and Historical Relationships in the Biblical Period*, ed. A. F. Rainey (Tel Aviv: Tel Aviv University Press, 1987), 137–161.

10. J. Philip Hyatt, *Exodus* (London: Marshall, Morgan, and Scott, 1971); John Van Seters, *The Life of Moses: The Yahwist as Historian in Exodus-Numbers* (Louisville, Ky.: Westminster/John Knox, 1994); William Propp, *Exodus 1–18*, ABC 2 (1999).

11. Alan H. Gardiner, "The Ancient Military Road between Egypt and Palestine," *JEA* 6 (1920): 99–116.

12. See note 10 for references.

13. Hyatt, *Exodus*, 150; Van Seters, *Life of Moses*, 130–131.

14. See sources cited in note 10 above.

15. Martin Noth, "Der Wallfahrtsweg zum Sinai," *Palästinajahrbuch* 36 (1940): 5–28.

16. Cf. George W. Coats, "The Wilderness Itinerary," *CBQ* 34 (1972): 135–152; Graham I. Davies, "The Wilderness Itineraries: A Comparative Study," *TB* 25 (1974): 46–81; Davies, *The Way of the Wilderness* (Cambridge: Cambridge University Press, 1979); J. T. Walsh, "From Egypt to Moab: A Source Critical Analysis of The Wilderness Itinerary," *CBQ* 39 (1977): 20–33; Davies, "The Wilderness Itineraries and Recent Archaeological Research," *VTS* 41 (1990): 161–175; Benjamin E. Scolnic, *Theme and Context in Biblical Lists* (Atlanta: Scholars Press, 1995).

17. For a detailed discussion of the Egyptian lists and comparisons with those found in the Pentateuch, see Hoffmeier, *Israel in Egypt: The Evidence for the Authenticity of the Exodus Tradition* (New York: Oxford University Press, 1997), 176–179. After the New Kingdom, some lists virtually drop out of usage, the major exception being the toponym list of Sheshonk I (Shishak of 1 Kings 14:25), which dates to ca. 925 B.C.

18. Charles Krahmalkov, "Exodus Itinerary Confirmed by Egyptian Evidence," *BAR* 20, no. 5 (1994), 56.

19. Martin Noth, *Numbers* (Philadelphia: Westminister, 1968); John Sturdy, *Numbers* (Cambridge: Cambridge University Press, 1976); Philip Budd, *Numbers*, Word Biblical Commentary 5 (Waco, Tex.: Word, 1984).

20. Lewis S. Hay, "What Really Happened at the Sea of Reeds," *JBL* 83 (1964): 399.

21. Jean Louis Ska, *Le passage de la mer: Étude de la construction, du style et de la symbolique d'Ex 14, 1–31*, Analecta Biblica 109 (Rome: Biblical Institute Press, 1986).

22. Barbara S. Lesko, "Edouard Naville," in *The Oxford Encyclopedia of Archaeology in the Near East*, ed. Eric Meyers (Oxford: Oxford University Press, 1997).

23. Edouard Naville, *The Shrine of the Saft el Henneh and the Land of Goshen* (London: EEF, 1887).

24. W. M. F. Petrie, *Tanis*, Part II, *Nebesheh and Defenneh (Tahpanhes)* (London: Egypt Exploration Society, 1888).

25. W. M. F. Petrie, *Hyksos and Israelite Cities* (London: School of Archaeology, 1906).

26. Alan H. Gardiner, "The Geography of the Exodus," in *Recueil d'études egyptologiques dédiées à la Mémoire de Jean-François Champollion à l'occasion du centenaire de la lettre à M. Dacier* (Paris: Bibliothèque de l'École des Hautes Études, 1922), 203–215; Gardiner, "The Geography of the Exodus: An Answer to Professor Naville and Others," *JEA* 10 (1924): 87–96; Édouard Naville, "The Geography of the Exodus," *JEA* 10 (1924): 18–39.

27. Quoted in Naville, "Geography of the Exodus," 18.

28. Alfred Lucas, *The Route of the Exodus of the Israelites from Egypt* (London: E. Arnold, 1938), 8.

29. There is some overlap between the types offered here and those presented by Clinton Bailey, "Bedouin Place-Names in Sinai," *PEQ* 116 (1984): 42–57.

30. For a detailed discussion of the brickmaking and the location of these cities, see my *Israel in Egypt*, 112–122.

31. Alan H. Gardiner, "The Residence of the Ramessides," *JEA* 5 (1918): 127–271.

32. Ibid., 266.

33. Max Müller, "A Contribution to the Exodus Geography," *PSBA* 10 (1888): 467–477.

34. Petrie, *Hyksos and Israelite Cities*; Petrie reiterated his view in *Egypt and Israel* (London: Society for Promoting Christian Knowledge, 1911), 33–34. Édouard Naville, *The Store-City of Pithom and the Route of the Exodus* (London: Egypt Exploration Fund, 1885). He subsequently defended his identification after a blistering attack by T. E. Peet and Gardiner; see Naville, "Geography of the Exodus."

35. Pierre Montet, "Tanis, Avaris, et Pi-Ramses," *RB* 39 (1933): 191–215.

36. Alan H. Gardiner, *Egypt of the Pharaohs* (Oxford: Oxford University Press, 1962), 258.

37. Labib Habachi, *Tell el-Daba I: Tell el-Daba and Qantir, the Site and Its Connections with Aravris and Piramesse*, ed. Manfred Bietak and Ernst Czerny (Vienna: Verlag der Österreichischen Akademie der Wissenschaften, 2001), 69–127.

38. See discussion and references in Hoffmeier, *Israel in Egypt*, 117–118; Manfred Bietak, *Avaris and Piramesse: Archaeological Exploration in the Eastern Nile Delta* (London: Oxford University Press, 1979); Bietak, "Tell ed-Dab'a," in *The Oxford Encyclopedia of Ancient Egypt*, ed. Donald Redford (New York: Oxford University Press, 2001), 351–354.

39. I owe this information to Kenneth Kitchen.

40. Donald Redford, "Exodus I 11," *VT* 13 (1963): 408–418.

41. Wolfgang Helck, "Ṯkw und Ramses-Stadt," *VT* 15 (1965).

42. Redford, "Exodus I 11," 403–407. See also Hoffmeier, *Israel in Egypt*, 119–121.

43. Yoshiyuki Muchiki, *Egyptian Proper Names and Loanwords in North-West Semitic*, SBL Dissertation Series 173 (Atlanta: Society of Biblical Literature, 1999). Kitchen has also pointed out that *samek* is the appropriate sibilant for the Hebrew writing of Egyptian *s*: Kenneth Kitchen, "Egyptians and Hebrews, from Ra'amses to Jericho," in *The Origin of Early Israel—Current Debate: Biblical, Historical and Archaeological Perspectives*, ed. Shmuel Ahituv and Eliezer D. Oren (Beer-Sheva: Ben-Gurion University of the Negev Press, 1998).

44. All of these Egyptian words containing an *s* that appear in Hebrew as *samek* were cited by me in *Israel in Egypt*, 118. All these examples have now been cited in Muchiki's above-mentioned study, *Egyptian Proper Names and Loanwords in North-West Semitic*, 207–258.

45. Redford, "Egyptological Perspective on the Exodus Narrative," 137–151.

46. John Van Seters, "The Geography of the Exodus," in *The Land That I Will Show You: Essays on the History and Archaeology of the Ancient Near East in Honour of J. Maxwell Miller*, ed. J. Andrew Dearman and M. Patrick Graham (Sheffield: JSOT Press, 2001), 255–276.

47. This study, interestingly, makes no mention of the absence of the prefix *pi* or the sibilant issue.

48. Israel Finkelstein and Neil Asher Silberman, *The Bible Unearthed: Archaeology's New Vision of Ancient Israel and the Origin of Its Sacred Texts* (New York: Free Press, 2001).

49. Niels Peter Lemche, "Is It Still Possible to Write a History of Israel?" *SJOT* 8 (1994), 172–174.

50. Edward Wente, "Rameses," in *ABD* 5: 617–618.

51. Manfred Bietak, *Tell el-Dab'a* (Vienna: Österreichischen Akademie der Wissenschaften Wien, 1975), 2:219–220; updated in Bietak, "Comments on the 'Exodus'," in *Egypt, Israel, Sinai: Archaeological and Historical Relationships in the Bible Period*, ed. A. F. Rainey (Tel Aviv: Tel Aviv University Press, 1987), 164.

52. Manfred Bietak, "Der Aufenthalt Israels in Agypten und der Zeitpunkt der Landnahme aus heutiger archaologischer Sicht, *ÄL* 10 (2000): 179–186.

53. Geoffrey Graham, "Tanis," in *Oxford Encyclopedia of Ancient Egypt*, ed. Donald Redford (New York: Oxford University Press, 2001), 348–350.

54. According to one scholar, this psalm dates to the period of the United Monarchy in Israel: Antony F. Campbell, "Psalm 78: A Contribution to the Theology of Tenth-Century Israel," *CBQ* 41 (1979): 51–79.

55. Van Seters, "Geography of the Exodus," 256.

56. James Hoffmeier, *Sacred in the Vocabulary of Ancient Egypt*, OBO 59 (Fribourg: University of Fribourg, 1985), 208–220.

57. Paul Barguet, *Le temple d'Amon-Rê à Karnak* (Cairo: IFAO, 1962), 37–38.

58. This translation is my own; cf. Hoffmeier, *Sacred in the Vocabulary of Ancient Egypt*, 215.

59. Text in Georges Posener, *La première domination perse en Égypte* (Cairo: IFAO, 1936), 14, lines 17–18. Translation in Hoffmeier, *Sacred in the Vocabulary of Ancient Egypt*, 217.

60. Eric Uphill, *The Temples of Per-Ramesses* (Warminster: Aris and Phillips, 1984).

61. Edgar Pusch, "Piramesse," in *Oxford Encyclopedia of Ancient Egypt*, ed. Donald Redford (New York: Oxford University Press, 2001); Edgar Pusch, "Towards a Map of Piramesse," *EA* 14 (1999): 13–15.

62. Alan H. Gardiner, *Late-Egyptian Stories*, Bibliotheca Aegyptiaca 1 (Brussels: Édition de la Fondation Égyptologique Reine Élisabeth, 1932).

63. KRI 2 (1979): 490.8–10; and *RITA* 2 (1993): 310.

64. Gardiner, "Geography of the Exodus," 211.

65. In the writing of *sḫt ḏꜥnt* in the Memphis temple inscription from Ramesses II's time, the city determinative is written; KRI 2 (1979): 490.8–10, and *RITA* 2 (1993): 310. This sign does not determine how large this settlement was, but it was probably relatively small, and after decades of excavations at San el-Hagar, the French have discovered no in situ New Kingdom remains.

66. Naville, "Geography of the Exodus," 32–36; Redford, "Exodus I 11," 403; Kitchen, "Egyptians and Hebrews, from Ra'amses to Jericho," 72.

67. Note the title of Naville, *Shrine of the Saft el-Henneh and the Land of Goshen*.

68. The references to Shur are found in Gen. 16:7, 20:1, 25:18; Exod. 15:22; 1 Sam. 15:7, 27:8. Most references indicate that Shur is a wilderness (*miḏbār*), and the way through it, presumably, is where the Way of Shur (*derek*) derived its name. Cf. Barry Beitzel, *The Moody Atlas of Bible Lands* (Chicago: Moody Press, 1985), 86–87, map 25; and *HAB*, 56–57.

69. Naville, *Store-City of Pithom and the Route of the Exodus*.

70. Petrie, *Hyksos and Israelite Cities*; W. M. F. Petrie, *Egypt and Israel* (London: Society for Promoting Christian Knowledge, 1911).

71. This is an important point, because Ramesside-period blocks, statues, and stelae made their way all over Egypt (including Tanis!) at later times. Only when there are ceramic or architectural remains that can be dated to Ramesside times can a certain date be assured. Hans Goedicke is the last Western scholar to work at Tell Retabeh, although publication of the material from the 1970s has not yet appeared. But he has written convincingly that this site was the major Ramesside-period defense structure in the Wadi Tumuliat. See Hans Goedicke, "Ramesses II and the Wadi Tumilat," *VA* 3 (1987): 13–24.

72. Manfred Bietak, "Comments on the 'Exodus,'" in *Egypt, Israel, Sinai: Archaeological and Historical Relationships in the Biblical Period*, ed. A. F. Rainey (Tel Aviv: Tel Aviv University Press, 1987), 168–169.

73. John S. Holladay, *Tell el-Maskhuta: Preliminary Report on the Wadi Tumilat Project 1978–1979*, Part 3, *Cities of the Delta*, ARCE Reports 6 (Malibu: Undena Publications, 1982).

74. John S. Holladay, "Pithom," *Oxford Encyclopedia of Ancient Egypt* (2000), 3:50–53; Holladay, "Tell el-Maskhuta," in *Encyclopedia of the Archaeology of Ancient Egypt*, ed. Kathryn A. Bard (London: Routledge, 1999).

75. Holladay, "Tell el-Maskhuta," 786.

76. Van Seters, "Geography of the Exodus," 255–276.

77. Ibid., 255–260.

78. Ibid., 260.

79. Ibid.

80. Georges Posener, *Ostraca hiératiques littéraires de Deir el-Médineh I/3* (Cairo: IFAO, 1938), 20, plates 43–43a.

81. KRI 2 (1979): 463. The 1987 conference was on the Exodus, sponsored by the Near East Archaeological Society on the occasion of the exhibit on Ramesses the Great at the Brooks Museum of Art. I also participated in that conference. The papers from that conference, unfortunately, were not published because of the untimely death of the organizer, Dr. James Power. Kitchen, "Egyptians and Hebrews, from Ra'amses to Jericho," 73.

82. Van Seters, "Geography of the Exodus," 262.

83. *LEM* 76.14; Hans Goedicke, "Papyrus Anastasi VI 51–61," *SAK* 14 (1987): 83–98; Goedicke, "Ramesses II and the Wadi Tumilat," 83–98.

84. Michael J. Fuller, "Tell el-Retaba: The Architectural and Depostional Sequence" (unpublished paper; Washington University, St. Louis, 1980). As of July 2003, Fuller had posted some of the information from his unpublished paper and photographs on a Web site, the address of which is http://www.stlcc.edu/fv/users/mfuller/Retaba/html.

85. Fuller, "Tell el-Retaba," 39–64.

86. Ibid., 22.

87. Ibid., 67–69.

88. Holladay, "Tell el-Maskhuta," 786.

89. See the regional survey by Carol Redmount, "On an Egyptian/Asiatic Frontier: An Archaeological History of the Wadi Tumilat" (Ph.D. dissertation, University of Chicago, 1989).

90. Karol Myśliwiec, "Le naos de Pithom," *BIFAO* 78 (1978): 171–195.

91. Naville, *Store-City of Pithom and the Route of the Exodus*, plates 9–10.

92. The translations are my own.

93. The first occurrence uses *nṯr nfr* instead of *c3 nṯr*, as is found in line 25.

94. Lit. "in the face of."

95. Naville, *Store-City of Pithom and the Route of the Exodus*, 4–10. Again, notice the title of this volume.

96. Hans Goedike may be right in proposing that the repetition of the name of the fort may be the result of dittography; Goedicke, "Papyrus Anastasi VI 51–61." The translation is my own, based on text in *LEM*, 76.

97. Bietak, *Tell el-Dab'a*, 88–90; see figures 28–36, especially 37.

98. Ibid., figure 45.

99. The sign as Naville read it could also be read *sri*; Alan H. Gardiner, *Egyptian Grammar: Being an Introduction to the Study of Hieroglyphs*, 3rd ed. (London: Oxford University Press, 1957), 443, sign A-17.

100. The text of this statue is found in Naville, *Store-City of Pithom and the Route of the Exodus*, 15–16, plate 4.

101. I say apparently because military titles from the Third Intermediate Period have not been studied thoroughly. Examination of New Kingdom military titles may offer help. It is thought that *idnw* + a military term like "chariotry" or "army" is definitely a military title of a high-ranking officer. But when *idnw* stands alone, it is uncertain whether the official is connected to the military or not; see Alan R. Schulman,

Military Rank, Title and Organization in the Egyptian New Kingdom, Münchner Ägyptologische Studien 6 (Berlin: Verlag Bruno Hessling, 1964), 34–35. However, the title *idnw ṯkw* is attested in Pap. Anastasi V, 25.2 and 26.2, with what can only have military intent (cf. *LEM*, 70–71). It seems likely that the Twenty-second Dynasty officer was the same as its earlier counterpart. The second title might be translated as "commander of Pharaoh."

102. Naville, *Store-City of Pithom and the Route of the Exodus*, plate 4, A, lines 1 and 3.

103. Holladay, "Tell el-Maskhuta," 786.

104. Naville, *Store-City of Pithom and the Route of the Exodus*, plate 3, B.

105. Kitchen, "Egyptians and Hebrews, from Ra'amses to Jericho," 76.

106. Herodotus, *Histories*, trans. A. D. Godley, vol. 1 (Cambridge: Harvard University Press, 1926).

107. Alan Lloyd, "Necho and the Red Sea: Some Considerations," *JEA* 63 (1977), 142 n. 1.

108. Naville, "Geography of the Exodus," 32–36.

109. Petrie, *Hyksos and Israelite Cities*, plates 19 and 20.

110. Eric Uphill, "Pithom and Ramses: Their Location and Significance," *JNES* 27 (1968): 291–316; and *JNES* 28 (1969): 15–39.

111. Uphill, "Pithom and Ramses: Their Location and Significance," *JNES* 27 (1968): 294–296.

112. Hoffmeier, *Israel in Egypt*, 116.

113. See ibid., figure 11.

114. On the use of mud brick in Egyptian architecture, see A. J. Spencer, *Brick Architecture in Ancient Egypt* (Warminster: Aris and Phillips, 1979). Concerning palaces, see W. Stevenson Smith and W. Kelley Simpson, *The Art and Architecture of Ancient Egypt* (New York: Penguin, 1981).

115. Karnak Temple is an excellent example of reusing blocks from earlier temples to establish sacred continuity between the earlier temples and their replacement. For a study of this phenomenon, see Gun Björkman, *Kings at Karnak: A Study of the Treatment of the Monuments of Royal Predecessors in the Early New Kingdom*, vol. 2 (Uppsala: Uppsala Studies in Ancient Mediterranean and Near Eastern Civilizations, 1971).

116. Gardiner, "The Ancient Military Road between Egypt and Palestine," 99; *RITA* 1 (1993): 13–14.

117. Redford, "Egyptological Perspective on the Exodus Narrative," 140–141.

118. Evidence and ideas not presented in this section were introduced in *Israel in Egypt*, 179–182.

119. It is also suggested that rather than being the name of a route, the Ways of Horus (*w3t ḥr*) is the name of the region; see Dominique Valbelle, "La (Les) route(s)-d'Horus," in *Hommages à Jean Leclant*, Bibliothèque d'Études 106 (Cairo: IFAO, 1994).

120. Mohamed Abd el-Maksoud, *Tell Hebuoa (1981–1991)* (Paris: Éditions Recherche sur les Civilisations, 1998); Abd el-Maksoud, "Tjarou, porte de l'oriente," in *Le Sinaï durant l'antiquité et le moyen age*, ed. Charles Bonnet and Dominique Valbelle (Paris: Errance, 1998), 61–65.

121. Muchiki, *Egyptian Proper Names and Loanwords in North-West Semitic*, 232–233.

122. Ibid., 233. The word may well have entered the Egyptian lexicon earlier in the New Kingdom, but presently, the reign of Ramesses II is the period for the earliest witness.

123. KB, 656.

124. Holladay, "Tell el-Maskhuta," 787.

125. Gardiner, *Egyptian Grammar*, 513. See also Kenneth Kitchen, "The Physical Text of Merneptah's Victory Hymn (the 'Israel Stela')," *JSSEA* 24 (1994): 71–76.

126. Kitchen, "Egyptians and Hebrews, from Ra'amses to Jericho," 73.

127. The texts of these are in *LEM*.

128. Kitchen, "Egyptians and Hebrews, from Ra'amses to Jericho," 74–75.

129. Helck, "Ṯkw und Ramses-Stadt," 35–48.

130. The text is in *LEM*, 166. The term for the runaways is *b3k*, which can be variously translated, as servant, slave, or worker: *CDME* 78–79. In a translation of this passage published in 2002, James Allen renders *b3k* as "workers." See Allen in "A Report of Escaped Laborers," *COS* 3, 16.

131. Gardiner considered the dating of the text to be suspect because the distance traveled in the course of one day was too great. He rightly pointed out that these Anastasi Papyri are schoolboy texts and may have contained mistakes. In defense of the dating, it should be pointed out that in 1924 Gardiner still thought that Pi-Ramesses was located at Pelusium, which would have made the trek even longer, and the routing made little sense, going from Pelusium south to Tjeku, only to make a U-turn and return back up to the Ways of Horus to pass by the Migdol of Seti I. To get around this problem, Gardiner proposed the departure point of Ka-Kem-Wer was closer to Memphis or Heliopolis (cf. Gardiner, "Geography of the Exodus," 89–91). Now that Pi-Ramesses is known to be at Qantir, travel from the capital to Tjeku could be achieved in one day, especially by chariot, and the dating need not be incorrect.

132. Chariot travel across the desert between the Delta and Wadi Tumilat might appear to have posed a challenge, but this possibility cannot be ruled out.

133. *LEM*, 76.

134. It is unclear to me why Allen's translation omits the word *mḥty* (north).

135. Gardiner, "Ancient Military Road between Egypt and Palestine," 109–110.

136. Ricardo A. Caminos, *Late-Egyptian Miscellanies* (London: Oxford University Press, 1954), 257; Edward Bleiberg, "The Location of Pithom and Succoth," in *Egyptological Miscellanies: A Tribute to Professor Ronald J. Williams*, ed. J. K. Hoffmeier and E. S. Meltzer, Ancient World 6 (Chicago: Ares, 1983), 24.

137. Kenneth Kitchen, "Ramesside Egypt's Delta Defense Routes the SE Sector," in *Studi di Egittologia e di Antichita Puniche*, ed. E. Acquaro and S. Pernigotti (Pisa: Istituti Editoriali e Poligrafici Internationali, 1998), 33–38.

138. Ibid., 34–35.

139. The translation is my own; the text is published in Abd el-Maksoud, *Tell Hebuoa (1981–1991)*, 271.

140. Though it is not recognized in A. Erman and W. Grapow in *Wb* 3: 352. See KB, 344.

141. Ellen Morris, "The Architecture of Imperialism: An Investigation into the Role of Fortresses and Administrative Headquarters in New Kingdom Foreign Policy" (Ph.D. dissertation, University of Pennsylvania, 2001), 8, and 637.

142. Hyatt, *Exodus*, 147.

143. Van Seters, *Life of Moses*, 128–134.

144. Brevard Childs, *The Book of Exodus* (Louisville, Ky.: Westminster, 1974), 219–220.

145. Propp, *Exodus 1–18*, 49–50, 461.

146. Henri Cazelles, "Les localizations de l'exode et la critique litteraire," *RB* 62 (1955): 358–359. He thinks that a mispronunciation of *ḫtm* may have resulted in the writing of *'tm*. J. Simons favors the connection between Egyptian *ḫtm* and *'tm*: J. Simons, *The Geographical and Topographical Texts of the Old Testament* (Leiden: Brill, 1959), 247. Most recently, see John Currid, *Ancient Egypt and the Old Testament* (Grand Rapids, Mich.: Baker Books, 1997), 130.

147. Kitchen, "Egyptians and Hebrews, from Ra'amses to Jericho," 78.

148. Muchiki, *Egyptian Proper Names and Loanwords in North-West Semitic*, 230.

149. P. Weimer, *Die Meerwundererzählung. Eine Redakionskritische Anallyse von Ex 13,17–14,31*, ÄAT 9 (Wiesbaden: Otto Harrassowitz, 1985), 264–265; Manfred Görg, "Etham und Pithom," *BN* 51 (1990): 9–10.

150. Muchiki, *Egyptian Proper Names and Loanwords in North-West Semitic*, 230.

151. Kenneth Kitchen, *On the Reliability of the Old Testament* (Grand Rapids, Mich.: Eerdmans, 2003), 259.

152. Alan H. Gardiner, *AEO*, 180–182.

153. In the Twelfth Dynasty, Sinuhe's day, Sneferu was venerated and worshipped, as can be seen in a stela from Serabit el-Khadim; see Alan H. Gardiner, T. Eric Peet, and Jaroslav Černý, *The Inscriptions of Sinai* (London: Egypt Exploration Society, 1955), no. 104.

154. KB, 101.

155. Hermann Kees, *Ancient Egypt: A Cultural Topography* (Chicago: University of Chicago Press, 1961), 113–114; Carol Redmount, "The Wadi Tumilat and the Canal of the Pharaohs," *JNES* 54 (1995): 127–135.

156. Amihai Sneh, Tuvia Weissbrod, and Itamar Perath, "Evidence for an Ancient Egyptian Frontier Canal," *American Scientist* 63 (1975): 542–548.

157. Ibid., 6A and p. 545.

158. Karl Butzer, *Early Hydraulic Civilization in Egypt*, Prehistoric Archeology and Ecology Series (Chicago: University of Chicago, 1976), 46 n. 2.

159. Holladay, *Tell el-Maskhuta*, 2–3; Eliezer Oren, "Migdol: A New Fortress on the Edge of the Eastern Nile Delta," *BASOR* 256 (1984): figure 2, p. 8.

160. Alan Lloyd, *Herodotus Book II, Commentary 99–182* (Leiden: Brill, 1988), 157; Lloyd, "Necho and the Red Sea," 142–155.

161. Naville, *Store-City of Pithom and the Route of the Exodus*, 2.

162. Pierre Montet, *Géographie de l'Égypte ancienne* I (Paris: Impremerie Nationale, 1957) 1:218–219.

163. Redmount, "On an Egyptian/Asiatic Frontier," 199–200; Redmount, "Wadi Tumilat and the Canal of the Pharaohs," 127–135.

164. E. M. El Shazly, "The Ostracinic Branch, a Proposed Old Branch of the River Nile," *DE* 7 (1987): 69–78.

165. Redmount, "Wadi Tumilat and the Canal of the Pharaohs," 133–134.

166. Georges Posener, "Le canal du Nil à la Mer Rouge avant les Ptolémées," *Cd'É* 13 (1938): 259–273.

167. Sneh, Weissbrod, and Perath, "Evidence for an Ancient Egyptian Frontier Canal," 546. Although this idea is only hinted at in their important study of the canal, Weissbrod has since studied the tectonics in the region and proposed this idea, which he communicated to me orally.

168. KB, 951.

169. Hoffmeier, *Israel in Egypt*, figure 2 and pp. 188–189.

170. Benjamin E. Scolnic, "A New Working Hypothesis for the Identification of Migdol," in *The Future of Biblical Archaeology*, ed. James K. Hoffmeier and Alan Millard (Grand Rapids, Mich.: Eerdmans, 2004), 97–99.

171. Umberto Cassuto, *A Commentary on the Book of Exodus*, trans. I. Abrahams (Jerusalem: Magnes Press, 1951), 159.

172. Simons, *Geographical and Topographical Texts of the Old Testament*, 242.

173. Linant de Bellefonds, *Mémoires sur les principaux travaux d'utilité publique executés en Égypte depuis la plus haute antiquité jusqu'à nos jours*, ed. Arthus Bertrand (Paris: Librairie Scientifique et Maritime, 1872–1873).

174. Sneh, Weissbrod, and Perath, "Evidence for an Ancient Egyptian Frontier Canal," 546.

175. Ibid., 542–545.

176. Otto Eissfeldt, *Baal Zaphon, Zeus Kasios und der Durchzug der Israeliten Durchs Meer* (Halle: Niemeyer, 1932); C. S. Jarvis, *Yesterday and to-Day in Sinai* (Edinburgh: William Blackwood and Sons, 1933), 161; and, for example, Siegfried Herrmann, *Israel in Egypt*, Studies in Biblical Theology 27 (London: SCM Press, 1973), 56–64.

177. D. Neev, N. Bakler, and K. O. Emery, *Mediterranean Coasts of Israel and Sinai: Holocene Tectonism from Geology, Geophysics, and Archaeology* (New York: Taylor and Francis, 1987), 83–84. See the extensive bibliography of Neev's work in North Sinai on pp. 121–122.

178. Eliezer Oren, "The 'Ways of Horus' in North Sinai," in *Egypt, Israel, Sinai: Archaeological and Historical Relationships in the Biblical Period*, ed. A. F. Rainey (Tel Aviv: Tel Aviv University Press, 1987), 79.

179. Pau Figueras, *From Gaza to Pelusium: Materials for the Historical Geography of North Sinai and Southwestern Palestine (332 BCE–640 CE)*, Beer-Sheva Studies by the Department of Bible and Ancient Near East 14 (Beer-Sheva: Ben-Gurion University of the Negev Press, 2000), 9–11.

180. Davies, "Wilderness Itineraries: A Comparative Study," 46–83; Davies, *Way of the Wilderness;* Davies, "Wilderness Itineraries and Recent Archaeological Research," 161–175.

CHAPTER 5

1. For a complete treatment of the source-critical and textual problems raised by the differences in the biblical manuscript traditions, see James Hoffmeier, *Israel in Egypt: The Evidence for the Authenticity of the Exodus Tradition* (New York: Oxford University Press, 1997), chapter 9.

2. The references in Isa. 10 and 11 are clearly early in date, whereas Isa. 63:11 is usually attributed by some scholars to so-called Deutero-Isaiah, and are dated to the exilic period.

3. D. N. Freedman and F. M. Cross, *Studies in Ancient Yahwistic Poetry*, SBL Dissertation Series 21 (Missoula, Mont.: Society of Biblical Literature, 1975), 31–33. For a more complete discussion of the dating of this song and a detailed bibliography, see *Israel in Egypt*, 201–203.

4. Georg Fohrer, *History of Israelite Religion*, trans. David Green (Nashville, Tenn.: Abingdon, 1972), 72.

5. John Roberts Towers, "The Red Sea," *JNES* 18 (1959): 151.

6. William W. Hallo, "The Limits of Skepticism," *JAOS* 110, no. 2 (1990): 189. He does add to the latter point, "but we can hope to know more than they chose to *tell*."

7. James Hoffmeier, "The Arm of God versus the Arm of Pharaoh in the Exodus Narratives," *Biblica* 67 (1986): 378–387.

8. Ibid., 386–387.

9. Richard Walsh, *Mapping Myths of Biblical Interpretation* (Sheffield: Sheffield Academic Press, 2001). See especially chapters 1 and 2.

10. Mircea Eliade, *Cosmos and History: The Myth of the Eternal Return* (New York: Harper Torchbooks, 1954), 104–105.

11. Ibid., 105.

12. Bertil Albrektson, *History and the Gods: An Essay on the Idea of Historical Events as Divine Manifestations in the Ancient Near East and Israel* (Lund: Gleerup, 1967).

13. Kenneth A. Kitchen. "The Battle of Qadesh—The Poem, or Literary Record," in *COS* 2:35–36.

14. James K. Hoffmeier, "The Gebel Barkal Stela of Thutmose III," in *COS* 2:17.

15. Richard H. Beal, "The Ten Year Annals of Great King Mursili of Hatti," *COS* 2:84. Mursili's texts are discussed in Albrektson, *History and the Gods*, 39ff.

16. H. W. F. Saggs, *The Encounter with the Divine in Mesopotamia and Israel* (London: Athlone, 1978).

17. For a recent study comparing it with Hebrew historiography, see Bill T. Arnold, "The Weidner Chronicle and the Idea of History," in *Faith, Tradition, and History*, ed. A. R. Millard, J. K. Hoffmeier, and D. W. Baker (Winona Lake, Ind.: Eisenbrauns, 1994), 129–148.

18. This problem is addressed in detail in my *Israel in Egypt*, chapter 9. Here I shall only review the main points.

19. KB, 652.

20. On the meaning of the Greek, see Henry Liddell and Robert Scott, *Greek-English Lexicon* (Oxford: Clarendon, 1968), 693.

21. H. Brugsch, *Hieroglyphische-Demotisches Wörterbuch IV* (Leipzig, 1868), 1,580–1,581; Max Müller, "A Contribution to the Exodus Geography," *PSBA* 10 (1888): 474; William Ward, "The Biconsonantal Root Sp and the Common Origin of Egyptian Čwf and the Hebrew Sup: Marsh (-Plant)," *VT* 24 (1974): 339–349; Yoshiyuki Muchiki, *Egyptian Proper Names and Loanwords in North-West Semitic*, ed. Michael Fox, SBL Dissertation Series 173 (Atlanta: Society of Biblical Literature, 1999), 251.

22. Alan H. Gardiner, *AEO*, 2:201.

23. Ibid., 201–202.

24. Leonard H. Lesko, ed., *A Dictionary of Late Egyptian* (Berkeley, Calif.: B. C. Scribe Publications, 1982), 1:168.

25. M. Vervenne, "The Lexeme *Sûph* and the Phrase *Yam Sûph*: A Brief Reflection on the Etymology and Semantics of a Key Word in the Hebrew Exodus Tradition," in *Immigration and Emigration within the Ancient Near East*, in *Festschrift E. Lipinska*, ed. K. van Lerberghe and A. Schooks (Leuven: Orientalia Louaniensia Analecta, 1995), 403–429. This article was published just after my *Israel in Egypt* went to press and thus I was unable to offer my critique of Vervenne's ideas.

26. Ibid., 427.

27. Ibid., 418 n. 74.

28. Ibid., 419.

29. In fairness to Vervenne, he does treat the Coptic versions of Exodus. I assume his lack of competence in Egyptian hieroglyphs from the fact that he does not discuss the Egyptian texts directly.

30. Alan H. Gardiner, *Egyptian Grammar: Being an Introduction to the Study of Hieroglyphs*, 3rd ed. (London: Oxford University Press, 1957), 478.

31. *Wb* 5:359. Cf. Anastasi III, 2.11–12 = *LEM*, 22.13–14; Sallier I, 4.9 = *LEM*, 81.7.

32. Gardiner, *Egyptian Grammar*, 481.

33. Vervenne, "Lexeme *Sûph* and the Phrase *Yam Sûph*," 427.

34. *Yām* is written with the directional *h*, indicating toward *yām sûp̱*.

35. In the following paragraph there is a discussion of references to *p3 ṯwfy* in a Demotic text.

36. It should be noted that Exodus 10:19 is usually attributed to J; see J. Philip Hyatt, *Exodus* (London: Marshall, Morgan, and Scott, 1971), 48.

37. Galit Dayan, "The Term '*P3 Ṯwf*' in the Speigelberg Papyrus," in *Jerusalem Studies in Egyptology*, ed. Irene Shirun-Grumach, ÄAT (Wiesbaden: Otto Harrassowitz, 1998), 133–135.

38. Ibid., 135.

39. Sarah I. Groll, "The Egyptian Background of the Exodus and the Crossing of the Reed Seas: A New Reading of Papyrus Anastasi VIII," in *Jerusalem Studies in Egyptology*, ed. Irene Shirun-Grumach, ÄAT (Wiesbaden: Otto Harrassowitz, 1998), 173–192; Groll, "Historical Background to the Exodus: Papyrus Anastasi VIII," in *Gold of Praise: Studies on Ancient Egypt in Honor of Edward F. Wente*, ed. Emily Teeter and John Larson, Studies in Ancient Oriental Civilization (Chicago: Oriental Institute, 1999), 159–162; Groll, "The Historical Background to the Exodus: Papyrus Anastasi VIII," in *Études égyptologiques et bibliques à la mémoire du Père B. Couroyer*, ed. Marcel Sigrist, *Cahiers de la Revue Biblique* (Paris, Cahiers de la Revue Biblique 36, 1997), 109–114.

40. Groll, "Historical Background to the Exodus," 159–160.

41. Ibid. 177 = Anastasi VIII, r. I, lines 6–8 and 16.

42. Anastasi VIII, r. II, line 10 = Groll, "Egyptian Background of the Exodus," 179.

43. Ibid., 191.

44. Ibid., 174–175, 191.

45. Ibid., 191–192.

46. Ibid., 192.

47. Vervenne, "Lexeme *Sûph* and the Phrase *Yam Sûph*," 424–425.

48. Bernard Batto, "The Reed Sea: *Requiscat in Pace*," *JBL* 102 (1983): 27–35.

49. Ahlström has subsequently argued for such a view. For my critique of Batto and Ahlström, see *Israel in Egypt*, 203–206.

50. Hoffmeier, *Israel in Egypt*, chapter 9.

51. Hans Goedicke, "Papyrus Anastasi VI 51–61," *SAK* 14 (1987): 96.

52. Hoffmeier, *Israel in Egypt*, 204.

53. Ibid., 204. Vervenne also discusses the Coptic versions and rejects the meaning "lake of reeds" (cf. Vervenne, "Lexeme *Sûph* and the Phrase *Yam Sûph*," 412–416.

54. James Hoffmeier, "The Possible Origins of the Tent of Purification in the Egyptian Funerary Cult," *SAK* 9 (1981): 167–177.

55. Janet Johnson, *Thus Wrote 'Ankhsheshonqy: An Introductory Grammar of Demotic*, Studies in Ancient Oriental Civilization 45 (Chicago: Oriental Institute, 1986), 4–5.

56. On the centrality of the sea crossing to the exodus tradition, see Samuel E. Lowenstamm, *The Evolution of the Exodus Tradition*, trans. B. Schwartz (Jerusalem: Magnes Press, 1992), 233ff.

57. Amihai Sneh and Tuvia Weissbrod, "Nile Delta: The Defunct Pelusiac Branch Identified," *Science* 180 (1973): 59–61; Manfred Bietak, *Tell el-Dab'a* (Vienna: Österreichischen Akademie der Wissenschaften Wien, 1975), 2:47–177.

58. For a picture of such an area, see Hoffmeier, *Israel in Egypt*, 76, figure 29.

59. Hoffmeier, *Israel in Egypt*, 207–212.

60. Pierre Montet, *Géographie de l'Égypte ancienne* (Paris: Impremerie Nationale, 1957), 1:216.

61. Since *p3 ṯwfy* is not attested before the Nineteenth Dynasty, one wonders if *km wr* might have included the Ballah Lakes during earlier periods.

62. Translation is that of Ricardo Caminos, *Late-Egyptian Miscellanies* (London: Oxford University Press, 1954), 307. The text is found in *LEM*, 8.6–7.

63. Alan H. Gardiner, *Late-Egyptian Stories*, Bibliotheca Aegyptiaca 1 (Brussels: Édition de la Fondation Égyptologique Reine Élisabeth, 1932), 35.

64. R. O. Faulkner, E. F. Wente, and W. K. Simpson, *The Literature of Ancient Egypt: An Anthology of Stories, Instructions, and Poetry* (New Haven: Yale University Press, 1973), 135.

65. The Arabic name of the site preserves the name of the the Pharaonic toponym. For the equation of Tell el-Balamun with the Island of Amun (*p3 iw n imn*), see Gardiner, *AEO*, 2:180–181*.

66. Ibid., 201.

67. Goedicke, "Papyrus Anastasi VI 51–61," 97.

68. Bietak, *Tell el-Dab'a*, 136–137. See also plates 10 and 23.

69. *LEM*, 21–22. Translations are available in Caminos, *Late-Egyptian Miscellanies*, 73–74. See, most recently, James Allen's translation in *COS* 3: 15. I am grateful to my colleague Dr. Lawson Younger, associate editor of the three *COS* volumes, for providing me with a copy of Allen's translation prior to the publication of the volume.

70. My own translation.

71. Groll, "Egyptian Background of the Exodus," 174–176.

72. Ibid., 173, 184.

73. Ellen Morris, "The Architecture of Imperialism: An Investigation into the Role of Fortresses and Administrative Headquarters in New Kingdom Foreign Policy" (Ph.D. dissertation, University of Pennsylvania, 2001), 489.

74. See Morris's index for scores of examples of this title: ibid., 1,199.

75. Gardiner, *AEO* 1:24.

76. Ibid., 2:202*.

77. Ibid., 2:122* and 44–45*.

78. Ibid., 2:201*–202*.

79. Ibid., 2:202*.

80. Vervenne, "Lexeme *Sûph* and the Phrase *Yam Sûph*," 419.

81. Bietak, *Tell el-Dab'a*, plates 10 and 23.

82. Ibid., 137, and plates 10 and 23. Others think that Shi-hor could be the Pelusiac branch of the Nile or Wadi el-Arish. See Arnold Betz, "Shihor," in *ABD* 5:1,212.

83. Bietak, *Tell el-Dab'a*, 137. See also Manfred Bietak, "Comments on the Exodus," in *Egypt, Israel, Sinai: Archaeological and Historical Relationships in the Biblical Period*, ed. A. F. Rainey (Tel Aviv: Tel Aviv University Press: 1987), 167.

84. Manfred Bietak, *Avaris: The Capital of the Hyksos: Recent Excavations at Tell el-Dab'a* (London: British Museum, 1996), 2.

85. Mohamed Abd el-Maksoud, "Tjarou, porte de l'orient," in *Le Sinaï durant l'antiquité et le moyen age*, ed. Charles Bonnet and Dominique Valbelle (Paris: Errance, 1998), 64–65.

86. These excavations are ongoing, but I have visited the site many times and have seen the port. Brief mention of the discovery of the Greco-Roman period at Tell Abu Sefêh has been made by Abd el-Maksoud, ibid.

87. This compares favorably with Bietak's map from 1975 (Bietak, *Tell el-Dab'a*, plate 23). The Israeli occupation of Sinai during the time when Bietak prepared his map would have prevented him from actually visiting Sinai during this period.

88. Gardiner, *AEO* 2:180–181.

89. The sibilant *š* in Middle and Late Egyptian becomes *th* in Coptic; Gardiner, *AEO* 2:66*.

90. Ibid., 2:35*.

91. Ibid.

92. Ibid., 2:177*.

93. Muchiki, *Egyptian Proper Names and Loanwords in North-West Semitic*, 251.

94. Eliezer Oren, "The 'Ways of Horus' in North Sinai," in *Egypt, Israel, Sinai: Archaeological and Historical Relationships in the Biblical Period*, ed. Anson F. Rainey (Tel Aviv: Tel Aviv University Press, 1986), 76; and "Sinai, Northern Sinai," in *NEAEHL*, 4:1,386–1,396.

95. Oren, " 'Ways of Horus' in North Sinai," 77–112.

96. Max Müller, "A Contribution to the Exodus Geography," *PSBA* 10 (1888), 467, 476–477.

97. KB, 659. I wish to thank Anson Rainey for drawing my attention to this possible etymology for Egyptian Tjaru.

98. Ibid.

99. The Semitic *samek* when it appears in Egyptian is written with *ṯ* (e.g., Succoth = Tjeku), and Semitic words with *lamed* are written in Egyptian with *r* (e.g., *isr3yr* = Israel), as the Egyptian language has no *lamed.*

100. William F. Albright, "The Town of Selle (Zaru) in the Amarnah Tablets," *JEA* 10 (1923): 6–8.

101. William L. Moran, *The Amarna Letters* (Baltimore: Johns Hopkins University Press, 1992), 331.

102. Gardiner, *AEO* 2:202*–203*.

103. For a recent critical edition of the text, see Wolfgang Helck, *Die Lehre des Dw3-Ḫtjj*, ed. Wolfgang Helck, Kleine Ägyptische Texte (Wiesbaden: Otto Harrassowitz, 1970), lines 3, 9f. Translation in Miriam Lichtheim, *Ancient Egyptian Literature I* (Berkeley: University of California Press, 1976), 2:185.

104. Wolfgang Helck, *Historisch-Biographische Texte der 2. Zwischenzeit und Neue Texte der 18. Dynastie*, ed. Wolfgang Helck, Kleine Inschriften (Wiesbaden: Otto Harrassowitz, 1975), 78, no. 113.

105. James K. Hoffmeier, "The Annals of Thutmose III," in *COS* 2:8.

106. Epigraphic Survey, *The Battle Reliefs of King Sety I*, University of Chicago Oriental Institute Publications 4 (Chicago: Oriental Institute, 1986), plate 6.

107. Kenneth Kitchen, "Battle of Qadesh—the Poem, or Literary Record," 33.

108. Hans-Werner Fischer-Elfert, *Die satirische Streitschrift des Papyrus Anastasi* (Wiesbaden: Otto Harrassowitz, 1983), 150–151.

109. The restoration of *ḥr* is quite certain. See Hans-Werner Fischer-Elfert, *Die Satirische Streischrift des Papyrus Anastasi I: Übersetzung und Kommentar*, ed. Wolfgang Helck, Ägyptische Abhandlungen 44 (Wiesbaden: Otto Harrassowitz, 1986), 232. Translation here by Edward Wente, *Letters from Ancient Egypt* (Atlanta: Scholars Press, 1990), 109.

110. Roland de Vaux, *The Early History of Israel*, trans. David Smith (Philadelphia: Westminster, 1978), 378–379.

111. Nahum M. Sarna, *Exodus*, ed. Nahum M. Sarna, The JPS Torah Commentary (Philadelphia: Jewish Publication Society, 1991), 69. Similarly, see Hyatt, *Exodus*, 149.

112. C. Küthmann, *Die Ostgrenze Aegyptens* (Leipzig, 1911), 38ff.

113. Alan H. Gardiner, "The Ancient Military Road between Egypt and Palestine," *JEA* 6 (1920): 99.

114. Alan H. Gardiner, *Egypt of the Pharaohs* (New York: Oxford University Press, 1962), 250.

115. W. M. F. Petrie, *Tanis, Part II: Nebesheh (AM), and Defenneh (Tahpanhes)* (London: Egypt Exploration Society, 1888), 97–108. The inscriptions are available in KRI 1:105–107 and 2:402–403, and were commented upon in *RITA* 1:13–14.

116. Petrie, *Tanis, Part II*, 97–98.

117. J. Clédat, "Nécroples de Qantarah (fouilles de Mai 1914)," *RT* 38 (1916): 21–31. Clédat discovered a Roman-period cemetery at Qantara, but nothing from the New Kingdom period.

118. Oren, " 'Ways of Horus' in North Sinai," 113 n. 3.

119. I have this information as verbal communication from several Egyptian colleagues who worked at the site.

120. See *RITA* 1:13–14. Kitchen expresses doubts about this identification on the basis of early work by Griffiths and more recent investigation by Oren, even before the Egyptian excavations began.

121. Alessandra Nibbi, "The Problems of Sile and Tjaru," *DE* 14 (1989): 69–78; Claude Vanderslayen, "Tjarou," *GM* 136 (1993): 85–87.

122. Vanderslayen, "Tjarou," 85.

123. David O'Connor has recently observed that "Ahmose first took Sile on the Egypt-Sinai border, thus cutting off contact between Canaan and Avaris, and then besieged and finally captured Avaris"; David O'Connor, "The Hyksos Period in Egypt," in *The Hyksos: New Historical and Archaeological Perspectives*, ed. Eliezer Oren (Philadelphia: University Museum, 1997), 45.

124. Nibbi, "Problems of Sile and Tjaru," 73–75.

125. Ibid.; see her map, figure 1.

126. Ibid., 72–73.

127. Mohammed Abd el-Maksoud, "Une nouvelle fortresse sur la Route d'Horus: Tell Heboua 1986 (Nord Sinaï)," *CRIPEL* 9 (1987): 13–16.

128. Mohamed Abd el-Maksoud, *Tell Heboua (1981–1991): Enquête archéologique sur la Deuxième Période Intermédiare et la Nouvel Empire à l'extrémité orientale du Delta* (Paris: Éditions Recherche sur les Civilisations, 1998); and Abd el-Maksoud, "Tjarou, porte de l'orient," 61–65. In this second article he also discusses the Roman remains from Tell Abu Sefêh.

129. Hoffmeier, *Israel in Egypt*, 185–187.

130. Abd el-Maksoud is publishing this important text.

131. Abd el-Maksoud, *Tell Heboua (1981–1991)*, 35–44.

132. Abd el-Maksoud, "Tjarou, porte de L'orient," 61.

133. Daniel Stanley and Vincent Coutellier, "Late Quaternary Stratigraphy and Paleography of the Eastern Nile Delta, Egypt," *Marine Geology* 77 (1987): 257–275; D. J. Stanley and G. A. Goodfriend, "Rapid Strandplain Accretion in the Northern Nile Delta in the Nile Delta in the 9th Century AD, and the Demise of the Port of Pelusium," *Geology* 27, no. 2 (1999): 147–150. See also the geomorphological work of Bruno Marcolongo, "Évolution du paléo-environnement dans la partie orientale du delta du Nil depuis la transgression flandrienne (8000 B.P.)," *CRIPEL* 14 (1992): 23–31.

134. Stephen Moshier, associate professor of geology at Wheaton College, has worked with me in Sinai since 1998. He has consulted with Stanley and Goodfriend, who were helpful to us. Dr. Goodfriend was especially helpful in looking at our data. We were saddened to learn of his untimely death in 2003.

135. During the 2001 season, our geological team identified a distributary of the Nile that actually passed between Fields II and IV at Tell el-Borg. This branch also emptied into this same lake. For further discussion regarding this feature, see below.

136. Maryvonne, Chartier-Raymond and Claude Traunecker, "Reconnaissance archéologique à la pointe orientale du delta campagne 1992," *CRIPEL* 15 (1993): 15, figure 1.

137. Hoffmeier, *Israel in Egypt*, 78, figure 2.

138. Donald Redford, "Report on the 1993 and 1997 Seasons at Tell Qedwa," *JARCE* 35 (1998): 45–49.

139. Eliezer Oren, "Migdol: A New Fortress on the Edge of the Eastern Nile Delta," *BASOR* 256 (1984): 7–44. According to Stephen Moshier, sites from the Persian through Greco-Roman times are built along the eastern shore of this lagoon.

140. Epigraphic Survey, *The Battle Reliefs of King Sety I*, Plates 2, 4, 5, 6. For the text of Anastasi I, see Fischer-Elfert, *Die satirische Streitschrift des Papyrus anastasi.* For the recent translations, see Wente, *Letters from Ancient Egypt*, 98–110; and James Allen, "The Craft of the Scribe," in *COS* 3:9–14.

141. Gardiner, "Ancient Military Road between Egypt and Palestine," 99–116. For a recent study of this travel route during the Ptolemaic through Byzantine periods, see Pau Figueras, *From Gaza to Pelusium: Materials for the Historical Geography of North Sinai and Southwestern Palestine (332 BCE–640 CE)*, Beer-Sheva Studies by the Department of Bible and Ancient Near East 14 (Beer-Sheva: Ben-Gurion University of the Negev Press, 2000).

142. This site is probably "Tell el-Ahmar," as named by the Egyptian Antiquities Organization; see "Projet de sauvetage des sites antiques du Nord-Sinaï," *DE* 24 (1992): 7–12. In W.M.F. Petrie, *Tanis II, Nebesheh (Am), and Defenneh (Tahpanhes)*, 97–108, Griffiths commented on the small size of this site and its apparent insignificance (107). Tell Semout is apparently another name for this site. That this site is not the same Tell Hebua that is being excavated by the SCA, see Abd el-Maksoud, *Tell Heboua (1981–1991)*, 24.

143. A member of the East Frontier Archaeological project, Benjamin Scolnic, has written a thorough study of Migdol, examining all available sources; see Benjamin E. Scolnic, "A New Working Hypothesis for the Identification of Migdol," in *The Future of Biblical Archaeology*, ed. James K. Hoffmeier and Alan Millard (Grand Rapids, Mich.: Eerdmans, 2005), 91–120.

144. Moran, *Amarna Letters*, 292–293.

145. Gardiner, "Ancient Military Road between Egypt and Palestine," 108.

146. Alan H. Gardiner, "The Geography of the Exodus," in *Recueil d'études égyptologiques dediées à la Mémoire de Jean-François Champollion à l'occasion du centenaire de la lettre à M. Dacier* (Bibliothèque de l'École des Hautes Études, 1922), 212.

147. T. E. Peet, *Egypt and the Old Testament* (Liverpool: University of Liverpool, 1922), 142.

148. Henri Cazelles, "Les localizations de l'exode et la critique litteraire," *RB* 62 (1955): 343–345.

149. Siegfried Herrmann, *Israel in Egypt*, Studies in Biblical Theology 27 (London: SCM Press, 1973), 60; Scolnic, "New Working Hypothesis for the Identification of Migdol."

150. De Vaux, *Early History of Israel*, 379.

151. J. Simons, *The Geographical and Topographical Texts of the Old Testament* (Leiden: Brill, 1959), 248 n. 14.

152. *BASOR* 256 (1984), 35.

153. William G. Dever, *Who Were the Early Israelites and Where Did They Come From?* (Grand Rapids, Mich.: Eerdmans, 2003), 19.

154. Redford, "Report on the 1993 and 1997 Seasons at Tell Qedwa," 55, 57.

155. Oren, "Migdol: A New Fortress on the Edge of the Eastern Nile Delta," 34–35.

156. Ibid., 31, 35.

157. Jean Clédat, "Notes sur l'isthme de Suez," *BIFAO* 18 (1920): 167–197.

158. Mohamed Abd el-Maksoud, "Fouilles récentes au Nord-Sinaï sur le site de Tell el-Herr," *CRIPEL* 8 (1986): 15–16.

159. Dominique Valbelle and Giorio Nogara, "La fortreresse du IVe siècle avant J.-C. à Tell el-Herr (Nord-Sinaï)," *CRIPEL* 21 (2000): 53–66. I visited Tell el-Herr in April 2002, and Dr. Valbelle indicated that nothing earlier than Persian times had been found. Also see Dominique Valbelle, "The First Persian-Period Fortress at Tell el-Herr," *EA* 18 (2001): 12–14.

160. *ANET*, 292. For references from the Greco-Roman period, see Figueras, *From Gaza to Pelusium*, 202.

161. *RITA* 1, 14.

162. Marcolongo, "Évolution du paléo-environnement dans la partie orientale du delta du Nil depuis la transgression Flandrienne (8000 B.P.)," 23–31. See especially figure 1, which shows a branch of the Nile passing between Hebua I and II before turning north and passing by the coastal ridge. A map based on this study by Marcolongo was included in Hoffmeier, *Israel in Egypt*, 73, figure 22. Now Bietak also believes that the Nile passed between these sites: Bietak, *Avaris*, figure 1.

163. D. Valbelle, F. Le Saout, M. Chartier-Raymond, M. Abd el-Samie, C. Traunecker, G. Wagner, J.-Y. Carrez-Maratray, and P. Zignani, "Reconnaissance archéologique à la pointe orientale du delta: Rapport préliminaire sur les saisons 1990 et 1991," *CRIPEL* 14 (1992): 17. A drawing of the pillar and a brief discussion of it is in Chartier-Raymond and Traunecker, "Reconnaissance archéologique à la pointe orientale du delta campagne 1992," 68.

164. I was able to visit Hebua II during the excavations in May 1999 and saw some of this material firsthand. The excavator has written a master's thesis in which he suggests that this site marks the second fort in the sequence, that is, the Dwelling of the Lion (see Abdul Rahman al-Ayedi, "Tharu: The Starting Point on the 'Ways of Horus'" [master's thesis, University of Toronto, 2000]). He claims that this Ramesside-period fort was built on the remains of earlier Hyksos-period occupation.

165. Dominique Valbelle and François Le Saout, "Les archives Clédat sur le Nord-Sinaï," *CRIPEL* 20 (1999): 71–73.

166. Oren, "'Ways of Horus' in North Sinai," 79.

167. James K. Hoffmeier, "Tell el-Borg in North Sinai," *EA* 20 (Spring 2002): 18–20; Hoffmeier and Mohamed Abd el-Maksoud, "A New Military Site on the 'Ways of Horus'—Tell el-Borg 1999–2001: A Preliminary Report," *JEA* 88 (2002): 169–197.

168. For some examples, see Epigraphic Survey, *The Battle Reliefs of King Sety I*. Numerous examples in W. Wreszinski, *Atlas zur altaegyptischen Kulturgesichte* (Leipzig: J. C. Hinrichs, 1935–1941).

169. Compare the Tell el-Borg piece with Epigraphic Survey, *Battle Reliefs of King Sety I*, plates 2, 4, 5, 6.

170. Ibid.; see plate 3, left side.

171. This piece is also carved on another surface and with a different orientation, showing the feet of a deity on a pedestal. At this point it is impossible to say which surface was carved first, but this block was clearly reused, which is not uncommon in ancient Egypt.

172. Alan R. Schulman, *Military Rank, Title and Organization in the Egyptian New Kingdom*, Münchner Ägyptologische Studien 6 (Berlin: Verlag Bruno Hessling, 1964), 30.

173. Alfred Lucas and J. R. Harris, *Ancient Egyptian Materials and Industries*, 4th ed. (London: Histories and Mysteries of Man, 1962; reprint, 1989), 50. In the excavations of the Akhenaten Temple Project in 1975 and 1977, in which I participated as a graduate student of Dr. Donald Redford, several reused fired bricks were discovered with the cartouche of "Men-kheper-re the first Priest of Amun" stamped on them (cf. Donald Redford, "Preliminary Report of the First Season of Excavation in East Karnak 1975–76," *JARCE* 14 (1977): plate X, nos. 1, 3, 5). This Twenty-first Dynasty priest-king ruled from 1045 to 992 B.C.

174. Hoffmeier and Abd el-Maksoud, "New Military Site on the 'Ways of Horus,'" 194–195.

175. KB, 492; *Wb* 2, 164.

176. Giacomo Cavillier, "The Ancient Military Road between Egypt and Palestine Reconsidered: A Reassessment," *GM* 185 (2001): 23–31.

177. Some of the scene has actually deteriorated during the past century. Now lost to us is the depiction of the Migdol of Menmaatre and the Dwelling of the Lion. But their presence was recorded by earlier epigraphers, so there is no doubt of their original placement or their names. Cf. Gardiner, "Ancient Military Road between Egypt and Palestine," 113; Epigraphic Survey, *Battle Reliefs of King Sety I*, 9–22.

178. Gardiner, "Ancient Military Road between Egypt and Palestine," 104.

179. Epigraphic Survey, *Battle Reliefs of King Sety I*, 16–17.

180. Amihai Sneh, Tuvia Weissbrod, and Itamar Perath, "Evidence for an Ancient Egyptian Frontier Canal," *American Scientist* 63 (1975): 542–548. See also my extensive discussion of the canal in *Israel in Egypt*, chapter 7.

181. In a personal communication, Eliezer Oren has indicated that he too thinks this feature is of a first-millennium date.

182. Chartier-Raymond and Traunecker, "Reconnaissance archéologique à la pointe orientale du delta campagne 1992," figures 2 and 3.

183. Epigraphic Survey, *Battle Reliefs of King Sety I*, 17. Morris, "Architecture of Imperialism," 502.

184. Morris, "Architecture of Imperialism," 502.

185. Fischer-Elfert, *Die Satirische Streitschrift des Papyrus Anastasi*, 150–151. Translation in Wente, *Letters from Ancient Egypt*, 109.

186. *LEM*, 69–70. Translation in Caminos, *Late-Egyptian Miscellanies*, 265–266.

187. The full name, of which the Dwelling of Sese is a shortened form.

188. Gardiner, "Ancient Military Road between Egypt and Palestine," 107; *RITA* 1, 14.

189. Stephen Moshier made this discovery and is preparing publication of the data. It appears that this is a minor branch of the Pelusiac that splits off, with the major branch emptying into the lagoon area east of Hebua I.

190. Further study of this Nile channel is planned. It is possible that some sort of bridge, as is shown in the Tjaru portion of the scene, might have been in place, but we have found no evidence to support this suggestion.

191. Oren, "'Ways of Horus' in North Sinai," 79, figure 4. Interestingly, most of the New Kingdom sites in North Sinai apparently were abandoned during the

Twentieth Dynasty, and show no occupation from Greco-Roman times. We attribute this to the changing environment as the Nile migrated north. Also mud-brick architecture did not stand up well in this area because of rainstorms that blew in off the Mediterranean. Consequently, the earlier sites could not be easily be rebuilt and fortresses reused, as they were in Nubia, where rain is rare indeed; there Middle Kingdom forts were reoccupied in the New Kingdom.

192. Gardiner, "Ancient Military Road between Egypt and Palestine," 113.

193. Morris, "Architecture of Imperialism," 1,084–1,085.

194. Ibid., 510.

195. Gardiner, "Ancient Military Road between Egypt and Palestine," 107.

196. Gardiner, *Egyptian Grammar,* 545.

197. Gardiner considered this possibility (ibid.). Fischer-Elfert, *Die satirische Streischrift des papyrus Anastasi I,* 233.

198. *RITA* 1, 16.

199. All these illustrations have been discussed in a recent study by Dag Oredsson, *Moats in Ancient Palestine,* Conciectanean Biblica, Old Testament Series 48 (Stockholm: Almquist and Wiksell International, 2000), 160–167.

200. Morris favors this identification in "Architecture of Imperialism," 520.

201. *LEM,* 67.4.

202. Schulman, *Military Rank, Title and Organization in the Egyptian New Kingdom,* 30. Schulman surmises that if a *pḏt* was an identifiable unit, it had to be larger than an *s3*, which was made up of 250 soldiers and junior officers, plus three high-ranking officers that would have included the *ḥry pḏt,* that is, "he who is over the archers."

203. KRI 5 (1983): 33, 16. See discussion in Morris, "Architecture of Imperialism," 943–947.

204. David O'Connor, "The Sea Peoples and the Egyptian Sources," in *The Sea Peoples and Their World: A Reassessment,* ed. Eliezer Oren (Philadelphia: University Museum, 2000), 100; Donald Redford, "Egypt and Western Asia in the Late New Kingdom: An Overview," in *The Sea Peoples and Their World,* 13.

205. Redford, "Egypt and Western Asia in the Late New Kingdom," 15 n. 36.

206. As believed by the geologists who discovered it: Sneh, "Evidence for an Ancient Egyptian Frontier Canal," 547–548.

207. For a discussion, see Hoffmeier, *Israel in Egypt,* chapter 7. For a good review of earlier interpretations, see Cazelles, "Localizations de l'exode et la critique litteraire," 350–357.

208. Donald Redford, "An Egyptological Perspective on the Exodus Narrative," in *Egypt, Israel, Sinai: Archaeological and Historical Relationships in the Biblical Period,* ed. A. F. Rainey (Tel Aviv: Tel Aviv University Press, 1987), 142–143.

209. Hoffmeier, *Israel in Egypt,* 170. For others who have recognized this interpretation, see William F. Albright, "Exploring Sinai with the University of California African Expedition," *BASOR* 109 (1948): 16; Cazelles, "Localizations de l'exode et la critique litteraire," 350–357.

210. Sneh, "Evidence for an Ancient Egyptian Frontier Canal," 547.

211. Hoffmeier, *Israel in Egypt,* 170. Based upon *CAD* 6:175–176.

212. Cazelles, "Localizations de l'exode et la critique litteraire," 331.

213. Gardiner, *Egyptian Grammar*, 491.

214. Noël Aimé-Giron, "Baal Saphon et les dieux de Tahpanhes dans en nouveu papyrus phénicien," *ASAE* 40 (1941): 433–460.

215. *Wb* 2:83.

216. This word is somewhat generic, with "reeds, rushes, papyrus, stalks, and plants" being possible translations. Lesko, ed., *A Dictionary of Late Egyptian* 1:52.

217. Caminos, *Late-Egyptian Miscellanies*, 74.

218. James Hoch, *Semitic Words in Egyptian Texts of the New Kingdom and Third Intermediate Period* (Princeton: Princeton University Press, 1994), 232.

219. James Allen, "Praise of Pi-Ramessu (Papyrus Anastasi III)," in *COS* 3:15.

220. Ibid., 15 n. 4.

221. Groll, "Egyptian Background of the Exodus," 189.

CHAPTER 6

1. Richard Clifford, *The Cosmic Mountain in Canaan and the Old Testament*, Harvard Semitic Monographs 4 (Cambridge: Harvard University Press, 1972), 1–3.

2. W. B. Kristensen, *The Meaning of Religion*, trans. J. B. Carman (The Hague: M. Nijhoff, 1960), 106–109, 370–373; Gerardus van der Leeuw, *Religion in Essence and Manifestation*, trans. J. E. Turner (Gloucester, Mass.: Peter Smith, 1967), 393–402.

3. Mircea Eliade, *Cosmos and History: The Myth of the Eternal Return* (New York: Harper Torchbooks, 1954), 12.

4. Mircea Eliade, *Patterns in Comparative Religion*, trans. Rosemary Sheed (New York: New American Library, 1958), 99.

5. Helmer Ringgren, *Religions of the Ancient Near East*, trans. John Sturdy (London: SPCK, 1973), 133.

6. Rami Arav, "Mount Hermon," in *ABD* 3: 159.

7. KB, 353–354.

8. KB, 354.

9. The root of Sharif is *šarufa* and, interestingly, *šaraf* means "elevated place," which is quite appropriate for this sacred area of Jerusalem; cf. Hans Wehr, *Arabic-English Dictionary* (Ithaca, N.Y.: Spoken Languages Services, 1976), 466–467.

10. Clifford, *Cosmic Mountain*, chapters 3 and 4.

11. Ringgren, *Religions of the Ancient Near East*, 24; Eliade, *Cosmos and History*, 13.

12. *CDME*, 7 and 185.

13. James Hoffmeier, *Sacred in the Vocabulary of Ancient Egypt*, OBO 59 (Fribourg: University of Fribourg, 1985), 172–173.

14. Text is in Adriaan de Buck, *Egyptian Readingbook* (Leiden: Nederlands Instituut voor het Nabije Oosten, 1970), 74.11. This translation is my own; for a translation of the entire stela, see Miriam Lichtheim, *Ancient Egyptian Literature* (Berkeley: University of California Press, 1973), 1:114–115.

15. For a drawing of the mountain and the surrounding temples, see Timothy Kendall, "Gebel Barkal," in *Encyclopedia of Archaeology of Ancient Egypt*, ed. Kathryn Bard (London: Routledge, 1999), 327.

16. Buck, *Egyptian Readingbook*, 61.7.

17. Kendall, "Gebel Barkal," 325.

18. Reads *d̲sr* plus dual strokes, which would be read as *d̲sry* and might mean "twice holy," or it might read *sp sn*, meaning *d̲sr d̲srw*, that is, "holy of holies"; see Hoffmeier, *Sacred in the Vocabulary of Ancient Egypt*, 195–196.

19. Ibid., 194–196.

20. Ibid., 196–197.

21. *NBD*, 1,168.

22. J. Philip Hyatt, *Exodus* (London: Marshall, Morgan, and Scott, 1971), 71; Georg Fohrer, *History of Israelite Religion*, trans. David Green (Nashville, Tenn.: Abingdon, 1972), 73; William Propp, *Exodus 1–18*, ABC 2 (1999), 198; Robert North, "Perspective of the Exodus Author(s)," *ZAW* 113 (2001): 497–499.

23. Bruce Waltke and Michael O'Connor, *An Introduction to Biblical Hebrew Syntax* (Winona Lake, Ind.: Eisenbrauns, 1990), 153.

24. KB, 350.

25. A. D. H. Mayes, *Deuteronomy*, The New Century Bible Commentary (London: Marshall, Morgan and Scott, and Grand Rapids, Mich.: Eerdmans, 1979), 115.

26. Nahum M. Sarna, *Exodus*, The JPS Torah Commentary (Philadelphia: Jewish Publication Society, 1991), 14.

27. Israel Finkelstein and Neil Asher Silberman, *The Bible Unearthed: Archaeology's New Vision of Ancient Israel and the Origin of Its Sacred Texts* (New York: Free Press, 2001), 61–68, 326–328; Charles Krahmalkov, "Exodus Itinerary Confirmed by Egyptian Evidence," *BAR* 20, no. 5 (1994): 54–62.

28. George W. Coats, "The Wilderness Intinerary," *CBQ* 34 (1972): 135–152; Graham I. Davies, "The Wilderness Itineraries: A Comparative Study," *TB* 25 (1974): 46–81; Graham Davies, *The Way of the Wilderness* (Cambridge: Cambridge University Press, 1979); Martin Noth, *Numbers* (Philadelphia: Westminister, 1968), 242–244; Eryl Davies, *Numbers*, The New Century Bible Commentary (Grand Rapids, Mich.: Eerdmans, 1995), 341–343; Baruch A. Levine, *Numbers 21–36*, ABC 4B (1993), 511–525.

29. Philip Budd, *Numbers*, Word Biblical Commentary 5 (Waco, Tex.: Word, 1984), 350–351; Davies, *Numbers*, 343.

30. Noth, *Numbers*, 242.

31. Davies, "Wilderness Itineraries," 78.

32. Ibid., 55 and 80.

33. Donald Redford, "A Bronze Age Itinerary in Transjordan (Nos. 89–101) of Thutmose III's List of Asiatic Toponyms," *JSSEA* 12, no. 2 (1982): 55–74. For a more detailed study of daybooks, their history and development in Egypt, see Donald Redford, *Pharaonic King-Lists, Annals and Day-Books: A Contribution to the Study of the Egyptian Sense of History*, SSEA Publications 4 (Mississauga, Ont.: Benben Publications, 1986). For the possible influence of the Egyptian daybook style on Hebrew military writing in the book of Joshua, see James Hoffmeier, "The Structure of Joshua 1–11 and the Annals of Thutmose III," in *Faith, Tradition, and History: Old Testament Historiography in Its Near Eastern Context*, ed. A. R. Millard, J. K. Hoffmeier, and D. W. Baker (Winona Lake, Ind.: Eisenbrauns, 1994), 165–179.

34. Redford, "Bronze Age Itinerary in Transjordan," 59–60.

35. Krahmalkov, "Exodus Itinerary Confirmed by Egyptian Evidence," *BAR* 20 n. 5 (1994): 54–62.

36. Ibid., 56.

37. Ibid., 54–62. See my discussion of this issue in James Hoffmeier, *Israel in Egypt: The Evidence for the Authenticity of the Exodus Tradition* (New York: Oxford University Press, 1997), 176–179.

38. For text and commentary, see Hans Werner Fischer-Elfert, *Die satirische Streischrift des Papyrus Anastasi I: Ubersetzung und Kommentar*, Ägyptische Abhandlungen 44 (Wiesbaden: Otto Harrassowitz, 1986); Fischer-Elfert, *Die satirische Streitschrift des Papyrus Anastasi* (Wiesbaden: Otto Harrassowitz, 1983). For recent translations, see Edward Wente, *Letters from Ancient Egypt* (Atlanta: Scholars Press, 1990), 98–110; James Allen, "The Craft of the Scribe (Papyrus Anastasi I)," in *COS* 3, 9–14.

39. William F. Albright, *Yahweh and the Gods of Canaan* (Winona Lake, Ind.: Eisenbrauns, 1968), 60, n. 36. Graham Davies does allow that Albright's suggestion might be correct (Davies, "Wilderness Itineraries," 50).

40. Brevard S. Childs, *The Book of Exodus: A Critical, Theological Commentary*, The Old Testament Library (Louisville, Ky.: Westminster, 1974), 342. Sarna, *Exodus*, 103.

41. J. Simons, *The Geographical and Topographical Texts of the Old Testament* (Leiden: Brill, 1959), 251.

42. Umberto Cassuto, *A Commentary on the Book of Exodus*, trans. I. Abrahams (Jerusalem: Magnes Press, 1951), 183.

43. John Lewis Burkhardt, *Travels in Syria and the Holy Land* (London: John Murray, 1822), 458–488.

44. Edward Robinson, *Biblical Researches in Palestine and the Adjacent Regions* (Boston: Croker and Brewster, 1841), 1:92.

45. Ibid., 95–110.

46. H. Clay Trumbull, *Kadesh-Barnea: Its Importance and Probable Site* (Philadelphia: J. D. Wattles, 1895), 71–74.

47. Barry Beitzel, "Travel and Communication (OT World)," in *ABD* 6: 646.

48. Graham Davies, "The Significance of Deuteronomy 1:2 for the Location of Mount Horeb," *PEQ* 111 (1979): 87–101.

49. Ibid., 93.

50. Ibid., 96.

51. Ibid., 97.

52. On directional *he* or *he* locale, see O'Connor, *Introduction to Biblical Hebrew Syntax*, 32.

53. *OBA*, 59.; *MBA*, 40.; *HAB*, 57.

54. Roland de Vaux, *Ancient Israel* (New York: McGraw-Hill, 1962), 2: §359.

55. For a discussion of these terms, see Levine, *Numbers 21–36*, 551–552.

56. Garth Bawden, "Painted Pottery of Tayma and Problems of Cultural Chronology in Northwest Arabia," in *Midian, Moab and Edom: The History and Archaeology of Late Bronze and Iron Age Jordan and North-West Arabia*, ed. John Sawyer and David Clines (Sheffield: JSOT Press, 1983), 39–40.

57. Beno Rothenberg, *The Egyptian Mining Temple at Timna* (London: University College London, 1988), 100–101.

58. Propp, *Exodus 1–18*, 215.

59. Manashe Har-el, "The Exodus Route in Light of the Historical-Geographic Research," in *Geography in Israel*, ed. D. Amiran and Y. Ben-Arieh (Jerusalem: Tzur-ot

Press, 1976), 388; Jon D. Levenson, *Sinai & Zion: An Entry into the Jewish Bible* (San Francisco: Harper and Row, 1985), 21.

60. Gösta W. Ahlström, *Who Were the Israelites?* (Winona Lake, Ind.: Eisenbrauns, 1986), 57–60; Frank Moore Cross, *From Epic to Canon: History and Literature in Ancient Israel* (Baltimore: Johns Hopkins University Press, 1998), 44–46.

61. S. R. Driver, *A Critical and Exegetical Commentary on Deuteronomy*, 3rd ed. International Critical Commentary on The Holy Scriptures (Edinburgh: T&T Clark, 1901), 3.

62. Ibid., 3–4.

63. John Thompson, *Deuteronomy: An Introduction and Commentary*, Tyndale Old Testament Commentaries (Leicester: IV Press, 1974), 81–82; Davies, *Way of the Wilderness*, 63.

64. J. G. Millar, "Living at the Place of Decision: Time and Place in the Framework of Deuteronomy," in *Time and Place in Deuteronomy*, ed. J. G. McConville and J. G. Millar (Sheffield: JSOT Press, 1994), 23–24.

65. Davies, "The Significance of Deuteronomy 1:2 for the Location of Mount Horeb," 97.

66. Trumbull, *Kadesh-Barnea: Its Importance and Probable Site.*

67. Martin Noth, *The Old Testament World*, trans. Victor I. Gruhn (Philadelphia: Fortress, 1966), 57.

68. KB, 1,075; Dale Manor, "Kadesh-Barnea," in *ABD* 4: 1; Martin Noth, *Das Buch Joshua*, Handbuch zum Alten Testament 7 (Tübingen: J. C. B. Moh; 1971), 150.

69. Manashe Har-el, *The Sinai Journeys: The Route of the Exodus* (San Diego: Ridgefield, 1983), 333.

70. Yohanan Aharoni, "Kadesh-Barnea and Mount Sinai," in *God's Wilderness: Discoveries in Sinai*, ed. Beno Rothenberg (New York: Thomas Nelson, 1961), 137.

71. C. L. Woolley and T. E. Lawrence, *The Wilderness of Zin*, Palestine Exploration Fund Annual 3 (London, 1914–1915).

72. I. Gilead, "Kadesh-Barnea: The Historical Sites," in *NEAEHL* 3, 841–843.

73. I. Beit-Arieh and R. Gophna, "The Early Bronze Age II Settlement at 'Ain el-Qudeirat (1980–1981)," *Tel Aviv* 8 (1981): 128–135; Beit-Arieh and Gophna, "Early Bronze Age II Sites in Wadi el-Qudeirat (Kadesh-Barnea)," *Tel Aviv* 3 (1976): 142–150.

74. Rudolph Cohen, *Kadesh-Barnea: A Fortress from the Time of the Judaean Kingdom* (Jerusalem: Israel Museum, 1983), 93–107; Cohen, "Kadesh-Barnea: The Israelite Fortress," in *NEAEHL* 3, 843–847.

75. Otto Eissfeldt, *Baal Zaphon, Zeus Kasios und der Durchzug der Israeliten Durchs Meer* (Halle: Niemeyer, 1932); William F. Albright, "Baal-Zephon," in *Festschrift Alfred Bertholet Zum 80. Geburtsag*, ed. O. Eissfeldt, W. Baumgartner, K. Elliger, and L. Rost (Tübingen: J. C. B. Mohr, 1950), 1–14; C. S. Jarvis, *Yesterday and To-day in Sinai* (Edinburgh: William Blackwood and Sons, 1933), chapter 9. It was noted above that the possibility of this route needs to be abandoned, since the land bridge on which the Israelites would have traveled did not connect to the mainland on the east side until some time in the first millennium (see chapter 5, §V).

76. Emmanuel Anati, *The Riddle of Mount Sinai: Archaeological Discoveries at Har Karkom*, Studi Camuni 21 (Valcamonica [Brescia]: Edizioni del Centro, 2001). On page 10, the author offers a list of his published monographs that attempt to connect Har

Karkom with Mt. Sinai, and pages 185–188 contain a complete bibliography of the excavations and various studies on Har Karkom. His ideas were introduced to an English-speaking audience in Emmanuel Anati, "Has Mt. Sinai Been Found?" *BAR* 11, no. 4 (1985): 42–57.

77. Anati, *Riddle of Mount Sinai*, chapter 5, 7.

78. Ibid., 15–16.

79. Ibid., 141.

80. William Stiebing, "Should the Exodus and Israelite Settlement Be Redated?" *BAR* 11, no. 4 (1985): 58–69.

81. Israel Finkelstein, "Raiders of the Lost Mountain—An Israeli Archaeologist Looks at the Most Recent Attempt to Locate Mt. Sinai," *BAR* 14, no. 4 (1988): 46–50.

82. Ibid., 48–49.

83. Aviram Perevolotsky and Israel Finkelstein, "The Southern Sinai Exodus Route in Ecological Perspective," *BAR* 11, no. 4 (1985): 27–41.

84. Joseph Naveh, *Early History of the Alphabet: An Introduction to West Semitic Epigraphy and Palaeography* (Jerusalem: Magnes Press, 1982), chapter 2. In the late 1990s, John Darnell of Yale University discovered what is now believed to be the earliest alphabetic Semitic scripts in the Wadi el-Hol in the Libyan desert in Egypt. These texts could push the beginning of the alphabet back to ca. 2100–2000 B.C. But even if these early dating observations prove correct, it would not help Anati's dating, as writing was at such an early stage of development that it is unlikely that laws of the sort found in the Torah would have been written.

85. Anati, *Riddle of Mount Sinai*, 51–53.

86. Har-el, "Exodus Route in Light of the Historical-Geographic Research," 373–396; Har-el, *Sinai Journeys*, 416–419.

87. Har-el, *Sinai Journeys*, 357.

88. Har-el, "Exodus Route in Light of the Historical-Geographic Research," 380–381.

89. Har-el, *Sinai Journeys*, 420–421.

90. Wehr, *Arabic-English Dictionary*, 60, 433. After coming to this linguistic conclusion on my own, I discovered that Graham Davies made the same observation in a footnote: Davies, *Way of the Wilderness*, 111 n. 31.

91. Har-el, *Sinai Journeys*, 419.

92. KB, 1,593–1,594.

93. In Arabic, Sinai is written as *sena'*.

94. Clinton Bailey, "Bedouin Place-Names in Sinai," *PEQ* 116 (1984): 42–57.

95. Ibid., 47.

96. Har-el, *Sinai Journeys*, 418.

97. Davies, "Significance of Deuteronomy 1:2," 97.

98. *OBA*, 59; *HAB*, 57; Barry Beitzel, *The Moody Bible Atlas* (Chicago: Moody Press, 1985), 87.

99. Ahlström, *Who Were the Israelites?*, 57–59; Cross, *From Epic to Canon*, 45–52.

100. D. N. Freedman and F. M. Cross, *Studies in Ancient Yahwistic Poetry*, SBL Dissertation Series 21 (Missoula, Mont.: Society of Biblical Literature, 1975), 3–4.

101. Ernst Axel Knauf, "Teman," in *ABD* 6: 347–348; Knauf, "Seir," in *ABD* 5: 1,072–1,073.

102. P. Kyle McCarter, *Ancient Inscriptions: Voices from the Biblical World* (Washington, D.C.: Biblical Archaeology Society, 1996), 106–109.

103. Ahlström, *Who Were the Israelites?*, 60.

104. Bernhard Grdseloff, "Édôm, d'après les sources égyptiennes," *Revue de l'histoire juive d'Egypte* 1 (1947): 69–99.

105. KB, 281; Patrick Miller, *The Divine Warrior in Early Israel* (Cambridge: Harvard University Press, 1973), 77–78.

106. Davies, "Wilderness Itineraries," 55 and 80.

107. Nili Shupak, "The God from Teman and the Egyptian Sun God: A Reconsideration of Habakkuk 3:3–7," *JANES* 28 (2001): 97–116.

108. Ibid., 109–110.

109. Aharoni, "Kadesh-Barnea and Mount Sinai," 167–169.

110. Charles Beke, *Sinai in Arabia and Midian* (London: Trubner, 1878). Colin Humphreys contends that originally Beke thought that Mt. Sinai was a volcano further to the south, but under pressure from colleagues who labeled his view heresy, pushed the location north to Mt. Biggir; see Colin Humphreys, *The Miracles of Exodus* (New York: Harper San Francisco, 2003), 326–328.

111. For a careful analysis of Paul's use of Hagar and the Arabic, el-Higra, see Graham Davies, "Hagar, el-Higra and the Location of Mount Sinai," *VT* 22 (1972): 152–163.

112. Beke, *Sinai in Arabia and Midian*, 47ff.

113. Ibid.; see his map at the back of the book for his reconstruction.

114. Alfred Lucas, *The Route of the Exodus of the Israelites from Egypt* (London: E. Arnold, 1938), chapter 2.

115. See the discussion of de Vaux on the history of the volcano interpretation: Roland de Vaux, *The Early History of Israel*, trans. David Smith (Philadelphia: Westminster, 1978), 433; Martin Noth, "Der Wallfahrtsweg zum Sinai," *Palästinajahrbuch* 36 (1940): 5–28; Jean Koenig, *Le site de al-Jaw dans l'ancien pays de Madian* (Paris: Libraire Orientaliste Paul Geuthner, 1971).

116. See Koenig's map: *Le site de al-Jaw*, figure 5.

117. De Vaux, *Early History of Israel*, 437–439.

118. Ibid., 436–437.

119. Bailey, "Bedouin Place-Names in Sinai," 44–45.

120. Itzhaq Beit-Arieh, "New Discoveries at Serabit el-Khadim," *BA* 45 n. 4 (1982): 13–18; Beit-Arieh, "The Route through Sinai—Why Israelites Fleeing Egypt Went South," *BAR* 14 n. 3 (1988): 28–37; Beit-Arieh, "Canaanites and Egyptians at Serabit el-Khadim," in *Egypt, Israel, Sinai: Archaeological and Historical Relationships in the Biblical Period*, ed. Anson Rainey (Tel Aviv: Tel Aviv University Press, 1987), 57–67; Beit-Arieh, "Serabît el-Khâdim: New Metallurgical and Chronological Aspects," *Levant* 17 (1985): 89–116; Beit-Arieh, "Fifteen Years in Sinai: Israeli Archaeologists Discover a New World," *BAR* 10, no. 4 (1984): 26–54; Har-el, *Sinai Journeys;* Ze'ev Meshel, "An Explanation of the Journeys of the Israelites in the Wilderness," *BA* 45, no. 1 (1982); Meshel, *Sinai: Excavations and Studies*, BAR International Series 876 (Oxford: Archaeopress, 2000).

121. Robert Cornuke and David Halbrook, *In Search of the Mountain of God: The Discovery of the Real Mount Sinai* (Nashville, Tenn.: Broadman and Holman, 2000);

Howard Blum, *The Gold of Exodus: The Discovery of the True Mount Sinai* (New York: Simon and Schuster, 1998).

122. Cornuke and Halbrook, *In Search of the Mountain of God*, 170.

123. Ibid., 170–172.

124. Ibid., 179–180.

125. Ibid., pictures shown between pages 120 and 121.

126. David Hackett Fischer, *Historians' Fallacies: Toward a Logic of Historical Thought* (New York: Harper and Row, 1970), 109.

127. Hoffmeier, *Israel in Egypt*, chapter 9.

128. R. I. Dorn and T. M. Oberlander, "Rock Varnish," *Progress in Physical Geography* 6 (1982). I am indebted to Stephen Moshier for this information and the reference cited here.

129. Cornuke and Halbrook, *In Search of the Mountain of God*, 65.

130. Ibid., 125.

131. Ibid.

132. Rothenberg, *Egyptian Mining Temple at Timna*, 27–64; Miriam Aharoni, "Arad," in *NEAEHL* 1, 84.

133. Cornuke and Halbrook, *In Search of the Mountain of God*, 124–125; see a picture of these pillars between pages 120 and 121.

134. Uzi Avner, "Sacred Stones in the Desert," *BAR* 27, no. 3 (2001): 31–41.

135. Rothenberg, *Egyptian Mining Temple at Timna*, 45.

136. Amnon Ben-Tor, "Tel Hazor, 2002," *IEJ* 52, no. 2 (2002): 256.

137. Gordon Franz, "Is Mount Sinai in Arabia?" *Bible and Spade* 13, no. 4 (2000): 101–113.

138. Humphreys, *Miracles of Exodus.*

139. For what it is worth, I met with Millard and Kitchen in April 2003, and they both told me that they had serious problems with Humphreys' views.

140. Humphreys, *Miracles of Exodus*, 317–319; Colin Humphreys, "The Number of People in the Exodus from Egypt: Decoding Mathematically the Very Large Numbers in Numbers I and XXVI," *VT* 48 (1998): 96–113.

141. Humphreys, *Miracles of Exodus*, chapter 6.

142. Ibid., 164–171.

143. Ibid., chapters 12–13.

144. Ibid., 154–160.

145. Ibid., 208–216.

146. Ibid., 234–235.

147. See plan in Rothenberg, *Egyptian Mining Temple at Timna*, 28.

148. Alan Schulman, Ibid., 114–115.

149. Ibid., 115.

150. Alan H. Gardiner, T. Eric Peet, and Jaroslav Černý, *The Inscriptions of Sinai* (London: Egypt Exploration Society, 1955), 11.

151. For a recent translation of the annals, see James K. Hoffmeier, "The Annals of Thutmose III," in *COS* 2: 8–11. That he was traveling by chariot is evident when the Egyptian army is described as moving through the Aruna pass "horses in single file, [his majesty] being at the head of his army" (p. 10).

152. Yohanan Aharoni, *The Land of the Bible: A Historical Geography*, trans. A. F. Rainey (Philadelphia: Westminster, 1967), 44.

153. Mohamad Abd el-Maksoud pointed out this road to me during visits to Hebua in 2001 and 2002. To my knowledge, the road has not been published in any form.

154. Humphreys, *Miracles of Exodus*, 313–316.

155. Avi Hurvitz, "The Historical Quest for 'Ancient Israel' and the Linguistic Evidence of the Hebrew Bible: Some Methodological Observations," *VT* 47 (1997): 316, see figure 19.1.

156. Davies, *Way of the Wilderness*, 66.

157. Barry Beitzel, "Exegesis, Dogmatics and Cartography: A Strange Alchemy in Earlier Church Traditions," *ABW* 2, no. 2 (1994): 10–21.

158. Robinson, *Biblical Researches*, 180.

159. Joseph J. Hobbs, *Mount Sinai* (Austin: University of Texas Press, 1995), 68.

160. Athanasios Paliouras, *The Monastery of St. Catherine on Mount Sinai* (Glyka Nera Attikis: St. Catherine's Monastery, 1985), 10.

161. John Wilkinson, *Egeria's Travels to the Holy Land*, revised ed. (Warminster: Aris and Phillips, 1981), 91–98.

162. Aharoni, *Land of the Bible*, 182–183.

163. G. Ernest Wright, *Biblical Archaeology* (Philadelphia: Westminster, 1957), 64.

164. Ibid.

165. Finkelstein, "Southern Sinai Exodus Route in Ecological Perspective," 33–35.

166. Beit-Arieh, "Route through Sinai," 28–37; Beit-Arieh, "Fifteen Years in Sinai 26–54; Beit-Arieh, *Archaeology of Sinai: The Ophir Expedition* (Tel Aviv: Nadler Institute of Archaeology, 2003).

167. Burkhardt, *Travels in Syria and the Holy Land*, 482.

168. Beit-Arieh, "Route through Sinai," 35.

169. Ibid.

170. Ofer Bar-Yosef, "Pre-Pottery Neolithic Sites in Southern Sinai," *BA* 45, no. 1 (1982): 9–18.

171. Perevolotsky and Finkelstein, "Southern Sinai Exodus Route in Ecological Perspective," 35.

172. Ibid.

173. Beit-Arieh, "Route through Sinai," 35.

174. Davies, "Significance of Deuteronomy 1:2," 101.

175. Ibid., 100.

176. Meshel, *Sinai: Excavations and Studies*, 99–117.

177. Ibid., 100–103.

178. Robinson, *Biblical Researches*, 140–141.

179. Ibid., 154.

180. Arthur Penrhyn Stanley, *Sinai and Palestine in Connection with Their History* (London: John Murray, 1856), 30.

181. Robinson, *Biblical Researches*, 154.

182. Stanley, *Sinai and Palestine in Connection with Their History*, 31.

183. Ibid., 74.

184. D. A. Randall, *The Handwriting of God in Egypt, Sinai, and the Holy Land: The Records of a Journey from the Great Valley of the West to the Sacred Places of the East* (Philadelphia: John E. Potter, 1869), 285.

185. Ibid., 286.

186. E. H. Palmer, *The Desert of the Exodus: Journeys in the Wilderness of the Forty Years' Wanderings* (New York: Harper and Brothers, 1872), 97–100.

187. Henry M. Field, *On the Desert: With a Brief Review of Recent Events in Egypt* (New York: Charles Scribner's Sons, 1885), 114.

188. KB, 666.

189. Field, *On the Desert: With a Brief Review of Recent Events in Egypt*, 98.

190. Burkhardt, *Travels in Syria and the Holy Land*, 607–609.

191. W. M. F. Petrie, *Researches in Sinai* (New York: E. P. Dutton, 1906).

192. Peter Grossman, "Firan in South Sinai," *EA* 10 (1997): 3–5.

193. Ibid., 3; Har-el, *Sinai Journeys*, 382–384. For a recent translation of Egeria's journal of her travels, see Wilkinson, *Egeria's Travels to the Holy Land*, 91–100.

194. Har-el, *Sinai Journeys*, 3, 378–379.

195. Grossman, "Firan in South Sinai," 5.

196. Henry Spencer Palmer, *Sinai: From the Fourth Egyptian Dynasty to the Present Day* (London: Society for Promoting Christian Knowledge, 1892), 131; Heinz Skrobucha, *Sinai*, trans. Geoffrey Hunt (London: Oxford University Press, 1966), 35.

197. Hobbs, *Mount Sinai*, 68.

198. Dewey M. Beegle, *Moses, the Servant of Yahweh* (Grand Rapids, Mich.: Eerdmans, 1972), 191. See Simons, *Geographical and Topographical Texts of the Old Testament*, 253; and Wright, *Biblical Archaeology*, 63–64.

199. Cassuto, *Commentary on the Book of Exodus*, 225.

200. Skrobucha, *Sinai*, 65–67.

201. Hobbs, *Mount Sinai*, 128–129.

202. Flavius Josephus, *Jewish Antiquities*, trans. Henry Thackeray (London: Heinemann; New York: Putnam's Sons, 1930), 4: 279, 355.

CHAPTER 7

1. I. Beit-Arieh, "The Route through Sinai—Why Israelites Fleeing Egypt Went South," *BAR* 44 (1988): 37.

2. For an excellent review of the Kenites, their origin and relations with Israel, see Baruch Halpern, "Kenites," in *ABD* 4: 17–22.

3. Daniel E. Fleming, "Genesis in History and Tradition: The Syrian Background of Israel's Ancestors, Reprise," in *The Future of Biblical Archaeology*, ed. James Hoffmeier and Alan Millard (Grand Rapids, Mich.: Eerdmans, 2004), 182–220.

4. Hans Wehr, *Arabic-English Dictionary* (Ithaca, N.Y.: Spoken Languages Services, 1976), 224.

5. Roger Cribb, *Nomads in Archaeology* (Cambridge: Cambridge University Press, 1991); Kay Prag, "Ancient and Modern Pastoral Migration in the Levant," *Levant* 17 (1985): 81–88; Israel Finkelstein and Avi Perevolotsky, "Processes of Sedentarization and Nomadization in the History of Sinai and the Negev," *BASOR* 279 (1990): 67–88; Israel Finkelstein, *Living on the Fringe*, Monographs in Mediterranean Archaeology

(Sheffield: Sheffield Academic Press, 1995); Steven Rosen, "Nomads in Archaeology: A Response to Finkelstein and Perevolotsky," *BASOR* 287 (1992): 75–85.

6. Finkelstein and Perevolotsky, "Processes of Sedentarization and Nomadization," 67.

7. Ibid., 68.

8. Ibid., 68–70.

9. Ibid., 75, 78.

10. Ibid., 72ff.

11. Rosen, "Nomads in Archaeology," 75–85.

12. Finkelstein, *Living on the Fringe*, chapters 1–3.

13. Israel Finkelstein and Neil Asher Silberman, *The Bible Unearthed: Archaeology's New Vision of Ancient Israel and the Origin of Its Sacred Texts* (New York: Free Press, 2001), 62.

14. William G. Dever, *Who Were the Early Israelites and Where Did They Come From?* (Grand Rapids, Mich.: Eerdmans, 2003), 161–165.

15. Ibid., 164–165.

16. Lawrence Stager, "The Archaeology of the Family in Ancient Israel," *BASOR* 260 (1985): 17.

17. Michael Homan, *To Your Tents, O Israel! The Terminology, Function, Form, and Symbolism of Tents in the Hebrew Bible and the Ancient Near East* (Leiden: Brill, 2002), 55.

18. James K. Hoffmeier, "The Annals of Thutmose III," in *COS* 2: 10. For a translation of the Battle of Kadesh texts, see Kenneth Kitchen, "The Battle of Qadesh—the Poem, or Literary Record," in *COS* 2: 32–40.

19. James K. Hoffmeier, "The Gebel Barkal Stela of Thutmose III," in *COS* 2: 16.

20. I owe this information to Alan Millard, who has served on the staff of the British School's excavations at Tell Nebi Mend.

21. Our workers demonstrated how they made bread in the sand, without using a pan of any sort and covering the sand with fire. The tasty bread was ready in less than 30 minutes, the time allowed for the breakfast break.

22. John Lewis Burkhardt, *Travels in Syria and the Holy Land* (London: John Murray, 1822), 464ff.

23. Edward Robinson, *Biblical Researches in Palestine and the Adjacent Regions* (Boston: Croker and Brewster, 1841), 1: 49.

24. Obviously this couple could have had more children. Girls and women are typically not mentioned in family histories and genealogies unless they play an important role in the story. Hence Miriam is mentioned because of her role in preserving the life of baby Moses (Exod. 2); she was identified as a prophetess (Exod. 15:20–21). She was also involved in a public confrontation with Moses, with the result that she became leprous (Num. 12). Whereas Genesis tells us of the two wives and two concubines of Jacob and the twelve sons, only one daughter, Dinah, is mentioned. Her inclusion was necessary because of the role she played in the story that she was raped by Shechem son of Hamor (Gen. 34). It is hard to believe that Jacob did not have other daughters from any of his four wives.

25. Nahum M. Sarna, *Exodus*, The JPS Torah Commentary (Philadelphia: Jewish Publication Society, 1991), 62.

26. Cf. Karl Butzer, *Early Hydraulic Civilization in Egypt*, Prehistoric Archeology and Ecology Series (Chicago: University of Chicago Press, 1976), 76–77. Butzer's figure is based on two different unpublished studies that he reviewed, by Klaus Baer and Fekri Hassan.

27. Edgar Pusch, "Towards a Map of Piramesse," *EA* 14 (1999): 13–15.

28. Exodus 14:7 actually reads: "he took six hundred picked chariots and all the other chariots of Egypt with officers over all of them." What this additional number is, we do not know.

29. I was able to obtain firsthand information about this find from the director of the German missions, Edgar Pusch. He kindly showed me the stone hitching posts during a visit in the spring of 2000. Reports of this important discovery were announced in the press; see news.bbc.co.uk/1/hi/world/middle_east/475347.stm.

30. KRI 2: 45.1, 135.7. For a translation, see Kitchen, "Battle of Qadesh," 34–35.

31. Alan R. Schulman, *Military Rank, Title and Organization in the Egyptian New Kingdom*, Münchner Ägyptologische Studien 6 (Berlin: Verlag Bruno Hessling, 1964). See also Andrea Gnirs, "Military," in *Oxford Encyclopedia of Ancient Egypt 2*, ed. Donald Redford (New York: Oxford University Press, 2001), 404. The figure of 20,000 is determined by the fact that during the Ramesside era, the army was made up of four divisions, named after the gods Re, Amun, Seth, and Ptah. There were 5,000 soldiers in a division. In a conversation with the late Alan Schulman many years ago, I pressed him on his estimate for the maximum size of the army during the New Kingdom. He thought that the Egyptian army was at its greatest size during the reigns of Thutmose III and Amenhotep II, and 25,000 was the highest figure with which he was comfortable.

32. For a preliminary report, see Steven Snape, "Ramesses II's Forgotten Frontier," *Egyptian Archaeology* 11 (1997): 23–24.

33. These figures are based on the translation of K. Lawson Younger, "Kurkh Monolith," in COS 2: 263–264. We cannot be specific about the number of troops from Siyannu, since the number of thousands is lost, so I have used the minimum of 1,000. Also, Shalmaneser claims that twelve nations were involved in the coalition, yet only eleven are mentioned. Thus one may have been omitted (cf. 234 n. 34). More than 53,000 is possible, but probably only than a few thousand additional troops can be added.

34. I reject the indigenous origins model.

35. Magen Broshi and Ram Gophna, "The Settlements and Population of Palestine during the Early Bronze II–III," *BASOR* 253 (1984): 45.

36. Magen Broshi and Ram Gophna, "Middle Bronze Age II Palestine: Its Settlements and Population," *BASOR* 261 (1986): 89.

37. Yigal Shiloh, "The Population of Iron Age Palestine in the Light of a Sample Analysis of Urban Plans, Areas, and Population Density," *BASOR* 239 (1980): 32.

38. Magen Broshi and Israel Finkelstein, "The Population of Palestine in Iron Age II," *BASOR* 287 (1992): 47–60.

39. Amnon Ben-Tor, "Hazor," in *NEAEHL*, 595.

40. Shiloh, "Population of Iron Age Palestine," 30.

41. The battle for Ai in Joshua 7:2–5 describes it as a small site that did not require the entire army, but there is no sense that the remaining forces attacked another city during the initial campaign against Ai, which was a debacle.

42. KB, 59–60.

43. William Holladay, *A Concise Hebrew and Aramaic Lexicon of the Old Testament* (Grand Rapids, Mich.: Eerdmans, 1971), 53–54.

44. KB, 59–60.

45. KB, 54.

46. J. W. Wenham, "Large Numbers in the Old Testament," *TB* 18 (1967): 25.

47. Walter Kaiser, *A History of Israel from the Bronze Age through the Jewish Wars* (Nashville, Tenn.: Broadman and Holman, 1998), 102; David Halbrook and Robert Cornuke, *In Search of the Mountain of God* (Nashville, Tenn.: Broadman and Holman, 2000).

48. J. Philip Hyatt, *Exodus* (London: Marshall, Morgan, and Scott, 1971), 139.

49. Ibid., 97–98.

50. David Fouts, "Another Look at Large Numbers in Assyrian Royal Inscriptions," *JNES* 53, no. 3 (1994): 277–287; Alan Millard, "Large Numbers in the Assyrian Royal Inscriptions," *Scripta Hierosolymitana* 33 (1991): 213–222. Millard shows that not all large numbers in Assyrian records are exaggerated.

51. Possibly this could be understood as 1,000 *elep̱*, that is, 1,000 units. For a discussion of the 2 Chronicles 14:9 text, see James Hoffmeier, "Egypt as an Arm of Flesh: A Prophetic Response," in *Israel's Apostasy and Restoration: Essays in Honor of Roland K. Harrison*, ed. Avraham Gileadi (Grand Rapids, Mich.: Baker Book House, 1988), 85–86.

52. Fouts, "Another Look at Large Numbers in Assyrian Royal Inscriptions," 205–211.

53. Hoffmeier, "Egypt as an Arm of Flesh," 85.

54. Umberto Cassuto, *A Commentary on the Book of Exodus*, trans. I. Abrahams (Jerusalem: Magnes Press, 1951), 147; Baruch A. Levine, *Numbers 1–20*, ABC 4A (1993): 139.

55. W. M. F. Petrie, *Researches in Sinai* (New York: E. P. Dutton, 1906), 207ff.

56. Some are R. E. D. Clark, "Large Numbers of the Old Testament," *Journal of the Transactions of the Victoria Institute* 87 (1955): 82–92; George E. Mendenhall, "The Census Lists of Numbers 1 and 26," *JBL* 77 (1958): 52–66; Wenham, "Large Numbers in the Old Testament," 19–53; Eryl Davies, "A Mathematical Conundrum: The Problem of the Large Numbers in Numbers I and XXVI," *VT* 45 (1995): 449–469; David Merling, "Large Numbers at the Time of the Exodus," *NEASB* 44 (1999): 15–27; Colin J. Humphreys, "The Number of People in the Exodus from Egypt: Decoding Mathematically the Very Large Numbers in Numbers I and XXVI," *VT* 48 (1998): 96–113.

57. Petrie, *Researches in Sinai*, 207–208.

58. Mendenhall, "Census Lists of Numbers 1 and 26," 52–66.

59. Ibid., 52.

60. Ibid., 60.

61. Ibid., 63.

62. Ibid., 65.

63. Ibid., 57.

64. Ibid., 6.

65. George E. Mendenhall, "Social Organization in Early Israel," in *Magnalia Dei: The Mighty Acts of God, Essays on the Bible and Archaeology in Memory of G. Ernest Wright*, ed. F. M. Cross et al. (Garden City, N.Y.: Doubleday, 1976), 147–148.

66. Metachronism is described by Fischer as the unwarranted practice of late-dating historical sources; David Hackett Fischer, *Historians' Fallacies: Toward a Logic of Historical Thought* (New York: Harper and Row, 1970), 133.

67. Norman Gottwald, *The Tribes of Yahweh: A Sociology of the Religion of Liberated Israel 1250–1050 B.C.E.* (Maryknoll, N.Y.: Orbis, 1979), 270–276; KB, 651.

68. J. David Schloen, *The House of the Father as Fact and Symbol: Patrimonialism in Ugarit and the Ancient Near East*, Studies in the Archaeology and History of the Levant (Winona Lake, Ind.: Eisenbrauns, 2001), 152–155.

69. Humphreys, "Number of People in the Exodus," 196–213; Merling, "Large Numbers at the Time of the Exodus," 15–27.

70. Humphreys, "Number of People in the Exodus," 196–213.

71. Yohanan Aharoni, *The Land of the Bible: A Historical Geography*, trans. A. F. Rainey (Philadelphia: Westminster, 1967), 51–52; *OBA*, 58–59; Barry Beitzel, *The Moody Bible Atlas* (Chicago: Moody Press, 1985), 86–87.

72. KB, 1,453.

73. Ibid.; J. Simons, *The Geographical and Topographical Texts of the Old Testament* (Leiden: Brill, 1959), §426; Aharoni, *Land of the Bible*, 130; Sarna, *Exodus*, 84; George Kelm, *Escape to Conflict: A Biblical and Archaeological Approach to the Hebrew Exodus and Settlement in Canaan* (Fort Worth, Tex.: IAR Publications, 1991), 81.

74. Graham Davies, *The Way of the Wilderness* (Cambridge: Cambridge University Press, 1979), 82.

75. *OBA*, 58–59 (interestingly, the third edition of this atlas has abandoned the turn north to cross in the Lake Manzelah region, and opts for a move southeast from Qantir to the Timsah-Bitter Lakes region for the crossing); *MBA*, map no. 47.

76. My translation. The text is found in A. M. Blackman, *Middle Egyptian Stories*, Bibliotheca Aegyptiaca 2 (Brussels: Fondation Égyptologique Reine Élisabeth, 1932), 13.

77. Burkhardt, *Travels in Syria and the Holy Land*, 465–472. I concluded this distance on the basis of two pieces of evidence in his book. First he states that it was 15¼ hours from 'Ayun Musa to 'Ain Hawara (p. 472). This time period did not cover travel in a single day but represented a day and a half of travel. Second, he reports departing Suez early on the morning of April 25 and after only 1¾ hour, he reached Hawara on April 27 (p. 472).

78. Robinson, *Biblical Researches*, 1:94–96.

79. Arthur Penrhyn Stanley, *Sinai and Palestine in Connection with Their History* (London: John Murray, 1856), 35; E. H. Palmer, *The Desert of the Exodus: Journeys in the Wilderness of the Forty Years' Wanderings* (New York: Harper and Brothers, 1872), 45–46; and see, for example, Cassuto, *Commentary on the Book of Exodus*, 183.

80. Burkhardt, *Travels in Syria and the Holy Land*, 473–474; Robinson, *Biblical Researches*, 1: 99–101.

81. Robinson, *Biblical Researches*, 1:100.

82. Manashe Har-el, *The Sinai Journeys: The Route of the Exodus* (San Diego: Ridgefield, 1983), 335; see map on p. 357; Kelm, *Escape to Conflict*, 82.

83. Wehr, *Arabic-English Dictionary*, 901.

84. Clinton Bailey, "Bedouin Place-Names in Sinai," *PEQ* 116 (1984): 46.

85. KB, 588.

86. Bailey, "Bedouin Place-Names in Sinai," 46.

87. Arie S. Issar, *Water Shall Flow from the Rock: Hydrogeology and Climate in the Lands of the Bible* (Berlin: Springer-Verlag, 1990), 109.

88. Simons, *Geographical and Topographical Texts of the Old Testament,* §427; Issar, *Water Shall Flow from the Rock,* 109.

89. Burkhardt, *Travels in Syria and the Holy Land,* 471.

90. Robinson, *Biblical Researches,* 1:90–91.

91. E. W. Davies suggests that it "means 'terebinth-trees,' and since these were commonly regarded as sacrosanct (cf. Gen. 12:6), it is sometimes suggested that Elim was an oasis with sacral associations"; Eryl Davies, *Numbers,* The New Century Bible Commentary (Grand Rapids, Mich.: Eerdmans, 1995), 345. One would expect that if such a tree or trees stood behind the name and were present that they would have been mentioned, rather than the palm trees!

92. Burkhardt, *Travels in Syria and the Holy Land,* 473–474; Palmer, D*esert of the Exodus,* 46; Stanley, *Sinai and Palestine in Connection with Their History,* 35, although he considers Wadi Tayibeh to be another possibility.

93. Robinson, *Biblical Researches,* 1:99–100.

94. Har-el, *Sinai Journeys,* 356–357.

95. Philip Budd, *Numbers,* Word Biblical Commentary 5 (Waco, Tex.: Word, 1984), 345; Davies, *Numbers,* 345; Simons, *Geographical and Topographical Texts of the Old Testament,* §427; Jacob Milgrom, *Numbers,* The JPS Torah Commentary (Philadelphia and New York: Jewish Publication Society, 1989), 173, 278.

96. Bernard Batto, "The Reed Sea: *Requiscat in Pace,*" *JBL* 102 (1983): 27–28.

97. James Hoffmeier, *Israel in Egypt: The Evidence for the Authenticity of the Exodus Tradition* (New York: Oxford University Press, 1997), 207–210. For a critique of the suggestion that *sûp̱* in the Exodus narratives should be read *sôp̱,* meaning "end," see *Israel in Egypt,* 202–203.

98. I have visited this site several times and am well aware that this spring would have been avoided by anyone seeking water to drink!

99. For a thorough study of fish and fishing in Egypt, see Douglas Brewer and Renée Friedman, *Fish and Fishing in Ancient Egypt* (Cairo: American University Press, 1989), 5–17.

100. Burkhardt, *Travels in Syria and the Holy Land,* 498; Petrie, *Researches in Sinai,* 249.

101. Stanley, *Sinai and Palestine in Connection with Their History,* 35; Simons, *Geographical and Topographical Texts of the Old Testament,* §428.

102. Robinson, *Biblical Researches,* 1:105–107; D. A. Randall, *The Handwriting of God in Egypt, Sinai, and the Holy Land: The Records of a Journey from the Great Valley of the West to the Sacred Places of the East* (Philadelphia: John E. Potter, 1869), 251; Henry Spencer Palmer, *Sinai: From the Fourth Egyptian Dynasty to the Present Day* (London: Society for Promoting Christian Knowledge, 1892), 203; David Seely, "Wilderness of Sin," in *ABD* 6, 47.

103. Burkhardt, *Travels in Syria and the Holy Land,* 625; Robinson, *Biblical Researches,* 1:104–105.

104. William F. Albright, "Exploring Sinai with the University of California African Expedition," *BASOR* 109 (1948): 5–20.

105. Dr. Mumford, in addition to directing the Markhah Plain project, is also assistant director for the Tell el-Borg excavations. The information regarding his work came through an unpublished report he kindly gave me. It is now published: Gregory D. Mumford and Sarah Parcak, "Pharaonic Ventures into South Sinai: El-Markha Plain 346," *JEA* 89 (2003): 83–116.

106. Davies, *Way of the Wilderness*, 84.

107. Concerning these wadis and their formation, see Ned H. Greenwood, *The Sinai: A Physical Geography* (Austin: University of Texas Press, 1997), 33–37, especially the map on p. 35 = figure 3.6. Greenwood in this map labels Wadi Humr as Wadi Baba. All other maps I have consulted know this valley as Wadi Humr, and when I traveled through it in 1997 to visit Serabit el-Khadim, our Bedouin guides called it Wadi Humr. The name of a wadi that leads from Wadi Humr to Serabit is called Wadi Beda', according to Robinson (*Biblical Researches*, 1:112).

108. Robinson, *Biblical Researches*, 1:107–109. On March 20, he recorded that his caravan entered the wadi at 12:15 P.M. and camped for the night at 5:10 P.M. On March 21, they continued at 6:20 A.M., arriving at Serabit around 1:00 P.M.

109. Mahmoud Abd el-Raziq, Georges Castel, Pierre Tallet, and Victor Ghica, *Les inscriptions d'Ayn Soukhna*, MIFAO 122 (Cairo: IFAO, 2002), 40–41.

110. KB, 229; BDB, 200; *Wb* 2:56. Baruch A. Levine, *Numbers 21–36*, ABC 4B (1993): 518.

111. *OBA*, 59; *MBA*, map #48; Carl Rasmussen, *NIV Atlas of the Bible* (Grand Rapids, Mich.: Zondervan, 1989), 89.

112. Lina Eckenstein, *A History of Sinai* (London: Society for Promoting Christian Knowledge, 1921), 67–68.

113. Simons, *Geographical and Topographical Texts of the Old Testament*, §428.

114. Davies, *Way of the Wilderness*, 84.

115. *Wb* 2:56; A. H. Gardiner, T. E. Peet, and Jaroslav Černý, *The Inscriptions of Sinai* (London: EES, 1955), 9–11, 41–42.

116. *Wb* 2:57; Gardiner, Peet, and Černý, *Inscriptions of Sinai*, 3.

117. Friedrich Junge, *Late Egyptian Grammar*, trans. David Warburton (Oxford: Griffiths Institute, 2001), 36.

118. Gregory Mumford, "Wadi Maghara," in *Encyclopedia of Ancient Egypt*, ed. Kathryn Bard (London: Routledge, 1999), 875.

119. Gardiner, Peet, and Černý, *Inscriptions of Sinai*, 97. Text is on plate XXVa.

120. This period is suggested on the basis of their departure from Egypt on 15 Abib (Exod. 12:18; 13:4), which is in March–April; they arrive at Rephadim, two stops before passing through the mining region, if our reconstruction is correct, at the beginning of the third month (Exod. 19:1), or six weeks later. This would mean they arrived at Mt. Sinai in the period of May-June.

121. Mumford, "Wadi Maghara," 875–878.

122. KB, 709. Thomas Lambdin, "Egyptian Loan Words in the Old Testament," *JAOS* 73 (1953): 152.

123. Yoshiyuki Muchiki, *Egyptian Proper Names and Loanwords in North-West Semitic*, SBL Dissertation Series 173 (Atlanta: Society of Biblical Literature, 1999), 251.

124. Alfred Lucas and J. R. Harris, *Ancient Egyptian Materials and Industries*, 4th ed. (London: Histories and Mysteries of Man, 1962; reprint, 1989), 404.

125. Hyatt, *Exodus,* 279; Brevard S. Childs, *The Book of Exodus: A Critical, Theological Commentary,* The Old Testament Library (Louisville, Ky.: Westminster, 1974), 529–530.

126. Yohanan Aharoni, *The Land of the Bible: A Historical Geography,* 3rd ed. Revised by A. F. Rainey (Philadelphia: Westminster, 1979), 54–57.

127. John Wevers, *Ezekiel,* The New Century Bible Commentary (Grand Rapids, Mich.: Eerdmans, 1969), 157.

128. Daniel I. Block, *The Book of Ezekiel: Chapters 25–48,* New International Commentary on the Old Testament (Grand Rapids, Mich.: Eerdmans, 1998), 106.

129. G. A. Cooke, *A Critical and Exegetical Commentary on the Book of Ezekiel,* International Critical Commentary (Edinburgh: T and T Clarke, 1936–1937), 316–317.

130. Moshe Greenberg, *Ezekiel 21–37,* ABC 22A (1997): 582.

131. BDB, 200; KB, 229.

132. Burkhardt, *Travels in Syria and the Holy Land,* 486, 487.

133. Robinson, *Biblical Researches,* 1:123–125.

134. Simons, *Geographical and Topographical Texts of the Old Testament,* §428; Gary Herion, "Alush," in *ABD* 1: 167; Dewey M. Beegle, *Moses, the Servant of Yahweh* (Grand Rapids, Mich.: Eerdmans, 1972), 172.

135. Davies, *Way of the Wilderness,* 84; Davies, *Numbers,* 345; Budd, *Numbers,* 355.

136. Levine, *Numbers 21–36,* 518.

137. Robinson, *Biblical Researches,* 1:175–180; Stanley, *Sinai and Palestine in Connection with Their History,* 38; Palmer, *Desert of the Exodus,* 21–22.

138. Aharoni, *Land of the Bible,* 199; Beegle, *Moses, the Servant of Yahweh,* 186–187; Aviram Perevolotsky and Israel Finkelstein, "The Southern Sinai Exodus Route in Ecological Perspective," *BAR* 11, no. 4 (1985): 27–45.

139. Cassuto, *Commentary on the Book of Exodus,* 200–201.

140. Sarna, *Exodus,* 93.

141. KB, 1,276; William H. C. Propp, *Exodus 1–18,* ABC 2 (1999), 604.

142. For many, aetiology signals a non-historical explanation for a name. This is not necessarily the case, as Alan Millard has shown, see Alan R. Millard, "Story, History, and Theology," in *Faith, Tradition and History,* ed. David Baker, Alan Millard, and J.K. Hoffmeier (Winona Lake, Ind.: Eisenbrauns, 1994), 37–64. Thus a genuine event may stand behind an aetiological story.

143. This is not the place to engage in a discussion about this Massah and Meribah story and its relationship to the one in Numbers 20, which takes place at Kadesh-Barnea. Whether these two stories reflect different events with similar consequences, and hence a case of déja vu, or if they indicate differing traditions about the same event, no one can say for sure.

144. Hyatt, *Exodus,* 180; Jo Ann Seely, "Rephidim," in *ABD* 5: 678.

145. Simons, *Geographical and Topographical Texts of the Old Testament,* §428.

146. Davies, *Way of the Wilderness,* 84.

147. Philip LaMoreaux and Hussein Idris, *The Exodus—Myth, Legend, History* (Tuscaloosa, Ala.: Word Way Press, 1996), 93, 95, figures 19, 20.

148. G. Ernest Wright, *Biblical Archaeology* (Philadelphia: Westminster, 1957), 65; Beegle, *Moses, the Servant of Yahweh,* 184. Beegle declares that this phenomenon does not occur in granitic rock, but only in limestone. Consequently he thinks that the

Numbers 20 episode at Kadesh-Barnea, a site in a limestone region, might be the original story that was applied to Exodus 17 (p. 184). Beegle was apparently unaware of the phenomenon that LaMoreaux discusses in his book.

149. Cassuto, *Commentary on the Book of Exodus*, 224; Sarna, *Exodus*, 103.

150. Donald Wiseman, "Calendar," in *NBD*, 158.

151. Finkelstein, "Southern Sinai Exodus Route in Ecological Perspective."

152. Manfred Görg, "Methodological Remarks on Comparative Studies of Egyptian and Biblical Words and Phrases," in *Pharaonic Egypt: The Bible and Christianity*, ed. Sarah Israelit-Groll (Jerusalem: Magnes Press, 1985), 61. *Mḥw.s* is a variant for the more common *šmᶜw.s* (*Wb* 2:125). For *psy*, see *Wb* 1: 551.

153. Görg, *Pharaonic Egypt*, 62; see *Wb* 5:494–495.

154. Robinson, *Biblical Researches*, 1:170.

155. F. S. Bodenheimer, "The Manna of Sinai," *BA* 10, no. 1 (1947): 76, 78, 80.

156. Hyatt, *Exodus*, 173.

157. Propp, *Exodus 1–18*, 590.

158. Cassuto, *Commentary on the Book of Exodus*, 191.

159. Alan H. Gardiner, *Egyptian Grammar: Being an Introduction to the Study of Hieroglyphs*, 3rd ed. (London: Oxford University Press, 1957), excursus C, 203–206.

160. Ann Macy Roth, "Work Force," in *Oxford Encyclopedia of Ancient Egypt*, ed. Donald Redford (New York: Oxford University Press, 2002), 523.

161. Gardiner, *Egyptian Grammar*, 472, sign G-42.

162. Patrick Houlihan and Steven Goodman, *The Birds of Ancient Egypt* (Cairo: American University Press, 1986), 75.

163. C. S. Jarvis, *Yesterday and To-Day in Sinai* (Edinburgh: William Blackwood and Sons, 1933), 259, 260, 264.

164. Ibid., 158–185.

165. R. K. Harrison, *Old Testament Times* (Grand Rapids, Mich.: Eerdmans, 1970), 138.

166. Flavius Josephus, *The Works of Josephus*, trans. William Whitson (Peabody, Mass.: Hendickson, 1736; reprint, 1987), 80.

167. Houlihan and Goodman, *Birds of Ancient Egypt*, 75–78.

168. Ibid., 77.

169. Budd, *Numbers*, 127.

170. Levine, *Numbers 1–20*, 321.

171. Hermann Kees, *Ancient Egypt: A Cultural Topography* (Chicago: University of Chicago Press, 1961), 77.

172. Barbara Mertz, *Red Land, Black Land: Daily Life in Ancient Egypt*, rev. ed. (New York: Dodd, Mead, 1978), 104.

173. Hans Schneider, *Life and Death under the Pharaohs: Egyptian Art from the National Museum of Antiquities in Leiden, the Netherlands*, trans. Julia Harvey (Leiden: National Museum of Antiquities in Leiden, 1996), 68, 120–121, 126–127 and elsewhere; Richard Fazzini, *Ancient Egyptian Art in the Brooklyn Museum* (New York: Thames and Hudson, 1989), 32, 33, 90.

174. The word translated as "leeks" (חָצִיר) does occur elsewhere in the Bible, usually meaning grass (e.g., 1 Kings 18:5; 2 Kings 19:26; Isa. 15:6, 40:6, 7, 8). Only here is the meaning "leeks" used.

CHAPTER 8

1. E. H. Palmer, *The Desert of the Exodus: Journeys in the Wilderness of the Forty Years' Wanderings* (New York: Harper and Brothers, 1872), 171–172.

2. Because no other evidence for the Old Kingdom was found at Serabit, it could be that the statue on which Sneferu's name occurs was transported from Maghara, when it was being phased out of use; Alan H. Gardiner, T. Eric Peet, and Jaroslav Černý, *The Inscriptions of Sinai* (London: Egypt Exploration Society, 1955), 38 and plate I.

3. W. M. F. Petrie, *Researches in Sinai* (New York: E. P. Dutton, 1906), 130, 131.

4. Ibid., vi.

5. Gardiner, Peet, and Černý, *Inscriptions of Sinai*, plates LXXXII–LXXXIII.

6. Alan H. Gardiner, "The Egyptian Origin of the Alphabet," *JEA* 3 (1916): 1–16.

7. Ibid., 13.

8. William F. Albright, *The Proto-Sinaitic Inscriptions and Their Decipherment*, Harvard Theological Studies 22 (Cambridge: Harvard University Press, 1966), 10–11.

9. Ibid., 6.

10. Ibid., 6–7.

11. Frank M. Cross, "Yahweh and the God of the Patriarchs," *HTR* 55 (1962): 236–241. Albright, *Proto-Sinaitic Inscriptions and Their Decipherment*, 24.

12. Frank M. Cross, "The Origin and the Early Evolution of the Alphabet," *EI* 8 (1967): 8*–24*; Cross, "Early Alphabetic Scripts," in *Symposia Celebrating the Seventy-Fifth Anniversary of the Founding of the American Schools of Oriental Research*, ed. Frank M. Cross (Cambridge, Mass.: ASOR, 1979), 1–20; Cross, "Newly Found Inscriptions in Old Canaanite and Early Phoenician Scripts," *BASOR* 238 (1980): 1–20.

13. Joseph Naveh, *Early History of the Alphabet: An Introduction to West Semitic Epigraphy and Palaeography* (Jerusalem: Magnes Press, 1982), 26–27.

14. Publication of some of the Egyptian texts has recently appeared: John Darnell, *Theban Desert Road Survey in the Egyptian Western Desert*, Volume 1: *Gebel Tjauti Rock Inscriptions 1–45 and Wadi el-Hôl Rock Inscriptions 1–45* (Chicago: Oriental Institute, 2002). Owing to the complex nature of the early Semitic-alphabetic texts, however, and because a team of scholars, including specialists in early Semitic scripts, are working together on the new texts, more time is required prior to the publication of these Semitic texts.

15. Dori Baker, "Finding Sheds New Light on the Alphabet's Origins," *Yale Bulletin and Calendar* 28, no. 16 (2000); John Darnell, "Journey to the 'Valley of Terror'," *Chicago House Bulletin, Epigraphic Survey of the Oriental Institute* 2 (April 1994:) 1–2.

16. I. J. Gelb, *A Study of Writing* (Chicago: University of Chicago Press, 1969); André Lemaire, "Writing and Writing Materials," in *ABD* 6: 999.

17. James Hoffmeier, *Israel in Egypt: The Evidence for the Authenticity of the Exodus Tradition* (New York: Oxford University Press, 1997), 142, 143.

18. Acts 7:22.

19. Moshe Kochavi, "An Ostracon from the Period of the Judges from 'Izbet Sartah,'" *Tel Aviv* 4 (1977): 1–13.

20. Cross, "Newly Found Inscriptions," 12–13.

21. Note the title of Kochavi, "An Ostracon from the Period of the Judges from 'Izbet Sartah."

22. Israel Finkelstein, *The Archaeology of the Israelite Settlement* (Jerusalem: Israel Exploration Society, 1988), 73–80.

23. Ibid., 78. Interestingly, the important 'Izbet Sartah ostracon is passed over in complete silence in his recent book: Israel Finkelstein and Neil Asher Silberman, *The Bible Unearthed: Archaeology's New Vision of Ancient Israel and the Origin of Its Sacred Texts* (New York: Free Press, 2001), 110–111. Over the past decade Finkelstein has moved into the minimalists' camp!

24. William G. Dever, *What Did the Biblical Writers Know & When Did They Know It?: What Archaeology Can Tell Us about the Reality of Ancient Israel* (Grand Rapids, Mich.: Eerdmans, 2001), 114.

25. Kenneth Kitchen, "Ancient Arabia and the Bible," *ABW* 3, no. 1 (1995): 28; see references in n. 6. Pierre Bordreuil, "The South-Arabian Abecedary," *Near Eastern Archaeology* 63, no. 4 (2000): 197. I was able to discuss the significance of this discovery with both Kitchen and Bordreuil in April 2003 at a conference in Liverpool.

26. Kitchen, "Ancient Arabia and the Bible," 28.

27. See above, chapter 1, §III.

28. J. Philip Hyatt, *Exodus* (London: Marshall, Morgan, and Scott, 1971), 208.

29. John Van Seters, *A Law Book for the Diaspora: Revision in the Study of the Covenant Code* (New York: Oxford University Press, 2003).

30. Brevard S. Childs, *The Book of Exodus: A Critical, Theological Commentary*, The Old Testament Library (Louisville, Ky.: Westminster, 1974), 344.

31. Julius Wellhausen, *Prolegomena to the History of Ancient Israel* (Gloucester, Mass.: Peter Smith, 1878), 392.

32. Martin Noth, *Exodus* (Philadelphia: Westminster, 1962), 155–194.

33. Ibid., 173.

34. J. Morgenstern, "The Oldest Document of the Hexateuch," *HUCA* 9 (1927): 1–138.

35. Robert Pfieffer, "A Non-Israelite Source of Genesis," *ZAW* 48 (1930): 66–73.

36. Georg Fohrer, *Introduction to the Old Testament*, trans. David Green (Nashville, Tenn.: Abingdon, 1968), 112, 133–134.

37. John Durham, *Exodus*, Word Biblical Commentary 3 (Waco, Tex.: Word, 1987), 259.

38. John Van Seters, *The Life of Moses: The Yahwist as Historian in Exodus-Numbers* (Louisville, Ky.: Westminster, 1994), 247.

39. Ibid., 248–252.

40. Van Seters, *Law Book for the Diaspora*.

41. Richard Elliott Friedman, *Who Wrote the Bible?* (San Francisco: Harper, 1987), 251.

42. For example, Rolf Rendtorff, *Die überlieferungsgeschichtliche Problem des Pentateuch*, *BZAW* 147 (Berlin: de Gruyter, 1977); Isaac Kikawada, *Before Abraham Was: A Provocative Challenge to the Documentary Hypothesis* (Nashville, Tenn.:

Abingdon, 1985); R. N. Whybray, *The Making of the Pentateuch: A Methodological Study*, JSOT Supplement Series 53 (Sheffield: JSOT Press, 1987); Thomas L. Thompson, *The Origin Tradition of Ancient Israel: The Literary Formation of Genesis and Exodus 1–23*, JSOT Supplement Series 55 (Sheffield: JSOT Press, 1987).

43. D. Patrick, "The Covenant Code Structure," *VT* 27 (1977): 145–157; G. C. Chirchigno, "The Narrative Structure of Exod. 19–24," *Biblica* 68 (1987): 457–479.

44. Joe Sprinkle, *The Book of the Covenant: A Literary Approach*, JSOT Supplement Series 174 (Sheffield: JSOT Press, 1994), chapter 1.

45. Ibid., chapters 2–4.

46. T. D. Alexander, "The Composition of the Sinai Narrative in Exodus xix 1-xxiv 11," *VT* 49, no. 1 (1999): 4.

47. Ibid., 20.

48. Wellhausen, *Prolegomena to the History of Ancient Israel*, 417–418.

49. KB 157; Kenneth Kitchen, "Egypt, Ugarit, Qatna and Covenant," *UF* 11 (1979): 453–464; Delbert R. Hillers, *Covenant: The History of a Biblical Idea* (Baltimore: Johns Hopkins University Press, 1969).

50. See William L. Moran, *The Amarna Letters* (Baltimore: Johns Hopkins University Press, 1992).

51. For some recent and important essays on diplomacy in the Amarna period, see the volume edited by Raymond Cohen and Raymond Westbrook, *Amarna Diplomacy: The Beginnings of International Diplomacy* (Baltimore: Johns Hopkins University Press, 2000). See also Zipora Cochavi-Rainey, *Royal Gifts in the Late Bronze Age, Fourteenth to Thirteenth Centuries B.C.E.*, Beer-Sheva Studies by the Department of Bible and Ancient Near East (Beer-Sheva: Ben-Gurion University of the Negev Press, 1999).

52. KB, 500.

53. William F. Albright, "The Hebrew Expression for 'Making a Covenant' in Pre-Israelite Documents," *BASOR* 121 (1951): 21–22.

54. On the importance of the sacrificial meal to the treaty ceremony, see D. J. McCarthy, "Three Covenants in Genesis," *CBQ* 26 (1964): 184–185; McCarthy, *Treaty and Covenant: A Study in Form in the Ancient Oriental Documents and the Old Testament*, Analecta Biblica 21 (Rome, 1963), 253–254.

55. D. J. McCarthy, *Old Testament Covenant: A Survey of Current Opinions* (Richmond, Va.: John Knox Press, 1972), 30–31.

56. Hillers, *Covenant*, 40–41, 57.

57. See also Baltzer's critique of Wellhausen's understanding of b^{e}*rîṯ* Klaus Baltzer, *The Covenant Formulary*, trans. David Green (Philadelphia: Fortress, 1971), 1–8.

58. Viktor Korošec, *Hethitische Staatsverträge; Ein Beitrage zu ihrer Juristischen Wertung*, Leipziger Rechtswissenschaftliche Studien (Leipzig: Leipziger Juristen-Facultät, 1931).

59. George E. Mendenhall, "Covenant Forms in Israelite Tradition," *BA* 17, no. 3 (1954): 32.

60. Gary Beckman, *Hittite Diplomatic Texts*, Writings from the Ancient World (Atlanta: Society of Biblical Literature, 1999).

61. See particularly the works of Kenneth Kitchen, *Ancient Orient and Old Testament* (Downers Grove, Ill.: InterVarsity Press, 1966), 94–102; Kitchen, *The Bible in Its World: Archaeology and the Bible Today* (Exeter: Paternoster Press, 1977), 80–85; Kitchen, "The Fall and Rise of Covenant, Law and Treaty," *TB* 40 (1989): 118–135, Kitchen, *On the Reliability of the Old Testament* (Grand Rapids, Mich.: Eerdmans, 2003), 283–294.

62. This is from the treaty between Suppiluliuma I the Hittite and Tette of Nuhashshi. Translation in Beckman, *Hittite Diplomatic Texts*, 54.

63. This from the treaty between Mursili II and Tuppi-Teshshup of Amurru; ibid., 59.

64. This is from the treaty between Suppiluliuma I the Hittite and Tette of Nuhashshi, ibid., 54–55.

65. Sharrupshi's grandson, with whom the treaty is made.

66. This is from the treaty between Suppiluliuma I the Hittite and Tette of Nuhashshi; Beckman, *Hittite Diplomatic Texts*, 55–57.

67. This is from the treaty between Suppiluliuma I the Hittite and Shattiwaza of Mittanni, ibid., 46.

68. Ibid.

69. This is from the treaty between Muwattalli the Hittite and Alaksandu of Wilusa, ibid., 91.

70. This is from the treaty between Suppiluliuma I the Hittite and Shattiwaza of Mittanni, ibid., 47.

71. This is from the treaty between Suppiluliuma I the Hittite and Tette of Nuhashshi, ibid., 58.

72. If damage has occurred to a tablet, it usually happens at the beginning or end of the text. Consequently some of the curses and/or blessings are lost.

73. This is from the treaty between Suppiluliuma I the Hittite and Tette of Nuhashshi, in Beckman, *Hittite Diplomatic Texts*, 58.

74. Mendenhall, "Covenant Forms in Israelite Tradition," 25–53.

75. Ibid., 25.

76. Ibid., 36–46.

77. Ibid., 43.

78. John Thompson, *The Ancient Near Eastern Treaties and the Old Testament* (London: Tyndale Press, 1963); McCarthy, *Treaty and Covenant*; Baltzer, *Covenant Formulary*; Hillers, *Covenant*; Kitchen, *Ancient Orient and Old Testament*, 90–102. For Deuteronomy, see Kitchen, *Ancient Orient and Old Testament*, 90–102; Kitchen, "Ancient Orient, 'Deuteronism,' and the Old Testament," in *New Perspective on the Old Testament*, ed. J. B. Payne (Waco, Tex.: Word, 1970), 1–24; M. G. Kline, *Treaty of the Great King* (Grand Rapids, Mich.: Eerdmans, 1967); Kitchen, *Bible in Its World*, 79–85.

79. Beckman, *Hittite Diplomatic Texts*, 96.

80. Hillers, *Covenant*, 31.

81. Translation from the German is that of Mendenhall, "Covenant Forms in Israelite Tradition," 33.

82. Hillers, *Covenant*, 31.

83. For example, Gösta W. Ahlström, *Who Were the Israelites?* (Winona Lake, Ind.: Eisenbrauns, 1986); Niels Peter Lemche, *Ancient Israel: A New History of Israelite*

Society (Sheffield: JSOT Press, 1988); Lemche, *Early Israel; Anthropological and Historical Studies on the Israelite Society before the Monarchy* (Leiden: Brill, 1985); Lemche, "Is It Still Possible to Write a History of Israel?" *SJOT* 8 (1994): 164–190; Finkelstein, *Archaeology of the Israelite Settlement*; Finkelstein and Silberman, *Bible Unearthed*.

84. McCarthy, *Old Testament Covenant*, 19.

85. Kitchen, *Ancient Orient and Old Testament*, 97; Kitchen, *Bible in Its World*, 81–82.

86. Delbert Hillers, *Treaty-Curses and the Old Testament Prophets*, Biblica et Orientalia 16 (Rome: Pontifical Biblical Institute, 1964), 30–42.

87. Kitchen, "Fall and Rise of Covenant, Law and Treaty," 123–128; Kitchen, *On the Reliability of the Old Testament*, 283–294.

88. Mendenhall, "Covenant Forms in Israelite Tradition," 43; Baltzer, *Covenant Formulary*, xii; Kitchen, *Ancient Orient and Old Testament*, 98–99.

89. Thompson, *Ancient Near Eastern Treaties and the Old Testament*.

90. Eberhard Gerstenberger, "Covenant and Commandment," *JBL* 84 (1965): 45.

91. Moshe Weinfeld, "Traces of Assyrian Treaty Formulae in Deuteronomy," *Biblica* 46 (1965): 417–427.

92. Ibid., 423.

93. Hillers, *Treaty-Curses and the Old Testament Prophets*, 42.

94. Moshe Weinfeld, *Deuteronomy and the Deuteronomic School* (Oxford: Clarendon, 1972).

95. McCarthy, *Old Testament Covenant*, 15.

96. Van Seters, *Law Book for the Diaspora*, 11–19, 172–175.

97. Donald J. Wiseman, "The Vassal-Treaties of Esarhaddon," *Iraq*, no. 20 (1958): 1–3.

98. Joseph Fitzmyer, "The Inscriptions of Bar-Ga'yah and Mati'el from Sefire," in *COS* 2:13–22.

99. This structure is based upon the recent work on the Sefire treaties by Fitzmyer, ibid., 213–217. The Assyrian structure is determined from Wiseman's publications.

100. One text is thought to have a fragment of an historical prologue, but this is from a broken text that makes it difficult to conclude whether this is a genuine historical prologue or a line connected to the preamble.

101. Kitchen, *Ancient Orient and Old Testament*, 94–102; Kitchen, *Bible in Its World*, 80–85.

102. C. F. Whitley, "Covenant and Commandment in Israel," *JNES* 22 (1963).

103. Hillers, *Treaty-Curses and the Old Testament Prophets*, 83.

104. Yehezkel Kaufmann, *The Religion of Israel: From Its Beginnings to the Babylonian Exile*, trans. Moshe Greenberg (New York: Schocken Books, 1972), 127–133; Fohrer, Introduction to the Old Testament, 75–86.

CHAPTER 9

1. For recent essays on the tabernacle that deal with literary, cultic, and structural questions, see Richard Averbeck, "Tabernacle," in *Dictionary of the Old Testament:*

Pentateuch, ed. Desmond Alexander and David Baker (Downers Grove, Ill.: InterVarsity Press, 2003), 807–827; Richard E. Friedman, "Tabernacle," in *ABD* 6: 292–300.

2. Julius Wellhausen, *Prolegomena to the History of Ancient Israel* (Gloucester, Mass.: Peter Smith, 1878), 36–37.

3. Ibid., 37.

4. Ibid., 8.

5. Berhard Pelzl, "These zur Entstehung des Zeltsbaurichtes von Ex. 25ff.," *UF* 8 (1976): 323–327; Pelzl, "Das Zelt Heiligtum von Ex. 25ff. die frage nach der Möglichkeit seinen Errichtung," *UF* 7 (1975): 379–388.

6. See Ezekiel 1:2 and 29:17 for the basis of the twenty-one-year prophetic career of this prophet.

7. KB, 1,496–1,497.

8. Brevard S. Childs, *The Book of Exodus: A Critical, Theological Commentary*, The Old Testament Library (Louisville, Ky.: Westminster, 1974), 540.

9. Manahem Haran, "The Nature of the 'Ohel Mo'edh' in Pentateuchal Sources," *JSS* 5 (1960): 50–66. There are some references that suggest that a "tent of meeting" was located outside the camp (cf. Exod. 33:7), where Moses encountered God in a direct way. For other indications of a prophetic tent outside the camp, see pages 54–55 in Haran's study.

10. KB, 557.

11. Ralph Hendrix, "*Miškan* and *'Ohel Môe̱d*: Etymology, Lexical Definitions, and Extra-Biblical Usage," *AUSS* 29, no. 3 (1991): 213–224; Hendrix, "The Use of *Miškan* and *'Ohel Môe̱d* in Exodus 25–40," *AUSS* 30, no. 1 (1992): 3–13.

12. Hendrix, "Use of *Miškan* and *'Ohel Môe̱d* in Exodus 25–40," 4, 7.

13. Ibid., 13.

14. Umberto Cassuto, *A Commentary on the Book of Exodus*, trans. I. Abrahams (Jerusalem: Magnes Press, 1951), 476.

15. Bruce Waltke and Michael O'Connor, *An Introduction to Biblical Hebrew Syntax* (Winona Lake, Ind.: Eisenbrauns, 1990), 211.

16. Translations vary considerably for this verse, hence I offer here my own rendition. The meaning of the word תחשים (*tᵉḥāšim*) is disputed and will be investigated below.

17. John Van Seters, *Abraham in History and Tradition* (New Haven: Yale University Press, 1975), 14, 38, 310.

18. Kenneth Kitchen, *The Bible in Its World: Archaeology and the Bible Today* (Exeter: Paternoster Press, 1977), 58–59; Donald Wiseman, "They Lived in Tents," in *Biblical and Near Eastern Studies: Essays in Honor of William Sanford Lasor*, ed. Gary Tuttle (Grand Rapids, Mich.: Eerdmans, 1978), 195–200.

19. Wiseman, "They Lived in Tents," 195–200.

20. Arno Poebel, "The Khorsabad King List," *JNES* 1 (1942): 251–252.

21. James Hoffmeier, "Tents in Egypt and the Ancient Near East," *JSSEA* 7, no. 3 (1977): 13–28. My study and that of Kitchen appeared the same year, but our conclusions were reached completely independently of each other. Although his treatment is much shorter than mine, as it is only a small section of a book, we nevertheless cite many of the same texts.

22. Ibid., 14.

23. Miriam Lichtheim rejected Gardiner's view that the Admonitions were written in the Middle Kingdom to reflect on the society upheavals of the First Intermediate Period, preferring to see it as a literary work of the late Middle Kingdom; Miriam Lichtheim, *Ancient Egyptian Literature* (Berkeley: University of California Press, 1973), 1:149–150.

24. John Van Seters, "The Date for the 'Admonitions' in the Second Intermediate Period," *JEA* 50 (1964): 13–23.

25. Translation in Hoffmeier, "Tents in Egypt and the Ancient Near East," 15.

26. Ibid.

27. *Wb* 1: 119; *DLE* 1: 49.

28. For references and discussion, see Hoffmeier, "Tents in Egypt and the Ancient Near East," 23.

29. KRI 4 (1982): 9.10–11.

30. *Wb* 1: 119.

31. Richard Clifford, "The Tent of El and the Israelite Tent of Meeting," *CBQ* 33 (1971): 221–227.

32. Ibid., 223.

33. Ibid., 224–225.

34. John Wilson, "The Assembly of the Phoenician City," *JNES* 4 (1945): 245.

35. Van Seters, *Abraham in History and Tradition*, 14.

36. Daniel Fleming, *Democracy's Ancient Ancestors: Mari and Early Collective Governance* (Cambridge: Cambridge University Press, 2004), 20–23, 47–49, 85–92, 148–157.

37. Ibid., 22.

38. KB, 322.

39. Richard E. Friedman, "The Tabernacle in the Temple," *BA* 43, no. 4 (1980): 241–248; Friedman, *Who Wrote the Bible?* (San Francisco: Harper, 1987), 174–187.

40. Friedman, "Tabernacle in the Temple," 241–244; Friedman, *Who Wrote the Bible?*, 177–181.

41. Friedman, *Who Wrote the Bible?*, 183.

42. For a recent example of this tendency, see Ralph W. Klein, "Back to the Future: The Tabernacle in the Book of Exodus," *Interpretation* 50, no. 3 (1996): 264–276.

43. Friedman, "Tabernacle in the Temple," 245.

44. Friedman, *Who Wrote the Bible?*, 184–187.

45. V. A. Hurowitz, "The Form and Fate of the Tabernacle: Reflections on a Recent Proposal," *JQR* 86 (1995): 127–151.

46. Ibid., 127, 131, 132, 142.

47. Friedman, "Tabernacle in the Temple," 241.

48. Michael Homan, *To Your Tents, O Israel! The Terminology, Function, Form, and Symbolism of Tents in the Hebrew Bible and the Ancient Near East* (Leiden: Brill, 2002), 170–177.

49. Susan Pollock, "Ur," in *The Oxford Encyclopedia of Archaeology in the Near East*, ed. Eric Meyers (New York: Oxford University Press, 1997), 5: 288–289.

50. William Murnane, "Luxor," in *The Oxford Encyclopedia of Ancient Egypt*, ed. Donald Redford (New York: Oxford University Press, 2001), 2: 310–311.

51. Ephraim Stern, "Jerusalem," in *NEAEHL* 2: 698–800.

52. Mircea Eliade, *Patterns in Comparative Religion*, trans. Rosemary Sheed (New York: New American Library, 1958), 368.

53. Cassuto, *Commentary on the Book of Exodus*, 316.

54. Childs, *Book of Exodus*, 508.

55. Myung Soo Suh, *The Tabernacle in the Narrative History of Israel from the Exodus to the Conquest*, Studies in Biblical Literature 50 (New York: Peter Lang, 2003), 98–100.

56. Ibid., 99.

57. It is worth noting that the tent that David made for the ark in Jerusalem (2 Sam. 6:17) is never called the "tent of meeting" or "the tabernacle." It clearly was a new and different tent set up to house the ark, while the old tent of meeting/tabernacle stood at Gibeon (cf. 1 Chron. 21:29; 2 Chron 1:3, 13).

58. By saying this I am not denying the importance of the theophany of 2 Samuel 24:16–17, which accounts for the particular spot where the temple was erected. Reference to the original Sinai tent does not preclude the possibility or even likelihood that in the course of the centuries some or all of the linens and skins were replaced.

59. Jon D. Levenson, *Sinai and Zion: An Entry into the Jewish Bible* (San Francisco: Harper and Row, 1985), 91.

60. Gun Björkman, *Kings at Karnak: A Study of the Treatment of the Monuments of Royal Predecessors in the Early New Kingdom* (Uppsala: Uppsala Studies in Ancient Mediterranean and Near Eastern Civilizations, 1971), 2: 58.

61. Text in Pierre Lacau and Henri Chevrier, *Une chapelle de Sesotris Ier à Karnak* (Cairo: IFAO, 1956), 44; my own translation.

62. *Wb* 3: 239–240.

63. Hugo Gressman, *Mose und seine Zeit* (Göttingen: Vanderhoeck and Ruprecht, 1913), 240–242.

64. Frank Moore Cross, "The Priestly Tabernacle," *BA* 10, no. 3 (1947): 209.

65. Ibid., 212.

66. Ibid., 213, 217–219.

67. Frank Moore Cross, *From Epic to Canon: History and Literature in Ancient Israel* (Baltimore: Johns Hopkins University Press, 1998), 92, 85.

68. Ibid., 92.

69. Mark S. Smith, *The Early History of God: Yahweh and the Other Deities in Ancient Israel* (San Francisco: Harper and Row, 1990), 3.

70. A. A. Anderson, *2 Samuel*, Word Biblical Commentary 11 (Waco, Tex.: Word, 1989), 117.

71. Some of the translations rendering הַיְרִיעָה as tent include RSV, NRSV, NIV, JB, and NJPS.

72. Clifford, "Tent of El and the Israelite Tent of Meeting," 221–227.

73. Ibid., 225.

74. Cross, "Priestly Tabernacle," 220.

75. Clifford, "Tent of El and the Israelite Tent of Meeting," 227.

76. Daniel E. Fleming, "Mari's Large Public Tent and the Priestly Tent Sanctuary," *VT* 50, no. 4 (2000): 484–498.

77. Ibid., 486, 487.

78. A. J. Spencer, *Early Egypt: The Rise of Civilisation in the Nile Valley* (Norman: University of Oklahoma Press, 1993), 63–65. On the development of Egyptian temples from earlier reed shrines, see Alexander Badaway, *A History of Egyptian Architecture: From Earliest Times to the End of the Old Kingdom* (Giza: Studio Misr, 1954), 1: 13–93.

79. Richard Wilkinson, *The Complete Temples of Ancient Egypt* (London: Thames and Hudson, 2000), 16–18.

80. Cyril Aldred, *Egypt to the End of the Old Kingdom* (New York: McGraw-Hill, 1965), 68–73.

81. Bernhard Grdseloff, *Das Ägyptische Reinigungszelt* (Cairo: IFAO, 1941); James Hoffmeier, "The Possible Origins of the Tent of Purification in the Egyptian Funerary Cult," *SAK* 9 (1981): 167–177.

82. William Kelly Simpson, *The Mastabas of Kar and Idu at Giza* (Warminster: Aris and Phillips, 1976), figure 24.

83. A. M. Blackman, *The Rock Tombs at Meir V* (London: EES, 1952), 52–54.

84. W. Stevenson Smith, *The Art and Architecture of Ancient Egypt* (Baltimore: Penguin, 1965), 48–50, and plate 30a.

85. Kitchen, *Bible in Its World*; Kitchen, "Some Egyptian Background to the Old Testament," *TB* 5 (1960): 7–13; Kitchen, "The Tabernacle—a Bronze Age Artifact," *EI* 24, Avaham Malamat Volume (1993): 119–129; Kitchen, "The Desert Tabernacle: Pure Fiction or Plausible Account?" *BR* 16 (2000): 14–21; Kitchen, *On the Reliability of the Old Testament* (Grand Rapids, Mich.: Eerdmans, 2003), 275–283.

86. Homan, *To Your Tents, O Israel!*, chapter 7; Homan, "The Divine Warrior in His Tent: A Military Model for Yahweh's Tabernacle," *BR* 16 (2000): 22–33, 55.

87. Hoffmeier, "Tents in Egypt and the Ancient Near East," 16, 18.

88. For the measurements and drawing of the frame structure, see Nicholas Reeves, *The Complete Tutankhamun* (London: Thames and Hudson, 1990), 100–101.

89. Hans Bonnet, *Die Waffen der Völker des alten Orients* (Leipzig: J. C. Hinrichs, 1926), 58.

90. Percy Newberry, *El-Bersheh*, vol. 1 (London: Egypt Exploration Fund, 1894), plate xiiii.

91. Homan, *To Your Tents, O Israel!*, 112.

92. Hoffmeier, "Tents in Egypt and the Ancient Near East," 18.

93. Ibid., 14, #14.

94. Homan, *To Your Tents, O Israel!*, 113–114.

95. This parallel was recognized by Homan, "Divine Warrior in His Tent," 113.

96. Homan, *To Your Tents, O Israel!*, 114.

97. Kitchen, "Tabernacle—a Bronze Age Artifact," 126*; Kitchen, "Desert Tabernacle: Pure Fiction or Plausible Account?" 15–21.

98. *Wb* 4: 520; KB, 1,473; Thomas Lambdin, "Egyptian Loan Words in the Old Testament," *JAOS* 73 (1953): 520; Yoshiyuki Muchiki, *Egyptian Proper Names and Loanwords in North-West Semitic*, SBL Dissertation Series 173 (Atlanta: Society of Biblical Literature, 1999), 256.

99. Muchiki, *Egyptian Proper Names and Loanwords in North-West Semitic*, 256.

100. Henry Spencer Palmer, *Sinai: From the Fourth Egyptian Dynasty to the Present Day* (London: Society for Promoting Christian Knowledge, 1892), 46.

101. Ibid., 47.

102. The altar was covered with bronze (Exod. 27:2).

103. Ziony Zevit, "Timber for the Tabernacle: Text, Tradition, and *Realia*," *Eretz-Israel* 23 (1992): 137*–143*.

104. Ibid., 137*.

105. Ibid., 140*–141*.

106. Ibid., 141*.

107. Ibid., 141*–142*.

108. David Hackett Fischer, *Historians' Fallacies: Toward a Logic of Historical Thought* (New York: Harper and Row, 1970), 109.

109. Zevit, "Timber for the Tabernacle," 141*.

110. C. F. Keil and F. Delitzsch, *Commentary on the Old Testament in Ten Volumes*, Vol. 1 *Pentateuch*, Pt. 2 (1869–1870; reprint, Grand Rapids, Mich.: Eerdmans, 1983), 178; Cassuto, *Commentary on the Book of Exodus*, 354; J. Philip Hyatt, *Exodus* (London: Marshall, Morgan, and Scott, 1971), 274; R. Alan Cole, *Exodus: An Introduction and Commentary*, Tyndale Old Testament Commentary (Downers Grove, Ill.: InterVarsity Press, 1973), 194–195; John Durham, *Exodus*, Word Biblical Commentary, (Waco, Tex.: Word, 1987), 366; Cornelis Houtman, *Exodus*, Historical Commentary on the Old Testament (Kampen: KOK Publishing House, 1996), 428. Houtman translates comaḏîm literally as "posts."

111. Christine Hobson, *The World of the Pharaohs* (London: Thames and Hudson, 1987), 76–77.

112. John Currid, "The Deforestation of the Foothills of Palestine," *PEQ* 116 (1984): 1–11.

113. Philip King and Lawrence Stager, *Life in Biblical Israel* (Louisville, Ky.: Westminster/John Knox Press, 2001), 112.

114. KB, 922; Lambdin, "Egyptian Loan Words in the Old Testament," 153; Muchiki, *Egyptian Proper Names and Loanwords in North-West Semitic*, 253.

115. *Wb* 4: 539; KB, 1,663; Lambdin, "Egyptian Loan Words in the Old Testament," 155; Muchiki, *Egyptian Proper Names and Loanwords in North-West Semitic*, 257–258.

116. For a detailed discussion of the Egyptian elements in the Joseph story, see James Hoffmeier, *Israel in Egypt: The Evidence for the Authenticity of the Exodus Tradition* (New York: Oxford University Press, 1997), chapter 4.

117. James Hoffmeier, "Flax, Linen," in *New International Dictionary of Old Testament Theology and Exegesis*, ed. Willem Van Gemeren (Grand Rapids, Mich.: Zondervan, 1997), 711.

118. Avi Hurvitz, "The Usage of *Šēš* and *Bûṣ* in the Bible and Its Implication for the Date of P," *HTR* 60 (1967): 117–121.

119. Ibid., 120.

120. Ibid.

121. Cross, "Priestly Tabernacle," 220 n. 21; *Wb* 5: 396. *Wb* shows that after the Middle Kingdom, the *ṯ* was vocalized as *t*, which fits its appearance in the Torah.

122. Cross, *From Epic to Canon*, 88.

123. Nahum M. Sarna, *Exodus*, The JPS Torah Commentary (Philadelphia: Jewish Publication Society, 1991), 157.

124. Cross, *From Epic to Canon*, 89.

125. Edward Robinson, *Biblical Researches in Palestine and the Adjacent Regions* (Boston: Croker and Brewster, 1841), 1: 171.

126. Ibid.

127. KB, 1,721.

128. Othmar Keel, *Symbolism of the Biblical World* (New York: Seabury, 1978), 190–192.

129. Nahman Avigad, "Samaria," in *NEAEHL* 4: 1,305; Max Mallowan, *The Nimrud Ivories* (London: British Musem, 1978), 26–43.

130. See Daphna Ben-Tor, *The Scarab: A Reflection of Ancient Egypt* (Jerusalem: Israel Museum, 1993); Nahman Avigad and Benjamin Sass, *Corpus of West Semitic Stamp Seals* (Jerusalem: Israel Exploration Society, 1997), for example, nos. 3, 4, 11, 29, 37, 44, 46, 59, 82, 85, 103, 104, 116, 126, 127, 135, 143, 146, 159, 160, 163, 168, 182; Keel, *Symbolism of the Biblical World*, 350–354.

131. Reeves, *Complete Tutankhamun*, 133.

132. Donald Wiseman, "Weights and Measures," in *NBD*, 1,246.

133. *Wb* 5: 26–27; KB, 173; Carol Meyers, *The Tabernacle Menorah: A Synthetic Study of a Symbol from the Biblical Cult* (Missoula, Mont.: Scholars Press, 1976), 22.

134. Alan H. Gardiner, *Egyptian Grammar: Being an Introduction to the Study of Hieroglyphs*, 3rd ed. (London: Oxford University Press, 1957), 529, sign W–15.

135. Meyers, *Tabernacle Menorah*, 65–69, 107–111.

136. Ibid., 182.

137. That these Semites were involved in metalworking is suggested by the fact that the donkeys are shown carrying bellows, which would have been used for smelting.

138. Meyers, *Tabernacle Menorah*, 184.

139. Manfred Görg, "Methodological Remarks on Comparative Studies of Egyptian and Biblical Words and Phrases," in *Pharaonic Egypt: The Bible and Christianity*, ed. Sarah Israelit-Groll (Jerusalem: Magnes Press, 1985), 61.

140. J. R. Harris, *Lexicographical Studies in Ancient Egyptian Minerals*, Deutsche Akademie der Wissenschaften zu Berlin Institut für Orientforshcung 54 (Berlin, 1961), 58.

141. *Wb* 1: 437.21; J. Černý, *Coptic Etymological Dictionary* (Cambridge: Cambridge University Press, 1976), 26.

142. Friedrich Junge, *Late Egyptian Grammar*, trans. David Warburton (Oxford: Griffiths Institute, 2001), 37.

143. Görg, "Methodological Remarks," 61.

144. Baruch Levine, "The Descriptive Tabernacle Texts of the Pentateuch," *JAOS* 85 (1965): 307–318.

145. KB, 491–492.

146. Ruth Amiran, "The 'Arm-Shaped' Vessel and Its Family," *JNES* 21, no. 3 (1962): 162–174.

147. *Wb* 5: 105.

148. *CDME*, 284.

149. Aylward M. Blackman, "Remarks on an Incense-Brazier Depicted in Thuthotep's Tomb at el-Bersheh," *ZÄS* 50 (1912): 66–68.

150. For a study of the development of the arm censer, see Henry Fischer, "Varia Aegyptiaca," *JARCE* 2 (1963): 28–34.

151. KB, 572.

152. *CDME*, 182.

153. Gardiner, *Egyptian Grammar*, §290.

154. The only time this word refers to garments of a nonpriestly figure is in Isaiah's denunciation of the steward Shebna for making himself a marvelous tomb (Isa. 22:15–20). The prophet announces that he will be replaced by Eliakim the son of Hilkiah, who would wear Shebna's robe and sash (Isa. 22:21). This would suggest that the sash was worn by individuals of special status.

155. KB, 8–9; Lambdin, "Egyptian Loan Words in the Old Testament," 146; Muchiki, *Egyptian Proper Names and Loanwords in North-West Semitic*, 237.

156. *Wb* 1: 465. This particular word survives into Greek as *βυνητος* and refers to "an Egyptian garment." See H. G. Liddell, R. Scott, and H. S. Jones, *A Greek-English Lexicon* (Oxford: Clarendon Press, 1996), 333b.

157. KB, 1,720.

158. Sarna, *Exodus*, 182.

159. James Hoffmeier, "Military, Materiel," in *Oxford Encyclopedia of Ancient Egypt*, ed. D. B. Redford (New York: Oxford Univesity Press, 2001), 2: 410.

160. Lambdin, "Egyptian Loan Words in the Old Testament," 155; Muchiki, *Egyptian Proper Names and Loanwords in North-West Semitic*, 258; *Wb* 5: 481.

161. *Wb* 2: 149.

162. Ezekiel 44:18, where it is also priestly garb.

163. KB, 581.

164. S. D. Sperling, "Pants, Persians, and the Priestly Source," in *Ki Baruch Hu: Ancient Near Eastern, Biblical, and Judaic Studies in Honor of Baruch A. Levine*, ed. R. Chazan, W. Hallo, and L. Shiffman (Winona Lake, Ind.: Eisenbrauns, 1999), 373–385.

165. Reeves, *Complete Tutankhamun*, 154.

166. The materials from the tomb of Kha are on display in the Egyptian Museum of Turin.

167. Ziony Zevit, *The Religions of Ancient Israel: A Synthesis of Parallactic Approaches* (London: Continuum, 2001), 47.

168. Ibid.

169. Cassuto, *Commentary on the Book of Exodus*, 257, 387.

170. *Wb* 5: 134; *CDME*, 286.

171. Lambdin, "Egyptian Loan Words in the Old Testament," 147. In Ezekiel 28:13, where the gemstones from the priestly breastpiece of Exodus 28 and 39 are listed, three of them have apparently dropped out of the Hebrew manuscript tradition but are present in the LXX. *'Aālāmâ* is one of the stones missing in Ezekiel, hence the only two references to it are in Exodus 28 and 39.

172. Muchiki, *Egyptian Proper Names and Loanwords in North-West Semitic*, 239.

173. Harris, *Lexicographical Studies*, 124.

174. Alfred Lucas and J. R. Harris, *Ancient Egyptian Materials and Industries*, 4th ed. (London: Histories and Mysteries of Man, 1962; reprint, 1989), 397.

175. Lambdin, "Egyptian Loan Words in the Old Testament," 152; *Wb* 2: 339–340. Concerning the interchange between Egyptian *n* and Hebrew *l*, see the discussion in the previous paragraph.

176. Muchiki, *Egyptian Proper Names and Loanwords in North-West Semitic*, 248.

177. Harris, *Lexicographical Studies*, 115–116.

178. *Wb* 2: 493; Lambdin, "Egyptian Loan Words in the Old Testament," 149; Muchiki, *Egyptian Proper Names and Loanwords in North-West Semitic*, 243.

179. Muchiki, *Egyptian Proper Names and Loanwords in North-West Semitic*, 282, 299.

180. Pierre Grandet, "Weights and Measures," in *Oxford Encyclopedia of Ancient Egypt*, ed. D. B. Redford (New York: Oxford University Press, 2001), 3: 493; Wiseman, "Weights and Measures," 1,246.

181. *Wb* 1: 49; Lambdin, "Egyptian Loan Words in the Old Testament," 147; Muchiki, *Egyptian Proper Names and Loanwords in North-West Semitic*, 239–240.

182. Grandet, "Weights and Measures," 493.

183. Marvin Powell, "Weights and Measures," in *ABD* 6: 899.

184. Gardiner, *Egyptian Grammar*, §266.2.

185. Full publication of these cubits is not yet available, but they are now on display in the special exhibit section of the Cairo Museum. Alain Zivie, who made the discovery, was kind enough to give me a copy of the article which mentions them as a part of the exhibit, but no photograph or drawing was included. See Alain Zivie, "Le vizier 'Aperl-El au musée," in *Egyptian Museum Collections around the World: Studies for the Centennial of the Egyptian Museum, Cairo*, ed. Mamdouh Eldamaty and Mai Trad (Cairo: American University Press, 2002), 1,261–1,274. My observations here are based on my study of the sticks and sketches made during a visit to the museum in January 2004.

186. For a discussion of this sign and the development of the meaning of holy/sacred, see James Hoffmeier, *Sacred in the Vocabulary of Ancient Egypt*, *OBO* 59 (1985).

187. The talatat building blocks of the Amarna period are proof of this length. We have found a number of talatat at Tell el-Borg, and they consistently are 52 centimeters long.

188. Wiseman, "Weights and Measures," 1,247.

189. Jeffrey Tigay, *Deuteronomy*, The JPS Torah Commentary (Philadelphia: Jewish Publication Society, 1996), 35.

190. *Wb* 5: 584.

191. Lambdin, "Egyptian Loan Words in the Old Testament," 149–150.

192. Muchiki, *Egyptian Proper Names and Loanwords in North-West Semitic*, 243.

193. KB, 81.

194. *Wb* 5: 562–563.

195. Philip Budd, *Numbers*, Word Biblical Commentary 5 (Waco, Tex.: Word, 1984), 106; Eryl Davies, *Numbers*, The New Century Bible Commentary (Grand Rapids, Mich.: Eerdmans, 1995), 87.

196. Jacob Milgrom, *Numbers*, The JPS Torah Commentary (Philadelphia: Jewish Publication Society, 1989), 72–73.

197. H. Hickman, *La trompette dans l'Égypte ancienne* (Cairo: IFAO, 1946), 3–15.

198. Ibid.

199. John Cooney, *Amarna Reliefs from Hermopolis in American Collections* (New York: Brooklyn Museum, 1965), 69.

200. Donald Redford, *The Akhenaten Temple Project*, Volume 2, *Rwd-Mnw and Inscriptions* (Toronto: Akhenaten Temple Project, 1988), 10, plate 31.

201. "An Unusual West-Semitic Loan-Word and a Possible Further Mention of Sea Peoples in the Twentieth Dynasty," *Cd'É* 71 (1996): 48–51. I am grateful to Kenneth Kitchen for this reference.

202. Carol L. Meyers, "The Elusive Temple," *BA* 45, no. 1 (1982): 37.

203. Ibid.

CHAPTER 10

1. Theophile J. Meek, *Hebrew Origins* (New York: Harper and Brothers, 1936), 32; Meek, "Moses and the Levites," *AJSL* 56 (1939): 118–120.

2. Martin Noth, *Die Israelitischen Personennamen im Rahmen der geminsemitischen Namengebung* (Hildesheim: Georg Olms, 1928).

3. John Spencer, "Aaron," in *ABD* 1: 1.

4. Manfred Görg, "Aaron—Von einem Titel zum Namen?" *BN* 32 (1986): 11–17.

5. Michael Homan, "A Tensile Etymology for Aaron," *BN* 95 (1998): 21–22; Homan, *To Your Tents, O Israel! The Terminology, Function, Form, and Symbolism of Tents in the Hebrew Bible and the Ancient Near East* (Leiden: Brill, 2002), 121–122.

6. Homan, *To Your Tents, O Israel!*, 122.

7. Ibid., 122–123.

8. Thomas Schneider, *Äsiatische Personennamen in Ägypstischen quellen des Neuen Reiches*, Orbis Biblicus et Orientalis 114 (Freiburg: Freiburg University Press, 1992), 105–106.

9. Eryl Davies, *Numbers*, The New Century Bible Commentary (Grand Rapids, Mich.: Eerdmans, 1995), 9; Baruch A. Levine, *Numbers 1–20*, ABC 4A (1993): 137; KB, 34.

10. KB, 32–34.

11. Yoshiyuki Muchiki, *Egyptian Proper Names and Loanwords in North-West Semitic*, SBL Dissertation Series 173 (Atlanta: Society of Biblical Literature, 1999), 207.

12. Martin Noth, *Die Israelitischen Personennamen*, 236.

13. J. Gwyn Griffiths, "The Egyptian Derivation of the Name Moses," *JNES* 12 (1953): 220.

14. This name is found in Egypt, according to Hermann Ranke, *Die Ägyptischen Personennamen* (Glückstadt: Augustin, 1935), 1:2. Muchiki has suggested that this Egypto-Hebrew hybrid name stands behind the name Ahimoth in 1 Chron. 6:25 (MT 10). There is a textual problem with this verse in the Chronicler, when compared with v. 35, suggesting that the name was actually Mahath. Even if 1 Chron. 6:25 does not preserve an Egypto-Hebrew hybrid name, it is, nevertheless, attested in Egyptian.

15. Muchiki, *Egyptian Proper Names and Loanwords in North-West Semitic*, 209.

16. This occurs at Ugarit; ibid., 278.

17. A significant number of Egypto-Phoenician hybrid names have been documented; see ibid., 14–21, 267.

18. KB, 73; Noth, *Die Israelitischen Personennamen*, 63. See also Meek, *Hebrew Origins*, 32.

19. Muchiki, *Egyptian Proper Names and Loanwords in North-West Semitic*, 208. For its Egyptian usage of both of these possibilities, see Ranke, *Die Ägyptischen Personennamen* 1:85. Muchiki also points out that a Hebrew root meaning "prisoner" is possible, but a name with such a negative connotation seems out of place.

20. Muchiki, *Egyptian Proper Names and Loanwords in North-West Semitic*, 208.

21. Ernst Axel Knauf, "Hori," in *ABD* 3: 288.

22. Muchiki, *Egyptian Proper Names and Loanwords in North-West Semitic*, 211; Ranke, *Die Ägyptischen Personennamen* 1:251.

23. Nahum M. Sarna, *Exodus*, The JPS Torah Commentary (Philadelphia: Jewish Publication Society, 1991), 95.

24. KB, 348; Muchiki, *Egyptian Proper Names and Loanwords in North-West Semitic*, 211.

25. James Hoffmeier, "The King as God's Son in Egypt and Israel," *JSSEA* 24 (1994): 29.

26. The root *mrr* has two meanings: the first is "strengthen" or "bless," and the second one is "bitter" (KB, 638). It might be recalled that Naomi, in the agony of her widowhood and the loss of her sons, asks that her name be changed to Mara, meaning "bitter" (Ruth 1:20). KB, 639, favors the meaning "strong."

27. Meek, "Moses and the Levites," 119. That the root means "beloved": see *Wb* 2: 98–101.

28. Meek, "Moses and the Levites," 118; Noth, *Die Israelitischen Personennamen*, 63; Kenneth Kitchen, "Phineas," in *NBD*, 934; Douglas Stuart, "Miriam," in *ISBE* 3, ed. (1986): 382; Muchiki, *Egyptian Proper Names and Loanwords in North-West Semitic*, 215.

29. Alan H. Gardiner, "The Egyptian Origin of Some English Personal Names," *JAOS* 56 (1936): 194–196.

30. Griffiths, "Egyptian Derivation of the Name Moses," 225–231; Muchiki, *Egyptian Proper Names and Loanwords in North-West Semitic*, 216–217; John Van Seters, "Moses," in *Encyclopedia of Religion*, ed. M. Eliade (New York: Macmillan, 1987), 115.

31. Ranke, *Die Ägyptischen Personennamen* 1:164–165.

32. James Hoffmeier, *Israel in Egypt: The Evidence for the Authenticity of the Exodus Tradition* (New York: Oxford University Press, 1997), 140–142.

33. *Wb* 2: 303.

34. Muchiki, *Egyptian Proper Names and Loanwords in North-West Semitic*, 222.

35. Ranke, *Die Ägyptischen Personennamen* 1:113.

36. KB, 918.

37. Muchiki, *Egyptian Proper Names and Loanwords in North-West Semitic*, 221.

38. Noth, *Die Israelitischen Personennamen*, 63; Meek, *Hebrew Origins*, 32; Muchiki, *Egyptian Proper Names and Loanwords in North-West Semitic*, 220.

39. Ranke, *Die Ägyptischen Personennamen* 1:121.

40. The nature and origin of the genealogies in 1 Chronicles are complex indeed, and discerning between ancient lists and postexilic ones is difficult, if not impossible.

41. Meek, "Moses and the Levites," 113–120.

42. Noth, *Die Israelitischen Personennamen*, 40 n. 1.

43. Richard Wilkinson, *The Complete Gods and Goddesses of Ancient Egypt* (New York: Thames and Hudson, 2003), 153–156.

44. Muchiki, *Egyptian Proper Names and Loanwords in North-West Semitic*, 207.

45. *Wb* 1: 73–74.

46. Ranke, *Die Ägyptischen Personennamen* 1:2.

47. Muchiki, *Egyptian Proper Names and Loanwords in North-West Semitic*, 207.

48. Martin Selman, *1 Chronicles; an Introduction and Commentary*, Tyndale Old Testament Commentaries 10a (Downers Grove, Ill.: InterVarsity Press, 1994), 117.

49. Muchiki, *Egyptian Proper Names and Loanwords in North-West Semitic*, 212; Ranke, *Die Ägyptischen Personennamen* 1:249.

50. Diana Edelman, "Harnepher," in *ABD* 3: 62.

51. Noth, *Die Israelitischen Personennamen*, 63; Meek, *Hebrew Origins*, 32; Meek, "Moses and the Levites," 118.

52. *Wb* 3: 74; Ranke, *Die Ägyptischen Personennamen* 1.

53. C. F. Keil and F. Delitzsch, *I & II Kings, I & II Chronicles, Ezra, Nehemiah, Esther*, Commentary on the Old Testament 3 (Edinburgh: T and T Clarke, 1890), 67.

54. Muchiki, *Egyptian Proper Names and Loanwords in North-West Semitic*, 212.

55. Ranke, *Die Ägyptischen Personennamen* 1:42.

56. Muchiki, *Egyptian Proper Names and Loanwords in North-West Semitic*, 213.

57. KB, 439; John Wright, "Jeremoth," in *ABD* 3: 741–740.

58. Muchiki, *Egyptian Proper Names and Loanwords in North-West Semitic*, 213.

59. *Wb* 1: 108–109.

60. On the meaning of *psš*, see *Wb* 1: 554.

61. Muchiki, *Egyptian Proper Names and Loanwords in North-West Semitic*, 222; Ranke, *Die Ägyptischen Personennamen* 1:137.

62. Muchiki, *Egyptian Proper Names and Loanwords in North-West Semitic*, 222.

63. Ranke, *Die Ägyptischen Personennamen* 1:297.

64. The current Coptic Orthodox patriarch, Shenouda III, derives from Shenoute, the fifth-century Egyptian monk.

65. Philip Budd, *Numbers*, Word Biblical Commentary 5 (Waco, Tex: Word, 1984), 181–186; Davies, *Numbers*, 162–168; Levine, *Numbers 1–20*, 405–406.

66. KB, 1,140.

67. *Wb* 1: 280–281.

68. *Sw'b* is the causative form of the verb, "to make pure." James Hoffmeier, *Sacred in the Vocabulary of Ancient Egypt, OBO* 59 (1985), 25–26.

69. Denise Doxey, "Priesthood," in *Oxford Encyclopedia of Ancient Egypt*, ed. D. B. Redford (New York: Oxford University Press, 2001), 3:73.

70. Serge Sauneron, *The Priests of Ancient Egypt*, trans. David Lorton (Ithaca, N.Y.: Cornell University Press, 2000), 36–37.

71. For a convenient review of some of the theories, see Mary Douglas, *Purity and Danger: An Analysis of the Concepts of Pollution and Taboo* (London: Routledge and Kegan Paul, 1966), 43–51; Edwin Firmage, "The Biblical Dietary Laws and the Concept of Holiness," in *Studies in the Pentateuch*, Supplements to Vetus Testamentum (Leiden: Brill, 1990), 177–208. Jacob Milgrom's commentary also offers an excellent review of various theories, including some from Jewish sages as well as recent scholarship: Jacob Milgrom, *Leviticus 1–16* (New York: Doubleday, 1991), 649–653 and 718–736. See also Edwin Firmage, "Zoology," in *ABD* 6: 1,133–1,134. In Simoons's monograph, chapter 3 is devoted to a thorough investigation of pork consumption in the Near East, Europe, Africa, and Asia; see Frederick Simoons, *Eat Not This Flesh: Food Avoidances from Prehistory to the Present*, 2nd ed. (Madison: University of Wisconsin Press, 1994).

72. Douglas, *Purity and Danger,* chapter 3. Subsequent to her classic work, Douglas has taken up this subject in other writings, most recently in Douglas, *Leviticus as Literature* (Oxford: Oxford University Press, 1999), chapter 7.

73. Douglas, *Purity and Danger,* 54.

74. Mary Douglas, *Implicit Meanings: Essays in Anthropology* (London: Routledge and Kegan Paul, 1975), 261.

75. Ralph Bulmer, "Why Is the Cassowary Not a Bird? A Problem of Zoological Taxonomy among the Karam of the New Guinea Highlands," *Man* (new series) 2 (1967): 23.

76. Douglas, *Implicit Meanings,* 272.

77. Gordon Wenham, *The Book of Leviticus,* New International Commentary on the Old Testament (Grand Rapids, Mich.: Eerdmans, 1979), 169, 171.

78. Firmage, "Zoology," 1,134.

79. Simoons, *Eat Not This Flesh,* 92–94.

80. Brian Hesse, "Pigs," in *The Oxford Encyclopedia of Archaeology in the Near East,* ed. Eric Meyers (New York: Oxford University Press, 1997), 4:347–348.

81. Raymond O. Faulkner, *The Ancient Egyptian Book of the Dead* (London: British Museum, 1985), 108.

82. Rami van der Molen, *A Hieroglyphic Dictionary of Egyptian Coffin Texts* (Leiden: Brill, 2000), 120.

83. Miriam Lichtheim, *Ancient Egyptian Literature* (Berkeley: University of California Press, 1973), 1:186.

84. A. D. Godley, *Herodotus I–IV* (London: William Heinemann, 1931), 2:47.

85. Patrick Houlihan, *The Animal World of the Pharaohs* (London: Thames and Hudson, 1996), 24–29; Patrick Houlihan, "Pigs," in *The Oxford Encyclopedia of Ancient Egypt,* ed. D. B. Redford (New York: Oxford University Press, 2001), 47–48.

86. *Urk.* IV, 75.15.

87. Wolfgang Helck, *Urkunden der 18. Dynastie: Historische Inschriften Thutmosis' III und Amenophis' III* (Berlin: Akademie-Verlag, 1955), 1,797.2.

88. Houlihan, *Animal World of the Pharaohs,* 28.

89. H. M. Hecker, "A Zooarchaeological Inquiry into Pork Consumption in Egypt from Prehistoric to New Kingdom Times," *JARCE* 19 (1982): 59–71.

90. Penny Wilson and Gregory Gilbert, "Pigs, Pots and Postholes: Prehistoric Sais," *Egyptian Archaeology* 21 (2002): 12–13; Hecker, "Zooarchaeological Inquiry into Pork Consumption," 61.

91. J. Boessneck, *Tell el-Dab'a III* (Vienna: Österreichischen Akademie der Wissenschaften Wien, 1976), 32–33.

92. Study of the faunal remains at Tell el-Borg were made by Dr. Michelle Loyet in 2002, and thus did not include the faunal remains of the most recent season. Her study will appear in *Tell el-Borg I* (forthcoming).

93. H. M. Hecker, "Preliminary Report on the Faunal Remains from the Workmen's Village," in *Amarna Reports I,* ed. Barry Kemp (London: Egypt Exploration Society, 1984), 154–164.

94. Hecker, "Zooarchaeological Inquiry into Pork Consumption," 62.

95. I have this information from Egyptian friends who worked with social agencies helping poor folk in Egypt.

96. Houlihan, *Animal World of the Pharaohs*, 29.

97. Brian Hesse and Paula Wapnish, "Can Pig Remains Be Used for Ethnic Diagnosis in the Ancient Near East?" in *The Archaeology of Israel: Constructing the Past, Interpreting the Present*, ed. N. A. Silberman and David Small (Sheffield: Sheffield Academic Press, 1997), 240.

98. Marvin Harris, *Good to Eat: Riddles of Food and Culture* (Prospect Heights, Ill.: Waveland Press, 1985), 74.

99. Hesse, "Can Pig Remains Be Used for Ethnic Diagnosis in the Ancient Near East?" 248.

100. Ibid., 238–264.

101. Ibid., 251.

102. William G. Dever, *What Did the Biblical Writers Know & When Did They Know It?: What Archaeology Can Tell Us about the Reality of Ancient Israel* (Grand Rapids, Mich.: Eerdmans, 2001), 113.

103. Milgrom, *Leviticus 1–16*, 870.

104. Manfred Görg, "Methodological Remarks on Comparative Studies of Egyptian and Biblical Words and Phrases," in *Pharaonic Egypt: The Bible and Christianity*, ed. Sarah Israelit-Groll (Jerusalem: Magnes Press, 1985), 61. One caveat should be noted: one would not expect the Egyptian *s* to appear as *š* in Hebrew.

105. Gabriel Barkay, "The Divine Name Found in Jerusalem," *BAR* 9, no. 2 (1983): 14–19; Gabriel Barkay, Andrew G. Vaughn, Marilyn J. Lundberg, and Bruce Zuckerman, "The Amulets of Ketef Hinnom: A New Addition and Evaluation," *BASOR* 334 (2004): 41–71.

106. For references, see Sharon Keller, "An Analogue to the Priestly Blessing," in *Boundaries of the Ancient Near Eastern World: A Tribute to Cyrus H. Gordon*, ed. Claire Gottlieb, Meir Lubetski, and Sharon Keller (Sheffield: JSOT Supplement Series, 1998), 338 nn. 1–2.

107. Ibid., 338.

108. Ibid., 342.

109. Ibid.

110. Dever, *What Did the Biblical Writers Know?*, 180.

111. David Noel Freedman, "Aaronic Benediction," *UF* 10 (1978): 16.

CHAPTER 11

1. See the following studies for reviews of the various theories and their adherents: Richard Hess, "Early Israel in Canaan: A Survey of Recent Evidence and Interpretations," *PEQ* 125 (1993): 125–142; James Hoffmeier, *Israel in Egypt: The Evidence for the Authenticity of the Exodus Tradition* (New York: Oxford University Press, 1997), chapter 2; William G. Dever, *Who Were the Early Israelites and Where Did They Come From?* (Grand Rapids, Mich.: Eerdmans, 2003).

2. J. Philip Hyatt, *Exodus* (London: Marshall, Morgan, and Scott, 1971), 79.

3. Herbert B. Huffmon, "Yahweh and Mari," in *Near Eastern Studies in Honor of William Foxwell Albright*, ed. Hans Goedicke (Baltimore: Johns Hopkins University Press, 1971), 283–289.

4. Hyatt, *Exodus*, 79.

5. Ibid., 80.

6. Brevard S. Childs, *The Book of Exodus: A Critical, Theological Commentary*, The Old Testament Library (Louisville, Ky.: Westminster, 1974), 64.

7. H. H. Rowley, *From Joseph to Joshua* (London: Oxford University Press, 1950), 149ff.; Martin Noth, *Exodus* (Philadelphia: Westminster, 1962), 30ff., 145ff.; William F. Albright, "Jethro, Hobab, and Reuel," *CBQ* 25 (1963): 1–11; Helmer Ringgren, *Israelite Religion*, trans. David E. Green (Philadelphia: Fortress, 1966), 33–34.

8. George E. Mendenhall, *Ancient Israel's Faith and History: An Introduction to the Bible in Context* (Louisville, Ky.: Westminster/John Knox Press, 2001), 44.

9. Patrick D. Miller, *The Religion of Ancient Israel*, Library of Ancient Israel (Louisville, Ky.: Westminster/John Knox Press, 2000), 1.

10. For the excavations at Timna, see Kenneth Kitchen, *On the Reliability of the Old Testament* (Grand Rapids, Mich.: Eerdmans, 2003), 214; Beno Rothenberg, *The Egyptian Mining Temple at Timna* (London: University College London, 1988); Beno Rothenberg, "Timna," in *NEAEHL* 4: 1,475–1,486; Beno Rothenberg, *Timna: Valley of the Biblical Copper Mines*, New Aspects of Antiquity (London: Thames and Hudson, 1972).

11. Rothenberg, "Timna," 1,483; Kitchen, *On the Reliability of the Old Testament*, 214.

12. P. Kyle McCarter, *Ancient Inscriptions: Voices from the Biblical World* (Washington, D.C.: Biblical Archaeology Society, 1996), 106–109.

13. Ziony Zevit, *The Religions of Ancient Israel: A Synthesis of Parallactic Approaches* (London: Continuum, 2001), 395.

14. Yehezkel Kaufmann, *The Religion of Israel: From Its Beginnings to the Babylonian Exile*, trans. Moshe Greenberg (New York: Schocken Books, 1972), 224.

15. Rowley, *From Joseph to Joshua*, 150.

16. KB, 1,264–1,265.

17. George E. Mendenhall, *The Tenth Generation: The Origins of the Biblical Tradition* (Baltimore: Johns Hopkins University Press, 1973); Norman Gottwald, *The Tribes of Yahweh: A Sociology of the Religion of Liberated Israel 1250–1050 B.C.E.* (Maryknoll, N.Y.: Orbis, 1979).

18. His views have been recently updated in Mendenhall, *Ancient Israel's Faith and History*, 50–54.

19. Gottwald, *Tribes of Yahweh*, 36–39.

20. Ibid., chapter 22.

21. One example of this school would be Gösta W. Ahlström, *Who Were the Israelites?* (Winona Lake, Ind.: Eisenbrauns, 1986).

22. J. David Schloen, "Caravans, Kenites, and Casus Belli: Enmity and Alliance in the Song of Deborah," *CBQ* 55 (1993): 18–38.

23. Mark S. Smith, *The Origins of Biblical Monotheism: Israel's Polytheistic Background and the Ugaritic Texts* (Oxford: Oxford University Press, 2001), 145.

24. Some recent advocates of the connection are William Propp, "Monotheism and 'Moses,'" *UF* 31 (1999): 537–575; and Lawrence E. Stager, "Forging an Identity: The Emergence of Ancient Israel," in *The Oxford History of the Biblical World*, ed. Michael Coogan (New York: Oxford University Press, 1998), 148–149.

25. The titles of the papers, which have been presented at academic conferences, are "The Hymns to Aten: Their Antecedents and Implications" and "Psalm 104 and the Hymns to Aten." These will probably be expanded in a monograph.

26. Stager, "Forging an Identity: The Emergence of Ancient Israel," 148–149.

27. Childs, *Book of Exodus*, 64.

28. *Wb* 4: 412; Raphael Giveon, *Bédouins shosou des documents égyptiens* (Leiden: Brill, 1971).

29. *Wb* 4: 412.

30. Thomas Lambdin, "Egyptian Loan Words in the Old Testament," *JAOS* 73 (1953): 155. This development of the word seems doubtful to Muchiki, however: *Egyptian Proper Names and Loanwords in North-West Semitic*, SBL Dissertation Series (Atlanta: Society of Biblical Literature, 1999), 257.

31. Edward Wente, *Letters from Ancient Egypt* (Atlanta: Scholars Press, 1990), 106–108.

32. For a discussion of all relevant texts, see Giveon, *Bédouins shosou des documents égyptiens*. For a recent review of different views about the Shasu, see William Ward, "Shasu," in *ABD* 5: 1,165–1,167.

33. For the reliefs, see Epigraphic Survey, *The Battle Reliefs of King Sety I*, vol. 4, *Reliefs and Inscriptions at Karnak* (Chicago: Oriental Institute, 1986), plates 2–6.

34. William Murnane, *The Road to Kadesh: A Historical Interpretation of the Battle Reliefs of King Sety I at Karnak, Studies in Ancient Oriental Civilization* 42 (Chicago: University of Chicago Press, 1985), 55.

35. Ibid., 57.

36. Art historical analysis of this scene by Jessica T. Hoffmeier is already under way. The reason for attributing a Ramesses II date to the relief is that several other blocks from the same group as this piece do have the cartouches of Ramesses II on them.

37. *LEM*, 76. For discussions of this text, see Manfred Weippert, "Semitische Nomaden des zweiten Jahrtausends," *Biblica* 55 (1974): 270–272.

38. Michael C. Astour, "Yahweh in Egyptian Topographic Lists," in *Festschrift Elmar Edel*, ed. Manfred Görg (Bamberg: *ÄAT*, 1979), 19. Other scholars have shown a possible northern location for this sequence of names: Weippert, "Semitische Nomaden des zweiten Jahrtausends," 265–280, 427–433.

39. H. W. Fairman, "Preliminary Report on the Excavations at ʿAmrah West, Anglo-Egyptian Sudan, 1938–9," *JEA* 25 (1939): 139–144.

40. Raphael Giveon, "Toponymes ouest-asiatiques à Soleb," *VT* 14 (1964): 239–255.

41. Astour, "Yahweh in Egyptian Topographic Lists," 19.

42. Bernhard Grdseloff, "Édôm, d'après les sources égyptiennes," *Revue de l'Histoire Juive d'égypte* 1 (1947): 69–99; Giveon, *Les Bédouins shosou des documents égyptiens*, 28.

43. Grdseloff, "Édôm, d'après les sources égyptiennes," 79ff.

44. Astour, "Yahweh in Egyptian Topographic Lists," 20–24.

45. Shmuel Ahituv, *Canaanite Toponyms in Ancient Egyptian Documents* (Jerusalem: Magnes Press, 1984), 122.

46. Donald Redford, *Egypt, Canaan, and Israel in Ancient Times* (Princeton: Princeton University Press, 1992), 272–273.

47. Albrecht Alt, *Die Landnahme der Israeliten in Palästina* (Leipzig: Reformationsprogramm der Universität Leipzig, 1925).

48. Manfred Weippert, *The Settlement of the Israelite Tribes in Palestine: A Critical Survey of Recent Scholarly Debate,* Studies in Biblical Theology: Second Series 21 (Naperville, Ill.: Alec R. Allenson, 1971); Weippert, "The Israelite 'Conquest' and the Evidence from Transjordan," in *Symposia Celebrating the Seventy-Fifth Anniversary of the Founding of the American Schools of Oriental Research (1900–1975),* ed. Frank M. Cross (Cambridge, Mass.: ASOR, 1979), 27–34.

49. Cf. Manfred Bietak, *Avaris and Piramesse: Archaeological Exploration in the Eastern Nile Delta* (London: Oxford University Press, 1979); and "Tell ed-Dab'a," in *The Oxford Encyclopedia of Ancient Egypt,* ed. Donald Redford (New York: Oxford University Press, 2001).

50. I was present at the Society for the Studies of Egyptian Antiquities annual meeting when he made public his findings. I am truly grateful to Frank for his thoughtful scholarly contributions over the years. He judiciously treated Egyptian and biblical issues surrounding early Israel.

51. Frank Yurco, "Merneptah's Canaanite Campaign," *JARCE* 23 (1986): 189–215.

52. Ibid., 197–203.

53. One scholar who questioned Yurco's reading of the usurped hieroglyphs is Redford, but few now doubt Yurco's conclusions; Donald Redford, "The Ashkelon Relief at Karnak and the Israel Stela," *IEJ* 36, no. 3–4 (1986): 188–200. Interestingly, Professor Kitchen was a participant in the same conference when Yurco disclosed his discovery. Kitchen was the first to stand and commend Yurco's work, as it had been assumed before that the usurped name was that of Ramesses II.

54. Yurco, "Merneptah's Canaanite Campaign," 199–200.

55. For a full discussion of the writing and its implications, see Hoffmeier, *Israel in Egypt,* 27–31; Hoffmeier, "The (Israel) Stela of Merneptah," in *COS* 2: 40–41.

56. Anson Rainey, "Israel in Merenptah's Inscriptions and Reliefs," *IEJ* 51 (2001): 68–74; Rainey, "Rainey's Challenge," *BAR* 17, no. 5 (1991): 58–60, 93; Rainey, "Unruly Elements in Late Bronze Canaanite Society," in *Pomegranates and Golden Bells: Studies in Biblical, Jewish and Near Eastern Ritual, Law and Literature in Honor of Jacob Milgrom,* ed. D.Wright, D. Freedman, and A. Hurvitz (Winona Lake, Ind.: Eisenbrauns, 1995), 481–496.

57. Rainey, "Rainey's Challenge," 59.

58. Frank Yurco, "Merneptah's Canaanite Campaign and Israel's Origins," in *Exodus: The Egyptian Evidence,* ed. E. S. Fredrichs and L. H. Lesko (Winona Lake, Ind.: Eisenbrauns, 1997), 41.

59. Rainey, "Israel in Merenptah's Inscriptions and Reliefs," 73–74.

60. Yurco, "Merneptah's Canaanite Campaign and Israel's Origins," 41.

61. Lawrence Stager, "Merneptah, Israel and Sea Peoples: New Light on an Old Relief," *EI* 18 (1985): 60*.

62. Rainey, "Unruly Elements in Late Bronze Canaanite Society," 494–495.

63. Stephen Harvey, "Monuments of Ahmose at Abydos," *EA* 4 (1995): 5.

64. For example, Ephraim Stern, "Pagan Yahwism: The Folk Religion of Ancient Israel," *BAR* 27 n. 3 (2001): 21–29; Zevit, *Religions of Ancient Israel;* Miller, *Religion of Ancient Israel,* chapters 1 and 2; Susan Niditch, *Ancient Israelite Religion* (New York: Oxford University Press, 1997), chapter 1; Mark S. Smith, *The Early History of God: Yahweh and the Other Deities in Ancient Israel* (San Francisco: Harper and Row, 1990).

65. He frequently uses this expression; for example, Smith, *Early History of God,* xxiv, xxxi.

66. Ibid., 53. His more recent study is equally tilted in favor of Ugaritic sources, while ignoring Egyptian ones: Smith, *Origins of Biblical Monotheism.*

67. Tryggve N. D. Mettinger, "The Roots of Aniconism: An Israelite Phenomenon in Comparative Perspective," *VT* 66 (1997): 219–233; Miller, *Religion of Ancient Israel,* 16–23; Ronald Hendel, "The Social Origins of the Aniconic Tradition in Early Israel," *CBQ* 50 (1988): 365–382.

68. William F. Albright, "What Were the Cherubim?" *BA* 1 (1938): 1–3; Roland de Vaux, *Ancient Israel* (New York: McGraw-Hill, 1962), 2:397–402; Othmar Keel, *Symbolism of the Biblical World* (New York: Seabury Press, 1978), 169–171.

69. Mettinger, "The Roots of Aniconism"; Hendel, "Social Origins of the Aniconic Tradition in Early Israel," 365–368.

70. Hendel, "Social Origins of the Aniconic Tradition in Early Israel," 374–382.

71. Othmar Keel, *Jahwe-Visionen und Siegelkunst* (Stuttgart: Katholisches Bibelwerk, 1977), 39–40. The translation here is that of Hendel, "Social Origins of the Aniconic Tradition in Early Israel," 372.

72. See discussion above, chapter 6 §IVB, *Midian-Arabia.*

73. Uzi Avner, "Sacred Stones in the Desert," *BAR* 27 n. 3 (2001): 40. See also Avner, "Ancient Cult Sites in the Negev and Sinai Deserts," *Tel Aviv* 11 (1984): 115–131.

74. Avner, "Sacred Stones in the Desert," 40.

75. Ibid., 32.

76. Ibid., 39.

77. Alan H. Gardiner, T. Eric Peet, Jaroslav Černý, *The Inscriptions of Sinai* (London: Egypt Exploration Society, 1955), 40.

78. The ratio figures are based on measurements I have taken.

79. Avner, "Sacred Stones in the Desert," 41.

80. William G. Dever, *What Did the Biblical Writers Know & When Did They Know It?: What Archaeology Can Tell Us about the Reality of Ancient Israel* (Grand Rapids, Mich.: Eerdmans, 2001), 273.

Index

Foreign Terms

Scriptures

CPSIA information can be obtained at www.ICGtesting.com
Printed in the USA
LVOW100350250112

265427LV00004B/3/P

9 780195 155464